SOUNDINGS IN ATLANTIC HISTORY

Latent Structures and Intellectual Currents, 1500–1830

EDITED BY

Bernard Bailyn

AND

Patricia L. Denault

HARVARD UNIVERSITY PRESS

Cambridge, Massachusetts

London, England

2009

Library of Congress Cataloging-in-Publication Data

Soundings in Atlantic history : latent structures and intellectual currents, 1500–1830 /
edited by Bernard Bailyn and Patricia L. Denault.

p.　cm.

Includes bibliographical references and index.
ISBN 978-0-674-03276-7 (cloth : alk. paper)
1. Atlantic Ocean Region—History.　2. Atlantic Ocean Region—Intellectual life.
3. History, Modern.　I. Bailyn, Bernard.　II. Denault, Patricia L.

D210.S68　2009
909′.09821—dc22　　　2008053246

Contents

Figures, Maps, and Tables

Maps

Tables

SOUNDINGS IN ATLANTIC HISTORY

Introduction
Reflections on Some Major Themes

BERNARD BAILYN

I

Historical accounts of events and developments that took place in the Atlantic world began to appear almost as soon as contacts were established between Europe and the Americas in the late fifteenth century. But Atlantic history itself—that is, the evolving history of the zone of interaction among the peoples of Western Europe, West Africa, and the Americas—was first seen as a distinct and cohesive subject of historical inquiry in the years immediately after World War II. References to Atlantic history as such were at first scattered, random, and incidental to studies of more limited subjects, gradually becoming more frequent and prominent, until, toward the end of the century, the outline, at least, of the evolution of this vast, interactive region of the globe could be glimpsed and efforts could be made to grasp its essential characteristics.

How Atlantic history emerged from a plethora of scattered, localized studies and casual terminology to become a defined subject with a distinctive course of development I have attempted elsewhere to describe.[1] In recent years the subject has flourished to a remarkable degree. Important contributions have now appeared in so many books, articles, special journal issues, and Web sites, the subject has been discussed in so many conferences and seminars in the United States and abroad, it is being developed in so many and diverse research centers, and the word "Atlantic" has appeared as a defining characteristic so frequently in so many contexts, that no comprehensive bibliography can be compiled. Though the subject, Professor Horst Pietschmann of the University of Hamburg writes, has been "methodically founded . . . as a historical sub-discipline . . . widely accepted in Western Europe and different parts of America," it is still emerging—shifting, quickly moving, and responsive to the impact of new information and new ideas.[2]

The main stimulus to the proliferation of studies in and references to Atlantic history has been the explanatory power and suggestive implications created by the vision of the Atlantic region as a coherent whole. In that large regional context, otherwise limited, local studies gain heightened meaning at a more general plane of significance. Context matters. Perspective matters. They shape meaning. Thus "early American" historiography—that is, studies of pre-Revolutionary British North America—though voluminous, exhaustively researched, and in many ways original and sophisticated, seems over the years to have been self-enclosed, a world of creative scholarship with surprisingly little resonance in or influence on the major strains of Western historiography, British or continental European. Integrating this dense but often isolated historiography into that of the larger Atlantic world of which it was a part results in enrichment, for the subject and for the context as well. And what is true of Anglophone history is equally true of aspects of Latin American, Iberian, Dutch, and French history.[3]

The concept of the Atlantic world as a coherent whole involves a creative shift in orientation, from nationalistic, longitudinal, and teleological structures toward "horizontal," transnational, trans-imperial, and multicultural views as the mind's eye sweeps laterally across the past's contemporary world rather than forward to its later outcomes. It is futile, a contributor to the American Historical Association's Forum on "Entangled Histories" writes, to study "historical phenomena that were transatlantic, hemispheric, and transnational within the limits of national narratives." The birth of the American nation-states in the independence movements of the late eighteenth and early nineteenth centuries was not the goal toward which Atlantic history had been inevitably tending, but the opposite: it marks not the fulfillment but the demise of the world that had gone before.[4]

Slowly, incrementally, "Atlantic" historical studies have appeared, drawing data from Spanish, British, African, Dutch, French, Portuguese, and Native American sources otherwise localized and segmented into larger units that are part of the region's greater history. Connections, parallels, and comparisons that help "surmount the complexity and tyranny of local detail" become revealing. But as John Elliott has shown in his magisterial comparative study, *Empires of the Atlantic World: Britain and Spain in America, 1492–1830,* while the differences between metropole and colony, between Iberians and British, between Catholic and Protestant, and between Africans, Europeans, and Native Americans are obvious, the connections and similarities are not. There is "a shock of recognition," a historian of the Caribbean writes, "as populations we assumed to be insular, and whose events we therefore explained in terms of local dynamics, are revealed to be above-water fragments of . . . submarine unities."[5] Gradually, as once "submerged" transnational structures and large-scale patterns are perceived, the outlines of an immensely complex but cohesive multicultural region come into view. But clarity and comprehension are difficult to achieve, especially in those subtler realms of experience that are close to the inner lives of the multitudes of people involved.

It is the purpose of this volume to explore as sensitively as possible some—a selected few—of the latent but revealing lines of coherence, some of the submerged linkages and structures that bound the region together, and the currents of ideas and patterns of belief that flowed from continent to continent, empire to empire, nation to nation. The essays that follow are probes in various modes of historical discourse, imaginative soundings, of certain themes in Atlantic history that have attracted historians aware of the scope and complexity of the region's history and that exemplify something of the broad coherence of this evolving early modern world, in terms both of public, objective, behavioral phenomena and of private, interior, subjective experiences.

It was a world, let it be said at the start, that was never entirely autonomous, never wholly discrete, self-enclosed, or isolated from the rest of the globe. In every major area—economic, cultural, political—there were extra-regional contacts, other worlds "impinging on and often shaping developments" in the Atlantic world. The question is not whether Europeans, Americans, and Africans had contacts and involvements in other regions of the globe—of course they did—or even whether those extra-Atlantic links did not at times significantly affect events in the West. How could they not? Diseases, like scientific knowledge and technology, spread inevitably from East to West as they did from West to East, and European trade with the Far East, established at least from the fifteenth century, formed "articulated" circuits that played, however irregularly, into the growing Atlantic commercial system.[6] The vital question is whether experiences in the Atlantic realm—in trade, in governance, in social and cultural life—were not essentially different from those elsewhere on the globe, and whether the early modern Atlantic world did not have distinctive characteristics that shaped the course of world history.

Extra-Atlantic contacts, however articulated with other circuits, were not constitutive of a global world. Globalism emerged, Patrick O'Brien writes in the inaugural issue of the *Journal of Global History,* "in the aftermath of the Revolutionary and Napoleonic Wars," developing through the nineteenth and early twentieth centuries as the West rose to world dominance, and climaxing after World War II. Expert economic analysts, working with voluminous statistical data and advanced economic theory, agree: "it was only after the early 19th century that globalization really took off."[7]

If one goes beyond these technical measures and thinks in terms of ideal forms, one can hypothesize, as the authors of a recent United Nations report have done, that in its full, ideal development a global world would be borderless, territory would have lost importance, and there would be an "international division of labour, financial transactions, and trade in goods." No such borderless world, or any approximation of it, existed in fact before the twentieth century, indeed before the late twentieth century.[8]

As Europeans scattered into all the accessible parts of the globe as merchants, missionaries, scholars, posted army officers, government officials, and errant wanderers, they discovered that experiences in one region of the globe could not be replicated in another.[9] East and West were fundamentally different. The Dutch assumed they would remain traders along the shores of the Hudson River just as they had done in Indonesia, and would coexist with the natives as they did in Batavia. But aggressive traders among them found they could easily penetrate inland for greater profits, and land-hungry settlers began seizing native lands—until both met resistance that resulted in spirals of exceptionally bloody warfare, the displacement of the natives, and the unanticipated spread of Dutch settlement. English plans for establishing traditional trading stations in Virginia were fruitless; a new strategy, of settlement, had to be devised. "In the East," Peter Coclanis tells us, "no successful colonies of settlement were established . . . by Europeans in the early modern period." There seemed to be similarities to what the English might do in India and in the Caribbean, but they soon discovered the differences. In India they came as traders, and "successful trade required insinuation into local networks and accommodation to local mores. Though Europeans fought with each other [there], they had to be careful in dealings with indigenous people, whose alliances and support promised the wealth that had initially attracted [them]. . . . In the Caribbean Europeans . . . turned the region into their own battleground and by the middle of the seventeenth century these endemic rivalries could be carried out without inconvenient concerns about the political interests of the dwindling indigenous populations." And while they neither needed nor wished for territorial conquests or colonies in West Africa, "the whole opening up of Africa . . . was the first major thrust of Europe overseas and the beginning of the age of Western domination, colonialism, and imperialism."[10]

Europe's penetration of Africa began as early as the mid-fifteenth century, when Christianity became the dominant religion in parts of central Africa and "the Portuguese language quickly became the basis of a trading patois that was spoken throughout the region." "By the eighteenth century rough spheres of influence had been established, with the English, Dutch, and the Portuguese most dominant as residents on the African coast with their permanent forts or factories. But no African area was totally closed to any European trader, and there was an extensive published contemporary literature and general European knowledge on the possibilities of local trade everywhere in western Africa." A mixed Afro-Portuguese Catholic free merchant class that emerged in Senegambia "not only occupied key settlements along the coast but often penetrated deep into the interior." Afro-English and Afro-French merchant groups followed—"racially mixed elites who intermarried with members of the local African establishments and were deeply involved with the regional African states and societies."[11]

In extra-Atlantic domains, however, except for the conquered parts of the Philippines, the Europeans remained "supplicants for the favors that would permit them access to valued commodities." They worked their way cautiously and precariously into the outer margins of Middle Eastern and Asian commerce, rarely penetrating into their cores, and they groped for some small purchase on the arcane and convoluted power struggles in those distant lands. But in the Western Hemisphere, "European settlers brought with them their customs and institutions, languages and religions, and founded neo-European offshoot societies. The prerequisites for this approach were created in the sixteenth century; by the seventeenth century such societies had crossed the threshold to irreversible stability nearly everywhere."[12] The Portuguese understood the differences particularly well. Any European empire in Asia, they knew, could be held together only by fleets and occasional fortresses. "The ancient civilizations of Asia, densely populated and firmly governed, did not suffer the incursions of foreigners easily." In Brazil, on the other hand, the Portuguese found a long coastline with access to a rich interior, sparsely inhabited by scattered tribes. There they were able to reproduce the agro-maritime economy they knew at home "almost independent of the local population."[13]

Only in the Atlantic did the Europeans find a maritime sphere without competition—without the adversaries of the eastern oceans: "Arabs, Chinese, Malays, and other maritime traders and pirates." Nor were there indigenous empires north or south that did not sooner or later fall to the military force of the European powers, however much they might resist and negotiate their submission. Since no effective forces challenged their ambitions, and since native populations were commonly decimated by foreign pathogens, the Americas seemed open to "unlimited possibility. . . . Only there was it possible to conduct one of the most ambitious experiments in social engineering of the early modern era: the establishment of slave plantations." For this Atlantic phenomenon—demographic, racial, cultural, and economic—there was no parallel on the face of the globe.[14]

The Atlantic world in the early modern era was one of several great regional entities. But how can one describe or define it? Nicholas Canny, a major scholar in the field, wonders what the subject entails, because he finds so many and so different approaches to it. Some of those he identifies as "Atlanticists" concentrate on the comparative history of Euro-

pean overseas expansion, others on the comparative study of transatlantic migrations, forced or voluntary; still others study pan-Atlantic
networks of various kinds (trade, ethnicities, religions), and others,
Canny writes, "take their inspiration from Fernand Braudel, believing
that there must be an Atlantic history . . . to match that fashioned by
Braudel for the Mediterranean" (though who these Atlantic Braudelians
might be is difficult to discover).[15] Still others are "historians of England
or of Britain seeking to construct a wider focus for their subject"; and
finally, he writes, there are historians of the United States seeking to escape from the claims of exceptionalism by tracing Atlantic interconnections, though mainly in the nineteenth and twentieth centuries.[16]

Except for the elusive Braudelians, Canny's categories are reasonable, and one can identify other approaches and other contributors who
might be included: students of the pan-Atlantic circulation of ideas, of
the diffusion of technological innovations, of the regional involvements
in constitutional reforms, and of the enlargement of mental horizons.
The subject is capacious, it allows for approaches from many directions,
but it is not a random miscellany of disassociated phenomena. Though
it includes all these aspects of life and others, it is a coherent subject,
and, unlike Braudel's Mediterranean, it is coherently historical, moving
from scattered beginnings to shifting lines of development, to phases of
fulfillment, and finally, with respect to its essential structures, to evanes-
cence as it melded, transformed, at the end of the eighteenth century,
into the modern, more global world.

Nor is its coherence or uniqueness diminished by the fact that people
in all centuries from all known cultural backgrounds have sought "to
migrate from their heartlands to populate new lands," or by the fact that
leaders from most human societies have sought to commandeer labor,
voluntary and forced, to perform "onerous and hazardous" work. So
they have. But *how* this happened in the Atlantic world, *why* it happened there, and what its consequences have been lie at the heart of this
regional history, and at the heart too of the emergence of global modernity. For while there were several great regional entities East and West, it
was the Atlantic region that proved to have the dynamic edge that
would account for the "great divergence" in economic development that
took place in the nineteenth century, the result in large part, Kenneth
Pomeranz has famously argued, of the availability to Europeans of the

resources of American land. It was there, in the Euro-American world, Christopher Bayly explains in his *Birth of the Modern World,* that economic dynamics coexisted with an assumed link between scientific theory and practical application, with a unique density of civil institutions, and with an equally unique information-richness, "in which inquisitiveness and cupidity turned information into tools for world exploration, and, later, world conquest."[17]

How that came about and what the main lines of integration were—those are stories yet to be told. But elements of it are clear, and none more so than the complex economic networks that bound the scattered sources of production and consumption into a broad if loose and erratic system.

II

But was there a discrete Atlantic economic "system"? Some have argued that there was no system, because "the economies of Europe, Africa, and the New World largely remained independent from one another," hence that "without the 'Atlantic system' the economies of Western Europe, West Africa, and the New World would not have been much different." Others, conceding that Atlantic history has linked up historians working in largely independent fields and has "enriched our understanding of the complex, intricately imbricated relationship among various parts of Western Europe, West Africa, and the Americas during the early modern period," note the importance of supra-Atlantic markets and exchanges—American silver ending up in China as well as Europe, Indian textiles feeding both African and European markets, Asian spices and chinoiserie prized by Western consumers. And indeed it is obvious that the economic life of the Atlantic world was never "discrete" in the sense of having been sealed off within rigid boundaries, its dynamics self-contained, confined, and comprehensive. How could it have been? Why should it have been? It naturally drew on and fed into—irregularly in time and place—regions far from the four ocean-fronting terrains.[18]

Villages in sub-Saharan Africa, markets in far northeastern Europe, Mediterranean ports and their hinterlands, trading factories in India and Indonesia, countinghouses in the Philippines and China—all felt the effect, strongly or weakly, directly or indirectly, of the Atlantic's dynamic outflows and fed substance back into the region's core. Yet, for all its reach, the Atlantic's economy was neither formless nor a minor dependency of other systems nor part of a functioning global system. During the seventeenth century and especially in the eighteenth century, Peter Coclanis, both a critic of Atlantic comprehension and a major scholar of the subject, concludes, "a unified, coherent, and increasingly cohesive Atlantic economy truly began to take shape. Underpinning and reflecting this process we see an emerging economic 'system' characterized by European and Euro-American domination and by increasingly sophisticated production complexes, commercial institutions and practices, and transportation and communications facilities." And it was a system of distinctive creative force, contributing uniquely, the leading economic historian of Latin America has written, to the development of modern capitalism.[19]

From Pierre Chaunu's monumental *Séville et l'Atlantique (1504–1615)* (eleven volumes, 1955–1959) to assessments, fifty years later, of Dutch, British, French, and Iberian Atlantic commerce, historians have identified some of the powerful networks that bound the scattered pan-oceanic production and consumption elements into a dynamic whole.[20] As Coclanis notes, these ties were not created at once, nor were they evenly distributed among the Atlantic powers. The assumption that the Dutch were consistently more deeply involved in commerce with the Far East than with the nearer West has recently been effectively challenged by studies of investment patterns, shipping, and capital markets.[21] Similarly, the irregular phases of French Atlantic trade, from the ancient northern fisheries to the late colonial exploitation of the Caribbean sugar plantations, have been traced, as have their complex involvements in the economies of Britain and Spain.[22] Both of those nations had vital interests beyond the Atlantic region, but for both the Western connections were pivotal. The elaborate ramifications of their economic linkages to their dependencies in the Western Hemisphere radiated, with different intensities at different times, through their entire economic systems. The West was a unique source of extractive and agricultural wealth and became a major market for the products of Europe, a market that grew rapidly with the increase in Creole and mixed-race populations; at the same time the metropolitan centers flourished as profitable transfer points between the American West and the European East.

Though the Euro-Atlantic states, competitors to the point of open
warfare for economic primacy, were involved in the commercial world
beyond the Atlantic region, those distant contacts did not create a global
network, as later, in the late nineteenth and twentieth centuries, they
would, nor did they subvert the integrity of the Atlantic economy.

Of that economy much is known, in terms of the magnitudes and
chronology of the flow of goods, the size of markets and productive ca-
pacities. But one wants to know more, not so much of statistical aggre-
gates as of the shaping circumstances, inner processes, and patterns of
entrepreneurship that developed in response to the opportunities that
appeared. Three approaches to these subtler questions are probed in the
pages that follow.

The first relates to the Atlantic slave trade, which its latest and most
precise analysts correctly describe as "the largest transoceanic forced
migration in history"—"a new phenomenon in the human experience"
whereby "relatively small improvements to the quality of life of a people
on one continent . . . were made possible by the removal of others from
a second continent, and their draconian exploitation on yet a third."
In the process this third continent, the Americas, was comprehensively
re-peopled, not initially with Europeans, but with Africans. "Prior to
1820, about four Africans arrived in the Americas for every single European."[23] The slave trade's pan-Atlantic enormity continues to stagger the
imagination. We now know that an estimated 12.5 million Africans were
seized and shipped out in slavery under appalling conditions; 10.7 million arrived in the Americas. These are the reliable estimates of the team
of scholars who have created *Voyages: The Trans-Atlantic Slave Trade*,
an immense statistical compilation drawn from a multitude of records,
public and private, that includes reliable estimates for the geographical
and ethnic origins of the slaves shipped from Africa, for the relative contributions to the trade by the various Atlantic nations, and for the destinations of the captives in the Western Hemisphere.[24] But hidden from
view, beneath the manifest enormity of the traffic, lay an intense world
of technical entrepreneurship, of the myriad business decisions that pro-
pelled the trade forward and that shaped its contours and consequences;
and beneath that lay the basic circumstance of the physical environment
that determined what could be done.

In an earlier paper Stephen Behrendt explained how extraordinarily fine-tuned, how delicately dovetailed were the functionings of the transaction cycles of the slave trade—how closely integrated the movements had to be among entrepreneurs and goods producers in Britain, slave dealers and transoceanic shippers in Africa, and plantation owners and labor managers in the Americas for profits to be made from the trade, and how little it took to pitch even the most carefully planned slaving venture into bankruptcy.[25] Now, in the present essay, he extends that analysis into deeper reaches—into the profound influence of climate and ecological seasonality on production and commerce on the continents involved in the slave trade, and into the nature of the delicately balanced networks that resulted as merchants and planters adjusted the transaction cycles to the dictates of nature.

Seeking to understand the basic circumstances that shaped the slave trade, Behrendt traces, in illuminating detail, the "rainfall calendars, temperature, and oceanic winds and currents—the underlying ecology of the Atlantic world," together with the agricultural practices, crop cycles, and seasonal patterns of nutritional supplies in West Africa, and he relates all of this to the recruitment and marketing of African slaves and to the labor needs in the Americas. Nothing was stable and little was predictable, but adjustments to the dictates of nature could be made and effective patterns devised. It is only by acknowledging the intricate calculations of the European merchants, African traders, and American planters struggling to coordinate intercontinental transaction cycles in the face of the ecological and climatological complexities of four continents and the oceanic basin, that one can fully grasp the depths of the Atlantic slave trade's inhumanity.

This realm of Atlantic geography, ecology, and climatology was latent with respect to the shipboard and plantation history of the Atlantic slave trade, and it is revealed only by quantitative analysis of conditions that participants would grope to understand. Also embedded in the information gathered on some 35,000 pan-Atlantic slave voyages are surprising aspects of the slaves' and slavers' manifest experiences: the peculiar ethnic and geographical determinants of the sex ratios and death rates among the enslaved Africans; the positive correlation between shipboard rebellions and female captives; and the unanticipated limitations imposed on the size of slave cargos by the costs of shipboard security, costs that would otherwise have been invested in larger car-

goes. A million Africans, it has been calculated, were spared captivity
by the diversion of investments to the hiring of larger, less vulnerable
crews.[26]

But if the slave trade database, which Behrendt, David Eltis, David
Richardson, and others have so carefully compiled and analyzed, has
revealed hitherto unknown aspects of the Afro-Atlantic slave system,
there is another, deeper background to this history, which is explored in
the essay by Linda Heywood and John Thornton.

That the Africans acquired by the slave traders did not simply appear
in undifferentiated groups on the West African coast but were drawn
from a wide range of identifiable regions and local cultures with their
own deep histories has long been known. To some extent the relocation
in the Americas of various African ethnic groups has been plotted and
the lasting influence of their original cultures assessed.[27] But beyond
that, there were also in the West African world political organizations
that were formally structured, even bureaucratic, and whose rules were
clearly articulated. Some were long-lasting empires, which can be found
as far back as the thirteenth century; others were kingdoms and organized states—"nations"—of lesser dimensions and degrees of stability,
ranging from ministates along the West African coast to clusters of village associations deep in the interior. Most of the larger entities had continuous contact with European powers or agents; all sought to manage
and profit by trade in whatever commodities were available—slaves
commonly but often only incidentally.

Powerful in the early modern period were the kingdoms of Kongo
and Dahomey (now Benin), which had been in contact with Portuguese
traders and Catholic missionaries since the late fifteenth century. In the
seventeenth and eighteenth centuries both kingdoms were scenes of organized struggles for power, of political alliances and deals, of dynasties
and successions, and of political manipulation of trade, especially the
slave trade. The two cases differed significantly. Kongo was a monarchical Catholic state; its leadership was repeatedly contested and ultimately
overcome by fratricidal struggles amounting to civil war. Dahomey, an
absolutist warrior state devoted to ancestor worship, was endlessly engaged in aggressive warfare. Its severe political system grew stronger as
Kongo's splintered and weakened. In both cases the nature of interior,
domestic politics and the persistence of armed conflict form the deep

background of the slave trade. Captives in political battles or scattered raids routinely became slaves, to serve as local laborers, to populate depleted armies, or to be sold, along with ivory, redwood, and copper, to European slavers in exchange for weapons, clothes, and other goods.[28]

Until "large-scale warfare in which obtaining slaves for the Atlantic trade was a major theme" became common in the eighteenth century, the available supply of captives varied in response to domestic war and politics, the vagaries of commerce, and to some extent ideology. Catholic Kongo, for example, resisted selling slaves to Protestants and other "heretics" for labor in Protestant lands, but evasions could be devised. The Dutch, though Protestant, were believed to be more likely than the English to deliver slaves to the Spanish than to the Protestant Indies. The English found many ways of overcoming such constraints, and after 1713 were empowered by award of the *asiento,* the license to supply slaves to the Spanish colonies. The far-flung trading networks whose outer fringes the European traders grasped, stretching far into the African interior, were created as much by local political struggles in the two realms as by the prospect of commercial profit. And in both cases the domestic political history in Africa, barely visible to historians focused on the Middle Passage and the fortunes of slaves in the Americas, helps explain not only the dynamics and the magnitude of the African Diaspora but also, as Heywood and Thornton explain, something of the slaves' self-identities, their inherited attitudes to authority, their responses to the world around them. In the case of the Congolese, the persistence of national identity seems clear; in the case of the Dahomeans it is much less so. But in their account of the political chronicles of the two states, Heywood and Thornton have shown the possibility of probing the recondite and complex political history of the African background of the Atlantic slave population, characterizing the self-identities they carried abroad, and thus enriching our understanding of the African population that became so vital in the subsequent history of the Western world.[29]

Just as Behrendt deepened and refined an earlier effort, so too in a different way does David Hancock. His *Citizens of the World* (1995) broke new ground by analyzing in detail the integration of the British Atlantic community as seen in the far-flung but coordinated activities of a group of Anglo-Scottish merchants who rose from the margins to prosper at the core of the developing Atlantic world, commercial and social.[30] Since then, he has moved into a larger dimension of Atlantic history through an analysis of the region-wide trade in Madeira wines. He now draws together European investors, Madeiran producers, syndicates of distributors, and consumers throughout the Atlantic world. The system that evolved from their combined activities was something new, unplanned, undesigned, and unformulated.[31]

Though efficient in eighteenth-century terms, that system was highly decentralized, and, far from being dominated by any kind of top-down management or limited oligarchy, it was essentially self-organizing at local levels—how local Hancock shows in this essay through the career of an obscure German storekeeper turned prosperous miller in backcountry Pennsylvania. The world of Atlantic commerce caught in Hancock's lens is composed of a multitude of small, scattered units organized into a loose but effective system that linked the Wine Islands to the West Indies, North America, and Western Europe. The units, he writes, were "self-organized. . . . No one designed or maintained them, and few were aware of them in their entirety. They were the result of decentralized agents individually but connectedly working out specific solutions through their networks to places, personalities, and situations one step beyond, where they were adopted and adapted."[32] Though subject to regulation and taxation by the various nations involved, there was little effective interference with the routings and flow of produce and payments. Where regulation existed it could often be evaded, as were so many other attempts at regulating, hence artificially shaping, the region's developing commerce.

How crucial to the operation of the entire Atlantic system such evasions were is shown in detail by Wim Klooster. He describes how free-flowing, how little managed and regulated the commercial system of the entire Atlantic region in fact was, despite the elaborate efforts of the imperial governments to exclude foreigners from the benefits of their commerce. So voluminous was contraband trade, so common at so many levels was smuggling in all sorts of products, and indeed of people, that in economic terms "smuggling" loses its meaning. It seemed that "everyone had a stake in the smuggling business." The implications run deep. Formally it was a world of competing European states tightly bound into their Western empires, each bent upon maximizing its economic advantages at the expense of all others, especially by forcing its competitors into dependency by excluding them from lucrative goods and markets and by maintaining positive balances of both payments and trade. But, though government officials and economic theorists in London, Paris, Amsterdam, and Seville could produce logically and legally convincing mercantilist designs to satisfy their nations' interests, they could not compel obedience on ocean voyages or in dozens of ports in both hemispheres and on offshore islands. The informal transnational linkages counted in some places as much as, in others more than, the formal connections from which the nations' statistical information was derived, and everywhere brought the Atlantic world together.

The mass of details matters. Klooster, drawing with equal linguistic skill on Dutch, Danish, French, English, Portuguese, and Spanish sources, sketches a world of endless transnational collusion, of multitudes of secret deals beyond, around, and beneath the law, of swarms of vessels from all the European powers probing successfully year after year the weaknesses of official barriers along thousands of miles of American and Caribbean coastlines. In the Caribbean, Jacob Price writes, smuggling was so central to everyday commerce that it created "another moral world in which normative and the norm have very little in common." The relationship between legal and illegal trade was so delicate and so difficult to maintain that at times it collapsed altogether. Some government officials actively encouraged their people to engage in smuggling; at one point the Portuguese in Brazil officially licensed a company for the express purpose of trading illegally with the Spanish province of Quito.

Though resident officials commonly recognized that the local economies depended on illicit transactions, Klooster writes, "to make up for the chronic undersupply and exorbitant prices" imposed by chartered companies and state monopolies, and that without them the quality of life would diminish substantially, the informal economy had no theoretical rationale. Both Spain and Britain, in the late colonial period, felt the need to relieve some of the restraints on trade by creating limited "free ports" within their own commercial systems; Britain's concessions extended to foreigners who traded in bullion or a very small number of specified goods. But the basic structure of their dual commercial economies, formal and informal, persisted. In time, however, and soon, there would be some who would see in the propulsive flow of clandestine trade among the Atlantic nations the natural workings of an invisible hand which, they believed, when fully released from artificial controls, would enhance the wealth of nations.[33]

III

In other, quite different realms, too, informal accommodations overcame the requirements of formal doctrine. That was especially true of religion, formally rooted as it was in credal definitions and prescriptive of both the forms of worship and behavior in everyday life. In Europe, orthodoxy, however defined, though faced with external challenges and inner deviations, could be maintained; when propagated abroad, to Christian settlers or indigenous people, it came under intense pressure to accommodate local circumstance. The result was a system of religious networks that spanned the Atlantic, orthodox at its sources but constantly adjusting and deviating at its western extremities in response to shifting pressures.

Two essays explore this process from two radically different points of view. One traces the fortunes of a single tightly disciplined Catholic order seeking to maintain and promote strict Counter-Reformation orthodoxy; the other explores the intersections of three loosely defined and overlapping dissident Protestant sects seeking to express their free-flowing spiritual passions in ways denied to them in Europe's dense social atmosphere, and to expand the boundaries of toleration. But different as they were, both Jesuit priests and Protestant sectarians were products of surges of religious zeal in the post-Reformation European heartland, both expressive of the explosive forces released by the break with Rome. Both struggled to maintain their integrity in the distant West; success in both cases depended on imaginative accommodation to local pressures; and in both cases the constant flow of communication among the scattered units and with the metropolitan centers, despite the great distances involved, nourished and helped sustain the religious life of their communities.

J. Gabriel Martínez-Serna gives us a detailed picture of the remarkable administrative organization of the Jesuit order. Supporting and binding together the great array of Jesuit missions, colleges, residences, and estates lay a tightly controlled system of procurators. Operating with remarkably efficiency deep within the order's inner workings, appointed for short periods, their performances in office closely monitored, and organized into a disciplined hierarchical structure that linked the local provinces to the Society's procurator general in Rome, ultimately to its General Congregation, the procurators were the managers of the order's immense properties, its real estate agents, salesmen, purchasers, bookkeepers, and often the intermediaries between the Society and Church and State. Some procurators held well-established, regular positions, but the system remained sensitive to shifting needs, and new ad hoc positions were created to deal with new problems and altered priorities.

While the structure of these administrative offices linked the American provinces to the European sources of authority, it also spread laterally across the New World, as it had across Europe, covering much of Catholic America in a network that stretched from the Great Lakes to Chile, Paraguay, and Brazil. Along the system's many intersecting lines of transnational, pan-Atlantic communication flowed orders, requests, reports, funds, goods, equipment, books, and people. More efficient than the agents of imperial government, the procurators made possible the Jesuits' remarkable success in carrying out their mission—often more successfully than the mendicant priests with whom they commonly competed—which was to advance the goals of the Counter-Reformation in Christian areas and to bring Christianity to the pagan peoples of America and other benighted lands.

Nothing could be more different from the Jesuits' disciplined, well-organized efforts to impose on a pagan world the pure doctrine of Counter-Reformation Catholicism than the sprawling, dynamic struggles of the Mennonites, Quakers, and Pietists to escape persecution in Europe and find in America the fulfillment of their sectarian aspirations. Products of the wave of evangelicalism that swept through Europe in the late seventeenth and early eighteenth centuries and that enflamed the outer fringes of English Protestantism, they were radical reformists, tolerationists, passionately devoted to nondoctrinal personal piety. The picture Rosalind Beiler sketches is that of a swirling world of harassed and passionate people in constant motion throughout Western Europe, dodging persecution, seeking help from their own parochial leaders, from local authorities, and from roving agents of similar groups, and es-

tablishing throughout the German- and Dutch-speaking world a series
of networks that would become migration corridors, some leading in
the end to transatlantic destinations. "Each group," Beiler writes, "developed regular transnational communication channels in their attempts
to fight religious discrimination or spread their ideas about reforming
society." She describes how in all these cases channels of information
served first to foster group identity and solidarity, then to serve the immediate needs of their imperiled co-religionists seeking the indulgence
of state authorities, and finally to provide a mechanism for the transfer
of groups of their people to settlements overseas.

It was a complex world, inconspicuous within the major flows of
European and British history, but vividly alive. There were designated
collection points for funds, information, and people, "correspondence
centers or hubs," and "fluid and flexible series of connections and intersections" that kept the dissenters' world in motion.

The sects shared the broad culture of radical Protestantism but they
had no common origins. Some were English, others were Dutch, most
were Rhineland Germans; but contacts among them were common. For,
although they shared no strict confessional discipline, their common
piety bridged linguistic, territorial, and national differences. They gathered in shifting, fluid congregations, each of which "carried its own utopia, and individuals moved easily from one circle into another, punctuat-
ing their advents and departure with appropriate religious revelation.
Men dropped in and out of groups, recanting previous errors, writing
confessions and testimonials . . . it was incumbent upon each of the radical sects to distinguish itself from the teeming mass, and much energy
was expanded upon touting the superiority of one future society over its
rivals."[34]

Seeking refuge from persecution, freedom of expression, and often
the realization of millennial hopes, they moved, as refugees, from place
to place. Potential settlers for sparsely populated borderlands and overseas colonies, they caught the attention of both British officials and
European promoters of migration, some of whom were benevolent benefactors of dissident religions, some agents for landowners seeking tenants, others predatory "Newlanders" seeking profits by exploiting the
Pietists' discontents. An immense intra- and intercontinental transit system developed, arching north from the lower Palatinate near the Swiss

border, through minor principalities from which local groups of emigrants moved into the streams of refugees that flowed north, east, and west to marginal lands and pockets of toleration throughout Europe, and to the emigration hub of Rotterdam, where they joined the Dutch, north German, and French Protestant refugees who gathered there. While some settled in Prussia or on small isolated principalities and the Danubian lands, others sailed west from Rotterdam to Southampton, where English recruits were waiting to join the dangerous ocean crossing and to settle in the near backcountry of North America, from inland New York south to the Shenandoah Valley.[35]

The Lutheran Pietists were especially well organized. From their headquarters at their remarkable theological, educational, and medical center in Halle, near Leipzig, dominated by the powerful presence of August Hermann Francke, they spun a web of their own. It stretched from lower Austria through central and northern Europe, across southern England where they shared in the philanthropic work of the Church of England, to colonies and scattered settlements in North America. Not only was the Pietists' transatlantic network a communication channel through which the experience of worship, the meaning of faith, and the interpretation of scripture could be shared and the community's identity reinforced, it was also a unique commercial arrangement. For from Halle the Lutheran Pietists managed a highly successful Euro-Atlantic trade in pharmaceuticals, distributing a broad range of medicines, medical ideas, and medical texts through Europe and the North Atlantic world. "An outgrowth of the enterprise of reform and transatlantic mission of a voluntary and independent religious foundation," the Pietists' pharmaceutical trade, flowing from Halle through routes pioneered by emigrants, penetrated markets and shaped medical practice wherever it touched, and carried with it a heavy freight of Pietist lore.[36]

Even more widespread through the Atlantic world were the once-despised and persecuted Quakers. By the end of the seventeenth century they were established in most of Britain's Atlantic colonies, and they flourished as well, after years of deprivation, at home. Scattered in units as small as families and households, they were seldom truly isolated. The coordination of their system of meetings—local (monthly), regional (quarterly), and general (yearly)—linked groups living on the far borderlands of European settlement with those at the metropolitan core.

And embracing them all was the "itinerant ministry," the traveling agents of the Society, male and female, whose ceaseless intercolonial and transatlantic voyages enabled them to transmit the experience of each individual and each group to all others. The flow of the itinerants' energies and confessional tracts constituted the "bloodstream of the transatlantic Society of Friends."[37]

More complex in their spread through the Atlantic world and no less interactive were the communities of Spanish and Portuguese Jews—professing Jews in British, Dutch, and French America; crypto-Jews, *marranos*, New Christians, and *conversos* in Spanish and Portuguese America. Their secondary migrations from the Netherlands and elsewhere in Europe led them to settlements in the Western Hemisphere where, located in small numbers throughout Latin America, in a few places in North America, and mainly in the Dutch Caribbean Islands, they formed networks of shared culture and commerce. Though they suffered civil disabilities ranging from inquisitorial persecution to special taxation, for much of the seventeenth and early eighteenth centuries they prospered. At the height of their prosperity, between one-quarter and one-third of the entire white populations of Suriname and Curaçao were Jews. Curaçao, "the Amsterdam of the Caribbean," "a bridge between Spanish America, English America, and French America," was their hemispheric center, "the principal hub of Jewish inter-American trade," which circulated through the island's main port of Willemstad to all of the West Indian and North American ports and, by way of co-religionists abroad, to major commercial centers in Western Europe as well.[38]

Was all of this uniquely Atlantic? The Quaker networks were almost entirely confined to Anglo-America and the Dutch and Rhenish principalities, and while the greater Jewish Diaspora had deep roots in eastern Europe, the Mediterranean coastal regions, and the Ottoman Middle East, the direct commercial contacts of the Jews in the Western Hemisphere rarely extended beyond the Atlantic and Baltic ports of Europe and the slaving stations of West Africa. Regionalists not globalists, the Jewish merchants in the Americas engaged in Asian commerce only indirectly. Their European kinsmen and other Sephardic and New Christian merchants intermediated, exchanging the Americans' sugar and other local products for such Asian imports as spices, cotton goods, silk cloth, and precious stones.[39]

But the Jesuits *were* globalists. The reach of their missions extended from central Europe to the Philippines, India, China, and Japan as well as to the Americas. And there remain in the Lutheran archives in Halle and elsewhere in Germany reports sent back to Europe by the Lutheran Pietists' missionaries in India, the first Protestants to proselytize the native peoples in Asia. In both cases the experiences East and West were radically different. Halle's leader Francke corresponded freely and fully with missionaries and co-religionists in Europe, England, and America, kept close contact with German emigrants and other pious transatlantic travelers, and with them all shared views on "every imaginable sphere, from general living conditions, such as food, climate, and geographical condition, to the affairs of the North American Indians and political conditions, to opportunities for earning a living through craft, manufacturing, and trade."[40]

He had no such communion with the Pietists' constituents in India. From his former students who led the minuscule Pietist mission in Tranquebar, near Madras and Pondicherry at the southeastern tip of India, he received only reports of struggles with the secular authorities of the small Danish colony in which the mission was located and with the feckless, at times barbarous adventurers and wanderers who gathered there. The missionaries' letters from India were both proud and piteous, ambitious and despairing. Nothing in their background or training for the Atlantic missions had prepared them for the obstacles they faced in Tranquebar and which they struggled to overcome: *theological* obstacles (they were baffled by the impressive heathenism of the Hindus); *confessional* (they were faced not only with "the spite and malice" of other, long-established Protestants in the trading community, but also with "the Roman horror" [*Römische Greuel*]); and *linguistic* (to reach the local populations they had to learn Danish and then Tamil through Portuguese translations). They rejoiced in small and unreliable successes in converting native peoples, and they constantly begged for support, in personnel and funds, explaining the miseries they were enduring, and hoping that they would not in the end regret the time and effort they were devoting to the souls of largely impervious heathens. In reply,

Francke could only remind them that "in India among the heathen you
are on a different field of battle than we are in Europe," urging them "to
teach and admonish" the other, wayward Christians as well as the pagans, and always to "preserve, wisely and carefully," their unique heritage of evangelical Pietism. The Indian mission was no replica of the
familiar Euro-Christian Pietist community or its extension in the American West, but a faint, scarcely palpable touch on an utterly remote
world beyond Francke's influence or comprehension.[41]

The Jesuits' missions in Asia were great achievements next to the
Pietists' marginal efforts, but their worlds East and West were no less
different. For them the American natives had long been an ideal population of pagans. Though they were "as divergent and mutually unrelated
as the Iroquoians of the Great Lakes, the Tupi-Guarani of the River
Plate and Amazonian regions, the Araucanians of Chile, and various
Uto-Aztec groups of northwestern New Spain and Baja California," together they formed in the Jesuits' minds what Martínez-Serna has called
a "distinct ontological category . . . a *tabula rasa* or a sort of *gens
angelicum*, i.e. a race of innocents ready to receive the Gospel."[42] All
their missionary efforts were based on that premise. But no one could
think the same of the Chinese, the Japanese, or the peoples of India. Nor
in those regions could the Jesuits reach, as they did in the Americas,
deeply and broadly into the lives of ordinary people.

In China and Japan they faced well-organized, self-protective, and sophisticated empires and kingdoms. They sought favors from the powers
in the land, including the elemental privilege of preaching. Never secure
in their positions or persons, subject everywhere to the whims of authorities (after years of proselytizing successes they were suppressed in
Japan in 1614, in China in 1724), they were rarely able to penetrate
deeply into the advanced and intricate cultures they faced. Often they
were in awe of the Asians' intellectual world; some were suspected of
having succumbed to its attractions. Their efforts "to integrate Christianity and the indigenous culture" led to the Chinese Rites Controversy, in which, in 1715 and 1742, the papacy, after a century of debate
and controversy, flatly outlawed the subtle "Confucian-Christian synthesis" that the Jesuits had so carefully devised. The papal prohibitions
crushed the Jesuits' efforts to draw the Chinese to Christianity by com-

promise, infuriated the Kangxi emperor, and led to the effective end of the Jesuits' mission.[43]

But even without the papal interdictions, the Jesuits' efforts to create effective compromises in Asia would not have succeeded. For beyond the fact that the Chinese, the Japanese, and other Asians could not be conceived of as a *tabula rasa*, Christianity was "inextricably linked to European culture," and few accessible Asians, even the most amenable, were willing to adopt "a eurocentric mental attitude." The argument of the Jesuits' ruling "visitor" in Japan that "becoming a follower of Christ does not mean becoming a European or ceasing to be Japanese" was unconvincing. In the end the Jesuits' community in China remained a harassed sect, largely of illiterate commoners, and in Japan subject to outright persecution, with attraction only "to people at the periphery of society."[44]

Though the global relevance of the prohibitions to all forms of compromise was obvious, their effect on the Jesuits' American missions, from the Great Lakes to Patagonia, was minimal. There, relieved of competition from effective native theologians and indigenous state power, the Jesuits' syncretism flourished, even when the Chinese rites edicts were explicitly invoked. The bishop of Québec, well informed on events in China and fearful of similar problems in New France, harassed the Jesuits in every way he could, condemning them for tolerating, even encouraging, "Christians who spoke no French, worshipped a Manitou, and lived like savages." Yet the Jesuits' belief persisted that "Indians could be good Christians and good allies without being assimilated to French 'civilization.'" The Indians, they insisted, could remain essentially as they were—semi-sedentary, outwardly "savage," preoccupied with dreams and other seemingly non-Christian ideas, and in that state, if properly instructed and disciplined, they might "achieve a kind of ideal primitive Christianity." So the religion of the Iroquois in New France, Allan Greer writes, "combined native and European elements in complex ways . . . an array of permutations and combinations: some synthesis, some unconsummated dialogue, some oil-and-water divergences." All of this the Jesuits, acutely sensitive and carefully responsive to cultural nuances—reacting with "cultural nimbleness unparalleled in its time in European civilization"—recorded in reports that, carefully edited for publication as *Relations*, together form a virtual textbook of closely observed comparative ethnography.[45]

What the Jesuits in Canada could consider ideal, others elsewhere in Catholic America accepted as intractable reality. In the Andes, official "extirpators" were dedicated to rooting out all evidence of indigenous religions and the cultures that nourished them. Working with "controlled ferocity," they followed approved protocols of interrogation, desecration, reconstruction, public shaming, and physical punishment. But often, after sweeping campaigns (*diligencias*) the extirpators were deeply discouraged; in some cases, they admitted failure. For despite their efforts, "indigenous gods and Andean religious organizations . . . survived the attempted spiritual conquest," and the result was various forms of "Andean Christianities" in which the Indians melded new forms of worship with ancient traditions, and so kept contact with their "rich ancestral mythology and [the] fundamental dimensions of their religious systems"—precisely the syncretism that had failed to develop in Asia.[46]

The unique bearing of Christian beliefs and ideas on Europe's engagement in the Americas is explored at a different level in Jorge Cañizares-Esguerra's discussion of the typological readings of the Bible, an epitome of his extensive research and writing on this subject. Latent in the thinking of Europeans—Spanish, Portuguese, Dutch, and English—was the instinct to enclose the transforming experience of Europe's discovery and conquest of the Americas within the grand narrative of Christian history. Typological readings of the Bible, both learned and popular, by relating current and impending events to what were assumed to be prefigurations in biblical lore and by viewing them as simulacra that could only have been intended as anticipations and models, made the strange new world familiar, illuminated the dark unknown, and legitimized the deepening encounters.

Thus for some, the exodus of the Israelites prefigured the wanderings of the Aztecs to Mexico where they built a temple destined to be destroyed. For others the Israelites' exodus was the clear anticipation of the migration of the Puritans to New England where they would create a new Jerusalem. The conquest of Mexico was clearly prefigured in Revelation 12; the reception of the image of Our Lady of Guadalupe was the fulfillment of Moses's reception of the Ten Commandments; and the grid plans of the Spanish-American cities were typologically the recreation of the city of Jerusalem (Ezekiel 40–47).

In the biblical culture shared by all the Christian Euro-Atlantic peoples, typological concepts, expressed in prose, poetry, and elaborate iconographic details, circulated across national and confessional boundaries. And at the highest theological level of millenarian, eschatological thought, a theme emerged that made the Atlantic connection uniquely important for an understanding of the entire Christian pageant. For both Catholic and Puritan theologians the indigenous peoples, being pagan, had long been the victims, the bondsmen and slaves, of Satan. America was the Devil's refuge. The word of Christ and the zeal of true Christians having driven Satan from the Old World, he had turned to "those barbarous nations dwelling upon the northern ocean (whither the sound of Christ had not yet come)," and there he had flourished, keeping the natives in the darkness of paganism and threatening with encroaching barbarism the souls of incoming Christian settlers. He was cunning, imaginative, self-protective, and aggressive, and he would survive in the New World despite the efforts to defeat him, until God's final triumph, led by his devoted missionaries, put an end to his dominion.[47]

It was a biblical reading, as much Iberian as Puritan, as clearly articulated by the Jesuit José de Acosta as by the Anglican Joseph Mede, that construed the Atlantic world and the great motions within it as a crucial and unique battleground in the struggle for Christian fulfillment. In this, the Old World and the New were closely bound together; their histories were entangled; the destiny of neither could be understood without the other.

IV

Cañizares-Esguerra has also explored a different and contrasting realm of Atlantic history in which Iberia, northern Europe, and the Americas were closely entangled. In "The Colonial Iberian Roots of the Scientific Revolution," he writes that the first efflorescence of empirical natural science appeared, however incompletely, not in the seventeenth-century Protestant world of the northwestern European pansophists, nor in London's fledgling Royal Society or in the Académie Royale des Sciences, but in the "Iberian colonial origins of key ideas" associated with the intellectual changes that would revolutionize the world. Francis Bacon, he suggests, "had the Iberians in mind when he wrote *The New Atlantis*," for in the texts of Spanish intellectuals like Andrés Garcia de Céspedes, Pedro Fernández Quiros, José de Acosta, and Juan de Cárdenas lay a deep fund of knowledge of botany, cosmography, natural history, natural philosophy, cartography, and the marvels and wonders of the New World that circulated among Europe's scholars and scientists and, though little noted thereafter, formed something of a substructure on which the North European empiricists could build.[48]

Cañizares-Esguerra's sources in his study of the Iberian roots of the scientific revolution are largely literary texts, but he refers as well, in passing, to the everyday work of Spanish pilots, apothecaries, mechanics, inventors, and artisans of all kinds. How their everyday work entered into and helped create the first major phase of the scientific revolution was sketched in theoretical terms in the 1930s by the Marxist historical sociologist Edgar Zilsel.

Modern empirical science, Zilsel argued, emerged, around 1600, from the creative interactions between, on the one hand, traditional humanist scholars trained in logic and the analysis of texts and abstract propositions, and, on the other, artisans—"artist-engineers"—working on the ordinary, real-world problems of "mechanics, chemistry, metallurgy, geometry, anatomy, and acoustics." There was, of course, nothing new in the coexistence of the empiricism of the crafts with the systematic rationalism of "university scholars and humanistic *literati*," nor in the philosophers' appreciation of craft inventiveness. But the "real science is born when . . . the experimental method of the craftsman overcomes the prejudice against manual work and is adopted by rationally trained university-scholars." The disdain of the *literati* for manual work and "the distinction between *understanding* and *doing*" persisted until intense demands were made for new and accurate knowledge of the world—especially knowledge of the New World, its nature, its people, and above all the possibility of its exploitation. It was then, toward the end of the sixteenth century and in the early seventeenth century, Zilsel wrote, that "the experimental method [was] adopted by rationally trained scholars of the educated upper class," and in that fusion "modern science is born."[49]

Zilsel's general insight, reflected in Cañizares-Esguerra's comments, has now been explored, expanded, and focused clearly on Spain's Atlantic world by Antonio Barrera-Osorio. Well before 1600, he explains in his book on the Spanish-American empire and the scientific revolution, Spain's exploitation of America demanded new technology and sophisticated scientific activities of all kinds. "With the establishment of the Spanish empire in the New World came the need for a practical understanding of the natural world there through institutions, practices, and mechanisms for exploring nature, mapping new lands and the oceans, and collecting commodities, curiosities, and information." For this, old practices had to be revised or reinvented; theory had to be brought to bear on practice and practice on theory; and new devices and procedures had to be devised—research expeditions, questionnaires, juntas of experts for organizing information and performing tests "to determine claims of truth." Funded by the Crown as well as by concerned economic interests, and refined by Spain's distinguished scholars and scientists, "empirical practices became the tool to study nature." The Casa de la Contratación, Spain's central agency for managing its overseas commerce, became "a veritable Chamber of Knowledge" as the nation's involvement with the Western Hemisphere grew and demand heightened for knowledge of American commodities, improved navigation techniques, better instruments for the exploitation of natural resources, and a more accurate understanding of the American people.[50]

In its sixteenth-century euphoria, Spain seemed confident, Barrera-Osorio writes, that by its might, flamboyant adventurism, and accumulation of practical knowledge it could control its Atlantic world. But by the seventeenth century the growing magnitude and complexity of the imperial problems, compounded by the nation's endless military engagements in Europe, overwhelmed that early confidence and drained resources and enthusiasm for projects it had once supported. Urgency faded for the pursuit of natural history and technology. But by then, Spain's American communities were developing their own scholars and scientists and creating their own territorial and cultural identities, thereby laying the foundation for what would become the Enlightenment in Latin America.[51]

Such, Barrera-Osorio writes, was the influence of the Atlantic connections on the development of sixteenth-century empirical science. Our understanding of the history of science is incomplete, he concludes, if it does not situate "the emergence of empirical practices in its Atlantic context"—however embedded they may have been in the continuing fascination with magic, monsters, and wondrous events.[52] But was the Atlantic context of early empirical science only an Iberian phenomenon? Something more general was at work. "There is a chronological coincidence between European expansion and the institutionalization of empirical practices in European kingdoms." And indeed, the Atlantic connections account in part for the emergence of several scientific academies in seventeenth-century Europe and America, "with the goal of obtaining power through knowledge: knowledge about routes, commodities, agricultural products, medicine, exotic animals, and wandering stars." Spain's successful model for the development of empirical knowledge "helped other Europeans to establish their own models of domination based on this type of knowledge, which would become the new science of the seventeenth century."[53]

That new science represented a shift from Spain to England and northern Europe, to the pansophists, and to the Anglo-European circles of John Dury, Samuel Hartlib, and Jan Comenius, who sought to mobilize and employ all of human knowledge for the reformation of everything from politics to agriculture and from commerce and poverty to law and the arts. It was the start of the great quest for the recovery of what Hartlib, that frenetic Anglo-German-Polish virtuoso of new knowledge and reform, called "man's lost dominion over nature."[54]

It had no national boundaries. Despite Spain's policy of keeping the details of its empire secret, word of the flora and fauna, the geography and natural history of Iberian America circulated widely, and in the ferment of expanding fields of knowledge, the Americas, Europe, and Africa continued to be intimately involved. It was as part of the expanding inquiry into new worlds of knowledge that in the seventeenth and eighteenth centuries sophisticated institutions of scientific inquiry sponsored explorations into the deep interiors of the Americas.[55]

Paris, with its salons glittering with famous scientists and scholars—Buffon, Cassini, the Bernouillis, Maupertuis, Bougainville, Condorcet, Helvétius, Quesnay, Réamur—and with its flourishing, state-supported Académie Royale des Sciences, was the epicenter of Europe's intellectual life and the major sponsor of scientific explorations. Challenged by England's Royal Society on the great question of the Earth's shape, the

Académie launched two official expeditions, to the Arctic Circle and to the viceroyalty of Peru, to settle the matter, and thereby initiated a series of famous scientific missions that bound the Old World and the New into a transnational community in search of the deeper mysteries of nature.[56]

Cooperative international scientific expeditions multiplied—twenty-four were dispatched to Peru before 1805, eleven of them French. Though Spain joined in the French expeditions as early as 1735, its independent involvements in what Charles III called "the methodical examination . . . of my American dominions . . . to promote the progress of the physical sciences" came in the 1770s and 1780s, concentrated on the fiercely competitive search for national commodities of value for trade and for relief from foreign suppliers. The French expeditions flourished, and their reports proved to be major documents in the intellectual history of the Atlantic world. From one of the first, and best publicized— the twenty-month descent, in 1744 and 1745, of the Amazon River to settle the debate on the shape of the globe—came a report, Charles-Marie de la Condamine's *Relation abrégée d'un voyage fait dans l'intérieur de l'Amérique méridionale,* which, Neil Safier has explained, circulated throughout Europe in several translations, and in Latin America as well. Though a record of endless mishaps and travails, it proved to be the first of "a long line of ethnographic works by French missionaries and explorers of Brazil and the rest of South America"; it led "several waves of Portuguese, Spanish, German, and Dutch explorers," Safier writes, "through the darkest folds of the Amazon jungle"; and it introduced "a broad public to a new world which, over the two-and-a-half centuries to follow, would become . . . a powerful metaphor for the richness and diversity of the Earth's plant and animal life."[57]

Scientific, as distinct from commercial and exploratory, expeditions were sent elsewhere as well—to the Mediterranean, to the Levant, and late in the century to the Pacific. But except for the rarely visited Pacific islands and the "terra Australis" whose settlement and exploration followed and were in part responses to the breakup of the Atlantic empires, these were not *terrae incognitae* in the same sense. Their mysteries—anthropological and ethnographic as well as botanical and natural-historical—had long been known and studied, and could not be considered, as could the deep recesses of the unknown American continents, as "ripe for the tools of Enlightenment science" and as an unrivaled laboratory for scientific experimentation.[58]

The Enlightenment, Neil Safier points out, was "an *itinerant* enterprise," its ideas "portable," flowing through networks that were not limited to a single empire or a single geographical center. So the Brazilian Hipólito da Costa, educated in Portugal's University of Coimbra, sought botanical specimens on behalf of the Portuguese government in Pennsylvania, the lore of tobacco production in Virginia and Maryland, the organization of the whaling industry in Nantucket, the sources of cochineal dye in Mexico, and knowledge of plants, trees, and shrubs wherever he went—New York, Québec, New England, and his native Brazil. And in the major phase of his career, as editor in London of the Lusophone journal *Correio Braziliense*, he promoted for the entire Portuguese/Brazilian world the litany of enlightened causes, from the virtues of a free press to the abolition of the slave trade and above all the supreme value of "rational discourses in religion, culture, and politics."

How important the Western Hemisphere was for the advance of medical science, how entangled the two worlds were, is vividly shown in Londa Schiebinger's study of the struggle to develop tropical medicine in the West Indies, "that cauldron of cultural upheaval," a region that proved to be a "fertile ground for scientific innovation." It was not a matter of knowledgeable, sophisticated European scientists devising and imposing treatment for severe tropical diseases among African slaves. Such treatments as there were emerged from "the mixing and hybridization, collecting, sorting, and extinctions of knowledge" among Amerindians, Africans, and Europeans. That blended scientific endeavor, involving strange experiments and counterintuitive, exotic approaches to healing and prevention, was profoundly Atlantic, as European-trained physicians seeking to identify the nature of tropical diseases and to devise effective cures competed and worked with African slave doctors, free black practitioners, knowledgeable overseers, and midwives of both races. The results of this creative pooling of traditions and cooperation among diverse practitioners would in time circulate across once-restrictive imperial and linguistic boundaries and become part of the scientific and cultural lore of the Western world.

In this process local, parochial developments in the treatment of tropical diseases entered into the cosmopolitan world and became part of broader cultures. But this process—the emergence of what has been called "provincial cosmopolitanism"—was not confined to medicine and science.[59] As the Euro-American communities matured, they pressed in many ways against the limits of their parochial origins, and expanded into the greater world of Atlantic cosmopolitanism.

V

There can be no better illustration of this vital process than the early history of Puritan Boston. The original community, a product of the distinctive though diverse views of zealous dissenters from the formal demands of Anglican worship, was utterly self-absorbed as it sought to define its own local orthodoxy and create some degree of stability in the disordered circumstances of the initial settlement. Struggling for two generations to establish its distinctive identity, the community, fissiparous in its nature, gradually resolved the diverse pressures within it. Emerging from its narcissistic turmoils, it reached out beyond itself to merge in significant ways with the greater, pan-Atlantic world.

How provincial cosmopolitanism developed in this one locality, what its range and limitations were, and how it affected many spheres of life are described by Mark Peterson. Typical in many ways of the experience of European communities throughout the Americas, Boston's local history can be transposed into different linguistic, cultural, and socioeconomic settings.

As Peterson explains, two distinct though overlapping lines of force emerged in the first century of Boston's existence. One was commercial, as the town's small patriciate found lucrative markets for regional produce, mainly in the Caribbean islands and the Iberian Peninsula. These commercial contacts, many of which depended, directly or indirectly, on the existence of plantation slavery, were secular, profit-oriented, and increasingly free of the asceticism that had dominated the lives of Boston's earliest Puritan traders. The new commercial leaders were Restoration adventurers, well aware of the greater world, alert to the possibilities of profits in far-flung trade and in the exploitation of undeveloped land. And they knew not only how to take advantage of existing networks abroad but also how to create their own private, pan-Atlantic webs, often secured by kinship links, within the intricate complexities of the overall Atlantic commercial system. Dominant in the community's commerce, they gained control of politics as well, and so formed a Creole oligarchy only lightly supervised from "home."

It was from this background that the Belcher family, tradesmen and tavern keepers at the start, rose to prominence and to the affluence that would allow young Jonathan to visit England, where he secured his family's interests, and to roam through Europe paying his respects to the monuments of Protestant success. There, remarkably, improbably, he established a personal relationship with the court of Hanover in general and in particular with the Princess Sophia, chatted for several hours with Leibniz in Berlin, and ultimately presented to the princess, as a token from America, an Indian slave boy, whom she found enchanting and kept by her side. What Belcher said of the boy could be said of himself: "If he behaves himself well, his fortune is made for this world." Jonathan indeed behaved himself well in this cosmopolitan world, returning to Boston where he advanced his family's fortunes and ended his career as royal governor, first of Massachusetts and New Hampshire, then of New Jersey. The associations he had secured with Europe's commercial and political regimes were secure and radiated through links to the Rhineland, Prussia, the Netherlands, and Britain.

In the same years, Peterson explains, Cotton Mather, a third-generation Boston-born preacher and scholar, was weaving his own web of associations in Europe, entering through his prolific writings (over 450 separate imprints) the pan-Atlantic Republic of Letters. Though nostalgic for the heroics of his Puritan ancestors, he was desperate to transcend the provincialism around him. So he read everything, from everywhere, in any number of languages, struggled to reconcile traditional Puritan theology with what he knew of advanced theories of man and nature that were sweeping through Europe, and secured, through correspondence, ties not with the courtly figures who fascinated Belcher but, we learn from Peterson, with the likes of Boyle, Starkey, and above all that key, ever-present figure in turn-of-the-century reform Protestantism, August Hermann Francke, in Halle.

It was his correspondence with Francke that not only gave Mather direct access to the cosmopolitan world of advanced Protestant thought but also inspired him to develop, on the eve of what he believed was the beginning of the end of time and the advent of universal redemption, his own version of the eternal principles of true Christianity. Relishing the opportunity offered by the correspondence with the "incomparable," the "marvelous" Francke, and convinced that, in this transnational, poly-lingual relationship, he was helping to end the estrangement of New England Puritanism from mainstream Protestantism while at the same time contributing to the spiritual revival movement in Europe, he began what proved to be fifteen years of zealous engagement with the most active centers of Pietism in Germany, Britain, and Switzerland.[60]

For Mather, Francke was the central, charismatic figure in an international program of moral reformation and spiritual renewal—in effect a second Reformation—and it was over the shared doctrines of ecumenism and the sacred mission of proselytizing the heathens that Mather could most easily join hands with "this great man . . . the wonder of Europe." Corresponding directly and through emissaries, they quickly agreed that the splintered Protestant churches should coalesce and that for two centuries the Reformation had neglected the sacred obligation to convert the pagan peoples. The time had come for such as they to fulfill the missionary obligation. Together they developed "a theology of missions" to be adopted by all Protestant churches. Both could point to useful efforts that had been made in that direction. Francke described Halle's mission in Tranquebar, while Mather wrote about John Eliot's "praying Indian" towns of New England.[61]

Their correspondence flourished. Francke, in Halle, eager to advance true Christianity in America and already well informed on the Pietists' settlements in Pennsylvania and to a lesser extent on missionary work in New England, sent Mather in Boston one of his treatises on true Christianity together with his personal prayers so that "at so vast a distance of places, our hearts will be, nevertheless, more and more united." His published description of the institutions he had created in Halle (*Pietas Hallensis,* 1705) overwhelmed the Bostonian. They included, Mather reported in his most learned style, a *"Collegium Orientale Theologicum,"* a *"gynæcium* for young gentlewomen," two *"cherotrophea"* for poor widows, a seminary for future teachers, an *"officina pharmaceutica* [where] the noblest remedies upon earth are known," an orphan house, schools to teach religion and "all sorts of good literature," a university, a hospital, and printing presses for biblical translations and cheap editions of Bibles and psalters. Intimidated by these "vast projects

. . . for religion and learning" that had been sparked by the "fire of God
which thus flames in the heart of Germany," and flattered not only by
Francke's general interest in "us obscure Americans" but by the inclusion of his personal letter to 'The Reverend Dr. Cotton Mather' in the
third edition of Francke's *Pietas Hallensis* (1716), Mather replied effu-
sively and self-consciously to his worldly correspondent.[62]

"We Americans here live beyond ultima Thule," he wrote, "in a country which was unknown to both Strabo and Caesar, but not unknown to
Christ." He was able proudly to describe the flourishing state of New
England's churches, refer to Boston's new orphanage, modeled, he said,
on Halle's, and to send Francke for his foundations a copy of his rhap-
sodic biography of Eliot, several theology treatises of his own, and
gifts of books, together with charitable donations in the form of bills
of exchange and a piece of gold, transmitted by "Mr. Belcher." And
with the help of Francke and intermediaries in London, Mather made
direct contact with the two principal missionaries in Tranquebar, sending them greetings and some of his publications, which he called "little
engines of piety."[63]

But if they agreed that all missions did the work of God, all missionary fields, Mather wrote, were not the same. While he praised Halle's
work among the heathens in India, he reminded Francke of the transcendent importance of America in the proselytizing of Christianity
in these last days. Invoking the geography of Satan's influence that
had been so thoroughly explored a century and more earlier—in effect
paraphrasing the words of the Jesuit Acosta—he rehearsed again, for
Francke's benefit, the widespread belief that the West, the Americas,
had been the preserve of the Antichrist, who, having been driven from
Christian Europe, had taken refuge in the Western continents. But the
Puritan missions in New England, he assured Francke, were now beginning to transform darkness into light—and just in time. For America,
where until now Satan had held his benighted people in bondage and
darkness, had been chosen by God as the site of his ultimate eschatological events, hence the urgency and transcendent importance of the Puritans' missionary labors. It was not easy work, but in the end it would be
saved by God's gift of the Holy Spirit "to those who ask Him for it."[64]

Boston, in which all this was stirring, was one small, provincial hub
among many that dotted the coastal regions of the Atlantic basin—nu-

clei "for the consolidation of the Atlantic commercial community and for the sociopolitical integration of the Americas," reaching out to the cosmopolitan centers. The town's radiating lines of contact formed subordinate networks within the arterial flows of the region's life. By the 1760s the town was alive with contentious views of public authority and acutely sensitive to the deeper motions of the Enlightenment's challenge to the traditional structures of power. It was from Boston that the first open challenges to Britain's monarchical authority were mounted, and from its presses, in the years that followed, came vital discourses on the uses and misuses of power, the moral foundations of public authority, and the acceptable limits of coercion. Little of this was original; most of these ideas and beliefs were the currency of liberal thought that was circulating throughout the Atlantic world, east and west, penetrating, however erratically, even the scholastic barriers of the Catholic Church.[65]

The sweeping influence of these ideas and the dynamics of constitutional and juridical reform, European in their origins, reached into the far recesses of the Western world. As the fires of reformist thought and revolutionary zeal swept across the enormous reaches of Latin America, the leading intellectuals of remote Buenos Aires, as Beatriz Dávilo explains, like their counterparts elsewhere, accepted the challenge of the new ideas and struggled, erratically, in the early years of independence to create a new political order dominated not by tradition, hierarchies, privilege, and arbitrary rule, but by the impersonal and universal ideals of reason, justice, and equality under law.

The two port towns, Boston and Buenos Aires—British and Spanish, Protestant and Catholic—were different in so many ways as to seem incomparable. But Boston had long been a vital hub of British-Atlantic commerce, and "within the Hispanic world," Susan Socolow writes, "perhaps no city benefited as dramatically from the development of the Atlantic world as did the port city of Buenos Aires." In the mid-eighteenth century the populations of the two commercial communities were of roughly equal size (though Buenos Aires's would grow much more rapidly); both were centers of contraband trade; their occupational structures differed, but approximately half of the population in both towns was engaged in "services" of one kind or another. While their exports differed greatly, both were transit points for the import and distribution of goods from Europe, and they were equally inefficient cogs in systems of imperial governance. Finally, in both cases the first forces of revolution would lead in similar ways to the displacement of one group of leaders—Crown officials and the merchant patriciate associated with them—by other, Creole elites, free of such entanglements. But there the similarities end, and the differences become revealing.[66]

Boston, relieved of imperial constraints, flourished as the capital city of a well-organized semi-autonomous province long used to open, competitive politics and a well-established legal system—one of thirteen contiguous and associated provinces that in less than two decades after independence willingly if cautiously came together into a formally constituted, federated nation-state. Their revolution was essentially a separation from the mother country followed by a wave of political reforms, not a fundamental social upheaval or a transformation of an inherited way of life. For Buenos Aires the separation from Spain meant the destruction of a complex social, political, and economic system that had existed for three centuries. While the North Americans idealized their past and sought to preserve and improve on its virtues, the Latin Americans, Dávilo informs us, "did not think that their society was the moral reserve of virtue, but rather the repository of vices inherited from despotism."

So Buenos Aires, the capital city of a recently formed and superficially governed viceroyalty, the Río de le Plata, stood alone in 1810 when the revolutionary movement began. As the leading administrative unit of a miscellany of provinces, intendancies, and cities, none of which had "horizontal" associations with each other, it led the long struggle to create, out of the sprawling jumble of Platine jurisdictions, a modern, enlightened nation-state infused with "new beliefs and a new style of behavior."[67] It was a nearly hopeless task. The several provinces of the Río de la Plata, which stretched for 2,000 miles from Upper Peru to Patagonia, had a multitude of conflicting interests. Several of the larger units had powerful desires to break away into their own autonomous states (Uruguay, Paraguay, and Upper Peru [Bolivia] would succeed), and there was no basic agreement on constitutional or political principles or on how the nation—if the old viceroyalty were to become a nation—should be organized.

The result was years of bitter disputes between centralists and au-

tonomists, *criolles* and *peninsulares,* moderates and radicals that ended in
sporadic warfare as the shifting leadership of the *porteño* centralists sent
militia armies to the outer frontiers to compel obedience to the ill-de-
fined and fragile central authority. It was predictable that diverse interests would clash throughout the former viceroyalty once the "vertical"
hierarchical links from the separate jurisdictions to the Crown were destroyed, but that the armed conflicts would be utterly savage could not
have been foreseen. *Porteño* armies invaded the farther provinces in
waves, met fierce resistance, terrorized the resisting communities, exiled
some of their leaders, executed others, and reduced whole districts to
ruin—until they were themselves overrun and devastated by equally
brutal royalist and provincial armies. Provincial loyalties deepened, and
with them a sense of despair that the fluctuating leadership in Buenos
Aires—juntas, triumvirates, councils, and proto-dictatorships—would
ever succeed in creating a viable modern state. Indeed it was an open
question whether the city of Buenos Aires would ever construct for itself a peaceable, workable, civil regime. The city's government as well as
the nation-state that it sought to create fell into constant disarray as one
junta, one constitutional convention, one legislative agenda followed another, creating a blur of bright initiatives, brief successes, and repeated
failures that led to phases of authoritarian rule. "By 1814, Buenos Aires
ruled over an increasingly rebellious domain, engulfed in a chronic and
indecisive war between cities, between the countryside and cities, and
between Spanish and Portuguese armies."[68]

Yet through the first two decades of independence, and especially in
the *feliz experiencia* of the early 1820s, Buenos Aires was the center of
an extraordinary effort to transform a deeply traditional, mixed-race society and an ancient, monarchical political system into an enlightened,
independent modern regime.[69] Amid all the confusion and violence, as
Dávilo explains, the city's leaders, convinced that the revolution was
"an Atlantic process . . . [and] that the North American, French, and
Hispanic American revolutions were different stages of a single process," scoured the Atlantic world for enlightened principles that might
best be employed to remodel Argentine politics and civic culture. In
those years of exuberant efforts "to balance coercion and consensus,"
the influence of Anglophone, and especially British, ideals and practices,
mores and cultural style, was dominant. The overwhelming success of

the British system was universally acknowledged. The Argentine leaders knew about Locke, Hume, Smith, Blackstone, De Lolme, and above all Bentham. But were the views of those men applicable to Argentina as an emerging nation or to Buenos Aires as its capital city? They knew also about Franklin, the *Federalist Papers,* Jefferson, and Paine. But was the United States, with its complex federalism and long tradition of effective provincial self-governance, a proper model? Could models be found in the other former Spanish colonies?

Bolívar, struggling to establish enlightened regimes in the Caribbean region and Venezuela, denounced the North American system as fatal to stability in any Latin American country ("it would be more difficult to apply to Venezuela the political system of the United States than it would be to apply to Spain that of England"), and he sought to establish, in the chaos of Central America's struggle for independence, an all-powerful central government. But others flatly disagreed. In Chile the provincial leaders believed that American federalism was an "archetype and example"; Ecuador's leading intellectual, the translator of North American state papers, believed that the U.S. Constitution was "the only hope of an oppressed people"; Uruguay's leaders modeled their first constitution on the Articles of Confederation; and in Mexico the quasi-independence of the provincial states was retained in the constitution of 1824, which combined elements of both the U.S. Constitution and Spain's innovative Cádiz constitution of 1812.[70]

The struggle continued, yet in Buenos Aires, amid the political turmoil that would end only in 1853 when Argentina succeeded in devising a viable constitutional system, much was accomplished in social reform. While the clamorous struggles for power continued, the initial *Junta Provisional* and its ruling triumvirate promoted education, the arts, industry, and agricultural reform; later assemblies abolished slavery and the slave trade, judicial torture, and the Inquisition. In the early euphoria of independence the press was declared to be free, and religious toleration was established and maintained.[71] How much a part of the pan-Atlantic circulation of meliorist ideas and enlightened ideals these efforts were, how much they reflected the *porteños'* emulation of European, British, and North American models in this age of reformist revolutions, Dávilo explores in detail in her essay.

But long before the fumbling, abrasive political experimentation of the Río de la Plata settled into the constitutional structure of modern Argentina, such ideas, circulating throughout the Atlantic world, had become commonplace. So too had the unspoken assumption that Europe, Africa, and the Americas constituted a naturally associated world. For Europeans, the Americas were extensions of their domestic domains, while for Creole Americans and those of mixed race the transoceanic east was the cultural metropolis with which, however distant, they were intimately involved.

VI

How deep these assumptions went, how broad their reach, is explored in Emma Rothschild's sensitive portrayal of the public career and inner life of David Hume. More than a biographical narrative, her essay probes the subjective worlds Hume lived in, the Enlightenment as he experienced it, the boundaries of his social and cultural perceptions, and the "oceanic connections" that bound his sensibilities into the "Atlantic milieu." Hume never ventured across the Atlantic, though he contemplated doing so, and at the outset of the Revolution declared himself to be "American in my Principles." But probing his experiences in Scotland, England, and France, Rothschild notes how far inland, for him and for the British people generally, the Atlantic world extended, how far "into the interior of provinces and into the interior of individual existence." However restricted Hume's physical movements, his mind's eye took in the broad panorama of Atlantic life and identified its distinctive characteristics. As both a government official and a well-connected, ultimately a world-famous intellectual, he knew much about the greater, global world with which Britain was becoming increasingly involved. But he knew too that all parts of the greater world were not the same, and that while Britain's engagement with the Far East, still marginal, was growing in importance, the Americas had a special meaning for the realization of ordinary Europeans' aspirations.

Hume lived deeply in his own interior world of ideas and sensibilities, but he also lived in Britain's everyday world, none of it more than 70 miles from the sea. "The oceanic world," Rothschild writes, a world of bustling port towns full of carriers, porters, ships and shops, loading and unloading, "was at the edge of the vision of almost everyone, as it was at the edge of David Hume's vision, in his childhood home in Berwickshire, or in his little room in La Fleche, as he looked toward . . . the Loire, and to Nantes and the Atlantic." And to that outward edge of cognition came floods of information, in conversations, personal letters, newspaper articles, rumors, reports of government officials, notices of commodities and prices—all of which formed a vision not of a singular global world abroad but of two quite different worlds that bore profoundly different meanings. One was a wildly exotic, heavily historic, sophisticated East Indian world "of satraps, bashaws, nabobs, nizams, and emperors" from which were being drawn magnitudes of personal wealth never before imagined but in relation to which the British were servants, dependents, at best diplomatic and military allies. The other was a primitive American world, apparently without history, seemingly empty, not ruled by bejeweled and sophisticated potentates but by stone-age tribal chieftains ruling primitive peoples who lacked any proper European sense of the meaning of possession. In Hume's eyes, both East and West were "uncivil societies," but the former drew from Europe agents of great corporations, Crown officials, and armed battalions that might ultimately challenge the satraps and seize the wealth of the land. The latter was a magnet not for officials and armies but for masses of ordinary people—tens, ultimately hundreds, of thousands—hoping to find in the West the ultimate object of their desires, a change of circumstance, expanded possibilities, above all independent and unencumbered ownership of land. "The romance of ownership of land and slaves," Rothschild writes, was "one of the defining conditions of the Atlantic world and one of the ways in which it was considered to be most different from the world of the East Indies." But the differences were larger than that. In Hume's world the Eastern empire, Rothschild writes, "represented corruption, and the Atlantic empire represented faction; the East represented superstition, and the American colonies enthusiasm; the shipping industry to the East Indies represented monopolistic power, and the shipping industry to North America . . . represented the unlimited competition of sects, or enterprises, or interests."

That Hume would be aware of these differences and would be acutely sensitive to their importance, is not surprising; the evidence was all about him. So too was the evidence, and influence, of slavery, which permeated his immediate world of the Scottish borderlands. However distant from the slave marts of Africa and the plantations of America, his world was "full of slaves," Rothschild writes, "of information about slaves, and of slaves' own information." And deeper than the commonplace and universal awareness of Atlantic slavery was the racism that underlay it, which Hume, however elevated and universalistic his view of humankind, deeply and almost casually shared. Rothschild's analysis of Hume's racism as a form of "insensitive empiricism" is not only a profound comment on the inner spheres of Hume's personal cognition but a comment as well on the latent assumptions of most Europeans on the Atlantic littoral, from the cold-eyed slavers Behrendt describes to benign humanitarians like Franklin who kept one or two for convenience, and sold them on occasion. Hume's acceptance, indeed endorsement, of the racist foundation of slavery was part of the world, the atmosphere, around him. So too was his awareness of the great motions of people responding to the magnetism of the West.

He did not need to be informed by Dr. Johnson, reporting famously on his tour of the Highlands in 1773, that there was an "epidemick disease of wandering" among the Scots that threatened "a total secession" from the ancient land. The numbers substantiated such fears. In the last fifteen years of Hume's life at least 125,000 farmers, laborers, and tradesmen and their families left Britain for America—including 3 percent of Scotland's total population as of 1760—together with 12,000 German-speaking emigrants from the Continent with the same hopes for unencumbered lives in the West. He knew all this well, as did the Scottish and Yorkshire landowners who were shocked that their tenants, crying "America that land of promise," were vacating the land and depriving them of rents.[72]

VII

These are soundings, probes, into the complexity of the Atlantic world as it developed from the first European contacts with the Americas to its mutation into a different, more global world three centuries later. The essays—efforts to search, in selected fields, beneath the surface of events for the latent structures and the underlying flow of ideas and beliefs that shaped the manifest world and bound it together—reveal the intricately woven webs of pan-Atlantic relationships. They were products not of rational designs but of multitudes of individual and group efforts to achieve limited personal and corporate goals.

There are cunning and calculating slave traders coordinating pan-Atlantic transaction cycles in the face of uncontrollable ecological, climatological, oceanographic, and demographic forces, and subject at the same time to the complex politics of the interior states of Africa. There are inland North American shopkeepers drawn half knowingly into the extemporized marketing systems of wine producers on islands thousands of miles away. There are swarms of smugglers of all nations, dealing in all sorts of contraband goods and multitudes of captive peoples, their legally subliminal transactions so voluminous as to form an independent economy that crossed all imperial boundaries and drew the commerce of rival nations together. Deep within the fabled missionary system of the Jesuits lay an integrated hierarchy of procuratorial agents that was more efficient than any of the imperial bureaucracies and that brought within the discipline of a single structure missionary establishments throughout Europe and the Americas, controlled by the order's leadership in Rome. And the fears and spiritual ambitions of scattered Protestant radicals seeking relief from persecution and some measure of independence generated informal migration patterns that linked the Rhineland and the Electoral Palatinate to Holland, England, and the far borderlands of North America. At the same time the flow of ideas— theological, scientific, sociopolitical—formed a pan-Atlantic intellectual world uniting London and Buenos Aires, Halle and Boston, Paris and Lima, Lisbon and Philadelphia. And in the exceptionally sensitive and capacious mind of one preeminent intellectual, David Hume, one can see how deep into the interior of contemporaries' awareness the distinctive Atlantic relationships went.

There were worlds beyond—Near East, Far East, Far West—with their own distinct structures and mentalities, never entirely remote from the Atlantic world. There were always points of contact among people, goods, and ideas in all of the globe's regions, but there was no global system. The Atlantic world remained distinct. In the ten generations from Columbus to Bolívar it had developed unique powers—in the propulsive, ruthless energy of its economies, the broadening enlighten-ment of its ideas, the sophistication and practical successes of its science, and the dynamics of its human diversity—that would create the culture of modernity and "the tools for world exploration, and, later, world conquest."[73]

1

Ecology, Seasonality, and the Transatlantic Slave Trade

STEPHEN D. BEHRENDT

On July 23, 1783, the African merchant Ekpenyong Ofiong wrote to inform his trading partners from Liverpool, Richard Wickstead and Company, that their captain John Burrows had anchored safely in the waters off Duke Town, Old Calabar, on May 4. During the previous eighty days Egbo Young (Ofiong's trade name) and other local Efik merchants had sold Burrows some slaves, but soon they would begin selling thousands of yams and greater numbers of slaves to Burrows to supply his ship and "tender."[1] Egbo Young stated that Burrows would send by his tender "340 or 330 slaves" and that Burrows himself would depart "with 450 or 460 Slaves aft[er] October." The African had confidence that he could meet the fall deadline, and thus that his British partners could expect to see their captain return from Kingston, Jamaica, in the early spring. As he continued: "I will not keep him long, and I think he will get back to Liverpool on the 15th or 20th day of March."[2]

In predicting months when Burrows would depart Old Calabar (in present-day Nigeria) and arrive in Liverpool, Egbo Young reveals how slave supply and demand linked to the seasonal production of African staples and American cash crops. Late July marked the beginning of the Upper Cross River's four-month yam harvest and, because ship captains purchased yams for their enslaved Africans, late July also marked the onset of Old Calabar's overseas trading season. Egbo Young believed that within three to four months he and other merchants would be able to supply Burrows with yams and slaves, as well as goods for the captain's secondary trade in ivory and palm oil.[3] By sending the captain from the Cross River in November, they would enable him to arrive at a West Indian slave market early in the New Year, during the beginning of the "in-crop" season, when planters demanded more laborers to harvest and process cash crops.[4] Egbo Young anticipated that Burrows would be able to sell his human cargo quickly and clear the West Indies in time to return to Liverpool by mid-March.[5]

Whereas Egbo Young and Richard Wickstead gauged slave supply and demand by determining the link between crop cycles and labor requirements in Africa and the Americas, historians who comment on slave trade seasonality have focused principally on New World planter demand for harvest workers.[6] The preponderance of slave trading sources written in Europe or the Americas helps explain this planter-focused discussion. Numerous letters mention planter preferences for slaves of certain ages or "ethnicities" and the best time to sell slaves in American colonies—months linked to harvests—and seasonal weather patterns.[7] Numerous shipping records document the dates when Guineamen arrived in specific American markets, such as those that place John Burrows's ship *Edward* in Kingston on December 29, 1783.[8] Few contemporary testimonies, however, identify "slaving seasons" in Africa or mention any links among African crops, farming labor, and slave supplies. Few African merchants kept written business records, and for those who did most of the papers are lost—Egbo Young's brief letter is one of the exceptions.

Though sources center on New World planters' optimal labor requirements, to understand the structure of the transatlantic slave trade one needs to examine African crops, their growth periods and their labor inputs, and to integrate this analysis with an assessment of cash crop work regimes in American markets. Slaving traders, after all, were shifting farmers between Atlantic agricultural systems: Egbo Young purchased enslaved Africans who came from farming communities; he then sold Captain Burrows yams, palm oil, plantains, and other local foodstuffs to keep those Africans alive on the Middle Passage; and of the captives who survived to arrive in Jamaica with Burrows, most would work as farmers on sugar or coffee plantations.[9] Identifying agricultural cycles and work requirements in various staple and cash crops allows one to predict both the months when African merchants would likely sell slaves and the months when American planters most demanded field labor.

In this essay I focus on African agriculture, but first I consider rainfall calendars, temperature, and oceanic winds and currents—the underlying ecology of the Atlantic world. Mariners could harness winds, but they could not alter their incidence, volume, speed, or direction. In the age of sail, downwind, leeward markets became last ports of call. In agricultural communities rains regulated when farmers cleared, planted, weeded, and harvested, and the volume of rainfall determined the types of crops they chose to grow. Rainfall dictated trading seasons, since merchants could not transport bulk goods profitably by land during downpours, which often closed dirt roads that connected ports to hinterlands. The stages in agricultural production, determined by ecology, demanded male and female farmers in shifting proportions, and those ratios relate to the incidence of slave raiding and warfare. Varying ecological realities in Africa and the Americas placed seasonal constraints on how slave buyers and sellers organized the transatlantic slave trade.

Winds, Currents, Rainfall, and Temperature

In his year-long voyage from Liverpool to Old Calabar to Jamaica and back to Liverpool, John Burrows traversed a North Atlantic world shaped by environment, climate, and physical geography. He navigated along the clockwise wind and current system that operated north of the equator. As he sailed downwind along the Bight of Biafra in April, early seasonal rains brought some relief from the 80-degree temperatures and high humidity; rains would double in volume and intensity as the summer months heated, making it almost impossible to keep people, trading goods, and foodstuffs dry. When he arrived at the Cross River estuary in early May, Burrows hired an African pilot to steer his small ship around dangerous sandbars and 45 miles upstream to Duke Town on the Calabar River. Most crewmen had never before seen the lush African tropical rainforest or dense mangroves banking the Cross and Calabar rivers. Departing Calabar (4–5°N latitude) in late October, Burrows plotted a 5,000-nautical-mile course to Barbados (13°N) and then 1,400 miles northwest to Kingston, Jamaica (18°N). Heavy equatorial rains followed the ship during the first month of its passage; they lessened in late December as the *Edward* approached the West Indies and the beginning of the five-month Caribbean dry season.[10]

The sun's heat and the earth's rotation, tilt, and gravitational constraints create regular wind, current, temperature, and rainfall in the Atlantic.[11] Warm air rises from hot equatorial latitudes and moves toward the cooler air of the poles, moving from high to low pressure. Differences in air pressure cause the winds, which bend because of the spinning of the earth. In the mid-latitudes of the Atlantic, 30–60°N and south of the equator, most winds blow from west to east. From the equator to 30°N, trade winds blow from the northeast; from the line to 30°S, they blow from the southwest. Winds drag surface water in their direction—creating currents.[12] Trade winds meet along the equator, an area of low pressure referred to as the Intertropical Convergence Zone (ITCZ), characterized by doldrums and heavy rainfall. The ITCZ moves seasonally with the sun's movement across the tropics—from 5°S in January to 13–15°N, the Sahara's southern boundary, in June. The shifting ITCZ causes most rain to fall in Atlantic summers—north of the equator from April to October, in south latitudes from January to April.[13]

Winds and currents ordered ports of call along the African Atlantic coastline. From southwest Europe, slaving vessels proceeding toward equatorial Africa sailed downwind and down current to Cape Ann. They then continued eastward into the Bight of Biafra, the western extent demarcated by pilot guides as Cape Formosa.[14] To depart the Niger or Cross River estuaries, captains steered southwest until they gained the westward-flowing equatorial current. Vessels charting from North Atlantic ports to the Angola coast, south of the equator, sailed toward the eastern promontory of Brazil (35°W longitude), tracked the Brazil Current south for one to two weeks until they could gain the West Wind Drift, and then sailed toward southern Africa and the northward-flowing Benguela Current. From the first major Angolan slaving market, Benguela, captains sailed downwind with the current to leeward markets near the Congo River estuary.[15]

Captains sailing from the African coast to the Americas also arrived first at windward landfalls. North of the equator, winds and currents cycled clockwise, positioning the Guianas, Barbados, and the Lesser Antilles as the first lands sighted. Running downwind and with the currents, sailors reached Saint-Domingue, Jamaica, Cuba (82°W), Florida and the

Carolinas (80°W), and then the Chesapeake.[16] When plantation agriculture developed in Maryland in the mid-1600s, that colony became the most leeward (38°N) major slaving market in the North Atlantic. The southern Atlantic's oceanic system rotates counter-clockwise: ships arrived off northeast Brazil and then steered downwind and downstream to Río de la Plata, the most southern major slaving market (34–35°S). To regain windward ports after reaching the Chesapeake and La Plata, masters needed to circle back thousands of miles into the Atlantic to recapture prevailing trade winds—a costly decision (see Map 1.1).[17] Winds and currents separated the Americas into North and South Atlantic systems, systems reinforced by the ability of the Portuguese to enforce their monopoly of the slave trade to Brazil. Guineamen did not sail from slaving markets north of the equator to Brazil or the Río de la Plata, or sail from South to North America.

Light or variable winds were the greatest concern to mariners in the slave trade. In Europe contrary winds delayed ship departures, as in the shallows (the Downs) off the Thames estuary. In general, light winds flowed over the African slaving latitudes (15°N–15°S) and often forced ships to remain in port, waiting for land breezes to assist departures. Entrapment in the equatorial doldrums or unusual summer westerlies and southwesterlies in the North Atlantic could double or triple the number of days on the Middle Passage, increasing the mortality risks for those on board.[18] Winter gales in the North Atlantic and occasional strong winds off the African coast challenged the most experienced mariners.[19] And captains eyed their summer calendars in the North Atlantic, knowing that a departure from Africa in July–September would place ships at risk of the Caribbean hurricane season, August 1–November 1.[20] The main threat during the hurricane season, however, was that Guineamen arriving in late summer might not have the option to freight cargo, because planters transported produce to port by mid-July to avoid increased insurance costs.

Africa's estuarial sandbars and American reefs posed hazards equal to those of marginal winds.[21] In West Africa there were deep-water anchorages only in the Lower Gambia, off the Iles de Los, and in the lower Sierra Leone River—and only the last location was sufficiently "commodious" for the largest ships.[22] In most Upper Guinea slaving outlets pilots negotiated sandbars at high tide; merchants sent ships there

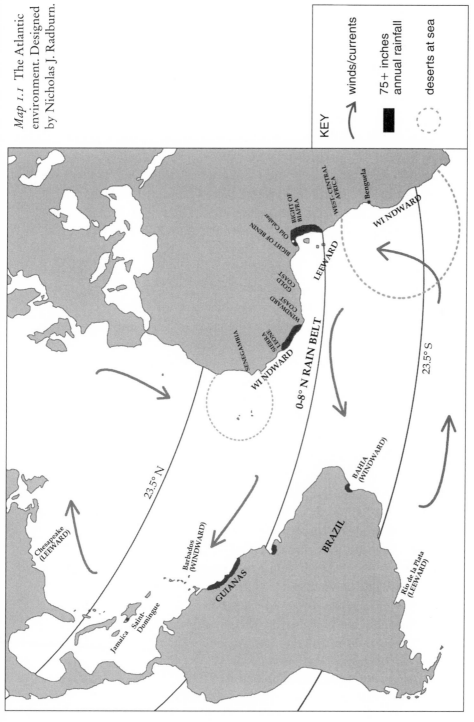

Map 1.1 The Atlantic environment. Designed by Nicholas J. Radburn.

KEY

→ winds/currents

■ 75+ inches annual rainfall

⟲ deserts at sea

WEST-CENTRAL AFRICA

BIGHT OF BIAFRA

BIGHT OF BENIN

Old Calabar

Benguela

WINDWARD

LEEWARD

GOLD COAST

WINDWARD COAST

SIERRA LEONE

SENEGAMBIA

WINDWARD

0-8° N RAIN BELT

23.5° S

23.5° N

BAHIA (WINDWARD)

Barbados (WINDWARD)

Chesapeake (LEEWARD)

Jamaica Saint-Domingue

GUIANAS

BRAZIL

Rio de la Plata (LEEWARD)

that drew no more than 12–14 feet of water—generally 125–225 British tons. In exceptional circumstances, low water levels or sediment buildup blocked some rivers in the dry season.[23] Sandbars protected the deep-water harbors in the bights of Benin and Biafra and trapped even experienced captains.[24] By contrast, slaving markets along the Gold Coast and the Angolan coastline, lacking sandbars or navigable rivers, proved less challenging to captains.[25] Pilot guides identified the numerous reefs in the Americas, particularly those in the Windward, Mona, and Crooked Island passages.[26] Late into the eighteenth century slave trade captains still hit well-known obstacles, such as Cobbler's Rock off southeast Barbados and the aptly named "Folly Reef" off Morant Bay, southeast Jamaica.[27]

Navigational dangers increased during the tropical rainy seasons in Africa, the Guianas, and northeast Brazil, and ships foundered if deck hands did not pump sufficient quantities of water. At the northern extent of the rainforest above Sierra Leone (8–9°N), 90 inches of rain fall on the coast in just two months, July and August.[28] Heavy summer rains continue from Sierra Leone to the Windward Coast, bordered by dense rainforests. Rainy season deluges resume along the eastern Bight of Benin and in the Bight of Biafra, with precipitation amounts increasing during the summer months as one sails toward the equator. The stretch of land from Conakry (in modern Guinea) to Bassa (Liberia) and the Douala estuary of Cameroon are the two rainiest areas in the Atlantic world. In the Americas, the greatest downpours occur in the spring–summer in the tropical rainforests of northern South America from Suriname (5–6°N) to Pará (1–3°S). By contrast, the wettest locations on the West Indian coastline reach only the precipitation levels of the driest rainy seasons in Atlantic Africa: those rainy months in Senegambia, the Gold Coast, and the coastline from Loango to Benguela. Intense downpours in almost all Atlantic slaving markets deliver at least double the volume of water from rainstorms in London, Nantes, or Lisbon (Table 1.1).[29]

The volume and intensity of African seasonal rains followed ships to the Americas, with the greatest Atlantic Ocean rains occurring from May to August between the equator and the northern limit of the rainforest, 8–9°N.[30] Encountering contrary winds in the Guinea Gulf in June 1591 "from 8 degrees of northernly latitude unto the line," James

Table 1.1 Comparative Rainfall in the Atlantic Littoral and Ocean

| | Approximate rainfall (inches)[a] | | |
Region/colony[b]	Annual totals	Rainiest quarter months/inches	Driest quarter[c] months/inches
Windward Coast (Liberia), Monrovia	202	May–July	98	Jan.–March	7
Guinea, Conakry	169	July–Sept.	119	Dec.–Feb.	1
Cameroon, Douala	158	July–Sept.	79	Dec.–Feb.	7
Sierra Leone, Freetown	141	July–Sept.	92	Jan.–March	1
Guyane, Cayenne	131	April–June	54	Aug.–Oct.	8
Atlantic Ocean, 4°N × 33°W	118	June–Aug.	38	Dec.–Feb.	21
Nigeria, Old Calabar	117	July–Sept.	50	Dec.–Feb.	6
Brazil, Pará, Belem	112	Feb.–April	48	Sept.–Nov.	13
Gabon, Douala (Libreville)	112	Oct.–Dec.	48	June–Aug.	1
Atlantic Ocean, 7°N × 20°W	98	June–Aug.	44	March–May	6
Nigeria, Bonny	93	July–Sept.	40	Dec.–Feb.	5
Guyana, Georgetown	90	May–July	34	Sept.–Nov.	13
Brazil, Maranhão, São Luís	89	Feb.–April	49	Sept.–Nov.	3
Suriname, Paramaribo	88	May–July	33	Sept.–Nov.	11
Brazil, Bahia, Salvador	83	April–June	35	Sept.–Nov.	14
Saint-Domingue (Haiti), Les Cayes	76	Aug.–Oct.	29	Dec.–Feb.	9
Dominica, Roseau	76	July–Sept.	28	Feb.–April	9
Guinea-Bissau, Bissau	74	July–Sept.	60	Dec.–April	0
Brazil, Pernambuco, Recife	71	May–July	33	Oct.–Dec.	4
Nigeria, Lagos	69	May–July	36	Dec–Feb.	4
Saint-Domingue, Cap-Français	61	Nov.–Jan.	26	June–Aug.	8
Benin, Porto Novo	55	May–July	28	Dec.–Feb.	3
Brazil, São Paulo	55	Dec.–Feb.	24	June–Aug.	5
South Carolina, Charleston	52	June–Aug.	20	Oct.–Dec.	9
Jamaica, Montego Bay	51	Sept.–Nov.	19	Feb.–April	7
Cuba, Havana	47	Aug.–Oct.	17	Feb.–April	7
Gold Coast, Cape Coast	46	April–June	26	Dec.–Feb.	3
Brazil, Rio de Janeiro	44	Dec.–Feb.	16	June–Aug.	6
Chesapeake, Annapolis	42	June–Aug.	13	Jan.–March	9
Río de la Plata	40	Jan.–March	12	June–Aug.	7
Saint-Domingue, Port au Prince	38	April–June	14	Dec.–Feb.	4
Jamaica, Kingston	36	Aug.–Oct.	16	Jan.–March	3
Gambia, James Island (Banjul)	34	July–Sept.	29	Nov.–May	0
France, Nantes	32	Oct.–Dec.	11	June–Aug.	6
Angola, Cabinda	31	Feb.–April	16	June–Sept.	0
Gold Coast, Accra	30	April–June	17	Dec.–Feb.	3
Atlantic Ocean, 13°N x 20°W	28	June–Aug.	12	March–May	2
Portugal, Lisbon	28	Nov.–Jan.	12	June–Aug.	1
England, London	24	Aug.–Oct.	7	Feb.–April	5

Table 1.1 Comparative Rainfall in the Atlantic Littoral and Ocean (continued)

	Approximate rainfall (inches)[a]		
Region/colony[b]	Annual totals	Rainiest quarter months/inches	Driest quarter[c] months/inches
Senegal, Dakar	20	July–Sept. 17	Nov.–May 0
Angola, Luanda	13	Feb.–April 10	June–Sept. 0
Atlantic Ocean, 8°S x 2°E	5	June–Aug. 3	Sept.–Feb. 0

Sources: www.worldweather.org; worldclimate.com; africaguide.com; remss.com; bbc.co.uk/weather/world
[a] Selection includes mostly 1961–1990 data and thus approximates totals for previous years.
[b] Includes a sample of major slaving markets.
[c] Three-month period unless no rain (Bissau, Gambia, Cabinda, Senegal, Luanda, Atlantic Ocean zones).

Lancaster experienced such intense rainfall and humidity that "we could not keep our men dry three hours together."[31] Pockets of the equatorial Atlantic might receive 2 inches of summer rain per day—totals similar to those in the African rainforests. Open ocean summer downpours continue up to 1,500 miles along this 0–8° latitude belt, though daily volumes decrease the further one sails from the African coast. By contrast, giant "deserts at sea" exist to the north and south in the latitudes of the Sahara and Kalahari deserts. If one sails due west from the African coast between 12 and 20°N from April to July, one encounters little rain for 1,000 miles—a 250,000-square-mile maritime desert. More impressively, almost no rain falls in the "Southeast Atlantic dry zone" along an 8–30°S latitude belt from the African coastline (12–15°E longitude) to about 20°W longitude—four million square miles.[32] Slaving captains departing Luanda would not expect significant rain in any month until they sighted the northeast Brazilian coastline (see Table 1.1 and Map 1.1).

Those purchasing and transporting human cargoes understood that there were seasonal water supplies in African ports and at sea. They knew that food and water intake related to health, but did not know that under normal conditions adults require two to three quarts of water per day and children two-thirds of that total.[33] Water supplies varied considerably by location and season on the African coast, and mariners noted specific watering locations in drier regions, such as along the Gold Coast.[34] Captains could load sufficient stocks during coastal rainy seasons and when they sailed their Middle Passage in 0–8°N latitudes.[35]

They would have no difficulty obtaining water along the rainiest coast-lines—from Conakry to Cape Coast and then from Lagos to Gabon. Slaving captains who planned to embark enslaved Africans from Senegambia or the Angolan coast, though, could not expect to purchase large quantities of water during the dry season or to collect much sailing west through maritime deserts. One expects that a disproportionate number of slaves who died from dehydration-related diseases would have been shipped from comparatively dry coastal and ocean latitudes.[36]

Captains encountered regular winds, currents, and rainfall patterns that dictated decision making in the transatlantic slave trade. Along the African coast and in the Americas they entertained the option of trading at windward markets before proceeding to leeward ports. The "Windward Coast" of modern-day Liberia provisioned many slavers heading to Lower Guinea, and ships often anchored first at Barbados to reprovision before sailing west. Captains needed to reach port quickly, because unwilling captives rebelled and mortality risks increased with voyage length. They loaded life-sustaining water on the African coast and supplemented stocks on the Middle Passage, quantities varying by location and season on land and over the ocean. The trade in human cargoes heightened the importance of Atlantic ecological realities.

Atlantic Farming Calendars and Trade Cycles

Atlantic rainfall further explains the distribution of crops, farming calendars, and optimal months to purchase foodstuffs for enslaved Africans and cash crops to freight back to Europe. Captain John Burrows arrived at Old Calabar in early May 1783 during the local "hungry season," two to three months before farmers harvested the first yams in the Upper Cross River savanna. Burrows would purchase most of his food supplies in the Bight of Biafra. He had stocked some rice, bread, and beans to supplement the thousands of yams he would need to buy to feed his enslaved Africans on the Middle Passage.[37] While Burrows advanced goods to Egbo Young and other Efik traders for future yam and slave deliveries, enslaved Africans in southeast Jamaica produced the season's last barrels of sugar. They then needed to plant foodstuffs and new cane during summer showers, and prepare for the two- to three-month "hungry time" when provisions were scarce and the hurricane season reduced fish and grain imports.[38] Burrows departed Old Calabar after the main yam harvest in October, and when he arrived in Kingston on December 29, most slaves in southern Jamaica had begun cutting the first canes of the season. Within a few weeks those canes would be processed into crystals, ready for shipment to England.

Captain Burrows planned to purchase agricultural commodities in two regions in the Atlantic world dominated by single crops—in the Bight of Biafra, the staple yam, and in the West Indies, the cash crop sugar. The Upper Cross River was in the southeast corner of the 500,000-square-mile "yam belt," which comprises lands from the Bandama River in modern-day Ivory Coast to the eastern Cameroon Mountains. Farmers cultivate four main yam species; the most widely grown yam, *Dioscorea rotundata,* is known as the "white yam" or "Guinea yam." Today, Nigerian farms account for 70 percent of world yam production.[39] From the mid-seventeenth to the mid-nineteenth century, world sugar production centered in the Caribbean islands. For those 4.5 million enslaved Africans sold in the West Indies from the 1620s to 1867, three in four would work on a sugar plantation.[40] In the early 1780s Jamaican sugar and its by-products molasses and rum totaled 80 percent of the island colony's export revenues, and cane occupied half the arable land.[41]

Yams and sugar grow in locations best suited ecologically for their propagation. Ideal conditions for yam cultivation include temperatures in the mid-80s°F, rainfall totaling 60 inches, divided evenly throughout the year, a two- to three-month dry season, sufficient light, and free-draining sandy loam soils. In Africa, 10°N divides the cereal from the root crop zone; lands to the north of this line lack sufficient rain to grow yams.[42] Yams do not grow well in coastal rainforests, because downpours leech soils of essential nutrients and tubers cannot tolerate waterlogging. In the Americas imported yams adapted to some biomes in the West Indies and South America.[43] Sugar thrives in the low-lying tropical Americas. Ideal growing conditions to propagate cane sweetening require temperatures of 75–90°F, seven to nine hours of sunshine per day, well-draining fertile soil, abundant water during the plant's main growth, and a three- to six-month dry season. In the Atlantic world the climate of Madeira, most of the West Indies, sections of the Brazilian coastline, and Louisiana proved optimal for sugarcane.[44] Farmers produced poorer quality sugar on lands with heavier rain and a short dry season, such as on São Tomé.[45]

Rainfall determines the agricultural calendar and export seasons for yams and sugar. In the southeast Nigeria forest belt, 100 miles north from Old Calabar, yam workers plant in March–April with the onset of the first rains, dig up "early yams" in July/August, and then harvest the main crop in late October, toward the end of the rainy season. The common white yam matures to its maximum size and nutritional capacity seven to eight months after planting. With proper pest management, yam farmers stored their annual crop without spoilage until February or even March.[46] From planting to harvesting, the cane cycle averages fourteen to eighteen months. In the West Indies cane planting generally occurred between August and November, and workers then cut and squeezed cane from December to May the following year. Dry seasons varied regionally within the larger islands of Jamaica and Saint-Domingue. In Jamaica southern planters took off the crop between December and June; those with estates along the rainier northern coast, who planted later, often harvested from March to November.[47] Jamaicans understood that seasonal rainfall and dry periods limited the production schedule to one annual crop.[48] Saint-Domingue planters timed sugar production to best suit rainy and dry seasons in the north, west, and south.[49]

Slaving captains identified an August–February yam season in the Bight of Biafra that sometimes stretched from July to March, depending on crop conditions and demand. In the late 1600s Jean Barbot placed the early New Calabar yam harvest in July–August.[50] Vessels sailing to Bonny, stated Simon Taylor at the turn of the nineteenth century, should arrive there "by the beginning of August when the Yams come in" or "about the month of September that being the time when yams are plenty."[51] In January 1790 Captain William Woodville, Jr., wrote to merchant James Rogers to expedite his departure from Liverpool, "because the season for provisions will be very far advanced although I have some hopes that yams may be had all March—I once sailed from Bonny late in March & then they were to be bought."[52] Captains who purchased "early yams" of the common species *D. rotundata* received smaller, immature tubers, as decreased dormancy restricts tubers' development.[53] Those loading the white yams in November, after the principal harvest, stowed the larger 7- to 10-pound tubers.[54]

Slaving merchants unable to organize voyages to the Bight of Biafra during the yam season needed to consider provision seasons in other African markets. Coastal dealers also sold millet, sorghum, rice, and maize to slaving captains and agents. The millet-sorghum zone in West Africa begins at the Gambia River (13°N) and the dry sub-humid region, and occupies the semi-arid and arid zones to the southern Sahara's limit of cultivation. In many villages millet and sorghum are the only crops grown in the 10–15°N belt, 300 miles inland from the African Atlantic coastline. The crops also thrive in the long dry seasons of the Congo savanna, and they may have grown farther west before being displaced by manioc in the seventeenth, eighteenth, and nineteenth centuries.[55] In the early modern era, West Africa rice lands began at the mouth of the Gambia River and extended to the Bandama River on the Ivory Coast, and in microclimates around Axim (western Gold Coast) and the Volta River estuary. Most rice fields were positioned near the Atlantic coast.[56] In precolonial Africa maize grew mostly in the south-central Gold Coast Fante states, exported to the coast in large quantities by the late 1600s.[57]

Hinterland merchants supplied most West African millet and sorghum to the Upper Guinea coast by March–May. Farmers plant the cereals during the first rains in June and in early November, at the end of the rainy season when floodwaters begin to recede. The short-season crops mature in 90–180 days, the harvests occurring in September–December and February–May, depending on location and rainfall.[58] Today in Sahel villages like Kita in western Mali, below-average rain during their short rainy season (June–September) limits the village to one annual crop, harvested in September and stored throughout the year.[59] During the era of the overseas slave trade, tons of millet and sorghum shipped downstream to the French and British trading posts in the lower Senegal and lower Gambia. British agents stored grain in James Fort, near the mouth of the Gambia, "at the Chief season, viz. March, April and May," as one factor wrote in March 1678.[60] Captains had difficulty trading for provisions in Senegambia in the summer, needing to rely on foods they transported from their homeports.

In Upper Guinea farmers grow rice during the summer–fall rains and market the cereal during the dry November–April months. Rice is the staple from the Lower Gambia south to Sierra Leone and along the Windward Coast, coastlines that receive heavy rain to allow rice to grow in its requisite water depth of 4–6 inches.[61] Europeans, in particular the Dutch, purchased Windward Coast rice for the Middle Passage in increasing amounts through the seventeenth century.[62] By the mid-eighteenth century, the Rice Coast from the River Nuñez southeast to Sestos on the Windward Coast annually provisioned fifteen to twenty European ships, with many sailing on to leeward markets.[63] In late February 1784 at "Young Sisters," near Sestos, Liverpool captain Peter Potter regretted his decision to spare two tons of rice to a fellow Liverpool captain en route to the Bight of Benin: "which I have sence paid Dear for; as the Scarcety commenst soon after oweing to the vast quantite of ships that stops here for rice."[64] The rice season "advanced" by the end of April, and captains knew that from May to October they would need to purchase provisions elsewhere on the African coast.[65]

Captains who arrived out of season along the Rice Coast in May or June would not find large supplies of maize in Gold Coast or Slave Coast ports until after the July–August harvest. Maize grows in six weeks and hence two crops can be harvested per year if there are two distinct rainy-dry seasons, as can occur along the Gold Coast and in the Bight of Benin.[66] African farmers begin maize planting at the March and September equinoxes, and cut the largest maize crop in July/August, the two months with the least rainfall. They often grow smaller crops of beans, yams, or potatoes in the maize fields.[67] Maize arrived on the Gold Coast in the mid-1500s and became a staple there at the turn of the seventeenth century.[68] By 1689 Anomabu, located 10 miles east of Cape Coast Castle, was the principal corn granary for British slavers.[69] The handful of fort administrators on the Gold and Slave coasts knew that they depended on local provisions and hence needed to maintain good relationships with African leaders or risk starvation.[70]

Testimony from surgeon Robert Hume illustrates how captains planned voyages around seasonal shortfalls in North Atlantic provisions. In November 1789 Hume mustered in Liverpool for two ventures to Bonny. On the first voyage he and his shipmates arrived in the Bight of Biafra in January 1790, still "the Season of the Year for Yams." After returning to

Liverpool in May of that year, they remained in port for eight months while the vessel underwent repairs. A late January 1791 departure from Liverpool to Bonny would place the ship at the end of the Biafran yam season—a risky proposition. The captain may not have wanted to provision only with warehoused rice and beans, which might have been in short supply in the Merseyside winter. Purchasing rice along the Windward Coast was an option; the rice season ended in April, however, and five to ten British ships were by then already on the Windward Coast. Similarly, few African merchants offered large quantities of maize for sale in the spring. The captain thus decided to purchase rice at South Carolina en route to the Bight of Biafra—one of the more unusual voyage patterns in the British slave trade.[71]

Whereas captains could purchase in-crop African foodstuffs north of the equator, they found few stocks offered for sale along the Congo and Angolan coastlines. Local foods included, in various quantities, cassava, beans, chickpeas, plantains, sweet potatoes, pumpkins, Indian corn, millet, sorghum, bananas, and yams.[72] All testimonies, though, point to frequent scarcities and suggest that slaving ships loaded provisions elsewhere. According to Captain John Adams, Angola merchants "have no superfluity of provisions to sell," and thus slaving ships "are compelled to bring with them, from Europe, sufficient food to feed the negroes while accumulating on board the ships, and during their passage to the West Indies."[73] In 1767, one Liverpool firm even advised their captain "not to give the Slaves too much Provisions, that is worse than too little, particularly for Angola Slaves that are acustomed [sic] to very little food in their own country."[74] Well into the nineteenth century, West-Central African droughts occurred every ten years.[75] Accordingly, British merchants purchased at home more than twice as many barrels of beans and rice on voyages sailing to Congo-Angola as they would on ships departing for the Bight of Biafra.[76]

Provisioning ships with local foods helped to maintain the health of enslaved Africans, and traders singled out the importance of purchasing yams in the Bight of Biafra. When a Bristol ship arrived in Jamaica from Bonny in August 1791, having lost 67 of 438 slaves, agent Francis Grant attributed the high mortality to "the Season of the Year" in Bonny. The ship slaved in the hungry May–June months, and Grant believed that "not one Cargo in ten comes in here in a healthy condition which is laid in at the time [the captain] got his." Writing in 1806, Simon Taylor stated, "if a ship goes [to Bonny] after the Yam season is over the cargo of slaves is in general sickly and therefore she ought to be kept so as to be there just as that season comes in."[77] In preharvest months enslaved Africans likely were malnourished and more susceptible to diseases.[78] Captains force-fed maize, rice, or beans to Africans from low-protein yam regions, and the shock to their digestive systems worsened health.[79] Data from the British and French slave trades at Biafra indicate that Middle Passage slave mortality varied by yam supplies. Vessels slaving in July–December during the in-crop yam season later lost 16 percent of their human cargo on the Middle Passage. Ships trading in January–June, when yam reserves had decreased, lost 26 percent of their captives.[80] Those Guinea captains in the Bight of Biafra during months of peak yam stocks purchased healthier enslaved Africans than those trading after the provisioning season.

As they planned their triangular voyages, captains were more concerned with seasonal food supplies than with freighting large quantities of New World produce. Guineamen indeed attempted to arrive in the Americas when barrels of sugar, coffee, tobacco, rice, or other plantation produce awaited transportation overseas. But captains also deemed these harvest months optimal because they occurred during the healthier dry season, when colonial provisions were available—encouraging slave purchases. As a Royal African Company agent in Barbados stated on August 30, 1715: "the best time for Negroes to arrive is between December & June, being a healthy time & affording plenty of provisions, and ye rest of ye Year being ye reverse."[81] Captains profited from higher slave prices during in-crop months, when planters demanded agricultural labor. They earned less money shipping colonial produce, and some transported only bills of exchange drawn on European merchants. Guinea commanders, particularly regular traders, could not afford to wait long in American ports, because delays increased the risk of missing seasonal provisions trades in African markets. Captains kept in mind the timing of return voyages to Guinea, "the Proper Season for the next Year's Service."[82]

Captains also ranked the availability of African staples above concerns about crew mortality. Because slavers needed to purchase yams in the Bight of Biafra, for example, they needed to trade during the rainy season. The harvest and coastal marketing occurred during heavy July–October rains (60 inches, on average) because of the yam growing cycle and because wet soils facilitated digging. To secure deliveries of food-stuffs captains needed to advance goods on credit to African merchants at Old Calabar, Bonny, or New Calabar. While moored in the heavy rains, mariners rigged temporary tarpaulins above deck to shelter crates of trading goods and their yam rooms.[83] These shelters did not protect sailors from bacteria and parasites transported and propagated by summer rainstorms and high humidity. Those on voyages to the Bight of Biafra died at the highest rates in the slave trade; dysentery or related gastrointestinal diseases were the biggest killers.[84] John Burrows lost eight of thirty-one hands while at Old Calabar from May to October 1783 and an additional sailor on the Middle Passage.[85]

Merchants, then, planned slaving voyages around the provisioning supply constraints in Atlantic Africa. Rains, soils, and temperature determined the types of crops that could grow and regulated their production cycles. In most Guinea markets north of the equator, African millet, rice, maize, and yams provided the calories to sustain slaves during their coastal confinement and Middle Passage. Some foods grew on or near the coast—Europeans and other visitors observed farmers in some West African rice lands, in microclimates such as the Gap of Benin (where the drier savanna breaks through the coastal rainforest), and in pockets along the Angolan coast.[86] Other crops grew inland. Captain John Burrows, anchored off the rainforest at Old Calabar, would not have witnessed workers harvesting the yams he purchased, as that activity occurred 100 miles to the north. He also would have known little about the origins of the enslaved Africans he purchased. From his experience trading with Egbo Young, though, Burrows would have understood that the annual yam cycle governed economic activity in the Cross River region, including the export slave trade.

Yam and Slave Trades in the Bight of Biafra

When Egbo Young and other Efik merchants received goods from John Burrows in May 1783, they began working with hinterland dealers to supply yams and slaves to enable Burrows to depart Old Calabar after October. Egbo Young's trading season began each summer, pegged to the July–October yam harvest, and ended in late March when yam supplies decreased. Hinterland merchants, middlemen brokers, and captains relied on yam stocks to provision slaves, whose value depended on their health and fitness for heavy agricultural work in the Americas.[87] During these in-crop months, foreign cloth, metal and glass manufactures, iron bars, copper rods, liquor, gunpowder, firearms, and beads flooded into Calabar. Egbo Young advanced European and Asian goods on credit to backcountry yam and slave traders, anticipating that more captains would arrive in the Cross River during the fall and winter. Ivory, dyewood, palm oil, and spice merchants also timed their exports to coincide with the expected arrival of overseas ships. In the Bight of Biafra, regional economic activity hinged upon the annual yam harvest.

Scattered testimonies from European traders demonstrate the link between yam supplies and the slaving season at Old Calabar. In the late 1600s Barbot placed the early Calabar yam harvest in July–August, and then demarcated August–September as the "fittest time for us to purchase slaves."[88] In late July 1785, Liverpool captain Peter Potter commented that he had "very little trade" at Old Calabar, but hoped "it will be beter soon as there is a grate many cannews gone in the country and this is the best time of the year for Slaves as well as Provisions."[89] Given that they expected yams and slaves to be delivered after July, captains needed to calculate precisely below-deck room to store tubers and imprison Africans: people and foodstuffs competed for the limited space. "I Hope you & the other good gentlemen will not reflect on me for not puting more slaves on board the *Juba,*" Captain Richard Rogers wrote in late July 1788, "but my Reson for it is that the *Juba* will be Crouded a Deal with 250 & will not have Room for her Yams."[90] Yams not only crowded out room for people, but also restricted the space to load barrels of palm oil.[91]

Antera Duke—kinsman and associate of Egbo Young in Old Calabar—described his travels north from Duke Town to purchase seasonal yams and slaves.[92] As he recorded in his diary, at midnight on November 3, 1785, he and a few other Efik traders and canoemen traveled four hours southwest to Seven Fathoms Point. They then paddled up the Cross River, and after a 40-mile journey they beached at Itu. Antera sent his brother 20 miles farther north to Umon, a yam distribution center, while he and the others remained to trade at Itu (see Map 1.2). His

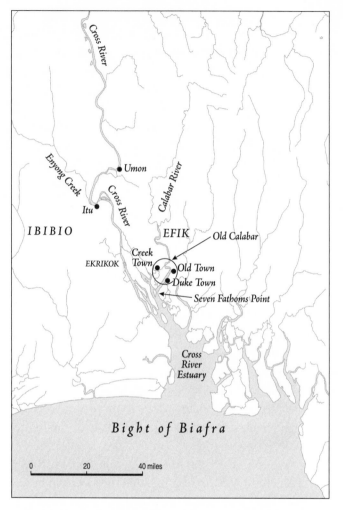

Map 1.2 Old Calabar and the Cross River region. Adapted by Nicholas J. Radburn from Randy J. Sparks, *Two Princes of Calabar: An Eighteenth-Century Atlantic Odyssey* (Cambridge, Mass., 2004).

brother returned with five slaves and a supply of yams—hundreds, one presumes—and on November 10 Antera Duke's expedition, his canoe and three small canoes, paddled downriver to Duke Town, arriving the next day after an all-night trip. Antera Duke, like Egbo Young, sold small lots of slaves to individual slave captains, spaced over several months. His trading journeys by river and land occurred mostly in the

November–March dry season. The May–October rains heightened water levels, facilitating later boat travel in minor tributaries; the November–April dry weather hardened pathways, easing overland transport.[93]

In his three-year diary, January 1785 to January 1788, Antera Duke reveals busy in-season yam and slave trading with ship captains. He steered his canoe to the moored hulls to gather captains' trading goods, as he did in January 1785 on board John Burrows's ship.[94] In late October 1785 Antera traveled downstream with five British slaving captains to meet a new ship that was cruising upriver from Seven Fathoms Point. On December 14, 1785, Antera, Esien Duke, and Egbo Young traveled down in three "big canoes" with 32 slaves and at least 6,000 yams. A week later he sent two canoes stocked with 1,500 yams to a Liverpool captain, who the next day departed Old Calabar with 484 slaves. Antera's diary records other dates when slaving vessels departed Old Calabar, and he usually states the number of slaves confined on board. In total, he enumerates 8,165 slaves shipped from twenty-two vessels, 4,592 (56 percent) of whom captains transported from Old Calabar in December–February, the three driest months in Calabar and three months when yams remained in stock.

Ship arrival and departure dates from the slave trade database, before and after the period of Antera Duke's diary, confirm Old Calabar's seasonal trade and that of other principal Bight of Biafra ports.[95] Estimated African months of departure are available for 687 vessels embarking an estimated 198,201 slaves at Old Calabar, 1638–1838. Three times as many slaving vessels departed the Cross River in October (in-crop) as did in June (out-of-crop). Ninety-three vessels departed Old Calabar in October, as John Burrows did in 1783, and carried an estimated 29,443 slaves. This peak export month contrasts to June's total of thirty-six Guineamen sailing to the Americas with 9,133 Africans. Similar seasonal patterns emerge from export slave trades from Bonny and New Calabar. October slave exports more than tripled those from the months before the main yam harvests. The September–November quarter represents the busiest in-season slave trading from the Bight of Biafra, whereas the fewest ships and Africans departed for the Americas in June–August (see Table 1.2).

How did hinterland merchants maintain regular summer–fall slave exports to outlets in the Bight of Biafra? The link between the yam and

Table 1.2   Seasonality in the Major Bight of Biafra Slaving Ports

Port	Months slaving vessels departed the Bight of Biafra (*n*) = number of voyages			
	Maximum slave exports		Minimum slave exports	
Bonny	October	48,246 (121)	June	17,305 (46)
Old Calabar	October	28,920 (91)	June	8,893 (35)
New Calabar	October	11,232 (40)	July	1,795 (8)
Bight of Biafra	*October*	*114,272 (340)*	*June*	*44,543 (159)*
Bonny	Sept.–Nov.	120,513 (324)	June–Aug.	58,593 (168)
Old Calabar	Sept.–Nov.	61,614 (210)	June–Aug.	32,279 (117)
New Calabar	Oct.–Dec.	27,030 (96)	June–Aug.	10,107 (35)
Bight of Biafra	*Sept.–Nov.*	*269,734 (846)*	*June–Aug.*	*146,482 (487)*

Source: *Voyages: The Trans-Atlantic Slave Trade Database*, www.slavevoyages.org.

slave seasons is suggestive. Arguably the majority of slaves who arrived in the major ports—Bonny, Old Calabar, and New Calabar—came from northern yam-growing regions and worked as farmers. We know that captains purchased a disproportionate number of women in the Bight, an imbalance that one recent study attributes to the dominant male role in yam cultivation.[96] Further, modern studies indicate that yam cultivation in Nigeria requires the greatest labor inputs during the clearing/planting (January–April) and harvesting (August–October) seasons, and the fewest hours of crop work during November, December, and January.[97] This evidence suggests that large numbers of slaves farmed yams and then were sold when their labor became redundant. Owners retained maximum numbers of agricultural slaves during essential land clearing and planting; they then sold slaves who dug the yams along with the yams they had harvested. Spotlighting Old Calabar's trade from 1660 to 1837, slave exports dropped during the period of yam planting and weeding (March–June), and then rose sharply in August as workers harvested yams, peaking during the main harvest in October (see Figure 1.1).

Further, given that large numbers of agricultural slaves from the Bight of Biafra entered the transatlantic trade, particularly after 1750, regular slave raids must have occurred each year.[98] Efik merchants abandoned large-scale attacks by the mid-eighteenth century, relying instead on dis-

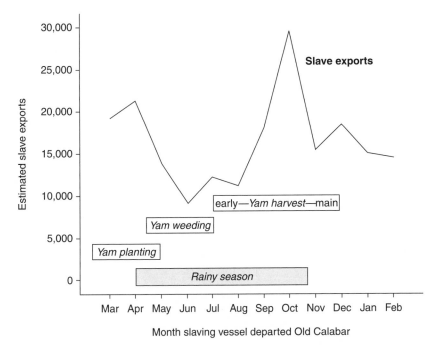

Figure 1.1 Seasonality in the Old Calabar slave trade, 1638–1838 (by month of vessel departure and yam-growing cycle). *Sample:* 687 vessels embarking an estimated 198,201 slaves, 1638–1838. *Source:* See Table 1.2.

tant slave suppliers. Aro merchants were the dominant slavers in the backcountry, but no studies discuss their seasonal slave trades or raids.[99] Since men raided and were essential workers in yam cultivation, one can predict that most raids occurred during the dry November–January months, after the yam harvest and before land clearing. Women and children weeded yam vines in June and July, freeing up two months when men could leave the farms and engage in warfare or skirmishes. Though late in the history of slaving, one northern Nigeria official wrote in mid-July 1900, "this is the season for slave raiding."[100] Hinterland merchants purchased, confined, and worked slaves during the planting, weeding, and early harvest seasons, their labor offsetting confinement costs. Coastal brokers then purchased slaves who had completed the crop harvest, aiming to meet the demands of ship captains.

Since African hinterland and middlemen slave owners needed large

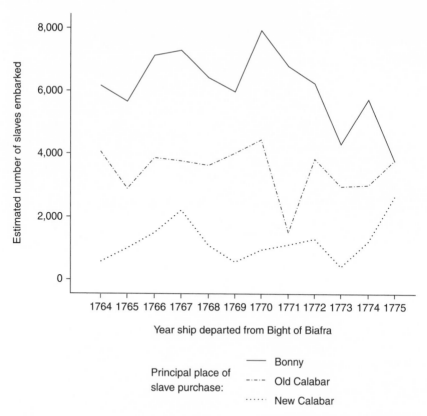

Figure 1.2A Annual cycles in the export slave trade from the Bight of Biafra, 1764–1775 (by port of departure). *Sample:* 403 vessels embarking an estimated 129,390 slaves, 1764–1775. *Source:* See Table 1.2.

supplies of seasonal yams to keep slaves alive, annual yam production relates directly to the number of slaves purchased in the hinterland and later sold into the transatlantic slave trade. The "economics of mortality" limited the number of slaves buyers would purchase; African slave owners and ship captains could not profitably keep large numbers of slaves in unsanitary compounds, pens, or below deck.[101] Changeable rainfall, whether in seasonal amounts or in the timing of the first-planting rains, caused yam supplies, needed to support slaves, to fluctuate. In the yam-dependent Bight of Biafra, merchants from Bonny, Old Calabar, and New Calabar competed for business from European ship captains, and each drew upon some common hinterland slave and yam

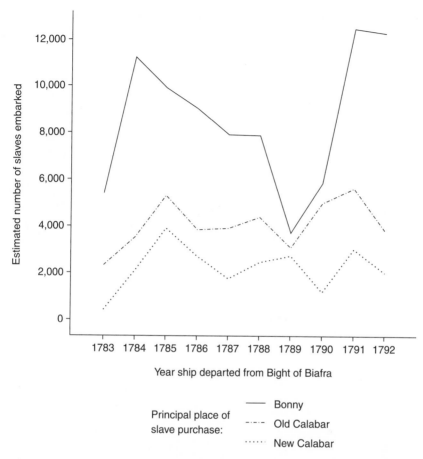

Figure 1.2B Annual cycles in the export slave trade from the Bight of Biafra, 1783–1792 (by port of departure). *Sample:* 408 vessels embarking an estimated 148,713 slaves, 1783–1792. *Source:* See Table 1.2.

supply networks. By the 1760s and 1770s, merchants from Bonny had begun aggrandizing the slave trade, a point not lost on the Efik traders of Old Calabar.[102] Yet annual cycles of slave exports, 1764–1792, from the three principal Biafran ports mirror each other, a pattern most apparent in 1783–1792 (see Figures 1.2A and 1.2B).[103] Parallel peaks and troughs in slave exports suggest that quantities of provisioning staples varied each year.

Ecological conditions created the seasonality in Egbo Young's yam and slave trades. Those Efik who wanted to profit from the trade in slaves needed to maintain yam-supply networks with Upper Cross River merchants. Old Calabar middlemen purchased local supplies of fish, plantains, and palm oil, but quantities were insufficient to meet the provisioning requirements of a large-scale export slave trade. Each year Egbo Young planned his business activities around the annual July–October yam harvest; he aimed to supply tubers and slaves to ship captains who anchored early in the trading season, as did John Burrows, or to those mariners who arrived later in the year with the onset of the winter dry period at Old Calabar.

Seasonal Provision and Slave Trades in Other African Markets

Just as merchants in the Bight of Biafra synchronized their slave trades to the July–March yam season, those in other African markets also organized their slave trades around the production schedules of local crops. Rains in Senegambia, which fall mostly during the three summer months, governed the planting cycle, water levels, and current flows in the Senegal and Gambia river systems, and they controlled access to overland pathways. In the wetter Sierra Leone/Windward Coast regions, slaving seasons were linked to annual rice supplies. Monthly slave export cycles compare with those in single-crop Biafra, but the trading season occurs later in the calendar, because farmers harvest rice four months after yams. Along the Gold Coast and in parts of Benin, rain falls more evenly throughout the year. With short crop cycles and two harvests, brokers could provision slaves in most months. South of the equator, though rainy January–April hindered some travel from Congo/Angola to Atlantic ports, traders did not identify major crop-related slaving seasons. Warfare and raids occurred most often during dry seasons, generally after major harvests, and those predatory activities supplied slaves to hinterland dealers and coastal middlemen at regular periods.

Comparing the Bight of Biafra's seasonal slave trade to that from other regions prompts analysis of how different African ecosystems linked to the Atlantic slaving world. Drawing on information in the consolidated online database and estimating the loading period, from Senegal and Gambia captains embarked three times as many slaves in February–June as in June–October.[104] Three-quarters of the trade occurred from November to June—reversing the Bight of Biafra pattern. The coastline along the Sierra Leone/Windward Coast regions, generally Guinea-Bissau southeast to Cape Palmas, also exhibited a seasonal trade: for every eleven slaves loaded during the December–April slaving season, seven departed the coast in April–July. Weaker seasonality characterized the regional slave trades from the Gold Coast, Bight of Benin, or West-Central Africa, though in each, coastal merchants loaded 30 percent more slaves in the highest three-month period than in the lowest quarter. With the exception of the Bights of Biafra and Benin, dealers supplied more slaves to the coast during comparatively dry months. Slave sales occurred year-round in all African coastal outlets, regardless of ecological constraints (see Table 1.3).

In Senegambia the pronounced rainy and dry seasons regulated the long-distance provision and slave trades by land and river. Eighty-five percent of all rain falls in July–September; markets dotting the Senegal and Gambia rivers experience the longest dry periods in the Atlantic world, beginning in November and lasting for six to seven months (see Table 1.1). Most transatlantic slaves shipped from Senegambia came from distant Sahel lands near the Upper Niger River. Caravans making thousand-mile journeys westward from "the merchants' country" of the Upper Niger generally began their trips in December or January, after the rains. Merchants purchased slaves, commodities, and foodstuffs during February–March fairs and aimed to reach the Upper Senegal or Gambia by March–April, when weak currents and strong tides aided westward navigation. The spring traveling months corresponded with the millet (March–May) harvest.[105] Forty percent of all Senegambian slaves forced across the Atlantic departed in May, June, or July; 64 percent sailed from February to July. In September–November, the scarcity of millet, sorghum, and rice reduced the volume of the export slave trade by two-thirds.

South of Senegambia, the slave trade along the Upper Guinea Coast centered on the November–May rice and dry seasons. Hinterland dealers marched slaves overland after the rains, aiming to reach the coast during the beginning of the rice harvest. On October 25, 1793, north of Sierra Leone, Captain Samuel Gamble received on board the first lot of slaves (five men) who "have come this season who have travell'd upwards of 1000 Miles." Two weeks later Africans marketed the first bas-

Table 1.3   Quarterly Slave Exports by African Region (arranged north–south)

African region[a]	Captains loading slaves[b]	Three-month period (greatest/lowest trade)		Index
		To depart *with*	Estimated slaves	
Senegambia	Feb.–June *(dry)*	May–July	94,880	2.95
	June–Oct. *(rainy)*	Sept.–Nov.	32,208	
		Sample	*250,291*	
Sierra Leone/	Dec.–April *(dry)*	March–May	105,962	1.63
Windward Coast	March–July *(wet)*	June–Aug.	65,100	
		Sample	*348,685*	
Gold Coast	Nov.–March *(dry)*	Feb.–April	158,638	1.29
	March–July *(wet)*	June–Aug.	122,888	
		Sample	*578,202*	
Bight of Benin	July–Oct. *(wet)*	Sept.–Nov.	290,568	1.37
	April–July *(rainy)*	June–Aug.	212,839	
		Sample	*1,012,381*	
Bight of Biafra	July–Oct. *(wet)*	Sept.–Nov.	272,293	1.85
	April–July *(rainy)*	June–Aug.	147,405	
		Sample	*808,750*	
West-Central Africa	Oct.–Feb *(dry)*	Jan.–March	349,824	1.30
Loango-to-Ambriz	Feb–June *(rainy)*	May–July	270,112	
		Sample	*1,250,815*	
West-Central Africa	July–Nov. *(dry)*	Oct.–Dec.	352,451	1.36
Luanda and Benguela	Jan.–May *(rainy)*	April–June	258,427	
		Sample	*1,235,608*	

Source: See Table 1.2.

[a]Excludes Southeast Africa.

[b]Approximate months when greatest number of slaves embarked. Guineamen averaged three to five months on the African coast, loading more slaves toward departure. Slavers loaded more quickly in the Bights of Benin and Biafra. Dry/rainy/wet indicates general four- to five-month conditions: dry = 0–10 inches of rain; rainy = 10–30 inches; wet = 30+ inches.

Sample: 15,464 voyages (imputed departure months) embarking 5,484,732 slaves.

kets of the season's rice crop. In March 1794, during his rice and slave trades, Gamble drew a "Representation of a Lott of Fullow's [Fula] bringing their slaves for Sale to the Europeans," and noted that their trade "generaly commences annually in December, or early in January, being prevented from comeing down sooner by the river being over- flow'd and their paths impassable, from the heavy rains which end in

November." Further, the Fula merchants' "Principal places of trade are Gambia, Rio Nunez & the Mandingo Country 1500 of them have been bought here in one Season, they are of[f] in May as the rains set in in June."[106] Hinterland slave dealers such as the Fula supplied their largest lots to the coast at the end of the trading season. In early May 1790, for example, a visitor noted how Rio Pongo agent John Ormond expected "that a thousand Slaves will very soon be brought to him in one Lot."[107] Those slaves unsold would need to be kept alive during the four- to five-month rainy season, as few European ships would arrive then.[108]

In contrast, double cropping on the Gold Coast enabled captains to provision and purchase slaves during most weeks. European visitors discussed seasonal rains, winds, and maize but do not cite the "best" or "worst" slave-trading months. Jean Barbot was one of many writers who believed that "It is possible to trade on [the] Gold Coast in any season."[109] The voluminous correspondence of English fort officials and ship captains in the 1680s and 1690s discusses the dry harmattan winds, intense deluges (particularly in April and May), weekly scarcities and surpluses of corn, and occasional days of "good trade," sometimes occurring in the aftermath of local African wars. They do not mention seasonal hinterland slave trades to the European coastal forts or to ships.[110] Similarly, merchants organizing slaving vessels to the Gold Coast do not identify seasonal constraints in the supply of human cargoes. In 1799 merchant Simon Taylor believed that slavers could depart London for the Gold Coast "whenever they can be gott ready"—there was no preferred departure time.[111] During typical years shortfalls in maize provisions delayed captains' slave trades on the Gold Coast for at most four to five weeks.

Each month African merchants supplied similar numbers of slaves to Bight of Benin ports and lagoon sites because there were adequate supplies of maize, rice, beans, and yams.[112] In 1685 a slaving captain at Ouidah identified October–March as "the best time of the year." During this six-month dry period, craft could better manage the pounding coastal surf; these months also correspond to peak yam supplies, as well as to the maize and bean harvests. More slavers departed Ouidah in April than in any other month; some of those ships would have provisioned Gold Coast maize and purchased slaves to windward as well.[113] Greater numbers of vessels loaded slaves in July–October from eastern ports such as Lagos, which lay closer to major yam-growing lands. Throughout the Bight, slave exports ebbed in early summer, the two months before yams and a second cereal harvest came to market. As in the Bight of Biafra, dominated by British traders, September-November equals the greatest ship departure quarter from the Bight of Benin, though that region was most frequented by Portuguese captains.[114]

Europeans at "Angola," the long stretch of coastline from Mayumba to Benguela, did not identify slaving or provisioning seasons. Visitors to the northern coast, such as Andrew Battell (1589) or Pierre van de Broecke (1608–1612), mention valuable commodities such as ivory tusks and dyewoods, and they specify where those goods might be purchased, but they do not mention seasonal trades.[115] Later commentators focus on the scarcity of foodstuffs and remind ship captains to load provisions en route to Angola. One reads about river levels, differences in vegetation in the wet and dry season, or periods of extended drought.[116] The Portuguese monopolized the slave trades from Luanda and Benguela, which together accounted for 1.5 million slave exports, and built forts to house their administrators, soldiers, and merchants.[117] One could argue that African dealers in the hinterland thus shipped equal numbers of slaves year-round to Portuguese coastal agents, men who had authority to purchase slaves every day. But there was little difference in seasonality in the slave trades from Loango, Melimba, Cabinda, and Ambriz—locations where the British, French, and Dutch did not build fort-castles to staff traders (see Table 1.3). The common conditions in the West-Central African hinterland appear to be frequent shortfalls of rain and harvest failures—failures exacerbated by raiding and warfare—that created ecologically and demographically fragile communities, feeding the export slave trade.[118]

Did monthly slave exports from these regional African markets relate to the season of the year when raiders attacked farming communities, as they did in the Bight of Biafra? Armies mustered farmer-soldiers, and they needed to pillage communities for people and food.[119] North of the equatorial rainforests, military excursions occurred often from August to May/June, depending on the crop cycle and timing of the dry season.[120] "I have had butt a verry small trade, towards the latter end of last month," wrote John Gregory on September 4, 1691, at Anomabu, Gold

Coast. "These country people are all gon to the wars."[121] Here a comparatively dry August coincided with the end of the major maize harvest in the Anomabu backcountry. In the Bight of Benin, Oyo military leaders favored cavalry attacks during the dry season, when horses survived longer and gunpowder weapons proved more effective. The Oyo invaded and torched Abomey, Dahomey's capital, in March 1728 and again in dry seasons in 1729 and 1730.[122] Botanist C. B. Wadstrom visited Senegambia in August–September 1787, a time that "was not the Season when the Slaves are brought down from the interior Country; during the Harvest Time the Country is generally at Peace; when the Harvest is over they frequently make War upon each other."[123] Other evidence points to dry season campaigns throughout Atlantic Africa, and these incursions would have occurred after staple harvests.[124]

Because military leaders mustered able-bodied soldiers during months when villages did not need farming labor, crop type plays a key role in understanding the seasonality of slave raids. A detailed study of Guinea-Bissau communities, drawing on French slave trade data, demonstrates the links among gendered agricultural work in one crop—rice—raiding and warfare, and slave supplies. Most raids occurred during the dry season months, November–May, the rice harvest period when fewer males were needed in production. Teenage males and young men provided most of the labor in rice agriculture during the heavy rains from July to early October. They cut mangrove trees, constructed wooden dikes to desalinate water pools, and transplanted rice to the paddies. Many African males continued their rice work throughout the plowing and harvest months, but others raided for slaves to meet the increased European demand in the coming New Year. Ship captains sold iron bars, an essential good for the iron-poor Guinea-Bissau region; blacksmiths forged iron tools to ease dike building and rice cutting. More than half of all French slaving vessels trading at Bissau in 1788–1794 departed for the Americas in April, May, and June. Nine in ten French slavers at Bissau and Cacheu, 1758–1780, sailed from the African coast between December and July.[125]

Seasonality in overseas slave exports relates to the timing and intensity of rainfall, crop type, and varied inputs of male and female labor during the agricultural cycle. Each crop demanded a different combination of slave workers—young and old, male and female. But all available farmers hurried to sow seeds during the season's first rains, an "urgent task," suspending other activities to try to increase future food supplies.[126] One suspects that few communities were attacked during the planting rains. In regions supporting cereal crops, women harvested during the dry season, while some men raided and merchants traded. Pronounced slave trade seasonality occurred in regions dependent on an annual crop, such as the rice and millet-sorghum lands in Upper Guinea.[127] In the Gold Coast and western Bight of Benin, two rainy seasons supported double cropping of short-growing maize and grains; two dry seasons prompted more frequent slave raiding, and the greater distribution of foodstuffs enabled merchants to buy and sell slaves throughout the year. The Bight of Biafra was unusual in its dependence on a long-growing root crop, yams, farmed intensively by men during the July–October rains. Finally, the ecological history of West-Central African communities was one of recurrent drought, disease, and famine, a destructive combination that encouraged year-round slave raiding and trading.

Though seasonal attacks ensured predictable monthly slave supplies, raiders and traders "harvested slaves" without concern for rainfall, soil conditions, or food stocks.[128] The lowest slave-export quarters throughout Atlantic Africa, which occurred generally in the hungry rainy or wet seasons, still provided 20 percent of all captives sold into the transatlantic slave trade.[129] African investors purchased these slaves during out-of-crop months to clear lands, drain swamps, fight in armies, hunt animals, mine gold, fix roads, or perform other work. These were usually hungry times, and keeping slaves alive would have been difficult.[130] But by maintaining slaves they might profit from Guinea captains who came outside African trading seasons, willing to pay premium prices.[131] Such captains arrived out of season, such as in the rainy July–September quarter in Upper Guinea, because two to three months later they would find merchant-planters in the Americas who wanted to purchase enslaved African labor.

Seasonality in the Americas and the Slave Trade

After departing Old Calabar in October, Captain John Burrows reached Kingston, Jamaica, on December 29, 1783, with 450 enslaved Africans.

This Calabar-to-Kingston voyage was not unique: between 1718 and 1807 at least a hundred British slaving voyages transported 27,500 agricultural workers from one port to the other. Considering broad slave-trading regions, from 1663 to 1808 an estimated 767 British Guineamen sailed from the Bight of Biafra to disembark 230,000 slaves in Jamaica. The Bight of Biafra became Jamaica's most important slave supplier by the mid-1700s because British captains dominated trade there, and the two- to three-month Middle Passage bridged the July–October yam and December–May sugar and coffee harvests. Forty percent of the Africans who were shipped from the Bight of Biafra, however, arrived in Jamaica during the June–November out-of-crop season. Moreover, many of these people would have sailed from Bonny, Old Calabar, or New Calabar from April to July when yam stocks were low or depleted. Planters imported slaves from all other African regions in the Jamaican summer and fall as well. In Jamaica and in most New World markets, investors were willing to purchase enslaved labor from any African region on any day of the year.

Nevertheless, as in Atlantic Africa, ecology dictated the monthly production cycles of New World cash crops and the weeks when planters demanded the greatest number of new farmers.[132] Whereas rainfall governed crop choice in tropical Africa, temperature and rainfall controlled where farmers could grow specific crops in the tropical and temperate Americas. Compared to many African Atlantic coastal markets, the American littoral lacks extreme wet-dry periods, and only South and Central American rainforests and mountainous islands or coastal regions experience weekly deluges. Precipitation in the June–August rainy season in rice-growing Carolina (20 inches), for example, equaled that of the November–February dry season along sections of the Rice (Windward) Coast of Africa. The frosts north of Carolina perplexed both Europeans and Africans—winters too cold to grow tropical crops such as sugar or yams. On both sides of the Atlantic, demand for farmers increased during intensive work periods, usually dry-season cane, fruit, berry, leaf, or cereal harvests, but also during rainier weeks, when slaves sowed and transplanted some crops.

Jamaica, like other New World regions specializing in sugar production, imported more slaves during the dry-season harvest. Most West Indies and Guianas harvests took place from December to May. Drier weather accompanies cane cutting and processing in November–January in Havana and Kingston, and then in December–February in Bridgetown, Barbados, Montego Bay, Jamaica, west-central Saint-Domingue (Saint-Marc and Port au Prince) and in the island's southwest (Les Cayes). In Cap-Français, the largest town in Saint-Domingue, the greatest slave import quarter occurred during the April–June dry period.[133] All of these ports front extensive sugar plains. Pernambuco and Bahia, Brazil's earliest (from the 1570s) and later (by the mid-1600s) cane centers, respectively, imported more slaves in the comparatively dry November–January period than in any other quarter, as did Suriname, the leading Guianas sugar producer (see Table 1.4).[134] In these major sugar-producing areas, the greatest slave-import quarter totaled between 29 percent (Cuba, Pernambuco, Bahia) and 44 percent (northwest Jamaica) of the region's annual slave trade. The lowest quarters, usually during the rainier planting season, accounted for one-fifth of the annual slave imports.

In the smaller non–sugar-growing regions of North and South America, captains disembarked comparatively large numbers of slaves in-season during rainier months.[135] Chesapeake tobacco planters demanded new migrant farmers during the April–May spring rains, when men and women transplanted tobacco stalks to the fields, and in the heat and humidity of August–September, when they cut and stripped tobacco leaves.[136] In the rice-growing Carolina and Georgia Lowcountry and in Maranhão, labor intensity increased in April–October, when workers sowed seed, hoed wet fields, and harvested and processed rice.[137] The Brazilian rice planting took place after the heavy February–April rains; farmers aimed to mill rice in time for the Lisbon ships that departed in August and September at the beginning of the dry season. Delays in the onset of the New Year's rainy season would push back the rice production schedule.[138] Perhaps three-quarters of the enslaved Africans disembarked in Río de la Plata ports were re-exported to Upper Peru or Chile, a movement facilitated by the rising December–February waters that allowed inland boat transport.[139]

Slave-trading seasonality in the Americas, whether during dry or rainy months, increased from windward to leeward markets. Approaching the Lesser Antilles in December 1783, John Burrows could have anchored in Carlisle Bay, Barbados, purchased provisions, and gauged local and

Table 1.4 Quarterly Slave Imports by American Region (arranged north–
south)

American region	Three-month period (greatest/ lowest trade)[a]	Sample slave imports (estimated)	Index
Chesapeake	June–Aug *(rainy)*	45,684	48.40
	Nov.–Jan. *(dry)*	944	
Carolinas/Georgia	May–July *(rainy)*	51,134	2.84
	Jan.–March *(rainy)*	18,024	
Cuba	Nov.–Jan. *(dry)*	183,622	1.38
	July–Sept. *(rainy)*	132,609	
Saint-Domingue, northeast	April–June *(dry)*	99,751	1.59
	July–Sept. *(dry)*	62,754	
Saint-Domingue, west-central	Dec.–Feb. *(dry)*	71,829	1.73
	Aug.–Oct. *(rainy)*	41,603	
Saint-Domingue, southwest	Dec.–Feb. *(dry)*	20,477	2.27
	Aug.–Oct. *(rainy)*	9,001	
Jamaica, northwest	Dec.–Feb. *(dry)*	18,143	3.70
	Aug.–Oct. *(rainy)*	4,907	
Jamaica, southeast	Nov.–Jan. *(dry)*	145,075	1.93
	Aug.–Oct. *(rainy)*	75,301	
Barbados	Dec.–Feb. *(dry)*	99,670	1.70
	Aug.–Oct. *(rainy)*	58,576	
Guianas	Nov.–Jan. *(dry)*	71,806	1.54
	Aug.–Oct. *(rainy)*	46,548	
	Equator		
Maranhão	May–July *(rainy)*	14,409	2.54
	Oct.–Dec. *(dry)*	5,666	
Pernambuco	Nov.–Jan. *(dry)*	34,944	1.52
	Aug.–Oct.*(rainy)*	23,039	
Bahia	Nov.–Jan. *(dry)*	169,129	1.58
	July–Sept. *(dry)*	106,896	
Rio de Janeiro	Dec.–Feb. *(rainy)*	292,077	2.01
	June–Aug. *(dry)*	145,215	
Río de la Plata	Dec.–Feb. *(rainy)*	17,139	3.76
	July–Sept. *(dry)*	4,561	

Source: See Table 1.2.

[a]Dry/rainy/wet indicates general three-month conditions: dry = 0–12 inches of rain;
rainy = 13–36 inches; wet = 37+ inches.

regional slave prices. He knew that prices increased from windward to leeward to compensate captains for longer voyages and increased risk from insurrections and epidemic diseases. Once he arrived at a leeward market, though, he could not profitably reverse course against currents and winds. He thus would need to make sure that he arrived at a leeward market during the harvest, when planter demand for labor was strongest. From Barbados he could sail downwind in three days to Dominica, an expanding coffee frontier in need of workers. Montego Bay, reachable downwind in two weeks, would be his last option, since the American Revolution had ended the slave trades to Carolina and the Chesapeake.[140] Montego Bay was a more seasonal slave-trading port than Kingston; Kingston in turn was more seasonal than windward Barbados. In Saint-Domingue, captains sailed from northeast to southwest toward more seasonal leeward outlets, and after captains reached Brazil's northeastern promontory they steered south from Pernambuco to Bahia to Rio de Janeiro. In the northern and southernmost leeward markets, the Chesapeake's strong summer demand for farmers mirrored Río de la Plata's concentrated summer labor mart. A rainy spring–summer tobacco production cycle in a leeward market made the Chesapeake the most seasonal slaving region in the Atlantic world (see Table 1.4 and Map 1.1).[141]

Spotlighting the British slave trades from the two most seasonal African slave-trading regions—Upper Guinea and the Bight of Biafra—demonstrates how captains sailed toward in-crop American markets. The November–April slaving-provisioning season in Upper Guinea positioned ships to leave the coast in time to reach the Caribbean during the sugar harvest. Of those mariners who departed Upper Guinea in May, half chose to sell in the West Indies and half decided to proceed to North American leeward markets (see Figure 1.3). Planter demand for rice and tobacco slaves began rising in the Carolina and Chesapeake summers. Captains slaving in Upper Guinea in May knew that with each month they delayed their departure, North American slave prices dropped. Few attempted to sell slave cargoes there in the winter, an out-of-crop period accompanied by an increase in the number of respiratory diseases that afflicted Africans. Similarly, captains departing the Bight of Biafra between January and May more and more often opted to sail for North American ports; after May, with each passing month they de-

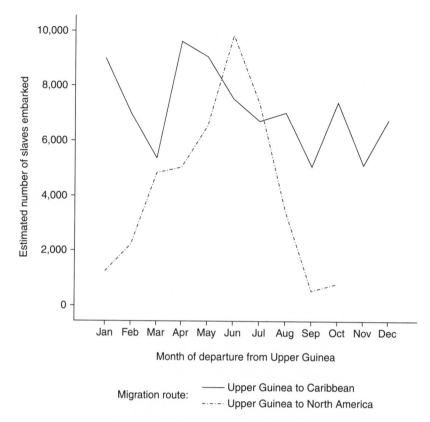

Month of departure from Upper Guinea

Migration route: —— Upper Guinea to Caribbean
---- Upper Guinea to North America

Figure 1.3 Forced migration from the Upper Guinea coast to the British Americas, 1663–1770 (by month of departure). *Sample:* 500 voyages from Upper Guinea to the Caribbean; 232 voyages from Upper Guinea to North America. *Source:* See Table 1.2.

cided increasingly to sell slaves in the British West Indies. Northern plantations rarely drew labor from the Bight of Biafra's fall slaving season (Figure 1.4).

The care that ship captains took to sell workers during harvests was not matched by any concern that planters preferred specific African ethnic groups or people with certain agricultural skills.[142] Captain John Burrows agreed to command a ship to Old Calabar because he knew that there were buyers for his human cargo, even though Jamaica planters did not prefer "Calabar slaves." Indeed, merchant-planters in North or South America never demanded Africans from this coastal enclave.

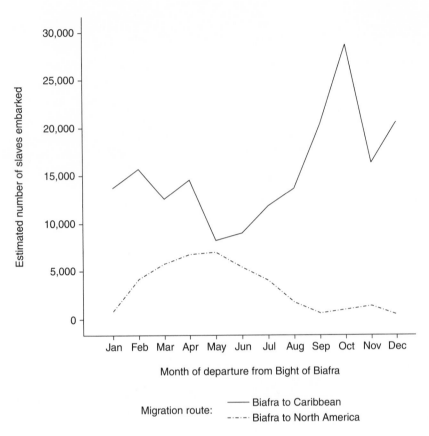

Figure 1.4 Forced migration from the Bight of Biafra to the British Americas, 1663–1770 (by month of departure). *Sample:* 614 voyages from Biafra to the Caribbean; 151 voyages from Biafra to North America. *Source:* See Table 1.2.

Nonetheless, from ca. 1650 to 1838 New World buyers purchased 275,000 Africans shipped from Old Calabar, and 30 percent arrived out of season. Planters expressed their preference by paying lower prices for Africans from Old Calabar, a valuation based on health and strength rather than on consideration of skills.[143] Though prices decreased out of season for Africans transported from Old Calabar or other markets, no shipload of slaves, regardless of provenance, went unsold in the Americas.

Interlocking structures created by commercial power, mercantilism, ecology, and social control explain better than planter preferences the geographical distribution of Africans in the Americas. Captain Burrows

and other Britons, for example, traded most competitively at Old Calabar because they offered the greatest range and quality of trading goods
demanded by Efik merchants such as Egbo Young. They assembled
these cargoes speedily in port, enabling their ships to arrive during the
yam-slaving months.[144] Burrows sailed to Jamaica because British military strength maintained control over the island, and mercantilist laws
stipulated that only British-flagged Guineamen could import slaves directly from Africa. Ecological conditions determined the yam-slaving
season at Old Calabar that positioned most captains to arrive in Jamaica
during labor-intensive sugar and coffee production. Sailing down to leeward Jamaica did not concern Burrows, because he arrived in the Lesser
Antilles early in the crop season. If the captain had been delayed, he
knew that Jamaican planters still would purchase his human cargo out-
of-crop—albeit at lower prices; in season or out, colonists relied on exploiting slaves to maintain the plantation complex and their position of
dominance in a racialized society.

The mix of factors explaining each transatlantic slave-trading pathway
differs. In the Portuguese slave-trading world, military rule in coastal
Angola and Brazil ensured a long-term migration stream that totaled
5,250 voyages and two million enslaved Africans between 1550 and
1850.[145] In the late 1500s Portuguese officials developed ports at Luanda
and Benguela and controlled them throughout the era of the slave trade,
except for the period (1641–1648) of Dutch occupation. Portuguese rule
in Brazil dates from 1500 to 1822, interrupted by the Dutch seizure of
ports in Pernambuco (1637–1654). Neither Dutch control nor Brazilian
independence in 1822 severed connections with Angolan entrepôts.[146]
North of Angola, Portugal's slave trade to Brazil centered on trading
forts in the Bight of Benin, a coastline of intense European competition.
Here the Portuguese were able to purchase as many as 800,000 slaves,
not because they controlled territories but because they supplied the
molasses-cured Brazilian tobacco demanded by African merchants. In
the mid-1700s the Portuguese Crown sponsored the monopolist Company of Grand-Pará and Maranhão to transport slaves from Portuguese
forts at Cacheu and Bissau to the rainforest ports Belem (Pará) and São
Luis (Maranhão). Over a twenty-year period most of the 21,000 Africans who arrived in northeast Brazil on Company ships worked on rice
and cotton plantations.[147] In this short-term pathway, the early-year

rice-slaving season in Guinea-Bissau linked to the May–July Maranhão in-crop season, which allowed some Brazilian planters to work with experienced African rice farmers.

Numerous transitory and long-term forced migrations occurred during the era of the transatlantic slave trade. Whereas Portuguese slavers concentrated in the Bight of Benin and the South Atlantic, Britons traded at all African Atlantic markets north of Luanda and throughout the West Indies and North America. The Old Calabar–Kingston pathway was one of fifty transplantations that, on average, moved a few shiploads of workers each year between Atlantic ports. As prices for agricultural commodities rose, so did planters' demand for laborers and their willingness to purchase human cargoes year-round from any African market.[148] British slaving merchants widened their operations on the African coast to meet planter demand, ensuring that every year different combinations of African peoples arrived in different West Indian and North American markets.[149] Similarly, French captains competed successfully to purchase slaves in most African Atlantic markets, and thus different groupings of African peoples arrived in Martinique, Guadeloupe, Guyane (French Guiana), and in northern, western, and southern Saint-Domingue.[150] These scatterings contrast with large-scale regular slave trades carried on by Portuguese-flagged ships between Ouidah and Bahia and between Luanda and Rio de Janeiro.[151]

Captain John Burrows sailed in 1783 from the Bight of Biafra to Jamaica on what had become one of the most regular routes in the British slaving world. This connection, like that between Upper Guinea and North America, developed and grew because the Middle Passage bridged complementary transatlantic crop cycles. African merchants created regular supply networks to deliver large numbers of agricultural slaves to Biafran ports in time to work later during Jamaican dry-season harvests. The volume of the slave trades in Bonny, Old Calabar, and New Calabar doubled in the 1740s and 1750s to help supply the new farmers needed to place more Jamaican acreage under cane. The slaving frontiers in the Nigerian hinterland and Jamaica expanded together; by abolition in 1807, the Bight of Biafra supplied half of Jamaica's new plantation farmers. Jamaicans, like planters and merchants in other New World markets, purchased greater numbers of slaves during in-crop seasons.

Even during rainier or colder out-of-crop seasons, though, colonists throughout the Americas bought slaves from any region in Africa. The African ethnic groups they purchased depended on captains' competitiveness in numerous markets along the African coast and on mercantilist laws that restricted trades to national carriers.

Conclusion

Ecology undergirded the organization of the slave trade in the early modern Atlantic agricultural world. The incidence and amount of rainfall determined the timing of crop cycles: farmers prepare soils at the end of the dry season, plant during the beginning rains, and then harvest toward the end of the rainy season or during dry months. European incursions did not alter seasonal rainfall patterns or agricultural rhythms. Varying rainfall amounts helped determine crop type and growing seasons in each African region. Optimal rainfall, temperature, and soil conditions enabled farmers to maximize staple- and cash-crop yields, increasing dietary intake. Rain-fed water supplies varied along the African coast and on the Middle Passage, a critical issue for those transporting human cargoes. Sequential stages in agricultural production require different mixes of men, women, and children. In Africa those ratios related to the incidence of warfare, slaving raids, slave supplies, and trading seasons; American planters purchased and hired seasonal workers at key production points. Marked seasonality characterized the slave trades from much of the Upper Guinea Coast, the Bight of Biafra, and leeward markets in the Americas. Greater year-round slave trades occurred at many Gold Coast and Bight of Benin settlements, along the West-Central African coast, and at first ports of call in the Americas. In shifting farmers between Atlantic agricultural systems, shipping merchants created numerous transatlantic migration patterns linking specific African and American ports, often moving farmers between dry seasons on the Atlantic littoral.

By examining ecology, particularly food production in Africa, one sees more clearly how transatlantic supply and demand factors shaped forced migrations. Consider the ecological histories of three African regions with long-standing ties to Europe and the Americas: the Gold

Coast, the Bight of Benin, and West-Central Africa. In the second half
of the 1600s maize began flourishing in Fante lands and in the Gap of
Benin. As a more diversified agricultural base developed along the Gold
and Slave coasts, African and European investors could support a
greater number of export slaves. New Atlantic powers attempted to establish coastal trading forts, tapping into expanding provisions and slave
trades that functioned year-round. Visitors commented that good African agriculturists farmed well-cultivated lands during two crop seasons.[152] More varied high-protein diets strengthened health, as reflected
in the comparatively high prices captains and planters paid for slaves
from these regions. In the Americas, from 1660 to 1820 six major slave-
importing markets controlled by four European powers—Pernambuco
and Bahia (Portugal), Barbados and Jamaica (Britain), Saint-Domingue
(France), and Cuba (Spain)—imported at least one in five slaves from
the Gold and Slave coasts. Competition along this stretch of the African
coast drove up prices and forced many European merchants to reori-
ent their business toward northern Angola's supply of lower-priced
slaves.[153] In this African region, however, the high volume of monthly
slave exports that began in the 1600s resulted not from comparative agricultural abundance, but from the frequency of drought and famine that
forced people into slavery and into the Portuguese, British, French, and
Dutch slave trades.

   Historians should study more closely the impact of varying ecological conditions on the size and seasonal regularity of transatlantic slave
trading pathways. In 1783–1784 Captain John Burrows purchased and
sold slaves during the Nigerian and Jamaican yam- and sugar-harvest
cycles, and he returned to Liverpool only one month later than predicted by Old Calabar merchant Egbo Young. If the yam crop had failed
due to insufficient rains or pest invasions, Burrows would have been
forced to purchase fewer slaves or to remain longer on the African coast.
If unpredicted wind directions or drops in air pressure had delayed his
Middle Passage, the captain would not have arrived in Kingston in late
December. If Jamaican planters had anticipated a poor sugar crop, Burrows would have had difficulty selling his human cargo and would not
have returned to Liverpool in the spring. The seasonal regularity of
slave-supply lines from the African interior to coastal outlets to Atlantic
ports depended upon optimal ecological conditions on land and at sea.

Non-optimal precipitation, temperature, or winds increased the likelihood that merchants and captains would not deliver slaves at predicted times, to predicted markets. Disruption in either trading diaspora—inland to coastal Africa, or from Africa to the Americas—forced traders to seek alternative markets and hence broadened the geographical distribution of African peoples in the Atlantic world.

2

Kongo and Dahomey, 1660–1815

African Political Leadership in the Era of the Slave Trade and Its Impact on the Formation of African Identity in Brazil

LINDA M. HEYWOOD AND

JOHN K. THORNTON

The slave trade was Africa's primary export and essential connection to the other corners of the Atlantic basin; it is therefore not surprising that studies of Africa during the early modern period have focused on that trade as the dynamic factor in Atlantic Africa. Although several major works on the slave trade published during the 1970s and 1980s explored its political dimensions, most of those appearing in the last two decades have emphasized the commercial aspects of the interaction, examining among other issues how money and credit were handled, the numbers of people exported, the nature of imports, and the demographic characteristics of the trade.[1] Concomitant with this, some scholars have made use of the studies of the trade to explore the cultural dimensions of the African Diaspora and have focused particularly on identity formation among enslaved Africans in the Americas.

The question of identity among enslaved Africans has been hotly debated in recent years. In this case, "identity" is conceived as self-perceived membership in a bounded community with cultural practices and customs that members recognize as distinctive. Among enslaved Africans in the Americas, identity was often defined by reference to "country" (*nation, nação, nación* in French, Portuguese, and Spanish) or to ethnic affiliations such as Congo, Mina, Coromantee, Calabar,

Lucumi, or Mandinga. Some scholars argue that these ethnic identities were continuations and modifications of earlier African distinctions.[2] Others believe that, because these ethnic names were connected variously to geographic areas, African political units, ports of exit, and languages, they were more the creation of Europeans than of the Africans themselves.

Resolving this question requires a fuller examination of the way in which identity was formed in Africa. Whatever the various elements that may have contributed to identity on the American side of the Atlantic, African states were important in the formation of identity among their subjects. States can create identity by defining boundaries, requiring common action such as military service or taxation, establishing a common ideology, or serving as a final arbiter of disputes. What we are calling states in Africa were polities that exercised a "monopoly of legitimate force within a given territory," to use Max Weber's classic formulation.[3] There have been various debates within African historiography about the concept of the state in Africa and the application of the term to precolonial polities. Robin Law, for example, has contended that the polities of the precolonial "Slave Coast" (modern-day Togo, Benin, and western Nigeria) meet the Weberian definition of states.[4] On the other hand, Joseph C. Miller believes that no states existed in precolonial Central Africa, and that the primary units were "small to moderate-sized village communities of kin, in-laws, clients, and others of familiar backgrounds," which grew by adding dependents who were loosely connected to other similar communities through trade.[5]

In fact, Africa had a wide variety of polities, ranging from micro-units to much larger areas like the Kingdom of Kongo and Ndongo. These entities were also constitutionally complex and varied, and they enjoyed varying degrees of legitimacy. Many underwent radical changes over time, all of which affected both the way their subjects or citizens viewed themselves and the role of the state in shaping their self-conception. Not all states were equally successful in shaping ideologies and conceptions that informed African identities in the Americas. In order to explore this variety, we will compare two African states, Kongo and Dahomey, to argue that the way the state functioned over time and the degree to which the subjects responded were crucial to the state's role in forming identities.

Kongo and Dahomey: Background

In the mid-seventeenth century Kongo ruled some half a million people living in a territory of over 100,000 square kilometers located in the region just south of the Congo River in modern-day northern Angola and western Democratic Republic of Congo. Most of its people spoke the Kikongo language, though the kingdom also ruled related Kimbundu speakers on its southern border. Kongo was already in existence when the first Portuguese navigators arrived on its Atlantic coast in 1483 and had probably been formed at least a century earlier. Dahomey, located in a gap in the West Atlantic rainforest in modern-day Benin, had far less surface area, only about 8,000 square kilometers, but its population probably numbered around 350,000 by the early eighteenth century. It came to prominence in that period, when leaders of the inland core province of Abomey conquered their neighbors in the closely related Fon- and Ewe-speaking region along the coast and in the farther interior. Both kingdoms contained enslaved people from outside their core zones as permanent residents.

A comparison between the states of Kongo and Dahomey during the long eighteenth century (1660–1815) provides interesting contrasts in state structure and history. Kongo and Dahomey are among the few Atlantic African states to have generated their own written documentation, primarily in the form of letters written by their kings. While there are important descriptions of the states written by outsiders—traders in the case of Dahomey, largely missionaries in Kongo—this insider's view brings another dimension to the comparison that is often lacking in African history.

The two states were major suppliers of the slave trade. West-Central Africa (including Kongo and its immediate neighbors) and the Bight of Biafra (including Dahomey and the areas with which it had diplomatic relations and against which it made military forays) supplied nearly 54 percent of all slaves leaving Africa for the Americas during the long eighteenth century. Dahomey and the area affected by its wars supplied about 20 percent of that total. Although exports from Kongo are more difficult to calculate, the kingdom probably supplied as much as 15 percent.[6] This regional differentiation was even more pronounced when seen from the viewpoint of Brazil, where Central African slaves, usually referred to as "Angolas" and "Congos," and slaves from the Bight of Biafra, called "Minas," accounted for as much as 80 percent of enslaved Africans. Given the dominance of these peoples in Brazil, it is reasonably certain that manifestations of African identity there would be informed by the ideas that Africans from Kongo and Dahomey brought with them. The impacts of the state on identity in Kongo and in Dahomey were not the same, however. The two states had very different histories between 1660 and 1815. Whereas Kongo had become a failed state by the 1660s after a century and a half of stability and centralization, Dahomey was reaching its height as a highly centralized and powerful state in the eighteenth century. These divergent histories played a vital role in the way that the identities of subjects of Kongo and Dahomey were shaped, and they would have implications for the manifestation of those identities in the Americas.

Ideal versus Reality: The Nature of Kongo Identity

During the period when the state was strong, the structure of the kingdom and the way in which the state functioned greatly informed a sense of Kongo identity. The most powerful influence was the Kongo monarchy, which had been created in the late fourteenth century.[7] A second feature of the state that was also at the core of Kongo identity—Christianity—had its origins in the conversion of Queen Nzinga a Nkuwu in 1491 and was bolstered by the efforts of later rulers to expand the faith throughout the kingdom and the region. Independent neighboring regions such as Loango, Malemba, Matamba, and Ndongo claimed origins in Kongo and sometimes identified themselves as Christian. The combination of ancient royalty and Christianity made the Kongo state unusual in Atlantic Africa.[8] The two themes persisted, albeit reinterpreted, even when civil wars caused the virtual collapse of the state and even when the kingdom being fought over was more symbolic than real. Ordinary Kongos accepted the idea of royalty and strove to have a Christian identity.[9]

The Kongo state reached the apogee of its centralization during the reign of King Álvaro I (1568–1578) and his successors until the reign of King António I (1661–1665). Álvaro pushed to intensify and strengthen Christianity throughout the kingdom. He wanted Kongo to be like the

Christian monarchies in Europe, and he successfully petitioned the papacy to have the kingdom declared an episcopal see in 1596, requested and had sent from Rome many relics and other Catholic paraphernalia, and changed the name of his capital to São Salvador from its Kikongo name Mbanza Kongo. He and his son Álvaro II also introduced such European titles as duke, count, and marquis for the nobility who were appointed to various offices in the kingdom. The kings insisted that they be treated with the same courtesy and ceremony as European monarchs received from their subjects, visitors, and foreign residents or religious personnel. The size of the kingdom and the rituals that embodied kingship during the period informed the conception of the state and the identity of future generations of Kongos. These ideas rested on the notion of a large and powerful kingdom, a king who exercised a range of functions, well-developed notions of royalty, and the central role of the Christian religion in the functioning of the state.

Kongo kings always publicly claimed that they ruled over extensive lands (Map 2.1). Garcia II, for example, proclaimed in a letter to the Dutch *stathouder* Moritz van Nassau in 1642 that he was: "Dom Garcia, by Divine Grace King of Congo, Angolla, Matamba, Ocanga, Cunde, Lulla, Sundi, Lord of the monarchy of the Ambundos, Lord of the Duchy and province of Bata, and of the County of Sonho and of the kings annexed to this, Angoyo, and Cacongo, and many other kingdoms and lordships confining this above and below the immense River Zaire."[10] Kongo kings conceived of themselves not only as powerful over wide-ranging territory, but also as benevolent protectors of their people in the name of their Christian faith. At his coronation in 1641 Garcia swore an oath that detailed exactly what the electors expected of the king. Before his coronation a herald enjoined the king: "You shall be king, be no thief, neither covetous nor revengeful, but be a friend of the poor: You shall also give alms for the release of prisoners or slaves and help the needy and be charitable to the Church, and always work to keep this kingdom in peace, and to observe the alliance with your brother in arms the king of Portugal."[11]

Garcia affirmed the Catholic basis of his rule when he emphasized in his letter to Nassau, in which he agreed to all the terms of a treaty of alliance to fight the Portuguese presented to him by Dutch representatives, except those allowing Protestant ministers to come and preach in the

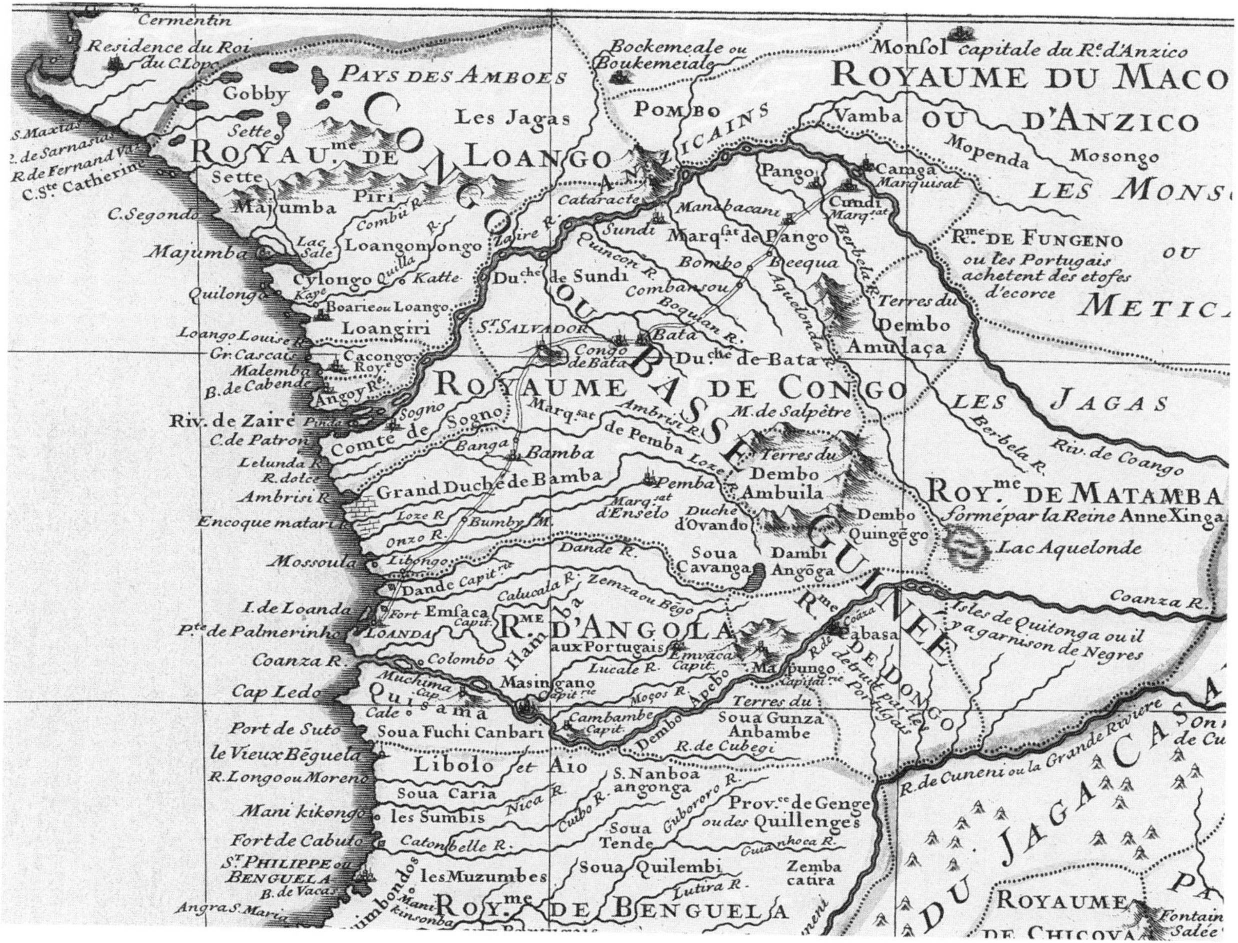

Map 2.1 Kingdom of Kongo, early eighteenth century. Detail, Guillaime de L'Isle, "Carte du Congo et du Pays des Cafres," *Atlas de géographie* (Paris), ca. 1718–1726.

country, "as I confess the true Catholic Faith and place myself under the obedience of the Holy Father, vicar of God, because the evil of the Portuguese, founded in ambition is not sufficient for me to abandon the Catholic Faith . . . there is no Catholic prince who would castigate me for this."[12] Moreover, in a 1648 letter to officials throughout the kingdom, Garcia laid out the Christian character of the realm. He wrote: "I wish you health and prosperity in our Lord Jesus Christ. . . . Great are the benefits that God has done for this kingdom . . . principally after this kingdom received the light of the Holy Gospel and the true Holy Roman Catholic faith."[13]

Seventeenth-century Kongo rulers not only promoted the idea of a strong unified kingdom with a Christian identity, but also had a centralized bureaucratic structure to go with it. However, neither the ideology nor the bureaucratic structure prevented rivalries within the ruling group from destabilizing the central authority, ultimately leading to the Kongo's collapse. Constant rebellions were fostered by claimants to the throne or their supporters, who often used a provincial appointment as a base for mobilizing against the king. Such rebellions were particularly pronounced in the early years of any king's rule and resulted in many short reigns, as kings failed to consolidate their power, remove rivals from provincial office, or integrate the province into their own loyal faction.[14]

The rebellions that disrupted the kingdom in the seventeenth century rapidly escalated into full-scale and long-term civil war after the 1665 battle of Mbwila, in which King António I sought to enforce his authority over a rebel province that had won the support of the Portuguese in the neighboring colony of Angola. The Portuguese won the battle, and António and many nobles were killed. The struggle to replace António was indecisive, and the country was left without a single recognized leader. By 1678 the capital had been sacked and abandoned, and many of the rivals had fled to fortified bases where they were protected and able to raise supporters from surrounding provinces.[15]

Although the capital was restored in 1709 and only three kings ruled until 1752, the kingdom's centralizing power had been essentially gutted, because the kings were unable to appoint or remove many of the most important officials. Rival kings and provincial nobles appointed some officials in the areas under their control, but their authority was limited to those regions, and in some areas rivals appointed different officials to the same province. Moreover, in many places the descendants of previous provincial rulers continued in their offices. Although these powerful local rulers never claimed independence, keeping their original titles of duke, count, or marquis, they exercised power more or less as if they were kings of their own area. At no time during the period was Kongo an aggressor state that attacked its neighbors, but it was overwhelmed by constant civil strife, which in some localities at times degenerated into chaos.

A visiting Portuguese missionary, Rafael Castello de Vide, observing the irreconcilability of the rival factions in 1781, described the Kongo royal family as being divided into three clans *(gerações)* from which "they elect the kings."[16] These divisions, in his opinion, led to continuous warfare, because "after the war . . . they cannot do anything, but the relatives of those who have died now want vengeance."[17] In the case of the election of Henrique I, whose coronation was handled by the Italian priest Raimondo da Dicomano in 1794, rivals presented themselves at the time of the election and declared war against the king, creating an opposition that the king could head off only by paying out a good deal of his wealth.[18]

Eighteenth-century kings continued to claim rights over extensive areas just as their early seventeenth-century counterparts had done, even when their authority was highly curtailed. Indeed, the titles were more grandiose than those of the seventeenth century. The claims that Pedro IV made upon his coronation in 1696, at a time when he controlled little more than the region around his fortified base at Mount Kibangu and was forced to flee from a rival the day after his elevation, provide an excellent example of this pretension. Pedro identified himself as "Emperor of the Kingdoms of Congo, Angola, Luango, Zongo, Angoi, Malemba, Engobella, Macoco, and of the immense River Zaire."[19] Even missionaries identified Kongo in these grandiose but hollow terms. Cherubino da Savona, an Italian Capuchin missionary who worked in Kongo from 1761 to 1776, identified the kingdom as "an empire because it has several diverse subject kingdoms and very many provinces, principalities and duchies."[20] Castello de Vide, writing in 1782, made similar claims that Kongo was "a great empire," while Afonso V (1785–1788) asserted that he was "the king of Congo and most powerful Dom Afonso the Fifth, lord of this part of Ethiopia."[21] These titles hardly described the real power of the kings, and indeed some of the more modest kings used considerably more realistic titles. Garcia V (1803–1830) claimed in 1804 to be simply "King of Congo Garcia fifth of that name," and in 1814 he began his letter to the governor of Angola with "I, Garcia am lord of [the] Mountain of Quibango," which was in fact his real domain.[22]

Cherubino da Savona's description of Kongo in the mid-1760s gives a good idea of the political organization at the time. He described the country as "the Kingdom of Congo, or to say it better, the Empire," which had "many various kingdoms subjected to it." He then listed four that had their roots in the division of the country following the battle of Mbwila.[23] Da Savona also described some twenty-two provinces that were under Kongo, variously ruled by princes, dukes, grand dukes, marquises, grand marquises, and dembos (an Angolan title). There seemed to be little question of the kings' appointing to these offices as they had in the seventeenth century, though some of the dukes and marquises were said to have other nobles subject to them. Some of the districts seem to have been connected by family ties, since marriages between Romano Leite, de Leão, and Agua Rosada clans were common.[24] Similarly, Castello de Vide, crossing Kongo in 1781, entered the "lands of the Queen," or the land that da Savona called Nkondo, located along the Mbidizi River; it included "many duchies and marquisates," including Mpemba, whose ruler Afonso de Leão was the brother of the king, José I.[25]

However much disorder there was in the kingdom, to the elite the ideas of the indivisibility of the kingdom and of its Christian character persisted. The Catholic identity of the monarchy and the king's role as benevolent protector were not affected by the political chaos. In the midst of civil strife, at the coronation of Álvaro XI in 1764, a priest invested the king, giving him a variety of regalia and exhorting him to be faithful to the "Holy Roman Church" and to remain "in peace with the king of Portugal," to "serve for the glory of God, for the defense of the Faith, and his people," to keep the roads open for evangelization, and finally to suppress idolatry and superstition.[26]

Even ordinary people continued to share this larger view of the kingdom and its rulers. Dutch visitors in 1642 observed that when ordinary people had a party, they might follow the party giver around crying

"Here comes the King of Kongo."[27] In celebrations of the feast of Saint James Major, Kongo's patron saint who was identified with the king-dom's conversion to Christianity, thousands of commoners flocked to public places to celebrate. In these celebrations they reenacted episodes of Kongo's early history, sang the praises of the kings and their power, and of the country and its splendor. In all of this a Christian tone pre-vailed, in which both Kongo and foreign priests played a prominent role.[28]

Moreover, in the aftermath of the civil wars that followed the battle of Mbwila, many tales of Christian devotion surfaced. One claimed that Afonso had buried his own mother alive for the sake of the Church, be-cause she had refused to part with a small idol she wore. The story re-mained current in the eighteenth century and was recorded in a brief history written in 1782 by a secretary of King José (1779–1785), along with other miraculous tales linking the origins of the three families who contested the throne and even the chivalric Order of Christ to Afonso and the conversion of the country.[29] Although recorded by the elite or priests, the story probably also had popular manifestations, being found in more recent times among clan mottos.[30]

Furthermore, all Kongo kings constantly reaffirmed their roles as de-fenders and supporters of the Church. Pedro IV (1696–1718), who sought to reunite the country in the early eighteenth century, signed his letter to the Capuchin priest Bernardo da Gallo "Dom Pedro IV, peaceful de-fender of the Holy Faith and its Restorer."[31] He saw himself as elected "by God and the People."[32] Manuel II (1718–1743) noted that "all my predecessors" had a "deep devotion" for the convent of St. Francis (in Kibangu), the home of Capuchins, where "dukes, counts, marquis, and titled knights have always had Capuchin religious as chaplains." He added that the late Capuchin missionary Bernardo da Gallo had refused to crown Manuel's deceased predecessor, Pedro IV, because he was not properly married. He hoped that a new crown, blessed by the Pope, that Kongo had been promised could be delivered to him. He contended that he was personally a great devotee of Saint Francis (and to a lesser extent, of Saint Anthony). He also believed that a banner of Saint Francis that da Gallo had given him was a crucial piece of regalia: "without that Holy Christ, the rebels against my crown would not obey because I would be abandoned."[33] Toward the end of the century, continuing in the same tradition, Afonso V called himself "the Christian King who" defends "the Holy Faith of God."[34]

The ruling group sought to live up to Christian ideals. A report on Kongo written by the Capuchin Bernardo Ignazio d'Asti in 1749 noted that Garcia IV (1743–1752) was "a good example of matrimonial fidelity who lives with his wife and castigates his subjects who live in concubinage." D'Asti also noted the piety of a widowed queen named Moconde, once the wife of a king, who "by a special impulse of the Holy Spirit" had worked as a missionary to the people in her district, so that when d'Asti arrived he was able to perform four thousand baptisms and a considerable number of marriages.[35] In his report on the mid-1760s, da Savona also pointed out that most of the inhabitants in the various provinces of Kongo were Christian, and most had churches or hospices, though commonly ruined by war or ecclesiastical neglect.[36] As part of their Christian identity, members of the elite wanted to be buried in churches, as Castello de Vide noted: "the grandees of the realm want to be buried in the churches of the Court [of which there were twelve] because even though they have fallen in, each one looks to have their tomb there."[37]

Throughout the eighteenth century, members of the ruling group competed to attract and hold missionaries in their areas to strengthen their claims to Christian legitimacy. Thus in 1782, when he wished to visit lands controlled by a faction hostile to King José I, Castello de Vide observed that the king was anxious that "we not go to the lands of the other faction [*parcialidade*]."[38] When he crossed Kongo in 1780, he lodged in Mbanza Nkondo, then held by José I, while awaiting an audience. During this time he received an impassioned and detailed letter from José's rival Pedro V requesting that he relocate to his lands, because he (Pedro) was "true king of Congo"; the letter was angrily dismissed by José's partisans as a trick.[39] José I initially wanted the missionaries to work only in his area, and not to visit or perform sacraments in the areas loyal to other leaders. Only when Castello de Vide threatened to leave the country did the king relent and allow the missionaries to travel freely.[40]

The ordinary people, although regarded as superstitious by the missionaries, also believed themselves to be Catholic and clamored to participate in Church rituals and sacraments. Membership in the Church indicated that they were a part of the Kongo state. They accepted the sacraments readily and sought out the missionaries and priests to obtain them. Detailed reports from 1752 show that each mission station performed thousands of baptisms, which were universally regarded in the country as a part of Christian identity. Devotion had grown since earlier times, as more people made confessions and joined in marriages, which Kongos previously had been less willing to do.[41] Da Dicomano, reflecting on his stay in Kongo in 1792–1795, said that he was glad to see "such a great multitude of people crowding in to give their children to the Father to baptize, and crying in a loud voice *anamungoa,* baptism," and he was overjoyed to see them "throw themselves on the ground and raise their hands to heaven in joy to see the missionaries and ask for a blessing."[42] While the sacraments were administered by ordained priests, the majority of whom were Italian Capuchin missionaries, along with a handful of secular priests (mostly mulattoes from Angola), the teaching was done by Kongo interpreters, whom the missionaries labeled "masters of doctrine." These masters were found all over Kongo; they taught the religious basics and contributed to the maintenance of the Christian identity of ordinary people.[43]

For much of the eighteenth century, the people of Kongo were a regular part of the human exports of West-Central Africa, whose numbers rose in the period between 1700 and 1799 from 109,780 in the first decade to 340,110 in the last.[44] Although we do not have statistics specifically on Kongo, we have estimated that for the period from 1780 to 1789 a total of 61,800 slaves were exported from Kongo alone.[45] These slaves went to English, French, and Portuguese shippers and then to every part of the Americas, and they carried with them their strong sense of Kongo Christian identity.

Elusive Identity: The Case of Dahomey

Whereas throughout Kongo's history rulers promoted the idea that royalty and Christianity lay at the base of the state, eighteenth-century Dahomey rested on the idea that the state's primary function was military, at times conceived to be offensive, at other times defensive. Thus the king's main role was to lead his army in warfare. Perhaps as an adjunct to their military role, Dahomey's rulers subscribed to an absolutist conception of the state, and to that end they developed a highly centralized bureaucracy directed by the king. In religion, Dahomey's rulers upheld the public worship of the royal ancestors, who were perceived as having a direct role in the success of the state, as opposed to the more universal gods of their religious tradition. The organization of the state gave Dahomey a radically different structure from that of Kongo in the eighteenth century, and this fundamentally affected how Dahomeans, people under Dahomey's military control like the Whydahs (Ajuda) and Allada (Ardra), and others who were variously enemies or allies of Dahomey (Mahee, Sabara, Nagos) conceived of their identity.

While Kongo was a long-established kingdom in the eighteenth century, Dahomey was building a new state from existing structures in which the consciousness of being subjects of a monarch was just emerging. Dahomey had probably once been an interior province of the Kingdom of Allada but broke away in the seventeenth century and began a series of conquests in the years that followed (Map 2.2).[46] The eighteenth-century kings of Dahomey contended that wars were necessary to create security, although some were clearly intended to impose a Dahomean regime on nearby regions. Dahomey faced few civil wars. When conflict broke out between competing lineages following the death of kings, it was short-lived and took place within the palace walls and not throughout the entire country.

The central role that warfare and the warrior tradition played in the eighteenth-century Dahomean kings' conception of the state is clear from letters that various rulers sent to Europeans and official statements recorded in their courts. In these attempts to explain how the state functioned, warfare took a prominent and explicit place. King Agaja (1708–1740) brought his state to the attention of European merchants at the coast when he conquered the coastal kingdom of Allada in 1724. The letter to King George I that he dictated to the English factor Bullfinch Lambe can be used as the official statement of Agaja's conception of the state and its role in this part of Africa.[47] Agaja wrote of the several wars he had undertaken and outlined a brief history of the conquests of his predecessors, noting that his own conquests exceeded theirs. The motive expressed for these wars was primarily to bring independent states in the region under Dahomey's control, culminating in the conquest of Allada. But Agaja did not think this was the end of his wars, for he

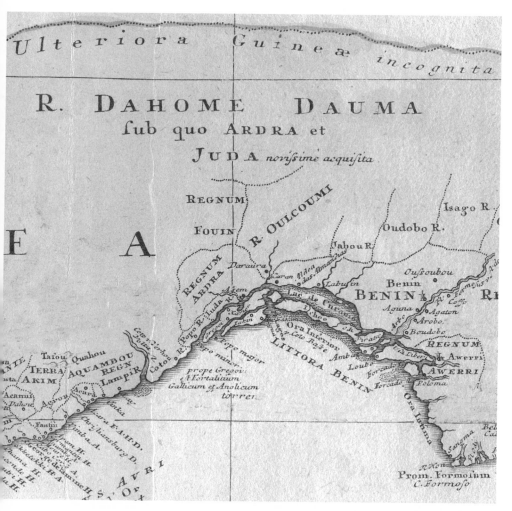

Map 2.2 Kingdom of Dahomey. Detail based on "Guinea proper, nec non Nigritiae vel Terrae Nigorum maxima pars," published by J. B. Homann (Amsterdam, 1743).

noted that the leaders of Whydah, another coastal state located west of Allada, "vainly think themselves above my power, but I'le let them see there is no withstanding Dawhomayns unless there gods fight against them." To emphasize the central role of warfare as a mechanism for governance, Agaja noted that "I can send near 500,000 armed and well skill'd man to battle, that being what all my subjects are bread to." He referred to his attempts to modernize the army by including firearms, which he felt had given him an advantage, and had plans to manufacture his own gunpowder.[48]

Agaja's successor Tegbesu (1740–1774) also represented himself as a warrior king who dominated the regions from the coast to the interior. When his ambassador had an official audience with the Portuguese viceroy of Brazil in 1751 in Bahia, he gave a speech in which he described Tegbesu as "a monarch of all the heathen nations from the coast to the far interior and among all the peoples of great courage the king of Dahomey exceeds all."[49] Although his successor Kpengla (1774–1789) left no letters, a chronicle of his reign written by Lionel Abson, a well-informed English trader who served in his court, also presented him as another great warrior, recounting his victories in detail.[50]

When Robert Norris, a slave trader with long experience on the coast, was shown the preserved body of one of Kpengla's enemies in autumn 1774, he commented on how carefully the king looked after the remains of a former enemy. Kpengla replied, "I am a warrior myself, and if I should fall into the enemies hand I could wish to be treated with that decency of which I set the example."[51] On another occasion Kpengla warned the subject king of Allada, whom he suspected of treason, that he should be careful, since "I am easy in my pace but always in pursuit."[52] In 1783 after his army lost a major battle to the neighboring small coastal state of Badagri, Kpengla swore at the religious ceremony held once or even twice a year to honor the ancestors of the ruling dynasty—called by the Europeans the "Annual Customs"—that "if he did not make a total conquest of Badagri he was unworthy to be called [his mother's] and Ahadee [Tegbesu]'s son."[53] In a long speech that he made to Abson upon learning of the parliamentary debates about the slave trade, Tegbesu explained his penchant for making wars by noting that Dahomey was surrounded by enemies and "obliged by the sharpness of our swords to defend ourselves from their incursions and punish the depredations they make on us."[54] Agonglo, the son of Kpengla who followed him to the throne in 1789, wasted little time in taking up the military tradition of his father, conducting three campaigns in 1790 that netted more than 1,500 captives.[55]

Adandozan (1797–1818), who succeeded Agonglo, wrote a letter to King João VI of Portugal in 1810 in which he too identified himself as a warrior. His detailed chronicle of his wars bears a remarkable resemblance to the kinds of military details found in the account kept for Kpengla earlier.[56] Adandozan began his letter expressing concern that he was too young to "go on dry land to give you some aid with my arms," and he described in minute detail the several wars that he had fought and won against neighbors both in the interior and along the coast.[57]

Though the warrior tradition may have created a sense of élan and duty in the subjects who served in the armies, it undoubtedly had less resonance with those subjects who had been drawn into the state through conquest. William Snelgrave, for example, noted in 1730 that, although Agaja had made great conquests, he was "only a king in name for want of subjects, by reason of his having destroyed in so cruel a manner the inhabitants of all the places he has conquered"; moreover, he had forced thousands more to flee elsewhere to be secure from "his rambling bands." Though Agaja promised to allow some of the refugees from Allada to return, "no sooner were these poor People settled, than the *Dahomes* surprised them and killed or took captive all that could not escape from them."[58] As late as 1750, French observers noted that Tegbesu was alienating his own subjects through his cruelty "toward his allies as toward his subjects . . . detaching the former from allegiance to him and depriving him of the latter through their desertion to the Whydahs."[59]

From this inauspicious beginning as heads of a ruthless state, Dahomean rulers of the later eighteenth century sought to increase their popular legitimacy. Robin Law concludes that by the 1770s the Dahomean rulers had "clearly won the consent of the conquered to [the] legitimacy of their rule."[60] Norris noted around 1760 that the Dahomeans "reverence [their king] with a mixture of love and fear little short of adoration." A Dahomean named Dakou told Norris that "my head belongs to the king, not myself; if he pleases to send for it, I am ready to resign it." Dakou was in fact sold as a slave by the king. Such strong loyalty to the ruler, even in the face of arbitrary actions that touched many people, could have been the basis for a Dahomean identity.[61]

Beyond the warrior tradition, Dahomean kings also presented Dahomey as an absolutist state. Agaja's letter of 1726 included ideas that showed his absolutist philosophy. "I have no disturbance or controversies whatsoever," he wrote, "either amongst my wives or other subjects, everyone knowing thare duty, place and station. For if one transgress against my laws or customs, or att least them of my forefathers, they must suffer death." He stressed that his jurisdiction was not entirely arbitrary, however, for he could not proceed without taking a body of existing law and practice into consideration. As he noted about those who were condemned, "it is not in my power to save them without violating the laws of my gods, kingdom and predecessors." He also recognized some sort of due process for the accused; as he observed, "I never give sentence without sufficient proof, or the gods convicting them by thare taking fetish."[62]

Agaja was proud of his status as an absolute monarch, describing the debasement of conquered kings, who could not come to him without lying on the ground and "rubbing their mouth nine times in the dust before they opens it to speak to me."[63] However, he still respected existing customs and leadership in the conquered regions. He recognized the line of the kings of Allada, and installed the son of the king he had defeated, as well as nine of Allada's dependent kings "with the same ceremony as formerly done by the kings of Ardah." The newly installed king, however, had to agree to submit to Agaja, acknowledge Dahomey as his ruler, and abandon all allegiance to Allada.[64] Later Dahomean kings would be installed in Allada, as a way of recognizing that Allada had once been their overlord, but now they were its inheritors.[65]

Such absolutist notions were institutionalized by a well-established and closely controlled bureaucracy. Agaja hinted that he had tight control over a great bureaucracy; in describing how he had managed to carry many cannons to his capital, he emphasized the role of merit in his appointments. He wrote, "I reward them well, and punish them well according to their deserts, a rule with me in government."[66] Norris, writing about the situation he observed after 1763, maintained that officials in Dahomey had "no hereditary claim, being appointed to them [offices] by the king's particular favor, arising from the opinion he entertains of their qualifications and abilities."[67]

The dependent nature of the bureaucracy was noted by most other observers of Dahomey in the years following Agaja's rule. Norris recorded how justice was meted out. When passing the marketplace of Grigwhee, he witnessed the execution of middle-aged women who had accidentally set the market on fire after wishing for a person's death. He observed that "the king himself had considered the offense and decreed the sentence."[68]

Luis Antonio de Oliveira Mendes, a Brazilian who learned of Dahomean customs first from slaves on his own estate and then from a wide range of Dahomean visitors and friends from the 1790s onward, made this more explicit. "The nobility is not hereditary," but becoming noble or titled was based on "putting in good works" or "being most free of crimes and vices," and also possessing wealth. The king "taking notice of this calls them to be his friends and makes them caboceiros [nobles and officials]."[69]

The long and detailed account of the country written by Vincente Ferreira Pires, a Brazilian-based priest who traveled to Dahomey in 1797 in hopes of converting King Agonglo, provides an excellent exploration of how Agaja and especially his successors built Dahomey into a despotic, bureaucratic state. At the Annual Customs, the king received gifts and gave return gifts to his officials. Although the value of the gifts the king received was twenty times greater than those given to the governors, the king also gave out positions and titles that surely compensated for the gifts.[70] Dahomey's government was "the most despotic in all the coast of Africa, and above all, hereditary." Pires believed that the king's will "is law without limit," and "all are his slaves and look upon him as upon Divinity, in such a way that all they are and they own . . . they received as if by a gift of the king."[71] Archibald Dalzel, who was a constant visitor to the coast of Dahomey from 1763 to 1802 and who served as the British governor of Whydah from 1763 to 1767, commented on how the people accepted the power that the Dahomean kings exercised. He observed that "so great is the veneration of the Dahomeans for their sovereign . . . [that] the most oppressive mandates of the monarch are submitted to without a murmur."[72]

The scope of the bureaucracy was also far-reaching. The king and his officials were engaged in supervising much of the economy. For example, an important official, the Topozú, was in charge of agriculture; his duties were to "divide the portions of land" according to the status of the recipient. But, if the recipient failed to develop the land "and giv[e] to the king a portion of all that he produces, the owner loses the right to the new possession and his goods are confiscated in favor of the king."

Such people also lost an exemption from military service and were sent to the wars.[73]

Commerce was also under close bureaucratic supervision, and foreign traders were carefully managed. Agaja noted in his letter to George I that he welcomed Muslim traders from the north, and "I have appointed a governor or petty king of their owne over them."[74] He would repeat this practice with Europeans who appeared at his court regularly, for he stated that Captain Tom, "who is one of the king of Jaquin's family who I took likewise at Ardah with him," would be appointed as Yewo Gah al[ia]s, Captain Blanco or the white man's caboshiere [a Dahomean official]."[75]

One way the king controlled trade was by guaranteeing security to the merchants, while also closely supervising them. In a 1790 letter to the governor of the state of Bahia in Brazil, King Agonglo, noting that the "continual wars" of his ancestors had led to the destruction and abandonment of the important commercial center and slave port of Jaquem, directed "all the necessary governors and commissioners and white boys who know how to read and write to correspond with the captains and to inform them of the state of the land."[76] In another letter to the governor of Bahia he presented himself as a ruler who could guarantee security to traders so that "they can be free of the persecutions and robberies which are customarily done."[77] His successor Adandozan directed a long letter to the Portuguese king explaining how his military campaigns at the coast had affected Portuguese merchants, outlining his provisions for securing trade, supervising traders, and settling disputes, and ensuring their proper behavior. In the same letter, Adandozan even asked for a ship, of which he would be captain, to conduct commerce on his own.[78]

Dahomean kings made no secret of their ability to purchase European imports in return for the slaves that came from their conquests. In his 1726 letter to King George I, Agaja noted that he had sent a present of forty slaves and that "if you desire it fourty [*sic*] times fourty." Moreover, in 1796 Agonglo in a letter to Fernando José of Portugal promised that if he received bigger rolls of tobacco and better Portuguese goods, he would pay "in good captives without increasing the price," and that he would buy "all the aguardente [liquor]" that they could send.[79]

Although constant warfare was the ultimate source of these slaves, the kings did not make a direct link between their military interests and the commercialization of the captives. Adandozan asserted that Dahomey's wars were defensive: "We Dahomeans are surrounded by enemies who make incursions, we must defend ourselves." Europeans "who alledge that we go to war for the purpose of supplying your ships with slaves are grossly mistaken. In the name of my ancestors and myself I aver that no Dahomean man ever embarked in war merely for the sake of procuring wherewithal to purchase your commodities." He made it clear that the slaves were not their own wives and children, as some Europeans claimed, but "a part of our prisoners. Are not all prisoners at the disposal of their captors?"[80]

These payments in slaves were the result not only of the constant wars but also of a bureaucratic method of procurement by the king and his officials. Pires observed that an official, the Sogân, "is the receiver of the captives which they make in war . . . he makes a fiscalization and no military official can hide anything without the consent of the said Sogân."[81] Oliveira Mendes contended that the king had rights to all slaves captured in wars; at the end of the war, "the victors carry to the king the defeated and [he] takes the slaves he wants." Although the kings—as Adandozan did—often talked of massive sacrifices of slaves in the Annual Customs, where captives were executed to be sent as messengers and servants to the royal ancestors or to honor them, Oliveira Mendes's informants believed that "most are sent to the edge of the water, where all have correspondents and sell their portion of slaves."[82]

The kings also promoted religion in the service of the state. The most notable elements were rituals connected to the kings' ancestors, who they believed were capable of intervening in the lives of their descendants.[83] While kings paid attention to the more universalist elements of Dahomean religion such as major deities who protected the community, including toleration and incorporation of the religions of the people they had conquered, worship of royal ancestors was regarded as essential for the proper functioning and protection of the state.[84] Agaja made note of the significance of ancestors in his 1726 letter, asserting that he recognized the role of his ancestors, "who we strongly believe, [have] a power of revenging any wrong to them by violating the laws and customs of thare country and ancestors, and that it is in thare power also to prosper us or frustrate our designs, nay, even to take away our lives."[85]

Royal ancestors therefore played a critical role in the state, as the super-natural powers behind the king's prosperity. Agaja first described the Annual Customs, noting that "I am obliged to go out at different times in the year and strow great quantities of food and money amongst the common people and make sacrifices to our gods and forefather, some-times of slaves."[86] In a letter of 1804, Adandozan wrote, "I ordered my lesser nobility to go and honor the house of my great god Leba [Legba]." Elsewhere, he connected Legba to the ancestral cult, for he said that "I have already sworn by my great god Leba, and sent to in-form my dead father that I have sent to him that message by 150 men that I ordered killed only to affirm to him that I have to be avenged."[87]

Continuity and Identity Formation in the Americas

Enslaved Africans in the Americas commonly evoked the symbol of the king of Kongo as a primary symbol of their identity. People from West-Central Africa who were not subjects of Kongo were also exposed to the idea of the symbolic power of the king of Kongo, since the king-dom was the dominant state in the region. The traditions of Loango, Ndongo, and Matamba, for example, traced their origins back to Kongo, and Kongo kings, as we have seen, claimed authority, however nomi-nal, over those areas. Language was another marker that West-Central Africans shared. Although West-Central Africans spoke several distinct languages, they were closely related, and it was not difficult to learn Kimbundu if one knew Kikongo, for example, or vice versa.[88]

In addition to Kongo as a royal symbol, West-Central Africans iden-tified with Christianity, as the religion was widely spread because of missionary efforts both by the Portuguese in the colony of Angola and by Kongo itself. Within Kongo and the colony of Angola, Christian ico-nography was prominent, and it could also be found far from the mis-sionaries and the courts of the kings, often among people with relatively little contact with either.[89] All these ideas would influence identities for people from West-Central Africa as they were carried as slaves to the Americas.

In the Americas, the links among the king of Kongo, Christianity, and identity can be seen in the pronouncement of Macaya, a Kongo-born re-bel slave during the Haitian Revolution. Macaya, when recruited by the

French Republicans to abandon his alliance to the Spanish king, asserted that he was the subject of "three kings . . . of the king of Kongo master of all the blacks, of the king of France who represents my father, the king of Spain who represents my mother . . . these three kings are the descendants of those who, led by a star, came to adore God made man."[90]

Brazil, the destination of so many enslaved Central Africans, provides many examples of the lasting impact of Kongo royalism and Christian identity in the Americas. As early as the mid-seventeenth century, West-Central Africans in Pernambuco elected an individual from among their fellow enslaved Africans to be their king, who with the leave of the authorities led celebrations in the city.[91] Our first account is vague about the celebration, having been left by a passing French traveler, but later documentation makes it clear that the celebration involved the coronation of a "King of Congo," and that the choice fell to the lay brotherhood of Our Lady of the Rosary. In fact, a chapter of Our Lady of the Rosary was functioning as early as 1595 in Kongo, and others were also organized in the colony of Angola.[92] In Pernambuco, where West-Central Africans made up the overwhelming majority of the slave population and where they were identified as "Angolans," the position of "King of Congo" was restricted to men of Kongo background.[93]

By the late eighteenth century, the "King of Congo" was considered dominant in the popular celebrations of both enslaved and free Afro-Brazilians, so much so that the authorities recognized him as such, and some of his role was written into the constitution of the brotherhoods. For example, in the 1782 constitution of the Brotherhood of Nossa Senhaora de Rosário dos Homens Pretos of Recife, the membership elected "A King of Congo and a queen" and the members were required to give an annual "alms of four milreis" to each.[94] Henry Koster, who visited Itamaraca, the earliest settlement in Pernambuco, in 1816, left a detailed description of the custom. He wrote that in "March took place the yearly festival of our Lady of the Rosary, which was directed by negroes; and at this period is chosen the king of the Congo nation, if the person who holds this situation has died in the course of the year, has from any cause resigned or has been replaced by his subjects. The Congo negroes are permitted to elect a king and queen from among the individuals of their own nation."[95] The "King of Kongo" figure became a powerful unifying symbol for Central Africans in general, and even for other African "nations"; Africans from other ethnic groups also adopted the custom of electing their own kings (Figure 2.1).[96]

The Christian identity of Kongos was also evident in other parts of Brazil as members of the group identified themselves, and were identified by Europeans and enslaved non-Kongo Africans, as Christian. Pedro "of the Congo nation," a slave in Itaubira in Minas Gerais, was brought before the Inquisition in 1768 for holding mass in a "synagogue" for a large group of slaves, including ten Mina women and one Mina man, as well as several other Africans whom the denunciants did not know. When confronted with the heretical content of his preaching, Pedro responded that he was teaching Christian doctrine, and he noted that for four "vinteis" the souls of dead Africans on the Mina coast would go to heaven.[97]

At about the same time Christian Georg Andreas Oldendorp, a Moravian missionary in the Danish West Indies, recorded that some Kongos on the island performed "a certain type of baptism on the bosals [recently arrived slaves] who desire it." He added further that it was "an imitation of the baptism that they have seen of the holy Catholic one or of blacks who are accustomed to it or heard of it and described it."[98]

If West-Central Africans were ready to invoke the king of Kongo as a symbol, Dahomean identity was less visible and more diffused among Africans who came from that part of the African coast. One reason for this was that Dahomey was still legitimating itself in the eyes of people it had conquered in the 1730s, a process that was far from complete. In addition, many of the slaves arriving in the Americas from the region came from areas that Dahomey had conquered, and they did not identify with their conquerors or invoke the king of Dahomey. Though, as we have seen, Dahomean identity with the king was strong, it was based on fear and submission rather than on reverence for a benevolent protector. Although there were undoubtedly some Dahomean subjects from the kingdom who had served in the army and who might still believe in the king of Dahomey, many others from the conquered provinces or who otherwise resented the absolute and arbitrary nature of royal rule did not identify with the kingdom.

Still, there was a common identity, however diffused, among the Dahomean subjects, conquered people, allies, enemies, and neighbors of the kingdom who were caught up in the slave trade. In Brazil they were

Figure 2.1 Carlos Julião, "Coronação de um Rei nos festejos de Reis," ca. 1750s. Courtesy of Fundação Biblioteca Nacional, Brazil.

all commonly called "Minas" by the whites, often having identified themselves as "naturales da costa da Mina" (natives of the Mina coast), the term "Mina" probably functioning as something of an overarching identity for various peoples in the region of Dahomey. Many also gave themselves a more specific ethnic identity as well. Thus when the free Mina woman Rosa Egipcíaca was brought before the Inquisition for religious offenses, she stated that she was "a native of the coast of Mina of the Curana [Lagos] nation." Similarly, in 1782 when the free black Joana Machado dictated her will, she declared she was "a native of the Mina Coast and of the Coira [Lagos] nation."[99] Although the origin of the term "Mina" is problematic, in the eighteenth century it clearly referred to a large linguistic group and the cultures associated with it, the language being a widespread lingua franca based on Ewe and Fon but including elements from the surrounding regions.[100] Dalzel, in his description of Dahomey relating to the 1760–1790 period, observed, "the language is that which the Portuguese call lingua geral or general tongue and is spoken not only in Dahomey proper but in Whydah and the other dependent states; and likewise in Mahee and several neighbouring places."[101] In Brazil a distinctive vocabulary of the American-born children of enslaved Minas was clearly evident in 1741.[102]

The reluctance of Mina slaves to identify more narrowly with Dahomey is revealed in a late eighteenth-century case involving a group in Rio de Janeiro, who, in common with many other African groups, formed a lay brotherhood dedicated to Santo Elesbão and Santa Efigênia. A contemporary sketch of the society's history noted that initially its kings were from "Dagombe," but that in 1762 the brotherhood was torn apart by internal conflicts, and several new ethnic-based alliances emerged, challenging the absolutist ideas of the Dahomean leadership. The new groups adopted terms such as "Sabaras" or "Curamos," indicating that they identified with regions to the north and south of Dahomey that had been forcibly integrated into the Dahomean state.[103]

Conclusion

Kongo's core markers of royalty and Christianity continued to inform Central Africans' identity in Brazil, where it survives in the widespread folk festival of the Congada, especially in Pernambuco and Minas Gerais.

Congada remains closely connected to the brotherhood of Our Lady of the Rosary as well and is today a multi-ethnic celebration. For their part, the people of the Mina coast also managed to survive culturally, but largely under the influence of the Yorubas, who arrived in Brazil in the nineteenth century. They bore not so much a state concept as a more universal religious tradition, which has become incorporated into Candomblé, Brazil's most recognized African-based religious practice.

The African political background figured prominently in the patterning of the slave trade, for state activities determined who was captured and where and to which European merchants they were sold, and thus ultimately where they ended up in the Americas. Moreover, the various conceptions of the state that African subjects had formed were critical to the way in which they reformulated their identities in the Americas. Not all states were equally legitimate in the eyes of their subjects, nor did all Africans draw from a common fund of traditions about the state. Knowing the particular histories of African states will go a long way toward improving our understanding of how Afro-Atlantic identities were formed.

3

The Triumphs of Mercury

Connection and Control in the Emerging
Atlantic Economy

DAVID J. HANCOCK

Few topics in Atlantic history have received as much sustained attention in the last few decades as the development of the economy jointly
built by the inhabitants of Europe, Africa, and the Americas. Scholars
have examined the growth of the population, the increasing complexity
of the labor force, the spread of settlement, the patterns of urbaniza-
tion, the divergence of wealth and welfare, consumption and consumer-
ism, exporting and importing, shifts in agriculture, and the intertwining
of business and government. Early Americans were remarkably open
to foreign partners, goods, and institutions—more open, perhaps, than
at any time before the 1860s or in the 1990s.[1] British and European peoples settled the New World, bought African slaves and European and
Asian manufactures, replicated English institutions, and spread Reformation and Enlightenment ideas. One contemporary, the scion of an Atlantic wine-shipping family whose operations connected Funchal, Lisbon, Bordeaux, London, Bahia, Barbados, and Philadelphia, responded
in 1810 to a question raised by a relative residing in France: "How Wide
was the Atlantick?" "From the forests of what we called Pologne [Po-
land]," he replied, "to the banks of the Mississippi."[2] This panoptic perspective is not captured by confining history to the limits of the nation-
states that became all-encompassing over the course of the nineteenth
century. The later, narrower perspective of most historians writing today misses the internationalism and porousness of early American life—
Hispanic, French, and Dutch, as well as British—the creativity of widely

dispersed American agents, and the continuous, conversational interaction among levels in a large, geographically diffused, and economically unbounded oceanic economy. These realities were not abstractions; they comprised the warp and woof of the lived American experience.

It is arresting to contemplate the extent of the Atlantic economic zone that contemporaries confronted, compared to the reach of pre-Atlantic Europeans.[3] Amsterdam (a common trading partner of London before 1500) was 225 miles from London, and Constantinople, 1,500 miles. By the mid-1600s, Londoners were trading with Bostonians and Rio de Janeirans, 3,000 and 6,000 miles away, respectively. Transoceanic trade was more demanding than intra-European, or even Baltic and Mediterranean, trade. The distances were greater, and so were travel times, shipping risks, communication lags, and financing requirements. Maintaining cultural continuity with settlers across the Atlantic created additional challenges—and not only those of distance. More people, vessels, goods, and information crossed the ocean, requiring more people to handle them and engendering more people to consume them. The recorded annual export of sugar from Jamaica rose forty-three–fold between the 1670s and the 1770s. An increase in the number of ships carrying sugar- and molasses-filled casks made the outflow possible, as did a proliferation of merchants, brokers, and other intermediaries as well as of commercial publications.[4] Yet, for all the difficulties that distance and scale created, the natural productivity of the Americas was a reason to persevere and find ways to meet the challenges. Inventors, merchants, and improvers of all types strove to do just that.

One result was an efflorescence of technical "improvements." Consider the trades in sugar and wine. Barbados sugar planters reduced the amounts of total cane acreage and introduced new and more valuable cane types, while Jamaica sugar planters adopted better manuring. Planters tinkered with the refining process, and planters and merchants invested in processing and warehousing facilities.[5] Wine Island grape growers, too, began replanting their stock more frequently with new varietals. Merchant-distributors developed new blends and sped production by introducing steam engine–related heating techniques.[6] Both commodities benefited from improvements in shipping and cargohandling. Between 1600 and 1800, Atlantic shipbuilders adopted the Dutch *fluyt* design that increased cargo carriage, introduced a wheel for steering at sea, extended triangular head sails to all manner of ships, and increased the size of ships. Though other periods may have seen greater technological changes, these innovations were nonetheless significant.[7]

Besides making technical improvements, participants in the early modern Atlantic economy responded to the increased distance and scale by making substantial changes in the organization of commerce and in the ways they connected to each other. Their alterations were as innovative as the new technical practices, and they bore some of the same traits: they required investment, and they were carried out by tinkering and by trial and error.

What did it mean for participants to have innovated in the organization of commerce? A few examples shed light on the matter. One of the principal institutions of the Atlantic trade after the second half of the seventeenth century was the commission merchandising system—colonial planters' use of handpicked agents in the metropolis to sell their raw products, buy plantation supplies and consumption items, and, in general, "tend to their business" in the city. Commission merchandising helped solve the problems that arose when agricultural goods like sugar and tobacco were grown by expatriate farmers thousands of miles from consumers. Although the system built on existing models in which correspondents were used, the institution of colonial principals in the colonies employing agents in the metropolis was not foreordained. Some enterprisers attempted to operate as principals from London, sending out agents to the colonies, whom they dunned with volleys of questions and instructions. Other individuals tried to play a peddler's role in North America and the Caribbean, sailing from port to port, selling metropolitan goods and buying sugar and tobacco. But by the 1670s the commission merchandising system was becoming the norm, and English merchant-agents assumed the tasks of providing metropolitan supply, finance, and sales links for producer-principals across the Atlantic. This approach emerged in part because of differing ability to control outcomes, differing information, and differing willingness and capacity to shoulder risk throughout the oceanic marketplace. As the system became established, metropolitan agents devised a number of subsidiary institutions that drew them closer to the planters who employed them: they spent time in the colonies, usually early in their careers; they owned land there, allying their interests with those of their customers;

and they adopted a comprehensive, full-service view of "merchandising." These tactics mediated and mitigated "the principal/agent problem" that inhered in any transoceanic relationship.[8]

Equally revealing were eighteenth-century European wine exporters, who built supply and distribution chains that included continental European and Wine Island producers for the raw must, continental Europeans for barrels and bottles, and North Americans for commodities to trade in exchange for the wine. Early on, the exporters sold wine to ship captains at the point of production; because this arrangement was not sufficiently reliable, they began consigning wine to agents among the customers, commissioning ship captains to transport the goods; later—again to increase their control—they started posting their partners to the consuming countries to manage sales and delivery. Parallel developments emerged on the North American continent, although access to customers there may have been as important as control: importers and retailers began by selling wine at their offices and shops; they expanded to riding a circuit to reach customers outside the city; and later they established stores in the backcountry for an ongoing relationship with customers.[9]

These two examples together suggest a "great leap forward" in organization over the course of the long century stretching from the English Civil War through the ravages of Napoleon. The known world that impinged on the peoples of the Atlantic rim was greater in 1815 than 150 years earlier, but the distances between communities were in some significant way smaller. Personal and commercial links connected every continent facing the Atlantic, moving across political and intellectual as well as economic and geographical boundaries. Citizens and subjects of Atlantic states and empires knew about each other, communicated with each other on a more regular basis, and traded with each other more intensively.[10]

Organizing the Atlantic

This essay highlights three key attributes of Atlantic organization—decentralization, networks, and self-organization—that emerged from the endeavor to meet the challenges of the scale increase in Atlantic trade. To do so, it draws upon the structures and experiences of those participating in the Madeira wine complex, a complex whose institutions and initiatives shared a great deal with other transatlantic trade structures.

Because of the increases in scale, the seventeenth- and eighteenth-century Atlantic world was, first of all, radically decentralized. Decision making and implementation were dispersed, often situated very close to the action. The governments in Philadelphia and Bahia, like those in London, Paris, Madrid, and Lisbon, impinged only indirectly on producers, distributors, and consumers working in the colonies and subject territories. In any empire, whether political or commercial, management had to be flexible, information had to be shared, control had to be dispersed, and authority had to be delegated to individuals, groups, and communities on the periphery. Lateral, conversation-driven relationships prevailed among agents, each of whom possessed the power to decline to participate in a transaction, a relationship, or a network if it did not meet his or her needs.[11]

Examples like the trade in Madeira wine complicate traditional understanding of states and empires by suggesting that the influence of government was considerably more indirect than historical analysis has allowed. Individual decisions within the commercial sector made throughout the Atlantic—about what was produced, where and how it was distributed, and how and when it was consumed—were more important than government decisions made in imperial capitals. This state of affairs runs contrary to much modern state-formation and empire-management theory and many historians' application of it. But it has the advantage of adhering more closely to actual experience. Imperial centers and structures certainly were important; where they could effect their will, they set the overall conditions for settlement and trade.[12] Britain's alliance with Portugal affected the relative economic prospects of English-speaking traders doing business with Lisbon, Porto, and Madeira, for instance, in contrast to those trading with Bordeaux or Cádiz. But it did not create a product, link commercial networks and institutions, or fix the associations between goods and sumptuary displays. The Atlantic wine complex was constructed not by the dictates of the metropolises or commercial centers of Portugal, Spain, or France, but rather by the actions of far-flung people who took advantage of the wine trade to further their own commercial and social goals in the context of their local situations. Producers and distributors responded to mercantilist master plans by taking advantage of the opportunities they created, if they created opportunities, and by tolerating, ignoring, or evading them if they did not. Central authorities affected the Atlantic world, but the extent of their influence is more often assumed than evidenced. In many cases, the influence was less efficacious, more diluted—more subject to interpretation—than one might expect.[13]

The power of individuals working within decentralized contexts also complicates traditional views of action and structure. Neither great, influential actors—strong, active, or disruptive individuals whose actions determine events—nor people and their actions fully embedded in their communities' social, economic, and legal structures—which both create and limit their freedom of action and thought—is viable as a dominant explanatory device. One must combine the two perspectives. Men and women in this highly diffused commercial arena produced and reproduced the worlds they inhabited, and those worlds in turn produced and reproduced the people, activities, and attitudes constituting them. The heads of sugar plantations in Barbados and Jamaica and of wine firms in Madeira and Porto often established themselves by setting up business in the West Indies or Wine Islands. There, they recreated the attitudes of prior cohorts—self-imposed exile was more honorable than living in financial embarrassment—and reproduced the "seeking his fortune" narrative that had driven their forebears to leave one town for another, or one country for another. Their actions created new economic and social contexts. They improved commercial communication across the ocean, provided models for commercial success that others could emulate, and instructed their customers (the same people they had left behind) on how to use the commodities they hawked to portray themselves as refined. Consumers modified and reinterpreted metropolitan styles, adapting them to their own situations rather than merely emulating them, or they invented styles of their own. The Monmouth Rebellion plotter Azariah Pinney of Dorset and Nevis and the bankrupt Richard Hill of Maryland and Madeira mediated, in their new environments, the influence of states and capitals by building "peripheral" institutions and networks that resembled, but did not replicate, the metropolitan institutions they left behind. In extended imperial communities and porous inter-imperial markets, authority derived from an extended and delicate process of negotiation in which peripheral inhabitants were principals.[14]

The Atlantic market economy, furthermore, was highly networked. Multiple linkages are common in highly decentralized environments, and the peoples of the Atlantic created networks to connect them. They built these structures with long-standing forms of commercial interaction they had inherited and adopted, but they adapted and modified them, as well as simply replicating them, to take advantage of the opportunities and to mitigate the risks that the unparalleled Atlantic scale presented. The networks they created linked and integrated them across economic sectors and imperial geographies. As historians like Christopher Bayly and social scientists like Michel Callon have suggested, network structures made possible the movement of people, objects, institutions, and ideas. These works describe activities within empires, yet Atlantic-wide networks also served as the integument of an emerging and evolving inter-imperial economy.[15]

Merchants were the people most conscious of networked approaches.[16] In order to exchange goods, merchants built networks from their family, neighborhood, and friendship connections, their oceanic travels, and their opportunistic alliances and joint ventures. They did so to marshal dispersed resources and to mitigate the swings in supply and demand, the fickleness of consumers, and the unreliability of suppliers. The commercial, informational, and social networks they created structured the groups and markets in which they worked, and connected them to other markets and the people of those markets. Networks allowed members to conserve on the information required in any one place, while making use of dispersed information about consumers' tastes, the successes and failures of other merchants, the prosecution or tolerance of infractions of commercial laws, and the like. They defined the space within which group conflicts could be resolved; within a network, members could cope with uncooperative, shoddy, or failing suppliers, hostile competitors, and adverse political and economic situations. Networks were collective attempts to solve problems raised by the heightened information and transaction costs of long-distance trade. They were not state responses; instead, they were the results of contacts and contracts among agents who worked and lived within contexts shaped by geography, climate, technology, and policy.

In establishing links and then building networks, Atlantic merchants created an infrastructure that bound them together reciprocally—as suppliers and customers, as partners, agents, and competitors, and eventually as compatriots. The networks they built were primarily commercial, constructed to sell goods from the inland settlements of North America to the eastern port cities and to the wider world beyond, and vice versa; these networks contained greater numbers of correspondents, operating over longer distances and with increasing functionality. Once established, these arrangements could be turned to extra-commercial purposes as well. When Londoners, Lisbonites, Madeirans, Bahians, Barbadians, and Philadelphians communicated about acquiring, transporting, and financing a cargo of wine, for instance, they also transmitted military and diplomatic news, shared their opinions on matters such as reform, independence, and revolution, and established guidelines for fiscal and moral probity, directly through instruction and indirectly through observation and opinion on the indiscretions of others. These "full-bodied" networks created a dense, integrated, inter-imperial set of social, economic, and cultural institutions out of seemingly disconnected actors, impulses, conditions, and opportunities.

By the early nineteenth century, the networks that members deployed were different in significant ways from those their forebears had appropriated and adapted two hundred years before—more dense with more links to more places much farther away; more specialized and at the same time more substantial, dealing routinely with more than matters of trade and the market; more interactive and thus more flexible; and ultimately more central to the process of trust building in what had become a vast marketplace. Networks were not new, of course, nor were the conversations that fueled them and the information that flowed along them. Yet some combination of an increasing scale of trade, an increasing density of distributors and consumers, and a thickening of information channels led to an efflorescence of and reliance upon them in the 175 years preceding 1815. This change took place just as another shift occurred, away from a narrow pre-1640 oceanic market geared to small-quantity, high-value goods like spice and gold (a market that paralleled the narrow information stream) and toward a broader oceanic market in which the people in the Americas with whom network members were communicating were largely colonists rather than expatriates. The growing preponderance and importance of settlers, rather than sojourners, changed the quantity, nature, and quality of the communication. As channels grew thicker, they also changed character. Large markets did exist long before, but people in them had not been privy to the volume of information and the range of purpose that would transform production, distribution, and consumption in the long eighteenth century. When nodes and links became as dense and thick as they did, networks changed in character.

Finally, the Atlantic market economy was self-organized. The existence of networks already suggests a significant degree of order, even if the market was not structured through central command and control. No state or person set out to create an Atlantic market economy or to articulate a particular commodity culture. Nor did anyone plan to develop Atlantic-spanning, inter-imperial institutions. Such structures were too grandiose and complicated to have been imagined in advance. Yet they came forth, and contemporaries recognized them. They were "emergent" phenomena. They emerged from the individual but connected actions of decentralized agents who were working out solutions to local problems and extending the solutions through their networks to places, personalities, and situations one step beyond, where they were adopted and adapted. Economies and societies built in this fashion can be called "self-organized."

The idea of self-organization—that "the internal organization of a system increases automatically without being guided or managed by an outside source"—is not new; it is at least as old as Descartes' *Discourse on Method* and eighteenth-century naturalists' drive to comprehend "universal laws of form." In its modern form, a self-organizing system is thought of as an entity that "changes its basic structure [and evolves] as a function of its experience and environment."[17]

This idea is not just another way of arguing that individuals organized themselves. Rather, the idea of self-organization explicitly addresses the connections between higher-order phenomena and the multitude of decentralized activities that create or comprise them. It concerns the origins and existence of higher-order, often impersonal, phenomena like

group behavior, professional norms and ethics, and occupational inter-
mediation and specialization. Understanding such phenomena as emergent removes the constraint of having to apply the same historical con-
structs to all levels of analysis.

Turning the spotlight on self-organization also allows historians to
explain the emergent features of Atlantic life by connecting them to
their constituent actors and actions. By the latter part of the eighteenth
century, to take just one example, a Madeira wine trade and culture had
emerged in the Atlantic; it was multinational and inter-imperial, one of
the first products to acquire these characteristics. The institutions of the
Madeira wine trade and the meanings of the Madeira wine culture—indeed, the trade and culture themselves—emerged as more people interacted more frequently, trading and conversing about what they were doing. In scientific language, there was a "phase transition" from a casual
state of sporadic and eccentric transactions to an organized state in
which individuals' interactions about Madeira wine were ordered by the
business processes of the traders, and the meanings they attached to the
wine, its rituals, and its paraphernalia became common among participants. The trade had become predictable and routine; commercial links
bound together people who did not know each other except through intermediaries; the wine was drunk in cosmopolitan St. Petersburg and
rustic, hinterland Angola, in polite aristocratic clubs in London and
rude military messes along the Mississippi River, in the homes of Baltic
Sea merchants and the palaces of Mughal lords in India, where similar
meanings of luxury and refinement attached to the drink and its consumption.

"Ich bin frei"

"Decentralized," "networked," "self-organized": these are abstract ad-
jectives. What difference did such things make in the lives of participants
in the early American marketplace? These concepts come down to earth
in the life and career of one fairly representative example: George Frey, a
storekeeper, tavern keeper, miller, and landowner in Middletown, Pennsylvania, who lived and worked during the second half of the eighteenth
century.[18]

Frey did not bear that name from birth. He was born Johannes Georg

Eberhardt in 1732 in the town of Sulz-am-Neckar, in the southwestern German principality of Württemberg, where he was baptized into the Lutheran faith. At 17, he emigrated to Pennsylvania, arriving in Philadelphia in early October 1749 with about 250 others from Württemberg, Swabia, and Darmstadt on the ship *Jacob,* which had carried them from Amsterdam and Shields (just east of Newcastle, England).[19] Of Eberhardt's early years in America, little is known.[20] He was a redemptioner. John Fisher, a prominent Quaker merchant in Philadelphia, paid for Eberhardt's voyage in exchange for his agreement to serve for a term of years helping Fisher's son George work a 696-acre farm that Fisher had recently been granted on the Susquehanna River. How long Eberhardt worked the farm is unclear; certainly, he redeemed himself "with a little fund" before the agreed-upon term was up and commenced work as a peddler, hawking goods in the developing frontier north and west of Lancaster.[21] A few years later, in 1754, he bought 25 acres and a spring just west of the Isle of Que, between Middle and Penn Creeks, 60 miles north of Fisher's farm (see Map 3.1).[22] Eberhardt tilled this land for nearly a year, until the massacre of several dozen white neighbors— whose extralegal "improvements" to ancestral lands along Penn's Creek had roused the local Delawares to murder—made it unsafe to remain.[23]

Homeless and stripped of his livelihood, Eberhardt descended on Lancaster, where he resumed peddling local produce and small imported manufactures. One day, according to a memoir that he wrote later in life, Eberhardt "encountered a party of soldiers from the garrison at Fort Hunter," whereupon they "arrested him as a runaway redemptioner." Ultimately, he convinced the soldiers "of his independence," repeatedly exclaiming "Ich bin frei," and "went with them to the garrison where he became quite a favorite," known as George Frey.[24] It is at this point that Eberhardt began using the surname Frey: the soldiers gave it and the peddler adopted it, he later recounted, to signify his freedom (Frey being an Anglicization of the German *frei*).[25] At this time he also married Anna Catherina Späth, the daughter of a family recently arrived in Lancaster from Württemberg.[26] After his marriage, Frey worked as a laborer in Lancaster Borough.[27]

The increasingly well-off itinerant in 1761 acquired from the son of his former master a plot of land adjacent to the one he once tilled. George Fisher was constructing Middletown on the banks of the Sus-

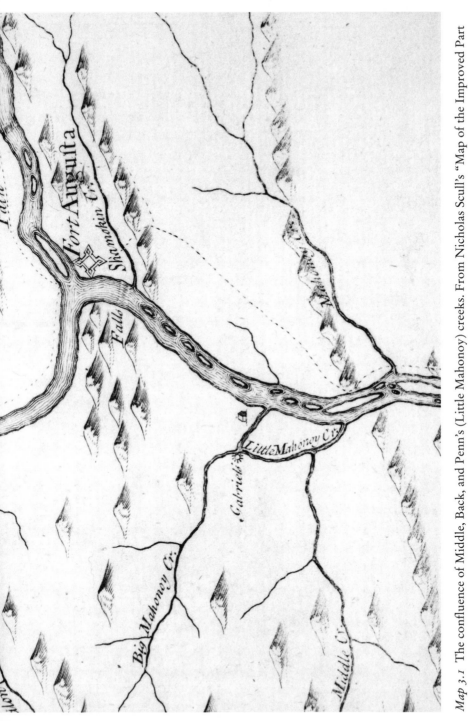

Map 3.1 The confluence of Middle, Back, and Penn's (Little Mahonoy) creeks. From Nicholas Scull's "Map of the Improved Part of the Province of Pennsylvania" (Philadelphia, 1759). Reproduced courtesy of the William L. Clements Library, University of Michigan.

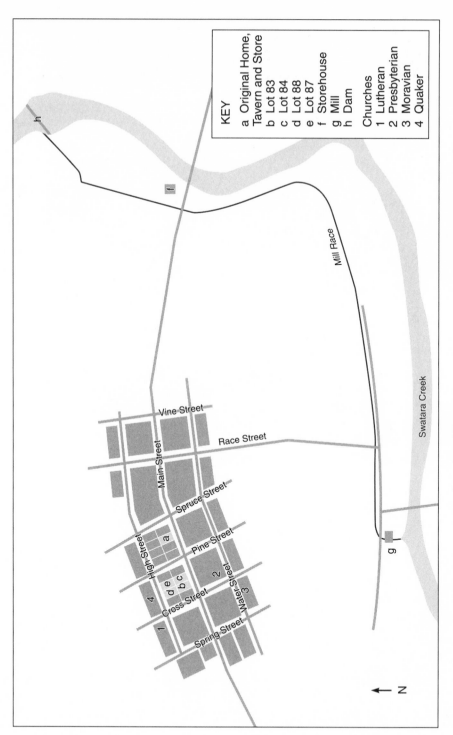

KEY
a Original Home,
  Tavern and Store
b Lot 83
c Lot 84
d Lot 88
e Lot 87
f Storehouse
g Mill
h Dam

Churches
1 Lutheran
2 Presbyterian
3 Moravian
4 Quaker

Figure 3.1 Street plan of Middletown, ca. 1765–1795. Created by Karl Longstreth.

quehanna—a utopian community both religious and commercial in scope on land given to him by his father. We do not know with what resources Frey secured his lot; prior acquaintance and good standing with the Fisher family might have earned him some credit. We do know that he flourished, building a small commercial empire in the country atop three complementary businesses: storekeeping, tavern keeping, and milling.

In 1761 Frey acquired the town's largest plot, Lot 98, which stood on the town's Main Street, two blocks east of the central square. On it, he erected a house and ran a combined store and tavern business (Figure 3.1, item a). Soon thereafter, he acquired two more lots (Lot 84 in 1768 and Lot 83 in 1775—items b and c) and built houses on them as well. Renting out Lot 98, he used the former as his home and the site for his retailing and the latter as his home after 1775, when he ceased "keeping a publick House of Entertainment in order to contract my Business as much as possible."[28]

Frey came to play a variety of economic roles in Middletown. In the late 1760s, he developed his store and tavern businesses. He was the first in town to open either type of establishment. He was the town's preeminent landowner, especially after the death of George Fisher in 1777; he acquired six properties of his own, managed roughly forty other lots, and bought up 6,000 acres in three counties.[29] Quitting tavern keeping just as American independence was declared, he moved into milling to complement his shopkeeping and landowning.[30] During the late 1770s, he built a storehouse on the east end of town along Swatara Creek (Figure 3.1, item f). In 1783, he and John Hollingsworth of Wilmington built a large mill on the southern edge of town (item g). The next year, they cut a race to enhance the work of the grist mill—an improvement that was "the only work of the kind" in the state. Then, in 1789, just as the partnership was dissolving, Frey gained approval from the state to build a new mill dam (item h). At the end of his life in 1806, Frey was the largest miller and milling agent in the state.[31]

Ordering the Interior

In the canonical history of early America, Frey would not be considered emblematic of much of anything. He was not a pioneer in the wilderness; he was peripheral to the debates and struggles for independence; he did not even found a commercial dynasty. Yet his experiences were similar in outline to those of many of the men and women who migrated to Atlantic peripheries in this period: he left Europe because avenues were closed to him there; in the New World, he had to cast about for ways to make a living; and he succeeded, to the extent he did, in a corner of that world, as a middleman, bridging the needs of sellers and buyers, an old world and a new. People like Frey were central to the creation and operation of a circum-Atlantic marketplace and, in fact, of an Atlantic world. How did the processes we have identified as central to the working of the Atlantic market—decentralization, networking, and self-organization—fit into the lives of ordinary people like him?

Life in a Decentralized World

The most important of Frey's enterprises were marked by dispersed deliberation and action. His own migration is a case in point. Frey moved to Pennsylvania from Württemberg as a redemptioner—that is, as an immigrant who gained passage from Europe by selling himself into indentured servitude as a way of reimbursing the captain or company that paid for the voyage. The recruitment of such immigrants and the process of redemption were managed by neither central policies nor royal officials; especially in the case of non-British migrants to British America, they were ad hoc processes open to the opportunism of continental European merchants and shippers and of American managers and to the needs of the receiving communities in America. These processes moved Frey to "Plantation Point"—the Fishers' farm—and to Middletown, both hinterland settlements over which the king of England wielded little palpable day-to-day power. And not just the English monarch: the authorities in Philadelphia were also remote. Middletown was a private venture begun and operated by a commercially opportunistic and idealistic young man. George Fisher's father received a grant from Pennsylvania's proprietors, imparting legal title to the land—or, at least, the white man's legal title. That title enabled the Fishers to do with the property as they saw fit, recruiting settlers, selling plots, and appealing to the local militia for protection. The Fishers depended on metropolitan power and its extensions to gain legitimate claim. But the owners having achieved that, the future development of Middletown as a place to live, work, and raise families rested largely in their hands and those of their grantees. There was no joint-stock or monopoly "British North America Company" to organize Middletown's production and lobby for favorable tax treatment of its products, or, of course, to impose its rules and take a cut of the earnings. The regulations that emanated from Philadelphia were likewise few, mostly limited to the administration of justice and the collection of taxes. Middletowners were, to a large extent, on their own and distant from the centers of established power in an age and region of slow transportation and uncertain communication.

Frey established himself by adhering to models of decentralized action like those that had ordered his migration, wandering, and settlement, and so did not rely solely on the epicenter of the English-speaking commercial world—London—or its colonial counterpart—Philadelphia. No one else directed his entrepreneurial schemes, as might have been the case had he been a factor in Virginia working in conjunction with a Glasgow or London tobacco house or even as an agent of a Philadelphia firm. If Frey wanted goods from Portugal or Spain, he wrote to Madeira or Tenerife merchants recommended by Dutch traders in Rotterdam; if he wanted items from Alsace or the Black Forest, with which he was more familiar, he wrote to acquaintances in the Upper Rhine Valley. Only if it suited his purpose did he go through people in the metropolises of Europe or America, and that rarely.

Frey's business was further decentralized in the following sense: rather than creating or participating in a hierarchical organization, with employees and supervisors, he created most of his relationships laterally, among equals, at least to the degree that each had the right to participate in a transaction and to exit from it. Power inequities of wealth and experience did exist, of course, but it was nearly impossible for traders to force a particular outcome. Frey's voluminous correspondence reveals very few authoritarian tiers or "levels" to his trading; almost everything was open to negotiation. The letters entice and cajole, rather than order and punish, in large measure because he had no legitimate organizational authority or power to resolve a dispute. Partly as a result, Frey shared information relatively freely with people who may have been, at different times, his partners, suppliers, and customers.

Life in a Networked World

Frey steadily expanded supplier and customer networks over the course
of his career. At first, he built his supply networks primarily from ethnic, kin, and friend relationships; as time passed, he placed greater emphasis on financial expertise and access to capital. He drew upon local
suppliers at the commencement of trading in Middletown in the mid-
1760s. Edward Shippen, Sr., and Colonel James Burd had opened a specialty wine shop in Lancaster the year before Frey commenced business,
for instance, and they began stocking Frey's cellar, bar, and storehouse.
For Frey, Shippen & Burd was an obvious choice, as the men had
known each other from the time of Frey's marriage in Lancaster roughly
ten years before. During the late 1760s, however, the firm lost interest or
grew frustrated with its specialty work, at a time when Frey needed a
greater variety of drink and a greater amount of credit. So Frey turned
to Philadelphia suppliers, as did most other backcountry retailers whose
custom was growing. (In part, the backcountrymen were responding
to Philadelphia wholesalers and retailers, who were beginning to side-
step the intermediary roles previously performed by the larger rural retailers.) By the mid-1770s, Frey was regularly calling on Philadelphia
traders: Samuel Miles & William Wister in Market Street for wine, for
instance, and Francis Hasenclever in Second Street and a few other
wholesalers for spirits.[32]

After Congress declared independence and war with Britain disrupted
transatlantic flows of liquor, Frey felt a need to move beyond the handful of his regular Lancaster and Philadelphia suppliers, but options were
few. A copybook of letters Frey wrote in 1781–1782 shows him dealing
with twenty-three wholesalers and service providers by the end of the
war (marked in light gray in Figure 3.2). Frey's suppliers shared a German heritage or, at least, a familiarity with German culture (as was the
case with the Scots-Irish of Lancaster County), so that they could deal
with German-speakers like Frey and his wagoners. Often, Frey knew a
Philadelphia supplier's brother or sister who lived in Middletown or
its environs, and Frey procured a letter of recommendation from the
neighbor to the supplier, which he personally handed to the Philadelphian. Paul Zantzinger of Lancaster, for instance, introduced Frey to
Zantzinger's brother Adam in Philadelphia. Similarly, Frey came to know

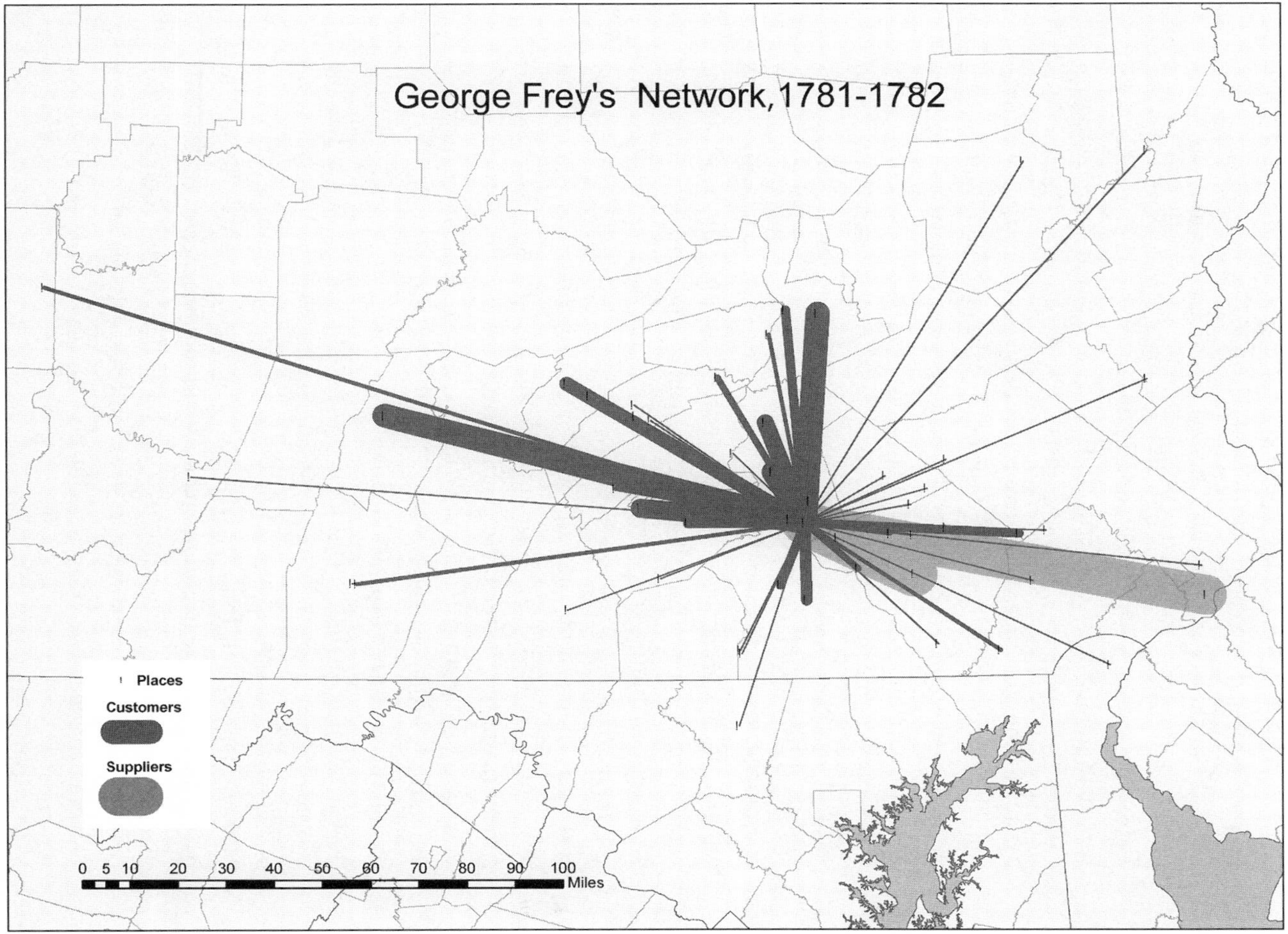

Figure 3.2 George Frey's supplier and customer network, 1781–1782. Created by Karl Longstreth.

James Patterson, Jr., of Lancaster through James, Sr., who lived along the Juniata River northwest of Middletown and routinely called on Frey for household goods and wine.[33]

Frey's customers (shown in Figure 3.2 in dark gray) were more scattered than his suppliers. Some 9 percent lived in Middletown; another 16 percent inhabited adjacent townships. The remaining three-quarters resided throughout Pennsylvania's hinterland, as far northeast as Wyoming County, as far northwest as Sunbury, and as far west as Tuscarora and Chambersburg, with most counties in between represented as well. Especially important were settlers in the new western communities of Cumberland County. Only one customer, the Anglo-Irish Quaker businessman John Hollingsworth, lived outside Pennsylvania, in Wilmington, Delaware, where he received the bulk of the grain and flour passing through Frey's mill. (A few years later, he would partner with Frey in a Middletown mill.) Thus, from a small store near the Susquehanna, Frey was supplying much of eastern Pennsylvania. Able to speak, read, and write in German, Dutch, and eventually English, he satisfied the needs of three different linguistic communities.[34]

Hollingsworth's Wilmington-based services were central to Frey's milling, which during the 1780s and 1790s outstripped his merchandising. The prospect of exporting, in fact, led the Middletown enterpriser into overseas trading generally, as he looked for markets for his grain and flour and in time for items desired by his grain suppliers and store customers. Before 1783, he had relied on Philadelphians to contact and deal with Europeans. But as soon as Portugal's ports were reopened to American shipping after the war, Frey backed his own "Adventure to Madeira" on the ship *Concord.* With the help of Dominick Joyce, a Sephardic Jewish merchant from Lisbon who had settled in Philadelphia during the war, Frey sent Middletown-area flour and beeswax to William Jenkins in Madeira, who then exchanged them for wine. Jenkins was no stranger to Frey. In the 1760s and 1770s, Frey had bought wine in Philadelphia from Henry Hill, the resident American agent of the Madeira firm Lamar, Hill, Bisset & Co., in which Jenkins's father had been employed and to whom Jenkins himself had been apprenticed. Moreover, Jenkins's father had become a partner of the Portuguese exporter Joaquim Jose Sanches in 1773, and had left Madeira to be the Sanches firm's resident agent in Pennsylvania, young Jenkins staying be-

hind to supervise its shipping and trading. In the year of Frey's first adventure to Madeira, 1783, Frey imported twenty pipes from Jenkins.
The next year he repeated the venture, again directing his orders to
Sanches and Jenkins's house. This time he sent some wax to the Jewish
Philadelphia merchant Aaron Levi, asking him to forward it to Madeira
"in the manner" already agreed upon; it was Frey's hope to have "the return made in good wine, either best New York or best London" grades,
for that is what backcountrymen wanted.[35] Overseas adventures like
these became an important component of Frey's trading, and in time he
linked himself to other trading centers. In the next decade, in fact, he
backed five similar Atlantic voyages—to France and Spain as well as
Portugal—in search of a market for flour and a supply of wine, fruit, oil,
and salt.[36]

Frey extended his network by wholesaling wine and other imported
goods to other backcountry traders, in addition to selling them at his
tavern and store and using them in his home. In principle, he could have
sold the imports in Philadelphia, but that market was extremely competitive and frequently glutted. Instead he looked to the less developed areas of the "frontier." In 1783 he sold quarter casks, hogsheads, and pipes
of wine to planters in Maryland and Virginia. By then it had become
cheaper to carry wine overland from Middletown to inland areas of the
Upper South than to transport it via river and coastal craft. Frey took
advantage of this development, as well as of the increased output of
grain in that region, to offload his wine and keep his mill busy.[37]

Frey's use of networks is revealing. Members of the networks he constructed were especially good at solving problems relatively quickly.
They did more than find a supply of wine or a market for wheat, although those were two of the most important functions they served.
They surveyed a market for him, as when local customers wanted
Rhenish wine in the 1770s but Philadelphia suppliers found themselves
without it and thought it impossible to obtain. In a matter of months,
European members of Frey's transatlantic network proved the Philadelphians wrong, informing Frey where, from whom, and when he could
get it. Similarly, they assessed customers' problems, as when a planter in
Virginia appeared to be avoiding repayment in the 1780s; or they provided unbiased information, giving several different perspectives on the
planter's unwillingness to pay. Finally, they proposed solutions more

appropriate to the handling of a problem in a faraway place than Frey could derive, as when a contact in Bordeaux counseled arbitration rather than a lawsuit, which was Frey's favored form of dispute resolution.[38]

Complementary evidence of Frey's networking is found on the shelves and cellars of his store. One of the effects that merchants like Frey had on the countryside was to widen the array of provisions. Rural retailers introduced foods, drinks, and manufactures into everyday life. While a markedly distant and even foreign mix of goods is what one expects today, it is not what historians have led us to believe prevailed in the eighteenth century. In Middletown, 62 percent of the items Frey sold his customers in the ten months between May 1773 and February 1774 were produced more than 100 miles from Middletown; nearly half of those (30 percent of the total) were imports into North America. Twenty-seven years later in 1800–1801, the shares had not shifted much: 57 percent of goods were nonlocal, although the share of foreign products had fallen slightly to 25 percent.[39] Such international items could have been found in any Philadelphia store, but here they were in a relatively remote region that was to have been, or so historians have suggested, mostly self-sufficient and limited, when reliant on outside goods at all, to British goods. Rural retailers regularly sold items from China, India, Morocco, Spain, Portugal, France, Holland, Germany, and Sweden, in addition to those from England and Ireland. In Frey's general store, one could find African pepper, Chinese tea, Brazilian fruit and candy, five kinds of Wine Island, Iberian, and French wine, and Swedish ironware. Middletown householders could buy "exotic" merchandise with relative ease. Stores like Frey's bound rural Americans to the outside world—to the next county, the next colony or state, the next empire, and the next continent.[40]

Life in a Self-Organized World

In his shipping, trading, and milling, Frey performed certain roles and adopted certain ideas and practices that were undeniably transatlantic. At the same time and in doing so, he helped institutionalize them. These roles, behaviors, and attitudes, like the trade and culture in which he participated, had emerged from the nest of relationships and the flurry of interactions among them that constituted his life and the lives of others like himself. One sees this self-organization at work in three different areas: commercial organization, supply management, and marketing focus.

Increasingly articulated commercial organization. Dealing with greater numbers of customers, agents, and partners across wider expanses of land and sea, providing more varied arrays of products obtained through longer voyages with heavier, more complex cargoes: these developments required increasingly complicated arrangements as the century progressed. Such operations were difficult to control, however, pressuring the individuals involved in them to innovate in the ways they organized business and deployed human and social capital. Activities that had been tasks shaped by particular needs and capabilities were elevated into roles, with titles and characterizations, and people stepped into them. Many of the new roles were intermediary: some were internal to firms, while others were performed by independent agents or brokers. Some of the new roles also involved increasing specialization by product or market.

Consider European exporters of wine like Hill and Sanches, who shifted in their approach to customers: from a correspondence-based relationship, they began sending trade missions to meet buyers face-to-face. A partner on a trade mission in the eighteenth-century Atlantic was absent from his home base for several years, but could be very successful in finding business. Observing this, some houses established resident expatriate agents, added traveling supra-agents, or appointed Creoles to do the same work. These roles were not completely novel, but their proliferation contributed to the emergence of a new type of participant in Atlantic trade.[41] American distributors innovated in similar ways. Like European exporters, they started visiting the counties and towns where their customers resided to ascertain their needs and tastes and to resolve problems. George Morgan of Philadelphia, for example, took a tour of New England in 1764 to drum up wine sales; a few years later, he traveled down the Ohio, as far west as Kaskaskia, doing the same. His competitor William Wister of Philadelphia visited Frey in Middletown on at least three occasions in the 1770s and 1780s to gather wine and spirits orders and to see that competitors did not wrest them away, even though Frey still regularly called on Wister in Philadelphia.[42]

A relatively new retailing role to emerge was the liquor specialist. Provisioning Americans with wine and spirits was as old as Atlantic trade itself, but the role of specialty liquor retailer first appears in newspaper advertisements, tax lists, and city directories in the 1750s. By the 1770s, it was a common feature of commerce. In Philadelphia, the first "wine store" or "wine shop" as a distinct establishment appeared in 1753. A handful of specialists worked there in the 1760s and early 1770s; along with Lancaster specialists Shippen & Burd, they supplied Frey during his first decade of store- and tavern keeping. During and after the Revolution, specialty merchants, coopers, vintners, stores, shops, and cellars all proliferated rapidly, and, as their numbers grew, so did rural retailers' reliance on them. By the 1780s, Frey received his wine from a handful of general merchants, liquor brokers, and specialty retailers, including Levi Hollingsworth, Wister & Miles, and Benjamin Poultney.[43]

Yet a third role, wholly new in America, arose in the aftermath of the French and Indian War: hired commission agents or brokers who brought importers, wholesalers, and retailers together. Only after 1765 does one find mention of a "commission store" in operation or a wine and spirits "broker" procuring drink for customers. In times of scarcity, such people became invaluable to rural storekeepers, whose clientele demanded specific types, varietals, and brands. One wine specialist favored by Frey was Philadelphia's first dedicated wine broker, Leonard Dorsey. Frey also utilized the brokerage services of Harris & Fergusson on several occasions when customary sources failed him, turning to the firm that would "purchase and find Goods of any Kind," including choice claret and old Lisbon wine, even if that meant going off in search of it at competitors' houses. In addition, he sent them Middletown-area produce and manufactures he had obtained in the course of trade, for they were "prepared to receive all kinds of Goods that may be sent to them, to sell on Commission," in America or overseas.[44]

The work of specialty suppliers and liquor brokers was complemented by that of branch retailers who, like the aggressive merchants, made direct forays into the rural hinterland. The branch system can be viewed as an analog to the Madeira firms' placement of partners in the American marketplace. Both were responses to the magnitude of the tasks required. Randle and John Mitchell of Philadelphia, merchants with whom Frey did business, devised a branch system to extend their custom well before the form is said to have taken hold in the nineteenth century. They established stores in Allentown, Reading, and Trappe in 1771, and in Caernarvon and Middletown in 1773—all places "well known for their good situation and considerable trade." In each, the proprietor was a partner or an employee who owned a share in the operation, not a relative. The arrangement combined a division of labor with a division of ownership in a form that had not been tried before. An advantage of their approach was that, in an emergency, when one store fell short, the storekeepers could call on each other, rather than appealing all the way back to the brothers in Philadelphia. Middletown could more readily draw upon Reading than restock itself from Philadelphia. Similarly, when "there was a great demand for" wine bottles at all the stores and Mitchell experienced difficulty procuring a shipment from his friend Caspar Wistar's New Jersey glass factory, the storekeepers could quickly go to Henry Stiegel's glasshouse in nearby Manheim and purchase the bottles there.[45] Coincidentally, the Mitchells acquired their store in Middletown from Frey, who had previously used it as his own store, tavern, and residence. In time, the Mitchells constituted Frey's most significant competition.[46]

Close management of supply. By far the most significant sources of wine for retailers were their local trading communities. They usually called on one or a few suppliers for each type of wine, depending on the importer-wholesaler's connections with Europe, the Islands, or the Caribbean; increasingly, they also drew upon local auctioneers. Philadelphia retailers found wine in Philadelphia; Middletown storekeepers found it in Middletown, Lancaster, or Philadelphia. Neither group bought drink from merchants in other American towns. Frey, for example, traveled to Philadelphia each autumn and spring to visit importers, wholesalers, and retailers, and frequently called on Shippen & Burd in Lancaster. He generally requested information from them about the prices of goods before paying them a call, as well as news about the market for barter goods he might carry with him.

A very few storekeepers also bought from overseas sources. Only those who had reliable connections overseas and enduring operations in America corresponded with exporters in the Wine Islands, Iberia, France, or the Netherlands directly, sending orders to exporters or accepting consignments from them. The most aggressive retailers sent out ships on their own initiative, assuming previously unacceptable risks and costs, in the hope of selling an inland cargo or exchanging it for wine. This is what Frey began to do in the 1780s. Other retailer-adventurers placed orders through middlemen in London, Amsterdam, Bordeaux, Lisbon, and Cádiz. The indirect middleman option was significant for wines that by law could not directly flow duty-free into Anglo-America, as could wines from Madeira and the Azores. Still, even if indirect, overseas sources were often the best way to procure the correct "brand mark" desired by one's customers.[47]

Frey paid attention to the variety and quality of the supply. He procured for his own customers Port, Madeira, "wine," cordial, brandy, gin, spirit, whiskey, peach brandy, beer, and cider. He insisted that the wine always be "genuine." When he asked his agent in Philadelphia to get "a doz. Bottles of Red French Wine," Frey insisted that they be "none but genuine" and "well packed per Bearer," as the wine was "to be used for medicine." When he ordered a tierce of wine and a hogshead of rum in 1782, he cautioned another supplier to send "no Lisbon wine and no [West Indian] rum [the man was also a distiller] but of the best quality, and, in case you have no tierces of wine, send . . . only a quarter cask of it, as a whole pipe would rather be too much, and the wagoner could not load it all." In case the agent found none, Frey instructed him to get it from competitors, "on the best terms going, and of the best quality that is to be had."[48]

Frey was extremely demanding of suppliers, as well. He insisted that, if an agent had "no opportunity to write" to Frey "by other people," then the agent should advise him "per Post, which sets off from Philadelphia on Thursday and by which" he could "receive the Letters Saturday or Sunday." It was "of great service," he knew, "to be "informed of the alteration of circumstances" (such as different measures of containers) as soon as possible. As his suppliers knew, Frey had no qualms about returning defective goods. He returned broken bottles to Stiegel's glassworks in Manheim, for instance, noting the broken casks that had been sent, which contributed to broken bottles and thereby "loss of wine." To forestall any debate, he wrote immediately after one pipe had broken: "the pipe really was defective, and had worm holes below the middle hoops." It was not, he opined, a pipe fit for holding cider, much less wine.[49]

An attention to marketing. Storekeepers increasingly called on and corresponded with customers, taking care to know their history, circumstance, and circle. When a buyer complained about the quality of goods purchased, the retailer would lavish attention on him or her—first with kind words, then perhaps with a humorous anecdote and an apology to defuse the tension, and ultimately with a promise to correct the matter. Storekeepers also became more flexible about customers' payments—allowing credit and longer periods of repayment. When a debtor defaulted, the retailer would complain discreetly to an appropriate person who had some influence over the buyer, rather than broadcasting the problem to the community. Increasingly, the customer was always right . . . even if he or she was not.[50]

Solicitous retailers like Frey, desirous of luring customers, expanded their product offerings beyond the wine, rum, and cider—each in only one variety—that were commonly found in stores and taverns earlier in the century. For his tavern patrons in the 1760s, Frey procured rum, brandy, burnt wine, Malaga, Madeira, "best wine," old and new unspecified wine, and beer. For his store customers, many of whom also frequented the tavern, he procured the same drinks, but in much larger volumes—pipes, hogsheads, quarter casks, and barrels. By the 1780s, he stocked not just Madeira and Malaga but also Rhenish, Canary, Sherry, Port, Lisbon, and several varieties of French wine, in addition to an expanded list of spirits.[51]

Frey did not rely on newspaper advertising to seduce would-be buyers—as did his urban counterparts—because his customers were beyond the ambit of Philadelphia's papers. Instead, he pursued them personally and with extreme consideration, writing letter after letter to acquaintance and stranger alike. When Robert Patton of Lebanon ordered two of Frey's best Barcelona handkerchiefs for the new store Patton was opening in Lebanon, Frey insisted that, if Patton did not like what was sent, he could return them. Much of Frey's attitude sprang from an awareness of mutuality. Like any rural retailer, Frey had to walk a fine line between customers and suppliers, for in the countryside they were often the same people. Rural storekeepers and tavern keepers "lived within communities where concerns other than commercial profit were often prominent, and maintaining good relations with their . . . neighbors and customers often meant that they could not engage in the same type of entrepreneurial activity" that they might with a stranger. When a would-be customer desired to sell Frey his produce, Frey would send one of his wagons for it. Even when he did not accept a customer's goods, he returned them, deferentially.[52]

An important new tool available to retailers of Frey's generation was the use of display. Everywhere it became customary for retailers to tempt customers through better design and outfitting, more vivid displays, and samples. Such had not been the case fifty years before. Frey's first store was a small, simple affair, with two stories, a stone façade, comparatively large ground-floor windows, and a center-entry door. But by the 1770s, he and other Middletown retailers were using large picture windows, glazed doors, and sign boards. These features were neither recent nor American innovations; they first appeared nearly a half century earlier in English cities. But American retailers started incorporating them as a matter of course during Frey's lifetime, and within a decade or so they became the norm. Frey introduced a large amount of pane glass (large, that is, for Middletown) on the front façade, so that passersby could see the goods within. Frey also hawked his wares with a hanging sign on which was painted a Phrygian cap—playing on both the goods within and the name of the owner, for to the Romans the goddess Liberty was generally depicted as wearing such a hat, and freed slaves were ceremonially capped with one. Frey used several signs during his long career. When his mood changed and his livelihood shifted into milling, he hung a board adorned with Mercury, the god of grain traders and all commercial activity.[53]

Shop contents and furnishings became more instrumental, targeted toward particular types of sales and buyers. This was true in the larger, more successful urban stores, but the change occurred in varying degrees in most establishments, including Frey's fairly modest shop. According to an inventory, the interior was filled with furniture for showing off the goods. Free-standing counters, cupboards, and tables allowed a customer to see more than one item at a time and to compare them— and thereby to rely on his or her own taste as much as, if not more than, on Frey's discretion. Some cupboards had pigeonholes so that many small items could be seen at a glance. Fixed shelves and drawers allowed similar visibility; goods could be laid out, rather than tucked away in a drawer. During the day, viewing was easy, given the significant expanse of window glass. At night, sconces, candlesticks, and candles enhanced visibility and allowed Frey to extend his hours. He and his wife kept wineglass pattern books under the counter and brought them out when need arose. They offered Madeira samples, served in small flint glasses made in New Jersey or Bristol and set upon silver trays or rubber mats, to ease a discussion or close a sale. As Frey seized on the relatively new architectural and display techniques of the day to keep customers entering and buying, he participated in (and in turn helped shape) a consumer-oriented business culture that no particular person or government organized, yet one that every participating retailer recognized.[54]

Conclusion

George Frey was a man of parts: immigrant, servant, peddler, tavern keeper, storekeeper, and miller; initial settler and first citizen; squatter, renter, owner, and landlord; laborer, enterpriser, employer, and philanthropist. The Fishers' primacy having diminished, Frey became the most important man in Middletown, connecting the new settlement to Lancaster, neighboring counties, Philadelphia, neighboring colonies, England, Holland, Germany, France, Portugal, and Spain. Master of three languages, he is said to have been working through an Italian pamphlet on the care of orphans at his demise. Childless, he left his fortune to his wife and, on her death, to a trust that would manage the building and maintaining of an orphanage "called 'Emaus'" at a place he chose "for that purpose" near his mill.[55]

Frey's story intersects with much of what gave the eighteenth-century Atlantic world its vibrancy. His carefully worded letters and meticulously kept accounts detail the commercial developments that transformed the economies of Pennsylvania and the other English-speaking settlements of early America. He was one of the new commercial intermediaries who emerged to link backcountry communities with cities of the coast and worlds beyond the sea. He and others like him built the distribution systems that supplied people on each side of the Atlantic with the products of the other. He was both a buyer and a seller in these systems. As a buyer he continually sought ways to reduce the costs of obtaining the goods he needed; as a seller he understood the other side of that relationship, as he endeavored to meet the increasingly exacting demands of his customers. He accomplished these things through the networks he constantly nurtured and pruned, gathering together humble neighbors in Middletown and commercial grandees in British and European port cities. By the time of his death, his contacts were legion. His networks tied Frey and Middletown to other people and places scattered around the Atlantic in ways that no planner in Whitehall or Leadenhall Street could have imagined or constructed.

Frey's story provides a stark contrast to the view that early American trade and life can be understood entirely as a relationship between the metropolis and its peripheries. If one sees only the links between the two, one loses much of what was important in any Atlantic state or region before 1815, especially the various and multiple exchanges that made empire such a porous construct. Everywhere—Bahia, Curaçao, Vera Cruz, Philadelphia, Québec, and Halifax—ongoing, reciprocal network interactions with people living all around the ocean complicated directives emanating from the governing centers of empire, drove and implemented local initiatives, and, in the process, built a market and a world where none like them had existed before.

4

Inter-Imperial Smuggling in the Americas, 1600–1800

WIM KLOOSTER

Although European travelers frequently commented on the ubiquity of contraband trade in the early modern Americas, few scholarly monographs on the subject have appeared.[1] My argument in this essay is that illicit trade was big business in many parts of the New World, often overshadowing legal trade between 1600 and 1800, the heyday of contraband trade in the Americas. Although the extent of the activity varied with time and place, every colony was involved in smuggling. The incidence increased steadily after France, England, and the Dutch Republic planted their flags across the Atlantic in the early seventeenth century, and contraband trade remained a staple of colonial life until the Age of Revolutions.

I will use "smuggling" and "contraband trade" interchangeably. Both denote the illegal movement of goods across national boundaries to evade payment of taxes; I also refer to it as "informal" trade.[2] I will deal with only one type of smuggling: inter-imperial or supranational trade (sometimes called "direct trade") that was illicit from the vantage point of at least one of the colonial powers involved.[3] Trade in which subjects of one empire transported products they had illegally extracted in another empire—such as the British logwood industry in Honduras and the Dutch salt-raking enterprise in Punta de Araya (Venezuela)—is also omitted here, because those activities did not involve commercial contacts between residents of different empires.

Let me begin with a truism: it takes two to smuggle. The initiative was usually taken not by persons residing near the site of the exchange, but rather by interlopers, either Europeans or colonial settlers. People domiciled in Europe dominated the early stages of the contraband trade, but by the last third of the seventeenth century settlers of the newly established northern European colonies in the Americas, especially in the Caribbean, began to transport their goods on small craft to commercially attractive areas, competing with merchants in Europe who, legally or illegally, also tried to tap foreign New World markets. The Europeans were at a severe disadvantage, as the ships that carried their goods took much longer to complete voyages, and traders were unable to react adequately and rapidly to local demand.

Careful to protect their valuable goods, the initiators of informal trade often chose to land their merchandise far from the watchful eyes of local officials. The governor of Massachusetts complained in 1737: "The Sea Coast of the Province is so extensive & has so many Commodious harbours, that the small number of Customs House Officers are often complaining they are not able to do much for preventing illegal Trade."[4] An official in Puerto Rico desperately cited a popular expression when he argued that illegal trade was difficult, if not impossible, to prevent: one cannot put gates in the countryside.[5] Elsewhere, it was not a long coastline that gave interlopers full scope, but rather numerous isolated coves, isles, and inlets or an escape route offered by rivers discharging into the sea (Map 4.1).[6]

The trading partners of the interlopers, of course, also took their precautions. An English captain reported about the people with whom he did business near Portobelo: "These Merchants frequently travelled in the Habits of Peasants, and had their Mules with them, on which they brought their Money in Jarrs, which they fill'd up with Meal [flour]; and if any of the King's Officers met them, nothing appeared but Meal, and pretended they were poor People going to Portobello to buy some Trifles; but they for the most Part went through the Woods, and not in the Road, in order to prevent their being discovered by the Royal Officers."[7] The term "merchant" may be misleading: on the receiving end, there was no prototypical smuggler. People from all walks of life participated in illicit trade with foreigners. The inhabitants of Massachusetts Bay, a New Englander wrote in 1781, "were notorious in the smuggling Business, from the Capital Merchant down to the meanest

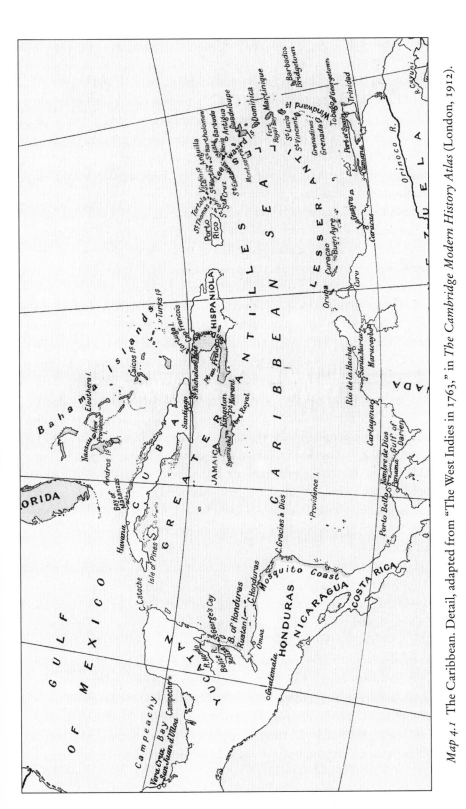

Map 4.1 The Caribbean. Detail, adapted from "The West Indies in 1763," in *The Cambridge Modern History Atlas* (London, 1912).

Mechanick."[8] Smuggling in the New World, as in coastal and border areas in Europe, was part of what Olwen Hufton has called "the makeshift economy of the poor." Seasonally or periodically, large sections of the population helped to move illicit goods in order to provide for their daily necessities.[9] The governor of Santo Domingo in the 1730s and his colleague in Spanish East Florida fifty years later were not alone in questioning the anti-smuggling laws when complaining to their superiors about the common man's lack of food and clothing.[10] But residents higher on the social ladder were also eager to take part in smuggling, tempted to buy better quality at a lower price rather than contenting themselves with the products available through legal channels.

It seemed, therefore, that everyone had a stake in the smuggling business. The governor of Saint-Domingue fretted that he had tried everything to destroy foreign contraband trade, but in vain: "I am alone against the whole colony."[11] In both Santa Marta and Cartagena (in New Granada), widespread involvement created a solidarity across class and racial lines that frustrated efforts to root out smuggling.[12] Similarly, in early seventeenth-century Cuba, a representative of governor Pedro Valdés found that the lieutenant-governor, the wealthiest *hacendados,* and "the entire people" in the southeastern town of Bayamo were guilty of smuggling.[13] Punishment under such conditions was impossible, as Valdés wrote to the Crown; the interior parts of Cuba "would be reduced to desolation" if the smugglers were penalized according to the severity of their crime. In 1606 King Philip III responded to Valdés's pleas by issuing a general pardon for smugglers in Hispaniola, Cuba, and Venezuela.[14]

In the British colonies, contraband trade also had a strong democratic element. Governor Richard Coney of Bermuda wrote in 1687 that his settlers "will not [give] evidence against each other in any publique concern; for they are all of them a kin both by Consanguinity and Villany."[15] The local population in British North America frequently intervened when officials arrested interlopers or seized contraband. In the 1760s, customs officials in Maryland had to "labour under great discouragements in doing their duty."[16] Similar examples abound for other parts of the eastern seaboard. The governor of New York, the Earl of Bellomont, reported to London in 1698 that "[t]he late Governor [Benjamin Fletcher] hath connived at those Lyberties of breach of the Acts of

Trade, and the Merchants here are so accustomed thereto, that on a small seizure I ordered to be made, just after my arrival here on some East India goods imported in an unfree bottome, the whole city seem'd to be in an uproar, and lookt on it as a violent seizing of their property."[17] In 1719, when the customs collector in Newport, Rhode Island, armed with a warrant from the governor and assisted by his officers, seized several hogsheads of claret, the townspeople rebelled. They seized the claret, stove the hogsheads open, "and with pailes drunke out, and carryd away most of the wine, and then threw the remainder into the streets."[18] Half a century later, a Newport mob dragged the boats of a coast guard vessel through the town and burned them, before destroying the vessel and freeing the two prizes it had captured.[19]

Restrictive measures could lead to full-blown rebellions, especially when such actions put an abrupt end to a period of unrestrained smuggling. The arrival of officials authorized to suppress contraband trade antagonized local populations everywhere in the Americas. The southern parts of Cuba were accustomed to "free trade" without official interference. The arrival of new authorities bent on enforcing the law led to three major revolts in which hundreds of people participated. In Venezuela, the appointment of a new justice of the peace had the townspeople of San Felipe up in arms. The new incumbent was authorized to proceed against officials in two neighboring places who had admitted to smuggling. When the residents realized that serious action against informal trade would be forthcoming, they launched a rebellion, which was soon crushed.[20]

In view of the economic importance of their activities, smugglers were rarely thwarted by their own imperial or colonial governments. Portuguese authorities in Brazil encouraged trade with Buenos Aires in order to obtain coveted silver from Potosí, while their English counterparts stimulated merchants in Jamaica to explore the nearby markets of Spanish America. The Dutch government on Curaçao exempted products brought in from the Spanish colonies from customs duties. Theoretically, foreign vessels—Spanish or other—were not allowed to sail within a mile of the coast of the French colonies. The arrival of Spanish ships, often carrying silver, in Barbados or Jamaica regularly created confusion in British imperial circles. Although Spanish bottoms were formally forbidden to unload Spanish (New World) products in English colonies, English law made an exception for any foreign ship laden with bullion. In many cases, therefore, Spanish trade was allowed to proceed.[21]

Throughout Spanish America, which was on the receiving end of much illicit trade, connivance was the rule. Contraband goods entered Spanish America with relative ease in part because officials realized how much local economies depended on illicit transactions. Without the illegal foreign connection the quality of life would diminish substantially. Condoning the introduction of illegal imports thus mirrored the official support of smuggling expeditions to Spanish America from the French, British, or Dutch colonies. Similarly, Portuguese officials routinely allowed the exchange of Brazilian gold for British textiles.[22] Still, risk was always involved, and there were few places where smuggling went on with impunity for lengthy periods.

When the opportunity presented itself, almost everyone purchased smuggled goods. As Adam Smith remarked:

> Not many people are scrupulous about smuggling, when, without perjury, they can find any easy and safe opportunity of doing so. To pretend to have any scruple about buying smuggled goods . . . would in most countries be regarded as one of those pedantick pieces of hypocrisy which . . . [would] serve only to expose the person who affects to practise them to the suspicion of being a greater knave than most of his neighbours. By this indulgence of the publick, the smuggler is often encouraged to continue a trade which he is thus taught to consider as in some measure innocent; and when the severity of the revenue laws is ready to fall upon him, he is frequently disposed to defend with violence, what he has been accustomed to regard as his just property.[23]

As we have seen, many officials, junior as well as senior, and often precisely those whose task it was to suppress contraband trade, connived at illegal exchanges. They were, after all, "members of the communities in which they resided and had to think of their personal relationships as well."[24] Other officials simply sought personal enrichment, like the governor of Texas, an interior province of New Spain, who was accused of sheltering French smugglers, or the agent of the Compagnie des Indes Occidentales who was not above accepting Dutch bribes for permission to introduce merchandise into the French Caribbean.[25] In Spanish America, even the most senior official joined the ranks of the smugglers. In 1717, the Spanish Crown created the viceroyalty of New Granada in an effort to end, once and for all, the participation in informal trade by officials in that region. Soon, however, the viceroy himself was implicated, supporting illicit trafficking by official decree and cooperating with like-minded Cartagena officials. He was arrested in 1722, and a year later the viceroyalty was abolished altogether.[26]

The Spanish Crown's decision to start selling offices on a large scale in the mid-seventeenth century may have been responsible for an increase in corruption.[27] The officials who purchased their posts tried to make as much money as possible during their tenure. A royal officeholder sent to the colonies from Spain "often had only a fixed number of years in the New World to pay off his debts and accumulate enough capital to live as was expected upon his return."[28]

The situation in British America was not fundamentally different. Customs officers had to pay servants certain sums of money from their incomes, and the temptation was therefore strong to squeeze as much out of their positions as possible, by arranging confiscations or accepting gifts or bribes. Without bribery and corruption, Massachusetts governor Thomas Hutchinson wrote, the customs collector "must starve." Parliament was therefore well advised when in 1767 it set the duty on molasses—the key ingredient of rum—lower than the average bribe paid to the customs officers. The large-scale administrative revamping of the English state after 1688 had left many existing institutions untouched, as John Brewer has shown. Newly appointed officials, to be sure, were paid salaries rather than fees and had the prospect of gradually climbing the career ladder.[29] But office holding for life or through royal patent continued, and the custom of using one's office to create patronage networks was equally ineradicable.

Officials, after all, did not operate in a social vacuum. Whether they had obtained posts in the colonial administration by appointment, election, or purchase, officials in all European colonies wanted to be accepted by the local elites.[30] In order to maintain good relations, they occasionally chose to disregard official regulations or to ask for their modification. Social connections between traders and officials often prevented the truth about the legality of commercial transactions from coming to light.[31] When the *corregidores* or other royal officials in Peru seized a cargo, they were either taking revenge on traders who had deceived them or apprehending personal enemies.[32] Bribes and gifts were hallmarks of the system, frequently blurring the distinction between the private and public domains in the colonial world.[33] Officials therefore gave preference to wealthy friends; when they did prosecute interlopers, they went after petty traders and minor consumers of smuggled goods.[34] In the French Caribbean, the few smugglers who were caught and condemned were almost invariably foreigners unconnected to the local population. We know about some smuggling operations and the involvement of officials elsewhere through the existence of contemporary denunciations, often made by members of a rival political faction trying to boost their own careers by condemning their opponents' illegal activities.[35]

Foreign merchants also depended on the whims of local authorities. On occasion officials decided to take law enforcement seriously, if only to impress their metropolitan overlords; at other times, they issued illegal trade permits to foreigners, sometimes invoking fake emergencies. In this way, English vessels received no fewer than ninety-four permits between 1721 and 1723 to conduct trade in Martinique and Guadeloupe.[36] In Brazil, foreign merchants faced confiscation of their ships and cargoes if they refused to have senior local officials act as intermediaries in illegal trade—that is, contraband trade was condoned if it took place on the terms of the local administration.[37] Elsewhere in the Americas, extant documentation offers glimpses of similar arrangements. Four merchants who carried African slaves from Angola to Buenos Aires without a license had agreed beforehand with royal officers in Buenos Aires to buy back their human cargoes after the officers had confiscated them. Although the ensuing pro forma trials increased the expenses for the slave smugglers, they still reaped a handsome profit.[38] Such settlements, which amounted to the whitewashing of illicit trade, formed a grey area between legality and illegality. Whitewashing was not only important for the local economy; it also helped fill the colonial treasuries. In New Granada, contraband seizures constituted 12 percent of the net income of the provincial treasury of Santa Marta in the years 1705–1760, twice the amount collected from import duties on legal trade.[39]

Lesser officers on the ground were not exempt from the pressures that higher-placed officials faced. The guards assisting the local *teniente* on Río de Matina in coastal Costa Rica facilitated trade from Jamaica by authorizing the English merchants to unload their merchandise and build a small shop next to the watch house. The *teniente* received 400 pesos per vessel, part of which undoubtedly trickled down to the guards.[40] Two customs officers in Guadeloupe were each rewarded with an African slave when they turned a blind eye to the importation by a French firm of two hundred slaves from Danish Saint Thomas.[41] In other instances, the amount spent on gifts was negligible. One merchant from Curaçao obtained permission from the *teniente* of Coro, Venezuela, to do business there with the gift of some good wine, a shirt, and new pants.[42]

Contraband trade flourished in the Americas, despite attempts by metropolitan authorities and some of their colonial counterparts to fight the multiheaded monster. Everywhere in the New World, smuggling waxed and waned according to economic, social, and political circumstances. Below I discuss the main hotbeds during eight twenty-five-year periods in the seventeenth and eighteenth centuries. For all the variety and changeability of inter-imperial relations, and despite the continuity of many commercial practices, illicit trade in each Atlantic generation had its own characteristics.

1600–1625: Smuggling under the Habsburg Cloak

The Iberian countries united under the Habsburg monarchy sought to curb foreign trade with their overseas colonies from the early days of colonization. The Casa de la Contratación, the Spanish House of Trade, which registered all ships, crews, equipment, and merchandise bound for the Indies, was established in 1503. It closely monitored foreign involvement in transatlantic trade, which was strictly forbidden. Portugal also applied a policy of national exclusivity to colonial trade, although in fact numerous licenses were issued to foreigners over the years. At times, the authorities proceeded rigorously, as they did in 1605. Not only were all foreign ships forbidden entrance to Portugal's Atlantic colonies, but all foreigners living in Portuguese possessions were required to move to Portugal within a year on pain of death. Subsequent measures were less stringent, including an edict issued in 1771 declaring that foreigners were allowed to sail only in official Portuguese fleets and to enter Portuguese ports only in case of a forced landfall.[43]

Mariners from coastal France were among the pioneers of the contraband trade in Spanish America. Their preferred location was Santo Domingo, where they exchanged Rouen linen for hides as early as the 1560s. In the 1590s, the French were joined by English and Dutch traders.[44] Spanish reports reveal that the northern Europeans drove a brisk trade on the north and west coasts of Hispaniola and often cooperated in the first years of the seventeenth century.[45] In the same decade, northern Europeans were active in the trade with Cuba, where they supplied linen, wine, and African slaves in return for hides. One pamphleteer estimated that annually around 1600, some twenty large Dutch ships with a total of 1,500 men imported hides from Santo Domingo and Cuba, a business that yielded a profit of 800,000 guilders (320,000 pesos). It is likely that most hides in these years were smuggled away from the Caribbean and never arrived in Spain.[46]

English and Dutch carriers were also found trading with the easternmost Spanish settlements on the mainland of South America and with the nearby islands of Margarita and Trinidad. The Dutch sent a flow of vessels in 1599–1605 to the peninsula of Araya, where crew after crew raked salt and returned to the United Provinces until direct Spanish military action and the erection of a fort put an end to the business. In Tierra Firme (the Spanish Main) and the islands offshore, tobacco was the main item purchased, with most transactions taking place at the port of Cumaná. Most local tobacco was carried by Dutch and English ships; twenty to thirty English ships sailed annually to the coast of Venezuela and to Trinidad for this purpose in the years around 1610. The Spanish Crown tried to stem the flow of contraband by ordering the depopulation of northern and western Hispaniola (1603) and Cumaná province (1606) and by forbidding tobacco cultivation in Margarita, Caracas, and Cumaná for ten years.[47]

Both the Dutch—*conversos* and Calvinists alike—and, to a lesser extent, the English were active in Brazilian waters, starting in the 1580s. The English initially were mostly privateers and the Dutch primarily traders, although rarely smugglers. Dutch mariners and vessels were integrated into the official Portuguese shipping system, which involved Portuguese ports of call and the payment of customs duties. The occasional direct, and therefore forbidden, navigation between Dutch ports and Brazil did not account for the large quantities of sugar that arrived in Middelburg and Amsterdam, spawning a refining industry that was unrivaled in Europe. Dutch participation in the Portuguese Brazil trade, with ships, crews, and investors, ended abruptly in 1621 with the renewed outbreak of hostilities between Habsburg Spain and the rebellious northern provinces, whose mariners especially targeted Portuguese shipping. Some English now stepped into the shoes of the Dutch, although again, few sailed in smuggling ventures.[48]

Despite the activities of northern Europeans, it was the Portuguese who dominated smuggling in Spanish America from 1600 to 1625. When Portugal came under the Spanish Crown in 1580, many Portuguese were already living in Seville; in the early seventeenth century, their number was estimated at two thousand. It is no coincidence, then, that more Portuguese by far were naturalized than were men of other nationalities.[49] Some Portuguese merchants settled in Panama, Lima, or Buenos Aires, while others sent agents. Many of their activities would not bear the light of day: bills of lading and import papers were forged, and Seville, Spain's designated port of departure, was bypassed.[50]

Can the informal Portuguese trade be considered an example of inter-imperial smuggling? Were Portuguese foreigners in the eyes of Spanish officialdom? When Spain's king in 1605 expressly forbade foreigners to do business in the colonies, Cuba's governor grappled with the same question. He was reluctant to expel the baker, the shoemaker, the wine merchant, the street vendor, and the many other Portuguese residents who were held responsible for the island's massive smuggling operations. But the king and his advisors maintained their stance and ordered another governor three years later to banish all the Portuguese from Havana, except those who were married and had lived there for at least ten years.[51] But this far-reaching measure was not executed, and the Portuguese were not actually excluded from trading. The same circumstances applied to Buenos Aires, where the Portuguese settled in appreciable numbers, making up around 370 of 1,500 residents in 1643.[52]

Some of the resident Portuguese were undoubtedly instrumental in facilitating illegal activities by their fellow nationals. The Portuguese commercial role in the Spanish Empire was conspicuously large prior to Portugal's independence in 1640, primarily because of the key position the Portuguese held in the transatlantic slave trade. Spain relied almost exclusively on its neighbor for slaves in this period. The Spanish Crown signed successive monopoly contracts with Portuguese merchants, who were handsomely rewarded for their services. Complaints about Portuguese transgressions abounded from the start of these *asientos* in 1595. Many Portuguese sailed to Spanish-American destinations after having secured a license, but then exceeded the quota that they had been allowed to transport. On average during the period 1595–1640, the number of slaves the Portuguese surreptitiously introduced was three times the authorized number.[53]

By the second decade of the seventeenth century, smuggling was rampant in the Spanish slave trade on both sides of the Atlantic, in part because Spanish metropolitan authorities reorganized the business in 1615. One consequence was that slaves were no longer required to be shipped to the New World via Seville. In Angola, soldiers, settlers, merchants, commanders, and the governor himself benefited from relaxation of some of the rules, while in South America the new and profitable outlet of Buenos Aires, the gateway to the mines of Potosí, became available. If underregistration was the most common form of slave smuggling in the Caribbean, outright smuggling of entire human cargoes was the rule in Buenos Aires. In 1621, for example, only three of sixteen slave ships anchoring in the port had valid licenses.[54] In response to the situation, one author proposed to the Casa de la Contratación that Buenos Aires be depopulated.[55]

Most ships that fraudulently offered slaves for sale arrived in Buenos Aires from Salvador da Bahia and other ports in Brazil, not directly from Africa, typically arriving with about a dozen slaves. It is unclear how many of the estimated 22,000 Africans who entered the city between 1595 and 1615 were smuggled in, but it must have been the overwhelming majority, because authorized slave imports for the entire period from 1586 to 1645 numbered only six thousand. By 1624, the Council of the Indies took action by declaring that all slaves who arrived illegally in the Río de la Plata would be free upon disembarkation. That decision, like many others, probably remained unenforced. Too many officials were implicated in a trade that—legal or not—accounted for about two-thirds of the value of all imports. Rarely was other merchandise introduced under the cover of the slave trade.[56] Whitewashing was very common on the receiving end, as officials in the Spanish colonies often decided to sell the smuggled slaves at public auctions. If we accept the estimates of one historian, more than half of all slaves were smuggled in. About one quarter entered illegally but were whitewashed, and just over a fifth were sold legally.[57] By the 1620s, Buenos Aires had thus become a slave entrepôt, as ships arrived with human cargoes from Brazil and—increasingly—Angola, and the Africans were sold to Potosí, Chile, Mendoza, and Paraguay.[58]

1625–1650: The Calm before the Storm

Contraband trade between residents of the Río de la Plata and Brazil continued unabated in the second quarter of the seventeenth century. A Dutch native who served the governor of Buenos Aires as chamberlain in the early 1630s reported that most of the wealth passing through the port went to Brazil, where Peruvian gold and silver were exchanged for sugar. Spanish merchants apparently preferred to ship sugar, since the Crown was known to confiscate cargoes of bullion arbitrarily upon a ship's arrival in Spain. Such seizures of privately owned Peruvian bullion were themselves the consequence of the growing practice among merchants of shipping unregistered silver, which forced the Crown on occasion to sequester 25 percent or more of the value of registered silver in order to compensate for the low levels of income collected from the *avería* (a tax levied on transatlantic trade in order to finance the fleet system).[59] Like Buenos Aires, Cartagena also emerged as a major hotbed of illicit trade. Even before disembarking Africans in Cartagena, ships made stops at smaller ports on the northern coast of South America to sell slaves and textiles.[60] After anchoring in Cartagena, traders used bribes, amounting to 10 or 15 percent of the value of their human cargo, to avoid paying taxes or risking confiscation. Others resorted to under-registration, as was confirmed by an inspection carried out by the local tribunal of the Spanish Inquisition on board eight ships in Cartagena in 1634–1635. For every arriving African slave who had been registered, two had not been recorded.[61]

Overall, however, American smuggling diminished between 1625 and 1650. The main reason was not the general crisis of the seventeenth century, which did not apply to the New World.[62] More mined silver remained in the New World than in the late sixteenth century, posing an even greater attraction for interlopers. The real explanation for the decline in contraband trade was the transformation that took place among the countries of northern Europe. Whereas those states had previously attempted to siphon off some of the American riches by engaging in illicit commerce with the Iberian colonies, metropolitan energy and investment after 1625 were directed toward settling, planting, and—for the Dutch—waging war. The decline of informal trade was also a consequence of rigorous Spanish attempts to root out the phenomenon, which in turn may have influenced the decisions of northern European investors to form colonies of their own.[63]

In this period, tobacco cultivation took off in Virginia and English settlement began in Saint Christopher (1624), Barbados (1627), and some other islands of the Lesser Antilles. The French claimed possession of Martinique and Guadeloupe in 1635 and expanded their Caribbean holdings to Saint Croix in the north and Grenada in the south, while the Dutch captured Curaçao (1634) and moved into other, undefended, Caribbean islands, including Saint Eustatius (1636). The Dutch West India Company, which had been founded as a commercial enterprise, was in practice more of a war machine, fitting out privateers and battling for Brazil against Habsburg and later Luso-Brazilian forces (1624–1625 and 1630–1654).

1650–1675: Dutch Dominance

Although officially excluded from Spain's fleet system, the *carrera de Indias,* some foreigners nevertheless participated illegally in the *flotas* and *galeones.* Dutch merchants sold their goods to a Spanish shipper and were usually paid in cash for one-third or one-half of the merchandise. The rest of the goods were bought on credit, on which the shipper had to pay interest. Alternatively, one or more shippers acted as supercargo, sailing with the foreign goods to the Spanish colonies and supervising the sales there. The goods were transported at the expense and risk of the foreigners. To disguise this type of illicit trade, foreign traders availed themselves of the services of a Spanish figurehead (or those of a Fleming residing in Seville or Cádiz), whose name was listed on the invoice and the bill of lading and who was used as a front when the goods were registered or cleared through customs.[64]

The Dutch actively began to use these methods once the Treaty of Münster put an end to their long war with Spain. The Dutch involvement was sometimes limited to the ownership of the ship and a small cargo to be sold in the Indies, making the venture largely a Spanish one. In other cases, however, the ship was Dutch-owned, -freighted, and -manned, and even accompanied by one or two shippers from the Dutch Republic.[65] In yet another scenario, Dutchmen, Flemings, or Frenchmen co-owned and co-freighted a ship before it sailed via Spain to the Americas.[66] The Dutch discovered a less cumbersome way to open up Spanish America: the "register ships" that sailed without convoy from Spain to individual ports in the Americas. A contract was usually concluded in Amsterdam with a Spanish merchant, who then undertook to transport a certain cargo across the ocean. The ship would drop anchor off the Canary Islands, where—for the sake of appearances—it would be sold to local traders by means of forged passports. But ordinarily this charade was unnecessary, because registers to sail to Havana or other Caribbean ports were granted without much ado.[67]

Dutch ships had used the Canaries as a port of call en route to Brazil since the 1590s, and by 1611 the Casa de la Contratación and the Council of the Indies were aware of French and "Flemish" ships also using the Canaries to obtain access to the Spanish Indies. By midcentury, Dutch vessels often picked up the sweet white wine that was a local specialty, encouraged by a measure the Spanish Crown introduced in 1641 (and renewed in 1656 amid protests about abuses): in light of the poor provisioning of the colonies, the Canaries were allowed to ship their wines without the usual strict controls.[68] Canary wine had been exported for decades to Brazil, Angola, and West Africa, but the secession of Portugal from Habsburg rule in 1640 enabled the Dutch to expand their Canary trade, albeit illegally. Realizing the advantages of having the ships seem to be Spanish, the Dutch merchants gave them Roman Catholic names.[69] If the arrangements were worked out beforehand, these ships could sail back and forth multiple times between Dutch ports and Spanish America via the Canary Islands.[70]

Occasionally, Amsterdam merchants would take the risk of bypassing the Canary gateway. One such venture offers an example of the places visited, cargoes bought, and the large sums of money invested in this Caribbean trade. The ship *De Liefde* left in 1664 with a cargo valued at 60,000 pesos, touching at the Cuban ports of Santiago and Puerto del Príncipe, before carrying on to Caracas, Maracaibo, and Ríohacha. The ship was back in Dutch waters in September 1665 with 30,000 pesos in cash, 200 canisters of Barinas tobacco, 2.5 million pounds of Campeche wood, 4,000 hides, some indigo, and assorted other items.[71]

Similarly lucrative was the trade, either direct or by way of the Canaries, with Buenos Aires. In several cases, the northern Spanish port of San Sebastián was also used in this traffic, enabling Basque captains to take part in the Indies trade. Dutch-owned ships clearly dominated foreign smuggling in Buenos Aires in this period, accounting for more than two-thirds of all cases. In the decade 1655–1665, no less than sixty-three large Dutch ships—often 400 tons or more—visited the Río de la Plata.[72] Curiously, this commerce fell off rapidly after 1675. In the next decade, only six Dutch ships are documented as having sailed to Buenos Aires and none after 1685. Lack of profitability seems not a likely explanation, if we go by data that the Spanish ambassador in The Hague supplied in 1665. He had been informed from Cádiz that a consortium of Amsterdam merchants had sent a Basque captain to Buenos Aires with three ships. The small fleet returned with 54,000 hides as well as a cargo in gold and silver valued at 1.6 million pesos.[73]

Similar transactions wreaked havoc with the *carrera de Indias.*[74] In 1660–1661, another ship fitted out in Amsterdam arrived in Portobelo with cargo valued at 300,000 pesos, an appreciable amount compared to the one million pesos traded at the Portobelo fair in early 1661—and that was a relatively good fair. The Dutch paid the governor a huge bribe of 60,000 pesos, apparently necessary to enable an unprecedented flow of contraband goods.[75] The value of the cargo shipped in 1664 by the aforementioned ship *De Liefde,* one of many such Dutch carriers active in Caribbean waters, compared favorably with the worth of the merchandise officially changing hands at that year's fair in Portobelo: 150,000 vs. 400,000 pesos.[76]

Dutch smuggling also extended to enslaved Africans. The end of the war with Spain came at a time when the shipping of slaves to Spanish America was in profound disarray. The Portuguese, who had possessed the legal monopoly of such slave shipments, lost the contract after becoming independent from Spain in 1640 and war ensued. Instead of a monopoly contract, the Spanish Crown issued thousands of small licenses to myriad individual traders, which led to an increase in smuggling. The Portuguese themselves were not averse to providing the colonies of their new enemies with laborers, sending at least fifteen ships to Buenos Aires between 1650 and 1675, nearly all slavers. Between 1648 and 1663, such ships were arriving not from Brazilian ports but directly from Africa; thereafter, direct shipments from Angola were exceptional.[77] Having gained experience in the slave trade during the brief period in which they controlled most of the area of sugar cultivation in Brazil (1635–1645), the Dutch were also eager to supply slaves to Spanish America. Eighteen Dutch slave voyages to Buenos Aires have been documented for the years 1657–1663, probably involving more than 2,000 slaves, while Dutch merchants sold another 3,800 slaves in Santo Domingo and Puerto Rico and on the north coast of South America.[78]

From the late 1650s onward, the Dutch used their colony of Curaçao as an entrepôt in the slave trade with Spanish America. The island's favorable location and the regular slave imports enabled the Dutch to become subcontractors of a new *asiento* drawn up in 1662. Their role in the *asiento* also led the Dutch to provide the designated ports of Havana, Veracruz, Cartagena, and Portobelo with more than human cargoes. No opportunity was lost to bring ashore all kinds of products. The Spanish ambassador in The Hague estimated that the returns of this trade amounted to 1.5 million guilders (600,000 pesos) in the year 1670 alone.[79]

If the Dutch were dominant in the period 1650–1675, English settlers were learning the ropes of contraband trade in the Americas. International commerce in the English colonies was virtually unrestrained until the adoption of a string of Navigation Acts, starting in 1651. These acts ordered that all trade between the colonies and the metropolis had to be carried in English vessels. English ships were allowed to conduct any trade in foreign colonies that was legal according to existing international treaties.[80] In addition, some New World products could be sent only to England. The products that were singled out in this way (the "enumerated commodities") included sugar, tobacco, cotton, indigo, ginger, speckle-wood, and dyewoods. The list was expanded in later years, as rice (1704) and furs (1721) were added.

As Spanish-American traders began to frequent Barbados in the early 1660s, trying to buy slaves and merchandise, the question of the legality of such trade arose. Although formally forbidden by the Navigation Acts, it was legalized by the Privy Council in 1663 in order to increase colonial income.[81] No such exceptions were to be made for the Dutch, however, who in earlier decades had been large-scale trading partners of the English colonies of Virginia, Saint Christopher, and Barbados. Despite the first Navigation Act, the Dutch presence at Barbados continued until 1655, when an English fleet seized many ships. Few Dutch shipowners dared to do business in Barbados thereafter.[82] Yet by the 1680s, one group had managed to restore the old link: the Jewish merchants of Barbados. Their co-religionists in Amsterdam sent ships to England, where their associates arranged for the cargoes to be entered in the names of Englishmen, thereby evading the heavy "alien duties." The sugar sent from Barbados in return escaped the alien duties in the same way. How long this surreptitious trade continued is unclear.[83]

In Virginia, the situation was different. After an initial attempt to enforce the Acts rigorously had led to a sharp drop in the price of local tobacco, Dutch traders were welcomed back. In the late 1650s and early 1660s, Dutch ships, perhaps with some token English sailors on board, still sailed directly to home ports such as Rotterdam, depriving the English Treasury annually of an estimated £10,000.[84] However, as more and more Dutchmen were naturalized and as metropolitan Dutch merchants gradually preferred other, less risky trades, the tobacco trade was left increasingly to the English and the Scots.

The French government had tried to curb the role of foreigners in overseas commerce from the early stages of Caribbean colonization, but their policies met little success as long as the Dutch dominated the coastal trade of France itself. Laws stipulating that foreigners could no longer load commodities in French ports, such as the Michau Law (1629) and the Grande Ordonnance de la Marine (1631) had no effect. Politically, moreover, it was not opportune to act against the Dutch until 1648, when their alliance with France against Spain came to an end.[85] The crucial role of the Dutch in French domestic commerce was mirrored by their activities in the French Caribbean, where several Dutch traders lived and owned property and others supplied large amounts of linens and unknown numbers of slaves. French minister Jean-Baptiste Colbert estimated that, among the 150 ships trading with the French islands, only three or four were French. A list stolen by an English ship from a Dutch bottom in 1664 shows that 637 residents of Guadeloupe were debtors of the Dutch.[86] In the same year, Colbert acted decisively against the Dutch, that "nation of herring mongers, of cheese vendors"—who, he believed, obtained annual returns worth 12 million *livres*.[87] But, although he outlawed colonial trade with the Dutch completely, Martinique, Guadeloupe, and Saint-Domingue were so dependent on Dutch supplies that colonial governors frequently defied the new regulations and connived at, or at least consented to, the import of "Dutch" slaves.[88]

In the long run, however, mercantilist measures forced the Dutch out of the French islands in the Caribbean. In the French part of Saint Christopher (Saint Kitts), over sixty well-stocked Dutch warehouses were set on fire in 1663. The following year saw the foundation of the Compagnie des Indes Occidentales, which would wield power and administer justice in the French Antilles for forty years. The colonies' gradual breaking away from metropolitan control had not passed unnoticed, and the founding of the company was intended to reestablish French authority. A royal ban on mercantile dealings with the Dutch, initially issued under the pretext of a plague epidemic in Amsterdam, led to revolts, first in Martinique and some years later in Saint-Domingue. The planters' wishes were not heeded, and Dutch traders abandoned the islands. The door was left ajar, however, for Curaçaoan traders, who transported large numbers of oxen and horses to the French colonies, where the animals were used in the sugar mills. After 1670, this trade also came to an end.[89]

1675–1700: Smuggling Into and Out of British America

Around 1670, a number of merchants in the Dutch Republic who had traded with Spanish America by loading goods on the Spanish fleets changed course. Henceforth, they would forward their goods to Curaçao, where their local correspondents would send the products on to the Spanish colonies, thus bypassing Spanish customs duties as well as the extra costs involved in fleet traffic, and their capital would not be tied up for years before seeing returns. Soon after 1680, merchants in England began to use Jamaica in the same way. Jamaica was to become for the English what Curaçao was to the Dutch: their Caribbean entrepôt. Following the Treaty of 1670, the English Crown had agreed with Spain that English subjects would not be allowed to trade in the Spanish West

Indies; nevertheless, commercial relations were maintained with most of the Spanish colonies. The Jamaican merchant fleet expanded from forty vessels in 1670 to about a hundred in 1688, about half of which were constantly used in informal trade away from the major ports in the Spanish Caribbean. Like the Dutch, the Jamaicans benefited from delays or cancellations of the *galeones,* and they were negatively affected by the arrival of a fleet.

The governors of Jamaica and other English colonies guaranteed that smuggling would proceed smoothly by lending passports to ship captains who then supposedly went fishing, but in fact went to trade with the Spaniards. Many of them went to Cuba, where they could undersell the Spaniards by one-third and obtain hides. Others went to the Mosquito Coast of Central America, where the English offered wine, brandy, and ammunition for sale. In Costa Rica and Guatemala, they paid with a variety of dry goods for cacao and indigo. The English were thus responsible for the vast expansion of smuggling in Spanish Central America after 1680. But the main focus of Jamaica's trade in the Caribbean in this period was on Portobelo and Cartagena. In 1689, bullion obtained in that trade and exported to England was worth more than the local sugar shipped to the metropolis. By 1700, the English themselves claimed that their trade in the southwestern corner of the Caribbean, where they sold linens, silk, ironware, liquor, and slaves, amounted to some 6 million pesos a year, though that was a gross exaggeration.[90] The combined Dutch and English contraband trade effectively killed Spain's southern fleet system. Initially there had been biannual trade fairs at Portobelo, but after 1682 long hiatuses were the norm. After 1686, only two more fairs were organized in the seventeenth century (in 1691 and 1698), at the first of which only 216,035 pesos' worth of goods were exchanged—the value of the cargo of a single richly laden Dutch or English ocean-going smuggler. Fairs held in the eighteenth century were invariably minor affairs.[91]

And yet, there was grumbling in Jamaica. The Navigation Acts still felt like a straitjacket to many inhabitants, who wished to trade at better rates with the omnipresent Dutch ships.[92] While Jamaicans dreamed about the possibility, other English colonies breached the Navigation Acts and received foreigners, to whom the islands became more interesting as they became more developed, particularly as sugar producers.

Foreign interlopers seem to have neglected Barbados, but concentrated on Saint Christopher and other islands. Dutch ocean-going ships, putting in under the pretext of an emergency, would lie in port for a week and openly strike deals with planters for their sugar. After seeing to the delivery of their merchandise, the captains would then sail to Saint Eustatius and wait for the promised sugar to arrive.[93] Scottish and Dutch merchants, meanwhile, collaborated in carrying Maryland tobacco to the colonies of Curaçao and Suriname in exchange for linens and other dry goods.[94] Contraband trade in proprietary Maryland reached such proportions in the 1680s that King James II, angry that the Crown was defrauded of customs duties, threatened to revoke the colonial charter. Although James did not take action, his successor King William III made Maryland a royal colony in 1691 after two customs collectors had been murdered within five years.[95] Farther to the north, Boston traded goods with ports in France and other parts of the Continent that yielded an estimated £60,000 in returns a year. For its part, Newfoundland had no lack of Spanish wines and iron, supplied by ships from San Sebastián in northern Spain in exchange for cod.[96]

At the same time, at the other end of the New World, a new chapter was opened in Luso-Spanish smuggling with the founding, in 1680, of Nova Colônia do Sacramento in Brazil (present-day Uruguay), directly across from Buenos Aires. Eager for direct commercial ties with Buenos Aires and access to Potosí, merchants from Lisbon trading with Rio de Janeiro shipped large amounts of French linen to Colônia. The Portuguese Crown not only supported the trade with Buenos Aires, encouraging the inhabitants of Rio to become involved, but also intended to keep the trade under strict royal supervision. Several English and French ships presented themselves as well, stopping first at Colônia before moving on to Buenos Aires, but the Portuguese used their own colony with much greater frequency, supplying textiles, paper, sugar, *cachaça* (an alcoholic drink made from distilled sugarcane juice), and African slaves. A 1694 Portuguese report estimated that the ships returning that year from Rio de Janeiro had brought in returns worth 200,000 pesos deriving from the trade at their new hub.[97]

Compared to those of the English, Dutch, and Portuguese, the French interloping trade was not yet a major affair. There was no lack of interest on Saint-Domingue for exchanging cacao and cash for English linens and other manufactures, but in practice virtually no contacts were established with the English islands. Nor was much French trade conducted with Spanish colonies. At the end of the century, France's metropolitan authorities tried to learn from English and Dutch successes as they planned to make Saint-Domingue into an entrepôt, similar to Jamaica or Curaçao, that could tap the riches of the Spanish Main. But the idea was not followed by concrete measures.[98] The unbridled contraband trade in Saint Croix, a French possession since 1650, did elicit uncompromising action. The inhabitants reportedly made a living by trading with passing ships of all nations. In a move reminiscent of the Spanish depopulation of some areas in Spanish America at the beginning of the century, a French force evacuated all residents, including 623 blacks and some 300 whites, in the year 1696.[99] Saint Croix thus exited the French Empire.

1700–1725: Contraband Trade Becomes Universal

In the early eighteenth century smuggling made a qualitative leap. Wherever there were ports, from New France to Buenos Aires and from Chile to Brazil, illicit trade occurred. Commercial contacts that defied mercantilist frameworks became especially frequent in the Caribbean, where so many colonies of different empires existed side by side. The growth of smuggling in the French colonies was especially remarkable. During the War of the Spanish Succession (1701–1713), an illegal fur trade linking Montréal and Albany that had thrived since at least the 1670s assumed larger proportions: French authorities believed "that from one-half to two-thirds of the beaver brought to Montréal found its way to Albany. This illicit trade does not seem to have declined after the war. . . . Even with frequent seizures, merchants in the smuggling business [lost] only about 10 percent on their furs."[100]

Hispaniola was an important center of French informal trade in the Caribbean. The few statistics that have survived relating to the transactions that took place between Saint-Domingue and the Spanish half of the island deal mainly with overland trade. Both parties gained by this trade: Santo Domingo obtained European commodities that Spain was unable to provide, and the French took delivery of cash and mules. Officials could be bribed with one or two pesos for the passage of each mule, which were imported for labor in the sugar mills as well as for their meat. Sugar was not sold to the Spaniards, but its by-products, rum and molasses, were.[101] One type of contraband trade involved subjects of three empires: every year during the War of the Spanish Succession, Jamaicans exchanged slaves for sugar and indigo at the southern part of Saint-Domingue; from there some were further transported to Santo Domingo, and from there to Puerto Rico and Cuba.[102] The Danes of Saint Thomas and the Dutch of Saint Eustatius also found customers for their slaves in Saint-Domingue, as they did in the other French colonies of Saint Christopher, Guadeloupe, and Grenada.[103]

Louis and Jerome Phelypeaux—father and son Counts Pontchartrain, who between them were in charge of the French Ministry of the Marine from 1690 to 1715—tried to encourage French smuggling operations in three regions: Peru, Venezuela/New Granada, and the Gulf of Mexico.[104] But Franco-Spanish smuggling remained modest compared to British and Dutch colonial trade with their Spanish neighbors, although it boomed during the War of the Spanish Succession, when France and Spain were allies. Spanish shipping grew so scarce that French vessels were allowed to enter ports throughout Spanish America. According to one French estimate in 1709, during the previous eight years more than 180 million livres (ca. 50 million pesos) had accrued to France from direct and indirect dealings with the Spanish Indies.[105] Most of this traffic involved French metropolitan rather than colonial ships. Shipowners in the Breton port of Saint-Malo were particularly active, fitting out dozens of ships to the Caribbean (of which sixty-four have been documented), two-thirds of which went to the Spanish possessions, especially to the mainland west of Caracas and south of Veracruz. Ships returned to Saint-Malo with holds full of Venezuelan cacao, Central American dyewood, Guatemalan indigo, Mexican cochineal, and hides from Cuba and the Río de la Plata. But the main item was bullion: gold dust from New Granada and the Isthmus of Panama and silver from Mexico and Peru, the overall value of which may have amounted to between 2 and 3 million pesos.[106] The bulk of this trade was illegal, often taking place in collusion with local authorities who had at first denied access to the French vessels. Officials sometimes formally confiscated and sold the smugglers' ships at public auctions that enabled the French to reap the profits. French shipowners fitting out ships to the Río de la Plata counted on a net gain of 75 percent.[107]

Ocean-going French trade with the Pacific coast of South America was even more significant than commerce with the Atlantic seaboard of Spanish America.[108] Between 1695 and 1726, 181 ships, more than half from 200 to 400 tons and a quarter between 400 and 600 tons, reached that destination. Most ships, including once again many from Saint-Malo and others from Marseilles, traded with Peru, but some tried their luck along the extended Chilean littoral. There were even reports of Frenchmen going ashore in Chile and selling their goods along the road from Valparaíso to Santiago. The local market was so saturated with linen that there was no reason for merchants at the next trade fair at Portobelo to plan to sell it in Chile.[109] Total French returns from the Pacific coast in the first quarter of the eighteenth century have been estimated at 47 million pesos, or 65 percent of Peru's foreign trade.[110] French merchants tapped the mineral wealth of Potosí until 1716 when, in their bid to maintain good relations with the other Bourbon state, French authorities made shipping traffic to the South Sea a capital offense. Thereafter, the contraband trade with Spanish America was a matter of secondary importance to metropolitan French merchants.[111] They concentrated on the *carrera de Indias* and on commerce with their own colonies of Martinique, Guadeloupe, and Saint-Domingue.

Like the Portuguese and Dutch before them, the French after 1702 also used the *asiento* slave trade as a front for smuggling, despite a set of rules that Spanish officials had devised to prevent illicit transactions. The French also discovered the profitability of doing business in Buenos Aires—which was officially off limits to the *asentistas*—where they exchanged African slaves for hides and cash. Although the *asiento* was discontinued in 1714, the French slave trade to Cuba, Santo Domingo, Cartagena, and Portobelo continued surreptitiously.[112]

On a smaller scale, but more intensively, French settlers in the Caribbean traded with their British neighbors. As we have seen, Jamaican ships introduced slaves to Saint-Domingue, as they did to other foreign colonies. Up to a third of all slaves arriving in Jamaica from Africa were re-exported to French and Spanish colonies in the first two decades of the eighteenth century. In Saint-Domingue, the slaves were left at abandoned sites, where residents awaited them and guided them through the woods to the plantations.[113] Other Franco-British trade took place on Saint Thomas, the Danish island that had first functioned as an entrepôt during the Nine Years' War. While the War of the Spanish Succession lasted, neutral Saint Thomas, and to a lesser degree non-neutral Curaçao, were furnished with rum, sugar, cotton, and indigo from the British Leeward Islands and with other provisions from Boston, Carolina, Pennsylvania, and New York. The French islands were thus provided with a wide variety of goods.[114] The governor of Barbados noted that the Danish island "in time of war ever has been and is the staple for all sort of indirect and illegal trade and commerce."

Barbados itself also dealt with the enemy during this war. Flags of truce, for ships that officially carried prisoners of war, were in practice used as a cover for intensive contraband trade between Barbados and Martinique. In this way, French liquors and other prohibited goods came into British possession daily by 1713.[115] Merchants in Martinique's main port of Saint Pierre also maintained close relations with Antigua and other British colonies. The extent of this smuggling remains invisible, since Martinique sugar was put in English barrels and sold in New England and Britain. Small wonder that it was hard for the island to adjust to legal business after the war. Indeed, old habits continued: a 1722 report mentions that New Englanders had brought coopers to set up their casks in the French Islands and that they emptied the sugar, molasses, and rum from French casks into their own.[116] The Peace of Utrecht (1713) heralded a new era of British smuggling in Spanish America. France's loss of the *asiento* was Britain's gain. Politicians set great store by the *asiento*, because the slaves were paid for in silver. The *asiento*, which according to a separate treaty was to remain in British hands until 1744, could thus be an alternative device to procure currency needed to conduct trade in the Baltic, the Levant, and the Far East, even if most bullion was still being imported from Portugal and Spain. Besides, the prospects for smuggling in slaves seemed favorable, because—unlike other merchandise taken to the Indies—it was not mandatory to have slaves registered or taxed by the Casa de la Contratación.[117]

By agreement with the Spanish Crown, the South Sea Company—holder of the *asiento*—was allowed to fit out one ship of 500 tons to trade each year in the Indies. Between 1715 and 1732, nine "annual ships" sailed to the Caribbean to carry on business in Cartagena, Portobelo, and the Mexican ports of Jalapa and Veracruz. These annual ships were also involved in unlawful transactions, introducing more goods than had been agreed upon and thereby creating competition with those British merchants who had shipped their wares with the fleets and galleons. In exchange for linens, silk, hardware, and liquor, the annual ships primarily received bullion.[118] In some places, no slaves at all were offered for sale, as Company agents realized that there was a better market for provisions. One agent set up business in Puerto Rico in the name of the Company. The profits from all this informal trade amounted to between £450,000 and £600,000 in the years 1730–1739. Not surprisingly, the *flotas* and *galeones* often found the markets of Peru and New Spain saturated and suffering from a shortage of silver.[119] The South Sea Company also smuggled on the Pacific coast of South America, where in 1725 the Spanish Crown authorized it to sell the slaves that could not be sold in Buenos Aires.[120]

The South Sea Company was very much a British metropolitan creature and as such not particularly beloved in Jamaica. Company ships sailed the same waters as Jamaica's interlopers, who had been protected during the last war by convoys to the coasts of mainland Spanish America. The trade was so important that in 1707 Parliament prohibited any interference with Spaniards in the area between Ríohacha and Chagres.[121] One Spanish source claimed that Britain benefited from the smuggling with Spanish America to the value of 6 million pesos, undoubtedly an exaggeration. The estimate of £250,000, or ca. 55,000 pesos, in annual returns (for the years 1706–1713) seems more realistic.[122] After the war, the Jamaicans successfully competed with the South Sea Company in the slave trade to the Spanish Main, and they were largely responsible for the low price of slaves. Only 10 percent of contraband seizures in or near Cartagena between 1715 and 1739 concerned the South Sea Company.[123]

British smuggling was not exclusively concentrated on the Caribbean's southern littoral. A Spanish prisoner in Jamaica reported 143 ships leaving Port Royal for Cuba in the course of nine months in 1719.[124] Apart from hides, British traders in the Caribbean were constantly on the lookout for dyewood, an article indispensable to the British wool industry. Initially Spanish ships with loads of wood were seized; then readily accessible coastal woodland was plundered; and finally English logwood camps were founded in Honduras, Campeche, Ríohacha, Río Magdalena, and along the Mosquito Coast. These remote and sparsely settled places proved to be highly suitable for illicit commerce with the neighboring population.[125] At the same time, the British obtained cacao on the coasts of Costa Rica and Venezuela, at times by offering slaves for sale.[126]

In Venezuela, however, the British came second to the Dutch island of Curaçao, located only 37 miles off the Venezuelan coast. Cacao was the main cash crop in Venezuela, which was the world's largest producer from the mid-seventeenth to the early nineteenth century. Curaçao's hold on the Venezuelan cacao trade was such that in the years 1717–1725, for every Venezuelan cacao bean entering Spain, sixteen or seventeen entered the Dutch Republic by way of Curaçao. In the first half of the eighteenth century, cacao accounted for 37 percent of the value of all Curaçaoan exports to the United Provinces.[127] Large amounts of tobacco were also funneled to Dutch metropolitan ports from Spanish America, especially Cuba. In some years, more non-snuff tobacco arrived in the Dutch Republic than in Spain.[128] Bullion, obtained largely from Portobelo and Cartagena, made up 28 percent of the value of the island's re-exports to the mother country. In addition, Dutch ocean-going ships routinely sailed to the Spanish Caribbean in this period, looking especially for gold and silver. One company alone fitted out twenty-three ships for this purpose between 1721 and 1744. Finally, more than half of all hides leaving Santo Domingo between 1700 and 1746 were bought by merchants from Curaçao.[129]

1725–1750: The Intensification of Smuggling

By about 1725, residents in colonial America had developed myriad techniques to bypass official commercial regulations. In both North America and the British West Indies, customs officers issued fake clearance papers to ship captains, who could then export colonial products to Saint-Domingue or Suriname, while customs books showed the destinations as other British colonies.[130] Ship sales to foreign colonies also went undetected. Along with the sloops that Bermudians sold to the Dutch of Curaçao and Saint Eustatius, they provided British registries, thus making it possible to sail legally in and out of British colonial ports. Likewise, ships built and registered in New England were sold to the French West Indies and to Spanish America.[131]

Abuse of licenses was another widespread phenomenon. In one common mid-eighteenth-century scenario, Cuban sea captains received licenses from the governor in Havana

> to fish from four to six months in water off Nova Scotia and Newfound-
> land. This, however, had become a cover for clandestine trade activities.
> Leaving Cuba with hidden cargoes of tobacco or sugar, Cuban sailors
> sailed for Charleston or another convenient harbor, where they exchanged
> their tobacco or sugar for goods like dishes, clothes, or furniture. They
> then went to another out-of-the-way port and sold these articles for spe-
> cie. With enough time still remaining to fulfill the terms of their license,
> the Cuban mariners sailed north to net a few cod and returned to Havana
> within the time prescribed by the governor's license.[132]

Tobacco, in particular, often left Cuba illegally, sold to British, Dutch,
French, or Portuguese ships. One historian has determined that smuggling accounted for 75 percent of the island's tobacco production from
1726 to 1740.[133]

British traders were now becoming actively involved in illegal bullion
imports from South America. British merchants in Lisbon and Oporto
obtained Brazilian gold through Portuguese intermediaries resident in
ports such as Rio de Janeiro.[134] And ocean-going British merchants discovered Colônia do Sacramento, the old smugglers' den opposite Buenos Aires. British trade there accounted for about £500,000, at a time
when all British imports combined were worth £8 million.[135] Until a
blockade by Spanish forces in 1762, British ships frequented Colônia,
which was better suited to unloading goods and receiving large ships
than was Buenos Aires. But the British were also successful in smuggling operations there. In exchange for monetary gifts, luxury dinners,
and social gatherings in the local warehouses of the South Sea Company,
officials charged with inspecting incoming merchandise apparently regularly allowed British vessels to engage in contraband trade.[136]

Smuggling in the trade linking French and Spanish colonial subjects
also intensified in these years. The goods bought in New Orleans by
Spanish vessels from Florida, Havana, Campeche, and other Mexican
ports between 1742 and 1744 were estimated at 150,000 pesos. Spanish-
French business at Saint-Domingue was even more profitable: at the
port of Cap-Français alone, 400,000 pesos arrived in cash in the years

1727–1729 (Figure 4.1). The contrast with the amount of cash entering France from Spain was dramatic: in the years 1723–1729 six ships brought no more than a total of 21,000 pesos.[137]

By this time, the annual ships had begun to compete successfully with Jamaica's smugglers in the southwestern corner of the Caribbean. The island's president, council, and assembly complained in 1735 that the local slave trade had formerly been "the means of vending considerable quantitys of British manufactures, and introduceing six hundred pounds per annum, which or the greatest part was re-exported to our Mother Country."[138] However, with the outbreak of the War of Jenkins' Ear in 1739, the *asiento* ended and no more annual ships would sail. Jamaicans, Curaçaoans, and Dutch and British ocean-going ships were the beneficiaries, especially in the regions of Santa Marta and Ríohacha. In 1737, the value of foreign smuggling on the coast of New Granada was probably 550,000 pesos, over ten times that of the cargoes on the Spanish galleons (47,400 pesos). At least as much contraband passed through Ríohacha as through any other single region in the Spanish New World.[139] Because the value of legal trade through Ríohacha averaged less than 1,800 pesos a year, Ríohachan consumers needed contra-

Figure 4.1 View of Cap-Français ca. 1790, detail. From Moreau de St. Méry, *Recueil de vues des lieux principaux de la colonie française de Saint-Domingue* (Paris, 1791). Reproduced courtesy of the John Carter Brown Library at Brown University.

band supplies. The contraband seized in whitewashing operations in 1743–1765 produced 250 percent more Treasury revenue than did all import duties combined.[140]

Anglo-French smuggling also grew significantly between 1725 and 1750, as great demand in British North America for French colonial sugar and its by-products provided a solution for French sugar cultivators, who had failed to sell rum and molasses in the mother country. Despite the British Molasses Act (1733), which imposed a heavy tax on all foreign rum, molasses, and sugar imported into British America, and the official proscription of this commerce by French law, regular rum trade continued between the French islands and New England, as French sugar planters invariably undersold their British counterparts in the West Indies.[141] The volume of this trade was so high because virtually no trader complied with the Molasses Act, and there were no repercussions. Customs officers were usually helpful in allowing false entry. Rhode Island was the preferred place to land rum, but it appeared everywhere in New England and the Middle Colonies. The extent of official neglect was shown in Salem, Massachusetts, where merchants rose in rebellion when customs officers began to collect 10 percent of the tax in 1758.[142]

British commercial vessels and warships, as well as some Dutch ships, purchased much of the rum in exchange for enslaved Africans. In Guadeloupe, for example, no French slavers arrived from 1740 through 1744. Around 1750, planters in the southern province of Saint-Domingue, also abandoned by metropolitan France, bought perhaps as many as 3,000 slaves per year from their Jamaican neighbors. Saint-Domingue's payments for the slaves, provisions, and dry goods sent from Jamaica were largely made not in sugar but in indigo, which was then sent to Britain labeled as a British colonial product.[143] Santo Domingo, the Spanish colony that shared the island of Hispaniola with Saint-Domingue, also benefited from the rapid economic rise of its neighbor. Throughout the second half of the century, sales of livestock across the border would constitute the colony's main source of income.[144]

Much of the Franco-British trade, in particular exchanges involving ships from the thirteen colonies, took place at neutral Caribbean islands such as Saint Eustatius, Saint Thomas, Curaçao, the British Virgin Islands, and Saint Lucia. In the 1720s, British ships also sold slaves to the French at Saint Lucia, which was only a few hours' sail from Martinique.[145] Dutch Saint Eustatius was much farther away from Martinique—a return trip took eight days—but functioned as a frequent meeting place between British and French merchants.[146] The governor of Saint Christopher wrote: "The pretence of the Dutch buying of the English and then selling to the French is a mere fallacy. The produce of all St. Eustatius is not above 500 or 600 of our hogsheads of sugar a year. . . . The English and French vessels meet there and deal together as principals, or they have their agents . . . for the purpose. The Dutch have no concern but to receive the company's [customs] duties." While acknowledging that this did not constitute a breach of the Navigation Acts, he condemned the massive northern trade at Saint Eustatius for French rum and molasses, since royal duties were thus lost.[147] Others complained about the captains of British vessels that arrived at British islands with lumber who refused to be paid in rum and molasses. Instead, they insisted on payment in specie, which enabled them to buy cheaper rum and molasses at Saint Eustatius, where resident Englishmen distilled French rum.[148] Finally, transatlantic merchants also placed Bermuda at the intersection of the French and British empires, and that of the Dutch as well. Not only ships—an old tradition—but slaves, sugar, textiles, foodstuffs, and other products were sold there for re-export to their final destinations.[149]

1750–1775: The Start of Free Trade

Smuggling between British and French subjects continued unabated before 1775. In 1767, 21,000 barrels of molasses were shipped from Saint-Domingue to New England. With every barrel weighing a thousand pounds, the shipments totaled over 20 million pounds.[150] Such trade had not been halted during the Seven Years' War (1756–1763), which found the two nations on opposite sides. Even Stephen Hopkins, the governor of Rhode Island (and later a signatory of the Declaration of Independence), seems to have been involved in importing French sugar and as governor refused to allow enforcement of the laws against smuggling.[151] A Creole author from Saint-Domingue asserted a dozen years after the war that if the trade with the Dutch and British had not taken place, 10,000 people would have lacked bread during the war and only a third of the colony would still be inhabited. He added that the foreigners also helped prevent the colony's ruin in the wake of the 1770 earthquake that destroyed the capital city of Port-au-Prince.[152]

The war created new business opportunities. Greg, Cunningham & Co., the most important Irish trading house in New York, fitted out privateers against the French, but also "carried on an elaborate contraband trade to the French West Indies, supplying the French forces, in at least one instance, with weapons and ammunition." The Browns of Providence, Rhode Island, also pursued both tracks.[153] As in previous wars, many merchants resorted to the flag-of-truce trade, especially shipowners in Rhode Island and Philadelphia. In Saint-Domingue and Martinique, British ships sold enslaved Africans, cod, and provisions for indigo, molasses, rum, and European products, with the balance settled in cash.[154] Although not documented, the British slave trade at Saint-Domingue must have assumed enormous proportions during the Seven Years' War. In spite of the sharp decline in French Atlantic shipping and the disastrous mortality rate among the colony's black population, the slave population increased between 1756 and 1763, from 176,192 to 206,539. British ships also anchored off Guadeloupe (the island was briefly in British hands during the war), which was not a favorite destination of French metropolitan vessels or foreign slavers. By 1773, the island's Chamber of Agriculture estimated that 48 percent of the value of sugar and cotton was smuggled out. Because no cash was circulating on the island, payments for foreign contraband had to be made in kind.[155]

Planters in the French West Indies preferred dealing with merchants from British North America because of their reliability, the quality of their products, and above all their low prices.[156] Saint Eustatius continued to accommodate the Franco-British trade, especially in war years, although Parliament adopted the so-called Rule of 1756, asserting that neutral ships trading in French ports would be considered enemy vessels. This was no empty threat, as numerous ships from the United Provinces were taken by British privateers, even en route from Dutch metropolitan and colonial ports, resulting in a loss of at least 23 million guilders in cargoes and carriers during the Seven Years' War.[157] But other neutral ports sprang up elsewhere, and by 1760 every firm in New York traded with the enemy through such ports. The neutral ports, open to flags of all nations, thrived in seasons of war. The port of Montecristi in Santo Domingo, established by Spain in 1749 to stop French encroachments from nearby Saint-Domingue, emerged as such a port during the Seven Years' War. Most business in Montecristi was conducted by Spanish and (Protestant) French intermediaries. But Montecristi differed from other neutral ports in one important respect: whereas Saint Thomas and Saint Eustatius levied customs duties, however modest, Montecristi did not even have a customs officer.[158]

Reform was the watchword all over Europe in the 1750s and 1760s, as political authorities, faced with rapid population growth, serious food shortages (at least in southern Europe), and demands for military expenditure to keep up with powerful neighbors, realized that traditional solutions no longer worked. A new way to overcome these problems, popularized by Scottish "moral" philosophers and French physiocrats, was to put one's trust in the international economy. Free trade was deemed the best way to feed the hungry at home and to attract trade from foreign colonies to one's overseas possessions. After the end of the Seven Years' War in 1763, France therefore introduced free ports in places that had routinely engaged in smuggling operations, including Castries in Saint Lucia, Pointe-à-Pitre in Guadeloupe, and Môle Saint-Nicolas in Saint-Domingue. Foreign traders could now do business there undisturbed, although within certain limits. North American shipments of horses, light wood, and planks were allowed, but their flour, fabric, linen, and furniture were not. The French colonies were also granted permission to buy foreign provisions with rum and molasses. An exception was made for sugar, all of which had to be sent to France.

Britain in 1766 introduced the Free Ports Act, an attempt to establish some of its Caribbean ports as entrepôts for the Spanish and French colonies.[159] The decision to create a free port in Dominica, ceded to Britain by France at the peace in 1763, was inspired by the success of Dutch Curaçao and Saint Eustatius and reflected a compromise between West Indian and North American interests. In an attempt to protect their sugar-growing interests, West Indies planters had successfully lobbied for Britain to give up Guadeloupe, which British troops had conquered during the war. They had also supported the Sugar Act (1764), which lowered the duty on molasses, but they stressed the need to enforce that tax. The move to establish a free port in Dominica in 1766 met the wishes of the North American merchants, who were thus given more access to sugar and its by-products from the French islands. At the same time, four free ports were opened in Jamaica to invite foreigners—especially Spaniards—to bring in bullion and any other colonial products except sugar, coffee, pimento, ginger, molasses, and tobacco. More free ports were later established in the British colonies of Antigua, the Bahamas, and Grenada.[160] The new policy in the end was not very successful, because the free ports failed to offset the much stricter enforcement of the Navigation Acts after 1763.[161]

Smuggling remained ineradicable in the Spanish colonies—for example, in Puerto Rico, where legal trade was negligible (6.3 percent in 1759), and where the Danes of Saint Thomas and Saint Croix proved good customers for sugar.[162] To Venezuela, nearby Curaçao was an equally important partner, as evidenced by the many Dutch vessels captured by Spanish privateers in the years 1755–1780: more than three-quarters of all coastal seizures involved Dutch carriers. The annual value of this trade amounted to over 500,000 pesos in 1769–1770.[163]

The illegal flow of merchandise from Buenos Aires to Colônia may have reached its greatest extension between 1750 and 1775. The author of a manifesto addressed to the king of Spain asserted that Potosí silver was overwhelmingly transported to Buenos Aires, not Lima. He added that Spanish register ships brought 300,000 pesos' worth of silver from Buenos Aires to the mother country, a trifling share compared to that of the Portuguese who, by way of Colônia, annually secured silver worth 4 million pesos. The silver was purchased chiefly with British manufactures, shipped via Portugal to Brazil, and with gold mined in Minas Gerais.[164] Spanish forces captured Colônia in late 1761; it was restored to Portuguese rule two years later in the Treaty of Paris, but the Portuguese were expelled for good in 1777.

With the growth of the consumer market in the thirteen colonies, foreign smuggling into North America gained ground rapidly. The governor of New York exaggerated, however, when he argued in 1752 that examination might show that "Holland and Hamburgh receive more benefitt from the Trade to the Northern Colonies, than Great Britain does." Still, large amounts of Osnabrück linen, Dutch tea and paper, and Dutch and German gunpowder found their way to North American markets before, during, and after the Seven Years' War. The mercantilist fence proved especially porous in Rhode Island, Connecticut, and

New Jersey.[165] The main item smuggled in was tea, usually imported from the Dutch Republic via Saint Eustatius. Historian Carole Shammas assumes that 75 percent of all tea in British North America was introduced illegally. That would place the value of illicit tea at 18.5 percent of all imports into the colonies; combining tea with other smuggled goods, Shammas arrives at the figure of 25 percent for the share of contraband trade in overall trade.[166] In one widespread form of smuggling, New York merchants loaded manufactures in ports in the Dutch Republic before heading to British America; their papers, however, gave Saint Eustatius as the destination. Prior to crossing the Atlantic, they filled out their cargoes in the Orkney Islands or another part of Great Britain with goods that could be shipped legally to British colonies, with those commodities serving as a cloak for the illegal manufactures.[167]

Given the scope of illicit trade in British North America, the acts approved by Parliament following the Seven Years' War left deep scars. While leaving little room for profit for the merchants importing French molasses, the Revenue Act of 1764 (popularly called the Sugar Act) added logwood, boards, staves, hides, and other commodities to the list of enumerated goods. The imperial crackdown on smuggling thus made it hard for colonial merchants to earn enough credits to pay for British imports. Beyond mercantile practice, a way of life came under attack in the port cities, provoking riots and protests that eventually transformed into revolutionary fervor.[168]

Spain's King Charles III also tried to curb informal trade in his American possessions, especially British smuggling, the scale of which was one of the main reasons behind his decision to go to war with Britain in 1762.[169] After the end of hostilities, the Bourbon monarch also introduced free trade, but of a peculiar kind. In 1765, the Crown ended Cádiz's monopoly on navigation with Spanish America and announced the start of "free trade"—meaning that Cuba, Santo Domingo, Puerto Rico, Trinidad, and Margarita were allowed to carry on trade with nine different Spanish ports instead of only with Cádiz. Since some of the European products now exported from Spain to the Caribbean islands ended up clandestinely in Mexico, thereby undercutting the *flotistas,* the free trade project was extended to the smuggling centers of Louisiana (1768), Campeche, and the Yucatan (1770). In 1778, following the sailing of the last *flota,* all of Spanish America was included in the new system of colonial traffic that came to replace the fleet system, with the exception of New Spain and Venezuela, which were kept out until 1789.[170]

Spanish-American smuggling with foreigners did not abate, however. The voyage by a single ship from Cap-Français to the south coast of Cuba in 1768 produced a return cargo of no less than 100,000 pesos in cash. By that year, Cuba exported 7,000 horses to Saint-Domingue (and the same number to Jamaica).[171] The French Antilles were also on the receiving end of a thriving mule trade with Venezuela, which was sending 8,000 of the draft animals each year by the 1780s. According to a contemporary estimate, Saint-Domingue received 4 million pesos in cash every year from its contraband trade with the Spanish colonies, but that figure is almost certainly inflated.[172] British subjects, still usually based on Jamaica, were active in almost every Spanish colony in the Caribbean, despite attempts by British officials during and immediately after the Seven Years' War to halt intercolonial contraband trade.[173] In 1767, the important fair in Jalapa, Mexico, was disrupted in part because British merchants had saturated the market. In Spanish Louisiana, for example, Britain controlled virtually all imports and exports in the years 1770–1777. An officer in the Spanish forces who drew up a report on Louisiana estimated the colony's legal trade at 15,000 pesos annually against 585,000 pesos (97.5 percent) in illegitimate commerce.[174] Jamaican supplies to the Spanish Main included Silesian linen, taffeta, woolens, pewter plates, crystal vases, cups, coffee- and tea-pots, knives, razors, and millstones.[175] Jamaican demand could even set off a rise in production in contraband crops, as happened in Guatemala, where the interlopers bought indigo in bulk.[176] Estimates for the 1770s are hard to come by, but in 1750, overall Jamaican trade in Central American products was valued at £28,000–£43,000, which paled compared to the trade in precious metals, which amounted to £3.25 million in the years 1748–1765.[177]

1775–1800: The Transformation of Smuggling in an Age of Reform and Revolution

The War of American Independence (1775–1783) bred a new type of smuggling, as it encouraged state-sponsored French contraband trade to the rebel colonies. France loaned one million livres tournois (ca. 167,000 pesos) to a trading firm that purchased military supplies and sold them to the Americans. Both on the high seas and in sight of the North American mainland, British privateers seized 154 French ships worth 16.4 million livres (2.7 million pesos). Dutch entrepreneurs, engaging in a potentially very profitable business (in part to camouflage French supplies), also provided arms and ammunition to the rebels. Until 1781, Saint Eustatius was probably the single largest source of gunpowder for the North American revolutionaries. The scale of this business is suggested by a punitive expedition carried out by the British Navy in the summer of 1777, in which fifty-four ships were seized on the outward or return voyage between ports in the Netherlands and Saint Eustatius.[178]

Once the American Revolution was secured, the French government essentially admitted the dependence of the French islands on imports from the United States, legalizing imports carried on foreign ships of wood, livestock, salted beef, rice, corn, and vegetables.[179] But illicit commerce with the United States did not disappear, and according to a contemporary estimate, 11.5 percent of the sugar exported from Saint-Domingue in the mid-1780s was shipped to North America.[180] North American ships also actively smuggled sugar out of the booming Dutch colonies of Demerara and Essequibo (in present-day Guyana), depriving the Dutch West India Company of 200,000 guilders in 1778 alone.[181] Ships from Boston and other U.S. ports were also found trading in the southern cone of South America, usually on the pretext of whaling, and increasingly on the continent's western coast, gathering specie and merchandise for the China trade.[182] While interloping thus continued to flourish, smuggling along the eastern seaboard declined significantly; the Navigation Acts were no longer applied, reducing the incentive to conduct illicit trade.[183]

Saint-Domingue's close relationship with Jamaica continued during the American Revolution. According to one contemporary estimate, three-quarters of the colony's cotton and more than two-thirds of its indigo were absorbed by the Jamaicans, who often paid with enslaved Africans. Saint-Domingue's cacao also found its way to Jamaica, where soldiers drank it for breakfast in such amounts that it was believed to have reduced their mortality and morbidity.[184] The revolution that began on Saint-Domingue in 1791 proved lethal for this commerce, and France's richest colony rapidly declined as a center of illicit trade.

Slaves introduced from Jamaica no longer sold; in the early stages of the revolution slaves actually went in the opposite direction, as Saint-Domingue's merchants sold Africans to their British neighbors in exchange for much-needed provisions. Soon privateers would end the trade with Jamaica almost completely.[185]

Smuggling in Brazil, in contrast, continued as before in this period, which saw the involvement of British and Dutch merchants in the informal trade of Brazilian diamonds. In 1785, a Portuguese minister complained that many consignments of high-quality diamonds were appearing in Amsterdam's marketplace.[186] Brazil's connections with its Spanish neighbors remained strong, with the captaincy of Rio Grande do Sul now becoming the major transit route for African slaves recently arrived in Rio de Janeiro and sold to the Río de la Plata. The overall magnitude of contraband trade in Brazil is, however, hard to estimate. Illegal slave arrivals in Buenos Aires—whether on *porteño* ships that had bought Africans in Brazil or on Brazilian vessels that docked in Buenos Aires—clearly increased dramatically in the last decades of the eighteenth century. In addition, new opportunities for smuggling opened up when trade with neutral countries was authorized.[187]

Did commercial reform in the Spanish Empire bear fruit in the last quarter of the eighteenth century? At least at face value, free trade was very successful. From 1782 to 1796 the average value of American exports to Spain was ten times greater than in 1778. Still, smuggling went on everywhere from Florida to the southern cone of South America, and overall it may have been larger than legal commerce.[188] The extent of the contraband trade in Buenos Aires may not have resembled that of earlier periods, but Potosí silver was still funneled to Portugal. And in mainland Spanish America, French ships imported 615,900 pesos and goods worth 3,720,734 livres (ca. 620,000 pesos) in the year 1786 alone. For Spanish-American trade with the British colonies, we have detailed information regarding the years 1788–1796. The total value amounted to about £700,000 in 1792, increasing to almost £1.4 million by 1795. These years saw the culmination of a trend that had begun at midcentury. If British ships had once overwhelmingly dominated British-Spanish colonial trade, 95 percent of the value of Spanish products (livestock, specie, hides, dyewood) shipped to British colonies was now introduced by Spanish-American vessels. The free ports were the main beneficiaries. Grenada was the chief importer of these products (42.8 percent), followed by Jamaica (15.1 percent) and the Bahamas (12.5 percent).[189] Trade with the British islands was hampered somewhat by the onset of the Anglo-Spanish war in 1796. Yet the British blockade of Cádiz was so effective that very few Spanish ships managed to reach America, forcing Spanish metropolitan officials to allow neutral vessels to supply the Spanish-American ports. Although the measure was revoked in 1799, the damage had been done. Both during the remainder of the war and after the arrival of peace in 1801, neutrals, particularly the United States, dominated trade with Spain's colonies.[190]

Conclusion

By focusing on the Atlantic seaboard of the New World, I have tried to show in this essay the variety of inter-imperial transactions that the central authorities in the mother countries formally forbade in the colonial Americas. Here and there, contraband trade dwarfed legal exchange, belying the idea, to which some economic historians adhere, that its extent has been exaggerated.[191] In reality, smuggling came naturally to settlers seeking affordable products and easy outlets. Settlers in colonies of different empires created long-lasting economic—and cultural—ties that defied metropolitan designs. The scope of their illegal commercial contacts was truly astounding (see Table 4.1).

For the metropolitan administrators who promoted restrictive commercial legislation, economic motives were paramount in the colonization of America. Unable or unwilling to appreciate the artificiality of organizing trade within a mercantilist framework, those officials de-

Table 4.1 The Importance of Smuggling: Examples by Period and Item

Place	Period	Item(s)	Smuggled (%)
Buenos Aires	1595–1615	African slaves	80
Cuba	1726–1740	Tobacco	75
Puerto Rico	1756–1763	All	94
British North America	1760–1780	Tea	75
Louisiana	1770–1780	All	97
Saint-Domingue	1770–1790	Cotton	75

Source: Data cited in this essay.

manded that the riches of the New World be channeled to the imperial centers. Although colonial settlers and Creoles had routinely ignored the imperial blueprints generation after generation, mercantilism met its end only with the demise of colonialism in the Age of Revolutions. The leaders of the American independence movements North and South viewed the forced trade with the metropolis as tyrannical. George Washington, for one, condemned the Navigation Acts in 1774, calling for "an entire stop forever put to such a wicked, cruel, and unnatural trade."[192] Free trade also featured prominently among the desires of Creoles in Spanish America and Saint-Domingue, who saw the prohibition of commercial relations with foreign empires as yet another example of their countries' subordinate status.[193] As early as April 1776, Jacques Turgot wrote in a memorandum that France and Spain could learn from the tumult in Britain's North American colonies. They had to reconsider the traditional relationship between metropolis and colonies. "Wise and happy," he wrote, "would be the nation which . . . would consent to see its colonies as allied provinces, and not as subjects to the metropolis."[194] That, as it turned out, was a vain hope.

5

Procurators and the Making of the Jesuits' Atlantic Network

J. GABRIEL MARTÍNEZ-SERNA

Early in the history of the Society of Jesus (also commonly referred to as the Company of Jesus, or the Jesuits), Ignatius of Loyola's successors established the post of procurator to deal with the Company's temporal affairs: to represent the order's interests to the outside world, to administer its properties, and to establish and maintain what became a remarkably extended and efficient administrative network. In fulfilling these obligations, the procurators adapted the religious rules of the Society and the material needs of its ministries to the political and economic realities of the secular world.

Procurators were crucial figures in the explosive growth of the order from the late sixteenth century until the second half of the eighteenth century, as the Society rapidly extended its geographical, financial, educational, and missionary reach. Yet, despite the vast historiography on the Jesuit order, few historians have considered the institutional role played by the Society's procurators, usually examining them only in relation to the order's economic activities.[1] As a result, although the Society's organization is known generally for its efficiency and centralized command, our understanding of its specific workings is vague. Studying the procurators' institutional role can provide greater insight into the inner mechanics that made the Jesuits' Atlantic network run so well.

Also rare in the historiography of the Society are comparative studies of secular imperial networks and the Jesuit organization. The contrasts are revealing. The high command of the Society in Rome did not have to negotiate with local Jesuits in the way that colonial administrators had to negotiate with their agents and their constituencies on the peripheries of empire. Secular administrators could seldom impose their will by decree or force, whereas the Society's members were well known for their obedience to superiors. The Jesuits had a more streamlined chain of command, which was the envy of imperial and diocesan authorities; in many ways the order's network ran more efficiently than the imperial states within which it operated. This achievement was the result of the diligent work of Jesuit procurators at various levels of the organization.

Taking a comparative perspective, this essay attempts to provide a broader understanding of the role of procurators in building and maintaining the Jesuits' far-flung network. Procurators existed in other religious orders and also in the diocesan church, but procurators in the Society of Jesus differed from their counterparts in the great amount of time they devoted to economic matters and to building a network to circulate information, people, and goods. Furthermore, whereas procurators within other orders became weaker as European states became more centralized, Jesuit procurators became more important over time.[2]

Despite the early Jesuit presence in the Indian Ocean and the Far East and the order's achievements there, the Society was not as successful in transforming those host societies as it was the Americas. The Company's Atlantic provinces—which included those of Spain, Portugal, the Low Countries, France, and England and their New World empires—were in some ways the most important elements of the Jesuit network.[3] Together, the Atlantic provinces employed a significant part of the order's manpower and wealth and included some of its most lasting endeavors, notably the missions to the Indians of Paraguay, Brazil, and northern New Spain. These activities also played a crucial role in the development of the colonial (and later national) identities of the New World societies.[4]

Jesuit Organization: Provinces and Procurators

The basic unit of the Jesuit network was the province, headed by a father provincial who was chosen directly by the Society's father general in Rome. A provincial usually served for three years, though he could be reappointed at the discretion of the father general. A provincial had under his orders the rectors and superiors of his province's colleges, residences, and missions (also triennial appointments), as well as the administrators of the rural estates that funded much of the Jesuit system. Overseeing these institutions' properties and corporate interests were the provincial's assistants, the provincial procurators, who also reported to the Society's procurator general. Located in Rome, the procurator general was one of the most important members of the Jesuit curia and an advisor to the father general; he was also the order's main intermediary with the secular powers and with the Holy See.

Within the Jesuit curia in Rome, the provinces were grouped into five assistancies, which generally corresponded to the major European states and their imperial possessions (Figures 5.1, 5.1A, and 5.1B). Each was headed by a father assistant, who served as advisor to the father general and who was expected to be informed about the legal and cultural issues that might affect the Society's affairs in the provinces within his jurisdiction, and to advise the father general on the most prudent courses of action.[5]

The provincial procurators oversaw the management of the material possessions of the province through a sophisticated accounting and review process. College and mission procurators who had distinguished themselves for their business acumen and administrative gifts would often move up to the post of provincial procurator. In addition to his administrative tasks, a provincial procurator also represented the Society's corporate interests to the outside world, and he was responsible for building and maintaining the Society's sprawling network through regular communication with counterparts from other provinces and with the Jesuit curia in Rome.

That link was secured by separate procurators who periodically traveled from the provinces to Rome. These representatives, called *Procuradores a Roma*, constituted the Congregation of Procurators—a corporate body distinct from the Society's ruling General Congregation—which dealt with issues common to all provinces that did not require changes in the Society's rules. In modern corporate terms, the General Congregation set policy for the Society, whereas the Congregation of Procurators dealt with the implementation and operational aspects of the policies established by the General Congregations and the orders of the fathers general.[6] Often, but not always, delegates sent to

Figure 5.1 "Horoscopium Catholicum Societ. Iesu," in Athanasius Kircher, *Ars magna lvcis et vmbrae in decem libros digesta....* (Rome, 1646), 645aa. Assistancies are shown as branches of the tree, provinces as semicircles in the branches, and colleges, missions, and residences within each province as leaves. I thank Michele Molina for calling this image to my attention.

the Congregation of Procurators were the provincial procurators themselves.

The procurator general and the provincial procurator are the only two procuratorial offices specifically mentioned in the Society's *Constitutions,* but over the order's first two decades, more procuratorial posts were created as the size, needs, and complexity of the Society increased.[7] These specialized posts included court procurators and procurators representing several Jesuit provinces collectively to the Society's headquarters in Rome.

Court procurators represented the various interests of the Society at the royal court of a particular monarch. For example, the post of court procurator to the Spanish court in Madrid was created in 1570 to "arrange in the court the affairs that concerned principally the Spanish provinces of the Order"—to serve as the primary mediator between the court of Spain and the Society of Jesus. Although the court procurator in Madrid had under his purview only matters relating to the Jesuit provinces in the domains of the king of Spain, he was quite conscious that his job could affect the larger interests of the Society. The procurator of the Spanish provinces in Rome *(Procurador en Roma)* looked after the affairs of the Spanish and Spanish-American provinces before the Holy See.[8]

When Ignatius of Loyola and the early Jesuits established the province as the basic unit of their organization, they were inspired only in part by the experience of other religious corporations. The mendicant orders also had provinces as their main administrative units, but the Jesuit province was different in several respects. Its members dedicated a significant amount of time and resources to the economic management of the order's material possessions (as opposed, for example, to the Franciscans' total reliance on alms for their operations). Other departures from traditional mendicant provinces appeared in the Society's *Constitutions.* Loyola eliminated regular communal assemblies in favor of a ministry with greater emphasis on individual prayer and mobility among inhabitants of the non-Christian world. Furthermore, the selection of Jesuit provincials was left to the father general, instead of to a provincial congregation as was the case with the mendicants; and a Jesuit provincial in turn appointed provincial procurators, rectors, and superiors for colleges, residences, and missions within his province. The Soci-

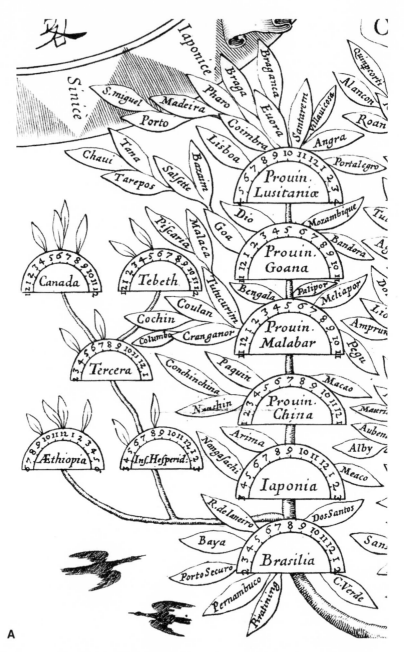

A

Figure 5.1A Detail from Kircher's "Horiscopium," showing a segment of the provinces of the Portuguese assistancy, including that in Brazil.

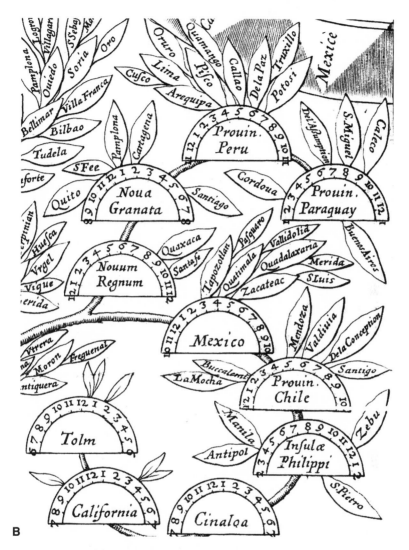

Figure 5.1B Detail from Kircher's "Horiscopium," showing the New World provinces of the Spanish assistancy.

ety's General Congregation (which met periodically, usually at the death of a father general) also had greater authority over its provinces, which had less power of self-determination than the provinces of the mendicant orders.[9]

The more centralized organization of the Jesuit provinces made for a more direct line of command. The Society's insistence on strict discipline and obedience to superiors had the practical effect of allowing directives from the father general in Rome to move rapidly and efficiently to the outer spokes of the network. Instructions from Rome were often more quickly and effectively implemented than were pronouncements by colonial administrators or imperial laws. Monarchical rhetoric notwithstanding, most empires were forced to negotiate continuously with their subjects in the New World to keep their colonial systems functioning, whereas the Company could circulate people, funds, goods, and ideas without contest or negotiation.[10] If Jesuit procurators had not built a system that compared so favorably with monarchical and diocesan networks, perhaps the Society would not have aroused such hostility among modernizing ministers in Portugal, Spain, and France, who eventually determined to humble or destroy a religious body that was rich, efficient, often immune from the state's fiscal and administrative reach, and responsive primarily to its own corporate interests.[11]

The Society's independence also aroused hostility from other ecclesiastics. Tension existed between the Society and the diocesan church throughout the Atlantic world, especially in dioceses on the peripheries. This was exacerbated when Jesuits assumed the role of administering the secular church, a fundamental canonical privilege of bishops—though they did so only for specific periods and under direct royal and papal orders. This was the case, for example, in the early colonization of Brazil and almost a century later in New France, when Jesuit superiors acted in place of bishops in a sort of frontier church. In these situations the efficiency of the Society's network allowed for easier communication with the metropolis than would have been the case with inchoate diocesan and colonial structures. Differences between bishops and the Society were only slightly less confrontational than those with secular ministers of state.

Special concordats negotiated between the Holy See and European rulers regulated the diocesan church's relationship with secular monarchies. Through these agreements, bishops came under special rules of engagement with those monarchies, and they were jealous of their hard-won concessions from Rome. Because of the canonical rights given to the order when it was created, however, such diocesan restrictions did not apply to the Society of Jesus.[12] Their independence from bishops became a double-edged sword for the Society. Many bishops, conscious of canonical prerogatives and potential tithes—from which the Company was also exempt—often sided with the secular state against the Jesuits. Feuds between bishops and the Jesuits were resolved on the part of the Society by its procurators, who acted in the name of their provincial.

The provincial procurators were the main administrators of a province's material possessions and the custodians of the Society's corporate interests, and they also had primary responsibility for setting up and maintaining communications with the Jesuit curia in Rome. Through the networks they established, procurators circulated people, funds, books, commodities, written reports, and manufactured goods across secular administrative units, both political and ecclesiastical. Through them, the order gradually created a remarkably fine-tuned network for satisfying the requirements of its educational and missionary efforts. The effectiveness and regularity of this network helped further the Society's interests and reputation, and made the Society one of the most dynamic religious corporations in the early modern world.

The Expanding Provincial Network

The Society of Jesus had been founded in the late 1530s and sanctioned by a papal bull in 1541; by 1553 it already had six provinces, with India being the only non-Atlantic province. Just three years later, the number of Jesuit provinces had grown to twelve: Italy (except Rome, whose residences and colleges were governed by the father general), Sicily, Lower Germany, Upper Germany, France, Aragon, Castile, Andalusia, Portugal, Brazil, India, and Ethiopia.[13] By the beginning of the seventeenth century, Spain had four provinces in its Iberian kingdoms (Castile, Aragon, Toledo, and Andalusia) in addition to two in its overseas empire (Peru and New Spain). In less than fifty years the Society had developed from a small organization of dedicated believers in Rome into an institution spanning the Atlantic and beyond. It soon had a global presence that spread throughout the Atlantic world as well as to India, China, Japan, Southeast Asia, and to the African and Arabian coasts of the Indian Ocean.[14]

The process of creating new provinces depended on internal Jesuit considerations as well as on the potential for the success of a ministry in any given region. By creating new provinces and appointing their re-spective procurators, the Society extended its administrative network exponentially in the first decades of its existence, especially in Italy and the Iberian kingdoms. Each new provincial procurator created a new spoke in the Company's organization, and as missions, colleges, and res-idences were established, procurators were appointed to each of them, thus extending the organizational structure that controlled the flow of goods, people, and written instructions and reports.

Portugal, the most precocious of the Jesuit assistancies, had one prov-ince in its European metropolis and the first province in the New World—Brazil, which was reached by Jesuits in 1549. A few years ear-lier the Company had tried to establish a mission in the Kingdom of Kongo at the invitation of its monarch, but the Jesuits were a fleeting presence because of the political turbulence in the region.[15] Although the Society would be somewhat more successful farther south in An-gola, where it established a college in Luanda, the two African missions were never as important as Brazil within the Portuguese assistancy's At-lantic network.[16] Portugal also had responsibility for the non-Atlantic provinces of Ethiopia, India, and Malabar, and nominally for the vice-province of China and the province of Japan. In longevity and cultural impact, however, Jesuit activities in the province of Brazil and its neigh-bor, the vice-province of Maranhão, had a greater influence on the his-tory of the host societies than the Jesuits in Portugal's African and Asian provinces had on theirs.

The Portuguese Jesuits also had a presence in the Atlantic islands of the Azores, Madeira, Cape Verde, and Saõ Tomé, and on the African mainland, which provided most of the slaves that worked in the Com-pany's estates in the New World.[17] Yet it was the Brazilian province that dominated this network. It served as the hub where the Com-pany received items from Asia, Africa, other American areas, and even the Azores before sending them on to Lisbon.[18] None of the Jesuit prov-inces in Spain's New World empire had a centrality in the Spanish assistancy comparable to that of Brazil in the Portuguese assistancy.

As the birthplace of Ignatius of Loyola and of many early Jesuits, in-cluding Loyola's two immediate successors as fathers general, Spain also took a leading role in expanding the reach of the Society and its net-work. In the late 1560s, the Spanish Jesuits sent off their first two transatlantic missions, under the direction of the province of Andalusia, to Peru and Florida. But problems arose when Phillip II voiced his intention to appoint a Mission Commissary to coordinate the order's missionary efforts in his overseas dominions, as he had for the mendicant orders. Differences also arose with aristocratic patrons such as the Dukes of Medina-Sidonia, because the Jesuits insisted on doing things "in our own way."[19] These problems delayed the organizational development of the Spanish Jesuits' overseas missions relative to those of the Portuguese assistancy, which had been helped in large part by the great fondness of the Portuguese king Sebastião for the disciples of Loyola.[20]

France was a relative latecomer to the Society, which was initially identified with Spain. Yet even though most of the first Jesuits were Spaniards, they had studied and taken their first vows in France, and the country was always central to the history of the Society. No sooner had the Company established a foothold in the dominions of the French Crown than it came into conflict with the Parlement, university, and archbishop of Paris. Eventually, France would have five Jesuit provinces, and over the centuries the country provided some of the most important Jesuit men of letters. Yet in comparison to those of the Iberian empires, France's overseas missions were small, particularly in terms of the monetary and human resources that the Iberian powers poured into their New World missions.[21] Administratively, the missions of the French Jesuits always depended directly on the Paris province, and they never established a full-fledged province in New France, Louisiana, or France's Caribbean possessions.[22] Yet the French Jesuits had many successes, and they were responsible for some of the most iconic chapters in European-Indian encounters in North America, famously recorded in the Company's publications describing its missionary endeavors, the *Jesuit Relations*.[23]

Another Atlantic province, the English, included, besides those in England proper, English Jesuits exiled in France, the Low Countries, and Iberia. At first organized as a mission, the English Jesuits became a vice-province in 1619 and a full-fledged province four years later. The English province was always peculiar, because it lived in almost continuous hostility with its nominal host government and because so large a number of English Jesuits lived and worked outside England. The English province also included the Maryland mission, where the economic base consisted of tobacco, livestock, and farm products—more like the output of other mid-Atlantic colonies than the products of typical Jesuit estates in New Spain and South America. The Maryland mission was threatened by Indians as well as by a hostile Crown and by neighboring Protestant settlers who more than once razed Jesuit properties in the colony. Indeed, the Jesuits of the Maryland mission often wrote in code in an effort to protect their activities. But like others conducting business in the British mainland colonies, the Jesuit procurators of Maryland had agents in London who managed their business affairs.[24]

The Belgian province included what is today the Netherlands and Belgium, and eventually split into the Flemish-Belgian and Franco-Belgian provinces. These two provinces were not metropolitan colonial centers in their own right, yet they contributed significantly to Jesuit missions in the New World by sending missionaries and goods.[25] The Flemish-Belgian province had under its jurisdiction the *mission hollandaise,* which ministered to Catholics in the Dutch homeland, and which also included perhaps the most modest transatlantic Jesuit missionary endeavor: an impoverished outpost in Curaçao.[26] This tiny mission was founded by the Bohemian Jesuit Father Michael Alexius Schnabel in the first decade of the eighteenth century, but it always lacked a firm economic base. It never possessed the rural estates (*haciendas,* plantations, tobacco manors) that funded its Iberian, French, and Maryland counterparts. Instead, the Jesuits in Curaçao encroached on the flock of a local Augustinian priest appointed by the bishop of Caracas. Father Agustín Caycedo, echoing the complaints against the Society by diocesan clergy in other areas, complained bitterly to the Caracas bishop: "The progress of our Holy Faith would be greater if the Jesuit fathers—who in their ambition and jealousy have unrightfully intruded in the mission— would not abuse our work. . . . They require fees from poor Catholics, and on Ash Wednesday set fixed prices: Blacks and mulattoes have to pay 2 reales for ash, whites 3 reales, and children 1½ real."[27] Like the Jesuits of England and Maryland, the Jesuits in Dutch Curaçao lived under constant threat of being expelled or imprisoned; Father Schnabel even had to disguise himself in layman's clothes when he went out in public. The Dutch West India Company, at first unaware of or indifferent to the presence of the Society in Curaçao, acted swiftly when some of the Dutch population and even garrison officials converted to Catholicism under Schnabel's direction. The West India Company's board of directors in Amsterdam ordered the removal of the Society from the island in 1720, though the Jesuit presence in Curaçao remained until 1742.[28]

Within the Atlantic empires, a Jesuit province was expected to be economically self-sufficient, and within the province each residence and college in theory had to be economically viable through endowments *(fundaciones),* which included rural estates, fixed-rate rents, or monetary gifts from aristocratic patrons. Sometimes a richer college or province could lend or even give money to a struggling part of the larger Jesuit enterprise. Royal funds were usually restricted to an American province's frontier missions or, in rare instances, to a particular college. Each provincial procurator had to gather the accounts of his provinces' properties regularly, collect any applicable subsidies from royal treasuries, and update the Jesuit curia in Rome about the financial state of his province.

The provincial procurators corresponded directly and regularly with the curia in Rome, keeping copies of their reports in the provincial archives and sending duplicates on different ships or overland on separate mules to increase the chances of delivery. They received in return a steady stream of orders from the father general, especially on issues of major importance. And they increased the reliability of this web of contacts by personally seeking out and hiring shipowners, mule drivers, and other merchants to fulfill their communication and transportation needs.[29]

Initially, Jesuit procurators were figures of secondary importance, but they became more important and powerful as the wealth and reach of the Society grew. Many of the scandals that plagued the Company involved procurators at one level or another, their Jesuit superiors and the larger corporation being shielded by the strict separation of functions and authority between procurators and provincials. These distinctions were sometimes lost on outsiders, who accused the Society of legalistic sophistry. Such arguments served to increase the Society's enemies, even among pious people, and helped spread pejorative terms like "Jesuitical" to describe excessively legalistic differences and responsibilities among members of the Society's leadership.

A notorious example of the manipulation of these internal categories to compartmentalize tasks and responsibilities and protect the Society was the Lavalette affair in France in the late 1750s.[30] Several large creditors in Marseille and Bordeaux sued to recover loans extended to Father Lavalette, the procurator of the French mission in Martinique, who for many years had been in charge of very profitable trading between the Caribbean and France. But after English corsairs seized ships containing his merchandise early in the Seven Years' War, those efforts ultimately resulted in the bankruptcy of the Society in France and the personal disgrace of Lavalette. Not satisfied with what they considered insufficient compensation from a debtor with a reputation for being the wealthiest religious corporation in Europe, Lavalette's creditors sued the entire Society in France. The procurator of the Paris province argued in court that the Martinique mission was solely responsible for the financial debacle; strictly speaking, the Paris province had never been involved with Lavalette, and creditors therefore could claim only the much less abundant assets of the Martinique Jesuits, not the possessions of the entire Society in France. Although this was a solid legal argument based on the order's structure, it enraged Lavalette's creditors. They then allied themselves with the Jansenists in the Parlement of Paris, who were sworn enemies of the Society, and accused the order of engaging in its infamous moral casuistry. Ultimately, the Lavalette defense backfired on the Company spectacularly; the scandal catalyzed opposition to the order and precipitated the Society's destruction in France in 1764.

The Jesuit Network: Contents

The best-known items circulating in the Society's network were written reports. The father general in Rome received annual reports from each provincial, who in turn expected regular reports from the superiors of each college, residence, and mission district within his province. Rome also received copies of specific legal documents relating to Jesuit properties in each province, which provided the procurator general in Rome with updated information on economic activities from each spoke of the system. In the other direction, instructions concerning general issues of importance to the entire Society, as well as those about specific matters involving a particular province or even a specific residence, college, or mission, flowed from Rome to the provinces. One of the tasks of the provincial procurators was to maintain the reliability of this communication flow.

Among the various types of reports sent by a provincial procurator to Rome were detailed catalogs of the province's personnel and material possessions; expense reports for his province, including individual accounts for each mission, residence, and college within the province; and various types of religious commentary, some of which had detailed ethnographic information that was passed on to Jesuits in other provinces or assistancies. The provincial procurators also edited the reports before sending them to Rome, and such reports sometimes made their way into print, usually in "relations" of the various missionary activities of the order. Copies sent to Rome were archived and available to the Jesuit curia. Using Jesuit-owned presses as well as commercial printers, the order published histories of its missionary efforts that were translated into many languages.[31]

Some of the published works written by Jesuits in one province were in part based on material from another province made available through the Society's network. The famous eighteenth-century French Jesuit historian Pierre-François-Xavier Charlevoix—who was considered by Enlightenment historians (not a group normally given to praising Jesuits) as having one of the best critical minds and the best grasp of historical method among his contemporaries—wrote an important history of the missions in New France, *Histoire et description générale de la Nouvelle France* (1744). But he also wrote the most widely read history of the Paraguayan reductions, using the Society's network to obtain pertinent documents, without ever setting foot outside the French dominions.[32]

Charlevoix's treatment of the nonsedentary Indians of New France and Paraguay fell within the categories that had been transmitted through the work of other Jesuits, including the natural historian José de Acosta. In his *Historia natural y moral de las Indias* (1590), Acosta had proposed a typology of Indian cultures based on whether or not they were sedentary societies. He placed the Aztecs and Incas in the higher category and the nomads of northern Mexico (generically called *chichimecas*) in the lower one.[33] This typology and the corresponding missionary strategies were used by the Society in its efforts among the nonsedentary Algonquians of New France, the Araucanians of the Chilean frontier, and the Guaraní and Tupí of Brazil and Paraguay. The reports, correspondence, and books written by Jesuits that circulated through the network were essential to the emergence of a distinct onto-logical category of "Indian" in the Jesuit imagination, as the works of Acosta and Charlevoix demonstrate.

A century earlier than Charlevoix, Athanasius Kircher, a Jesuit poly-math who resided at the papal court, used the same network to access reports from distant lands. He wrote about the history of the biblical lands of the Middle East and about myriad exotic topics, even though he never traveled outside Europe. Kircher, who is also credited with assem-bling the first museum, the *Musaeum Kircherianum,* in Rome, would not have been able to write on so many topics, collect so many rare items, or become so famous for his learning without the Society's net-work to support his eclectic, baroque scholarship.[34]

Books were widely delivered throughout the Company's organiza-tion. Often, crates of books constituted the main cargo in shipments from a procurator in Europe to his counterpart in the New World. The ability to circulate books proved to be one of the most important factors in making Jesuit colleges so highly regarded as educational institutions. Books written by Jesuits themselves made up a large part of these ship-ments; requests from American colleges often included books by fa-mous Jesuits like Acosta, Kircher, and the ethicist Baltasar Gracián. The provincial procurator of New Granada received a shipment of over 120 books for a single college in 1654.[35] The procurator of New Spain in 1673 received five crates of books, including volumes by Acosta, Gra-cián, and various devotional and statutory Jesuit works.[36]

The tiny Jesuit college in the oasis frontier town of Santa María de las Parras in northern New Spain had for many decades perhaps the most isolated library in North America; it had over two hundred books by the middle of the seventeenth century, a significant portion of which had been written or published by Jesuits.[37] By the time of the expul-sion of the Jesuits in 1767, the Parras college library had added hundreds of other volumes, including books in Portuguese, Italian, Latin, and Nahuatl, and works by authors such as Ovid, Cicero, Francisco de Quevedo, Francisco Suárez, Antonio Vieira, and Miguel de Cervantes.[38] Despite its remoteness, moreover, this lonely Jesuit outpost was known to readers throughout the Atlantic world. The Córdoba-born Pérez de Ribas had been mission superior on the northern frontier of New Spain in the 1620s, then provincial of New Spain in the 1630s, before becoming a Procurador a Roma in the early 1640s. While in Rome, he so impressed the father general with his knowledge and eloquence that the father general commissioned Pérez de Ribas to write the massive *Historia de los Triunfos de Nuestra Santa Fe* (1645), which contained an entire section dedicated to the pacification of the local Lagunero Indians.[39]

Far from the remote northern frontier, in New Spain's viceregal court, the Society was at the center of intellectual debates largely as a result of the circulation of books within its network. Carlos de Sigüenza y Góngora and Sor Juana Inés de la Cruz, two of the most important intellectuals of seventeenth-century New Spain, were avid readers of Kircher's books. Sor Juana, who considered herself a daughter of the Jesuits, even coined the term "Kircherize" to mean discussion of the famous Jesuit's work.[40] One can picture Sor Juana and Don Carlos discussing the latest Kircher book, which would have been sent to New Spain by a Jesuit procurator. Sigüenza (who had been expelled from the order but always remained close to it) had a famous dispute with the Tyrolese Jesuit Eusebio Kino on the nature of comets.[41] Chosen as a missionary to the northern frontier, Kino saw the comet of 1680 as he was waiting in Seville to embark on his trip to the New World; he continued to record observations throughout his transatlantic journey, explaining to his readers that he had studied with one of Kircher's protégés in Ingolstadt. Sigüenza challenged Kino's explanation of the meteorological phenomenon by claiming that his own reading of Kircher was more accurate.[42]

Sor Juana's most famous poem—"Primero Sueño"—is a departure from her religious poems and plays. It is a "metaphysical dream" involving a cosmic traveler who flies over pyramids and mythological landscapes—imagery clearly inspired by the work of Kircher, whose "curious books" she frequently cites in her letters.[43] But Sor Juana's access to Jesuit books in the end led her to grief. The Luso-Brazilian Antonio Vieira, one of the titans of Portuguese literature, had had his sermons translated into Spanish and published in Madrid in the second half of the seventeenth century. Those editions were available to Sor Juana, who commented unfavorably on one of Vieira's sermons in her "Carta Atenagórica." That criticism precipitated her censure by the Church and her subsequent depression, illness, and death.[44]

Such examples testify to the efficiency of the Jesuit network in circulating letters, reports, and books throughout the organization. Not only did these materials facilitate the general transatlantic movement of ideas and practices—from Europe to the remote Santa María de las Parras as well as to the viceregal court in Mexico City—but they also disseminated important ethnographic, scientific, and linguistic information among Jesuit missionaries in outposts around the world.

In addition to written reports and books, the Company's network also circulated people, money, religious paraphernalia, manufactured goods, and commodities. Some of these items were more often circulated within a province—for example, agricultural produce, animal hides, and even cotton goods from rural estates were sent to urban markets to raise cash for running a college or mission. Sometimes "vertical integration" allowed for a more secure and profitable intraprovincial network. The Jesuits of Tucumán, on the southern Spanish American frontier, shipped produce from rural estates to the markets of Buenos Aires, Asunción, and Salta, and they had a lucrative role in raising and selling the mules that transported much of the region's commerce.[45] The neighboring Jesuit province of Paraguay used *yerba mate* (also known as "Jesuit tea") as a cash crop. The popularity of *yerba mate* in the southern cone generated the profits that made possible the building of the so-called Jesuit Republic among the Guaraní.[46] In Maryland, the Company planted tobacco on its rural manors, which it then shipped across the Atlantic to representatives in London for sale.[47] The Jesuit estates of coastal Brazil cultivated sugar, while those of Mendoza, the coastal valleys of Peru, Santa María de las Parras, and southern Chile produced wine and brandy for barter and trade.[48] In 1584 the Jesuits from the Brazil province received permission from the government of Phillip II to ship brazilwood through Seville—a unique exception to commerce that was otherwise limited to Lisbon—possibly in a bid to gain the Jesuits' confidence after Phillip's assumption of the Portuguese throne in 1580.[49]

Other important commodities that circulated in the Company's network were drugs for Jesuit apothecaries. Most of the Society's colleges had an apothecary, usually a member of the order with one or two of the four vows a full Jesuit takes. Called brothers and spiritual adjuncts (as opposed to fathers and priests), Jesuit apothecaries depended on *materia medica* that procurators circulated through letters, manuscripts, a few published works, and word of mouth. The apothecaries of the St. Antão College in Lisbon (the main Jesuit institution in Portugal) learned of tropical remedies through contact with their Brazilian counterparts.[50] Huron, Pima, Guaraní, and Tupí medical knowledge, having crossed provincial and imperial boundaries, was readily available in Jesuit colleges throughout the Atlantic world.[51] Canadian ginseng was popularized by the Jesuits in New France, who learned of the root's properties from Jesuits in China, where ginseng was becoming scarce; the French Jesuits developed a trade in the American variety, eventually exporting it to China. Similarly, the Jesuits of the Quito province popularized *cinchona* as a fever remedy.[52]

One of the most common transactions within the Company's network was the transportation of manufactures. From European imperial hubs like Lisbon, Seville, Cádiz, Bordeaux, and La Rochelle, Jesuit procurators sent manufactured goods across the Atlantic for the American provinces—textiles for missionaries' clothes or church draperies, bronze crucifixes, religious medals, bells, wax for candles, printed devotional engravings, compasses, musical instruments, sand clocks, and even processed agricultural items like wine and oil not yet produced in the Americas. A request from the procurator of New Granada in 1654 included dozens of crates with many different types of textiles.[53] The products of the famous Brazilian sugar *fazendas* Sergipe do Conde and Santana were traded across the Brazil-Lisbon commercial axis.[54] Orders for goods sent by procurators of colleges, residences, or missions were carefully evaluated by their provincial counterpart before being forwarded to procurators in Europe.

Along with the requests for goods and commercial activities went payments, for another important part of the Company's network involved moving funds. The transmission of media of exchange was particularly important where no efficient financial institutions existed.[55] Most of the funds the Company circulated, usually in the form of bullion, were payments for specific items requested by procurators, but the Jesuits also transported money as favors to individuals or to other religious corporations. At other times, funds were sent for the payment of religious rituals such as masses for the soul of a wealthy patron or his family in a particular church in Europe, or for the canonization of individuals important to the Society, such as the Luso-Brazilian Jesuit Joseph de Anchietta, one of the pioneer missionaries of the Brazilian province.[56] Funds were also transferred for sustaining the Society's bureaucracy, although provinces were rarely ordered to send funds directly to Rome. Procurators did have to be on guard against royal schemes for tapping into Jesuit wealth concocted by ministers charged with increasing revenues and minimizing the drain of bullion from transatlantic trade and imperial economies.[57]

The funds in the Company's network also circulated as loans or gifts from one province to another, but only with explicit permission from Rome. Provincial procurators were independent when managing their own funds, but sometimes a province made an investment in the finances of another province that offered higher rates of return or a safer legal environment. The English province, though always cautious about moving funds into the territories of a hostile monarch, invested considerable resources in the Paris province. As a result, the English province became embroiled in the Lavalette affair, and its finances were devastated, a debacle from which it took decades to recover.[58]

The transportation of people was one of the most complicated tasks the Jesuit procurators faced; the process usually entailed sending members of the order to the New World—European missionaries or *visitadores,* personal envoys of the father general regularly sent to inspect and audit a province. But Jesuits also moved regularly in the other direction, particularly Procuradores a Roma traveling to Rome for a Congregation of Procurators.

When an American province asked for missionaries from Europe, usually manpower for a specific task within a mission rectorate, the request was channeled to Rome, where the Jesuit curia always weighed the political considerations attached. Mindful of the turmoil and political situation in Phillip IV's court after the Peace of Westphalia, for example, in 1655 the father general instructed the provincials of Spain to send only missionaries from their own provinces to the procurator of New Spain, Diego de Monroy, since it was at the time "forbidden to give them subjects that were not Spaniards."[59] Individual Jesuits sometimes applied repeatedly over several years to be sent to the frontier missions of the New World, but European provincials were often reluctant to grant those petitions; doing so required them to give up precious man-

power in which long, costly training had been invested, human resources who would otherwise remain in their own provinces.

Transporting missionaries was expensive as well as logistically complex. The province of New Spain in 1617 detailed the provisions requested for each Jesuit making the trip from Seville, enumerating at least
eighteen items, of which eleven were textiles of various types for daily
living or religious rituals, as well as shoes, hats, cases for the missionary's personal books, for a total cost per missionary of 10 ducats.[60] The
French Jesuits asked their procurator in Paris to send similar items for
their brethren in the Illinois missions, including over ten different types
of textiles.[61] For a trip from Lisbon to Madeira, each Portuguese Jesuit
was given 32 kilograms of ship's biscuit, six loaves of bread, dried and
fresh fish, a half-dozen chickens, 7.25 kilograms of sugar, and the same
amount of fruits and vegetables.[62] The procurators' web of contacts in
the ports of departure made waiting more comfortable and the trips and
their preparations faster and less expensive than would have been the
case if each missionary had been required to compare shipping prices,
find lodgings and meals, and gather the various permits for his overseas trip.

Atlantic Procurators: The Spanish Example

To extend and maintain their growing network, and because of the importance of the New World in the Jesuit missionary and educational enterprise, the Society of Jesus soon established special procurators with a
distinctly transatlantic view. Indeed, it was primarily the importance of
the American Indians in the Jesuit imagination that created the need for
special procurators to coordinate the Company's transatlantic efforts.
By 1561, the Lusitanian Jesuits had created the *Procurador do Portugal
e missões ultramarinas,* a post with a significant Atlantic component,
though technically the office also dealt with Portugal's missions in the
Far East and around the Indian Ocean. The Portuguese office served as a
model and precedent for similar specialized procuratorial posts in the
Spanish and French assistancies.[63] The equivalent post for the French Jesuits in North America and for their counterparts in the Caribbean missions was the *Procureur des missions de l'Amérique Septentrionale.*

For the Jesuits of the Spanish assistancy, evangelizing the Indians on the periphery of Spain's American empire became one of the order's most consuming endeavors, more important even than the similar efforts of the Portuguese. Moreover, the geography and size of Spain's colonial empire in the Americas dictated the need for a land network to complement maritime links in a way that was not the case for the Portuguese Procura do missões or their French counterparts. Spain's colonial empire, much more than that of France or Portugal, was an essentially Atlantic enterprise, and its *Procurador de Indias Occidentales* was perhaps the most distinctly transatlantic office of procurator in the entire Company.

In the late 1560s the Spanish Jesuits, following the example of their Portuguese brethren, undertook their first overseas missions. The Florida mission of 1566–1571, the order's first on the Spanish-American frontier, ended in disaster when most of its missionaries were killed in modern-day Virginia.[64] The Jesuit curia concluded that the debacle occurred in large part as a result of the absence of a mission procurator and the corresponding supply and support network. But the failure of the Florida missions also convinced the curia that a more detailed and specialized effort was needed, a dedicated structure to assist the Jesuits in the New World and to coordinate the efforts of the American procurators.

The result was the creation in 1574 of a Procurador de Indias Occidentales for the Spanish Jesuits. The office, loosely modeled on the Portuguese Procurador do Portugal e missões ultramarinas, was meant to expedite and better organize Jesuit connections between Spain and its New World colonies.[65] The number of Jesuit provinces in the Spanish New World grew from two in the 1580s (Peru and New Spain) to six by the middle of the seventeenth century, when the Philippines, New Granada, Paraguay, and Quito had been added.[66] The Procurator of the West Indies resided in Seville (by 1720 in Cádiz) with an assistant. In 1587 a branch of the office was established in Madrid to further expedite permits needed from the Spanish Crown.[67] The Spanish-American provinces were ordered to contribute yearly fees for the upkeep of the procurador and his staff, who had their own distinct quarters within Seville's Colegio de San Hermenegildo.

The incumbents of this procuratorial office became the Company's experts on Spain's byzantine imperial bureaucracies. They were knowledgeable about all the legal requirements needed to sail to the Americas, such as permits from the Consejo de Indias and the Casa de la Contratación. They also became experts in shipping prices, the schedule of *flotas,* and the cost of goods needed in the American provinces. Their responsibilities included the delivery of transatlantic correspondence and the organization and equipment of mission expeditions, as well as hosting foreign missionaries until they were ready for the transatlantic crossing, buying goods and keeping a stocked warehouse for provisioning the New World enterprises, selecting ships for the voyages, and acting as spiritual advisors to those about to make the arduous trip.[68] In addition, the procurator kept five different sets of accounts to document his responsibilities, including one chronologically listing all papal and royal bulls, acts, bills, laws, or other legal documents that involved the exemptions and privileges of the Society. These records were part of the post itself, and each retiring procurator was audited, either by his successor or by a *visitador,* at the end of the three-year tenure.

Before embarking for the New World, missionaries from other provinces stayed at the San Hermenegildo college at the considerable expense of the Andalusia province and Seville's college. This thorny matter was temporarily resolved by strictly recording the expenses that each missionary incurred and charging that amount to the office of the Procurator of the West Indies, who in turn covered the cost by using royal subventions for frontier missions and the funds charged to the American provinces for the upkeep of his office. Eventually the matter was settled by the creation of a special hospice for waiting missionaries, the Hospicio de Indias de Nuestra Señora de Guadalupe, founded at 1686 in Seville (it moved to Cádiz in 1720, along with the procuratorial office).[69] The hospice, like a Jesuit college or residence, had its own endowment, including rural estates in Andalusia, to cover expenses, though part of the costs continued to be paid by annual contributions from the American provinces.[70]

The case of New Spain illustrates the way in which the Jesuit provinces depended on the secular networks of their respective empires for the efficient functioning of the Society's operations. The procurators' schedule was built around the yearly *flotas* arriving at Veracruz from Spain. For months before the ships left Seville or Cádiz, the Procurador de Indias Occidentales was busy housing the missionaries traveling to the New World, buying necessities for the trip, fulfilling requests from American procurators, obtaining the necessary permits from the imperial bureaucracy, and collecting and editing reports coming from the Americas to Europe or out from Rome to Jesuits in the field. Once in Veracruz, the missionaries, correspondence, and goods were received by the provincial procurator there. The missionaries were housed and fed until they reached Mexico City, from where they traveled north to Tepozotlán, the forward operating base for the northern missions of the Society. Imported items were taken to the capital and placed in warehouses until the procurators could hire a mule driver to take them to their respective *colegio* or mission.

The Jesuit network was a tightly integrated, efficient system unmatched by those of rival religious orders, the diocesan church, or even royal officials, especially in dealing with goods or persons destined for the northern periphery. Considering the vast distances involved, and the hazards involved in sea and land travel at the time, the regularity, efficiency, and intricacy of the work done by the Procurator of the West Indies and the network of other procurators constitute a monumental achievement. A system that started haphazardly in the 1560s in response to the debacle of the Florida mission had grown into a formidable supply and support network for the transatlantic activities of the Spanish assistancy.

The specific protocols for the secular networks used by the Company in the French and Portuguese assistancies differed from those of the Spanish assistancy (most obviously, for example, neither France nor Portugal had the *flota* system). But in most respects the tasks of French and Portuguese procurators were similar to those of their Spanish counterparts. Differences in the secular setting for the various transatlantic enterprises of the Society were negotiated and integrated into an organization that functioned according to its own dynamics.

The Maturing of the Procuratorial System

By the middle of the seventeenth century, the post of Procurador de Indias Occidentales, like other procuratorial offices, was firmly established, though its work was still being refined; by the mid-eighteenth century the procurators' roles seemed to need little clarification. One can trace the process in the changes in the tone and content of the instructions given to the procurators in the Spanish assistancy. Brother Pedro Salinas, assistant to the Procurator of the West Indies, summarized the various tasks of the office and made four suggestions in a 1651 essay. The first was that a new *visitador* look at old annuities to see if they were still "good credit" and adjust the accounts accordingly; second, he should hire a helper specifically charged with collecting the various payments owed to the Company, leaving the procurator and his assistant free to do other things; third, the Procura should be split into three different offices, one for Peru and New Granada, another for Paraguay and Chile, and the third for New Spain and the Philippines, each with its own procurator and assistant; and fourth, these posts should be filled by Jesuits from the Indies, not by peninsular Spaniards, and each should be appointed in his own province by knowledgeable superiors.[71] Nothing suggests that these recommendations were ever implemented, but the document provides a clear indication that the organization of the Procura was not yet set in stone.

Seventeen years after Brother Salinas's essay, Father General Juan Pablo Oliva (1664–1681) found it necessary to write another lengthy instruction for the Procurator of the West Indies and his assistants. He spelled out twenty-two items, including the need to keep "a big book in which will be written the names of everyone going to the Indies with the day, month, and year and from which Province, lands, age, time in the company, studies, talents, noting also the day they left their college because from that day on his meals are paid for by the King. It will also be noted in said book the various laws and dispatches from the King and the [House of the] Contratación, specifying what is being provided for and how it was used as well as the amount given to each one for clothing and baggage, and how much was paid for dresses and clothes."[72]

The post of Procurador de Indias Occidentales was further defined over thirty years later, when another document recapitulated the orders and instructions of previous fathers general. In response to abuses in recent fleets, and to contain any further damages to the Society's reputation, a 1709 directive was written with detailed instructions, because of the "importance that the good administration and government of the affairs of the Indies in Seville and Madrid" held for the Company. In this document the Father General Miguel Angel Tamburini (1706–1730) spelled out twenty-one points to be followed. Worried about the potential damage to the Company's reputation that might ensue from the increasing volume of goods and crates transported by the *Procura,* the father general specifically asked for prudence from the various procurators:

> So that any type of negotiation or rumor are avoided that ours practice [illegal trade] founded on the many crates, business affairs, and dependencies that they see coming on the care of Our Procurators that come and go to the Indies, [and] renewing the orders and penalties imposed by our predecessors, . . . I hereby order . . . to every Procurator that comes from the Indies and their adjuncts, that come with them, that they do not take care of any business of any of ours, nor for any secular, nor the transport of gold, marked silver, or silver to be marked, nor any other type of merchandize. And if those errands have to be made because someone [in the province] [owes a favor] to someone of great authority or a great Benefactor of the company whose gratitude cannot be denied, so far as the good correspondence of said affairs, I hereby order that they not be accepted without the approval of the Provincial, so I order and take from him the power to give the approval by himself and that it should only be accepted in case that together with his ordinary advisors and *ad graviora* they resolve by majority of votes that such license should be given to admit such an errand and affair. And such cases they shall put in their list of businesses to do carried by the Procurator, which should be signed by the Provincial, his secretary, and the Province's Procurator; this list should come in triplicate with the appropriate signatures: two of them will be given when the Procurator arrives at Cádiz to the Superior of the Hospice and in case he is not there to the rector of the College so that he remits one of these to said Office, and keeps the other, in order to execute its orders.[73]

The specificity of this instruction, in contrast to the earlier, more comprehensive structural concerns, reflects the maturing of the Procura de Misiones. By the early eighteenth century, the general structure of the Spanish assistancy's transatlantic network had stabilized; it remained more or less constant until the expulsion of the Jesuits a few decades later.

Similarly conclusive in this respect are the instructions given to Jesuit procurators assigned to the Congregation of Procurators in Rome. The instructions for a Procurador a Roma from New Spain for the Congregation of 1663 spelled out what he must do on every leg of his journey from Mexico City to Rome. In Puebla, the procurator was to take care of, among other things, the proposed sale of some crumbling houses that were part of the endowment of one of the city's colleges. In Havana, the procurator was to collect several *réditos* (annuities from an investment) from the Company's properties there and send the amount through a *libranza* (bill of exchange) to the accounts of the provincial procurator in Mexico City. Once in Seville, he was to pay the annual fee that the province contributed for the upkeep of the Procura de Indias Occidentales, and also send some crates to specific people by order of the provincial or provincial procurator. The traveling procurator was also to check on some business in nearby Xérez de la Frontera, and when he arrived in Madrid, among other things he was to review the accounts of the province with the procurator in Madrid, and "follow the instructions of said father, presenting his official papers before him and following these affairs with the due diligence that we expect." Once in Rome the procurator was personally to inform the father general of the decisions of the recent Provincial Congregation. He was also to raise the issue regarding the privileges accorded to missionaries traveling through the province on the way to the northern frontier, and obtain the necessary papal dispensations in order to avoid problems with the frontier bishops. The procurator was also to see if the curia might close some of the missions in the Sierra of Topia and Tepehuanes to concentrate on other missions, "because these missions were more troublesome and had fewer Indians to subdue . . . and distract from the main and more glorious endeavors that this Province has."[74]

Eleven years later, in 1674, the procurator of New Spain, Juan de Monroy (brother of the previous procurator, Diego), wrote another directive for the procurators about to embark on their transatlantic trip. He specifically detailed the various jurisdictions of the Procurador de Indias Occidentales, court procurator, and Procurador a Roma, taking care to place the appropriate precedent for the court of Madrid before the papal court. In the instructions he stressed only two main goals for the traveling procurators: to plead for more European missionaries to convert Indians, and to bring to conclusion some pending litigation regarding tithes.[75]

In June 1681, the provincial of New Spain, Bernardo Pardo, wrote a pair of instructions for two procurators traveling to Rome. The first was devoted to bitter complaints about the bishop of Nueva Vizcaya, but two days later Father Pardo wrote another more general directive about the provincial affairs to be resolved at the courts of Madrid and Rome.[76] Thereafter, for the next several decades, no written instructions for either a Procurador a Roma from New Spain or for the Procurador de Indias Occidentales seem to exist, suggesting that the Atlantic network of the Spanish assistancy had achieved maturity by the first quarter of the eighteenth century. Hinting that this was the case are the last three surviving instructions for Procuradores a Roma from New Spain, which date from the first half of the eighteenth century. In 1726 the provincial wrote a one-page document with brief and general instructions for the procurators. He listed only four items, which read like bureaucratic platitudes and contrast notably with the detailed instructions of decades past. The document says that procurators should first get their permits from Madrid before moving on to Rome; that they should ask for a license in order to bring non-Spanish Jesuits into Seville; that they should register all money, commodities, and merchandise they bring from the New World with the appropriate bureaucracy; and last, that they should bring back medals and other devotional objects to be distributed throughout the province.[77] The last instructions for Procuradores a Roma in the archives of the province of New Spain—the instructions to the Congregations of 1734 and 1743—are also one-page documents, replacing the long and detailed instructions of the seventeenth century.[78] Rather than precise protocols and elaborate directives reminding the traveling procurators of their tasks, the later documents seem instead to be designed simply to pave the way with officials in ports of call. The absence of more detailed instructions for procurators is at odds with traditional patterns of documentation found in colonial archives, where normally more documents can be found for the eighteenth than for the seventeenth century. Thus by the mid-eighteenth century the procurators of the Spanish assistancy were following standard procedures, even as the volume of reports, goods, and people they moved across the Atlantic on behalf of the Society increased dramatically.

Conclusion

By the second half of the eighteenth century the Atlantic network of the Society of Jesus created and maintained by Jesuit procurators was a mature system that had been working efficiently for decades without major changes. It was nevertheless destroyed by a quick succession of devastating blows, culminating in the order's suppression in all Catholic countries by order of Pope Clement XIV in 1773. First, in 1759 the Marquis de Pombal struck at the Society in Portugal and its dominions in a single blow. Then, in 1764 in the wake of the Lavalette affair, the Duc de Choiseul maneuvered a reluctant Louis XV into issuing an edict, following the lead of the Parlement of Paris, dissolving the Society in France and its dominions. Finally, in 1767, Spain's Carlos III, following advice from the counts of Campomanes and Aranda, summarily expelled the Society from his kingdoms. The royal ministers of enlightened despots perhaps did not resent the expanding para-state in their midst so much as the independent network that circulated the necessities of the Jesuits' idiosyncratic and multifaceted enterprise more smoothly than those of the states themselves.

The Jesuits' growth and organizational power would have been impossible without the considerable work done by various procurators over two centuries of the Society's transatlantic activities. The network for which the procurators were in large part responsible facilitated the flow of ideas, scientific and medical information, and ethnographic views that influenced not only the Jesuits but the Atlantic world as a whole. Further study of these seldom-mentioned actors would provide a much better understanding of the internal dynamics of the Society of Jesus and its relation to the secular and imperial structures in which the Jesuit network was embedded.

6

Dissenting Religious Communication Networks and European Migration, 1660–1710

ROSALIND J. BEILER

On August 5, 1677, a large crowd gathered at Geertruyd Dirck's house in Amsterdam to hear prominent English and Scottish Quaker missionaries George Fox, William Penn, Robert Barclay, and George Keith debate with Dutch clergy. The audience included people from different parts of the Netherlands and was made up of "presbiterians, socinians, baptists, seekers, etc."[1] As the religious leaders engaged in a vigorous, five-hour discussion, Benjamin Furly and Jan Klaus translated their Latin exchanges into Dutch and then conveyed audience questions into English for the missionaries.[2] Through their extensive knowledge of languages and their translating skills, Furly and Klaus linked several far-flung communication networks that were both transnational and ecumenical. They participated in conversations among Quakers in England, Scotland, and Ireland; Mennonites, Quakers, and members of the Reformed Church in the Netherlands; and Lutheran and Reformed Pietists as well as Anabaptists throughout the German and Swiss territories.[3] Although their religious beliefs differed considerably, those who joined the discussions were connected by common interests in reforming society through individual piety, appeals for relief from religious persecution, and efforts to lend economic aid.

This essay explores the forces linking Mennonite, Quaker, and Pietist communities and the effectiveness of the communication networks that emerged in the second half of the seventeenth century.[4] A "communication network" as used here is a set of links providing regular communication through various media (oral communication, manuscript letters, printed and published texts). Networks include the individuals sending information, one or more agents facilitating the flow of information, and the persons receiving it. Mennonite, Quaker, and Pietist networks eventually became semi-institutional. Dutch Mennonites established the Commission for Foreign Needs to coordinate relief efforts; Quakers formed Meetings for Sufferings to manage lobbying activities on behalf of imprisoned members; and Lutheran Pietists at Halle created regular correspondence networks linked to the pedagogical institutions of the Franckesche Stiftung. Communication networks also include those individuals who were linked to these more formal systems but who had correspondents of their own and thus created intersections between the different religious networks.

This essay examines why the dissenter networks evolved, the kinds of people who participated in them, and the ways in which individuals with different interests capitalized on them to recruit immigrants for various colonization schemes. Religious persecution was critical in shaping the multiple conversations that cut across political and cultural boundaries. Dutch Mennonites sent financial assistance to Palatine Anabaptists to aid fellow believers exiled from Switzerland. Similarly, English Quakers raised money for and lobbied on behalf of imprisoned Friends in the German states along the Rhine. Each group developed regular transnational communication channels in their attempts to fight religious discrimination or to spread their ideas about reforming society.[5] Each also sought contact with people from other religious communities sympathetic to their cause. Consequently, men and women from a variety of dissenting groups and from a broad social spectrum participated in the networks. English and Scottish Quaker missionaries sought converts among Mennonites and Pietists living in the Netherlands and Germany and as far east as Poland and Bohemia.[6] Protestant merchants, the "middling sort," the nobility, members of royal courts, and European heads of state participated in these ecumenical conversations about religious toleration and social reformation, and they sought correspondence with other like-minded people.

The correspondence networks of religious dissenters provided the means for legitimizing dissenters' positions with state authorities. Mennonites, for example, subscribed to their own confessions of faith and developed institutional structures in the seventeenth century—processes of confessionalization occurring in official territorial churches—in order to defend against accusations of heresy and to argue that they were obedient citizens.[7] Quakers also organized in the face of intensifying persecution following the restoration of the Stuart monarchy. In the second half of the seventeenth century, Quakerism shifted from a radical reform movement to a religious sect with its own organizational structure and hierarchy to define membership and maintain discipline.[8] And while Pietists in Prussia became a part of the state-building efforts of the monarchy in the eighteenth century, radical and separatist Pietists (considered dissenters) also created confessional identities in the late seventeenth and early eighteenth centuries.[9] In each of these cases, regular channels of correspondence evolved in response to the group's minority status. They allowed dissenters to create confessional identities—processes similar to those occurring for continental Lutheran, Reformed, and Catholic churches—but outside the institutions of the state.

The religious communication networks of Protestant dissenters also became effective channels for information about migration and colonization. As Mennonites, Quakers, and Pietists recognized the possibilities that migration held for obtaining relief from discrimination, they capitalized on their connections to begin relocating people. European heads of state were interested in colonization for economic and geopolitical reasons. Looking for settlers to rebuild regions devastated by seventeenth-century wars, Protestant political leaders offered immigration incentives to dissenters forced out of Catholic and other Protestant lands. The English, Dutch, and Prussians welcomed Huguenot immigrants following the revocation of the Edict of Nantes in 1685.[10] Similarly, Dutch Mennonite leaders negotiated with heads of state in the Netherlands, Denmark, Prussia, and Hesse to resettle exiled Swiss Mennonites.[11] In addition, those who joined these discussions perceived the potential of overseas colonization for achieving their own goals and, thus, extended their connections across the Atlantic. British colonial proprietors and governors solicited religious dissenters from Britain and Europe in their efforts to people the American colonies. As people with a variety of interests—not all of them religious—funneled information through the networks, these channels became a dynamic force for

Religious Dissenters' Networks, 1670-1730

North Sea

Baltic Sea

Danzig▾

■Emden

FRIESLAND▾

Lübeck○

■Hamburg

Altona■

Elbe River

PRUSSIA

BRANDENBURG

Amsterdam■○

▾Utrecht

Rotterdam▾■

▾Herford

○ Berlin

POLAND

Nijmegen▾

○ Krefeld

NETHERLANDS

Brussels■

Cologne▾

Rhine River

○ Halle

HESSE

Frankfurt▾

Main River

Alzey■▾

Kriegsheim▾

Worms■

Heidelberg○

Mannheim■▾

Nuremberg●

BOHEMIA

PALATINATE

LORRAINE

Neckar River

Strasburg▾

Stuttgart●

Danube River

BADEN

WÜRTTEMBERG

Augsburg●

ALSACE

BAVARIA

Montbéliard●

Basel■

■ Zurich

■ Bern

TYROL

Geneva▾●

SWISS CONFEDERATION

Adriatic Sea

Legend

■ Mennonite Community

○ Pietist Community

▾ Quaker Missionary Visit

● City

Map 6.1 Religious dissenters' networks in Europe, 1670–1730. Map by Lindsey McNellis.

migrations within Europe that also extended to the British American colonies.

This study provides the broader European context for Atlantic migrations by examining how Mennonite, Quaker, and Pietist connections disseminated information about continental as well as American destinations to potential immigrants, and it reveals why the number of immigrants from German-speaking areas rose significantly in the eighteenth century while the number from England declined.[12] By the end of the seventeenth century the transnational and ecumenical communication networks created by Mennonites, Quakers, and Pietists to deal with religious persecution and to spread their messages took on new roles as channels of information for a variety of colonial schemes in both Europe and America.

Mennonite Networks: Their Evolution and Structure

Mennonites provide the starting point for assessing why these networks evolved and how they were structured. By the mid-seventeenth century, Dutch Mennonites, Swiss Brethren, and Anabaptists living in the Palatinate and Alsace all traced their origins to the radical Reformation. In the early 1520s, several Swiss university students broke away from Zurich's Protestant reformers over several theological issues, one of which was baptism. The Swiss Brethren, as they called themselves, replaced infant baptism with adult or believers' baptism; consequently, they became known as Anabaptists (rebaptizers).[13] They also stressed individual piety, refused to swear oaths, and shunned military service, all of which political authorities viewed as insubordination. In addition, the Swiss Brethren's insistence on membership in their own congregations rather than in established churches challenged religious orthodoxy. By the late seventeenth century, Anabaptists throughout Europe were called "Mennonites" (after Menno Simons, a sixteenth-century leader who worked to unite north German Anabaptist congregations), "Anabaptists," or "Baptists" interchangeably.[14]

The Anabaptist movement spread rapidly throughout Europe. Persecuted by Catholics and Protestants alike, the dissenters moved frequently from one place to another, seeking refuge in Moravia, the Palatinate, Strasburg, and the Netherlands. Harassment and toleration continued in cycles into the eighteenth century, depending on the religious affiliation of ruling governments throughout the region. In Switzerland, the government stopped executing Anabaptists in the 1570s but continued until the early eighteenth century to imprison them for life, banish them, or sell them as galley slaves.[15] In the Netherlands persecution ended in 1579 following independence from Spain, and Dutch Mennonites participated actively in the commercial life of the country throughout the seventeenth century. They became involved in shipbuilding, in the lumber, food, and textile industries, and in overseas trade. Within a century, Dutch Mennonites obtained a high degree of education and wealth. University-educated ministers led churches with the aid of lay leaders (elders and deacons) who were well-established physicians and merchants.[16]

Dutch Mennonites, Anabaptists in southern and central Germany, and the Swiss Brethren began corresponding regularly in the late 1630s, when Swiss officials passed measures banishing Anabaptists from Zurich. In response, Dutch Mennonites started lobbying the city's officials and sent money and supplies up the Rhine River to aid in resettling the exiles in the Palatinate and Alsace among small Anabaptist communities there.[17] Twenty years later Mennonites in Amsterdam and Krefeld assisted refugees from Jülich-Berg when the government systematically banished them.[18] In 1670, new measures sent another wave of Swiss Brethren into the Rhine Valley. The following year, Jacob Everling, an Anabaptist minister from Obersülzen in the Palatinate, sent a letter to the Mennonite congregation in Amsterdam describing the poor condition of the refugees. He reported that two hundred people had already arrived and, while they were making lodging arrangements for those, an additional sixty arrived, "among whom were many old people, also young children and people who were crippled or lame, traveling with a bundle on the back and children on the arms."[19] Once again, Dutch Mennonites collected money, food, clothing, and tools to distribute to the refugees. By January 1672, 640 Swiss Brethren had settled in communities on the east and west banks of the Rhine, where Anabaptist congregations were helping them establish new homes. The exiles had brought little property or money with them, and therefore posed a heavy financial burden on their Palatine benefactors. According to one report from Kriegsheim in the Palatinate, the refugees' assets totaled only 1,654 Reichstaler and a few household goods. Consequently, they relied heavily on the financial assistance of the Dutch Mennonites.[20]

The networks that evolved in response to persecution were headed by a handful of leaders who lobbied governments and solicited information, goods, and money. In the Netherlands, Hans Vlamingh, a wealthy merchant from Amsterdam and a deacon in "the Sun" congregation, began early efforts to assist Swiss exiles.[21] Throughout the 1660s he corresponded with a series of Swiss officials, businessmen, and intellectuals to urge toleration on behalf of fellow believers in Zurich and Bern. He also recruited other leading Protestants to argue that even though they, as Reformed theologians, disagreed with Mennonite beliefs, it was wrong to coerce people to change their religious views.[22] In addition, he kept careful accounts of the money collected and expended while lobbying on behalf of Swiss and other Mennonite refugees.[23]

While Vlamingh lobbied intellectuals and religious leaders, other church and lay leaders from congregations in Amsterdam solicited money on behalf of religious refugees. On January 20, 1672, two congregations in Amsterdam collected all kinds of coins as well as a gold chain, a gold ring with a diamond, and several silver medals. Those charged with keeping the accounts noted that they had already remitted more than 700 Reichstaler to assist the Swiss Brethren. They also requested contributions from other congregations nearby.[24] By 1689, when Palatine Mennonites sent news of the French plundering their homes, Amsterdam lay leaders had expanded their efforts. In 1690 they solicited money from congregations in more than thirty locations scattered throughout Holland, Zeeland, and Friesland.[25]

A committee with representatives from churches throughout the Netherlands met periodically in Amsterdam to determine who needed assistance and to carry news home to their congregations.[26] Coordinating information and keeping careful accounts of the money collected and expended, the group sent men traveling up the Rhine to deliver money and to assess the needs of the refugees. Committee members gave careful instructions about whom to contact, the kinds of information to gather, and how to distribute funds. One group sent to the Palatinate in 1672 went with merchants traveling to the Frankfurt Fair and used their connections to draw bills of exchange on merchants there.[27] After their arrival, the traveling committee members drafted detailed accounts of how they spent the contributions. They noted, for example, that they delivered one mattress and pillow, sheets, cloth for men's clothing, money to have clothes made, women's shoes and socks, and household equipment to Peter Fredrick, aged 66, and his wife, the same age, at Eychtersheim. Commissioners also noted with care the age and occupations of the refugees and of those who were considering moving to the Netherlands.[28]

While Dutch urban areas functioned as collection points, several cities and towns along the Rhine became important distribution and communication centers. In the Palatinate, congregations in Kriegsheim and Mannheim provided shelter for refugees fleeing Switzerland. In 1671, Jacob Everling reported to Amsterdam that families in Obersülzen had housed sixty of the exiles, many of whom were very old or very young. Fifty others had gone to Mannheim. The following year a church council met at Kriegsheim to determine how to assist the influx of recent arrivals.[29] Valentin Huetwohl, a minister in Kriegsheim, and Georg Liechti, the leader of the Swiss refugees, spent four days traveling from village to village constructing a census of the seventy-six Swiss families scattered among the Palatine Mennonites. Farther down the Rhine, Mennonites in Krefeld also contributed money and supplies to aid the cause and passed on information about refugees in the Palatinate to Dutch Mennonites.[30]

In each place, those who joined the efforts to help religious refugees had been earlier targets of religious discrimination. Mennonites living in the Palatinate and along the Rhine enjoyed limited toleration, but their situation always remained precarious. Karl Ludwig, Elector Palatine (1649–1680), granted Mennonites, Hutterites, Sabbatarians, Huguenots, and Jews the right to worship privately as part of his recruitment effort to rebuild following the Thirty Years' War.[31] Nevertheless, local and religious authorities frequently disregarded official policy. In 1660, Mennonites in Kriegsheim complained to Karl Ludwig that their neighbors kept them from purchasing property because of their religious identity.[32] In 1680 they sought his aid again because of misunderstandings about their worship services. The local inspector maintained that only twenty people could attend meetings for worship, whereas they understood that their congregations could include all members of twenty families.[33] Farther down the Rhine, Mennonites in Gladbach had moved to Krefeld in search of religious toleration in 1654.[34] Forty years later, when officials imprisoned thirty men, women, and children from the Mennonite congregation in the neighboring town of Rheydt, some of those former refugees collected 8,000 Reichstaler in bail money to purchase the prisoners' release.[35] For European Mennonites, responses to religious discrimination created shared identities that crossed political, cultural, and linguistic boundaries from the Netherlands to Switzerland.

Religious persecution, therefore, was a key factor in the emergence of Mennonite communication networks beginning in the 1630s. Although Dutch, German, and Swiss Mennonite clergy had exchanged letters before in their attempts to find common religious ground, they began corresponding regularly in response to the physical and material needs resulting from intolerance. Church leaders in different cities collected information about fellow believers who were imprisoned, threatened with death, or exiled for their religious views. They also solicited aid from congregants in the Netherlands and northern Germany and funneled money and household goods to those in need. Several key cities in the Netherlands, along the Rhine, and in Switzerland functioned as collection and distribution centers, while committees traveled between communities with Mennonite congregations. They worked with well-connected government officials to alleviate persecution and to negotiate terms of exile and resettlement. For European Mennonites, participation in these mutual aid networks and migration between congregations solidified the sense of belonging to a larger transnational religious community.

Quaker Networks: Their Evolution and Structure

Like the Mennonites, early Quakers developed regular channels of communication in their efforts to aid those being imprisoned and persecuted because of their religious beliefs. Originating in northwest England in the wake of the English Civil War, the Quaker movement sought to reform the world by preaching a message that urged individuals to seek the "light within."[36] Members believed that the light of God, directed at individual consciences, would expose people's sinful natures and convince them of their complete dependence on God.[37] Quakers first referred to themselves as "children of the light" and called one another "friends" as early as 1652. They considered themselves to be members of the gathered Christian church rather than a separate sect. George Fox, an early Quaker leader, traveled throughout northern England in the early 1650s spreading his message. His missionary zeal also character-ized other early converts, who felt an overwhelming need to "publish the truth." Friends traveled in pairs of men or women, speaking to any-one who would listen. They rapidly fanned out from northwest England to all parts of the country.[38] Within a few years, Quakerism spread into Ireland, Scotland, Europe, the West Indies, and the American mainland colonies. By 1660, the total number of Friends had reached approxi-mately forty thousand.[39]

The early Quakers' style of "speaking the truth" threatened estab-lished churches and the social order. Friends claimed to receive messages directly from God, spoke openly against the hypocrisy and failures of the clergy, and refused to demonstrate accepted forms of deference (by using the informal "thee" and "thou" and failing to remove their hats to their social superiors). Because of their refusal to swear oaths, attend es-tablished churches, and pay tithes, Quakers were persecuted by secular and religious officials alike. They were hanged, whipped, imprisoned, fined, exiled, and often had their property seized or destroyed.[40] In the social and political upheaval that characterized England in the 1650s, the persecution of Quakers was uneven and depended on local cir-cumstances. However, the restoration of Charles II in 1660 and the es-tablishment of the Church of England marked the beginning of a pe-riod of systematic persecution that lasted twenty years. The Clarendon codes, a series of acts passed by an Anglican-dominated Parliament and aimed at curtailing the rights of all non-Anglicans, established the legal basis for religious persecution aimed at all dissenting groups. They dis-placed clergy who would not use the Book of Common Prayer weekly, excluded non-Anglicans from city councils, and prohibited meetings for worship outside the Church of England. As a result, 8,600 Quakers were imprisoned during the first five years of Charles II's reign.[41]

Quaker correspondence networks evolved rapidly in response to both persecution and missionary efforts. Traveling ministers began exchang-ing letters to report their movements and their success. In the earliest years, Swarthmore Hall, the Lancashire home of Margaret Fell—one of Fox's earliest converts and later his wife—functioned as a communication center as Friends sent constant news to Fell.[42] Between June 1652 and December 1660, more than 563 personal letters from 148 different writers arrived at Fell's home.[43] Correspondents exhorted one another, reported on the progress of their missionary efforts, passed on news of fellow Quakers in other places, and described their "sufferings." William Ames, for example, wrote to Fell from Utrecht in 1656 about his trip to Holland. He reported on the meetings he had held en route with Baptists at Harwich when his ship was forced to wait out bad weather. He also described how, some time after his arrival in Amsterdam, he was called before the magistrates, who apparently had nothing to "alledge against us, only we would not put off our hats." Ames claimed that "the Lord made me as a brasen wall against them. They were a light company of men, but in the power of the Lord, their folly, in wisdom and moderation, was witnessed against, through which they were confounded." The magistrates, after several interrogations and Ames's refusal to leave the city, imprisoned the traveling minister and his companion. Several days later, after repeated questioning failed to convince the Friends to leave, officials escorted them out of the city and threatened severe punishment if they returned. From there Ames went to Rotterdam, where he "had two pretty meetings, and Friends were reached, and those who had run out and lost themselves in measure, were brought to see their loss and the cause of it, it being shewn them."[44] Reports like Ames's allowed Quaker leaders to stay in regular contact as they traveled to spread their message. They also helped to foster a cohesive group identity among the fledgling Quaker communities.[45]

A second center of communication, in addition to Swarthmore Hall, developed by 1675 after Quakers formed the London Meeting for Sufferings. By this time the Quakers had already established a system of weekly and monthly meetings for worship and for business that grew out of their response to persecution. What began as meetings of ministers to organize missionary efforts became regularized, as Friends responded to the physical needs of families whose members were in prison and worked to obtain freedom for those who were incarcerated.[46] The London Meeting for Sufferings was organized specifically to combat the legal codes that enforced persecution. It consisted of twelve London Friends who met weekly and established regular correspondence between the local meetings and London. The Meeting for Sufferings requested local monthly meetings to send representatives to London regularly and to submit reports of "sufferings" or persecution and discrimination in their communities. By spring 1677, they had compiled and submitted to Parliament a "Book of Sufferings" with evidence of persecution.[47] Through the London Meeting for Sufferings, Quakers lobbied the English courts and Parliament on behalf of the thousands of Friends who were imprisoned during the 1670s and 1680s.[48]

In addition to fighting against legal discrimination in the courts, Quakers also petitioned heads of state to establish official policies of toleration. William Penn, an English gentleman of means with a legal education and strong connections to the Stuart court, had become a Quaker by 1667. In events characteristic of Quaker ministers' experiences, Penn was arrested in Ireland in 1667, incarcerated in the Tower of London for blasphemy in 1668 and 1669, arrested again for preaching in 1670, and imprisoned in Newgate in 1671.[49] Penn's first appeals were on his own behalf, but he soon began to use his social and political connections to call for policies of toleration. In 1670, he published *A Great Case of Liberty of Conscience,* in which he made a political and philosophical argument for toleration. He and other Friends repeatedly petitioned the king and his ministry to change their religious policies.[50]

In Europe, English and Dutch Quakers also lobbied for religious toleration on behalf of recent converts suffering from persecution. In Kriegsheim, Friends were fined and imprisoned as early as 1658 for refusing to perform military service or pay war taxes. Two years later, after protesting an increase in the fees required to secure relief from military duty, seven men in the very small Quaker community were arrested.[51] Several English Quaker women who preached publicly also created problems for the community of Friends there when they visited Kriegsheim in 1678, for Palatine women did not preach in public or play a leadership role in their churches. Peter Hendricks, a Quaker button maker in Amsterdam, came to the defense of the Palatine Quaker congregation by engaging in a lively exchange of pamphlets with the Reformed pastor from a neighboring village.[52] English Friends also repeatedly petitioned the Elector Palatine to uphold his policies of religious toleration and to protect the fledgling congregation from local clergy, magistrates, and other citizens. In addition, they used their friendship with the Elector's sister Elizabeth, the granddaughter of James I, to try to influence his position.[53]

Farther down the Rhine, Quakers in Krefeld experienced similar episodes of discrimination beginning in 1679. Hendricks, in Amsterdam, reported to English Friends that "Concerning ye Crevelt friends, they have been banished and sent away twice with a threatning from ye deputie of Crevelt the last time if they come in againe, they should be whipt and burnt on theire backs, sweareing by his soules salvation he should do it." In spite of threats, however, they had returned and "have been theire again peacably a prettie while, about 6 or 7 weekes." One man "was beaten greiveously of late, by 2 of his neighbors, when he was passing by them."[54] As they had done for the Kriegsheim Quakers, English and Dutch leaders wrote petitions to government officials on behalf of the Krefeld Friends. Furly, Hendricks, and Arent Sonnemans wrote from Holland to local officials, while Penn wrote to the Prince of Orange requesting toleration for fellow European Friends.[55]

Thus, in the process of responding to religious persecution, Quakers, like the Mennonites, established the means for exchanging information. They created regular channels of communication and mobilized resources for influencing governments to change their policies. Two correspondence centers or hubs—Swarthmore Hall and London—emerged by the end of the seventeenth century. In Europe, Quakers in Amsterdam linked English Friends to fledgling meetings on the Continent. To facilitate the exchange of information and to coordinate lobbying efforts, Quakers created a system of regular meetings that reported persecution and the needs of members. Like those of the Mennonites, the webs of relationships they built reached across political, cultural, and linguistic boundaries; they helped to shape transnational identities based on common religious experience.

Network Participants: Missionary Work and Ecumenical Intersections

Even as they provided a way of sharing information and aid, the religious networks of the Friends functioned as avenues for their missionary efforts. As Quakers spread their message, they sought people who they believed were receptive to their interpretation of Christianity. Above all, they wanted to meet with others who shared their emphasis on a personal, unmediated relationship with God and a desire for pious living. Quakers' attempts to reach out to anyone who was willing to consider their message or who was open to similar religious practice expanded their communication channels not only across political and cultural divides, but also across confessional, social, and gender boundaries. By the end of the seventeenth century, participants in these religious networks were men and women from different social classes who came from a wide variety of religious backgrounds.

Quaker missionaries sought to convert people from religious backgrounds with whom they shared common ground. In England, Scotland, and Ireland, they sent traveling ministers to convert Anglicans, Presbyterians, Baptists, and a variety of sectarians.[56] Foremost among the groups that Quakers targeted in Europe were Mennonites. They recognized similarities in practice and belief in the Mennonite refusal to swear oaths and in their emphasis on personal religious experience, and they hoped to convert them to Quakerism. Missionary work in the Netherlands began as early as 1655, when "the word of ye lord came to John Stubbs . . . to go to Holland, & was shortly after revealed to William Caton . . . to go along with him."[57] Between then and 1661, Caton and William Ames worked feverishly to convert Mennonites in Amsterdam, Rotterdam, Flushing, Middleburg, and Utrecht.[58] In 1658 Ames traveled even farther to Friesland, Hamburg, the Palatinate, Bohemia, Brandenburg, Danzig, and Poland. The same year and again in 1661, he went as far up the Rhine as Kriegsheim, where he made converts among the Mennonite congregation before meeting with the Elector Palatine in Heidelberg. As a result of their missionary efforts, by the mid-1660s traveling Friends established meetings with Mennonite converts in Amsterdam, Emden, Hamburg, Danzig, Friedrichstadt, and Kriegsheim.[59]

Quakers also worked to convert Labadists, followers of Jean Labadie who lived in Middleburg from 1666 until 1669, when discrimination forced them to move.[60] Like Friends, Labadists stressed the importance of regeneration through the Holy Spirit and practicing godly living. Princess Elizabeth of the Palatinate had become acquainted with two of Labadie's followers while she was living in the Netherlands. When they were banished, she invited them to Herford, where she took them under her protection. In 1671, Penn, Furly, and Thomas Rudyard traveled there to visit the Labadists.[61] In 1676 Furly traveled a second time on a missionary trip to Herford.[62] The following year, when he went with Penn and George Keith on a month-long tour of western Germany and eastern Holland, the missionaries visited their friends at Herford twice.[63] Although their missionary efforts failed to produce converts, the Friends began a correspondence with Anna Maria von Schurmann and the Dutch countess Anna Maria van Hoorn, two of the Labadists, which continued throughout the 1670s. They also exchanged letters regularly with Princess Elizabeth.[64]

The princess and the Labadists at Herford connected the Quakers to another set of correspondents to whom they soon sent missionaries. These aristocratic women participated in a larger network of European intellectuals seeking to reform society through individual piety and devotion. One of their correspondents was Philip Jacob Spener, an early German Pietist leader who was in Frankfurt in the 1670s.[65] Spener and his friend Johann Jakob Schütz began weekly meetings in their homes to read and discuss devotional literature. The focus of their *collegium* (devotional group) was to promote personal piety. The Frankfurt Pietists were deeply influenced by Labadie's ideas of a philadelphian community in which members demonstrated an experience of rebirth and lived in close fellowship with one another. Schütz, in particular, corresponded with von Schurmann. By the late 1670s, these philadelphian ideas led to a split between Spener and Schütz, and the latter formed a group that became known as the Saalhof Pietists.[66] On their 1677 missionary journey, Penn, Keith, and Furly met with the Frankfurt Pietists. Penn reported that "they rec'd us with gladness of heart, & embraced our Testimony with a broken & reverent spirit; thanking god for our Coming amongst them, & praying that he would prosper this work in our hands."[67] Among this group were Johanna Eleonora von Merlau, Juliane Baur van Eysseneck, Johann Wilhelm Petersen, and Jacob Vanderwalle, a merchant with whom the missionaries lodged. They corresponded with others throughout Europe who were seeking further religious reform.[68]

In each case, Quakers linked intersecting correspondence networks and began conversations with people interested in reforming the Protestant church and society through religious practice. Those who joined

their networks came from a wide array of Protestant religious perspectives. Spener, for example, worked to bring about religious reform
within the established Lutheran church, but he corresponded with religious seekers who lived throughout Europe and held religious views
that differed significantly from his own.[69] Schütz exchanged letters with
Reformed and Lutheran Pietists throughout Germany; intellectuals such
as Christian Knorr von Rosenroth and Franziscus Mercurius van Helmont, who explored the more mystical elements of the Cabala; and sep-
aratists like von Schurmann, von Merlau, and Petersen, who had become leaders among the German philadelphians by the first decade of
the eighteenth century.[70] Penn, Furly, Barclay, and other leading Quakers joined these conversations, which focused on personal piety and
attempts to unify the Protestant church through spiritual practice.[71]
Through their missionary work, Quakers fashioned a kaleidoscope of
ecumenical connections with men and women from a variety of social
backgrounds. They visited and corresponded with one another in their
attempts to find common ground. In the process, they tapped into other
networks that provided them with current information on the status of
others working to reform the Christian church.

The Uses of Networks: Quakers and Pietists

The communication networks and lobbying mechanisms the Quakers
established in the interests of spreading the gospel and achieving religious toleration gained a new purpose when Friends became involved
in American colonization projects. In 1674, in an effort to solve a London merchant's credit problems, a group of Quaker investors purchased
shares of West Jersey on the Delaware River, where they decided to promote a Quaker colony. William Penn, one of the investors, was intimately involved in these colonizing efforts between 1676 and 1681.
During those same years, he was traveling in Europe on his missionary
journey and petitioning various heads of state there and in Britain for
religious toleration.[72] He clearly was thinking about colonization projects and Quaker settlements when he wrote to the Elector Palatine on
August 24, 1677, that, had he been able to visit him, Penn would have
conversed with him about "what encouragmt a Colony of virtuous and
industrious familys might hope to receive from thee, in case they should

transplant themselves into this country."[73] Three years later Penn submitted a proposal to the English Privy Council for a colony on the west side of the Delaware River and on March 4, 1681, he received a charter for Pennsylvania. Historians have debated the extent to which Penn intended his colony to be a religious haven for persecuted Quakers or an economic enterprise.[74] Penn likely saw no contradiction between religious and commercial purposes; he wrote that the colony was meant for "the service of God first, the honor and advantage of the king, with our own profit."[75]

Regardless of which purpose dominated Pennsylvania's founding, Penn clearly capitalized on his Quaker connections and the economic resources they offered to find settlers for his province. His original plan for the colony relied on investors whom he solicited largely from among Britain's wealthy Quaker merchants. To promote his enterprise and recruit immigrants, he depended on well-placed Friends with their own commercial networks to act as agents. In London, James Claypoole, a Quaker merchant with interests in the West Indies and the Baltic, sought investors for the proprietor. In Scotland Penn relied on Barclay, his missionary companion and a leading minister among Friends with powerful political connections, to aid his endeavors. And in Rotterdam, Furly acted as an agent, recruiting European investors in the land, translating promotional pamphlets, and arranging transportation for immigrants to the colony.[76]

Furly's activities as Penn's agent illustrate the way the Quaker colonizer relied on the ecumenical and transnational European networks in which he participated. They also demonstrate Furly's role as an information broker. His first task as Penn's agent was to translate and distribute promotional literature in the Netherlands, the German states, and France. At least fifty-eight broadsides, books, and pamphlets were published in English, Dutch, German, and French to promote Pennsylvania.[77] When Penn wrote the pamphlet *Some account of the Province of Pennsilvania in America; Lately Granted under the Great Seal of England to William Penn, &c,* Furly translated it into Dutch and German and had it printed in Rotterdam and Amsterdam. To strengthen the appeal of the pamphlet for his continental audience, he appended Penn's 1674 letter to the mayor and council of Emden, in which Penn had lobbied against the persecution of Quakers there. By adding Penn's letter, Furly signaled the founder's concern with religious toleration—a concern Penn did not address explicitly in his pamphlet.[78] Furly also added a glossary to the German edition to define some of the terms he left untranslated, thereby mediating English legal culture for potential German-speaking immigrants.[79] He then distributed the literature to Quaker and Mennonite communities along the Rhine, in northern Germany, and in the Netherlands, some of which he had visited on his earlier missionary journeys.[80]

Furly also recruited investors in Penn's American land; between 1681 and 1700, he sold almost 50,000 acres in Pennsylvania.[81] Among the first European purchasers were thirteen families from Krefeld, mostly Quakers.[82] Furly sold them land as individuals but promised to have it surveyed in adjoining lots so that they could establish their own settlement within the colony.[83] He also sent private letters to the Saalhof Pietists he had visited in Frankfurt just four years earlier, encouraging them to migrate to Pennsylvania.[84] As a result of his efforts, the Frankfurt Company purchased 15,000 acres of Penn's land from Furly. The company's investors included Van de Walle, Petersen, von Merlau, and Schütz, all Pietists whom Furly had met in 1677.[85] In late spring 1683, Francis Daniel Pastorius, acting as the agent for the company, set out for Pennsylvania. On his way, he stopped at Kriegsheim, where he visited with Furly's friends among the Quakers and Mennonites there, and in Krefeld, where he met the investors to whom Furly had sold Pennsylvania land. These early European contacts proved useful after Pastorius arrived in the colony. When it became clear that the other Frankfurt investors were not joining him, Pastorius worked with the immigrants Furly had recruited from Krefeld and later arrivals from Kriegsheim to establish Germantown, Pennsylvania.[86]

Furly continued to act as a broker of information for potential immigrants by passing news about the colony to his European correspondents. Having gained firsthand experience in the voyage and settlement process, Pastorius wrote letters and reports to Furly, who then funneled them, along with manuscript and print copies of Penn's promotional literature, to his own contacts.[87] One of Furly's correspondents was Jaspar Balthasar Könneken, a Pietist bookseller in Lübeck who had hoped to migrate to the colony but decided against it because of his age. Könneken and his close associate, Balthasar Jawert (also an investor in the Frankfurt Company), in turn disseminated the manuscripts through their own communication channels.[88] In this way, Furly spread personalized, eyewitness accounts of the new colony to an audience with their own interests and connections scattered throughout Europe.

Another set of immigrants Furly recruited through his religious networks were linked to Johann Jakob Zimmerman. Zimmerman was a Lutheran Pietist minister from Württemberg who was dismissed from his position for his millennial views. In Germany, he organized a "Chapter of Perfection," a group of intellectuals, mostly Lutheran Pietists, who believed that the establishment of the Kingdom of God was imminent. After his expulsion from Württemberg in 1685, Zimmerman lived for a brief period with Schütz, by that time an investor in the Frankfurt Company and Furly's correspondent.[89] In 1693 Zimmerman gathered a small group of forty immigrants in Rotterdam en route to Pennsylvania, but he died before they set sail. Nevertheless, Furly assisted the remainder of the immigrants on their journey to the colony under their new leader, Johannes Kelpius.[90] Their settlement in Pennsylvania, located close to Germantown, became known as "the Society of the Woman in the Wilderness" because of their particular religious views. The group mixed mysticism, scientific experimentation, and monasticism in their attempts to live their lives in preparation for Christ's return. By the time Kelpius died in 1708, most of the group had disbanded or joined other churches, but several members maintained connections to their European correspondents.[91]

In 1699, Daniel Falckner and Heinrich Bernard Köster, two members of Zimmerman's group who had left the "Society," returned to Europe to collect money for a new church, recruit immigrants, and solicit a pastor for the Lutherans in Pennsylvania.[92] While there, Falckner visited August Hermann Francke, the renowned Lutheran Pietist who had recently established the orphanage and educational foundations at Halle that would become the center of eighteenth-century German Pietism. The two men had corresponded before Falckner left for Pennsylvania.[93] Among the topics Falckner and Francke discussed was the potential for establishing an American Pietist colony. Francke, committed to expanding the reach of Lutheran Pietism, was interested, and posed a series of 103 practical questions about the people and conditions for colonization in Pennsylvania, which Falckner answered exhaustively in *Curieuse*

Nachricht von Pensylvania . . . (1702).[94] Although neither man succeeded in founding a Pietist colony in Penn's province, Falckner's pamphlet helped to spread practical information about the British colonies
in Europe at a time (1709–1710) when thousands of German-speaking
immigrants left their homes in search of better conditions. Many of
those immigrants moved to New York and a few eventually made it to
Pennsylvania.[95]

All of Falckner's activities—the return trip to Europe to recruit immigrants and the comprehensive and detailed *Curieuse Nachricht*—reflect
the importance of Penn's transnational religious networks, through which
he and Furly funneled literature, letters, and people. Others used the
network to pursue their own goals—whether to secure religious toleration, land for their families, investment opportunities, or the chance to
create utopian communities.

The Uses of Networks: Mennonites

Like the Quakers and Pietists, Mennonites also capitalized on their correspondence connections when they became involved in colonizing
schemes. Their participation in the practical aspects of migration, however, was directly linked to issues of religious toleration, at least initially.
As they helped to resettle Swiss refugees, Dutch and Palatine Mennonites sought returns for their own individual purposes as well as those
they were assisting. In contrast to Penn, who used dissenting religious
networks as an individual colonizer to recruit immigrants for his province, those representing Swiss refugees became involved in colonization
as they sought the best resettlement opportunities for the exiles.

Mennonites did not initially seek to settle refugees in new colonies
but began by lobbying appropriate authorities on behalf of fellow believers suffering from persecution.[96] At times they directed their petitions for tolerance to local and regional officials, as was the case in 1660,
when Rotterdam Mennonites convinced city officials to write to the city
of Bern on behalf of Swiss Anabaptists who had been banished.[97] In
other cases, they appealed to heads of state, as the Kreigsheim Mennonite church leaders had done in 1680 when they petitioned the Elector
Palatine to clarify his policy about meetings for worship.[98] They also
recruited other Protestant rulers and members of the nobility sympa-

thetic to their cause to apply pressure on appropriate political leaders. In 1694 Krefeld Mennonites solicited the help of the English king and the Dutch States General in their efforts to free imprisoned congregants from Rheydt, a village that belonged to the Elector Palatine. By this time, the electorate had passed to the Catholic Neuberg branch of the family. Both the Protestant king and the States General sent letters to the Catholic Elector Johann Wilhelm pressuring him to change his policies concerning the Protestant dissenters.[99]

The lobbying efforts of Dutch Mennonites became even more critical in 1709 and 1710, when Swiss officials in Bern organized another concerted effort to banish all remaining Anabaptists. By that time, Dutch Mennonites had formalized their mutual aid activities. They had created the Commission for Foreign Need, a committee of representatives from the various branches of the Mennonite church scattered throughout the Netherlands, to make decisions and solicit funds and household goods on behalf of religious refugees. Because they recognized the need to act quickly, the commission established an executive committee of five or six ministers and deacons in Amsterdam and Rotterdam who could meet on short notice.[100] Commission members corresponded regularly with other congregational leaders throughout the Netherlands, northern Germany, and the Rhine Valley.[101]

Negotiations for religious toleration and migration schemes were linked explicitly in 1710. In January, Johan Ludwig Runckel, the representative of the Dutch States General in Switzerland, sent news that Bern's officials had intensified their attempts to imprison and banish all of the Mennonites there, and he indicated his willingness to assist the commission's lobbying efforts.[102] Bern's government, hoping to send the exiles so far from home that they could not easily return, had contracted with George Ritter, a Bernese merchant, to transport them to England, from where they were to be sent to the American colonies. Proceeds from their confiscated estates were to pay for transportation costs.[103] When commission members received news of the Swiss plans, they petitioned the Dutch States General, asking it to intercede with the Bern government on behalf of the refugees.[104] On March 15, 1710, the States General petitioned Bern officials to free the imprisoned Mennonites. They maintained that the Dutch government, like the Swiss, believed the "Reformed religion is the best and the true religion," and that they wished "the Mennonites here with us as well as there with you could be brought over to the same religion." They thought, however, that there was "no other means to do this than to convince them with conversation and witness and that the method of force is no longer permissible or appropriate to be used in matters of conscience," but rather that each individual was accountable to God for his or her beliefs. The Dutch also argued that in "a land pretending to be a republic . . . each person has a right to exercise his own free will and belief" rather than being controlled by an established religion.[105]

The Dutch petition arrived too late to help the first set of Swiss refugees, who left Bern in mid-March 1710.[106] By the end of the month a ship carrying fifty-six prisoners arrived in Mannheim, where twenty-eight were permitted to disembark because of illness and age.[107] Government officials who organized the trip, however, made a critical mistake: they failed to secure the appropriate passport for the refugees to travel through Holland en route to England. When the Swiss representative in The Hague requested a passport, the States General decided to send a message of disapproval to Bern and refused to grant it.[108] On April 6, when the ship with the remaining exiles arrived at Nijmegen on the border of the Netherlands, Mennonite leaders there negotiated with the prisoners' guards to release them. Consequently, the Swiss scheme to transport the refugees to the American colonies failed. Some of the prisoners made their way to Rotterdam and Amsterdam; others went to the Palatinate in search of family and friends who had migrated earlier or had disembarked in Mannheim.[109]

Meanwhile, the commission used its influence with the Dutch government and Runckel's connections in Switzerland to improve the lot of those Mennonites still being imprisoned and persecuted in Bern. Hendrik Toren and Jan van Gent, two commission members from Rotterdam, repeatedly communicated with the clerk of the States General, who, in turn, negotiated with the Swiss representative in The Hague. Throughout the spring and summer of 1710, they also lobbied Queen Anne of England and her secretary through the English ambassador at The Hague. By July, the Prussian king had joined the English and Dutch in urging the government of Bern to stop persecuting the Mennonites there.[110] Outside pressure, however, seemed only to increase the resolve of the Swiss; in response, officials in Bern published a broadside threatening to behead any Mennonite exiles who chose to return to their homes and to whip publicly anyone granting lodging to the fugitives.[111]

In spite of intensified persecution, the lobbying of the Dutch Mennonites began to produce other results. Friederich I, king of Prussia, invited the Swiss refugees to his lands, where he promised them religious toleration in exchange for their assistance in his project to drain marshes.[112] The king of Denmark and the count of Hesse also offered to let them settle on their lands.[113] And the queen of England considered several petitions for colonizing schemes to send some of the refugees to Virginia or North Carolina with other "poor Palatine" immigrants who had arrived in London the previous year.[114] In November 1710, the Commission for Foreign Need proposed its own plan to resettle the Swiss exiles in several communities in the Netherlands.[115]

By early 1711, Runckel, the Dutch ambassador in Switzerland, succeeded in obtaining an agreement from the Bern government to free Mennonites who had been imprisoned and grant them amnesty until they could organize their migration from the city. He also negotiated permission for them to take along any money they received from the sale of property.[116] Runckel then used his channels to distribute circular letters from the commission to the Swiss Mennonites (written in Swiss dialect), persuading them to migrate rather than hold out for an end to persecution in Bern.[117] To carry out the proposed migration, Runckel and the commission secured five ships to transport 500–600 refugees down the Rhine to Amsterdam. They hired Ritter to direct the migration because he was familiar with the route. In addition, they assigned assistant directors for each ship to deal with customs houses, tolls, passport presentation, and the procurement of food. Runckel also worked to obtain the necessary passports from the city of Bern, the French and Prussian kings, the imperial court in Austria, and the heads of state in Württemberg, the Palatinate, Mainz, Trier, Hesse, Cologne, and Cleve.[118] By July, he reported that he had received the last of the passports and that the exiles were scheduled to leave on July 13.[119]

The success in rounding up exiles and arranging for their amnesty and the sale of their estates was a significant accomplishment. In addition to the complex negotiations with the Bern government to free those in prison and to allow the remainder to leave, the organizers faced the reluctance of the Swiss refugees to move from their homes. The group continued to hope for an end to persecution so that they would not need to uproot themselves. Internal conflicts and disputes over biblical interpretation also threatened the migration project. Some refugees refused to travel on the same ships with those who disagreed with their views. In the end, only 346 people of the estimated 500–600 made the trip down the Rhine in late July.[120]

Even as they left their homes, the Swiss refugees continued to consider their resettlement options. They were not altogether happy with the conditions the Prussian king offered. Some expressed concerns about an outbreak of the plague; others suspected the king wanted only the wealthy exiles to settle on his lands. Eventually, they decided against moving there. The majority of the refugees accepted the commission's proposal and went to the Netherlands, where they settled in colonies in Harlingen, Groningen, Kampen, and Deventer. The commission members, who had funded most of their transportation expenses through collections from Dutch and German congregations, agreed to assume the full costs of relocating the Swiss refugees. They promised to help them establish households and to supply provisions for the coming winter. In the Netherlands, of course, the exiles were granted religious toleration.[121]

The colonizing schemes of the Mennonites who were trying to relocate Swiss religious refugees demonstrate, like those of the Quakers, the ways in which participants capitalized on religious communication networks for funneling information about migration. In this case, however, it was those representing the immigrants seeking the best settlement opportunity rather than a colonizer seeking potential immigrants. They negotiated with political leaders and the refugees until they found the option for resettlement that best served the needs of the parties involved. The key information brokers were Runckel, a political diplomat, and commission members with access to politicians at The Hague. Whereas Furly had represented primarily the interests of Pennsylvania's Quaker proprietor, Runckel and the commissioners worked on behalf of the immigrants. In both cases, the same connections that had been used for religious purposes became conduits for logistical information about moving people from one place to another.

The colonizing schemes of the Mennonites who were relocating the Swiss religious refugees also demonstrate, like those of the Quakers, the ways in which other individuals intersected with the religious networks and capitalized on them for their own interests. Toren and van Gent, the two commission members who regularly lobbied Swiss, English, and Prussian officials at The Hague, had previous experience with English officials that no doubt aided their cause.[122] Toren was a Mennonite minister in Rotterdam who was also involved in the iron trade with England.[123] During the summer of 1709, the two men contracted with James Dayrolle, the British secretary of state at The Hague, to transport the thousands of "poor Palatine Protestants" who arrived in Rotterdam en route to England. They were responsible for collecting and distributing the charities given on the Palatines' behalf, caring for them, and arranging for their transportation.[124] Their participation in Commission for Foreign Needs activities likely made them good candidates for organizing the distribution of charitable funds for the Palatines, and that, in turn, strengthened their role as lobbyists the following year on behalf of the Swiss Mennonites.

Like Toren and van Gent, Ritter, the entrepreneur who transported Swiss refugees to the Netherlands, also brought valuable firsthand knowledge to his tasks. Ritter first became involved in a series of colonizing schemes when he formed a joint-stock company with François Louis Michel and Johann Rudolf Ochs, two other Swiss entrepreneurs, in early 1703. Michel had just returned from his first trip to Virginia and was on his way back to explore Pennsylvania, Maryland, and the Carolinas. First, however, he stopped in London, where he negotiated with Penn on behalf of Ritter and Company to settle Swiss immigrants in Penn's colony.[125] Between then and March 1710, when Ritter oversaw the first transport of Swiss Mennonite refugees down the Rhine, the three entrepreneurs proposed a series of colonizing schemes to the city of Bern, Queen Anne of England, the English Board of Trade, the Carolina Proprietors, and the governor of Virginia. In each case, the planners laid out the logistics and costs of transporting and resettling large numbers of immigrants from Switzerland to America.[126] Ritter's familiarity with the requirements of moving groups of people down the Rhine and across the Atlantic, a process that required crossing numerous political boundaries and obtaining passports from at least eleven governments, made him the perfect candidate for the commission's purpose.[127]

In both cases, the entrepreneurs participating in the Mennonite networks facilitated migration streams that eventually spanned the Atlantic. Several thousand of the immigrants whom Toren and van Gent assisted on their way to England continued to New York in 1709 and 1710.[128] And, while the Swiss Mennonites whom Ritter transported down the Rhine did not initially make it to the British colonies, many migrated to Pennsylvania beginning in 1717.[129] Internal migrations within Europe extended across the ocean as parts of colonial projects.

Like entrepreneurs, political leaders also recognized the benefits of the religious networks and refugees for recruiting settlers. The British government saw the possible advantages that toleration offered for expanding imperial goals, in part because of the lobbying efforts of Quakers and other religious dissenters.[130] When, in the summer of 1709, Queen Anne and her Privy Council considered whether or not to fund the transportation of 13,000 German-speaking immigrants to various parts of the empire, they knew that the potential settlers were not all "poor Protestants" from the Palatinate. But those advocating the immigrants' cause used the rhetoric of religious toleration, the examples of wealth other states had gained by welcoming French Protestant refugees, and popular ideas about a state's population as a source of wealth to justify supporting the "poor Protestant Palatines." By fashioning a new fictional identity for the immigrants that played on English anti-Catholic and anti-French sentiment, their supporters succeeded in raising over £100,000 in private and public funds.[131] The British Empire gained its first significant influx of German-speaking immigrants.

Thus the communication networks crafted by religious dissenters in their efforts to establish religious toleration and to spread their version of the gospel provided access to new groups of potential immigrants that had not been available before. By 1710 the connections began to take on a life of their own, as they intersected with the colonizing impulses of their participants. Individuals within the religious networks pursued the benefits of colonial enterprises for their own interests while continuing to use the information channels that dissenters had established. The British queen, like other European heads of state, took advantage of the networks and their rhetoric to increase the empire's population and

thus its wealth. Colonial proprietors and governors continued to recruit immigrants through the same channels, even after religious toleration no longer played a role. Many of the Swiss Mennonites who migrated to the Palatinate and the Netherlands in 1710 and 1711 moved to
Pennsylvania and Virginia beginning in 1717. Individual entrepreneurs
like Furly and Ritter sought the commercial profits of migration. And
the immigrants themselves, regardless of why they chose to leave home,
continued to rely on knowledge and news dispensed by participants
in those same networks to inform their decisions and secure transportation to the colonies. By providing advantages to participants and others
who recognized their benefits, the networks proved critical in shifting
sources of immigrants from England to Europe by the turn of the eighteenth century.

The communication channels that dissenters created were an integrative force.[132] They crossed political, cultural, and religious boundaries to
create conversations that eventually expanded beyond those interested
purely in religious issues. In the process, they facilitated the flow of information and people throughout Europe and the British Atlantic. They
were, however, a kaleidoscope—a constantly fluid and flexible series of
connections and intersections—rather than a stable set of links. All of
the players involved acted in their own interests and for their own purposes. The connections that began in an effort to alleviate religious persecution or to carry out missionary work took on a life of their own as
various participants capitalized on them for their own ends. Ultimately
the networks connected Great Britain and Europe in a way that allowed
colonizers of British America to recruit immigrants from the Continent.
But they did not remain constant. By the 1730s the intersections among
Quaker, Mennonite, and Pietist groups fostered by Quaker missionary
work began to disintegrate, and the recruitment of immigrants to the
British colonies was carried out by a handful of private merchant firms
with their own information networks.[133] Nevertheless, the integrative
force of the dissenters' networks lasted long enough to provide the dynamic for the settlement of radical dissenters throughout northern Europe and in coastal North America.

7

Typology in the Atlantic World

Early Modern Readings of Colonization

JORGE CAÑIZARES-ESGUERRA

"Typology"—the Christian tradition of reading contemporary events and actors as the fulfillment of older biblical episodes—drew on an ancient tradition first introduced by the Gospel writers themselves.[1] Although the Bible was an important, if not the most important, text on which Europeans drew to make sense, at the highest level, of their contemporary world, the tendency to read and think typologically extended not only to biblical but also to classical sources. Patristic writers did not entirely dismiss pagan sources as demonic. They often read classical myths as divinely inspired anticipations of the Christian narrative of salvation, a tendency that continued through the Middle Ages, as scholars transformed ancient myths into biblical types.[2]

The function of typological thinking was not simply to justify contemporary events and projects by locating them in the great Christian pageant, but to render them familiar, to domesticate them, to bring them into the confines of the great Christian and mythological epistemology that every literate person understood. For the Europeans encountering the strange new Western world and seeking justification for and understanding of the struggles that resulted and loomed ahead, typology was an ultimate intellectual reference with great explanatory power. This essential mode of understanding was expressed in prose, poetry, and above all in visual representations in which a host of ideas and references could be packed into limited space and from which networks of implications could be extracted by those familiar with the world of Christian iconography.

The "Mirror of Human Salvation" *(Speculum humanae salvationis),* a medieval illustrated Bible for the poor, offers clues to the workings of typology in the early modern period (Figure 7.1). Color images of events in the New Testament are paired with black-and-white illustrations of texts, mostly from the Old Testament but occasionally also from classical sources; the color illustration is the fulfillment of the Old Testament and classical prefigurations. According to the author of the *Speculum,* the epic battle of Revelation 12 between the woman of the Apocalypse and the multiheaded dragon had already been prefigured twice in the Old Testament: when Judith, the Israelite heroine, beheaded Holofernes, general of the Assyrian king Nabuchodonosor, and when Jael, another Israelite heroine, drove a tent peg through the brain of Sisera, general of the Canaanite king Jabin. Interestingly, the author also maintains that Revelation 12 was prefigured by the beheading of the

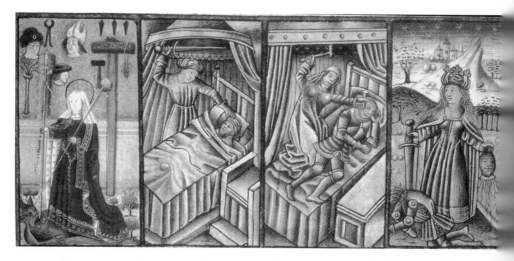

Figure 7.1 Prefigurations of Revelation 12 in the French translation of the *Speculum humanae salvationis* by Jehan Mielot, "Le miroir de l'humaine salvation," Glasgow University Library, MS Hunter 60 (T.2.18), fol. 43v. The image on the left, the woman of the Apocalypse battling the dragon, represents the culminating point prefigured by the other images: Judith beheading Holofernes; Jael killing Sisera; Tomyris beheading Cyrus. Reproduced by permission of Glasgow University Library, Department of Special Collections.

Persian king Cyrus by Tomyris, queen of the Massagetae, an episode described in Herodotus's *History,* not in the Bible.[3]

During the Renaissance and in the long seventeenth century, numerous treatises of biblical scholarship based on the study of classical mythology appeared.[4] This revitalized genre particularly affected the typological readings of early modern European expansion into the New World. All of the European colonial powers—the Portuguese, English, French, Dutch, and Spanish—found biblical and classical prefigurations of their involvement in the Americas, and quite similar examples can be traced across national and imperial borders. Unlike traditional historiography, which attempts to squeeze trans-imperial and hemispheric phenomena into national imperial narratives, the study of typology takes the Atlantic world to be a space of porous imperial boundaries, in which peoples, ideas, and commodities from four continents came together on certain vital issues to create a common, complex, hybrid culture.

Typology and Atlantic Colonization

To illustrate the scope and trans-imperial nature of typological readings, I examine illustrations from an iconic sixteenth-century work by Juan de Castellanos and from three seventeenth-century authors: Gaspar de Escalona Agüero, Antonio de Leon Pinelo, and Samuel Purchas. I also present images from two later works, both concerning the Jesuits, as evidence of the continuity of the typologies employed.

I have elsewhere discussed at length the frontispiece of Juan de Castellanos's *Primera parte de las elegías de varones illustres de Indias* (Elegies for Illustrious Great Men of the Indies, Part One) (1589).[5] It is nevertheless worth reexamining here, because the image epitomizes the use of biblical typology in portraying the colonization of the New World. It is a Spanish text, but in the way that the conquest is portrayed, as freeing the natives from a New World controlled by Satan, the frontispiece uses imagery that resonated throughout the Atlantic world of the period and that had considerable longevity. In a much later image from Mathias Tanner, *Societas Jesu usque ad sanguinis et vitae profusionem militans* (1675), the embodiment of the Jesuits, the bride of the Lord, stands on an anvil surrounded by monstrous creatures and demons wearing Amerindian feather headdresses (Figure 7.2). The bride

PERMANENT IMMOBILES VITÆ PEREÑIS GRATIÆ

ADAMAS DEI IN ANV

JESV EVAN CHRGELI STI VM

Sociat. IESU inter Americæ persecutiones, in pretiosum Adamantem Annuli DEI dura-
tur.

holds fast to a diamond wedding ring, while demons try to destroy diamonds through hammer blows and fire or by feeding them to the New World dragons and monsters, a subtle reference to Matthew 7:6: "Give not that which is holy unto the dogs, neither cast ye your pearls before swine, lest they trample them under their feet, and turn again and rend you." Good angels hold a banner with an Ambrosian hymn celebrating Jesuit martyrdom in the kingdom of Satan: as the bodies of saints are flayed and their blood splattered, their souls remain unmoved, experiencing everlasting grace ("permanent immobiles vitae perennis gratia").[6] Notice that Leviathan makes its appearance as a dragon with a crescent-moon for tail. It is striking that some hundred years after the publication of the Castellanos frontispiece, the same motifs were chosen in Bohemia to represent the struggles of militant Catholicism to tame demonic America, namely, a maiden locked in a battle with the dragon of Revelation 12.

We find the trope of the knight slaying Leviathan in an even broader context several decades later, in Lorenzo Ortiz's *El principe del mar, San Francisco Xavier, de la Compañia de Jesvs, Apostol de el Oriente, y Patron de sus navegaciones, y aora nuevamente de las del Sur, y su comercio* (1714) (Figure 7.3). Here the image is used to explain the timing of the European expansion in Asia. Known for his preternatural exploits calming storms unleashed by demons in the Indian Ocean, Saint Francis Xavier stands on Neptune's shell as he wields the Jesuit trident to slay the satanic enemies of Christianity.

In the Castellanos frontispiece (Figure 7.4), the faithful maiden Spain ("Hispania Virgo fidelis"), bearing a cross and the Bible, slays the dragon Leviathan, which has prevented the crossing of the Atlantic.[7] The dragon bites its own long tail, which encircles both the ocean and the two continents, and its Amerindian allies shoot arrows at Hispania, who stands on a shell in the middle of the ocean. Angels and the Holy

---

Figure 7.2 (opposite page) Martyrdom of Jesuits in America, the kingdom of Satan. From Mathias Tanner, *Societas Jesu usque ad sanguinis et vitae profusionem militans, in Europa, Africa, Asia, et America, contra gentiles, Mahometanos, Judaeos, haereticos, impios* (Prague, 1675). Reproduced courtesy of the Harry Ransom Humanities Research Center, University of Texas at Austin.

LA MILAGROSA IMAGEN DEL
PRINCIPE DEL MAR S. FRANCISCO
XAVIER.

Figure 7.3 Saint Francis Xavier riding the sea horses of Neptune in the Indian Ocean. In Lorenzo Ortiz, *El principe del mar, San Francisco Xavier, de la Compañia de Jesvs, Apostol de el Oriente, y Patron de sus navegaciones, y aora nuevamente de las del Sur, y su comercio* (Seville, 1714). Courtesy of the James Ford Bell Library, University of Minnesota.

Figure 7.4 Frontispiece, Juan de Castellanos, *Primera parte de las elegías de varones illustres de Indias* (Madrid, 1589). Reproduced courtesy of the John Carter Brown Library at Brown University.

Spirit descend on the New World. The Spanish king's coat of arms unites the two halves of the composition, in which the fauna and flora of the Old and New worlds stand at opposite sides. The words around the coat of arms proclaim "Philip II, Catholic and pious king" as the "Defender of the Church over seas and lands." A crucified Christ above the coat of arms is flanked by references to "King of kings and Lord of lords": a vengeful lord with a "sharp sword" for a mouth, who is about to "smite the nations" of the New World.[8] At the center of the composition, there is a quotation from Psalm 33:5: "The earth is full of the goodness of the Lord." The escutcheon of Hispania is held up by an Old World lion and by what appears to be an American "tiger." For every Old World animal, there is one from the New; thus the peacock, for example, stands opposite the turkey. On the ground, right center, below the escutcheon and next to the European rabbit, lies a dismembered Amerindian corpse, a symbol of the terrors that Hispania must overcome. Hispania arrives with a message of liberation, for written on the leaves and trunks of the American palm are passages from Psalms: "I waited patiently for the Lord; and he inclined unto me."[9] References to other Psalms adorn the Old World olive tree: "But I am like a green olive tree in the house of God"; "All nations whom thou hast made shall come and worship before thee, O Lord, and shall glorify thy name"; "The Lord hath made known his salvation: his righteousness hath he openly shewed in the sight of the heathen."[10] Engraved around the escutcheon are passages from the New Testament: "Come unto me, all ye that labor and are heavily laden, and I will give you rest"; "And other sheep I have, which are not of this fold; them also I must bring, and they shall hear my voice, and there shall be one fold, and one shepherd."[11]

Banners billowing beside Hispania's head contain fragments of Isaiah and Psalms: "Lift up thine eyes round about, and behold: all these gather themselves together and come to thee. . . . Thou shalt surely clothe thee with them all, as with an ornament, and bind them on thee, as a bride doeth"; and ". . . And in thy majesty ride prosperously because of truth and meekness and righteousness; and thy right hand shall teach thee terrible things."[12] The images and texts together form a basic worldview of Spain's role in the conquest and salvation of the New World. The densely packed typological references present the view that the part Spain is to play has been long prefigured in biblical sources.

The next frontispiece illustrates a more mundane but no less complex topic; it comes from *Gazophilatium Regium Peruvicum* (1647),
by far the most influential commentary on taxation written in Spanish
America. The author, the Creole Gaspar de Escalona Agüero, was a former *corregidor* of the province Xauja-Peru and *alcalde* of the city of
Castrovirreina who became a leading legal scholar in Peru. The ideological underpinnings of this erudite study can be found in the typological
reading of Old Testament and classical sources, with the main arguments
depicted in the book's frontispiece (Figure 7.5).

The inner central image in the frontispiece is divided into three. The
upper third has Philip IV seated on the *arca limensis,* the Peruvian treasury, as on Moses's Ark in the Tabernacle, the latter represented as a tent
unveiled by two angels. Peace and War also help as they kneel over excerpts from Tacitus's *History:* "there is no peace without armies, and
there is neither peace nor armies without tribute."[13] The composition
has millenarian undertones, for on top of the tabernacle there is banner with text from Daniel 11: "and the fourth shall be far richer than
they all." Philip IV appears therefore as the fourth monarch of Daniel's
prophecies, far more powerful than the previous three (Persian) kings.
His power rests largely on the mines of Peru, whose mountains with
several deep shafts are presented as crowned by the sun and the moon.[14]
On top of the mountains is an excerpt from the *Epistles* of Pliny the
Younger, pointing to the multiple sources of fiscal wealth, which in the
Indies are not limited to its mines: "there is certainly no more just return
than what is won from the soil, climate, and seasons."[15]

The millenarian message is reinforced in the middle third by several
images: two ships approach a beach crowded with an ulcerous Job, a
cow, and a false paradise guarded by a dragon. The nearer of the ships
carries a text from 2 Chronicles: "the king's ships went [to Ophir],
bringing gold and silver." Solomon and Ophir, therefore, become prefigurations of Philip IV and the New World.[16] The two vessels are buffeted and led by the omnipotent power of God, whose two angels blow
"treasures of snow" and "bring forth wind out of his coffers."[17] "More
pain comes from defending wealth [than from creating it]," announces
an excerpt from Juvenal's *Satire* embroidered on the trees of the orchard
of the Hesperides, which is guarded by a dragon. The image of America
as a false paradise that could lead officials to dishonesty and temptation

Figure 7.5 Frontispiece, Gaspar de Escalona Agüero, *Gazophilatium regium peruvicum* (1647). From the collection of the author.

is reinforced by another text from Pliny the Younger's *Epistles* next to the image of Job: "but this method requires strict honesty, keen eyes, and many pairs of hands."[18] In America, despite all travails and temptations, the officers of the state need to be as honest and as pious as Job.

The lower area of the central image displays the coat of arms of the president of the Council of the Indies, Don Garcia de Haro y Avellaneda, lord of Castrillo, to whom Escalona dedicates the treatise, flanked by a fully dressed America and by Neptune. Accompanied by a llama and a shaft of corn, America is cast by Escalona as the fulfillment of the sinful land of silver and gold that Isaiah once prefigured: "Their land also is full of silver and gold."[19] Neptune, on the other hand, lies supine above a text from Juvenal's *Satire* that recounts a scene in which the miserable fisherman Alab willingly gives to the Emperor Domitian the only fish he has caught: "whatever is noteworthy and beautiful in the entire sea belongs to the imperial treasury."[20]

Escalona's frontispiece is framed by twenty-two new Alabs: anthropomorphic representations of the tributary regions of the viceroyalty of Peru. Most of the images carry either a biblical or a classical text providing insights on tributary policy. Inspired by the story in Macrobius's *Saturnalia* of the wretched Greek who surrenders his money to the emperor Augustus, "Guanuco," like another Alab, urges the poor to hand in their meager savings to the authorities.[21] Drawing on the *Justinian Codex*, "Arica" calls on all men to pay tribute. "Paita" also draws on the *Justinian Codex* to urge each to give knowingly to the treasury. Tapping into the *Justinian Digest*, "Castrovirreina" warns functionaries not to impose inflated tributes. Inspired by Juvenal's *Satires*, "Cailoma" suggests that the treasury should be "frequented by men skillful in computing accounts, and the exchange of money." The adamant "Vilcabamba," carrying a text from the epistles of Cassiodorus, announces her willingness "to defend the tributary rights of the state." Like the general Haman who offers millions to the treasury of the Assyrian king Xerxes in exchange for the right to exterminate the Israelites, "Oruro" also announces her willingness to contribute millions to the state treasury. Finally, "Chiquiavo" quotes Matthew, urging each to "render therefore unto Caesar the things which are Caesar's."[22]

The anthropomorphic figures of Peruvian regions also invite a typological reading of the Bible and the classics. Thus the role of "Guancavelica," the source of mercury, whose alchemical properties are needed for the amalgamation of silver in Potosí, appears to have been prefigured in Psalm 74: "I bear up the pillars of it," for the liquefying power of mercury literally bears the pillars of the empire.[23] The immense riches of "Cusco," on the other hand, appear prefigured in Horace's *Satires:* "but I have large revenue, and riches ample for three kings."[24]

Escalona's typological readings of Peru's regions were not unique in Peru; they formed part of a much larger tradition. In 1656, for example, the civil and religious authorities of Lima organized a parade to dedicate the city to the Immaculate Conception. Images of Aristotle, Plato, Euclid, and Archimedes led the procession; the *empresas* and floats that followed sought to draw moral connections between pagan deities such as Mercury and Minerva and the Virgin Mary.[25]

Another part of that tradition lies in a legal compilation by Escalona's contemporary, Antonio de Leon Pinelo—his influential *Tratado de las Confirmaciones Reales de Encomiendas* (1620). This commentary on the laws on *encomiendas* has a frontispiece that succinctly captures the typological meaning that underlay most legal arguments on indigenous tribute in seventeenth-century Peru (Figure 7.6).

On the left, beneath the image of Peru—an Inca carrying a replica of Potosí, flanked by the arms of Peru and a llama—is a crisply carved text from Genesis: "and bowed his shoulder to bear, and became a servant unto tribute."[26] The reference, to Issachar, one of Jacob's twelve sons, would not have been lost on Leon Pinelo's readers. The dying Jacob summons Issachar to foretell his future: strong as an ass, Issachar will be destined to work and pay tribute. In Leon Pinelo's treatise Peruvians appear either as the descendants of Issachar or as the fulfillment of Genesis 49:15.[27] The Mexicans do not fare any better. They are represented in the right panel by a fully clad woman flanked by a condor and the arms of Tenochtitlan. She carries flowers and is accompanied by a hovering hummingbird, the symbol of Huitzilopochtli, the Aztec god of the sun and of war. The woman (Mexico) has her tributary conditions spelled out in Deuteronomy: "that all the people that is found therein shall be tributaries unto thee, and they shall serve thee." Again, the reference is clear. Deuteronomy 20 prefigures the rules of battle that followed the defeat of Tenochtitlan and sealed the fate of the Aztecs: when approaching an enemy city, first offer terms of peace. If the terms are accepted,

PRO INDIARVM · REGIO SENATV

IVS · VLTR

TRATADO
DE
CONFIRMACIONES REALES
DE
Encomiendas, Oficios i
casos, en que se requieren
para las Indias
Occidentales.
A Don Lorenço Ramirez de
Prado del Consejo del Rey
N.S. en el Supremo de las
Indias i Iunta de Guerra
dellas; i en el de Cruzada i
Iunta de Competencias.
Por el Lic. Antonio de Leon
Relator del mismo
Consejo de las
Indias.
Con Priuilegio.

I. de Courbes F

PERV.

NOVA HISPANIA

Et supposuit humerum suum ad portandum factusque est tributis seruiens. Gen. C 49.

Cunctis populus qui in ea est, saluabitur et seruiet tibi sub tributo. Deuter. C. 20.

En Madrid. Por Iuan Gonzalez, 1630.

Figure 7.6 Frontispiece, Antonio de Leon Pinelo, *Tratado de las confirmaciones reales de encomiendas* (Madrid, 1630). Reproduced courtesy of the John Carter Brown Library at Brown University.

open the gates and the people will serve as forced labor; if the terms are refused, fight and kill every man but spare the women, children, and livestock.[28]

Such biblical arguments were pervasive; they featured prominently in the origins of the infamous *requerimiento,* the document read aloud by conquistadors to Amerindians giving natives a choice between immediate conversion or war and enslavement. Although scholars have presented it as a contrived, ludicrous Spanish strategy to cast the conquest in the legal language of the "just war," the *requerimiento* is better explained as part of a larger typological interpretation of colonization. For the jurists who drafted the document, the conquest was the fulfillment of Joshua 3:7–13 and 6:16–21: Israelites/Spaniards gave the Canaanites/Indians an ultimatum to clear the Promised Land or face destruction.[29] Thus Leon Pinelo drew from a well-established legal tradition of justifying colonization, violence, and forced labor systems through typological readings of biblical texts.

The biblical and classical foundations invoked by Samuel Purchas, a leading proponent of British activity in the New World, to justify the colonial expansion of the British Empire are remarkably similar to those deployed by his Peruvian contemporaries.[30] The structure of Purchas's elaborate frontispiece in *Hakluytus Posthumus* (1625) resembles Escalona's in important ways (Figures 7.7 and 7.7A). It is also divided into three self-contained narratives along a vertical axis. The upper third offers a millenarian, typological interpretation of the British monarchy during Atlantic expansion. The middle third presents travel, peregrination, and colonization as foreordained both in the Bible and in the historical narratives of nations, empires, and travelers: from Noah, to Ulysses and Aeneas, to Alexander and Julius Caesar, to the apostles and Joseph of Arimathea (the rich merchant apostle who allegedly first converted the English), to Magellan and Pizarro, to the medieval kings of England and Scotland, to Mandeville and Columbus, and to Francis Drake and Sebastian Cabot. The bottom third presents travel and ex-

---

Figure 7.7 (opposite page) Frontispiece, Samuel Purchas, *Hakluytus Posthumus* (London, 1625). Reproduced courtesy of the John Carter Brown Library at Brown University.

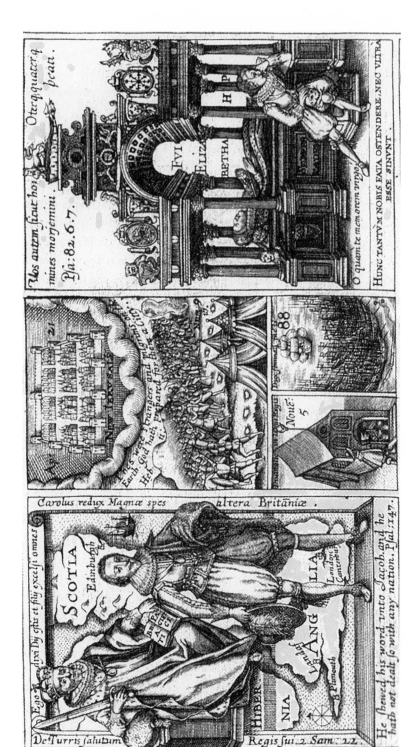

Figure 7.7A Purchas frontispiece, detail.

pansion as foreordained in human nature and the structure of the cosmos itself.

In the upper third of the frontispiece, typological readings of both biblical and classical sources are used evenhandedly. In the image to the left, King James stands next to his recently crowned son, Charles I, "the returning second hope of Great Britain," who is holding a Bible opened to Matthew 5:9, "blessed are the peacemakers." Both are introduced as new Davids, elected by God to carry out his will: "He is the tower of salvation for his king." The text underneath transfers this sense of election to the British people as a whole: "He shewed his word unto Jacob and he hath not dealt so with any nation."[31]

The biblical foundation of the British as God's elect is also the theme of the image in the middle upper third: British troops become the historically errant Israelites always in search of an unfulfilled divine promise of deliverance. God has a heavenly city in store for them, a New Jerusalem: "They were strangers and pilgrims on the earth. God hath prepared for them a city."[32] Directly below the errant troops, image and text present the denouement of the Gunpowder Plot as a result of James I's powers of augury: "A divine sentence is in the lips of the king."[33] In the small image to the right, the text calls forth the image of Dido, the Carthaginian queen who in the *Aeneid* defeats the tyrant Pygmalion, as the prefiguration of Elizabeth defeating Philip II: "the leader of the coup was a woman" (Figure 7.7A).[34]

In the right upper panel, Elizabeth surfaces again, this time with quotations that prefigure her both as a corpse and as the fulfillment of Venus, mother of the hero Aeneas, who cannot hide her divine origins in front of her son as she seeks to pass as a humble hunter: "How should I call you, lady?"[35] Elizabeth and the mourning Prince Henry, who would also die, are cast by Purchas as two of the "thrice, four times, blest" heroes who died defending Troy and whom Aeneas praises while about to drown off the coast of Carthage. Henry does not go quietly: Purchas suggests that he is the fulfillment of Marcellus, Augustus's nephew and adopted son, who, after having excelled in combat against the Gauls, unexpectedly died young: "he would only be shown to the world and then snatched away." Elizabeth's and Henry's mortality also appears as having been anticipated in the Bible: "I have said, Ye are gods; and all of you are children of the most High. But ye shall die like men."[36]

In the lower third of the frontispiece, Samuel Purchas, "age 48," appears as the "creator of the plate," *Pars sua Celum* (an anagram of "Samuel Purchas"), deeply aware of his own mortality and that of the rest of humanity. Written on the banner atop his bust and in the Bible he holds are excerpts from Psalm 39: "verily every man at his best state is altogether vanity," and "for I am a stranger with thee, and a sojourner, as all my fathers were."[37] It is this notion of human mortality and wanderlust that leads Purchas to include maps of the two hemispheres recording the circumnavigations of Francis Drake, Thomas Cavendish, and Ferdinand Magellan and crisscrossed by caravans of merchants and platoons of soldiers: "Soldiers and Merchants [are] the world's two eyes to see itself." Next to the bust of Purchas are images of a lodestone and a snail. The lodestone bespeaks the power of God: "I deliver and offer [my service] both at sea and on land. I preach [the power] of heaven," and "Everywhere it points and foretells; it works in every small box." The snail, on the other hand, also stays put and moves, like the lodestone. The snail, like the travelers whom Purchas studies, is a sojourner, carrying a house on its back. As it carries the earth on its shoulders, the snail is led by the stars.[38]

Purchas uses the lodestone and the snail in the same way that he used the Bible and the classics in the rest of the frontispiece—as a text to be read typologically. As Neil Kamil has argued, the traveling snail became a powerful symbol in the early modern period. The Huguenots, for example, interpreted it typologically to draw important lessons on how to behave during the Wars of Religion. Like the snail, the Huguenots traveled lightly and built inner fortifications around the soul through mechanisms of self-protection and deception. The snail/Huguenots crisscrossed the Atlantic as they avoided public worship, sublimating their piety into the artisan transformation of nature, from corrupt matter to crafted perfection.[39] Purchas's use of the snail as a prefiguration of the traveler is a window into forms of typological reading of nature relatively well known in Protestant scholarship but unnoticed in the Catholic world.[40]

There are many parallels to Purchas's very British millenarian narrative in Spanish sources. A common misconception is that the Bible in the Spanish world was the preserve of a small priestly elite and so did not circulate widely among Catholics there. But in reality, as Jaime Lara has recently shown, the Franciscans, along with cadres of native converts, saw themselves building new Temples of Solomon and new Golgothas in every mission. The grid plans of Spanish cities in the Indies originated in Christian dreams that sought to recreate in America the city of Jerusalem as laid out by Ezekiel.[41] Clearly biblical narratives and typological readings circulated widely in the Spanish Empire, affecting architecture, urban design, rituals, political philosophies, and patriotic identities. The Bible was everywhere, relentlessly displayed in objects, buildings, images, and sermons. As the texts discussed here suggest, typology colored all aspects of colonial culture.

Typologizing Amerindian History

One of the most important images of New Spain revolved around the patriotic cult of Our Lady of Guadalupe. Since the Virgin allegedly appeared in 1531 to a Nahua commoner, Juan Diego, near a hill a few miles north of Mexico City, the vision has been invested with a multiplicity of meanings. A shrine and growing numbers of devotees followed soon after 1531, but the image began to take on new dimensions, cutting across racial and class differences and becoming a distinctly Mexican national symbol, after Miguel Sánchez published his *Imagen de la Virgen María de Dios de Guadalupe* in 1648. Sánchez asserted that Saint John's image of a woman and an archangel fighting a dragon in Revelation 12 was a prefiguration of the conquest of Mexico. Far from being a development at the margins of the Catholic world, the miracle of Our Lady of Guadalupe had universal import: crucial episodes of the confrontation between good and evil described by Saint John in Revelation were taking place in Mexico. In the typological imagination of seventeenth-century Creole theologians, the reception by Juan Diego of the image of Our Lady of Guadalupe at Mount Tepeyac became the fulfillment of the reception by Moses of the tablets of the Ten Commandments at Mount Sinai. Thus the canvas of Our Lady of Guadalupe became a document in "Mexican hieroglyphs" that recorded a new covenant between God and the Mexican elect.[42]

In one mid-eighteenth-century engraving, for example, Oriental patriarchs, kings, angels, apostles, martyrs, and virgins offer crowns to the image of Our Lady of Guadalupe, while a seated Pope Benedict XIV and Mexico (an Indian woman carrying the kingdom's coat of arms) assent to the coronation below (Figure 7.8). The cartouche offers a textual narrative in Latin and Spanish of four scenes of the miracle to the right and left of the composition (the three apparitions of Guadalupe to Juan Diego and the transformation in front of the bishop of flowers collected by Juan Diego in his *tilma*). Passages from the Bible are interpreted typologically throughout. On the top right, for example, Our Lady of Guadalupe expels two demons from a possessed woman; a shield with a spike lies to the side with "contra demoniacos" carved on it. Genesis 3:5, "it shall bruise thy head," thus prefigures the power of the Madonna to crush the serpent. "Non fecit taliter omni nationi" (Psalm 14:20) appears on top of the entire composition, while Our Lady of Guadalupe calms the winds and the seas in a storm, as prefigured in Matthew 8:27, "the winds and the sea obey (her)."[43]

From the late seventeenth century, the motto "Non fecit taliter omni nationi" (He hath not dealt so with any nation) has accompanied most illustrations of Our Lady of Guadalupe.[44] Purchas used this same motto to justify the sense of the British under James I and Charles I that they were God's elect (Figure 7.7, bottom of upper right panel). In addition, Queen Elizabeth was often presented in her battles against the Spanish "Antichrist" as the fulfillment of biblical prefigurations. Thus in the eyes of some writers Elizabeth became the anti-type of the woman of the Apocalypse, confronting the multiheaded dragon that was Philip II (Revelation 12), a typological reading similar to Sánchez's analysis of the Virgin of Guadalupe. A poorly understood image designed by John Dee himself, the frontispiece to his *General and Rare Memorials pertaining to the Perfect Arte of Navigation* (1577), casts Elizabeth as the fulfillment of the woman of the Apocalypse (Figure 7.9). Like "Hispania, Virgo Fidelis" (Figure 7.4), Elizabeth is fully in control of the ocean; she steers the ship of Europe.[45] On the coast of England an almost naked "Opportunity" and a kneeling, fully clad "Britannia" both lure and implore Elizabeth to build a powerful navy to wrest the seas from the hands of the (Spanish) Antichrist. Elizabeth should find her allies across the English Channel among the French Huguenots and Dutch Calvinists. The composition is unmistakably inspired by Revelation 12: the Archangel Michael, flanked by sun and stars, wields a sword against the enemies of the woman, the Spanish fleet heading north.

Figure 7.8 Joseph Sebastian Klauber and Johann Baptist Klauber, *Pope Benedict XIV confers an Office and Mass in the Liturgical Calendar to Our Lady of Guadalupe as Patron of New Spain.* Engraving, ca. 1754. Reproduced courtesy of the Museo de la Basilica de Guadalupe, Mexico City.

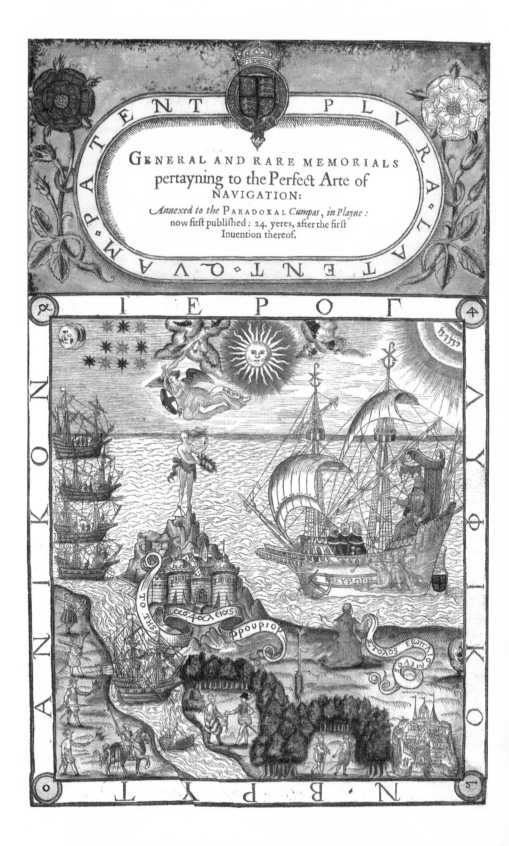

GENERAL AND RARE MEMORIALS
pertayning to the Perfect Arte of
NAVIGATION:
Annexed to the PARADOXAL *Cumpas, in Playne :*
now firſt publiſhed : 24. yeres, after the firſt
Inuention thereof.

The Marian tone of the composition is made explicit not only by Elizabeth's newfound mastery over the seas (the fulfillment of the classical deities Diana/Selena, a moon fully in control of the tides)—similar to that claimed for Our Lady of Guadalupe—but also by the references to the rose of Sharon of the Song of Songs in the upper third of the frontispiece. The two roses invite the reader to interpret the image typologically, for there is as much hidden as is made explicit *(plus latent quam patent)*.

Three decades after the publication of Sánchez's work, Carlos Sigüenza y Góngora, one of the leading polymaths of Mexico City, published *Teatro de virtudes políticas* (1680), written to explain the typology behind the triumphal arch he designed for the arrival of the new Viceroy of Mexico and his wife, the Marquis and Marquise de la Laguna.[46] Sigüenza's is an important text, for it suggests that by the seventeenth century typology was a technique appropriate for reading not only the Bible, classical sources, and nature, but also Amerindian history. As early as 1616, Guaman Poma de Ayala deployed the same psalm that Escalona would use a few years later to present the mercury mines of Guancavelica as "the columns" upon which the entire edifice of the empire rested (Figure 7.5). "I bear the pillars" of Psalm 74:4 was for Guaman Poma a biblical prefiguration of the providential role of both Potosí and the legitimate heirs of the Inca in Peru. In his image of the city of Potosí, he has the Inca and the four rulers of the Tawantinsuyu ("Four Quarters") supporting the columns of Hercules of the Habsburg monarchy (Figure 7.10). Thus, according to Guaman Poma, Psalm 74:4 bolstered the view of Bartolome de las Casas (and his own) that authority should devolve to the Andean native rulers. Guaman Poma's Latin altered the "ego confirmavi columnas eius" of Psalm 74:4 into "ego fulcio collumnas eios." Yet the point is the same: legitimate Andean lords from the four *suyus* (quarters) of Peru ought to be in charge of extracting the silver of Potosí. In Guaman Poma's typological imagination

---

Figure 7.9 (opposite page) Frontispiece to John Dee's *General and Rare Memorials pertayning to the Perfect Arte of Navigation* (London, 1577). From the collection of the author.

Figure 7.10 Potosí, from Guaman Poma de Ayala, *Nueva corónica y buen gobierno* (ca. 1615–1616). From the collection of the author.

Potosí and the Inca were very much in the mind of David when he uttered the psalm.[47]

This is not the place to attempt a synthesis of the uses of biblical and classical typologies in reading Amerindian history. Suffice it to say that the incorporation of indigenous texts into a network of typological readings was first tried by the Inca Garcilaso de la Vega in his *Comentarios reales* (1609), the most influential early modern history of the Inca. In the seventeenth century, Jesuits like Athanasius Kircher incorporated alien texts and historical traditions worldwide into a network of typological relations already deployed to read the Bible, the classics, and nature. In the New World, this tendency culminated in the work of Joseph-François Lafitau, who found in Huron and Mohawk histories the same prefigurations that medieval and Renaissance scholars had already found in classical antiquity.[48] Sigüenza is, therefore, representative of a larger Atlantic Catholic tradition.

Like Guaman Poma for the Inca, Sigüenza argued for the inclusion of Aztec history into typological display. His arch would not draw on classical mythology, for lessons for the prince should not to be found in the "shadows" of pagan mythology. Pagan deities were neither moral allegories nor prefigurations of Christian virtues, but rather the product of derelict satanic imaginations, as Saint Augustine had once suggested. Since the prince was the soul of the body polity and the very image of God on earth, to interpret classical myths as prefigurations of the prince's Christian virtues was to cast shadows on the very altar of the Lord, thus contravening the injunction in Deuteronomy 16:21 not to locate altars near the shadow of trees: forested darkness belonged to pagan cults, clarity and brightness to Christians. To replace classical mythology, Sigüenza argued, Mexican patriots should turn to their own Aztec history and stop looking to the pagans for inspiration; it was now time to read Aztec history prefiguratively. The deeds and names of Aztec princes, Sigüenza asserted, held as many lessons as did the French lilies and Habsburg eagles in the coat of arms of the Marquis and Marquise of Laguna (Figure 7.11).[49]

As Sigüenza struggled to design Alciato-like *empresas* to greet the arrival of the Viceroy Laguna and his wife, he fixed on the names and deeds of twelve Aztec rulers.[50] The etymologies and actions of these rulers, he argued, both fulfilled biblical texts and prefigured important

Figure 7.11 Detail of panel "Cortés visits Moctezuma." Miguel González and Juan González, 1698. The scene is part of a 24-panel series on the conquest of Mexico painted on canvas with mother-of-pearl inlay by two Japanese artisans resident in Mexico. The emblems of the Aztec rulers are strikingly similar to those first designed by Sigüenza y Góngora eighteen years before (of which no images are known to exist). The painting interprets the rulers, left to right, as follows: "Acamapich: Interpreta Cañas e la mano [it means canes in the hand]"; "Huitzilihuitl: Pajarito de pluma Rica [little bird of rich feathers]"; "Chimalpopoca: Rodela que hecha humo [smoking shield]"; "Itzoatl: Culebra de Navajas [snake of razor blades]"; "Motecuhzuma I: Señor enojado q. Flecha el Cielo [angry lord that shoots arrows to the sky]"; "Axayacatzin: Cara aguada [watery face]"; "Tizoc: Pierna tras pasada [pierced leg]"; "Ahuitzol [no description]." Reproduced courtesy of the Museo de América in Madrid.

virtues for the prince to emulate: piety, hope, clemency, self-sacrifice, prudence, fortitude, temperance, munificence, liberality, audacity, and constancy. Sigüenza represented Huitzilopochtli, for example, as a Moses-like figure who had been deified by the Aztecs. Since the name meant "hummingbird," "magus," and "left arm," Sigüenza designed an *empresa* in which the Moses/Huitzilopochtli followed a torch, which, along with a hummingbird, was held by a left arm sticking out of the clouds: Huitzilopochtli's name prefigured the religious foundations of all polities. The second leader, Acamapich, "handful of canes," stood for hope, which was meaningful only when maintained under duress. Ac-

cording to Siguenza, Acamapich dreamed up the future glory of Tenochtitlan under the worst of all possible circumstances—namely, when
the only available land to establish the city was a swamp covered with
wild canes. In fact, Siguenza argued, the reference to "emptiness and
void" in Genesis 1 was a prefiguration of the swamp where the Aztecs
had first settled. "Handful of canes" thus prefigured both the fragility
of all monarchical scepters, buffeted by fortune, and the prolific potential of all humble seeds. Acamapich was the New World equivalent of
the Old Testament Seth, the third son of Adam and direct ancestor of
Christ. Acamapich, "handful of canes," also prefigured the harmony of
the polity, for wild canes were the origin of music.

The vision of Acamapich catapulted the Aztecs—a nation of tall war-
riors whose land would be ravaged by floods and trampled upon, as
prefigured in the book of Isaiah (Isaiah 18:1–3)—from miserable origins
into future glory, for Mexico City had become the epitome of all great
historical urban complexes. Tizoc, "feet pierced by thorns-arrows,"
stood for peace and temperance. Despite having been an Aztec general
who engaged in bloody warfare to expand the empire, Tizoc became a
temperate emperor once he gained power. Tizoc turned away from war
and discord to embrace peace, a transition more difficult than "walking
on thorns." His name and his deeds thus fulfilled Isaiah 52: 7: "How
beautiful . . . are the feet of him . . . that proselytized peace." Finally,
Motecohzuma, "angry lord," stood for munificence. A man with a reputation for being fearsome and distant became a liberal host to Cortés and
his army. Thus, according to Sigüenza, Motecohzuma fulfilled Judges
14:14: "out of the strong came forth sweetness."[51]

Trans-Imperial Typology

A historiography that has rested satisfied with nationally defined narratives might find novel this account of common uses of biblical and classical symbols across empires. But the "Atlantic" as a category should
deliver narratives on the circulations of peoples, staples, and ideas, defining in the process a distinctly transnational space.

It is true that the circulation of typological readings was not a
uniquely Atlantic phenomenon, and that reading biblical passages as
prefigurations of current events was not a technique used only by early

modern Europeans to justify their colonial expansion.[52] Typological readings had helped Muscovites muster popular support in their expansion to central Asia and the crusading knights to launch their campaigns against Muslims, heretics, Jews, and pagans. In the Middle Ages they often contributed to architectural design, and they were the tool of choice to elucidate doctrinal and political conflict.[53] There seems, however, to be something distinctively "Atlantic" about the use of typology in the intellectual and cultural history of Europe's expansion. Typology became a particularly effective way of understanding the two worlds' encounters across time and space. The Bible, the classics, nature, and the Amerindian past could all be read together prefiguratively, cast into a net of relations reinforcing discourses of possession and colonial legitimacy. Early modern readers of empire and expansion, moreover, brought into the already dense network of typological relations alien historiographies and natural objects, thus creating new and often more complex texts.

The Atlantic was a common, shared space in which peoples, commodities, and ideas circulated across porous imperial boundaries. One needs to transcend the narrow constraints of national historiographies to understand events that were in their essence transnational, bred in the broad culture of Christianity.

8

A Courier between Empires

Hipólito da Costa and the Atlantic World

NEIL SAFIER

An isolated jailbreak may seem an unlikely event to alter the fate of a transoceanic empire. But the fugitive who escaped in the dead of night from a Portuguese prison and made his way through the dark alleys of Lisbon in the spring of 1805 would eventually come to play a pivotal role in the events that shaped Portugal's destiny as an imperial power. At the time of this man's escape, the Prince Regent João VI (1767–1826) was more preoccupied with Napoleon's threats to invade the Iberian Peninsula (and with preparing for his own family's eventual flight from Portugal to Brazil) than with the security of the Lisbon Inquisition's secret prisons. But perhaps he should have paid closer heed to the roster of prisoners: this refugee from inquisitorial justice would go on to formulate a highly effective and sustained critique of João's imperial administration and to contribute through his journalistic writings—directly or indirectly—to the weakening of the bonds that tied the Brazilian colony to the Portuguese metropole.

Hipólito José da Costa (1774–1823) was an iconoclastic and divisive figure. Through the *Correio Braziliense,* a monthly periodical he edited and published in London without interruption from 1808 to 1822, he caused continual consternation for the Portuguese monarchy during the period it reigned from Portugal's largest and most prosperous overseas colony.[1] An open forum for political dissent and a clarion for liberal policies on a British parliamentary model, the *Correio Braziliense* served as a conduit for expressing the political principles Hipólito had developed during his travels throughout the Atlantic: from Coimbra, where he studied in a newly reformed university, to Philadelphia, where he was sent early in his career to observe North American agricultural practices, to the Caribbean, where he may have traveled surreptitiously to procure agro-industrial commodities, and to London, where the *Correio Braziliense* would be published in the final two decades of his life as an imperial exile. Exposure to societies with free presses and frequent association with networks of freethinking agents—including Freemasons as well as naturalists—in both the New World and the Old led him to reject the Catholic Church's intransigent scholasticism and instead to support calls for the unhindered circulation of ideas. Because it was published outside the territorial limits of the Portuguese Empire, the *Correio Braziliense* carried its message free from the crippling constraints of the monarchy's censor—to the great chagrin and preoccupation of the Portuguese court in Rio de Janeiro.[2]

Hipólito da Costa and his *Correio Braziliense* were also heirs to the reformist spirit of the Enlightenment, the cultural and philosophical movement that offered direct inspiration not only for many of the worlds through which Hipólito passed—from the University of Coimbra to the Masonic lodges of Philadelphia—but also for a historical period that was seen as culminating in the explosion of independence movements throughout the Americas: the age of Atlantic revolutions. To an earlier generation of scholars, however, and especially prior to the renascence of interest in Atlantic studies, the writings and ideals of the Enlightenment appeared to be little influenced by intellectual tides from beyond Europe's shores. The ocean connecting Europe, Africa, and the Americas seemed to have scant effect on a "little flock of philosophes" printing pamphlets and plotting revolutions in European capitals. These limited interpretations had a particularly egregious impact on the history of the Iberian world, as they tended to portray Portugal, Spain, and Ibero-America as weak receptors of ideas whose origins lay elsewhere, rather than seeing those regions as active participants in a pan-European intellectual movement that also stretched beyond Europe's borders.[3]

In response, scholars have more recently challenged and moved beyond this oversimplified diffusionist model, arguing that important philosophical and natural historical investigations were also taking place independently in Ibero-America and throughout the Iberian world. Ideas that inspired European thinkers to embrace reason, empiricism, and political self-determination as motors of historical change were also prevalent among groups of erudite Americans who saw themselves in dialogue, if occasionally also in conflict, with their European counterparts. Some scholars have argued for a distinctively Latin American Enlightenment embodied in figures such as Francisco José de Caldas, the polymath self-instructed naturalist from Popayán (Colombia) who corresponded with Alexander von Humboldt about his theories of biogeography, or the physician and author Hipólito Unanue from Lima, or the Mexican Jesuit Francisco Xavier Clavijero, who was expelled from the New World but took refuge in Italy, where he composed a history of ancient Mexico that integrated colonial history with a study of indigenous cultures. The specific conditions of the Americas, they argue, provided a rich substrate within which Ibero-American intellectuals could formulate their ideas, including such elements as climate, natural resources, and indigenous history. And all of these savants—and there were many others—participated in what has come to be known as a hemispheric experiment in Enlightenment ideas, bringing a particularly American spirit to an endeavor that earlier scholars had characterized as exclusively European (and mainly French) in its origins, form, and character.[4]

Hipólito da Costa was one such cosmopolitan figure who was both marked by and a contributor to this experimental ethos. And if his beliefs during the later phase of his life were often in marked contrast to those of the Portuguese sovereign, earlier in his career he exemplified an entire generation of Portuguese subjects who loyally served the Crown. His cohort, which came of age in the final decades of the eighteenth century, included individuals who were familiar with the latest European literary and philosophical ideas of the Enlightenment and whose political and intellectual careers seamlessly crisscrossed the Atlantic (as well as other oceanic spaces).[5] Born in 1774 in the Portuguese colony of Colônia-do-Sacramento (present-day Uruguay), Hipólito, like many of his colleagues, first crossed the ocean to pursue a formal education in Portugal. At the University of Coimbra, he and a group of young Brazilian colleagues were instructed under a reformed curriculum that emphasized empirical studies in the natural sciences as well as the more traditional subjects of law and philosophy. They read the works of

Montesquieu, Voltaire, the Benedictine friar Benito Jerónimo Feijóo, and the Portuguese physician António Nunes Ribeiro Sanches, absorbing in the process the agro-economic principles of French physiocracy. They were also influenced to no small degree by the example of their protector, Dom Rodrigo de Sousa Coutinho (1755–1812), son of a Portuguese diplomat who had been a colonial governor in Angola. Having traveled widely as a child, Sousa Coutinho received his education at the College of Nobles in Portugal, and he embarked at the age of 23 on his first diplomatic mission, during which he spent a year touring important European capitals, including Turin, Madrid, and Paris. "Dom Rodrigo" (as he was often called to distinguish him from his father) was in regular contact with such Enlightenment luminaries as Jean d'Alembert, Pierre-Simon Laplace, and the Abbé Raynal. Sousa Coutinho's role at the Lisbon Academy of Sciences, and his *memórias* on subjects ranging from mineralogy to the use of sugarcane, molded this generation of enlightened Luso-Brazilian emissaries, individuals inspired to acquire practical and theoretical knowledge of the natural world on behalf of their political and intellectual mentor.[6]

As minister of naval and overseas affairs, Sousa Coutinho was responsible for selecting Hipólito da Costa for a diplomatic mission to North America only months after the young Brazilian native had completed his degree at Coimbra in June 1798. Using Philadelphia as his base, Hipólito was to study and collect botanical specimens throughout North America that might yield valuable agricultural resources to bolster the Portuguese economy. This was part of Sousa Coutinho's pragmatic reformist program, which aimed to introduce "new agricultural specimens and new agricultural products" *(novos artigos de cultura e de novas produções)* as part of a broad set of institutional, agricultural, and economic reforms.[7] Hipólito settled in Philadelphia and came into contact with an important group of the American cultural elite: the naturalists William Hamilton, John and William Bartram, and Humphry Marshall; the painter and collector Charles Willson Peale; Columbia College's professor of chemistry Samuel Mitchill; and Elias Boudinot, then director of the U.S. Mint. Hipólito later toured Montréal, Québec City, New England, the Carolinas, and, possibly, Mexico. The experiences in Philadelphia—both his personal contacts and the writings he found there—

encouraged him to challenge the absolutist censorship and religious persecution that still reigned in the Portuguese capital.

Upon returning to Lisbon late in 1800, he was invited by Sousa
Coutinho to be one of the literary directors of the newly constituted
Casa Literária do Arco do Cego printing house. This officially sponsored venture was designed to advance the "rural economy of specimens
already cultivated and others that may be introduced" by publishing
texts and treatises that would later be sent to governors and ministers
in outlying provinces.[8] During the year that Hipólito served in this capacity, he carried out his duties faithfully, publishing his own treatise on
the sugar maple tree and translations of several important texts he had
come across during his North American sojourn. But shortly thereafter,
Hipólito's career took a course that was anything but typical for a loyal
Crown agent. Having joined a lodge of Freemasons early in his stay in
Philadelphia, Hipólito became a target of reactionary forces in Lisbon
that eventually led to his persecution and incarceration. After a mission
to London to buy books and typographical machinery for the Arco do
Cego, he was detained by the Lisbon inquisitors for nearly three years,
accused of openly conducting business on behalf of Masonic lodges in
Portugal.[9] The fierce and unrelenting Pina Manique, intendant-general
of the Lisbon police, had insisted on keeping his captive under lock and
key for six months, a period that would be extended once Hipólito was
handed over to the inquisitors and their guards. It was only in April
1805 that the accused was able to slip from the watchful eye of his
jailors, hide out in a Lisbon safe house until he could leave the city, make
his way across Portugal and southern Spain to the port city of Gibraltar,
and board a ship bound for London, where he would begin a new chapter in an eminently transatlantic life. Three years later, he would publish
the first edition of the *Correio Braziliense*, a periodical he used as a platform to express his disgust at the regressive practices of Dom João's administration (not to mention the retrograde activities of the Inquisition
in nineteenth-century Lisbon).

Thus, at the time of his escape from the Inquisition's secret prisons in
Rossio, Hipólito da Costa had been incarcerated long enough to build
up a healthy dose of resentment toward the monarchy. By the time he
began to edit the *Correio Braziliense* in 1808, the Portuguese monarch

was already established in Rio de Janeiro's Quinta da Boa Vista palace, secure (with Britain's help) from the long reach of Napoleon's navy but nevertheless susceptible to (and doubtless incensed by) the monthly attacks of the *Correio Braziliense.* Given the extraordinary situation of the Portuguese court's presence in an erstwhile colony, it is no surprise that Hipólito began writing on themes of political and cultural import to the Lusophone community on both sides of the Atlantic. The fate of the monarchy and its relationship to the colonies it governed were paramount among his interests.[10]

Disaggregating the circulation of ideas from the political movements they were thought to foster is essential to comprehending the multiple paths of intellectual and scientific ferment in the period encompassed by Hipólito da Costa's life—1774 to 1823. His case represents an important contribution toward answering a series of central questions in the context of Atlantic history. How did ideas travel at the turn of the nineteenth century? What mechanisms were there for conveyance? In addition to periodicals and printed texts, how, if at all, did these ideas cross the seas in a revolutionary age? Although Hipólito began his career firmly within the orbit of the metropolitan "center" as a protégé and servant of his mentor Sousa Coutinho, the circumstances of his life led Hipólito to take a different path, one that placed him at a distance from the metropolitan authorities where, owing to his earlier experiences, he could write critically of the monarchy and help develop the ideas, ideologies, and forms of political dissent that were making their way from one side of the Atlantic to the other.

Hipólito da Costa's trajectories illuminate this process of intellectual transition and engagement across imperial lines. This essay will focus on his experiences in North America as a way of understanding how his earliest Atlantic itineraries contributed to two important phases later in his career: as literary director at the Casa Literária do Arco do Cego in Lisbon and as editor of the *Correio Braziliense* in London. But we begin on a winter's day in southeastern Pennsylvania.

A Luso-Brazilian in Early Republican Philadelphia

On the chilly morning of January 9, 1799, in an era when the Delaware River still froze over in the winter and ferry boats traversed the Schuylkill, carrying passengers and cargo to and from the city, a young and dapper Portuguese traveler sat for his portrait in Philadelphia. Not yet a month after arriving in the bustling capital of the nascent United States after a "rather uncomfortable voyage" of fifty-nine days aboard the corvette *William,* Hipólito da Costa made his way to the house of an equally young French émigré named Charles Balthazar Julien Févret de Saint-Mémin (1770–1852). Saint-Mémin had established his reputation as an artist by tracing profiles of prominent Philadelphians and providing them with small and convenient reproductions. Twenty-five dollars would purchase twelve impressions, the plate, and small and large versions of the pencil portrait. According to the journal Hipólito kept assiduously over the fourteen-month period between his departure from Lisbon on October 11, 1798, and December 1799, Saint-Mémin drew his subject's likeness by taking "the profile against the wall using a shadow [and] filling in the outlines with a pencil. . . . [H]e then reduces [this larger image] and engraves a small plate," which he later used to make impressions of the individual reproductions (Figure 8.1). On the reverse of the image he made of Hipólito on that January day was written "Drn. with the Physiognotrace & engrd. St. Memin. Philada." The physiognotrace was the eighteenth-century equivalent of the Kodacolor snapshot, and this previously unattributed image of Hipólito captures the young traveler during a period that was a formative moment in his future literary and political career; it is also one of the few physical vestiges of his passage through Philadelphia that exist today.[11]

The instructions Hipólito had been given by Sousa Coutinho were clear: he was to travel throughout North America and provide the court with detailed information about a host of potentially lucrative commodities. Tobacco varieties from Virginia and Maryland were among the products Hipólito was to examine, and it was expected that he would later write a report on the cultivation and preparation of those plants in order to compare them with tobacco specimens already being cultivated in Brazil. Hemp was another important specimen to be observed and collected, as were various grains, potatoes, and "guinea grass," an imported weed originally from Africa (also known as *panicum maximum*) that the English surveyor Nicholas Robson described as a swift-growing and "valuable" grass used primarily as stock feed on late eighteenth-century Jamaica plantations.[12]

Figure 8.1 Physiognotrace of Hipólito da Costa, by C. B. J. Fevret de Saint Mémin. Reproduced courtesy of the Corcoran Gallery of Art, Washington, D.C.

Most important to Sousa Coutinho, however, was the insect responsible for the production of cochineal dye, the most widely known of which was to be found near Veracruz in Mexico. Sousa Coutinho emphasized to Hipólito that he should "hide the main object that would take him into Spanish territory" as he acquired documents related to the quality and composition of the insect. He was also to obtain specimens of its host cactus and, if possible, a "considerable portion of said Insect that can be sent along with instructions . . . to Rio de Janeiro," from which it was hoped an "immediate benefit [might] be garnered."[13] Hipólito's attempts to acquire a passport to enter Spanish dominions hit some early snags, forcing him eventually to undertake his voyage incognito, but within two months of his arrival in Philadelphia he was already making good on his other commitments to the Crown. By early February, he had provided the newly established Portuguese ambassador there with a case of 192 native plant, tree, and shrub species that he reckoned would be of interest to the scientifically curious back in Portugal (to whom he referred as the "amadores da sciencia"). The case included samples of eight different pine trees, as well as cedars, hemlocks, nettles, and magnolias, trees he hoped would be "extremely useful in Civil Architecture, in the Arts, and in Medicine," and which would allow the king's garden at Ajuda to flourish with the scent of American evergreens.[14]

Hipólito was quite familiar with the gardens and museums in Portugal from his years at the University of Coimbra, which had undergone sweeping changes put into place by Sebastião José de Carvalho de Melo, the Marquis of Pombal (1699–1782). These innovations and reforms had been overseen by the Italian naturalist Domenico Vandelli (1730–1816), handpicked and imported from Italy by Pombal. Vandelli was a collaborator of the so-called *estrangeirados*, a generation that had attempted to bring Portugal in line culturally, politically, and intellectually with other European nations, especially through support for the foundation of the College of Nobles and Lisbon's Royal Academy of Sciences.[15] The next wave of reform-minded savants, instructed this time under Vandelli, may have been somewhat more eclectic than the prior generation, but more often than not they shared a common birthplace: Brazil. Born in the New World, they traveled to Coimbra to pursue an education and often spent the rest of their careers shuttling between cities along the Atlantic littoral—and inland as well—and adapting to the diverse conditions and circumstances in both colony and metropole. In later years, they would become scientists and philosophers, lawyers and poets, colonial administrators and revolutionaries.[16] Most of the individuals who comprised the "Generation of the 1790s" in fact found no dichotomy between their colonial and metropolitan identities. Brazil was merely one territorial possession of the greater Portuguese Empire, a land rich in resources but bereft of two critical hallmarks of European civilization: the printing press and the university.

As a member of this university generation trained in Coimbra,

Hipólito would doubtless have opened, in preparation for his arrival in Philadelphia, José António de Sá's *Compendio de observaçõens* (1783), a guide that instructed travelers to study the local character of the peoples and institutions they would visit on extended missions both within and outside Portuguese dominions. Study of Sá's text reflected a practical orientation for seeing new spaces—rural as well as urban—and also provided instructions on visiting museums. In his guide, Sá had written that it was important for the observer to record whether or not "there are public or private Museums in [a given] province, how many [there are], how many rooms they contain, [and] in what kinds of natural products they are the most rich."[17]

Following Sá's advice, in Philadelphia Hipólito first turned his attention to Peale's renowned museum of natural history, making a series of observations that related directly to Sá's list of queries. Peale had founded his Philadelphia museum to serve as a "world in miniature," organized according to Linnaeus's classification scheme in order to showcase Peale's own democratic, physiocratic, and moralistic tendencies.[18] Through civic pride and public support, the Philadelphia museum was vaunted in North America as a public curiosity constructed according to modern (which at the time meant European) standards. As such, Peale's cases of natural curiosities came to be seen as reflective of the American nation as a whole, a civic institution in private vestments, which, together with the American Philosophical Society, reflected the broadest ambitions to which North American savants and statesmen aspired.[19] Hipólito, however, found the rooms in Peale's museum to be small, its mineral collections minute, and the entire institution "without order or system of any kind . . . although in all the public papers you read just the contrary of what I observed."[20] This critical stance toward an important museological icon of the early republic was typical of some of Hipólito's more negative observations of North American culture, for which he used curt language and a tone of disdain both in his journal and in official correspondence. From an early age, it seems, the young traveler from Portugal was not shy about expressing his opinions on the most commonly held public assumptions, credos, and beliefs.

In addition to being home to the early republic's most esteemed natural history museum, Philadelphia was also a seaport and administrative center with connections throughout the Americas and overseas. Hipólito's list of personal contacts bears witness to the international networks that linked the city with the outside world. In the wake of the French Revolution, Philadelphia had welcomed French émigrés such as Moreau de Saint-Méry, La Rochefoucauld-Liancourt, and Saint-Mémin.[21] There were also Dutch, Germans, and Spaniards whom Hipólito encountered at social events throughout his stay. Through dinners at the residence of the Portuguese ambassador Cipriano Ribeiro Freire, Hipólito made the acquaintance of the British ambassador Robert Liston and his wife, with whom he continued to meet and correspond during his time in the United States.[22]

For Hipólito, establishing his credibility through social connections was essential for carrying out his mission to acquire knowledge of the natural world. His decision to stay through the winter following his arrival in Philadelphia was based on precisely such considerations: as he later wrote to Sousa Coutinho, "several months' residence in this city where members of Congress from all parts of the Union will be present . . . would provide me with the friendship of individuals who might later make the acquisition of knowledge far easier."[23] As an agent of the Crown, Hipólito saw it as his duty to befriend as many members of the community as possible and in turn to use those contacts to further his own (and Sousa Coutinho's) agenda. But he also seems to have taken these social duties seriously in and of themselves. While visiting New York, he dined in the house of Joaquim Monteiro, a businessman from Madeira, "where they played music after dinner." He even rented a piano for his own apartment during the time he spent in New York. On occasion, these social events allowed him to make particular observations that related indirectly to his broader mission. In one instance, Hipólito wrote about attending an orchestral concert in Philadelphia honoring a French musician where he was able to observe an American Indian in the audience who was dressed in English attire and whose "color, eyes, bodily shape . . . gestures and speech patterns were nothing if not those of an Indian from Brazil."[24] Though little more is said of this Amerindian (other than that he laughed aloud when the singer performed a high staccato trill), Hipólito was interested enough in Amerindian culture to include some important treatises on native populations among the books and manuals he sent back to Lisbon. Although native peoples play a minor role both in Hipólito's visit to Philadelphia and in his more mature political writings, these informal observations indicate at the very least an attention to the cultural diversity of the early United States and its potential for comparison to social and cultural dynamics in Portuguese America.

Not all of his visits were suffused with such moments of sociability, however. Hipólito had business interests to care for, and he took advantage of contacts on the ground to construct a network that included many of the individuals who were instrumental in making late eighteenth-century Philadelphia a center for botanical exchange.[25] From the earliest days of his journey, Hipólito visited the most important botanists and naturalists of the Philadelphia region. Soon after his arrival, he made the acquaintance of Thomas Parke, a doctor at the College of Physicians and a member of the Library Company of Philadelphia.[26] The two were in contact by early February, for it was Parke who forwarded a letter at Hipólito's behest to Humphry Marshall, a well-known Quaker naturalist and physician from the Brandywine River Valley of southeastern Pennsylvania, whose botanical garden was known in Europe and beyond.[27] After receiving no return correspondence from Marshall, Parke sent another letter asking him to respond to "a Gentleman from Portugal who has some knowledge of Botany."[28] Hipólito was likely familiar with Marshall's *Arbustum Americanum*, or perhaps the French translation *Catalogue alphabétique des arbres et arbrisseaux*, which was published in 1788 and enjoyed more popularity in Europe than the American version.[29] Marshall's text stated explicitly that "the foreigner, curious in American collections, will be hereby better enabled to make a selection suitable to his own particular fancy," and it listed "Dr. Thomas Parke, in Philadelphia" as the agent to whom all inquiries were to be addressed.[30] It was presumably from reading the *Arbustum Americanum* that Hipólito saw fit to use Parke as an intermediary to procure an invitation to meet Marshall.

Several months into 1799, Hipólito's efforts to make contact with the members of Philadelphia's botanical community began to bear fruit, and his social calendar began to be filled with meetings of both a personal and a professional nature. That year, he at last met Humphry Marshall and spent an evening in Germantown with Benjamin Smith Barton, with whom he had collected botanical specimens earlier in the day.[31] In the house of William Hamilton, a member of the Philadelphia gentry whose Woodlands estate contained one of the region's most important greenhouses, Hipólito dined with the German pastor Henry Muhlenberg, whom Hipólito considered to be "the best botanist in the United States." Yet he also recorded in his journal that he had found Muhlenberg's manners to be "crude and gross" and his company nearly "unbearable" for that reason.[32] Through Hamilton, in whose house Hipólito dined on several occasions, he also began a useful correspondence with a certain James Wiles of the Liguanea botanical garden in Jamaica, who was later to provide Hipólito with seeds of the breadfruit tree that had been brought by William Bligh to the Caribbean earlier that decade.[33] This connection with the Caribbean was no coincidence, since Hamilton's Woodlands estate was to Hipólito an emporium of all the world's botanical treasures. He wrote that Hamilton "had in his house many plants from China and Brazil," including a kind of sugarcane that originated from one of the Pacific islands and that was already being cultivated in Mexico. The precise conditions under which Hipólito came to meet and correspond with these naturalists were not always indicated in his journal, but it is clear that he used the friends he had made through diplomatic circles as intermediaries who facilitated his connections and provided him with the social standing to visit gardens throughout the greater Philadelphia area and to acquire important botanical knowledge as a result.

A year after his arrival, however, Hipólito no longer seemed to require the assistance of intermediaries, and he began to communicate more directly with his botanical contacts. On January 14, 1800, after he had returned to Philadelphia from an extended journey through New York, Québec, and New England, he "took the liberty" to write directly to the economist and former assistant secretary of the treasury Tench Coxe with questions on the whaling industry, on agriculture generally, and on hemp cultivation in particular. In his letter, he made reference to the "reunion of the Assembly's members at Lancaster" and to the possibility of receiving information directly "from some practical farmer" who had direct knowledge of the questions at hand.[34] This was no longer the demure and reticent individual who had awaited permission from his betters. Hipólito now presented himself as a self-assured and assertive emissary willing to take a more active role in procuring information related to his charge.

Whether Hipólito had actually met Coxe before writing to him is unclear from his journal; however, he was already familiar with Coxe's
View of the United States. In his journal entry of December 27, 1798,
Hipólito cited William Cooper's statistical portrait of the sugar maple
tree that Coxe had reproduced in his discussion of maple sugar. Hipólito
made no further explicit reference to Coxe's account. However, this
very chapter of Coxe's *View* contained a paean to the freedom of the
press in early America that might have reaffirmed Hipólito's admiration
for a society that valued the uninhibited circulation of ideas. In the
chapter "Containing some information relative to maple sugar, and it's
[*sic*] possible value in certain parts of the United States," Coxe had written: "The disposition of the people of America to examine and discuss
the topics of the day, the increased intercourse among the states since the
late war, and the diffusion of knowledge through the channels of their
numerous gazettes, naturally occasion information, which used to be local, to be much more generally extended."[35]

This kind of discourse emphasized the important role that "increased
intercourse" and the "diffusion of knowledge through . . . numerous gazettes" could play in expanding the circulation of information throughout the public sphere. The context to which Coxe refers is obviously
North American. But the fact that his text was being read by a Portuguese emissary in America meant that its circulation went beyond what
even Coxe himself might have imagined, and indeed confirmed Coxe's
argument regarding the "extended" circulation of knowledge through
the public conduit of print. Such early American texts and periodicals
evidently provided Hipólito with useful examples of the advantages of a
free press, ideas that he would later use to persuade his own Portuguese-
language readers of the paramount importance of the "diffusion of knowledge" through an uncensored public sphere.

Similarly, Coxe's discussion in the same text of the relationship between sugar maple cultivation and the diminution of African slavery in
the colonies may have contributed, if indirectly, to Hipólito's later dis-
avowal of the slave trade as a permanent solution to the lack of human
labor in the Americas. For, while Coxe had written that "a very large
proportion of the unsettled lands of [Pennsylvania] abound with this
valuable tree," and had discussed the potential importance for Europe of
the North American maple, he had also commented on its relation to the

Quakers' moral outrage at the practice of African enslavement: "The great and increasing dislike to negro slavery, and to the African trade, among the people of [Pennsylvania], occasioned this new prospect of obtaining a sugar, not made by the unhappy blacks, to be particularly interesting to them."[36] Hipólito's immediate interest in acquiring information regarding the *acer sacharinum* presumably had little to do with the "prospect of obtaining a sugar not made by the unhappy blacks." But the presence of enslaved peoples of African descent in Philadelphia certainly influenced the literary world with which we know Hipólito was familiar, which included notices of fugitive slaves in periodical journals such as the *Aurora* and the *Daily Advertiser.* Coxe's belief that knowledge was diffused "through the channels of . . . numerous gazettes" was a theme to which Hipólito referred frequently in later years, but we do not know whether the Quakers' antislavery discourse ultimately contributed to his later views about Portugal's role in the Atlantic slave trade. We do know, however, that he read this section of Coxe's account, and that he was aware of the arguments made in favor of agricultural products that did not rely predominantly on the forced labor of "unhappy blacks."

This reading of Coxe's *View of the United States* exemplifies another task Hipólito was charged with carrying out in Philadelphia, in addition to socializing and making personal contacts: reading and reporting on the most recent publications related to North American agriculture and industry. Scattered among his journal entries are references to a wide range of published texts, some of which Hipólito shipped back to Lisbon alongside crates of seeds and other exotic specimens. One shipment Hipólito sent to Portugal, for example, included a collection of gazettes (the *Aurora,* a periodical he described as the "most well-run paper of the opposition party," and the *Gazette of the United States,* which he called "a journal of the government"); the *Observations on the Commerce of Spain with Her Colonies,* an anonymous tract originally written by a Spaniard in Philadelphia; several "reports" to Congress, which Hipólito described as "very interesting"; and two texts by Benjamin Smith Barton, *Fragments of the Natural History of Pennsylvania* (1799) and *New Views of the Origin of the Tribes and Nations of America* (1797).[37]

Many of these books and periodicals, in fact, had been provided to

Hipólito by his North American botanical contacts. William Hamilton gave Hipólito a short book entitled *Letters to Sir Joseph Banks ... on the Subject of Cochineal Insects,* published in Madras in 1788, a text he received soon before he purportedly traveled to Mexico to examine cochineal in person. This collection of five letters from the physician James Anderson referred to the cochineal insect found upon the grasses of Madras, and included engravings of a Mexican cochineal plantation copied from Hans Sloane's *History of Jamaica,* with a textual citation indicating that the image was designated "for the use of Country Gentlemen who may be disposed to make Plantations, and are not in possession of that Work."[38] Hipólito relied on these texts to compose memoranda on the maple tree, the preparation of ginseng, and silkworms. Indeed, he seems to have become fascinated with silkworms following a discussion with Bartram, who attempted to convince him of the superiority of native silkworms over European varieties; Hipólito concluded from this discussion "that we must stimulate the culture of silkworms in Brazil."[39] He also had some peculiar suggestions of his own. At one point, he recommended sending American buffalo to mate with Portuguese cows, which he believed would produce an "extremely strong race extremely well suited for agricultural work."

The cosmopolitan nature of early republican Philadelphia thus provided a fertile field within which Hipólito da Costa was able to collect information from a range of local sources. From John Bartram and Tench Coxe to William Hamilton and Humphry Marshall, Hipólito took advantage of his social contacts in order to further his own knowledge regarding productive species that could serve Sousa Coutinho's broader economic goals.[40] But well into his stay in North America, Hipólito had been unable to acquire one of the most coveted specimens: Veracruz cochineal. And the personal contacts he had made in North America had not yet provided a convenient conduit. So, at least according to the report he composed to Sousa Coutinho, Hipólito took it upon himself to leave the United States and to travel surreptitiously to a region that was still under Spanish colonial rule: Mexico.[41]

In his mission to procure cochineal, Hipólito's original intent was to contact the Spanish ambassador in Philadelphia to procure a passport for safe transit through the ports of the Spanish Caribbean. Believing that there was no direct connection between Philadelphia and Mexico,

Hipólito thought it would be necessary to pass through Havana, but "without the plant and the insect being recognized" by Spanish authorities, who prohibited such transfers under great penalties. Hipólito suggested that he go "disguised, changing my name and transforming myself into a Spaniard, and putting myself on board a ship with any old occupation." This may have been a reaction to the Spanish minister's decision that he would not provide a passport for travel to Havana for anyone who was not a Spaniard, upon explicit instructions from Madrid. These imperial rivalries—and the likelihood that the Spanish suspected Hipólito of being a spy—required him to change his route, rather than his clothes and accent, in order to accomplish the mandate he had been called on to carry out.

His modified itinerary to reach Mexico meant sailing aboard an American merchant vessel, a journey of which there is no concrete record. In his final report to Sousa Coutinho, he claims to have traveled secretly to a place on the Gulf of Mexico near Veracruz called "Puerto Falso." According to advertisements in various early American periodicals such as the *Daily Advertiser,* there was an active trade between New York and Veracruz at this time and the cargo often contained cochineal, among other commodities to be sold on the American market. Once arrived in Mexico, Hipólito set out to accomplish his mission by going overland in search of the insect cultivation sites: "In fourteen days that the ship stayed there, I went into the interior of the countryside to some plantations where they cultivate cochineal, in order to collect as much information as possible in the brief time that I had."[42] Hipólito apparently succeeded in transporting the cacti and *coccus* (the cochineal insect) back to Philadelphia using three large crates, inside which he placed glass plates to cover the insects. The guards on board ship, understandably thinking Hipólito eccentric, considered his cargo as "something of a mere curiosity" and did not interfere with what would have been considered contraband goods. The greater challenge, however, was getting such fragile specimens to Brazil, since Portuguese Crown policy forbade direct commerce with Brazilian ports that did not first pass through Lisbon. In theory, taking cochineal to Brazil would have involved sending specimens from Veracruz to Philadelphia, from Philadelphia or New York to Lisbon, and then from Lisbon back to Brazil, their ultimate destination. Hipólito posited that it would be "impossible that after so many journeys the insect would still be alive."[43] And, indeed, his experience bore this out—or so he claimed. Having managed to get both the cactus and the insects back from Mexico to Philadelphia, he was nevertheless forced to write to the Portuguese minister that a cold spell during three days in November caused the death of the small insects, as well as of several breadfruit trees that he had received from Wiles in Jamaica.

In the wake of his reported visit to the Mexican plantations, Hipólito made the intriguing suggestion to Sousa Coutinho that the Crown consider opening Brazilian ports to North American commerce, precisely in order to facilitate the circulation of natural products that required a direct trade route to ensure their survival. "I have no doubt," he wrote, "that it would be possible to obtain [insects] again from Mexico, or at least the plant, as long as we have made arrangements in advance to conduct them [directly] to Brazil."[44] And there is some evidence that Sousa Coutinho attempted to carry through with Hipólito's suggestion. In a letter of February 1800, Dom Rodrigo asked whether the intendant-general of police might find an owner of a Portuguese ship who would be willing—for a "comfortable" price—to carry plants from Philadelphia to Rio de Janeiro, although further details of Sousa Coutinho's inquiry are not available.[45] Hipólito's insistence on seeing Brazil as an equal trading partner with other American and European nations, however, foreshadows his later writings, in which he would argue for a constitutional monarchy shared by Portugal and Brazil on equal terms.

The interest in hemispheric interchange extended as well to Hipólito's observations regarding the North American whaling industry, a sphere of commercial activity that was not listed in his formal instructions but one that appears to have become an important area of interest during his mission. Hipólito wrote that it would take no more than two years for Portugal to outstrip the United States in the capture of whales, although the United States was already clearly a leader in this industry: "My plan would be to invite a number of [North] American fishing families, principally those from Nantuket [*sic*], have them establish themselves in two different places in Brazil, add some Portuguese sailors, and connect them to the business dealers of the country."[46]

Hipólito's suggestion to recruit Americans to move to Brazil in order to establish and run a whaling industry alongside Portuguese mariners speaks once again to the possibility of activating Atlantic connections along a North–South axis.⁴⁷ In his final report to Sousa Coutinho, noting that the Americans had attempted to profit from the collapse of the Dutch fishing trade by supplying Europe with whale oil and other whale products caught in part off the coast of Brazil, Hipólito argued that Portugal could easily overtake the Americans in whaling. Portuguese sailors received lower wages, and they would have easier access to Brazilian waters and Brazilian ports, where ship repairs could be made and other needs fulfilled. There is no evidence that such a scheme was ever attempted. But the idea that Portugal's problems could be mitigated or resolved by encouraging migration of skilled workers to Brazil was a theme to which Hipólito would return, especially when he realized that attracting American and European workers might move the Portuguese monarchy closer to abolishing one of its most shameful practices: the forced transit and enslavement of African laborers.

Labor migration was one way in which, Hipólito believed, Brazilian society could be improved from without; he also recognized the central role that a free press would play in encouraging positive change from within. Upon his arrival in Philadelphia, he had marveled at the printed announcements hanging on the walls of the post office, recognizing that "because the press is free, everything is printed, which facilitates [communication]."⁴⁸ He also remarked on the role of print in the political process, referring during his stay in New York to the "printed pamphlets that circulated in order to deteriorate the character of those who were up for election, who in turn printed other [pamphlets] to defend themselves." He went on to say that "the gazettes were filled with the same [material]."⁴⁹ Throughout his North American sojourn, in fact, he seems to have stayed actively interested in American periodical literature, and his journal was filled with frequent references to this or that gazette. On January 24, 1799, he made his initial subscription to the *Aurora,* and he resubscribed at regular intervals during his stay. He apparently was also a habitual reader of the *Medical Repository,* chemistry professor Samuel Mitchill's magazine, to which he contributed an article on the effluvia of Lisbon.⁵⁰ In Boston, he purchased a printed description of the city and its environs, choosing to annotate the printed text rather than describing the city from scratch. Although he was far more explicit about the positive role of the free press during his exile in London, his numerous observations clearly show that it was in the nascent

United States that he first recognized the overwhelming importance of print in fostering communal identity within a new nation. This recognition of the centrality of print would mark his career in profound ways, first in Lisbon, then in London.

After Philadelphia:
A Journey from Imprisonment to Exile

When Hipólito returned to Lisbon sometime in the fall of 1800, he was recruited by Sousa Coutinho to work as a literary director at the Casa Literária do Arco do Cego. In the course of its two-year existence, the Lisbon printing house founded in 1799 produced a host of texts related to natural history, economics, and politics. This brief chapter in Hipólito's career solidified his nascent interest in the use of print to communicate knowledge across imperial boundaries and illustrates another way in which Hipólito himself served as a conduit for transporting ideas between the Americas and Europe—in this case through the translation of texts that had originally been published in languages other than Portuguese.

The Arco do Cego, with which Hipólito became deeply involved, was the brainchild of naturalist Frei José Mariano da Conceição Veloso (1742–1811), a native of Minas Gerais who was also a member of the Capuchin order. Following over a decade spent in Rio de Janeiro collecting plants at the behest of viceroy Luís de Vasconcellos, Conceição Veloso had come to Lisbon in the 1790s to participate with Vandelli in a project that sought to create a "Natural History of the [Portuguese] Colonies."[51] Conceição Veloso's most significant work, the *Fazendeiro do Brazil* (1798–1806), was a ten-volume agrarian manual meant to provide instruction to farmers and naturalists on both sides of the ocean; it was perhaps the most important Portuguese treatise on agronomy in the early nineteenth century. While he was compiling materials for this text, before Hipólito's journey to the United States, Conceição Veloso provided Hipólito with information relating to American species and specimens. Indeed, the *Fazendeiro do Brazil* had chapters on both the *acer saccharinum* (sugar maple) and cochineal. In his chapter on the tree, Conceição Veloso wrote that the announcement of a sugar tree (*árvore assucareira*) "will not be disagreeable to our readers in Brazil . . . which should make up for the lack of sugar canes and sugar itself caused by repeated frosts."[52] The exchange of information between Hipólito, then a recent graduate of Coimbra, and Conceição Veloso, a more mature member of Sousa Coutinho's inner circle, represents an important generational moment and an unwritten chapter in the pan-Atlantic circulation of ideas and cultural practices related to natural history.[53]

Just as for Conceição Veloso, the translation and publication of texts became for Hipólito activities through which he was able to link different sites and disciplines within the Atlantic world. Upon his return from Philadelphia, and after assuming a position as one of the Arco do Cego's literary directors, he translated several books, including Benjamin Smith Barton's treatise on goiter, *Memória sobre a bronchocele, ou papo da América septentrional* (1801); the *História breve e authentica do Banco de Inglaterra* (1801), a text originally written by Thomas Fortune; and a collection of essays by Benjamin Thompson, published in 1801 as *Ensayos politicos, economicos, e philosophicos.* The Arco do Cego also published two of Hipólito's own texts, the *Descripção da arvore assucareira, e da sua utilidade e cultura* (1800) and the *Descripção de huma maquina para tocar a bomba a bordo dos navios sem o trabalho de homens* (1800), dedicated to the Royal Portuguese Navy. These works by Hipólito served the broader aim of the Arco do Cego, which was to produce texts that would contribute to Sousa Coutinho's political and economic project (Figure 8.2).[54]

But Hipólito's activities as a Freemason earned him a different fate: three years as a prisoner in the secret jails of the Lisbon Inquisition. He was accused of dubious crimes and held in solitary confinement, despite his protests that neither in Portugal (where he was incarcerated) nor in the United States (where he had been accepted into a Masonic lodge) was membership in such a society held to be a criminal act. Fortunately for him, he was able to escape under circumstances that remained unclear to the Inquisition guards who reported his flight to the authorities on April 19, 1805.[55] After his escape from the Inquisition's clutches, likely with the assistance of the Duke of Sussex—the sixth son of George III and an active Freemason—Hipólito immigrated to England, where his service to the Portuguese communities on both sides of the Atlantic increased in scope and visibility. He no longer participated directly in projects supported by the Crown, either within Portugal or

Figure 8.2 Frontispiece, *Hymnus Tabaci*. Raphaele Thori's 1625 Leiden edition of the *Hymnus Tabaci* was reprinted at the Arco do Cego in 1800, as were numerous editions of agronomical texts that were meant to effect Sousa Coutinho's reformist vision of the Portuguese and Brazilian economies. Hipólito's contributions while working at the Arco do Cego fit well within the utilitarian and pragmatic emphasis of Sousa Coutinho's program. Reproduced courtesy of the John Carter Brown Library at Brown University.

outside its boundaries, but his experience as a literary director for the Arco do Cego would enable him to use his literary and typographical skills in a new and ultimately more influential undertaking: the *Correio Braziliense*. Within the pages of that journal, he maintained a strong sense of patriotic duty toward the Portuguese nation, but insisted that Brazil be considered an equal partner.

The consistent support for a unified Portuguese and Brazilian monarchy was guided by Hipólito's belief that responsibility should be vested in the individual subject rather than in a broader political organization. For Hipólito, the fate of the Portuguese Empire depended entirely on the activities of its citizens, who were obliged to contribute in whatever way they could to the advancement of the nation. "A human being's first duty in society is to be useful to that society," Hipólito wrote in the inaugural issue of the *Correio Braziliense* in June 1808, "[and] the light that an individual spreads [as a useful member of society] leads those whom ignorance has ensnared in the labyrinth of apathy, ineptitude, and error out from the darkness."[56] Hipólito believed that his nation *(nação)* was shared by all Portuguese, whereas his homeland (his "pátria") was more narrowly conceived as the place where he was born, a sentiment expressed eloquently by his fellow Coimbra graduate José Joaquim de Cunha de Azeredo Coutinho. Writing of the "riches that the land in which I was born [Brazil] possesses and is capable of [possessing]," Azeredo Coutinho considered himself a "blind man impassioned by his homeland *(pátria),*" even though he was willing to reveal those features of his native land "to my sovereign and to my nation *(nação).*"[57] This formula ultimately produced what one scholar has called "an imperial idea, Luso-Brazilian in inspiration, which moved beyond nationalism to a broader imperial solution, and sought to defuse metropolitan-colonial tensions."[58] Hipólito believed that citizens could serve this imperial effort and create utility for the *nação* through print; from 1808 forward, Hipólito's journal served both symbolically and literally as the vehicle to convey those ideas on the printed page.

The 1808 arrival of a printing press in Rio de Janeiro—part of the cargo that the Portuguese royal family brought with them from Lisbon as they escaped from Napoleon's advancing armies—also ushered in a new era of intra-imperial communication, a phenomenon that some scholars have seen as the initial phase of a distinctively Brazilian En-

lightenment.[59] Indeed, with the eventual proclamation of a free press
in 1820, the raison d'être of the *Correio Braziliense* diminished considerably, since its hallmark was the author's ability to write freely and
openly about topics that otherwise would have been censured. But
by the time a free Brazilian press was proclaimed, the influence of
Hipólito's widely circulating London journal and its discussion of topics that would have been anathema under a closed, monarchical regime
had already made censorship unthinkable—or at least untenable.[60] In
the *Correio Braziliense*, Hipólito had frequently and strenuously asserted that a vibrant polity would prevail only if truth were allowed to
flourish, for "truth could never be harmful to human society." Criti-
cizing the despotic nature of regimes that governed through lies and
illusions, he explained that "deception requires additional deceit to sustain it, and a system based upon governing populations through illusions always brings along with it a series of disgraces, of which the pages
of history provide us with abundant examples."[61]

A free press was crucial in this process, and Hipólito's experience in
England clearly played a central role in his understanding of its importance. "Having become used to seeing people in England publicly discuss the measures of the Government," Hipólito wrote only three years
after arriving in London, "and recognizing the advantages that result
from this process in favor of the Nation, it makes it difficult to accept
the principle of extreme submission to the opinions of the Government."[62] Contestation of the policies of the governing body, whether
embodied in a parliamentary system or a constitutional monarchy,
would ensure that arbitrary and despotic actions were checked through
the uninhibited commerce of ideas: "where there is not freedom to
speak and write," wrote Hipólito, nature provided few simple remedies
"to fix the errors of Government."[63]

A free press was certainly one of the ideas that Hipólito's experiences
in England and North America encouraged him to support. But he also
sought to incorporate the local councils *(câmaras municipais)* into the
full functioning of the government in order to reduce the possibility of
arbitrary rule by the sovereign. He believed that the commercial monopoly of Portugal's allies should be broken, and that agriculture should
be developed as a source for newfound wealth. He argued that Portugal
should recruit skilled laborers, particularly Europeans, to immigrate to

Brazil, thus reducing Portugal's dependence on the importation of African labor. And, finally, Hipólito wished to encourage the establishment of a university in Brazil, as well as schools to instruct the Brazilian nation in basic skills. All of these things, Hipólito wrote, comprised "the measures which we consider essential in developing a national character," and he toiled toward those ends during the fourteen years he dedicated to the *Correio Braziliense*.[64]

Vigorously advocating the free circulation of printed matter, Hipólito also became a staunch advocate for the free circulation of labor, an idea that formed the basis for his vocal support of the abolition of the slave trade in the South Atlantic. After the passage of an ineffectual law against the trade in 1831, Brazil finally acceded to British pressure to end its involvement in slave trafficking once and for all in 1850, with the ratification of an act that required vessels departing from Africa to declare openly that they were not involved in the trade and that established admiralty courts to try those who flouted this law (slavery itself would not be abolished in Brazil until 1888).[65] But there were already movements afoot by the early nineteenth century to suppress the trade, largely the result of English pressure after the 1807 passage of the Abolition of the Slave Trade Act.[66]

Hipólito's own contributions to this effort came in two forms: the publication in Portuguese of official documents from Britain that were related to the "illicit traffic in slaves" and several articles of his own revealing the pernicious effects of the slave trade on the conscience of the Brazilian nation. "It is a contradiction," Hipólito exclaimed in his most explicit article relating to the issue, "to want a nation to be free, and if it manages to be [free], to proclaim everywhere and at all times how free it is, and [at the same time] to maintain slavery within [that nation], that is, the very custom that is directly opposed to freedom." Hipólito did not, however, advocate the immediate abolition of the trade, but rather a "gradual and prudent extinction" which, he argued, would be easier to accomplish, because slavery was inextricably "linked to the actual system of society as it is presently constituted" and therefore potentially precarious to dismantle with one swift blow.[67] But he did ally his interest in abolition with broader economic and social issues, making it clear that the continuation of slavery would bring only further woes upon a society already burdened by its political, economic, and ethical contradictions. And, in the final pages of the *Correio Braziliense,* published in December 1822, he wrote that, "since the American revolutions are founded on principles of liberty, the preservation of slavery is obviously incompatible [with such principles]."[68] Liberal principles, and not only principles related to political independence, would lead in Hipólito's vision to the abolition of the slave trade as merely "a preliminary step toward the total annihilation of slavery."[69] The promotion of his anti-slavery platform through journalism, and its impact in the broader context of the Luso-Brazilian world of print, may be traced further in the Portuguese-language periodicals that circulated in London and across the Atlantic during this period.

The extraordinary range of Hipólito's intersecting trajectories—from the traversal of imperial spaces in pursuit of cochineal and cetaceans to the advocacy of a free press and the free circulation of labor in Brazil—underlines the importance of following the eclectic itineraries of individuals as they moved against the grain of common or entrenched currents within an Atlantic system.[70] Although the publication of Hipólito's ideas and theories did not always lead to their direct implementation, his individual experiences were broadcast to a broad audience, despite the intransigent strategies of Portuguese censorship still in place early in the nineteenth century. In Hipólito's thought, exigencies of the natural historical world influenced schemes to open Brazilian ports to North American commerce, while projects to encourage whaling and maple tree cultivation would have the collateral effect of diminishing the Portuguese monarchy's dependence on the Atlantic slave trade. The interconnected nature of these examples demonstrates that only an approach that integrates such disparate threads is capable of portraying the multiform and dynamic fabric linking one side of an ocean to the other.

Conclusion: A Brazilian Courier

This essay has attempted to show several Atlantic contexts that were crucial for the incubation of Hipólito da Costa's political and natural historical ideas. Prior to publishing the *Correio Braziliense* in London, Hipólito had already crisscrossed the Atlantic on multiple occasions and in several directions. He had traveled from Porto Alegre in southern Brazil to pursue his studies in Coimbra, the seat of a newly reformed

Portuguese university. He returned to the Americas to take up residence in Philadelphia, capital of a recently independent United States, and he traveled throughout North America and possibly to Mexico to visit a Spanish colonial city in the Caribbean renowned for a dye-producing insect that flourished nearby. He later returned to Lisbon, the seat of a European empire that would soon be abandoned by its own monarch, who opted for an extended exile across the Atlantic. And although he never left England after his arrival there in 1805, his monthly periodical journal traveled in his stead, reaching provinces and captaincies in Portuguese America that Hipólito himself would never live to see. Hipólito's dizzying itinerary thus speaks to a less common set of Atlantic connections and associations than is usually contemplated by historians of the Atlantic system. If one is to "sound" the inner workings of the Atlantic world at the dawn of the modern era, Hipólito's career has much to commend it. The interconnecting phases of Hipólito's life analyzed in this essay—from Coimbra to Philadelphia to Lisbon to London—help to explain why Hipólito ultimately became something of a renegade: originally a faithful servant in the inner sanctum of the monarch's service, but increasingly independent from those very imperial ministers who carefully sought to control his comings and goings on the Atlantic stage.

Hipólito's induction into Freemasonry also clearly transformed his personal and professional trajectory, yielding ripple effects when his opinions and experiences were broadcast widely through his London journal.[71] But if the *Correio Braziliense* represented the culmination of his career, the earliest phases of Hipólito's service to the empire deserve equal weight. In the final issue of the journal, in December 1822, Hipólito confirmed that his late eighteenth-century experiences in the nascent United States had molded his ideological interests both politically and metaphorically: "For many years, the United States of America has formed a nation that is conspicuous for its power, and while for many other reasons it may not deserve consideration, its having given the rest of America an idea of its own independence is alone sufficient [for praise]."[72]

For Hipólito, this "idea" of independence forged during the period he spent in North America contributed strongly to his overall trajectory. Having witnessed firsthand the advantages of the free circulation of ideas during a period of his *own* independence at the age of 25, he was able to transform these early impressions into an ideology of political expression that formed the base of his broader critique of Portuguese culture and empire in the first two decades of the nineteenth century. Although he only begrudgingly accepted the idea of an independent Brazilian republic at the end of his life, and remained committed to monarchical government both in theory and in practice, his vision of a Brazilian state unencumbered by some of Portugal's most burdensome traditions was deeply indebted to those earliest moments along the icy riverways of Philadelphia, which in turn extended to the ports of the Caribbean, the Arco do Cego in Lisbon, and ultimately to another printing house on London's Paternoster Row.

Colonial subjects such as Hipólito have historically been portrayed as regional informants to broader metropolitan efforts rather than as cosmopolitan travelers and thinkers in their own right. That is, the emphasis placed on the local nature of their education and contacts has tended to confirm an eighteenth-century metropolitan prejudice that saw colonial agents—be they botanists, astronomers, or statesmen—as providing local material to the imperial center, often unidirectionally. In addition, a nationalist historiography in many Latin American countries has frequently insisted on a stark division between metropolitan and colonial identities, a rift that is belied by the crossings and interconnections omnipresent in the colonial world. Those tendencies seem to have discouraged modern scholars from seeing the Enlightenment as an *itinerant* enterprise, a project for which movement and mobility were constitutive elements. It is thus insufficient merely to study the local origins of ideas, in Latin America or elsewhere; instead, we must turn to examine their itinerant nature across broader geographical spaces.[73]

These connected histories of Hipólito's Atlantic crossings and the circulation of his ideas stress the role of unique individuals, historical contingency, and highly particular local contexts in forging connections between transoceanic spaces. This essay has sought to emphasize the mobile, cross-cultural characteristics of the pursuit of knowledge, features that are often obscured when examined from a limited geographical or linguistic point of view. An Atlantic perspective focuses one's attention on the portable character of ideas: it encourages one to examine the contacts between peoples of different origins, allegiances, and creeds, and it leads to understanding cultural exchange in a trans-imperial frame, since rarely did knowledge flow through networks that were limited to a single empire in isolation. In short, it seeks to breathe life into the itineraries of those less visible bearers of ideas: unheralded couriers of sociocultural practices whose trails have been hidden from our view.

An Atlantic account of Hipólito's career—with attention paid to local contexts and inter-imperial contacts—helps us to see currents that move beyond the simple flows from center to periphery, entrepôt back to metropole, or colony to nation. Whether in Rodrigo de Sousa Coutinho's sending one of his Coimbra-trained agents to Philadelphia, or Hipólito's suggestion that the Crown encourage North American whalers to settle in Brazil, or even Hipólito's early interest in opening Brazilian ports to North American products, one finds innovative ideas that pointed toward a reformulation of natural, political, and geopolitical relations. Later in his career, Hipólito would argue that the new political constellation in the Americas following the American Revolution had transformed power dynamics in the Old World as well: "Here in the new hemisphere is a power that is unconquerable for European forces."[74] But it is also likely that Hipólito believed such power could be vested in yet another of America's emerging nations, a country whose colonial past had been tightly bound to Portugal's metropolitan interests but whose political maturity was only beginning to bear and profit from its own fruit. Hipólito's message of political empowerment for Brazil was to gain adherents on both sides of the Atlantic, even though the messenger himself would never again see the land whose political fate he had done so much to guide.

9

Scientific Exchange in the Eighteenth-Century Atlantic World

LONDA SCHIEBINGER

Pierre-Louis Moreau de Maupertuis, president of the Königliche Akademie der Wissenschaften zu Berlin, surely overstated his case when he claimed in 1752, "It is quite by accident and only from savage nations that we owe our knowledge of specifics [medicines]; we owe not one to the science of the physicians."[1] Maupertuis's statement nevertheless highlights how much Europeans profited from gathering medicines, plants, animals, minerals, and peoples from around the globe. Historians and theorists of colonialism have developed various models for understanding colonial science (of which medicine is a part). Traditionally, these models have placed Europe at the epicenter of knowledge making—Europe is viewed as the gravitational metropole sucking in goods, knowledge, and profits from distant peripheries. According to this paradigm, knowledge exchange in the eighteenth century was empire-based with metropolitan hubs serving as repositories and clearinghouses—what Bruno Latour has called "centres of calculation."[2] But this is only part of the picture. Shifting our perspective from a colonial, periphery-metropole model to an Atlantic world model brings to light more complex understandings of knowledge exchange, at least between the Old World and the New.

This essay brings to light the knowledge and practices of three groups: Amerindians—the peripatetic Arawaks, Tainos, and Caribs, who moved much knowledge and many plants from place to place in the Caribbean basin; African slaves—both males and females—who transported African flora and knowledge of its uses with them to the West Indies; and Europeans—mostly males—who actively bioprospected in both Europe and the West Indies for useful and profitable cures. While in the past historians have focused on European colonial science, here I highlight—to the extent possible—the mixing and hybridization, collecting, sorting, and extinctions of knowledges among the three groups, attempting to understand the contributions of each to what we today call tropical medicine. Because of their geographical location, Amerindians and Africans already knew something about tropical medicine when they encountered Europeans in the West Indies. Europeans, in contrast, suffered extraordinary morbidity and mortality in the Torrid Zone and turned to others for their very survival.

With all eighteenth-century history we face the problem of imperfect sources removed from us by several centuries. Historical knowledge of eighteenth-century scientific exchange is no exception. Europeans have been the focus of colonial science and medicine because they wrote extensively about it (and in the languages that U.S. and European historians commonly read). Amerindians and African slaves, in contrast, left no written documents detailing their use of plants and medicines. Hence, our access to their practices is filtered through European texts and, although we can glean much from such sources, many of the African and Amerindian naturalists active in these areas remain faceless and nameless—often referred to as a "slave doctor," a "native," and the like. Nonetheless we can know something about scientific exchange in the Atlantic world of the eighteenth century.

This essay examines Amerindian, African slave, and European medical practices as they mixed in that cauldron of cultural upheaval known as the West Indies. The West Indies is a fascinating setting for this study because in the eighteenth century a robust mixing of and competition among the scientific traditions of Amerindian, African, and European—and increasingly, of their Creole descendants—still existed. I will compare practices in the French and British West Indies, especially Saint-Domingue (the most profitable Caribbean colony in this period) and the neighboring island of Jamaica (a prime British holding) across the whole of the eighteenth century. The first section of the essay focuses on Amerindian knowledge as it developed in the West Indies and was transmitted to Europeans. The next several sections explore slave medicine, again looking at how Europeans collected and evaluated this information (because that is what we can know). Here I bring to light European experiments with African medical techniques. Throughout these sections it is important to emphasize that European practices in the Caribbean mirrored those in Europe. Europeans mobilized similar bioprospecting techniques among the lower classes in Europe and among diverse populations in the West Indies. They deployed similar regimes of medical testing and, though they collected much new empirical data, they often filtered it through the conceptual grids that guided their practices at home.

The essay's final section theorizes the circulation of scientific knowledge in the Atlantic world. To a large extent, knowledge in the Atlantic world circulated within empires—from Africa to West Indian colonies to metropoles and back again. This is surprising, given that many physicians seeking cures for tropical disease in Jamaica, for example, had more in common with physicians in Saint-Domingue than with their colleagues back in Europe. But, as we shall see, scientific exchange in the Atlantic world also went well beyond limits of empire. On the ground in the West Indies it was rich and multicentered. The West Indies was not just a colonial periphery supplying profitable drugs and knowledge of their use to the metropole, but itself fertile ground for scientific innovation. Here we investigate how African and Amerindian cures entered this economy of knowledge, how colonials often insisted upon and developed local knowledge economies, and how knowledge leaked through increasingly impermeable national borders.

Amerindian Knowledge

Before the onset of rampant racism in the nineteenth century, many Europeans valued the knowledge of indigenous Americans, Africans, and peoples of India and the East Indies. Richard Drayton has argued with respect to eighteenth-century England that racist tendencies were tempered by a recognition that inhabitants in the colonies—in the West Indies, Amerindian, transported African, or African or European Creoles—often held knowledge worth recruiting. This was also true in earlier centuries: Harold Cook has discussed how seventeenth-century Dutch physicians in Java valued local medical information, and Richard

Grove has written that the *Hortus Indicus Malabaricus* (1678–1704) pre-pared by Hendrik Adriaan van Reede tot Drakenstein, the East Indies Company governor in Malabar, was "a profoundly indigenous text," a compilation of South Asian botany "without equal." One might argue that, with respect to natural history, an epistemological shift took place over the course of the sixteenth and seventeenth centuries away from Europeans' reliance on the "summa of ancient wisdom" (Dioscorides, Pliny, Galen) toward their valuing (or at least appreciating) the authority of native peoples encountered through global expansion. European phy-sicians no longer defined their task as simply verifying the effectiveness of ancient medicines (or merely identifying local substitutes); instead, they took as their starting point for empirical investigation the drugs, dyes, and foodstuffs suggested to them by native "informants."[3]

Who were the local informants in the West Indies to whom Europe-ans turned for information concerning useful foods and medicines? When Christopher Columbus arrived in Hispaniola in 1492, the island was densely populated by the Tainos. The earliest Spanish and subsequent Dutch, French, and British documents, as well as archeological finds, show uniformity among plants and their uses throughout the Caribbean basin. This floral uniformity might have been created by nature—the winds, currents, and bird bellies that distribute seeds throughout an eco-logical niche. Yet the similar uses that Amerindians made of plants for food, medicine, shelter, rituals, household technologies (in the form of pottery), and trade goods also suggest that much knowledge migrated with the Saladoid peoples, the forebears of the Tainos. These peoples es-tablished gardens (called by Tainos *conucos*) for the cultivation of their most prized foodstuffs and medicinal herbs. When the Spanish arrived, physicians sometimes enjoyed especially close ties with the descendents of these migrating Amerindian naturalists. Antonio de Villasante, for ex-ample, learned the virtues of plants in Hispaniola from his Christianized wife, Catalina de Ayahibx, a Taino chief (or *cacica*).[4]

By the sixteenth century, Taino populations in the Caribbean had been decimated by conquest and disease. The Caribs had run the Arawaks out of the Lesser Antilles; the Spanish had crushed both peoples. A 1660 peace agreement among the English, the French, and the Spanish exiled the remaining warring Caribs to the islands of Saint Vincent and Dominica. A report issued in 1687 found only 111 Caribs living in

Martinique. The larger islands such as Jamaica or Hispaniola, heavily inhabited by Europeans and Africans, were left with perhaps even smaller
populations of Amerindians.[5]

European physicians nonetheless gleaned what information they could
from the few survivors. Their interest in Amerindian cures was not in
the service of value-free science: much European bioprospecting in the
eighteenth century was fueled, as it is today, by the vast fortunes to be
made. We should remember that chocolate was first popularized in England as a medicine—good for stomach ailments and consumption—by
Sir Hans Sloane. Edward Long, Sloane's compatriot in Jamaica seventy
years later, reminded his readers that those men and women who immigrated to the West Indies did so not for the purpose of compiling natural
histories, but "avowedly for the purpose of accumulating money."[6] The
most pressing motivation for investigating tropical medicines, however,
was to keep European troops, planters, and eventually slaves alive in the
colonies. Colonial botany was crucial to Europe's successful control of
tropical areas, where voyagers from temperate zones became sick and
died in alarming numbers.

Jean-Baptiste-René Pouppé-Desportes, a French royal physician in
Cap-Français, Saint-Domingue, from 1732 until his death in 1748, made
an elaborate study of what he called Carib medicines. In efforts to increase his success in patient treatment, he supplemented his mainstay of
remedies sent from the Hôpital de la Charité in Paris (often old and ruined by transport) with local "Carib simples." Because the first Europeans who came to the Americas, Pouppé-Desportes wrote, were afflicted
by illnesses completely unknown to them, it was necessary to employ
remedies used by "the naturals of the country whom one calls savages."
The third volume of his *Histoire des maladies de Saint Domingue* presented what he called "an American pharmacopoeia," offering an extended list of Carib remedies used to cure disease. Europeans had begun
producing *pharmacopoeia*, official compendia of medicinal drugs for
each major city, in the sixteenth century in an effort to secure uniformity
in remedies. Pouppé-Desportes's *pharmacopoeia* is one of the first to
record Amerindian remedies. As was typical of these works, he cross-
referenced plant names in Latin, French, and the vernacular Carib.[7]

Attitudes among Europeans toward Amerindian knowledge across
the Caribbean, of course, were not uniform. The French royal botanist

Pierre Barrère, working in Cayenne along the coast of Guiana from 1722 to 1725, did not think much of native cures. The good health the Indians (he named twenty-four peoples living there) enjoyed, he claimed, resulted from their careful diet, frequent bathing, and moderate indulgence in pleasure. In a word, he wrote, "our Indians are completely ignorant of how to compound medicines. The few remedies they know they have learned from the Portuguese and other Europeans."[8] He nonetheless recorded several Amerindian plant names and their medical uses.

Even in this era when many Europeans valued the knowledge of Amerindian naturalists, mythologies of drug discoveries suggested that knowledge traveled up an anthropo- and Euro-centric Chain of Being, from animals (with their instinctive cures), to Amerindians, to the Spanish and, according to Charles-Marie de La Condamine, ultimately to the French. La Condamine, who traveled extensively in present-day Ecuador and Peru, recounted the ancient legend that South American lions suffering from fevers found relief by chewing the bark of the *cinchona* tree. Observing its curative powers, the Indians, too, began treating malaria and other "quartan" (recurring) fevers with the bark. The Spanish then learned of the cure from the Indians, and the French, the self-appointed keepers of universal knowledge in the age of enlightenment, learned of it from the Spanish.[9]

A number of eighteenth-century historians of medicine subscribed to the notion that brute animals were the first discoverers of many beneficial cures. Pouppé-Desportes offered two further examples in this genre—one from Martinique and another from Saint-Domingue. In the first, a potent antidote to snake bite had been discovered by the lowly grass snake. "Unhappy enough to live on the serpent-infested island of Martinique," wrote Desportes, the snake learned to employ a certain herb when attacked by a venomous serpent. The effect was so wonderful that the natives called the plant *herbe à serpent,* or snake herb. In similar fashion, Amerindian naturalists had discovered the excellent qualities of the "sugar tree" by observing wild pigs shredding the tree's bark with their tusks when hurt and rubbing their injuries with its sap. For this reason the sap was called "wild pig balm." As Edward Long in Jamaica put it, "brutes are botanists by instinct." He reasoned that humans, too, in their "rude state" possessed a similar instinct to recognize herbs, balms, and salves necessary for their preservation. Robert James in London concurred and, like Maupertuis, disparaged European physicians for their ineffectualness in developing lifesaving cures. Drugs, he wrote, are discovered by "savages" by a "natural instinct perceivable both in man and beast," or by "madmen" (by whom he meant the alchemists) who, from time to time, "blunder" upon some cure by accident.[10]

Whatever their attitudes may have been, Europeans' opportunities to learn from Amerindians declined precipitously. By the 1770s Nicolas Bourgeois complained that "of the prodigious multitude of natives of which [the Spanish chroniclers] speak, not a single of their descendants can be discovered whose origin has been conserved pure and without mixture." By the 1790s, a chronicler of the revolution in Saint-Domingue bemoaned the fact that no trace of a "single native" remained.[11]

African Knowledge

With the decline of indigenous populations, slave medicines took on an unexpected importance in the West Indies, even though in the first half of the eighteenth century Africans on the big sugar islands were no more native to the area than Europeans (at least 80 percent were born in Africa). Unlike Europeans, however, Africans knew tropical diseases, their preventions, and cures. The Scottish mercenary Lieutenant John Stedman living in Suriname, for example, worked alongside a number of African slaves. One old "Negro," named Caramaca, had given him the threefold secret of survival: never wear boots but instead harden your bare feet (which Stedman did by incessantly pacing the deck of his boat); discard the heavy European military jacket and dress as lightly as possible; and bathe twice a day by plunging into the river. Some of these directives were distressing to Europeans, especially the last, given their distaste for bathing. In contrast to his intimate relations with African populations in Suriname, Stedman had only vague trading relations with the Arawaks and Caribs—both groups having been driven inland into the mountainous areas far from Dutch settlements.[12]

Nicolas Bourgeois, a longtime resident of Saint-Domingue, was one of those Europeans who appreciated slave medicines. Considering health a matter of state importance, he eulogized the "marvelous cures" abounding in the islands and remarked that *les nègres* were "almost the only ones who know how to use them"; they had, he wrote, more knowledge of these cures than the whites *(les blancs)*. According to Bourgeois, slave doctors were remarkably skilled. "I could see immediately," he wrote, "that the negroes were more ingenious than we in the art of procuring health. . . . Our colony possesses an infinity of negroes and negresses [*negres & meme des negresses*] who practice medicine, and in whom many whites have much confidence. The most dangerous [plant] poisons can be transformed into the most salubrious remedies when prepared by a skilled hand; I have seen cures that very much surprised me." What most surprised Bourgeois was that the Africans rebuffed two mainstays of European medicine: bleeding and purging. "If left to themselves, the negroes do not bleed patients or administer enemas."[13]

It is impossible to know with precision how much African herbal knowledge was transferred into the New World by slaves; this is a topic that requires more research. Displaced Africans must have found familiar medicinal plants growing in the American tropics, and they must have discovered—through commerce with the Amerindians or their own trial and error—plants with virtues similar to those used back home. Bourgeois confirmed that there were many "doctors" [*médecins*] among the Africans who "brought their treatments from their own countries," but he did not discuss this point in detail.[14]

Confidence among whites in African naturalists' cures was at times so high that when Sir Henry Morgan, lieutenant governor of Jamaica, became dissatisfied with his physician Hans Sloane's treatment of his disease, he sent for a "black doctor." Late in the eighteenth century, Jamaicans still sought the cures of "Negro Doctors." James Knight wrote that "many secrets in the art of physick, may be obtained from the Negro Doctors, were proper methods taken, which I think is not below our physicians to enquire into, as it may be of great service to themselves, as well as mankind."[15]

Even as late as 1799, amid the chaos of the Haitian Revolution, French botanist Michel Descourtilz learned much about plants and their uses from a "mulatress." Well into the nineteenth century, French physicians praised women of African origin living in Saint-Domingue for their extensive knowledge of medicines. Initially suspicious, the mulatress told

Descourtilz nothing, but eventually, by wooing her with his drawings of the plants from the Artibonite Valley, "which she coveted," Descourtilz was able to obtain many recipes from her. These he "corrected" as he experimented with them. His efforts, he wrote, "were crowned with very satisfying results."[16]

Others in and around the Caribbean also valued slave cures. David de Nassy, a Jewish physician working in Suriname in the latter part of the eighteenth century, remarked that the "negroes" played a large role in the health of the colony, with their "herbs and claimed cures." But he also noted that their cures were "more valued among the Christians than among the Jews."[17]

Others were less convinced that Africans were adept healers. Although Sloane in Jamaica took care to collect what the Africans told him, he did not find their cures in any way "reasonable, or successful." What they knew, he wrote, they had learned from the Indians.[18] Edward Long found "Negro cures," as he called them, unhelpful. "Negroes," he charged, apply their herbs "randomly" and, like monkeys, receive their skill only from "their Creator, who has impartially provided all animals with means conducive to their preservation."[19]

Europeans, for the most part, prospected for African or Amerindian cures. We do, however, have an instance where peoples of African origin adopted European techniques. Mesmerism, which took Europe by storm in the eighteenth century, also became popular in Saint-Domingue, not only among plantation owners but also among people of color. Historian James McClellan has reported the case of the mulatto, Jérome, and his black assistant, Télémaque, who set up a business promoting mesmerism and magical treatments. Their activity ended when the local government outlawed the practice in 1786 and punished the men.[20]

Secrets

Europeans were often curious about Amerindian and slave medicines and eager to learn, but the indigenes and slaves were less eager to divulge this knowledge to their new masters. Along with miraculous cures came the silence of secrets. Nicolas Bourgeois in Saint-Domingue characteristically remarked that, though "the negroes treat themselves successfully in a large number of illnesses . . . most of them, especially the most skilled, guard the secret of their remedies." Physician Philippe Fermin confirmed that the "negroes and negresses in Suriname know the virtues of plants and offer cures that put to shame physicians coming from Europe . . . but," he continued, "I could never persuade them to instruct me."[21] James Grainger on Saint Christopher found a "maroon negro" who cured lepers using an ingenious remedy; but Grainger could not "discover the secret of his art."[22]

The guarding of secrets from colonial aggressors occurred worldwide and certainly throughout the Atlantic world. In his influential 1577 *Joyfull Newes out of the Newe Founde Worlde,* Nicolás Monardes told the story of a company of Spanish soldiers patrolling in Peru who were curious about bezoars, gastric concretions used at that time in Europe as antidotes to poison, scorpion stings, worms, melancholy, and plague. The soldiers inquired about the stones of "certain Indians" hired to serve them, but, because the Indians considered the Spanish their enemy, they refused to reveal their secrets. After a while, a 12-year-old Indian boy, sensing that the soldiers truly wished to know about these stones, showed them that they came from the "stomachs of beasts." Immediately, the boy was killed by his compatriots "for the advice that he gave." Little had changed a century later when Alonso de Ovalle, a Jesuit writing from Chile, reported that "here are many plants of great virtue in physic known only to the Indians called Machis, who . . . are their doctors. Yet they conceal these plants, particularly from the Spaniards. If they do reveal the knowledge of one or two of them, it is a great mark of their friendship." In eighteenth-century Peru, La Condamine commented that "the naturals," as he called the Incas, had guarded the secret of *cinchona* from the Spanish for some 140 years (some said for more than 200 years).[23]

Naturalists in the West Indies devised various methods for wresting secrets from unwilling informants. Bourgeois attempted to win slaves' confidence with friendship. Failing this, he offered money "to be instructed in the details of all that they know," but again without success. Fermin in Suriname, anxious to save the colony from the cost of foreign drugs and the malfeasance of ill-intentioned slaves, attempted to learn from the "black slaves" their knowledge of plants, "but these people are so jealous of their knowledge that all that I could do," he wrote, "be it with money or kindness [*caresses*], was of no use."[24]

Europeans also used a variety of tricks when dealing with other Europeans in the West Indies. Nicolas-Joseph Thiery de Menonville, a French bio-pirate, tried flattery on the Spanish while maneuvering to steal cochineal (the beetle that produces a prized red dye). Landing in Cuba, he let it be known that he was a botanist and had come to herborize. Upon hearing this, the people of the country asked if the French did not have plants in their own country. Thiery de Menonville acknowledged that France and its colonies were not deficient in that respect, but, playing to "Spanish vanity," added "that the herbs of Havana have the reputation of possessing superior virtues." Europeans also threatened and coerced reluctant informants. Sloane tells how Europeans learned about *contra yerva*, the potent antidote to poisoned arrows. The story was told to him by an English physician named Smallwood, who had been wounded by an Amerindian's poisoned arrow while fleeing the Spanish in Guatemala. Not having much time, he took one of his own Indians prisoner, tied him to a post, and threatened to wound him with one of the venomous arrows if he did not disclose the antidote. Fearing for his life, the Indian (of an unnamed people) chewed some *contra yerva* and placed it into the doctor's wound, which healed soon thereafter.[25]

The effort to secure secrets against enemies or competitors was not unique to the vanquished in the colonies. Europeans, of course, had many secrets of their own. Historian William Eamon has discussed medieval and early modern literary texts that purported to reveal "secrets of nature." These texts supposedly held esoteric teachings associated with nature's occult forces. Many of the books did indeed divulge recipes, formulas, and "experiments" associated with various arts and crafts, such as instructions for making quenching waters to harden iron and steel, recipes for mixing dyes and pigments, cooking recipes, and practical alchemical formulas used by jewelers and tinsmiths.[26]

More commonly, trade secrets protected profitable knowledge all across Europe. In the medical domain, physicians and apothecaries often protected their remedies by keeping their recipes secret until they could sell them for a good price. In a celebrated case, the apothecary Robert Talbor of Essex (1639–1681) garnered fame and wealth from his "marvelous secret" that cured fevers. His *remède de l'Anglais* secured him a knighthood in England and an annual pension of 2,000 livres from Louis XIV, enough to live like a rich nobleman.[27]

The great trading companies of the early modern period guarded their investments through scrupulously protected monopolies. Carl Thunberg, traveling with the Dutch East India Company, recounted how the Company held a monopoly on the spice and opium trades in this period: "If any one is caught smuggling," he warned, "it always costs him his life, or at least he is branded with a red hot iron and imprisoned for life." Though many naturalists caught passage on Company ships, the Dutch East and West India companies cautioned scholars not to reveal too much of their findings in their publications. The French Compagnie des Indes also admonished authors to limit published information, and it blocked British efforts to buy Michel Adanson's papers treating the natural history of Senegal. After the British took the West African port of Saint Louis in 1758, few French academic papers dealing with that part of the world were published. Adam Smith pointed out that a monopoly granted to a trading company had the same effect "as a secret in trade or manufacturers."[28]

Drug Prospecting in Europe

It is important to emphasize that European scientific practices in the colonies and in Europe were similar. Beginning in the late seventeenth century and throughout the eighteenth century, academic physicians prospected for drugs inside Europe itself, using techniques similar to those employed by their colleagues in the colonies. From Sweden, Linnaeus remarked, "it is the folk whom we must thank for the most efficacious medicines, which they . . . keep secret." In England, Joseph Banks's interest in botany was kindled when, as a youth in the 1750s, he watched women gathering "simples" for sale to druggists. In encounters strikingly similar to those in the West Indies, European medical men cajoled their countrymen and -women into disclosing the secrets of their indigenous cures. Sometimes persuasion, at other times the power of the purse, yielded the secret of some purported magically efficacious ingredient. As with colonial plants, physicians began testing on the basis of ethnobotanical clues and then later (sometimes) published the results. The fashionable seventeenth-century London physician Thomas Sydenham provided a popular rationale for these new practices: any "good citizen," he wrote, in possession of a secret cure was duty-bound "to re-

veal to the world in general so great a blessing to his race." Medical experiments were to benefit the public good (not only physicians' purses)
for, as Sydenham continued, "honors and riches are less in the eyes of
good men than virtue and wisdom." Not everyone would have agreed.[29]

Physicians cast their nets widely in the search for effective cures at
home. Published instructions encouraged travelers inside and outside
Europe to question and learn from people of all stations and sexes—
from statesmen, scholars, and artists as well as from craftsmen, sailors,
merchants, peasants, and "wise women." European women in the sixteenth and seventeenth centuries were still widely acknowledged healers. Upper-class women were routinely educated in medicine; Thomas
More's daughters in England, for example, were educated in religion,
the classics, and practical medicine—the distilling of waters and other
chemical extracts along with the use of minerals, herbs, flowers, and
plants. Diaries and books on housewifery reveal that women who administered large households routinely dressed wounds, administered
medicines, distributed herbs from their gardens, and attended childbirth. Several of these women left books of family "receipts." Among
the lower classes, women served as unlicensed healers of all sorts. In
1560, surgeon Thomas Gale estimated that sixty females were actively
practicing medicine in London (in a population of some 70,000). Of the
714 unlicensed practitioners prosecuted by the College of Physicians of
London between 1550 and 1640, more than 15 percent were women.
These women treated males and females alike and often specialized in a
particular kind of cure. Female practitioners generally purchased their
drugs from apothecary shops and were distinct from the herbwomen
who supplied those shops.[30]

University-educated physicians in Europe were anxious to gather the
knowledge that many women held, including their traditional cures. In
the sixteenth century, Charles de l'Ecluse, who worked in Vienna and
Leiden, praised country "women root cutters" *(rhizotomae mulierculae)*
who supplied him with information about the medical properties of
plants and the names of indigenous varieties. Thomas Sydenham declared, "I know an old woman in Covent Garden who understands botany better [than any academic]."[31] The process of collecting information
from women "root cutters," older women, or particularly successful female healers was strikingly similar to that of prospecting abroad, a kind

of internal bioprospecting. A common strategy was to buy the cure, and often the government put up the money. One woman who did well for herself was the spinster Joanna Stephens, daughter of a gentleman of good estate and family in Berkshire, England. She was paid £5,000 by the king's exchequer on March 17, 1739, for her drug—an eggshell and soap mixture reported to dissolve bladder stones. Her cure for this "painful distemper" was highly prized because the only other option was surgery, known as "cutting for stones."[32]

Stephens's was a celebrated case. Most of the women, however, whose cures were eventually adopted and published in the various European *pharmacopoeia* remained nameless, as was true also of most of the West Indian indigenes or slaves who offered cures. The story of the development of digitalis provides a celebrated example of a medicament still in use today that came originally from an unnamed "old woman."[33] As with informants in the West Indies, we have little access to the women's own reactions to their encounters with academic naturalists. Historian Lisbet Koerner has highlighted an article in a 1769 Stockholm magazine purporting to give voice to "wise women." It was not uncommon in the eighteenth century for articles like these to be written by men under female pseudonyms. Nonetheless, the wise women's assertions echo complaints that appear in other women's writings from this period. The women noted their "joy and pleasure" when a physician, standing by a sick child's bed, ruled that "here no other help can be had than that of finding an experienced wise woman." They complained that physicians "exert themselves to both smell and taste our pouches, creams and bandages," attempting to divine the secrets of the medicines. The women, like so many at the time, ended by asking to be admitted to professional training, in this case to Stockholm Medical College, "for we are after all considered as highly as the gentlemen [physicians] in the homes into which we are called." Like most Africans, they were not admitted to European institutions of higher learning in this period.[34]

Experiments with Slave Medicine

Wise women, folk healers, slaves, and indigenous Americans no doubt tested their cures and even exchanged information in an organized fashion, but those activities have gone unrecorded. Testing, recording, and publication of cures—whatever their provenance—were carried out in uniform fashion throughout European territories by European-trained physicians. Even West Indian Creoles, when educated in Europe, employed standard European protocols in their work.

Historian Richard Sheridan judged the Jamaican plantation doctor James Thomson to be the physician in the West Indies who did the most to bring together the best elements of African and European medicine. Thomson indeed saw himself as following in the footsteps of ingenious men—Hans Sloane, John Bartram, Rev. Griffith Hughes, Patrick Browne, and Rev. Robert Robertson—all of whom had collected useful remedies from slaves, Amerindians, or other informants, whether Spanish or French, friend or foe. He also criticized Sloane and the others, however, for their methods, writing that their work failed for the want of a "correct mode of proceeding." Thomson was keen to develop proper experimental methods to determine the true efficacy of the many remedies he encountered. To this end, he implemented European-style drug testing, learned at the University of Edinburgh, in his work in Jamaica. This included numerous "trials," as he called them, of potentially effective Caribbean drugs—such as Capsicum peppers, *Zanthoxylum* (prickly yellow wood), quassia, unroasted coffee, and the bark of the lilac or hoop tree and the bullet-tree—first on himself in a healthy state and then on diseased subjects who might benefit from the cure. After the tests, he used these "country remedies" regularly in his practice, noting that the doses given to "negroes" must sometimes be greater than those given to whites.[35]

Thomson reported learning a particular cure from a "sensible negro, who had charge of the hospital on a large estate." This man often mixed drugs for Thomson and seems to have accompanied him on some of his calls to white patients. One day Thomson was called to treat a patient who had been seized with a "dreadful obstinate vomiting" that often proved fatal in the tropics. Thomson went to work with his medicines— an elixir of vitriol, effervescing draughts, and others—all with no effect. Because of the "robust habit" of the person, he dared not administer opium. Despairing, Thomson was at a loss (something, he wrote, that happened to "most medical men" in the tropics). At this point, the slave at his side recommended a strong decoction of adrue (Guinea Rush, or *Cyperus articulatus*) "as a last resource." The patient took a wineglass full along with some camphorated julep every half hour. The vomiting ceased within an hour and never returned. Thomson noted that after learning of the effectiveness of the adrue root, he used it frequently and "never without the greatest benefit." Africans' knowledge of medicine was considered of such value that European physicians in the West Indies often recommended that an "intelligent" slave—male or female—be put in charge of a plantation's hospital to dispense medicines, fix dressings, and the like. John Williamson, a surgeon in Jamaica's Saint Thomas in the Vale parish, noted that these slave practitioners "form very important acquisitions to every estate."[36]

In the British Atlantic, in particular, Europeans tested slave cures, often on plantations, and evaluated them vis-à-vis their own medicines. One extraordinary experiment pitting slave cures against European treatments took place in 1773 in Grenada. The experiment had to do with yaws, a form of the highly contagious treponemal infections that include pinta and syphilis. A nonvenereal disease, yaws produces horrid ulcers and lesions in its victims, and pain in the bones, and it is accompanied by a high fever. In advanced stages, yaws causes excruciating pain, especially in the hands and feet. The disease occurs primarily in tropical areas where overcrowding and poor sanitation prevail. Needless to say, slaves throughout the West Indies were plagued by the disease. Planters took note because slaves with yawsy feet often could not walk and hence could not work. As Thomson wrote, "any proprietor of negroes is well aware of the loss he sustains from the yaws. . . . The finest looking slave will . . . in a few months become a burden to himself and his master."[37]

Yaws—also known in the West Indies as *Framboeise* (for its raspberry-like appearance), *pian,* and *buba*—was so common among slaves that many West Indians considered it an African disease carried by "dirtily disposed good-for-nothing Negroes." The physician Thomas Trapham, writing in 1679, taught (incorrectly) that yaws gave rise to gonorrhea and syphilis, and he imagined that the disease originated in the "unhappy" coupling of humans with beasts. Indignantly, he denounced males—both Native American and African—who allowed their "humane seminals" to be wickedly and wantonly "suckt" into and caressed by the "vastly unsuitable matrices" of female malmasets, baboons, and drills. Such couplings—egregious sins against both God and nature—

wrought this "plague of morbid pollutions" known as yaws. Benjamin Moseley, surgeon-general in Jamaica, agreed that yaws was of a "bestial origin" and an African disease. Although by the 1790s most physicians took issue with such notions, Alexander Anderson, botanist and chief gardener in Saint Vincent's, persisted in the belief that yaws arose from the carnal "connections" of "Indians and Negroes" with "some species of monkeys."[38]

For these reasons, great shame attached to whites who contracted the disease. Succumbing to the yaws infection revealed European (mostly) males' otherwise surreptitious affairs with slave women. Yawsy whites were banned from elite society until completely cured, but even after all traces of the disease had disappeared, the lingering stigma "blasted away" any prospects for social advancement. Marriage to respectable females was out of the question.[39]

A first concern of physicians was to teach planters how to detect the disease and to stop its spread. Jamaican physician Thomas Dancer taught whites how to recognize the first signs of the disease among their "domestic negroes" so that they could banish infected persons—in the same way the "Jewish law" banished lepers—from their households. He warned that slave wet nurses often tried to hide their disease to avoid being discharged. But he also assured distraught parents that a child could not be infected through a nurse's milk, and that the child was safe until the nurse broke out with pustules.[40]

The standard treatment for slaves suffering from yaws was banishment to a yaws hut built in some remote corner of the estate. Here the patient might be cared for by an old slave woman, too infirm to work in the fields, who was employed to keep the sores clean. Or, more likely, infected slaves were sent away to the seaside, a plantain walk, or a provision ground in the mountains to act as guards while fending for themselves. The whole operation was calculated to transpire "without any expence to the estate." Moseley painted a bleak picture of a slave's prospects for recovery: "A cold, damp, smoky hut for his habitation; snakes and lizards his companions; crude, viscid food, and bad water, his only support; and shunned as a leper;—he usually sunk from the land of the living."[41]

European practitioners were horrified when called to attend a yaws patient. Fearful of catching the disease, they viewed patients from afar and offered their opinions in a hurried and perfunctory manner. Those who dared visit the yaws house were advised to cover their faces and hands as protection against infection. William Wright emphasized that, "should a medical man contract this filthy disease, his fortune and future prospects are ruined."[42]

Despite the dangers, practitioners gradually became interested in yaws and its cure. Because yaws was seen as an African disease, experiments were done primarily on slaves. One of the most interesting trials tested the relative efficacy of African and European treatments for yaws. We learn of the trial in a letter from A. J. Alexander, a planter in Grenada, to Joseph Black, a physician and professor of chemistry at Edinburgh, subsequently published in *Medical and Philosophical Commentaries.* Alexander detailed how in 1773 he returned to his extensive properties after a considerable absence, to find thirty-two of the slaves afflicted with yaws and confined to his plantation hospital. Some had been there for years, and those who had been sent away as cured, he lamented, generally returned soon again with a new outbreak of the foul disorder. Because yaws was assumed to be a venereal disease, his surgeon had employed the standard mercurial treatment which, Alexander complained, when taken over the course of several years, left slaves' health "broken."[43]

Alexander resolved to take matters into his own hands by conducting a well-conceived, well-executed experiment. He heard that one of his trusted "negroes" knew how to treat yaws, having learned the techniques in his "own country." European physicians elsewhere in the Caribbean had speculated that Africans had a cure for yaws, because slaves arrived in the West Indies with few marks of the disease (though these physicians also thought it possible that traders selected slaves free of defects in order to fetch higher resale prices in the islands). Alexander was lucky to be told of this African cure. William Hillary, working some thirty years earlier in Barbados, wrote that "Negroes have by long observation and experience, found out a method of curing this disease" (which involved various plant preparations taken internally and applied externally). This, he continued, they keep "a secret from the white people, but preserve [it] among themselves by tradition with which they sometimes perform notable cures."[44]

Whether this African cure was reliable or not, Alexander felt he had nothing to lose by running his experiment. He put two yawsy slaves under the care of the unnamed African doctor and four under the care of his surgeon. As reported in Alexander's letter, the African doctor sweated his patients twice a day by placing them in a "cask, in which there was a little fire in a pot." He (Alexander identifies him as male) also increased the sweat by giving them decoctions of two woods that Alexander identified as *bois royale* and *bois fer.* It is interesting that Alexander used the French terms for the medicines; the slave may previously have served French masters, and certainly still identified medicines in the French way, even though he may have learned about them originally from the Amerindians. In addition, the unnamed African applied an ointment made of iron rust and lime juice to the patients' sores.

The plantation surgeon treated his four patients with drugs (diaphoretic antimony) to induce sweats. To their sores he applied a number of noxious substances: *sacharum saturni* (sugar of lead), green vitriol (heptahydrate of ferrous sulfate), antimony (antimony trichloride), and corrosive sublimate (mercuric chloride).

The outcome: The African doctor's patients were cured within a fortnight; the surgeon's patients were not. Alexander, a man of science, consequently gave the African four other patients, who were also quickly cured. Thereafter he put the African in charge of all yaws patients in his plantation hospital, and at the end of two months all but about ten of the original thirty-two had been cured. The results of this experiment made a deep impression; Dancer in Jamaica mentioned it in the third edition of his book on Jamaican medicine published in 1819. And Thomson, who also experimented extensively with yaws, as we shall see, noted that the "use of woods employed by the natives," coupled with good nutrition from a "generous diet," alleviated the symptoms of yaws more effectively than the standard European mercurial treatments.[45]

Experiments with Yaws Inoculation

In addition to treating yaws, plantation owners were keen to prevent it. By the 1760s West Indian physicians had learned that Gold Coast Africans inoculated their children against yaws, and experimenters set out to learn whether inoculation yielded the wonderful lifetime protection for yaws that it did for smallpox. The great success with smallpox inoculation had been that, although it induced disease, it rarely resulted in death. Europeans experimented extensively with yaws in an effort to understand the modes of transmission and control and the course of the disease. The ultimate goal was to purge the plague from the islands.[46]

Learning whether inoculation in yaws could have the same success as inoculation with smallpox was of immediate importance to planters. Yaws was listed second (after tetanus) in the most common causes of mortality among slaves in Jamaica in the British House of Lords hearings on "Trade and Foreign Plantations" in 1788. Moreover, planters were well aware that a slave who had formerly had the yaws was more highly valued—by as much as a third of the price. And planters needed to be on their guard. Hillary reported the pernicious frauds practiced by surgeons on slave ships, whereby at the first appearance of yaws they applied strong repellents, such as the juice of roasted limes mixed with iron rust, and sulfur or gunpowder, to erase the outward signs of the disease. Ship captains then rubbed the slaves' skin with palm oil to make them look fresh and healthy for sale. Within a few days or weeks, however, the yaws erupted with renewed vigor, and planters were often burdened with a poor investment.[47] If, however, slaves could be inoculated with yaws, suffer a mild case, and then enjoy lifetime immunity, planters would secure their labor force. Thomson's experiments had great potential to bolster the Jamaican economy.

Physicians were pressed by masters to find quick and effective cures or—in the case of inoculation—preventions for yaws. Many West Indian physicians understood that a plentiful and healthy diet, comfortable homes, and protection from hard labor provided the surest protection. Masters, however, considered themselves "inconvenienced" by these slow and costly measures. Some pressed physicians to use solutions of corrosive sublimate much recommended by Gerard van Swieten, the great experimentalist in Vienna, and doctors employed them at times against their better judgment and, in their words, with "repugnance." After seeing thirty slaves on one plantation die within two years from these medications, some physicians refused to administer them further. Thus, the race was on to find new cures.[48]

James Thomson joined a long line of yaws experimenters. Both Wright (one of Thomson's mentors) and Benjamin Moseley regularly inoculated for yaws, given that "no habit, age, sex, or country" was immune to the scourge, though neither of them discussed first testing these rather

invasive interventions. In 1773 a Jamaican doctor, one Macgrudan, published his results of testing yaws inoculation in the first volume of the
Parisian *Journal de physique.* As subjects he chose a young "negro"
man—who "vigorously" pled to be inoculated—and an infant. The man
suffered an extremely painful case of yaws; the infant did not. Although
eager to continue his *expériences* (as the French journal rendered his
words), Macgrudan was forced to leave the islands because of bad health.
Experiments of this sort were continued by Thomas Dancer, who made
trials, as he reported, in "upwards of fifty" persons (probably slaves,
although he does not note the race or status of his subjects). Dancer
designed his experiments to test Joseph Adams's finding concerning the
best time in the course of the disease to take variolous matter from a
sick person for inoculation and whether smallpox had any effect on
yaws (since inoculation often induced both diseases in patients at the
same time).[49]

Dancer did not detail his experiments in his publications, but Thomson
did. Like others before him, Thomson went well beyond therapeutic
measures to engage in pure scientific study, drew his subjects for these
experiments exclusively from African slave populations, and chose to
include a number of children. Although whites occasionally contracted
yaws, to my knowledge none numbered among Thomson's subjects.

Thomson's first set of inquiries investigated the time from the initial infection to the onset of the disease—a key piece of information
if physicians were to inoculate effectively. This was something John
Hunter in England, among others, had recommended be put to the
test.[50] Thomson also wished to refute the celebrated case of a Danish nobleman who claimed to have experienced his first symptoms some ten
months after having left the West Indies and any likely source of infection. As in many experiments, Thomson's first observations responded
to a chance occurrence: a number of slave children who had been living in isolation in the mountains were moved to a sugar plantation.
After mixing with others on the estate, they were seized by the fevers
and pains of yaws. Soon thereafter eruptions appeared all over their
bodies. Within seven to ten weeks all the children showed symptoms of
the disease.

Not satisfied with this "accidental experiment," as Thomson called it,
he set to work inoculating—that is to say, willfully infecting—a child

(we can assume a slave) with the disease. Thomson ordered yawsy matter to be taken from the ulcers of an infected patient and inserted into five different punctures made for the purpose on the child's healthy body. Although inoculation with yaws was commonly undertaken in the West Indies, it was dangerous and subjected a child who might have escaped the disease entirely to certain infection. Again, the latent period in this child ran approximately seven weeks. Thereafter the child's body was fully covered with "foul ulcers"—and he or she (the sex was not recorded) did not recover for nine months.

Thomson made a second set of experiments to determine whether inducing yaws produced a milder form of the disease, as was the case with smallpox. Thomson's experiment began when, during inoculations for smallpox, he accidentally took live matter from a child also suffering from yaws. He observed that the child came down with both smallpox and yaws, but that the yaws inoculation did not have the desired effect of producing a mild form of the disease. Seeking more insight into the question, Thomson inoculated four more children with yaws, taking blood from an infected person and inserting it into five punctures made for that purpose on different parts of their bodies. Thomson found again that inoculation indeed spawned yaws, but not a benign form of the disease. From these experiments, Thomson concluded that—against common practice in Jamaica—slaves should not be inoculated against yaws.

Thomson made a third experiment with several slave children before abandoning his project. Wishing to know if inducing smallpox or chicken pox in children already sick with yaws would speed their recovery, he ordered several yaws children to be vaccinated with cowpox. Seeing that this intervention yielded no positive effects, he went no further. "I did not feel myself warranted in doing so," he noted simply.

Thomson did a few more experiments—one to see if yaws could be transmitted to a rabbit, a dog, and a "foul" (probably a chicken). It could not. Further he "endeavoured, by every means" to discover whether the disease was passed by mothers to their infants *in utero*. Thomson did not report what these means were. Perhaps not satisfied with his results, he asked "old negro women," who in the Caribbean were most often in charge of slave birthing, about their experience. They assured him that a child born to a woman with yaws was born free of disease—but Thomson dismissed them with the words, "no reliance can be placed on their testimony." Nor did he believe the "negroes" who told him that children delivered by women who have had the disease in pregnancy were secure from it afterward.[51]

Practitioners generally agreed that having yaws bestowed lifetime immunity to the disease. Thomson reported that he confirmed this through "numerous experiments" in which he had attempted to induce yaws via inoculation in persons who had already successfully recovered from it. The exceptions were mothers nursing yaws-infected infants. Even if a mother had had yaws before, she inevitably developed ulcers on her nipples and breasts, which, if not continuously treated, quickly proved fatal. Should the mother die, the child also perished because, as Thomson reported, it was "abandoned by every person." Williamson cautioned planters that "ill disposed" slave mothers sometimes infected their own babies with yaws as a form of infanticide.[52]

From his lengthy study, Thomson concluded that no particular precaution or treatment helped in yaws. "The practice now generally adopted in this island," he reported, "is to leave the disease to the efforts of nature." An infected slave should be fed well during the course of the disease and given only light work. If a slave were particularly weak, the physician might offer decoctions of "woods used by the natives" (those used by Alexander's slave doctor) along with flowers of sulfur or antimonial preparations.

It would seem from Thomson's records that he had the free run of plantations and a free hand in conducting experiments of his own choosing. There were, however, some limits to his practices. Thomson wrote of a case of "a fine negro boy, 10 years of age," who died suddenly of worms, a common affliction. He noted that "the body was not allowed to be opened, though requested." Who denied the physician's request, we do not know.[53]

Obeah and Vodou

While Europeans avidly collected and tested African medicines and techniques, they set strict limits on the types of knowledge they were willing to consider. They were eager to incorporate African herbal remedies or medical interventions such as inoculation, but they dismissed out of hand spiritual aspects of slave medicine. Obeah and vodou both worked by combining various herbal remedies with some sort of spirit possession or trance; they were invoked both to benefit and cure and to induce physical or social harm.[54]

The English were curious and collected information about obeah (although they also recognized that slaves took care to "keep secret their supposed arts, particularly from the whites"). Individual physicians reported on obeah, and the British government collected intelligence on its practices from each of its West Indian possessions in the extensive 1788 inquiry into the "present state of the African trade." Benjamin Moseley considered obeah akin to quackery, but he also recognized its extraordinary power. If a slave was "bewitched," he or she surely died, though of a "disease that answers to no description in nosology." Thomson also noted the "intimate union of medicine and magic in the mind of the African" and admonished "those interested in their welfare" (medical men and plantation owners) to understand the hold obeah had over Africans in order better to relieve their disorders and illnesses, especially chronic illnesses. A "medical man" hardly stands a chance, he wrote, in the management of disorders where obeah is involved.[55]

The 1788 government report included a story illustrating the power of obeah. A plantation owner returning to Jamaica in 1775 found that many of his slaves had died during his absence, and of those who remained at least one-half were "debilitated, bloated, and in a very deplorable condition." The mortality continued after his arrival; frequently two or three were buried in one day. The worried plantation owner employed every medicine and the most careful nursing to preserve the lives of his slaves—but in vain. He and his physician suspected obeah but could not prove it.

Finally a "negress," who felt that she would soon die, revealed the "great secret" and identified her stepmother, a woman over 80 years old, as the obi causing the trouble. As soon as the other slaves on the plantation heard the news, they ran to the master to confirm that the old woman had terrorized the "whole neighbourhood" since her arrival from Africa. The master took six white servants to the old woman's house, forced open the door, observed the whole inside of the roof and every crevice of the walls adorned with the "implements of her trade, consisting of rags, feathers, bones of cats, and a thousand other articles." The house was immediately razed. As for the old woman, the master did not bring her to trial but "from a principle of humanity" gave her to some Spaniards who transported her to Cuba. From the moment of her departure, the plantation was free from death and illness. The master estimated that over the course of about fifteen years he had lost a hundred slaves to obeah.

Rather than seeking to understand the obis' purported power, Europeans attempted to destroy it (as they did witchcraft in their own countries) by every means possible: through baptizing slaves into the Christian faith and convicting, executing, or deporting practitioners. This is remarkable, because Europeans themselves recognized the power of the mind to heal or destroy the body. John Gregory, in his *Lectures on the Duties and Qualifications of a Physician,* noted the power of sympathy alone to relieve a patient and contribute to a swift recovery. Further, English physicians had long debated whether the truth should be kept from a dying patient because any hope for survival depended on keeping spirits high.[56]

European physicians recognized the power of the imagination and its hold on the body in other contexts as well. In this period, interestingly, mothers' imaginations were deemed one factor contributing to skin color: black babies might be born to white families as a result of maternal impressions during conception or pregnancy. It was said that Lot's daughters saw smoke as they fled burning Sodom and that their imaginations fixed that color upon their children. At the same time, an African queen who dreamed of snow was said to have borne a white child.[57]

Eighteenth-century European physicians even experimented with what we today call placebos. In 1799 John Haygarth reported experiments done with a device fashioned by Elisha Perkins of Connecticut known as Perkins's tractors—metallic conductors of electricity used to cure a variety of diseases—that had become all the rage even, Haygarth reported, among "persons of rank and understanding." To test the validity of the miraculous cures, he and his colleague William Falconer fashioned a pair of "false," wooden tractors, painted to resemble the true, metallic device as closely as possible. Which were the "true" tractors was to be kept secret not only from the patient but from everyone involved in the experiment. Results from each device were to be recorded with complete impartiality and in the patients' own words. As subjects, Falconer provided five appropriate patients—each suffering from some sort of chronic rheumatism or gout—from the General Hospital in Bath (England). First the false tractors were employed. Four of the five patients assured the physicians that their pain was relieved. "One felt his knee warmer, and he could walk much better." "One was easier for nine hours." The next day the same patients were treated with the "true metallick Tractors of Perkins" and, again, four of the patients were much "relieved." Remarkably, both the false and the true tractors yielded the same results.[58]

According to protocol, Haygarth's "trial" was witnessed by Falconer, the hospital's surgeons, and the apothecary. Haygarth concluded that the experiment proved that the "whole effect" of the tractors depended upon the power of the "patient's imagination" to cause, as well as cure, disease. The experiments were repeated by doctors in London and Bristol with similar findings. Physicians found that other random objects, even those lacking the magic "patent" stamp (pieces of bone, iron nails, pieces of mahogany, slate pencils, and tobacco pipes), yielded cures. Interestingly, one of the experiments in Bristol was done on an African subject, Thomas Ellis—again, with similar results. Haygarth approvingly quoted James Lind, who wrote concerning his use of fictitious scurvy remedies: "an important lesson in physic is here to be learnt, viz., the wonderful and powerful influence of the passions of the mind upon the state and disorders of the body. This is too often overlooked in the cure of diseases."[59]

Physicians often depended on what they called "medical faith" to sustain their reputations. Haygarth noted that he "never wished to have a patient who did not possess a sufficient portion of it." Richard Smith, surgeon at the Bristol Infirmary, operated on a difficult case (of paralysis of the flexor tendons in both hands), which he feared would prove a "stumbling-block" to his reputation. To increase the possibility of success, Smith employed Perkins's tractors. In the end, the patient recovered the use of his hands so that he could almost clench his fist. Smith implied that the man's faith in the tractors augmented, and perhaps surpassed, the results produced by surgical technique. Haygarth noted that the marvelous cures ascribed to "empirical remedies," which he alleged were commonly "inert" drugs, relied on the power of patients' imaginations to cure. Haygarth also recognized that great cures required pa-

tients to believe in their physicians. Herein, he continued, lay the value
of a physician's medical reputation: the same remedy will do more to
cure a patient when prescribed by a "famous physician" than by a person of lesser standing. By the same token, a physician's ability to cure
depended to a great extent on his own faith in his remedies.[60]

But the English did not often see (or at least did not note) the conti-
nuities between their beliefs and practices and those of obeah doctors.
The term "obeah" in the West Indies came to denote practices that
whites understood as combining medical practices with witchcraft or
sorcery. Obeah "professors," according to testimony amassed from British holdings throughout the Caribbean, came directly from Africa. Europeans acknowledged that obeah could include good medicine. Charles
Spooner, agent of the islands Saint Christopher and Grenada, testified
that obeah doctors often performed "extraordinary cures in diseases
which have baffled the skill of regular [European] practitioners." "I have
myself," he continued, "made use of their skill . . . with great success."
Adair, writing from Antigua, drew analogies between West Indian obeah
and European "animal magnetism," noting that in both cases the "arts
and means" employed operated on the mind rather than on the body.
Although Adair suspected that obeahs often employed poisons, he emphasized that the diseases induced by obeahs resulted from "depraved
imagination, or a powerful excitement or depression of the mental faculties."[61]

But what was diagnosed as "imagination" in Europeans was judged
"superstition" in Africans. "In proportion as the understandings of the
negroes are less cultivated and informed and consequently weaker than
those of the white men," Spooner judged, "the impressions made on
their minds by obeah are much stronger, more lasting, and attended
with more extraordinary effects." Europeans were disgusted by African
slaves' superstition and by the stuffs used in obeah: grave dirt, hair, teeth
of sharks and other animals, blood, feathers, eggshells, images in wax,
bird hearts, mice livers, and potent roots, weeds, and bushes.[62]

John Williamson, however, indicated that obeah men and especially
obeah women often had the confidence of the whites as well. Indignantly, he wrote that, despite the efforts of European doctors to introduce more effective medical practices in the islands, "many negroes" put

great faith in "old women" whom they imagine to be gifted with "supernatural powers." This, he suggested, might be expected of slaves, but when those "of whom better might be expected" lend their "assent, approbation, and confidence to such ignorant pretenders," European medical men simply cannot do their jobs. Old women, he barked, "intrude themselves so often to the sick-room."[63]

But the struggles between European and African medicine in Jamaica and other Caribbean islands went far beyond those over professional turf. In the violence endemic to slave societies, whites overwhelmingly came to fear the power of obeah. Whether slaves turned obeah to ill in the West Indies as part of their struggle against slavery, we cannot know. Whites, however, emphasized the evil powers of obeah to "bewitch" people, to "consume" them in lingering illnesses, and to poison with greater skill even than the Amerindians, all this calculated to bring on dreadful deaths in hours, days, weeks, or even years. Their powers were for the most part leveled against slaves in the islands—the property of masters whom obis wished to harm. Moseley wrote that the victims of this "nefarious art" were numerous. "No humanity of the master, nor skill in medicine," he continued, "can relieve a negro, labouring under the influence of Obi." And, as in the case of empirics in Europe, obis were accused of being greedy and selling their nostrums in a "lucrative" trade.[64]

Government hearings listed obeah as one of the reasons slaves did not replenish their populations on plantations. Referring specifically to Jamaica, island agents judged that a "very considerable portion of the annual mortality among the Negroes" must be attributed to "wicked acts." But, worse, obeah was blamed for the power behind the slave revolt of 1760, known as Tacky's Rebellion. The British quickly captured some of the obeah men and sentenced one of them to death. At the place of execution the obi shouted that it was not within the power of white people to kill him. The crowd of "negro" spectators, the report continued, was astonished when they saw him expire. This rebellion led to the outlawing of obeah in Jamaica in 1760.[65]

In a grisly end to this affair, "experiments" (we are not told the details) were made with "electrical machines and magic lanterns" to punish the other captured obeah men. The report of the experiments noted that these "produced very little effect," except on one man who, after receiving "many severe shocks," acknowledged that the white man's obeah exceeded his own.[66]

The Circulation of Knowledge

Traditional scholarship on colonial science and medicine has emphasized a Latourian model of periphery and metropole, where European cities such as Amsterdam, Paris, and London served as "centres of calculation" to process the rich data of empire. Stretching forth from great metropolitan hubs were elaborate networks of collectors, informants, and experimental scientists who relished making their marks by having their "finds" scrutinized, catalogued, theorized, and stockpiled in the great European storehouses of knowledge.

We have seen, however, that Atlantic world models of scientific exchange are rich and multicentered. The examples presented in this essay reveal the West Indies as not simply a colonial periphery supplying profitable drugs and knowledge of their use to the metropole, but as a fertile ground for scientific innovation. The Saladoids arrived first carrying plants and cures from South America into the Caribbean islands. Slaves brought medicines and knowledge of their use from Africa. Europeans carried profitable and medicinal plants from colony to colony, often across vast stretches of ocean. Amerindians and Africans in the islands often supplied Europeans with knowledge; they also selectively adopted European medicines as their own.

In the hothouse of the West Indies, Amerindians, Africans, and Europeans mixed culturally and even racially. New biological entities—both plants and peoples—formed through contact. And knowledge from diverse cultural heritages readily traveled and blended. We do not know exactly how these processes worked, but we do have some direct evidence of the mixing of Amerindian and slave knowledges from Edward Bancroft's discussion of the "gulley-root" *(Petiveria alliacea),* also known as garlic weed or henweed. The abortive qualities of this plant were known to the indigenous peoples of the Amazon, where the plant is native. By the mid-eighteenth century, knowledge of the gully-root's many uses (including abortion) had reached Barbados, where Bancroft worked before moving on to Guiana. Bancroft wrote of the gully-root in the context of slave abortions, which he considered ruinous to the colonies. At some point, slave women—of mixed ancestry or not—learned from the Arawaks (who still resided on nearly every plantation in Guiana) how to prepare the plant as an abortifacient.[67]

Hybrid peoples also facilitated bicultural communications throughout the Atlantic. We get a glimpse of this through Pierre Campet, a physician working in Guiana in the 1760s, who was anxious to collect Amerindian information concerning tetanus, a disease that attacked African newborns throughout the Caribbean and dashed European hopes of breeding Creole slave populations. Campet, whose 1767 "Traité du tétanos" detailed his treatment of twenty-five cases of tetanus, primarily among slaves held by the French there, had been assured by the "Indians" of both sexes *(l'un et de l'autre sexe)* that their own newborns never suffered from this terrible disease. Anxious to discover their secret—which he suspected lay in a certain thick balm applied to the umbilical cord—Campet found "an old Indian and his wife" whom he wished to question on this matter but whose language he did not speak. Among a company of Amerindians newly arrived from the hinterlands, he found a "mulatto" *(malatre)* who could translate (the man's mother tongue was no doubt a mixture of Creole and Indian languages; his father tongue—like his father—was probably French).[68] Earlier conquest and colonial mixing in this case facilitated Campet's medical query.

But there were also numerous barriers—physical, cultural, intellectual—to knowledge exchange. Even when Africans wished to learn from Amerindians or vice versa, the "noise"—intellectual interference—was often deafening. Loudest perhaps was the cacophony of languages. Europeans usually only scratched the surface of Caribbean peoples' knowledges of plants and remedies, because they were often unable or unwilling to speak local languages. Bancroft in Guiana bemoaned that fact that he was "but little acquainted with the Indian languages" necessary for "acquiring that knowledge of the properties, and effects of the several classes of Animals, and Vegetables, which experience, during a long succession of ages, must have suggested to these natives." Though he endeavored to overcome these difficulties through the use of interpreters, he remarked that his efforts were largely "in vain."[69]

La Condamine, Pouppé-Desportes, and Alexander von Humboldt were all keenly interested in local New World languages. La Condamine spoke of what he called "the Peruvian language" and even owned a 1614 "quichoa" (Quechua) dictionary—which he used to study etymologies (of "quinquina," or quinine, for example). Dictionaries of various South American languages (Taracso, Quechua, Náhuatl, and Zapoteco) had been available since the late sixteenth century, prepared mainly by Spanish Jesuits. These typically consisted of some three hundred entries "useful to persons traveling in the area for commerce, to cultivate the land or to win souls." Humboldt, who traveled extensively in present-day Venezuela and Colombia, prepared dictionaries of the Chaymas language that consisted of only about 140 words.[70] One has to wonder if Europeans had sufficient knowledge of diverse languages for effective scientific exchange.

Humboldt was keenly aware of the problems of communication and the power relations involved in privileging one language over another. He commended the Amerindians for their facility in learning new languages, especially Spanish, and remarked that, because the Cassiquiare, Guahibo, Poignave, and several other peoples inhabiting the missions did not understand each other, they were forced to converse in Spanish—the language of the mission but also that of the occupying civil power. Humboldt admired the Jesuits for attempting to make Quechua the universal language of South America. Humboldt knew that most Amerindians did not understand specific Quechua words, but he supposed that they were familiar with its structure and grammatical form. He held this proposal to be much wiser than one made by a provincial council in Mexico that the various Native American peoples communicate with one another in Latin.[71]

The problem of language in the West Indies was not merely one between people of far-flung cultures. In the course of his travels to Saint Vincent, Jean-Baptiste Leblond happened upon an English doctor, Mr. Johnston, age 30. He knew not a word of French, and Leblond not a word of English. "I wished to speak to him in Latin," Leblond wrote, "but we could not understand each other because of the differences in pronunciation." In the end, they communicated in written Latin. Leblond stayed with Johnston two years, helping him run the hospital and pharmacy and learning the local island medicine.[72]

Communication across cultures was sometimes ameliorated by the native populations in the Caribbean who served as active linguists. The Caribs, for example, created "a jargon," through which they dealt with the French in Saint-Domingue, that was a mixture of "Spanish, French, and Caraïbe pell-mell [all] at the same time."[73] African slaves in Suriname created a language that served as common currency there called "Negro-English," composed primarily of English, with some Dutch, French, Spanish, and Portuguese.

But problems of communication did not arise simply from lack of knowledge. Charles de Rochefort in 1658 placed the problems of language in the context of war and conquest. "Some of the French have observed," he wrote, "that the Caribbeans have an aversion to the English tongue; nay their loathing is so great that some affirm they cannot endure to hear it spoken because they look upon the English as their enemies." He noted that the Caribs had, in fact, assimilated many Spanish words to their own language, but that this was done at a time when relations between the two nations were friendly. De Rochefort noted further that the Caribs shied away from teaching any European their language "out of a fear that their [own] war secrets might be discovered."[74] Knowledge exchange may have foundered on similar shoals.

Within the bounds of European empires, knowledge circulated swiftly (by the standards of the times). Europeans moved knowledge, plants, and peoples across impressive territories. Networks of scientists and correspondents sped knowledge from the East Indies to London and on to the West Indies. The route, if rapid, was not always direct. A Mr. Scott in Bengal, a correspondent of Joseph Banks, sent the important news that nitric acid could be substituted for mercury in the treatment of "fatal fevers." Banks made Scott's report "public," no doubt reading it at a session of the Royal Society of London, of which he was president. James Currie, trained in Edinburgh and a working physician in Liverpool, hearing of this hopeful new cure, made "trials" of it. Pleased with the results, he in turn suggested its use to some practitioners in the West Indies who used it with good effect. Via this route, experimental knowledge from Bengal passed into Europe and on to the West Indies.[75]

Information also moved rapidly between colonies—especially when no imperial border stood in the way. In the British West Indies results concerning cures for dysentery, for example, were collected from Saint

Vincent and Grenada. Williamson in Jamaica noted that "wangle" or "vangla," a plant whose leaf when crushed in spring water produced a glutinous matter, had been much used in those islands, especially in African regiments, among whom it was known by its French name, *zi zigree.*[76] Knowledge also transferred through conquest. As we have seen, the slave doctor in Alexander's experiment also identified his woods and decoctions by French names.

Military medical men stationed in ports throughout each empire were active agents of scientific exchange. The French naval surgeon and physician, Jean Barthélemy Dazille, who worked in Madagascar, l'Ile-de-France, the Mascareignes off the coast of Africa, Cayenne, the West Indies, and Canada, developed a global view of health issues. As he noted, these "fecund sources" made him Europe's expert at the time on tropical medicine.[77]

Although knowledge flowed rapidly within the bounds of empire, it moved more sluggishly between Caribbean islands—even when these islands, like Jamaica and Saint-Domingue, were separated by only 125 miles. Difficulties getting learned journals, books, and paper, and the rigors of travel often cut colonials off from potentially rich collaborations in developing tropical medicine. European colonial physicians, it should be remembered, were primarily practitioners who rode from plantation to plantation caring for up to 4,000 slaves at any one time. Consequently, physicians in the French West Indies often knew little of what was going on in the British West Indies and vice versa.

Toward the end of the eighteenth century, West Indian physicians organized intellectual circles within their national enclaves to promote their research. (Unlike the Spanish territories, the French and English West Indian colonies for the most part had no universities, teaching hospitals, and the like, which meant that their focal point for organized medical research remained in Europe throughout the eighteenth century.)[78] The Cercle des Philadelphes, the major scientific circle founded in Saint-Domingue in 1784, enjoyed foreign members such as Benjamin Rush and Benjamin Franklin from Philadelphia and Franz Joseph Märter, the imperial botanist from Vienna—but none from neighboring Caribbean islands such as the medical experimentalists William Wright, John Quier, or Thomas Dancer.[79] Although knowledge gathered from men and women of African origins may have been discussed in these colonial academies, it remains to be seen whether Africans themselves were present.[80]

Competitive animosity also impeded communications between colonials, as it did elsewhere in Europe. British physicians who cited French contemporaries often did so to criticize them. Benjamin Moseley, surgeon-general in Jamaica and more interested in things French than many of his colleagues, admonished English legislators to follow the French example of becoming self-sufficient in all foodstuffs and luxury goods by cultivating cloves, cinnamon, juniper berries, nutmegs, and pepper in their colonies, thus keeping in view the grand political maxim of "selling to all the world"—and buying from none. Moseley also appreciated French physicians of an earlier generation, such as Pouppé-Desportes and his early account of yellow fever. Yet even Moseley sharply refuted his contemporary and professional counterpart in Saint-Domingue, Dazille, and the public health measures that Dazille so passionately promoted. Criticism of the French was common among the British. Grainger reported that the French warned against opening a yaws pustule with a lancet only to refute the idea. "I can see no danger," he wrote, "from the use of steel." Picking up on Lind, Moseley criticized his French colleagues Antoine Poissonnier-Desperrières and Jean Chevalier for their lack of experience in the tropics, and he wrote of the Dutch physician Lewis Rouppe that there was nothing original in his account except his errors.[81]

Knowledge exchange in the Atlantic world, then, was multivariate and complex; the topic requires more research. What we can know comes largely from European resources. We know that Europeans actively bioprospected, investigating Amerindian and enslaved Africans' cures to aid in their own survival and to sell for profit around the globe. We can suspect that Amerindians and Africans exchanged information about plants and their uses as their populations mixed and sometimes interbred in the Caribbean basin. We know that, occasionally, slaves or free people of color showed an interest in European medicines imported into the colonies.

As older models have emphasized, much knowledge circulated within empires. But the West Indies was not simply a colonial periphery—a supplier of botanicals and a consumer of knowledge. Knowledge was forged in the crucible of the Atlantic exchange of peoples and cultures. On the ground in the West Indies, Amerindian, African slave, and European medical practices mixed—sometimes productively, sometimes explosively—to produce new knowledge and medicines.

10

Theopolis Americana

The City-State of Boston, the Republic of Letters, and the Protestant International, 1689–1739

MARK A. PETERSON

On the night of January 1, 1686, Samuel Sewall, Boston merchant and aficionado of apocalyptic speculation, had a dream. Earlier that day, he had finished reading a four-volume commentary on the book of Revelation written in the 1610s by "the Godly Learned ingenious" David Pareus, professor of divinity at the University of Heidelberg.[1] That night, his head filled with millennial thoughts, Sewall dreamed "that our Saviour in the dayes of his Flesh when upon Earth, came to Boston and abode here sometime, and moreover that He Lodged in that time at Father Hull's"—that is, at the home of Sewall's late father-in-law. The next morning Sewall remembered two reflections he had had during his dream: "One was how much more Boston had to say than Rome boasting of Peter's being there. The other a sense of great Respect that I ought to have shewed Father Hull since Christ chose when in Town, to take up his Quarters at his House. Admired the goodness and wisdom of Christ in coming hither and spending some part of His short Life here."[2]

Sewall's dream is a vivid example of early Bostonians' subconscious pride of place, but the general sentiment was by no means atypical. From the city's founding in 1630, when John Winthrop claimed that "the eyes of all people are upon us," to Oliver Wendell Holmes's 1858 assumption that he lived at the "hub of the solar system," the people of Boston became accustomed to asserting their importance in extravagant terms, and they developed oversized ambitions to accompany their inflated self-image.[3]

During the first significant period of the colony's existence, however, these ambitions were to a great extent thwarted. From its founding in 1630 to the revocation of its original charter in 1685, the year preceding Sewall's strange dream, Boston had suffered under the distant control of a government it despised. The imperial ambitions of the Stuart monarchs, their affinity for Roman Catholicism, and their admiration of Bourbon absolutism were anathema to Bostonians, who generally refused to join in any of the royal projects and consistently resisted the Stuarts' efforts to rein in the colony's radical republican polity and independent church governance. Even during the long decade of parliamentary rule in midcentury, when Oliver Cromwell and his Puritan allies offered a position ostensibly more sympathetic to Massachusetts, Bostonians avoided involvement in the protector's overseas ventures, steering clear, for the most part, of the Western Design and dawdling over the prospect of joining an assault on New Netherlands until the peace treaty ending the first Anglo-Dutch war made it a moot point.[4] This is not to say that Bostonians under the first charter lacked imperial ambitions, but their aggressive assault on the territory of New England's native population, their participation in new colonial ventures from Connecticut to New Hampshire to the incorporation of the district of Maine, their construction in 1643 of the New England Confederation as a defensive alliance, and their development of Atlantic trading networks from Acadia to Africa were all do-it-yourself projects, unaided and frequently opposed by the Stuart monarchy.[5]

In the few turbulent years that followed Sewall's dream of Christ's coming to Boston, all this changed. Angered by the despotic approach to colonial government taken by Sir Edmund Andros, James II's vice-regent for the Dominion of New England, the people of New England rose up in arms, arrested Andros and his coterie of royal officials, and sent them back to England. Of course, their rebellion was spurred by the news that James II had fled to France and that Parliament had invited William of Orange to succeed him. But after an anxious period of waiting and negotiation to discover how the new king would react to colonial rebellions, William's favorable response, in the form of a new charter for Massachusetts, opened new vistas for imperial cooperation for those Bostonians able to comprehend the magnitude of the revolution. By forming an alliance with the Protestant kingdoms of northern

Europe and implementing an aggressive strategy to counter the ambitions of Louis XIV, William made it possible for Bostonians to believe that their own ambitions might no longer be limited to their remote corner of the Atlantic world. For decades they had imagined themselves to be a saving remnant of Protestantism, on the run from tyranny, Catholicism, and the Antichrist in Europe, Africa, Asia, and in Spanish and French America. Now, with a militant Dutch Protestant patriot on the throne of the united kingdoms of Britain, they could finally link their aspirations to a powerful political and military force that they could plausibly imagine might turn dreams into reality.[6]

This essay explores how Bostonians took advantage of these new opportunities in the half century after 1689. It separates, somewhat artificially, some of the strongest forces in Massachusetts into two categories: politics and trade on one hand, and religion and culture on the other. As I have argued elsewhere, this division is essentially illusory, for these two forms of endeavor sustained each other to make Massachusetts a vital and dynamic entity in the seventeenth century, despite the colony's relative lack of material resources and its political isolation.[7] Furthermore, some figures such as Samuel Sewall, his father-in-law John Hull, and Sewall's friend and contemporary Increase Mather, the clergyman who negotiated with the Crown for the new Massachusetts charter, encompassed leadership roles that spanned trade, politics, and religion. And, as Bernard Bailyn demonstrated, the political and commercial leaders of New England were closely intermarried with the clerical and cultural elite, so that control over those interlinked endeavors often remained within households or families, if not in the hands of the same individuals.[8]

Nevertheless, the artificial separation of Bostonians' new imperial ambitions into the two aspects reflects the beginning of a division of labor in the more complex and specialized world that New Englanders explored in the wake of the Glorious Revolution. For the purposes of this essay, such a division makes it possible for us to follow two prominent figures as they developed Boston's connections with the world opened for them by the accession of William III—the Dutch and German Protestant states, kingdoms, and principalities, which offered new alliances, new potential for trade, and new models of religious and cultural reformation to which Bostonians could aspire and to which they could contribute their own ideas and examples, as they took their place in the Republic of Letters and the Protestant International.

The evidence for the links between Boston and greater Germany in this period forms an intricate web, spun out through a series of transatlantic journeys, mutual friendships, letters exchanged, and correspondence networks maintained across the decades. To attempt to replicate the entire network here would be hopelessly confusing. But the general outline of these connections can be seen most clearly through the experiences and ideas of two men who played as large a part as any in this "Dutch moment," Jonathan Belcher and Cotton Mather. Belcher, an ambitious merchant and politician, was one of the wealthiest and most powerful figures in Boston during the first half of the eighteenth century; his role in shaping the life of the city has long been underappreciated. Mather was equally ambitious, and, though his role in Boston's religious life has never been underestimated, it has often been misunderstood.[9] As the generation of New England leaders dominated by men like their fathers began to give way in the eighteenth century, Belcher and Mather stood (in their powdered wigs) at the center of an expansive network of people whose contacts and experiences in the Netherlands and Germany gave a new cast to the ambitions of Bostonians in the Atlantic world.

The two men moved through this network in very different ways. Belcher went where fate and his interests led him, with the result that his experience has a haphazard, accidental quality. Mather, on the other hand, was a systematic thinker who seldom left Boston and never crossed the Atlantic. Unimpeded by any confusing encounters with the messiness of external reality, Mather could contribute to the construction of an organized, imaginative Protestant Atlantic network. Rather than direct experience, what made it possible for Mather to perform this imaginative construction was one of the most remarkable material artifacts of the early modern Atlantic world, the library amassed over several generations by the extended Mather family, housed in the Boston North End home that Cotton inherited from his father. This essay first follows Jonathan Belcher on a tour through the Netherlands and Germany, then turns to Cotton Mather and follows his mental journey across the same territory, a journey that requires an excursion through the family's enormous library to explain the shape, dimensions, and meaning of Boston's Atlantic world in the early eighteenth century.

Jonathan Belcher's "Dutch" Tours

Andrew Belcher, Jonathan's father, started life as a tavern keeper, but he began to amass a fortune in the 1670s by provisioning the colonial military during King Philip's War, then later by outfitting expeditionary fleets during the wars of the 1690s. By 1699, when Jonathan graduated from Harvard College, his father was one of Boston's leading merchants and seeking to become still grander.[10] He sent Jonathan to England after the outbreak of the War of the Spanish Succession, hoping that his son could secure even more profitable military contracts. At the age of 22, Jonathan Belcher set sail for London, where he proved to be quite adept at advancing his father's interests (Figure 10.1).[11] Mission accomplished, the son went on holiday, and from July through October, 1704, he visited the principal cities of the Netherlands, then headed eastward across the Rhine to Hanover and Berlin. Throughout this trip, he kept an extensive journal, which reveals how the young man's travels shaped his developing sense of identity as a Bostonian in an Atlantic context, and how the issues that would be central to his subsequent career were foreshadowed in his journeys.[12]

Belcher's Dutch tour began at Rotterdam and proceeded from there to Delft, The Hague, Leiden, Haarlem, and finally Amsterdam. In his experience of urban life in the Netherlands, three principal themes emerge: first, a strong desire for an imaginative association with Dutch Protestant patriotism; second, a curiosity about the practice of religion in a Calvinist yet tolerant state; and third, an interest in the moral and social problems of commercial cities. None of these interests was unique to Belcher—his sightseeing agenda fell squarely within the well-established itinerary followed by many English travelers to the Netherlands.[13] But as a Bostonian, Belcher's cultural baggage was different and so the meaning of his Dutch experience would be different as well.[14]

Unlike some contemporary English travelers, Jonathan Belcher was unencumbered by any ambivalence toward the House of Orange, and his visits to its historic sites were occasions for outbursts of patriotic

Figure 10.1 Jonathan Belcher, mezzotint engraving by John Faber after R. Phillips, 1734, when Belcher was governor of Massachusetts and New Hampshire. Reproduced courtesy of the Massachusetts Historical Society, Boston.

emotion.[15] Belcher had been only 7 years old when news of William III's triumphal entry into Britain had prompted Boston's rebellion against Edmund Andros, in which his father had played a significant role, and it was through supplying expeditions during King William's War that the Belcher fortune had been made.[16] Belcher dutifully visited and admired the late king's palaces, but his strongest connection to the House of Orange was forged at Delft, where he was moved by the monument to "the great Nassau," William the First, great-grandfather of the late king. He then visited the palace where William was assassinated in 1584 and vividly recounted the details of the death of "this glorious prince, . . . the first deliverer of the Dutch from Popery," done in by the "cursed villany," the "folly and madness," of a "Frenchman" who "recd money from the Spaniards" to commit murder "on so great, so good a man."[17] This powerful identification with Dutch patriotism would stay with Belcher throughout his life. On his return to Boston, Belcher named an avenue he laid out through his family estate "Nassau Street," and fifty years later, as governor of New Jersey, he named the main building of the fledgling college at Princeton "Nassau Hall."[18]

Dutch Protestantism and toleration were also among Belcher's major concerns. Belcher grew up during the transitional period when the new Massachusetts charter mandated official toleration for all Protestant denominations. Staunch Boston Puritans like Jonathan's father had put up a united front of hostility toward the Anglican newcomers, fearing that contact with lax forms of worship would corrupt New England's traditions.[19] In this light, Andrew Belcher commissioned the minister of Boston's Old South Church to preach a private family sermon for Jonathan's benefit on the eve of his departure for England, warning him to cling to his ancestral faith throughout his travels.[20] But Belcher's Dutch experience subtly transformed his religious opinions in unexpected ways. He attended the services of many different faiths, noting the novel or surprising things that pleased or upset him. Unlike the New England congregational churches, Dutch Calvinists sang hymns accompanied by an organ "play'd very delightfully"—Belcher liked music. Yet they used a "form of prayer not altogether unlike the Church of England"—Belcher disliked "stinted" worship.[21] At no point during his excursions through Dutch churches (and synagogues) did Belcher seem remotely in danger of wavering in his beliefs. After his journey, when he reflected on the advantages and disadvantages of travel, he did see danger to religion as the main drawback to life on the road, but not in the way that his father and minister had feared. It was not doctrinal heterodoxy but rather waywardness in the "duties of religion" that was bred by a transient life. Being away from home and associating with strangers who were themselves uprooted tended to undermine the steady habits necessary to maintain a vital faith.[22] Belcher had now seen at first hand a range of possible confessional routes to attaining such a faith, and he had come to believe that the *practice* of piety within any one of them was the essential basis for salvation. His encounter with the varieties of Dutch religion set Belcher on the way to becoming an ecumenical Protestant Pietist.

In addition to patriotism and Protestantism, Belcher's interests embraced a third feature of Dutch life, the ethical and social obligations of a commercial society. Boston at the time was rapidly expanding its involvement in the Atlantic economy, to the point where it stood among the leading provincial ports in the British Empire, and its population had doubled since the time of Belcher's birth.[23] With this boom came unfamiliar problems—those that plagued merchants most, like commercial risk (especially in wartime), bankruptcy, chronic currency shortages, and the absence of banking, as well as poverty, crime, and the dependency of widows, orphans, and the chronically or mentally ill.[24] Belcher kept a watchful eye on Dutch approaches to these problems. In Amsterdam, he visited the "Great 'Change" in the main square, which he compared favorably to the London Exchange, but what impressed him most was the "civility" of the Dutch merchants who entertained him at dinner. Upon his return to Boston, Belcher would become a leader in the movement to regulate and introduce greater civility to Boston's chaotic public markets.[25] He also toured the Bank of Amsterdam in the magnificent Stadhuys (a "glorious pile," he called it) and remarked on its value to the city: "the money of their bank is much better than their curr[en]t coin, in that they receive no money into the bank but what is the best silver and of such a weight." Here, perhaps, is the beginning of Belcher's development as a hard-money man, framing the position he would consistently maintain in the endless controversies over currency and banking schemes that dominated his political career in Massachusetts.[26] Belcher also admired the absence of poverty and misery in the cities he visited, for which he gave credit to Dutch advances in charity and philanthropy. He was particularly impressed by the hospitals in The Hague and Amsterdam, including huge establishments for orphans and widows, where the inmates were "very well provided for" and lived with great civility amid gardens and orchards. In his subsequent career in Boston, Belcher took part in the establishment of similar institutions.[27]

Belcher visited Dutch palaces and courts as a tourist, making little contact with the country's rulers. But while stopping by the English embassy at The Hague, a chance encounter changed his fortunes. There he met Baron Johann Kaspar von Bothmer, envoy from Hanover, who gave Belcher a letter of introduction to Princess Sophia, presumptive heir to the English throne and mother of the future George I.[28] When Belcher set out eastward from Amsterdam for Hanover, his expectations were high for a direct encounter with courtly society. Reality, in this case, exceeded his fondest hopes. At Hanover he would meet with nobility on intimate terms, learn the rituals and manners of courtly life, and assess at close hand the glories and ravages of royal power.

Belcher's letter of introduction brought him to the center of Hanoverian courtly life, the Electoral palace at Herrenhausen, where he was swept away by his meeting with Princess Sophia, who became his ideal of a pious, educated ruler (Figure 10.2). She spoke six languages fluently, loved painting, music, and history, and, raised a Calvinist, was especially sympathetic toward the Pietists.[29] During his two-week stay, Belcher frequently dined at Sophia's table, accompanied her on long walks through the palace gardens, and played cards with her in the evening. Coming from Boston, where cards were played only in disreputable taverns, Belcher needed instruction on proper etiquette. "When one gives the cards to the Electress, you rise & give them with Ceremony, but they that play often, do it only the first 2 or 3 dealings." Belcher lost, of course, "the game being new to us," and then learned "tis the custom here never to give the money you loose the same night, but the first after."[30] In other words, it was uncouth for the loser to pay up immediately; a gentleman waited until the next day to make good his losses.

Not all courtly customs seemed so gracious. Belcher enjoyed the twice-weekly "Consort of Musick" that the Elector sponsored until he heard an appalling story: "one of the hautboyes, a young boy and the best player had run away . . . , which was the 4th time he had done so. The 3d he was taken, he was kept 15 dayes in prison and fed on bread and water, and now the Elector sent him word if he would promise to run away no more, he'd only cut off 2 of his fingers. His answ: was he wd run away a thousand times, if he did not hang him. The hautboyes

Figure 10.2 Electress Sophia of Hanover (1630–1706), ca. 1701, by Andreas Scheitz. Courtesy of Historisches Museum Hannover, Germany.

are all slaves, the Elector buyes 'em from one at Cassel, who breeds them up and sells 'em afterwards."[31]

Yet these same musicians performed beautifully in the elaborate service held in the court chapel "to give thanks for the victory" at the battle of Blenheim, the news of which was received at court the day Belcher arrived. The Duke of Marlborough's triumph became for Belcher, then, not merely a general moment of pride in a Protestant victory but a personal event as well—he was there to witness the Princess Sophia fretting over the fate of her younger son on the battlefield.[32]

On the whole, Belcher relished his chance to mingle with power and wealth. He enjoyed the dizzying sense of favor and would profit from it in the long run. He also marveled at the curiosities of the far-flung world brought to the European court, taking note of the two dark-skinned Turkish servants kept by the Elector, one of them a wartime captive.[33] And his admiration of the Princess Sophia never wavered. Upon his departure, she presented him with her portrait, which was thenceforth prominently displayed in the council chamber of the Town House in Boston.[34] But he was not without ambivalent feelings about the moral effects of royal power and the wealth it commanded, feelings that his further travels in Germany would bring out more strongly.

As he continued on his journey from Hanover to Berlin, Belcher stopped to visit a Benedictine monastery that had become a refuge for English Catholic gentry. Here Belcher had his encounter with the Catholic "other," an experience that became something of a set piece in the careers of many pious Bostonians who ventured into the Atlantic world.[35] In this case, it took the form of a debate with the "fathers" in the monastery's library, where Belcher found "none of the best works" of the Pietist writers, whereupon "the fathers fell out against the Pietists at a most prodigious rate & told us several stories of their madness & folly." Ever the patriotic Protestant, Belcher also observed with disdain several relics given to the monastery by the Stuart monarchs, including a skirt that Charles II had allegedly worn to disguise himself in his flight after the battle of Worcester. Nor did Belcher think that monastic life weaned the monks from worldliness: "they live retir'd from the world, but for ought I saw, their concern & care for it, is as great as if they liv'd in it."[36] Belcher's encounter with Catholicism reinforced the limits of his toleration. His ecumenical impulse would be confined within Protestant boundaries.

The next major stop on the way to Berlin was a visit to the famous silver mines in the Hartz Mountains, where guides took him down into the enormous underground city, with "towns and streets below as well as above ground and every mine has a name." Belcher watched the dangerous drilling and blasting, and later paid close attention to the intricate process of refining silver from raw ore. The use of "great quantities of wood to increase the heat" made "some of these fires . . . frightful and terrible to look at, [and] brought to mind the fire of Hell, *and who can dwell in everlasting burnings.*" He was equally dismayed by the disparities in wealth created by the labor system. Most of the silver went directly into the coffers of the Elector, and the mine's director lived like a prince. The workers, by contrast, "are at prodigious labour, but it is for others, not themselves tho they have the silver in their own ground, & dig it with their own hands." More curious still, when the miners were paid, "they agree with the greatest and Debauchees, in that they spend all the time they have to themselves in gaming and drinking." From witnessing the brutal labor required to extract silver, as well as the profligacy with which it was spent by lords and laborers alike, Belcher concluded that "nothing is harder come at, and nothing easier parted with, yet would make a man a miser to be a month or so at the mines."[37] From the Amsterdam Exchange to the Hartz silver mines, Belcher's Dutch progress was an education in the value of hard money.

When Belcher finally arrived at Berlin, he met with further examples of lavish courtly wealth, and with the aid of his letter from the Princess Sophia, was soon on familiar terms with her daughter, the queen of Prussia.[38] But his most intriguing encounter in Berlin occurred by chance while touring the royal library, "where we met with one Mr. Leibnitz." This "mighty civil and obliging man," the philosopher and polymath Gottfried Wilhelm Leibniz, was then serving as president of the Academy of Sciences in Berlin. There is no record of the topics covered in their several hours of conversation, though their mutual interest in Protestant ecumenism may have occupied their time.[39] But Belcher does tell us that "we chanc'd to fall upon the subject of Chymistry," and that Leibniz told him a story "that lately hapned at Berlin" of an apothecary's apprentice who had discovered the secret of producing gold from lead. The king of Prussia had tried to capture the apprentice, who fled, only to be seized by the king of Poland and imprisoned at Dresden, "where he now continues" making gold for the king of Poland, "but not enough for him."[40] Alchemy, or "chymistry," as it was interchangeably called, was still very much a live issue in the scientific world, and Leibniz's curious story seems to have been told in earnest. It reflects the philosopher's ambivalence over his hopes for experimental science as a transforming power in the world, a kind of alchemical utopianism, set against a deep concern that such power might be perverted by the imperial ambitions of Europe's feuding monarchs.[41]

From Berlin, Belcher retraced his steps to the Netherlands, crossed the Channel, and then returned to Boston, where his experiences made him an instant celebrity. He dined out on his adventures for months and circulated his manuscript journal in polite Boston society. Four years later his father's interests sent him back to London, and once again, having accomplished his necessary business, Jonathan set off for the Continent.[42] He had promised to send the Princess Sophia an indigenous product of the New World, and now he meant to make good on it. He brought (along with some green candles), an Indian slave, a boy named Io, whom he presented to Sophia as a gift. The princess was overjoyed: "she took a great liking to the boy, she kept him at Court in his own habit, and [he] always stood with a plate behind her chair at table." In addition, she "immediately put him to school to learn to speak and write high Dutch and French and told me would have him instructed in the Christian religion." Belcher's comment on the Indian's fate is telling: "If he behaves himself well, his fortune is made for this world."[43] The Princess Sophia now had her own exotic servant to match the two Turks her son possessed. And like that of his Indian slave, Belcher's worldly fortune was made; the royal family now thoroughly embraced him. The next day he dined with the princess and her family, dandling on his knee her great-grandson, the infant Prince Frederick, "who doubtless will be King of Great Britain."[44] When he finally departed, Sophia gave him a medal bearing her likeness, along with the promise that "it may some time be in my power or some of mine to do you some service, when you may be sure you will not be forgotten."[45]

Cotton Mather, the Mather Library, and the Republic of Letters

It was just at this time, in the early eighteenth century, that the active phase of Cotton Mather's involvement with Germany was beginning (Figure 10.3). Mather, unlike Belcher, was no traveler. But Mather brought a powerful organizing intelligence to his own "Dutch" correspondence, and through it constructed a vision of Boston's place in the Atlantic world that Belcher's experiences had only vaguely foreshadowed. Imagi-

Figure 10.3 Cotton Mather, portrait by Peter Pelham, 1727. Reproduced courtesy of Houghton Library of Harvard University, Cambridge, Mass.

nation and intelligence alone would not have been enough to sustain Cotton Mather's efforts. In the absence of direct experience and personal contacts with his religious and cultural peers in England and continental Europe, contacts of the sort that his father had sustained through his repeated transatlantic travels, Cotton fed his mind and built his world on what he read in books. To understand Cotton Mather's approach to the Protestant International and the Republic of Letters, one needs to know what kind of library the Mather family collection was, and what specifically it contained.

The American Antiquarian Society in Worcester, Massachusetts, possesses the largest remaining fragment of the library assembled by members of the Mather family: roughly two thousand volumes of what may once have been a seven- to eight-thousand-volume library, one of the largest private libraries in early British America. The library has posed a frustrating challenge to scholars; it is not the writings *of* the Mathers (which are dauntingly voluminous in their own right), nor is it a set of books *about* the Mathers, but rather a somewhat random collection of the books that the Mathers happened to own, arranged in no particular order. Only recently has the Antiquarian Society systematically cataloged the collection, which has been sitting for two centuries on its shelves. The collection was built by four generations of the family, beginning with Richard Mather, who arrived in Boston in the 1630s, the emigrant patriarch of the clan of Puritan clergymen. His sons, grandsons, and great-grandsons fanned out from Boston across New England and back across the Atlantic to the British Isles. Increase Mather, Richard's most prominent son, acquired the largest number of volumes in the collection during several extended trips to England, where he haunted the London book markets. But the close connections that Increase maintained with the two brothers who returned to England and served out their careers as dissenting ministers, as well as with countless correspondents across Britain and the Continent, meant that the Mather family home in Boston's North End became the de facto capital of the Republic of Letters in its North American provinces.

Although we may be tempted to call the Mather's library "private," private is not really the word to describe the functions it served in early Boston. The marginalia written in the flyleaves and endpapers of these volumes, as well as the diaries kept by various family members, reveal that this was a circulating library, its volumes available to members of the greater Boston community, depending on the station of the borrower and the social or cultural capital that such lending and exchange might bring. The endpapers often bear signatures, dates, and places of exchange, and there is other evidence that many hands thumbed these volumes, including manuscript poems, jokes, hand-drawn illustrations, and the inevitable underscoring. During the library's heyday, from the

time Increase Mather returned to Boston after the Restoration of Charles
II to the death of Cotton Mather in 1727, the city of Boston was the
dominant entrepôt, the material and cultural broker, for virtually all relations between Europe and North America. If one lived in America at
this time and wanted to acquire European books, chances are that they
would come by way of Boston.[46] An essential function of this library,
then, was its strategic importance in the organization and dissemination
of knowledge that was critical to the construction of authority in early
America.

In using the phrase "Republic of Letters"—the collective body of
those engaged in the world of scholarly pursuits in the early modern
era—I want to call particular attention to the significance of the word
"republic." It was not an empire of letters, or a kingdom of letters: there
was no centralized hierarchy to it, no single metropole or court. The
learned world was an open elite, ready to accept participation from
many regions and aspirants. Nor was it an episcopacy of letters: from
the Reformation onward, the dissociation of many ancient universities
from Roman Catholic connections and the development of scholarly
communities outside the structures of the church in both Catholic and
Protestant countries made sure of that. But neither was it a Democracy
of Letters. Different communities, regions, or provinces had their dominant figures, their power brokers, their chosen leaders who dominated
local affairs and represented their region to the larger world, all the
while acting, by their own lights, for the general good of the whole.[47] In
England, this self-appointed task was taken on by the nabobs of the
Royal Society. In Boston, in New England, and for colonial British
America, the Mathers were among those prominent individuals who
occupied the role of power brokers in the Republic of Letters. Their
library was both an asset and a tool that helped them maintain this
position.

Yet to say that it was a republic is not to say that the world of knowledge and scholarly authority was egalitarian or uniform. Some people
and places were more powerful and more richly endowed than others.
The Mathers came from the Protestant evangelical wing of this republic,
and they represented a small, poor, and remote district, with limited resources but high aspirations. These conditions are important when one
considers the politics of the Republic of Letters, and the role that the

Mathers played in that arena, as a way to understand why questions of temporality, continuity, knowledge, and authority were constructed differently in early America than they were in contemporary Europe. All politics is local, even when the political prizes at stake are thought of as universal truths and eternal verities. The Mathers' connection to a transatlantic conversation among fellow intellectuals invested in the advancement of learning does not necessarily imply that this world of knowledge was uniform or consistent throughout the Atlantic world.

The contents of the Mather library can best be described as a conglomerate artifact of Atlantic culture from the fifteenth through the eighteenth centuries, but at the same time, a distinctive one, shaped by the interests and connections of the family that assembled it. A selective sampling of the shelves on which the volumes are organized reveals some striking features. First is the sheer weight and size of the collection. When examined shelf by shelf, the Mather library reminds one of the physicality of books. Legend has it that, when the collection was acquired for the Antiquarian Society early in the nineteenth century, the original shelf order in which they were arranged at the time of purchase was preserved. Until the recent opening of the Society's new storage vaults, that is how they remained. The Mather library was both big and personal. The books and pamphlets were a form of extended and distributed personhood—they helped make the Mathers who owned them larger, weightier, more extensive and ubiquitous.[48]

Another noteworthy feature is the breadth of the collection. A sample set of one shelf, containing forty volumes, bears titles that range from a Latin Bible printed in Venice in 1476, barely into the Gutenberg era, to English pamphlets of the 1720s. Of the forty volumes, eighteen titles are British imprints (London, Oxford, and Edinburgh), while another eighteen are from continental Europe, including Frankfurt, Amsterdam, Leiden, Paris, Basel, Rotterdam, Westphalia, Antwerp, and Hamburg. Four have no indication of place of printing. There are no American imprints. In terms of subject matter, the Mather books cover a wide spectrum, from systematic divinity and ecclesiastical politics to travel guides and geographical gazetteers, from the published volumes of European royal societies to alchemical and hermetic medical manuals, from commercial handbooks and treatises on Semitic languages to English political tracts and Machiavelli's *The Prince*.

But the most striking feature of the Mather collection is the impression it creates that, in the eyes of this one family of clergymen, intellectuals, and political leaders, no periods, no distinctive breaks or turning points, existed between their own experiences as Europeans in North America and the extended continuous past of Western Christendom. The holdings and patterns of usage of three of the most prominent genres or categories of knowledge found in the Mather library convey this most clearly: works on science, medicine, and natural history and philosophy; works on controversial theology and church history; and works on politics and government in the turbulent British kingdoms under the Stuarts.

In the constellation of subjects that we today might categorize as science, the Mather library contains many works published from the sixteenth to the eighteenth centuries. Left in these volumes are marginalia and other odds and ends (buttons, dead bugs, notes pinned to flyleaves) that demonstrate remarkable continuity over time in the usage of these works, despite dramatic developments in theory, method, and practice that historians of science have often described as revolutionary. Medicine provides a useful starting point. The Mathers as a family were avid amateur medical practitioners, the type of learned men to whom New Englanders turned in the absence of university-trained physicians. They collected titles that would aid them in their efforts, from practical guidebooks of general medical practice such as Jean François Fernel's *Universa Medicina* (1554; the Mathers' copy was a Utrecht reprint from 1656) to such up-to-date works as Robert Boyle's *Memoirs for the Natural History of Humane Blood* (1684), which Increase Mather acquired in London in the late 1680s.

It seemed not to matter to them that some authors (like Fernel, who specialized in reviving the study of ancient Greek physicians) prescribed medical practices defined by the humoral theory of medicine known since the ancients, while others, such as Jean Baptiste van Helmont, *Ortus Medicinae* (Amsterdam, 1652), or the Danish healer Ole Borch, *Hermetis, Aegyptiorum, et chemicorum sapientia* (Copenhagen, 1674), offered alchemical and hermetical theories on the causes and cures of disease that challenged the Galenic system. This apparent indifference to changing theory and practice is most clearly evidenced in those texts, such as *Chemia Rationalis* (Leiden, 1687), by the mysterious "P. T., Med.

Doct.," which several generations of Mathers indexed in their own hand on the front or back flyleaves, creating a working palimpsest of medicinal recipes, methods of treatment, and signs for recognizing unusual symptoms or dangerous diseases (Figures 10.4 and 10.5).

The Mathers were not merely passive recipients and distributors of knowledge created and tested elsewhere. They saw themselves as active participants in an international scholarly world, and their books were the means, the tools, that made such participation possible.[49] For instance, their copy of Robert Hooke's *Lectures and Observations on Comets* (London, 1678) contains, pinned into the inside cover, a manuscript copy of Increase and young Cotton Mather's own observations of a comet seen in Boston in April 1677, the same comet Hooke had observed before writing his treatise (Figure 10.6). Together, the Mathers' notes and Hooke's text create a scholarly dialogue on astronomy. Building on this dialogue and on future observations, such as the 1682 visit of the comet we know as Halley's, Increase Mather then went on to write and publish his own treatise, *Kometographia, or a discourse concerning comets, wherein the nature of blazing stars is inquired into, with an historical account of all the comets which have appeared from the beginning of the world unto the present year* (Boston, 1683).

Increase Mather has been criticized as a sort of scientific Luddite for his failure to accept in its entirety the so-called scientific revolution, the Copernican/Newtonian system as applied, in this case, to comets. Mather continued to insist that comets had providential meanings and were directed by the hand of God, even if Hooke's work could help to explain mathematically the regular paths of their orbits, and thus make it seem less likely that an interventionist deity could use comets as warnings or omens. But the Mathers did not see scholarly discovery, the shedding of new light on old questions, as a revolutionary or transformative process requiring the rejection of the old in favor of the new. Instead, the growth of knowledge was for them an unsteady, wavering process, the halting addition of information, the gradual, sometimes unexpected, and not always trustworthy revelation of the secrets of God's divine creation.[50] In this sense, the methodology behind Mather's *Kometographia* was remarkably consistent with the Baconian program for the "new" natural philosophy laid out in the *Novum Organum* (1620). Mather was attempting to assemble a complete catalog of

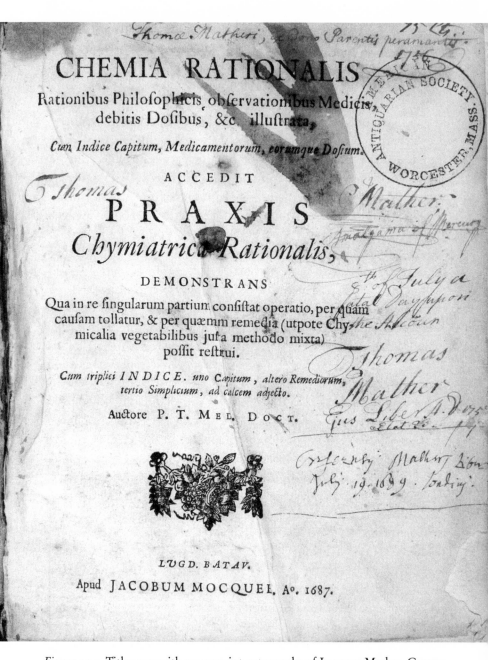

CHEMIA RATIONALIS

Rationibus Philofophicis, obfervationibus Medicis, debitis Dofibus, &c. illuftrata,

Cum Indice Capitum, Medicamentorum, eorumque Dofium.

ACCEDIT

PRAXIS

Chymiatrica Rationalis,

DEMONSTRANS

Qua in re fingularum partium confiftat operatio, per quam caufam tollatur, & per quæmm remedia (utpote Chymicalia vegetabilibus jufa methodo mixta) poffit reftrui.

Cum triplici INDICE. uno Capitum, altero Remediorum, tertio Simplicium, ad calcem adjecto.

Auctore P. T. MED. DOCT.

LUGD. BATAV.

Apud JACOBUM MOCQUEL, Aº. 1687.

Figure 10.4 Title page with manuscript autographs of Increase Mather, Cotton Mather, and Thomas Mather, in P.T. Med. Doct., *Chemia Rationalis*, 1 (Leiden, 1687); copy in the Mather Library, American Antiquarian Society, Worcester, Mass. All images from the Mather Library are reproduced courtesy of the American Antiquarian Society.

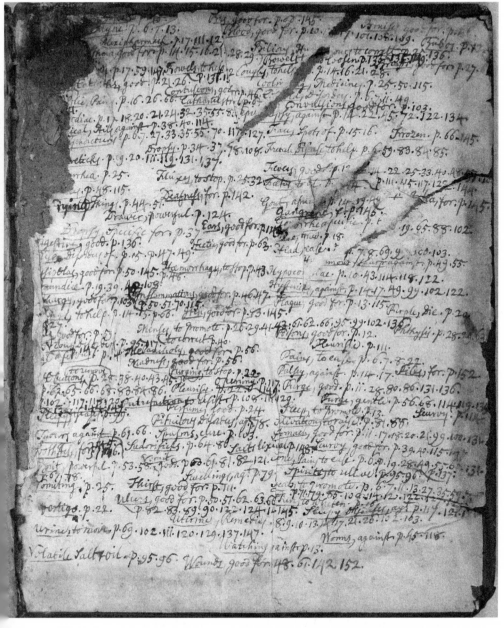

Figure 10.5 Manuscript index, rear endpapers, P.T. Med. Doct., *Chemia Rationalis*, Mather Library. This working index on the back flyleaves was constructed by several generations of the Mather family who used *Chemia Rationalis* as a practical medical guide. The dense palimpsest of notations shows the Mathers' intense engagement with the text and the continuity of its usage across time.

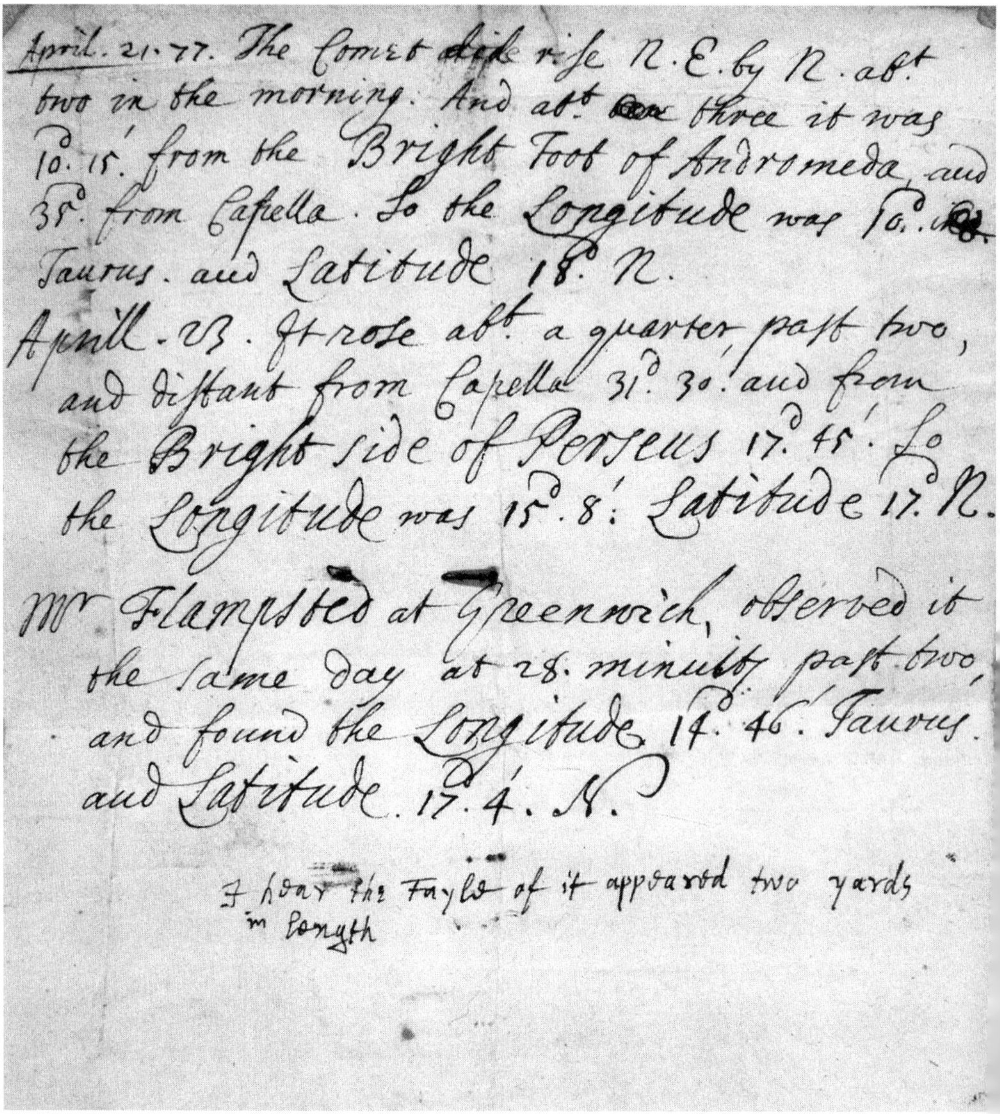

April. 21. 77. The Comet did rise N.E. by N. ab.t
two in the morning. And ab.t three it was
10. 15. from the Bright foot of Andromeda, and
35.° from Capella. So the Longitude was 10.°
Taurus. and Latitude 18.° N.

April. 23. It rose ab.t a quarter past two,
and distant from Capella 31.° 30.' and from
the Bright side of Perseus 17.° 45.' So
the Longitude was 15.° 8.' Latitude 17.° N.

Mr Flamsteed at Greenwich, observed it
the same day at 28. minutes past two,
and found the Longitude 14.° 46.' Taurus.
and Latitude. 17.° 4.' N.

I hear the Tayle of it appeared two yards
in Length

Figure 10.6 Manuscript notes of Cotton Mather and Increase Mather, pinned
to reverse of title page, Hooke, *Lectures and Collections*. Mather Library. The
single sentence at the bottom of the page was written by Increase Mather. The
remaining notes are in the hand of the young Cotton Mather, who was 14
years old at the time these observations on the comet of 1677 were made. The
Mathers' observations were made in dialogue with the contemporary English
astronomers (Robert Hooke, John Flamsteed) who informed their studies.

the available evidence, a record of every instance in recorded history where the appearance of comets seemed to portend important events. In Mather's eyes, his work assembled the factual background, the natural history, that was necessary before the more speculative or theoretical work of natural philosophy could be further developed.[51]

Where Mather differed from some of his contemporaries was in his reluctance to accept in its entirety the "mechanical philosophy," the metaphor that nature worked like a machine (such as a clock) that, once set in motion by its creator, required no further intervention or interruption. In this opinion, Mather was not alone. Both Francis Bacon and Robert Boyle were skeptical about the applicability of mathematical or mechanical accounts of nature "in its concrete particularities." Those investigators most thoroughly committed to the sufficiency of the mechanical metaphor tended to be those most likely to insist that their science was utterly new, a radical break from the Aristotelian past.[52] That Mather was not among them makes him neither less rigorous nor more retrograde than his European contemporaries; it simply places him along a spectrum of plausible positions for the investigation of nature in the late seventeenth century, and one which, as we shall see, accorded well with the politics of knowledge and authority in Boston.

In religious politics and Christian history, the most striking feature of the contents of the Mather library and the way its owners used it lies in its collective depiction of Christian continuity, from apostolic times to the unfolding present. Although the Mathers obviously tended to favor authors, both continental and British, in the reformed tradition, from John Calvin, Martin Bucer, and Henry Bullinger to William Ames, Richard Sibbes, and Richard Baxter, they also owned, read, and annotated the works of their ecclesiastical enemies (Richard Hooker), of English Catholics (Sir Kenelm Digby), of leading figures in contemporary Roman Catholicism (Cardinal Bellarmine), and of the church fathers stretching back through Aquinas to Augustine. The works they owned and favored with intensive and repeated readings define their allegiances clearly, but they do not suggest that the Mathers were given to stark periodization or rigid divisions in Christian history or church politics.

The Mathers, like all Protestants, were fully aware of the cataclysmic upheaval in European religion that Martin Luther, John Calvin, and other sixteenth-century reformers began, but it is nevertheless the case that, in the way they collected, used, and read their library, and in the way they presented their own immediate religious tradition and its history, there is very little sense of the Reformation as a sharp break, a bright dividing line, in the history of Christianity, so much as an ongoing struggle to preserve true Christianity from worldly powers that would corrupt and diminish it. No single reformer is unduly favored or singled out as the standard-bearer of religious truth; in this sense, the word "Calvinist" is a misnomer for New England's Puritans. Rather, many different reformers were read as champions of the godly cause, though all were human and fallible. As in the realm of the sciences (a distinction that the Mathers themselves would not have made), the emphasis in their collections and annotations of works on Christian history falls on gradual revelation, the slow accumulation of truth, and the sufferings of martyrs in defense of the faith and in the correction of Romish errors.[53] This attitude was similarly reflected in Jonathan Belcher's statement in 1704, while visiting the palace where William the Silent was assassinated, that William had been "the first deliverer of the Dutch from Popery." It conveyed the notion shared by Bostonians that Roman Catholicism had been a millennium-long captivity during which the true faith lay bound and hidden, but that true believers (like themselves), the saving remnant of the saints, had always managed to preserve it.

This emphasis helps explain the presence and purpose in the library of a work in French by Antoine du Pinet, published in Lyon in 1564, a work that describes the church polity of reformed congregations in a series of French cities. Appended to this text are dozens of pages of manuscript notes taken at synods held in the Channel Islands of Jersey and Guernsey in the late sixteenth century. Increase Mather may have acquired the book, and sewn in the manuscript notes, during the late 1650s when he served for a short while as minister to an English garrison on the island of Guernsey.[54] Although there are few books written in French in the library, this work fits the collection perfectly as part of the Mathers' compendium of knowledge of the historical revelation of the true church. Further research may reveal the utility of these records in Boston after 1685, when Huguenot refugees after the revocation of the Edict of Nantes began arriving in the Bay Colony. In other words, as citizen power brokers of the Protestant wing of the Republic of Letters, the Mathers in their scholarly practices contributed to sustaining the health and strength of the whole.

One of the few works in the collection that does reveal an intense concern among the Mathers with the periodization of Christian history is a title that makes a mockery of orthodox schemes of providential history, Catholic or Protestant. Isaac la Peyrère's *Men before Adam, A System of Divinity* was published in London in 1656, during the radical religious ferment of the interregnum. La Peyrère, a French Calvinist from Bordeaux, was a fellow traveler in the Republic of Letters, if one of its more disreputable and less well-equipped citizens. An autodidact, he had large ambitions, but no proper scholarly training. Like many of his contemporaries, he was a polymath, his interests ranging widely across natural, human, and historical spheres, but his most compelling concern involved the reconciliation of the Bible with other ancient and classical texts, not only Greek and Roman, but also works by the "Caldeans, Egyptians, Scythians, and Chinensians."[55] It was this effort that inspired *Men before Adam,* an attempt to argue, as the title suggests, that the two versions offered in the first two chapters of Genesis actually describe two different creations—the first of humanity in general, the second of the Jews as God's chosen people, meaning that there were many men and women long before Adam and Eve.[56] Peyrère's pre-Adamite argument so troubled Cotton Mather—like Peyrère, a polymath, but one with proper academic training and credentials—that on page after page of the text, Mather crossed out the word "DIVINITY" from the running heads and replaced it, in ink, with "HERESY." He also took the time to create an index of subjects at the end of the text that he could then systematically refute (Figure 10.7).

If we turn from Christian history to secular politics (another stark division that the Mathers would not have acknowledged), a brief glance at a single volume, of a type that constituted a significant subset of the collection, reveals a similar approach. The Mather library contains dozens of examples of composite books, collections of small pamphlets on related political subjects stitched together and bound to create a kind of homemade magazine, a running conversation among numerous authors on a single theme. What is striking about these compilations is that the publication dates of the individual pamphlets are often widely dispersed;

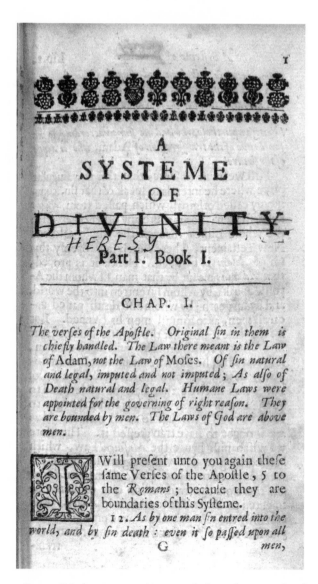

A
SYSTEME
OF
~~DIVINITY~~
HERESY
Part I. Book I.

CHAP. I.

The verses of the Apostle. Original sin in them is
chiefly handled. The Law there meant is the Law
of Adam, not the Law of Moses. Of sin natural
and legal, imputed and not imputed; As also of
Death natural and legal. Humane Laws were
appointed for the governing of right reason. They
are bounded by men. The Laws of God are above
men.

I Will present unto you again these
same Verses of the Apostle, 5 to
the *Romans* ; because they are
boundaries of this Systeme.

12. *As by one man sin entred into the*
world, and by sin death : even it so passed upon all
G *men,*

Figure 10.7 Cotton Mather manuscript emendation, chapter 1, book 1, of La Peyrère, *Men Before Adam*, Mather Library. Here, and on the running heads of dozens of the subsequent pages of *Men before Adam*, Cotton Mather crossed out "Divinity" and scribbled "Heresy" in its place. Although this may seem a juvenile response to La Peyrère's argument, Mather also compiled, at the back of the text, a detailed alphabetical index of the points he wished to refute, demonstrating a mature seriousness of engagement with newly emergent forms of biblical criticism.

titles from the reign of James I are sewn in beside works published under James II. The impression conveyed is that, although individual rulers and regimes come and go, and the fortunes of the godly ebb and flow with dynastic shifts, the universal human condition and its relationship to worldly power continues on essentially unchanged.

How do we explain the Mathers' stubborn insistence on the unbroken unity of the world of knowledge in all its separate realms, and the unbroken continuity of the past with the present, when we have become accustomed to believing that the era in which they lived was one of scientific revolutions, intellectual enlightenment—in short, of a dawning modernity, led by pioneers who were the Mathers' associates, correspondents, fellow delegates to the Republic of Letters? My inclination is to turn for assistance to work in science studies, by historians, sociologists, and anthropologists of science. Steven Shapin, Simon Schaffer, and other scholars have examined and uncovered the social and political work through which men like Robert Boyle created the context in which they could argue convincingly that their work was revolutionary, a purification of knowledge that required a sharp break with the methods and sureties of the past, and in particular, the removal of scientific facts from speculation about the role of divine providence in human affairs and natural occurrences.[57]

Robert Boyle was in many ways part of the same world that the Mathers occupied. He was in age a near contemporary of Increase Mather, and the two men became friends during the elder Mather's sojourn in England. Boyle's work in chemistry was strongly influenced by George Starkey, an early Harvard College graduate and secretive alchemist, who published his works under the mysterious pseudonym "Erineus Philalethes."[58] Boyle served for many years as one of the commissioners of the New England Company, responsible for raising funds to promote Indian conversion and education in New England. The Mathers read and absorbed Boyle's works, from *The Usefulness of Experimental Natural Philosophy* (1663) to *The Christian Virtuoso* (1690).

But in Boyle's particular environment of Restoration England there were good reasons to want to advance the necessity of a break in the unity of knowledge, of a distinctive discontinuity between past and present methods in science, and to distance inquiry into the natural world from contentious disputes about religion, providence, and politics. The general crisis of authority that marked the bloody first half of the seventeenth century in the British Isles, the near complete breakdown of consensus on the articles of faith and the sources of political authority, ending in regicide, religious anarchy, and finally counterrevolution—all this provided incentives for Boyle and his cohort in the recently founded Royal Society to make science something new and different, to reconstitute its authority on experimentally produced facts, and to downplay the interpretation of nature as a method for reading the purposes of God in human affairs.

Christianity still held an important place, indeed an essential one, in the cosmology and mental universe of Boyle and his cohort—the world was as much God's book of nature as the Bible was his revealed word. Furthermore, the authority on which scientific practitioners like Boyle rested their claims to speak the truth about God's nature lay as much in their demonstration of an irenic and charitable godliness as in their gentlemanly honor and integrity. Yet in the wake of the violence and fanaticism fostered by religious belief in portents and providence in the mid-seventeenth century, Christian virtuosos and natural philosophers in England tended to leave wonders, signs, and marvels of nature aside as they assembled their natural histories into a new philosophy.[59] In the context of Restoration England, Boyle and his Royal Society cohort found this stance effective and powerful, and the chief proponents of the new method used it to gain positions of power. It was no more an accident that Isaac Newton spent his last years holding two offices, president of the Royal Society and director of the Royal Mint, than that he eventually published his mathematical and mechanical philosophy but kept his alchemical and religious speculations to himself.[60]

To understand the politics of Boston's participation in the Republic of Letters, it is vital to remember where Boston was and the significance of both time and place in politics, even the politics of science and knowledge and the authority on which truth is based. For the Mathers, as colonial Creole elites, there was no incentive to break away from the past, to claim a newfound purity in the knowledge they were absorbing and helping to create. Rather, they had every reason to sustain the idea of continuity. Their possession and absorption of the volumes of scholarship that contained and replicated the knowledge of past ages and distant regions was, in the circumstances of colonial Boston and of early

British America generally, the source of their power and authority as cultural brokers, as delegates for New England to the Republic of Letters. They knew their constituency well, knew its devotion to biblical truth, and its belief in an active God who frequently intervened in human affairs to show his pleasure or dismay at the behavior of his chosen people.[61] Absent the revolutions that shook English life, the covenanted society of Massachusetts had not lost its faith in the civil authority of godly magistrates. Given such a constituency, it would have been folly, even intellectual treason, to announce that scholarly advances, new experimental methods, or strange new facts required a scientific revolution that must bring providential interpretations to an end. The Mathers did not embrace the concept of a scientific revolution because nothing in their immediate world gave them any reason, any incentive, to do such a thing. This makes them not lesser thinkers than Boyle, Hooke, and the other luminaries of the Royal Society, but the same kind—scholars who knew their own circumstances and interests, and bent their research, their investigations, and their conclusions to comport with those needs.

The local importance of this intellectual continuity can be seen in the politics surrounding the 1721 introduction of smallpox inoculation in Boston, when the contest over knowledge and authority erupted into a full-blown and violent public controversy. Thousands of people were infected by the deadly scourge, hundreds died, and in the midst of it all, Cotton Mather and his colleague, the self-trained "Dr." Zabdiel Boylston, began experimenting with the new process of inoculating the uninfected with live smallpox matter—it might well prevent the disease, or it might deliberately spread the deadly infection to otherwise healthy people. Some applauded and embraced these efforts, others denounced them, threw bombs into Mather's window, and mobbed Boylston's house.[62]

To reach the decision to try inoculation, Mather did what he had always done: he read about it—in this case from reports sent in by trained physicians working in Italy and the Levant to the *Transactions* of the Royal Society.[63] He also read reports in the Danish equivalent of the Royal Society *Transactions*, as is evident from Mather's marginal notations in articles on variolation, as inoculation was often called.[64] He had been, on his own, charting the course of smallpox epidemics in New England for years, and he knew that the region, including his own children, lay in danger of devastation when the next outbreak occurred. Beyond his reading and his timetables, he also spoke to those around him, including his West African slave, Onesimus, who had been inoculated in his homeland and described the process to Mather.

Boylston and Mather's chief opposition came from several quarters. The poor and frightened crowd, of course, constituted an expected group of opponents. But of the others, one was Dr. William Douglass, the only physician in New England with training at a European university, Edinburgh. The other was James Franklin's new satirical newspaper, *The Courant*, which consciously adopted the coffeehouse wit, the tone of sophisticated discernment and secular mockery of clerical earnestness, first advanced by Joseph Addison in *The Spectator*, Richard Steele in *The Tatler*, and their fashionable English contemporaries.[65] Taken together, Douglass and *The Courant* (in which Douglass published his diatribes against inoculation) represented voices of the so-called Enlightenment, of the scientific revolution, in that they had imbibed the culture of a world in which amateur clergymen/medical practitioners and self-trained stonecutters were ridiculed and in which the experimental philosophy had supposedly made folk medicine obsolete. But of course, the hidden reason for accepting the experimental testing and laboratory results that Boyle and his contemporaries had promoted—the valid testimony of acceptable authorities, gentlemen of good reputation and appropriate training—still lay behind the triumph of the experimental fact. And in this case, although it was Mather and Boylston who were hewing most closely to the actual practice of experimental medicine, they now lacked the political authority to sustain their claims, because a new form of challenge had entered the local picture. In the eyes of Douglass and the *Courant*, Mather's authorities and credentials were not good enough. The Royal Society reports came from physicians in ungodly and exotic places—Italy and the Levant. An African slave's testimony was obviously beneath contempt. Douglass, the *Courant*, and their large Boston audience refused to credit such disreputable authorities, and would not "buy" the pox inoculation, as the slang of the time described it.

Mather and Boylston were willing to risk what Douglass denounced because it was consistent with what they had always done, as delegates to the Republic of Letters who were fully convinced that knowledge could be discovered in the provinces just as well as in the metropolis. It was not that the quality of the science had changed, but rather that a new form of the politics of authority to speak the truth in science, triumphant in London for reasons distinctive to London, had now been brought to America and applied in a place where it previously had been out of place.

The Protestant International: The Charles Meets the Rhine

The challenge for Cotton Mather, then, and for intellectuals like him who were seeking to link their local traditions and conditions to the new potential for an integrated Protestant Atlantic, was to find like-minded people with whom to organize their often parallel intellectual projects into a coherent whole. Their task was as much a political as an intellectual one, and if the fashionable world of London intellectuals and coffeehouse sophisticates rejected or belittled their aspirations, there were other places to turn for allies. And so, like Jonathan Belcher, but through the medium of books and correspondence rather than through immediate experience, Cotton Mather made contacts in the intellectual centers of power that were opening up to him in the post-Stuart era, and found his interests and ambitions mirrored in the aspirations of German Pietism. In 1709, a year after Jonathan Belcher's second trip to Hanover, the first evidence appears of Mather's awareness of the Pietist institute at Halle developed by August Hermann Francke (Figure 10.8). Versions of the works of Francke published in London in 1707 had found their way into Mather's hands, and the following year he resolved in his diary to send some of his own recent publications, which he described as "the true American Pietism," to "Dr. Franckius, in Saxony."[66] Francke and his works were a revelation to Mather, and also a challenge. The two men were exact contemporaries—born a month apart in 1663, they died eight months apart in 1727—and they were extraordinarily similar in many ways. Both were sons of prominent, highly educated, and devoutly pious families. They shared a practical pietistic faith and were equally extravagant in their ambitions, with a vast range of interests, massive correspondence networks, and unbounded energy. In Francke, Mather had finally discovered someone whose intellect, ambition, piety, and energy surpassed his own, which fascinated him and brought out his competitive instincts as well. He began an eager correspondence with

Figure 10.8 August Hermann Francke, ca. 1730. Reproduced courtesy of the Franckesche Stiftungen, Halle, Germany (Staatsbibliothek zu Berlin—Preußischer Kulturbesitz, A. H. Francke Foundation).

Francke and his Halle connections that would last through the remainder of the two men's lives.[67]

But to understand the full significance of this correspondence requires a bit of backtracking down some tangled and circuitous paths, for Cotton Mather's connection with German Pietism had been at least twenty years in the making. In 1687, his father, Increase Mather, had corresponded with Johannes Leusden, professor of Hebrew at Utrecht, to whom he sent a description of John Eliot's efforts to convert the Indians of Massachusetts.[68] Cotton Mather used his father's letter as the basis for his own considerably longer biography of John Eliot, published in Boston and London in 1691 under the title *Triumphs of the Reformed Religion in America*.[69] The younger Mather's Eliot biography received wide acclaim among dissenters and Pietists in Britain, and it influenced the work of a fellow of the Royal Society named Patrick Gordon, whose *Geography Anatomiz'd* of 1693 was revised in 1699 in order to promote missionary activities, like those of John Eliot, throughout the expanding empires of Europe's Protestant nations.[70] Gordon's *Geography* was, in turn, one of the spurs that led to the formation in 1699 of the Society for the Promotion of Christian Knowledge (SPCK) in London, a voluntary organization committed to missionary endeavors and the publication of Bibles and pious tracts.[71]

In its early days, the SPCK, seeking connections throughout the Protestant world, made August Hermann Francke a corresponding member.[72] When Queen Anne came to the English throne in 1702, her husband George, prince of Denmark and a great supporter of Halle Pietism, installed Francke's protégé Anton Wilhelm Boehm as court chaplain in London, and thenceforth Boehm became the principal conduit between Halle Pietism and its British sympathizers.[73] In 1705, the year Boehm was made court chaplain, the SPCK's leading position was filled by Henry Newman, who remained the Society's secretary for the next forty years and became intimate friends with Boehm.[74] Newman, as it happens, was a Bostonian, Harvard College class of 1687, son of a Puritan minister and grandson of Samuel Newman, among the greatest of New England's founding clergy.[75] Although Henry Newman was drawn toward the Church of England, he never lost his dissenter's sensibility or his New England connections, maintaining lifelong friendships with Cotton Mather, Benjamin Colman, Thomas Prince, and Jonathan

Belcher. Through Newman, Boehm, and the SPCK, the initial links between Francke in Halle and Mather in Boston were forged, and over the
next two decades they would grow stronger and more elaborate.[76]

Cotton Mather's earliest letters to Francke went awry in the transatlantic journey, but a later effort in 1714 received a gratifying response.
Francke wrote Mather (in Latin) a seventy-page account of the history
and accomplishments of the Halle institute, which Mather then summarized in English and published in Boston in 1715.[77] Francke mentioned
that he owned a copy of a letter to Johannes Leusden written by one
"Crescentius Mather," who he guessed (correctly) must be a relative of
his correspondent, and he described how John Eliot's work among the
Massachusetts Indians had influenced Halle's missionary work in India, which must have been enormously gratifying to both Mathers.[78] In
response, Cotton Mather sent off to Francke, by way of Boehm in London, "a large Number of Packetts, which had in them scores of American Treatises, besides a few small presents in Gold" for Francke's orphanage—the gold was in part a gift from Jonathan Belcher. Mather
urged Boehm to hurry these on to Halle and to send some of the tracts
into the hands of the "Malabarian missionaries; And if you can do it,
send them into France; yea, excuse me, if I say, procure them to be translated into as many Languages as you can."[79] Not content to rely on
intermediaries, Mather then corresponded directly with Halle's missionaries at Tranquebar, on the southeast coast of India, the ministers
Ziegenbalg, Plütschau, and Gründler, with whom he traded ideas and
strategies. Mather then used this correspondence as the basis for a 1721
pamphlet entitled *India Christiana,* a lengthy discourse in which he outlined a series of principles for the conversion of pagans in both the East
and West Indies.[80]

During these first two decades of the eighteenth century, as his contacts with German Pietism increased and as the works of Johann Arndt,
Philip Jacob Spener, Boehm, and Francke became available in English,
Mather read them frequently and urged his wife, his family, his church,
and the members of the religious societies he organized in Boston to do
the same.[81] But the influence of these connections went beyond the level
of personal piety. For Mather, their great value lay in the way that German Pietism complemented and confirmed a range of ideas he had independently been developing. In this period Mather's interest in practical

piety, reform, and benevolence was at its height. His most famous work in this vein, *Bonifacius: An Essay Upon the Good* (1710), bears reference to Halle Pietism in its penultimate chapter.[82] In this work and many others of the same period, Mather laid out his ambitious ideas for social and religious reform, ideas that were reinforced by the works of other contemporary Bostonians, both clergy and laymen. The interlocking array of issues and subjects for pious reform he presented constituted a developing vision of the ideal society that Boston could come to represent, a vision that was shaped by the transatlantic conversation with continental Pietism.[83]

First and foremost in this constellation of concerns came individual conversion, the experience of the "new birth," which for Mather and all Pietists formed the groundwork for useful social action. Only those individuals whose hearts, through a kind of divine alchemy, had been converted from love of sin to love of God could be expected to persevere in the work of the Lord. This belief underlay Pietism's intense commitment to evangelical efforts: the need to increase the number of converts was a necessary step in the creation of a godly society.[84] The interest in missionary work among pagan peoples on the frontiers of an expanding Christendom was obviously part of this concern, and the transatlantic conversation on this subject was perhaps the issue on which Bostonians made the greatest contribution to the Pietist movement, though their influence did not stop there.[85] Another issue embraced by Mather and other Boston Pietists at this early date was opposition to the slave trade. Although slavery per se was not attacked by Mather, who promoted genuine efforts by masters to convert slaves, the slave trade as a system that ignored or perverted the missionary imperative became an increasingly common target.[86]

In addition to "pagans" of the East and West Indies and the plight of African slaves, Mather's concerns extended to those suffering persecution within the Christian world, especially refugees from Catholic tyranny. At the time Mather began writing in this vein, the Huguenot population fleeing after Louis XIV's revocation of the Edict of Nantes was the main concern, but in the eighteenth century the plight of various German refugee groups would move to center stage.[87] Together with the desire to aid the afflicted came a vitriolic form of anti-Catholicism, which included a fierce devotion to the Protestant succession in Britain and a constant awareness of the fate of Protestant forces in the wars of the eighteenth century.[88] Yet amid the intellectual currents swirling about the north Atlantic, these seemingly disparate subjects could become oddly entangled and intertwined. A peculiar document in this vein was written by Paul Dudley, another Bostonian with extensive Atlantic contacts, whose *Essay on the Merchandize of Slaves & Souls of Men* combined a rabid critique of Roman Catholicism with an assault on any form of trafficking in human merchandise.[89]

The intense passion of this opposition to popery was fueled in part by envy. Mather and his Pietist colleagues were jealous of the success of Jesuit missionaries, and they also envied the doctrinal and practical unity that Roman Catholicism could enforce.[90] Another major aim of this evolving Pietist program, then, was an attempt to counteract the divisive tendencies within Protestantism in order to compete with Roman Catholic efforts. The chief subject of Mather's conversation with the Halle missionaries in India was his attempt to reduce the tenets of Christianity to a few simple principles that all Protestants might agree on as a way to overcome national and confessional differences, principles that would be easily grasped by people unfamiliar with Christian doctrine.[91] And the final linchpin in these efforts to promote an expansive Protestant ecumenism came in the realm of language and communications. Just as Leibniz spent much of his career searching for a basis for a universal language, so Mather and his Pietist colleagues invented ways to make their ideas universally known and understood.[92] The aspect of Francke's work that Mather found most breathtaking was the translating and publishing business. As Mather put it: "Within a few Years, and since the light of Evangelical Piety thus breaking forth in the Heart of Germany, there have been more Volumes of the Scriptures vended, than in the whole Period of the Time, from the Reformation until Now; and never were they so cheap since the World began."[93] Halle's success became a model for Mather's own efforts to publish and broadcast his American Pietism as widely and accessibly as possible.

Still another element in this constellation of concerns was the need for reform at home, to construct model communities at the centers of Protestant Christianity that would be examples to the unconverted world as well as ideal training centers for missionaries. For Mather in Boston, this meant first of all attending to immediate social problems, for which

Halle again provided a useful model—orphanages, homes for widows and destitute women, hospitals, poor relief, and schools where poor as well as rich could learn Christian piety and be trained for missionary work.[94] But Mather's idea of a perfectly reformed society went beyond these more common forms of charitable activity to include a range of things that we would call, roughly, scientific, including medicine and healing (Halle's hospitals and pharmaceutical business were particularly important in this light) and alchemy, which was intimately linked to the healing arts.[95] Still another of his favorite notions, supported by friends and colleagues, was a belief in commercial and market reform. For Boston to become a model community, its commercial transactions would have to be conducted as fairly, openly, and charitably as possible, so that commerce would be a benefit to all rather than a means for the rich to cheat and oppress the poor.[96]

This last position was not a diatribe against commerce itself, but a collective vision of commercial friendship and prosperity that Mather advanced most powerfully in a pamphlet entitled *Theopolis Americana: An Essay on the Golden Street of the Holy City*, preached before the Massachusetts General Court in 1709. This essay, based on a text from the book of Revelation and built around an explicitly alchemical metaphor, explored the question of how the streets of a godly city might be converted into "pure gold." Here, in a single text, Mather combined virtually all the issues just described—the importance of individual conversion, the need for market regulation (according to the golden rule), an attack on the slave trade, a virulent anti-Catholicism, the urgency of missionary activities, the quest for ecumenical Christianity (including apologies for Massachusetts's earlier persecution of Quakers and suspected witches), and the promotion of education—with the ultimate purpose of suggesting the millennial potential of all these efforts. He concluded by paraphrasing a pagan writer of ancient Greece: "who says that in Times long preceding his, there was a Tradition, that Europe and Asia and Africa, were encompassed by the Ocean; But . . . beyond the Ocean, there was a great Island . . . [where] there was an huge City, called Theopolis, the Godly City. In that City, Sayes he, they enjoy all Possible Peace and Wealth, and Plenty, and . . . have God marvellously coming down among them. I know not what well to make of a Tradition so very Ancient, and yet having such an American Face upon it. [But] there are many Arguments to perswade us, That our Glorious Lord, will have an Holy City in America; a City, the Street whereof will be Pure Gold."[97] Although Mather was not bold enough to identify Boston as that luminous place, the implications for his audience must have been obvious. In conversation with other Bostonians and in his correspondence with German Pietists, Mather had assembled the jumble of issues and concerns that Jonathan Belcher had stumbled his way through in his Dutch travels into a coherent program for ushering in a Protestant international millennium, with high hopes for Boston's role in the process.

These millennial ambitions, partially homegrown but greatly amplified by Bostonians' emerging dialogue with German and Dutch sources, provide a background for the social, political, and religious reform movements that occupied Boston in the critical decades of the late seventeenth and early eighteenth century. Though the millennium did not arrive in Boston when Cotton Mather had hoped it would, he noted as the year 1715 drew to a close that Louis XIV had finally died, and he wrote to Boehm in London that "I apprehend the Time is now coming on apace, for the Empire of Antichrist and Satan . . . to come unto its promised period, and the Kingdome of our Saviour to be Exhibited with glory to God in the Highest, and on earth Peace, thro' Good Will among Men."[98] For Mather, the integration of Boston and Massachusetts into the cultural realm of international Protestant Pietism, as well as into the reconfigured British Empire and its strengthened continental alliances, was becoming clear.

In 1730, Jonathan Belcher's long-standing relationship with the House of Hanover finally paid off in his appointment as royal governor of Massachusetts.[99] The following year, the Catholic archbishop of Salzburg, trying to suppress a Pietist revival within his principality, ordered the expulsion of all Protestants, sending some 20,000 refugees north toward Prussia, where the Halle Pietists played a major role in organizing their wide-ranging resettlement.[100] Halle reached out to its English connections at the SPCK, and through the guidance of its secretary, Henry Newman, late of Boston, several hundred Salzburgers were transported to the new British colony at Georgia.[101] With Newman as go-between,

Jonathan Belcher and Benjamin Colman, minister of Boston's Brattle Street Church, began a correspondence with Halle's missionaries to Georgia and their superintendent, Samuel Urlsperger, the Lutheran senior of Augsburg.[102] Had Cotton Mather lived to see this day, he would clearly have relished the opportunity to develop new links in the chain of Pietist connections that *India Christiana* had described.

On their journey to Georgia, the Salzburger refugees were accompanied by the Baron Philipp von Reck, a young Hanoverian nobleman (nephew of George II's leading diplomat) and an ardent Pietist, who acted as a commissioner overseeing their settlement. Once the Georgia establishment had taken shape, Baron von Reck set off overland through British America to drum up support for the refugees. In his tour of the colonies, he was repeatedly shocked at the depredations of the slave system, especially the slaves' ignorance of Christianity, which he blamed on their masters. But of all the places he visited, including Philadelphia and New York, the Baron von Reck was most impressed by Boston, "the largest and most imposing commercial city in all of English America, . . . as favorably situated for commerce as any city in the world." He was entertained, of course, by Jonathan Belcher, whom he described as "Jonathan Belcher, Knight, Commander-in-Chief and supreme Governor of New England. . . . who can be put before all people in America as an example of honesty, good conduct, and love." Belcher must have been extremely flattered by the visit, especially by the way in which it mirrored his own experiences thirty years earlier. Here was the young Hanoverian nobleman coming to Boston, and paying flattering attention to the same sorts of things that Belcher, the young merchant prince, had observed in his Dutch travels. In particular, Baron von Reck noted that in Boston: "Many Christian provisions have been made here for the poor and the orphans. There is, for example, a corn house in which a large quantity of corn is stored every year when prices are lowest and where, when food gets expensive in the winter and people begin to starve, they can buy the corn they need for the price at which it was bought. There are, likewise, a hospital, four schools for poor orphans, etc. Four English miles from Boston is the University of Cambridge [Harvard College] where 200 students are enrolled."

The baron also admired the beauty of the streets, especially "Hanover Street, so named by the governor," and the distinctive quality of religious life in the city. By the time he left, Baron von Reck was laden with gifts and correspondence for his German contacts; he had also received promises from Belcher for two sloops loaded with wood to be sent to Georgia for the construction of an orphanage, and he had formed elaborate plans with a group of Boston merchants for the further settlement of Salzburg refugees in America.[103]

Theopolis Americana

It is easy to be dismissive of the hopes and aspirations of Mather, Belcher, and their seemingly naive fellow Bostonians, to compare them, for instance, with the Rosicrucian enlightenment described by Frances Yates: an incipient movement that never fully materialized, a moment—partly fictional but powerfully symbolic—of extraordinary intellectual, religious, and political promise centered around the Electoral court at Heidelberg in the 1610s. Indeed, there are not merely structural similarities but direct connections between Heidelberg and Boston, including the alchemy theme in Belcher's and Mather's experiences, and the relevance to readers like Samuel Sewall, dreaming of Christ coming to Boston, of reading David Pareus, who was a leading theologian at Heidelberg during that utopian interlude in 1612 when the Princess Elizabeth, daughter of James I of England, married Frederick, the Elector Palatine. As Frances Yates described it, the "chymical wedding" of Elizabeth and Frederick, the marriage of the Thames and the Rhine, was a brief moment when a new alliance between the leading Protestant powers of Europe gave rise to dreams of a unified Christianity, a revival of piety, a flourishing of the arts and sciences, emanating from a European courtly center that would be a model of Christian charity for the world to emulate.[104]

Those dreams, of course, were crushed on the Continent by Frederick's failed bid to seize the Bohemian throne and by the thirty years of brutal warfare that followed. For like-minded people in England, the portentous rise and disastrous fall of Cromwell's Commonwealth and the creeping Catholicism of the later Stuarts crushed their fervent millennial aspirations as well, leaving only faint traces of that earlier utopian moment, which Yates detected in the early enthusiasm of the Royal Society's founders for alchemy, cabalism, and hermetic science, an enthusiasm that was hidden and suppressed after the Restoration of Charles II.[105] The course of imperial state building in Europe left these earlier dreamers skeptical, if not cynical, about the possibility that earthly kingdoms could be made to serve the kingdom of God.

But people in Boston, spared the experience of defeat in their provincial isolation, found it possible to harbor utopian dreams longer than their European counterparts. Throughout the seventeenth century and well into the eighteenth, New England remained a hotbed of alchemical studies and millennial speculation, and the dream of a holy city remained alive there as well.[106] The 1688 crisis that placed a Dutch Protestant on the throne of England was followed in 1701 by an Act of Parliament settling the royal succession upon Belcher's future patron, Sophia of Hanover, the last surviving descendant of the Princess Elizabeth and the Palatine Elector Frederick.[107] There were people in Boston who imagined that at the moment of this remarriage of the Thames and the Rhine, the Charles River could also add a small trickle to the rising tide of an emerging Protestant Atlantic community. And so they reached out into that world, directly, as in the case of Jonathan Belcher, or through correspondence and imagination, as in Cotton Mather's case, until they made contact with those elements that were congenial to their way of thinking.

Dreams of a utopian Protestant international no longer lay at the center of European state politics, if indeed they ever had, despite the occasional illusion created, for instance, by Marlborough's victory at Blenheim, announced on the very day that Belcher arrived in Hanover. But there was still sufficient encouragement—indeed, growing encouragement—for such beliefs on the margins of Europe's centers of power, in voluntary societies like the SPCK, in quasi-independent organizations like Francke's institute at Halle, and in the revivalist Protestant Pietism that they promoted beyond the bounds of state churches and confessional orthodoxy. In those circles, Bostonians felt the most comfortable and had the most to contribute, for their century-long history as a marginal community, a voluntary society dedicated to the promotion of evangelical Christianity, built on a highly independent commercial foundation, gave them a wealth of experience to contribute to the growing transatlantic conversation.

When W. R. Ward tried to assemble this vast and unwieldy material into a single magisterial study, he saw a powerful force for the creation of evangelical awakenings emerging first in the heart of Europe, in Silesia, Bohemia, and Moravia, spreading south into Salzburg and Austria, north to the Baltic, west to the Rhineland, then crossing the Channel to Britain, and finally jumping the Atlantic to brush the North American coast as well.[108] But when one looks at this network from a Bostonian point of view, it seems less like a core-and-periphery, metropolis-and-margins model than an evolving conversation, a kind of transatlantic echo chamber, as ideas and practices generated indigenously in every corner of this expanding realm of communications began to merge. As Cotton Mather contemplated the world opening before him, he exclaimed, "O wide Atlantick, Thou shalt not stand in the way as any Hindrance of those Communications! Verily Our Glorious Lord will have Dominion from Sea to Sea."[109] That was the hope of the Bostonians who imagined the Charles River joining the Thames, the Rhine, and the Elbe, all flowing together to form a Protestant Atlantic world in which *Theopolis Americana* would prosper with a glory that would give Boston more to boast about than Rome had ever had.

11

The Río de la Plata and Anglo-American Political and Social Models, 1810–1827

BEATRIZ DÁVILO

Revolutionary leaders in the Río de la Plata, like those in the other regions of Hispanic America, confronted the task of founding a modern nation on the ruins of Spanish monarchical and colonial domination. Each political community (the viceroyalties, the provinces, and even the cities) had held a hierarchical and bilateral relation with the Crown without institutional ties among themselves. They were not eager to replace their subordination to the king with a structure that subordinated them to one another.[1] Moreover, the "republican solution" to the challenge of building a new order—the common option for those opposing a monarchical metropolitan power—was a double-sided problem. Politically and institutionally, the legitimacy and the organization of the new state required a constitutional and juridical tradition that had not been strongly developed in Hispanic America. Socially, the success of republican experiments would be dependent on a law-abiding citizenry committed to the principles of the new regime, whereas the colonial system had relied on the obedience of subjects accustomed to accepting—at least in a formal sense—the will of the king.

With revolution, Hispanic American elites confronted both the failure of Hispanic juridical culture to provide them with tools adequate to establish a new institutional organization and a citizenry without training in republican politics. From revolution onward the new governments claimed to express the sovereignty of the people.[2] But who were the "people" in whom sovereignty resided, and to what extent might they participate in government? Did "the people" refer to freely associated individuals or to the separate corporate political entities that previously formed the viceregal and monarchical governing structure?[3] Did the concept of 'popular sovereignty' entitle men to participate directly in politics, or did it imply the mediation of representative institutions? In the former viceroyalty of Río de la Plata the resolution of these questions required almost half a century of debates, conflicts, and war.

To mold both new institutions and citizens capable of membership in societies governed by those institutions, the elites of Río de la Plata looked to the North Atlantic countries. Argentine historiography has emphasized the importance of France and French Enlightenment philosophy for the Río de la Plata revolutionary process, while neglecting the importance of English and U.S. political thought and institutions. Notwithstanding the influence that French political philosophy and French revolutionary experiences had among its members, the dominant elite of Buenos Aires believed that Britain and the United States provided illuminating examples, completely different from the Spanish colonial tradition, of how to organize the state and to enlighten a society. Britain was the hegemonic nation of the age, projecting an image of never-ending economic growth and political stability. The United States was a pioneer in the struggle against colonial domination and in the creation of a modern republic. But what most filled the Buenos Aires elite with admiration was the success of those nations in harmonizing freedom and order, an outcome that was believed to result from habits and traditions forged over time by the nurturing of specific cultural and political values. They therefore believed that the introduction of those values, together with the institutions that supported them, would overcome the Spanish political and juridical legacy and clear the path to modern politics for Río de la Plata society.

Two ideas clearly express what the Atlantic discourse meant to the groups engaged in South American state-building: that the Atlantic region was a "formidable laboratory of political debate" and that it was a "reserve of experience." The political thought of Montesquieu, Jean-Jacques Rousseau, Edmund Burke, the North American pamphleteers and constitutional designers, and the authors of *The Federalist* was extensively discussed from about 1770 to 1830, as Darío Roldán shows.[4] But it was not only the theories that spread from the North Atlantic

Map 11.1 The viceroyalty of Río de la Plata, ca. 1780.

world to Latin America, but also the models of social, political, and institutional behavior.

In the Río de la Plata, the Buenos Aires elite—the leading *porteños*—searching for social, political, and cultural models in the greater Atlantic world, especially in Britain and North America, consisted of a comparatively small group: perhaps about 5 percent of the 40,000 inhabitants of the city. It included traders and landowners engaged in leather production, young and middle-aged lawyers, military officers, and priests who also took a leading role in the post-revolutionary political process.[5]

Buenos Aires became the capital city of the several provinces of the Río de la Plata in 1810, following on its role (1776–1810) as the capital of the viceroyalty of Río de la Plata. The small but dominant group of the city's elite shared the view that post-revolutionary institutional organization should take the form of a centralized government, though they sometimes differed on the means to achieve that aim. But by the end of the first decade of effort, when all the attempts to keep the far-flung provinces together had failed, some began to shift toward a loose confederative system. At that point the group broke into two factions—one defending confederation and the other continuing to support a centralized system.

Both factions were in touch with the intellectual and political debates that were taking place in the Atlantic world, though after 1820 the supporters of confederation were less inclined to transfer North Atlantic social and institutional models to the local society. From 1810 to 1827, the group defending a centralized government seemed to have followed a straighter path than those who came to support confederation.

Attempts to Establish a Government: An Overview

From 1810 to 1827, the main feature of Río de la Plata's history was the continuous struggle to establish a central government after the end of Spanish colonial domination. In 1810, an autonomous "junta" of Buenos Aires notables was installed in the city in the wake of the institutional collapse that resulted from the abdication in conquered Spain of King Ferdinand VII in favor of Joseph Bonaparte, the emperor's brother. The installation of this junta began a process that started as a movement intending to preserve the rights of the king and the continuing involvement of the American states in an expanded Hispanic monarchy, but ended in the revolution that finally severed ties with Spain.

From 1810 to 1820, Buenos Aires was the seat of a weak central government whose decisions rarely were accepted by the local provincial powers. Not only were the major outlying provinces—Upper Peru (Bolivia), Paraguay, and Uruguay—reluctant to obey the central government, but some of the villages that previously had been subordinated to larger cities sought their own autonomy. To a certain extent, this was the result of the political structure of the Spanish monarchy. During the seventeenth century, the monarchy had been seen to rest on a complex network of reciprocal rights and obligations between the king and the viceroyalties. These mutual rights and obligations were considered to be inherent in the condition of political subjects. Sworn obedience to the king in turn brought his acknowledgment of the various privileges enjoyed by the viceroyalties and the provinces. Those privileges could be related to economic activities, to judicial proceedings (guaranteeing regions special treatment when they had to appeal to the courts to resolve a conflict), or to preference in political negotiations.

The Bourbons and the intellectual elite associated with them supported an ideal of monistic sovereignty residing in the king. No rights inhered in political subjects; rather, rights were privileges that expressed the will of the king, who could grant them or abolish them. Thus, the power of the king was directly exercised over the subjects, eliminating all forms of mediation. The program of political and administrative reforms launched during Bourbon rule was designed to put these principles into practice. A bureaucratic administration formed by specialized Spanish officers was set up to replace the structures based on the sale of public offices. In Hispanic America, this meant that the Creole elite would no longer be able to hold public offices.[6] Of course, there was a gap between legislation and reality, a frequent occurrence in the Hispanic world; the gap is clearly exemplified in the phrase "se obedece pero no se cumple" (I obey but do not comply), so frequently used in the colonies to justify the failure to implement royal decrees. But the very existence of the decrees hindering Creole participation in the colonial administration gave rise to discontent and met stiff resistance, especially in the last decades of the eighteenth century.

In this context, in the vast borderlands of the Río de la Plata, the revo-

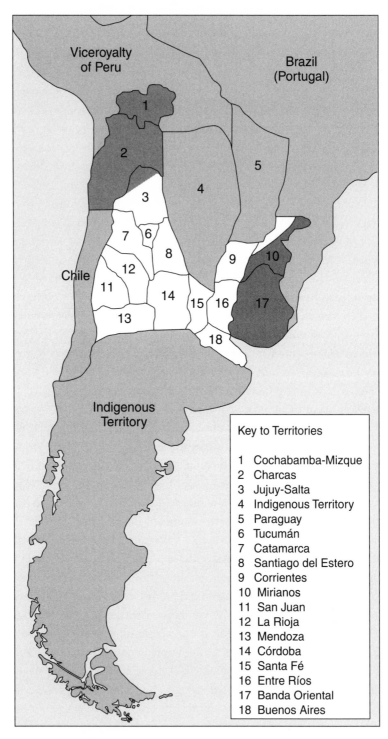

Map 11.2 The United Provinces of South America, ca. 1816. Based on a map at www.wikimedia.org.

Key to Territories

1 Cochabamba-Mizque
2 Charcas
3 Jujuy-Salta
4 Indigenous Territory
5 Paraguay
6 Tucumán
7 Catamarca
8 Santiago del Estero
9 Corrientes
10 Mirianos
11 San Juan
12 La Rioja
13 Mendoza
14 Córdoba
15 Santa Fé
16 Entre Ríos
17 Banda Oriental
18 Buenos Aires

Viceroyalty of Peru

Brazil (Portugal)

Chile

Indigenous Territory

lution cleared the way for a reaction against any form of centralized power. Claiming to be imbued with sovereign rights, most of the cities with a *cabildo*—a sort of city council—struggled to become the head of their surrounding territories, which could encompass either a small piece of land or larger areas including several villages. Although the usual decision-making process at the cabildos was restricted to a group belonging to the elite, there were extraordinary occasions when the cabildos were opened to the participation of all men who owned a parcel of land and a house in the city—the *vecinos* (neighbors), who were allowed to take part in "open cabildos." The revolutionary process strengthened the role of cabildos and open cabildos in legitimating political action: the revolution challenged the absolute monarchy on the grounds of the rights of the people, and the cabildos were the main institution of popular political activity. Over time, the obstacles posed to the establishment of order began to be attributed to these mechanisms of direct political participation, which came to be characterized as "tumultuous" and "anarchical." But at the beginning of the revolutionary period, the ordinances issued by the cabildos were viewed as incontestable, even when they defied the central government.

From 1810 to 1827 three constitutional congresses were convoked in an effort to create a stable and unified political organization that would encompass the whole former viceroyalty. All three failed. The Assembly that met from 1813 to 1815 was convened for the purpose of drafting a comprehensive constitution, but from the beginning of the sessions it was clear that the deputies of the provinces would not reach an agreement about a new system of government. The *caudillo* José Gervasio de Artigas, who favored a confederation, exerted a powerful influence, mainly in the provinces neighboring the Banda Oriental (present-day Uruguay), where Artigas had his political base. The Buenos Aires elite allied with the central government realized that it would not be able to impose its will, but they were determined not to accept the program of those who supported a confederation. Therefore it was decided to discuss none of the main constitutional proposals, and instead to draw up legislation on specific issues such as justice, individual rights, and the recruitment of military forces.

This Assembly faced an insurmountable obstacle that would reappear in the subsequent congresses: the problem of political representation.

Although many of the Buenos Aires deputies wanted to establish national representation not based on the provinces, the deputies of the inland provinces were subject to an ancient rule, the imperative mandate, which set strict limits on their powers of independent action. After a fierce debate, the Assembly declared that the deputies were representatives of the nation as a whole.[7] The vote was meaningless, however, as the deputies continued to act as representatives of the provinces that had appointed them. Indeed, those who accepted the resolution were brought to public trial by the provincial authorities after the Assembly was dissolved.

The second attempt to organize the Río de la Plata provinces met a similar fate. The Congress that met from 1816 to 1819 formally declared independence and promulgated a constitution that established a centralized system of government. But this constitution was rejected by most of the provinces, and again the representatives who had ratified it were brought to trial for disobeying the imperative mandate.

The rejection of the 1819 constitution pitched the provinces into a brief but decisive war that overthrew the central government established in Buenos Aires—or what remained of it, since during the whole decade it had been powerless by force or persuasion to enforce its decisions. At the beginning of 1820, each of the provinces became a sovereign state linked to the others only through a sort of "friendship league." But in 1824 the possibility of attaining diplomatic recognition from Britain and the prospects of going to war with the Portuguese then occupying the Banda Oriental moved the Buenos Aires leaders to undertake a new attempt to unify all the provinces and draft a constitution. That effort was thwarted both by the obstinacy of those who insisted on establishing a centralized system of government and by the resistance of the provinces, which rejected the transfer of their power to a central authority. With the failure of the unification project, the state of affairs by mid-1827 was similar to that in 1820: the provinces reacquired the status of sovereign states, which they kept for the next twenty-five years.

Developing the Social Underpinnings of Government

Despite the resistance of the inland provinces, from 1810 to 1827 the leading porteños continued to support the idea of a centralized state and tried to implement such a polity. Because the resistance was rooted in the Hispanic juridical and political tradition, after the revolution this elite turned its eyes outward to the greater Atlantic world for theories, institutional models, and patterns of social behavior that could counteract the burden of the Spanish legacy.

It was a natural instinct, since the revolution itself was thought to be part of an Atlantic phenomenon. In the Río de la Plata, many revolutionary leaders believed that the North American, French, and Hispanic American revolutions were different stages of a single process. Bernardo de Monteagudo, a Río de la Plata politician and journalist of radical opinions, expressed his faith in the progress of the "world revolution," which would stir the "plains near the Ocean," the "Baltic coasts," the "Mediterranean countries," and "the banks of the Thames."[8] And Gregorio Funes, a priest who represented the province of Córdoba in the three Río de la Plata constitutional congresses, regarded the Hispanic American revolutions as the necessary consequence of an Atlantic movement begun with the North American and French revolts, which had "revived" the rights of man.

If the revolution was an Atlantic process, it was in the Atlantic world that remedies for the problems raised by the revolution would be found. The constitutional efforts made in the Río de la Plata can be related to a cycle of Atlantic constitutionalism. After the successful constitutional experience of the United States in 1787, France promulgated four different constitutions—in 1791, 1795, 1800, and 1814; in Spain, a liberal constitution was approved in 1812 and restored in 1820; Portugal and Greece approved their constitutions, also of liberal design, in 1822. These efforts, along with the continuous struggles of the Hispanic American countries to draft viable constitutions, have led historians to conceive of a single, broad "Atlantic constitutional experiment."[9]

The determination to draft a constitution, which the porteños shared with other Hispanic American elites, reflects the extent to which constitutionalism itself had become a basic institutional strategy and a political value as well. Each summoning of a constituent assembly or congress expressed renewed confidence in a constitution as the most fitting device to overcome the obstacles facing the state-building process.

Other political and cultural goals also reflected widespread Atlantic values: religious tolerance, freedom of the press, philanthropy, polite manners, and the comforts of a civilized life. The means through which these values were spread throughout Latin America were also widely shared: travel, public education, newspapers, and theater.

Travel, in the revolutionary years, was assumed to provide useful social, commercial, cultural, and political apprenticeship. In Buenos Aires, youths belonging to important families involved in Atlantic trade traveled to London, where, like their British counterparts, they began their careers in distant countries before settling at the home office.[10] Through their frequent voyages to Europe and the United States, leading members of the Buenos Aires elite became acquainted with a new and totally different atmosphere, whose characteristics they would try to transfer to their own society. The case of Vincente Pazos Kanki is one of the most remarkable examples. A priest and newspaper editor, he relocated to London when the government accused him of using his newspaper, *El Censor*, to foment social unrest and suspended publication of the paper. In London, Pazos Kanki learned a great deal about British institutions, which he very much admired. The religious tolerance of London society led him to reflect on the sternness of Catholicism, and on his return to Buenos Aires after four years in England, he was no longer a priest and had married an Englishwoman.[11]

Over time, travel to foreign nations became a deliberate strategy to help the members of the local elite learn how other societies were organized and governed. An "Anonymous Englishman" who lived in Buenos Aires from 1820 to 1825 pointed out in his memoirs that both the native notables and the British merchants who had settled in the city strongly encouraged young lawyers and politicians to visit London in order to witness firsthand the workings of English political and judicial institutions.[12]

The connections between Buenos Aires and the city of Baltimore were peculiarly important. After the outbreak of the South American revolutions, Baltimore traders had expanded their commercial activities to Buenos Aires, and Baltimore may have sheltered Río de la Plata revolutionary leaders who dissented from the government's policies.[13] In 1817, Manuel Moreno, Pazos Kanki, and Pedro José de Agrelo—three prominent members of Buenos Aires intellectual circles, all editors of newspapers—were exiles in Baltimore, where they wrote a manifesto against the Río de la Plata government known as the "Baltimore libel."

In1817, *El Censor* published an article saying that, among all the people of the United States, the citizens of Baltimore were the most enthusiastic supporters of independence for the Río de la Plata, contributing to the cause, they believed, through a boycott on commerce between Spain and North America.[14]

But alongside the occasional experiences of transoceanic travels, there was a great deal of everyday contact that familiarized the Buenos Aires elite with the North Atlantic world. The nets of sociability woven with foreign traders, especially with the British, were fundamental to the promotion of social transformation.

Generally, foreigners were warmly received in the Río de la Plata. Alexander Caldcleugh, who visited in 1821, wrote that foreigners had quickly risen in the esteem of the Buenos Aires elite, to the point of being preferred over natives.[15] Upon leaving Tucumán, Captain John Andrews blessed its inhabitants for their generous hospitality.[16] Alexander Gillespie, a member of the British army, expressed his gratitude to the Buenos Aires population in his chronicle of events following the British defeat, and Edmund Temple remarked on how friendly the people of Córdoba were to overseas visitors.[17]

The revolution that ended Spanish domination made the Buenos Aires elite even more eager to receive foreigners, especially British traders. Spain had forbidden commerce with the British, but after 1808 that trade increased enormously. In 1810, when the revolution broke out, there were sixty-six British merchants in the city. By 1822 there were 3,500 Britons in Buenos Aires city and its hinterland.[18] The predominance of the British among the foreign migrants was incontestable: John Murray Forbes, the U.S. consul in Buenos Aires, complained bitterly about the overwhelming influence exerted by the English. He stated with disappointment that it did not seem to matter how much North America had done to enhance the moral prestige of the Hispanic American emancipation enterprise; the British would still occupy the first place in the esteem of both the government and the people.[19]

British trade to Buenos Aires was voluminous and reached into the daily lives of the entire population. Not only fabrics, iron objects, and porcelain but pianos, hats, saddles, socks, jackets, clocks, knives, and shoes flowed into the now open port, creating, the U.S. envoy Henry M. Brackenridge wrote, a great many artificial needs.[20]

Trade being the main source of income for the Río de la Plata, foreign traders had easy access to the highest ranks of the political establishment. Thus William Miller, who wanted to join the army fighting against the Spanish Crown, was introduced through a British trader to Juan Martín de Pueyrredón, director of the Río de la Plata—the highest rank in the local government.[21] And in Mendoza, a city located close to the Andes mountains, Robert Proctor, a merchant whose business connections reached Buenos Aires, Santiago de Chile, and Lima, was well received in the circle of General José de San Martín, the most prominent Río de la Plata military leader.[22]

As Buenos Aires was the communication center for all the interior provinces, it was the city in which British traders chose to settle, and their influence was found everywhere. According to the Scottish trader John Parish Robertson, British shoulder-straps and hats were frequently seen in Buenos Aires, and it was common for British citizens to encounter compatriots in the city.[23] There were British tailors, shoemakers, and hatmakers; there were also three British doctors, two pharmacists, a printer, a music teacher, and a carriage maker. Two inns were managed by English immigrants, and one Briton owned a circus.[24] Even a Buenos Aires school—where many members of the local elite chose to send their children—was directed by an Englishwoman.[25]

The most prominent families of the city organized *tertulias*—social gatherings where the main political issues of the day were discussed, and where foreigners were eagerly received. Tertulias were common in all large Hispanic American cities (Figure 11.1).[26] Caldcleugh stated that every respectable family had "its tertulia," and that they were remarkably cordial toward strangers.[27] Samuel Haigh reported that women at these tertulias treated the foreigners with utmost courtesy.[28] Some celebrated women organized their own tertulias.[29] John and William Parish Robertson described the tertulias organized by Mariquita Sánchez de Thompson, Ana Riglós—whom they called the "female leader of Buenos Aires' *tory* party"—and Melchora Sarratea, a woman of "*whiggish* principles," as a circle that, though not "political" was undoubtedly public, in that the philosophy and politics of state affairs were debated there by statesmen and other members of the upper classes. Because Signoras Sánchez de Thompson, Sarratea, and Riglós strongly favored

Figure 11.1 Charles H. Pellegrini, "Tertulia porteña," watercolor, ca. 1831. Reproduced from *C. H. Pellegrini: Su obra, su vida, su tiempo* (Buenos Aires, 1946), plate 123.

political alliances with European countries and North America, their tertulias were commonly frequented by diplomats.[30]

Foreigners and members of the Buenos Aires elite also met at public celebrations. In the parties organized to commemorate the revolution or a successful battle against Spain, an important place was reserved for foreign traders.[31] Similarly, when British subjects celebrated the king's birthday or a festival of Saint George, the local authorities and notables were invited.[32] The celebration of the battle of Ayacucho—in which Símon Bolívar's army won a decisive victory against the Spanish in Peru—generated a contest between the English and North American citizens settled in the Río de la Plata over who would offer the most striking celebration. Haigh thought that the party given by the North Americans was "magnificent." But an "Anonymous Englishman" emphasized the superiority of the British feast, which gathered people of the highest rank and featured entertainment by an orchestra, although he had to admit that the banquet offered by the "North-American gentlemen" was "splendid and dazzling."[33]

This fluid intermingling with foreigners was believed to be one of the most important vehicles for the transmission of habits and fashions from "the most advanced nations," as it was usually phrased, and for the acquisition of foreign languages.[34]

Fluency in English became increasingly important for the local elite.[35] At the beginning of the revolutionary decade, knowledge of English was limited to those who were regularly engaged in Atlantic commerce.[36] But by 1815, the teaching of English was making substantial progress in the upper levels of the population at large.[37] Although French was more widely studied, announcements of English classes taught at the *consulado*—the institution dealing with commercial affairs—became more frequent in the local newspapers.[38]

Contact with British traders also nourished the local elite's concern with education. The Lancasterian method of teaching, which involved having advanced students teach less advanced ones, was then in vogue in England. The method was adopted in Buenos Aires at the beginning of the 1820s, and a Lancasterian Society, composed of many members of the local elite as well as British traders, was created to further the education of youth under that system.[39] The British Lancasterian educator

James Thompson settled in Buenos Aires and set up two schools, one in Buenos Aires city and the other in Patagones, a village located on the frontier with an Indian population.[40]

Together with social and cultural patterns, contact with British and North American merchants acquainted the Buenos Aires leadership with political values considered typical of the Anglo-American world. Interaction with non-Catholic British merchants after 1808 evidently lessened the effects of religious differences, which in any case never posed major obstacles to the social or commercial intercourse between the two groups. As the Robertson brothers said, the upper classes were concerned with economic success to an extent incompatible with the principles of Roman Catholicism, a view they confirmed by observing that regular religious ceremonies were attended only by old women and people from the lower classes.[41]

In Buenos Aires, social interaction with Protestants probably helped to strengthen a "spirit of tolerance in religious affairs" that was noted by many travelers, including Caldcleugh and the Robertsons.[42] It may also have led the city's younger generations to adopt a "Voltairian" profile, as the "Anonymous Englishman" characterized their attitude toward religion.[43] In his opinion, Roman Catholicism was a "religion of the senses," whereas Protestantism was the "religion of the brain." The former priest Pazos Kanki shared this view of Catholicism, which he believed encouraged intolerance and repression. He criticized the practice of confession, for example, which allowed the clergy to know "the most secret thoughts of the people," and he remarked "that a system of religion which obliges its professors to act as self-accusers, and to regard the doctrines and counsels of their priests as oracles of Heaven is, without doubt, the most potent engine of despotism."[44]

It was believed that Protestantism, in contrast, had stimulated freedom and progress in the countries where it was the dominant religion. Pazos Kanki was certain that the early contact with Englishmen during the British invasions of Buenos Aires had made the local elite "more liberal in their opinions, and particularly in matters of religious worship." He hoped that acquaintance with the values inherent in Protestantism could release the Río de la Plata from the burden of the Hispanic Catholic heritage. For he believed that the Reformation had generally contributed "to the progress of light and liberty in the world," especially in the United States, where "religious liberty" and the "rivalry of different sects" had maintained "the morals of the people in their purity."[45]

Religious tolerance was not the only means of instilling public morals within society. The press was considered a powerful instrument for changing people's social and political behavior and a vehicle for the enlightenment of society. Echoing Thomas Jefferson's view, the learned people of the city said (though they did not always act accordingly) that the best way of contradicting error was to let free debate bring the truth to light.[46]

Freedom of the press was one of the most important topics of revolutionary discourse and political strategy. The first ordinance on this subject was issued in 1811, and many further revisions were undertaken by successive governments. The model for all such regulations was said to be England, although the 1811 ordinances were in fact very similar to those enacted by the Cortes of Cádiz in 1810.[47] Every statement on this topic—even the most divergent—claimed to be supported by the English experience of freedom of speech. The *Gaceta de Buenos Aires,* for instance, accompanied the publication of the 1811 ordinances with a detailed analysis of the press as a tribunal of public opinion that expressed the will of the nation. As in England, the free press could uncover plots, refute falsehood, and educate the people.[48]

The press aligned local society with the dynamics of the Atlantic world. The Buenos Aires newspapers were nourished by the foreign press. Occasionally pieces of news were obtained through travelers, but generally everything published in the local newspapers was related to articles that had appeared in the North Atlantic press, especially British publications, and hence provided channels of communication for philosophical and political ideas. Especially because the beginning of the nineteenth century was "an age without books," as the Argentine politician Juan Bautista Alberdi remarked in the 1850s, journalists' writings were the main sources of information about contemporary political thought.[49]

Another type of British publication, the review, played a similar role. These early magazines devoted to scientific, literary, and political issues were well known in Buenos Aires. Some were available in the city, and others received commentary in the local newspapers.[50] Though at times the local press criticized British reviews as a "frivolous fashion," they attracted the elite's attention, especially the *Quarterly Review* and the *Edinburgh Review*, and they contributed to establishing the intellectual fashions that the elite would attempt to follow.[51]

A particularly influential publication was *El Español*, a monthly journal issued in London from September 1810 to April 1814 by the Spanish émigré Joseph Blanco White. The circulation of *El Español* was supported by the British Foreign Office, which bought copies and distributed them freely in Hispanic America.[52] According to David Brading, the Foreign Office encouraged British companies trading with Hispanic America to take five hundred copies for distribution to the local population.[53] Blanco White's views were clear: he was strongly in favor of British intervention in Spanish politics, even suggesting that command of the Spanish troops and military operations against the French be transferred to the British government, because everyone would acknowledge the superiority of an army organized by England.[54] Reciprocally, the Foreign Office always took into consideration the opinions on Hispanic American affairs that appeared in *El Español*.[55]

Through newspapers, journals, and reviews, the Buenos Aires elite grew more closely acquainted with Anglo-American intellectual and political ideas. Local newspapers devoted many pages to British parliamentary discussions on the freedom of the press and on the suspension of habeas corpus, which were known in the first place through British papers and journals.[56] And when James Monroe became president of the United States, the press of Buenos Aires followed the details of the election attentively and published a biography of Monroe.[57]

The Buenos Aires notables were especially concerned with both official and general opinion in Britain and North America about Hispanic American independence. The vagaries of public opinion deserved as much attention as messages delivered to the British Parliament or the U.S. Congress, especially when that opinion was favorable to South American emancipation. *El Censor*, for instance, reprinted an article from *Bell's Weekly Messenger* stating that South America could no longer remain "in slavery."[58] The speeches delivered by Henry Clay to the U.S. House of Representatives also aroused enthusiasm among the local elite. Because Clay championed South American emancipation, his positive opinions were taken as proof of the success of revolutionary policies.[59]

The Buenos Aires press also expressed satisfaction with the firm condemnation by several newspapers, such as the *Baltimore Register* and the Philadelphia *Aurora,* of the U.S. government's decision not to give open support to Hispanic American emancipation.[60] On the other hand, when the British and North American press criticized the course of action of the South American independent governments, local editors countered by saying that the writers of those articles did not understand the situation of the newborn countries.[61]

The idealized images of Britain and the United States were to a great extent created by the press. The first articles comparing Spain and Britain that appeared in a Buenos Aires newspaper were attributed to a series written by the Spanish intellectual and politician Gaspar Melchor de Jovellanos, who signed the essays as "The Spanish Patriot." In these articles, Jovellanos reflected on the characteristic traits of the "British model," which would later be debated by the Buenos Aires elite: the liberty of the British people, the efficacy of the (unwritten) British constitution in eliminating any risk of despotism, and the importance of freedom of the press as an instrument for educating the people so that they became capable of wisely using "the traditional British freedom." Jovellanos warned Spain—now invaded by the French—that the world would respect the country only if it evolved into a free nation as had England.[62]

The success of the United States was thought to be a consequence of the inheritance of the British tradition of liberty, quite the opposite of the legacy of submission and "slavery" transmitted to Hispanic America by Spain.[63] The most admired traits of North American society were religious tolerance, an open attitude toward immigrants, and the extent of education—the latter a result of both state policy and the individual interest of people of diverse religious beliefs who wanted to be able to read "the Bible and the newspapers."[64]

Legitimating Constitutional Government

One of the most inspiring political devices provided by the Anglo-American world was representation, which came to be seen as not only an institution but also a political value that compelled the personal engagement of many members of the Buenos Aires elite. As Pazos Kanki pointed out, the progress of revolution resulted, to a great extent, from the free intercourse with other countries, which in less than a decade had allowed people who were previously "ignorant of the representative system of government" to become familiar with it and to begin to adopt "the republican institutions of the United States."[65]

Their interest in the institutional organization of the Río de la Plata provinces moved the patriciate of Buenos Aires to look for philosophical and political sources that could provide legitimacy for their proposals. Jovellanos—who can be considered the archetype of the Spanish "enlightened" man—studied the work of John Locke and David Hume. The writings of Benjamin Franklin were freely available as were fragments of *The Federalist,* and Paine's *Common Sense* and *The Rights of Man.* Thomas Jefferson's inauguration speech was also known in Buenos Aires.[66] British political and literary traditions were even better known. The complete works of Alexander Pope were available at the Buenos Aires Public Library, and the novels of Samuel Richardson had, according to Henry Brackenridge, a growing audience who became deeply engaged with the plots.[67]

Adam Smith's *Inquiry into the Nature and Causes of the Wealth of Nations* had been translated in Spain in 1794 and was known in Buenos Aires, as was William Blackstone's *Commentaries on the Laws of England.* In 1817, a translation of Robert Bisset's *Sketch on Democracy*—a fervent defense of the British political system—sold well in local bookstores.[68] And the government that was established in Buenos Aires in 1820 encouraged and subsidized a translation of James Mill's *Elements of Economy,* which appeared at the end of 1823. And from Blackstone and Jean de Lolme, in particular, the local newspapers had probably borrowed the rhetoric of what they called the "happy constitution of England." The *Gaceta,* for instance, quoted a fragment of de Lolme's *The Constitution of England,* together with a commentary from the editor, who wrote about the "happy circumstances" of the British government.[69] And *El Censor* referred to the British judicial system as an institutional network that guaranteed "happiness."[70]

Jeremy Bentham's utilitarian philosophy, which was remarkably well known in the Río de la Plata from 1820 onward, deserves special attention. We know little about the circulation of Bentham's works from 1810 to 1815, but we know that the library of the radical journalist and politician Bernardo de Monteagudo contained a copy of the *Traités de législation civil et pénal.*[71] During the 1810s, the main channel for access to Bentham's theories was *El Español:* in September 1810 it reviewed Bentham's *Tactique des assemblées législatives,* written in 1790 for the French National Assembly; in January 1811 it published Bentham's project on the freedom of the press conceived for Venezuela and requested by Francisco de Miranda; in February 1814 it reviewed Bentham's *Théorie des peines et des récompenses;* and in April 1814 it translated some paragraphs of *Principes politiques et économiques sur les colonies,* which Bentham had addressed to the French Assembly to suggest the emancipation of France's colonies.[72]

After 1820, both the compelling need for order and the personal acquaintance of Bentham and the Buenos Aires politician Bernardino Rivadavia, the chief minister of Buenos Aires from 1821 to 1824 and the first president of the Río de la Plata provinces (Argentina) in 1826, made Bentham's works widely known. And, again, the most important vehicle for disseminating them was the local press. The *Abeja Argentina,* a journal devoted to the educated public, serialized Bentham's *Book of Political Fallacies.*[73] And *El Centinela,* a paper aimed at a wider range of readers, referred to the "sublime" Bentham and quoted his writings.[74]

To some extent, Britain stood as proof to the Buenos Aires elite that human progress was the result of an intellectual task properly focused on the transformation of society. Very early in the revolutionary process, many voices claimed that British history demonstrated the importance of intellectual and cultural development for the prosperity of a nation. The *Gaceta,* for instance, stated that Isaac Newton, John Locke, Edward Clarke, David Hume, and William Robertson had exerted a remarkable influence on Britain's rise to dominance, not only in the political and intellectual spheres but also in the economic arena. According to the *Gaceta,* it was the contribution of those great men that made England stand out among the most cultivated and prosperous European nations.[75]

This complimentary attitude toward England resulted in part from the necessity of staying on good terms with the most powerful nation of the age. Certainly, the local elite were aware of the weight of British political decisions on the international scene. The government established by the 1810 revolutionaries expressed the hope that Britain would find the Río de la Plata's revolutionary policy advantageous, in light of Buenos Aires's rebellion against Napoleon.[76]

Yet the fascination exerted by the British model among the elite engaged in Río de la Plata political organization was accompanied by feelings of perplexity, deception, and even rejection as a result of England's foreign policy. The British government's reluctance to engage more actively in the Hispanic American independence enterprise aroused considerable indignation among some members of the local elite. Monteagudo wished that the revolutionary movement would overwhelm the "St. James cabinet" and that France would remain armed against England.[77] Pazos Kanki grew agitated about the "tricky strategies" of a country that refused to support the revolution openly because "it would prefer that the Río de la Plata became its own colony."[78] The alliance between Britain and Spain provoked disgust. In 1812, *El Censor* wondered what benefits Britain could obtain from an alliance that required "the great island" to undertake enormous economic and political expense.[79] After the restoration of Ferdinand VII, the British attempt to reconcile the Spanish and Hispanic American positions was interpreted by the local press as a policy unsupportive of Hispanic American emancipation.[80]

Paradoxically, this was the only moment when the British model had a real chance of adoption. The constitutional debate held in the Congress that met from 1816 to 1819 took place with a view toward the antirevolutionary stance of the Holy Alliance in Europe. Monarchy being the only political system granted legitimacy by the Holy Alliance, the adaptation of the British system to the local situation appeared to be a solution to the long-standing problem of external recognition. Moreover, some people believed that the establishment of a political order similar to that of Britain would incline the British government to accept Río de la Plata's independence.[81]

The Buenos Aires government sent a secret mission to Europe in search of a king for a society without royalty or aristocracy. The options were varied, but all of them now seem equally bizarre: candidates included the Prince of Luca, the brother of King Ferdinand VII, or the "Americanist" possibility of crowning a descendant of the Inca.[82] To some members of the Buenos Aires elite, a monarchical regime seemed the most favorable outcome of a revolutionary process that, by the middle of the 1810s, had not been able to secure either internal order or the formal acknowledgment of other nations.

Arguments in favor of the British monarchical model had in fact begun in 1814, when Ferdinand VII was restored to his throne. The summoning of the 1816–1819 Congress offered the supporters of an "English-style" political system a concrete opportunity to put forward and discuss such proposals. But secrecy surrounded the mission sent to Europe by the government, and the plan received a lukewarm welcome within the Congress. It was, however, taken seriously by the Buenos Aires press and even championed by some editors. *El Censor,* for instance, suggested that, because the Río de la Plata was so far from the conditions that made the U.S. republic a success, the possibility of a monarchical government deserved at least to be debated.[83] *El Observador Americano* was decidedly in favor of a constitutional monarchy. The editor of the newspaper, Manuel Antonio de Castro, argued against those who insisted that the exercise of freedom required a republican government. His example was of course England, where, he said, a "bloody revolution [had] sought fruitlessly to obtain freedom through a republic," but the country finally achieved it under the monarchy.[84] In Castro's view, the United States had inherited the part of the English tradition of freedom that had allowed self-government to develop in the colonies, where there was no deep "difference in the distribution of fortunes." Thus the United States could not be a model for the Río de la Plata provinces, which had received no similar foundation from Spain. Furthermore, the adoption of a monarchical system similar to England's would help reform the habits of the local society.[85]

In *El Independiente,* Pedro de Agrelo also suggested that England had discovered the "secret of freedom": that the people, the legislature, and the executive "simultaneously" enjoyed rights, and thus the three of them "gave life to the state-machinery."[86] This "secret" having been revealed, it was useless for the Río de la Plata Congress to devote time and energy to drafting its own constitution. It would be enough to adapt the British one to the circumstances of the provinces. But the adaptation proposed by Agrelo was complex. For him, the monarchy was the lesser problem: he did not believe that the Río de la Plata needed to have a king to follow the British model, because any single executive exercising the functions of kingship would be an adequate analogue. It was the English legislative power that was more distant from the social and political traditions of Río de la Plata society. The Río de la Plata did not have a formal aristocracy and, contrary to Castro's opinion, did not have extreme differences in the distribution of wealth. Agrelo's solution was an intricate institutional device that granted representation in a High Chamber to corporate groups such as the Church and the universities and to men who had won "any kind of distinction," and a Low Chamber where the representatives would be elected via suffrage established through a property census. To avoid despotism, Agrelo would endow an Ecclesiastic Chapter with the right of veto over the executive.[87]

The monarchical choice was doomed to fail. What was the point of transforming the legislative power into a mixture of corporative distinctions, when the Río de la Plata was far more homogeneous in regard to social ranks and wealth than the rest of Hispanic America? The constitution promulgated in 1819 by the Congress put aside the "monarchical solution" and instead tried to encompass what were considered the best features of the British scheme: a strong executive whose decisions were almost incontestable, a Senate that combined corporative representation for the clergy, the military forces, and the universities, together with senators elected indirectly by the provinces, and a representative chamber selected from a census of property owners.

The provinces rejected this constitution, precipitating a war between the forces of Buenos Aires and the resistant provinces that ended in 1820 with the fall of the Buenos Aires central government. This result had been predictable. While creating artificial social differences, the constitution avoided dealing with the main problem, the provinces' determination to maintain their autonomy and their unwillingness to be gathered into a centralized political organization. In this context, the North American experience, rather than the British, became more relevant.

The United States was considered a sort of "natural" ally of Hispanic America, and all the U.S. expressions of support were enthusiastically received in Buenos Aires. The *Gaceta,* for example, hailed the message sent by the U.S. Congress to the Caracas revolutionary leaders declaring that the news about their revolution had aroused optimistic expectations.[88] But the most substantial contribution that the United States made to the emancipation enterprise was its own political experience of breaking the colonial links with Britain and organizing as an independent state. In this sense, for Hispanic American countries, the constitutional path followed by North America to become a free and sovereign nation seemed to mirror the complexity of their own political circumstances. As Bernard Bailyn suggests, North American constitutionalism was a "reserve of experience."[89] And from this "reserve of experience," the Río de la Plata elites took selectively what was most convenient in each moment and circumstance. Throughout the 1810s, the United States provided an instructive example of how the division of powers could work effectively.[90] After the rejection of the 1819 constitution, the relationship between the U.S. central government and the federal states seemed most striking and admirable to those in the Río de la Plata.

From the outbreak of the revolution, both the Articles of Confederation and the 1787 Constitution of the United States were known in the Río de la Plata.[91] Nevertheless, the uses of the words "federation" and "confederation" were often conceptually imprecise. It is possible that the novelty of the U.S. experience impeded the Río de la Plata elites' full comprehension of the actual workings of either of the two types of organization and also made them cautious about the future of the northern republic. There were many who said that, because the U.S. Constitution had had such a brief history, its ultimate success or failure was difficult to predict. As Castro pointed out, forty years was not enough time to prove the success of a constitution.[92] Others believed that the U.S. federation imposed weak ties among the states, and so would not work in the Río de la Plata provinces, which were already loosely bound and therefore needed stronger links to become unified.[93]

But the ambiguities in the meanings assigned to the two words—"federation" and "confederation"—were also a consequence of the changing political situation in the Río de la Plata. A strategic use of words allowed the actors to maneuver between conceptual precision and political necessity, but often they abandoned theoretical coherence for practical efficacy. A clear example of the selective appropriation of different theories, terms, and political experiences is provided by the deputy representing the province of Tucumán in the 1813–1815 Assembly. Nicolás Laguna rejected a centralized system of government, arguing that there is a difference between the words "union" and "unity," the former meaning the gathering of different elements and the latter the substantial identity of the constituent parts of a body. "The Anglo-American United States, whose constitution I have in my hands right now, form a union," stated Laguna in confronting the proposals of many Buenos Aires deputies who were urging the provinces to accept unity. Seeking endorsement for his ideas in Jean-Jacques Rousseau's criticism of representation, Laguna argued that representation in a unitary government was a betrayal of the will of the people, a statement that could not easily be reconciled with the North American constitutional model.[94] In the new Congress of 1816 the references to the U.S. model were dropped by those intent on vindicating the provinces' sovereign rights, notwithstanding the practical advantages that the North American federal state clearly offered.

Nevertheless, events in the Río de la Plata during those years continued to show the potential of recent U.S. history as a "reserve of experience." The press stressed the importance of the political and institutional process that had led to the 1787 U.S. Constitution. *El Censor,* for instance, devoted many issues to the study of the various state constitutions.[95] Clearly with an eye on the recalcitrant provinces, the editor explained that the state constitutions had been drafted prior to the federal one and therefore had to be reconciled with the conditions imposed when they became part of a national state, though they never abandoned the liberal foundations on which they had been built.[96]

The attention paid to historical events in the United States highlighted the peculiarities of the North American case and the impossibility of transferring to the local society any kind of theoretical recipe. The U.S. constitutional trajectory proved what would *not* work in the Río de la Plata. As would soon be demonstrated, if the provinces were set loose to establish individual constitutions similar to those of the North American states, there would be no chance of reaching a consensus around a national charter.

After the failure of the 1819 Constitution, the provinces developed as sovereign states. For its part, the Buenos Aires government focused on the modernization of its own institutional structures and the cultural transformation of society. In this period, the *feliz experiencia* (1820–1824), the province's local leadership sought to establish in Buenos Aires what they most admired in both the North American and the British models: a mechanism for representation whose efficacy would guarantee that political participation did not degrade into chaos, an organizational structure capable of absorbing the demands of political participation and, at the same time, able to restrain disorder. The creation of a representative chamber whose debates were regulated through rules taken from Bentham's *Tactique des assemblées législatives,* an electoral system that essentially established universal male suffrage, and the fostering of the press as an instrument of consolidating civil society through public opinion—those were the main ingredients of a regime that would successfully combine freedom and order.

But this order, which appeared to fit the social and limited geographical scale of the province of Buenos Aires, collapsed when the local elite attempted to extend it to the rest of the Río de la Plata. From 1824 to 1827, the meeting of a new Congress seeking to bring the provinces into a national government revealed fundamental contradictions in the distribution of power among provincial and central authorities. References to the United States were mostly used as rhetorical weapons, often supporting opposite proposals. Those who adhered to a centralized regime praised the attributes of the U.S. national government, such as the power to set fiscal policy or to control a national army.[97] Those who defended a confederation pointed to the elements of that system that they believed survived in the U.S. Constitution, such as the Senate, in which all the states were equally represented.[98] The federal system, as it worked in the United States, was perceived to grant too much or too little to the central power, depending on which side of the dispute one stood. The provinces that advocated sovereign rights saw a federal system that would weaken them; supporters of a centralized regime saw a federal model that kept too many vital attributes under the control of the provinces, which they believed were refuges of "barbarian" incivility.[99]

Educating the Citizenry

If the provinces were the refuge of barbarian incivility, it would be necessary to "educate the sovereign" to make any political system work. This meant reforming citizens in both the upper and the lower classes, a task that also mirrored events and ideas around the North Atlantic world.

The elite of Buenos Aires developed strategies of social pedagogy that had either a civic or a civilizing aim. Though the two goals were generally mingled, there were distinct cycles in which one or the other prevailed. From 1810 to 1815, during the apogee of the revolution, the group was mostly engaged in the task of creating virtuous citizens, and the cultivation of habits was subordinated to that aim. By the mid-1810s, the conflicts arising from the competing political positions of the provinces, and of opposing factions within each of them, generated a pessimistic view about the natural condition of the Río de la Plata people. The strategy then shifted to guarantee that the cultivation of habits could make, if not virtuous citizens, at least obedient people inclined to conform their conduct to the commands of law.

In all of these endeavors, references to foreign nations were abundant. Because the Buenos Aires governments desperately sought diplomatic recognition from Europe and North America, virtue was associated with the possibility of attaining "the rank of a nation." As the *Gaceta* put it, the Río de la Plata "would gain the respect of other countries" when the virtues of an "austere and industrious people" grew among the inhabitants of the provinces, and when love for the "patria" became a shared virtue, prompting the citizens to fight against "difficulty and danger."[100] Such rhetoric continued to be deployed even when hope faded of molding the local population into upright citizens. In 1817, *El Censor*, supposedly quoting George Washington, asked: "Could Providence make the prosperity of nations not depend on virtue? Doubtless, prosperity relies on all the noble sentiments that embellish human kind."[101]

In 1815 the dissolution of the first Assembly led to charges that the population possessed a "moral ineptitude" that made it incapable of living under an independent government. While the second attempt to draft a constitution for the Río de la Plata was taking place, in 1816, *La Prensa Argentina* suggested that gaining the "respect of the cultivated nations" and transferring to the Río de la Plata their habits and virtues would be a "chimaera" unless the authorities appointed by the Constituent Congress strove not only for the observation of the law but also for the moral reformation of society.[102]

By the second half of the 1810s, and especially after 1819, views on creating a virtuous citizenry were much less ambitious than they had been at the beginning of the revolutionary process. But if men could not become virtuous citizens, at least they should be civilized in their habits, manners, and behavior, and thus inclined to accept the rule of law—not a minor concern in a society where violence remained an accepted means of resolving political differences.

Of course education was thought to be an appropriate and reliable instrument to achieve the goal of civilizing habits and manners. The formal system of education established after the revolution aimed to reach all the classes, and it actually increased the opportunities for elementary instruction, especially with the adoption of the Lancasterian method.[103] But, in fact, the most intensive attempts were addressed to the members of the upper classes: the Academies of Jurisprudence, Drawing, Mathematics, and Medicine, created during the 1810s, and the University of Buenos Aires, founded in 1821, were clear examples of the resources and energies that the cultivation of the upper classes absorbed within the framework of educational strategy.

The enlightenment of the upper reaches of society was a compelling task for the building of a representative republic, and this became more evident in Buenos Aires province during the *feliz experiencia,* when great efforts were made to establish republican institutions. In the government's view, these institutions would work only if there were an "enlightened" opposition, built on the basis of rational debate: "[the Buenos Aires government] wishes the Opposition was capable of forming free and rational judgment as everyone going ahead matched with civilization does; contenders with enlightened judgment, prone to admit the majority's opinions . . . ; an Opposition approving or disapproving an idea according to the voice of their conscience or to the opinion they have formed through rational debate, and not in the hope that its members will receive at home ten priests kissing and embracing them for being godly."[104]

In addition to formal education, a great many informal practices were considered to be equally fruitful in the creation of a civilized people. Charity work was significant, because it helped develop humane feelings toward other people and at the same time strengthened the social hierarchy. And here, once again, the Atlantic horizons of these social and cultural patterns are visible. The model was England, where the social responsibility of "those Protestants" toward the poor was viewed as worth imitating. *La Prensa Argentina,* for instance, noted enthusiastically that in London there were about two hundred relief houses, supported by individuals and private societies, that performed an "admirable task." On both sides of the ocean, philanthropy was thought to provide the upper classes with a mark of social distinction.[105]

Theater was another vehicle of social transformation highly esteemed in the Río de la Plata. If during the 1810s theater mainly attempted to spread republican values, after 1820 in Buenos Aires it became a means to educate the taste of local elites.[106] In 1817, for instance, many took part in the creation of the *Sociedad del Buen Gusto Teatral* (Society for Theatrical Good Taste). As conscious of their provincialism as the North American founders, these men and women sought to meet cosmopolitan literary standards.[107] Especially from 1820 onward, they began to discuss the narrative style of authors, the stage settings of plays, and the performances of actors and actresses.

The transmission of good models of social behavior was a major concern of the Buenos Aires leadership, especially regarding the lower classes. Since the theater was a very popular mode of entertainment, it was expected to help provide examples that could mold the audience's views of right and wrong. Thus, during the revolutionary period, the plays that showed "honorable actions" of men and women willing to die for the *patria* or to reject personal benefits in favor of those of the community were enthusiastically received by both the government and the press. After 1820, tolerance, rational intercourse among people holding differing views, and polite manners were the main topics on the local drama's agenda.

But the most serious challenge posed to the government was the reform of the habits of everyday life. When Buenos Aires became a sovereign state, the group of self-proclaimed "liberal reformers" who came to power made this issue a top priority. Sanitation at the local market became subject to regulation, together with selling practices. The press congratulated the government for trying to eradicate the stand-holders' practice of shouting raucously to attract clients for their merchandise: the resulting cacophony was thought to cause disorder. The noise, coupled with the ugly appearance, led the authorities to move the market to a peripheral area where it would not disturb the city's life or tarnish its image, especially in the eyes of foreign visitors.[108]

The celebrations of carnival were also on the government's agenda, because they were considered "uncivilized." During carnival, revelers threw water over people walking along the streets, a practice that, though considered "absurd and vile," could not be controlled through prohibitions. One Buenos Aires newspaper, *El Centinela,* suggested introducing new forms of amusement to the mob in order to "counterattack" these "corrupt habits."[109] One urban ordinance intended to help control the violence gave names to the streets and numbered the houses—a procedure that not only improved the image of the city among foreigners, but also allowed the authorities to locate inhabitants more easily.[110]

Implicit in all of these programs was the effort to reconstruct and enforce political obligation. After years of revolutionary instability during which the problem of legitimacy had fostered disobedience among those who contested the central authorities, Buenos Aires in 1820 began to consolidate the government through a combination of coercion and consensus, attempting to establish laws and punishments to control transgression. There were codification projects and proposals for building a prison following Bentham's Panopticon.[111] But the efforts of the government and the elite of Buenos Aires were primarily concentrated on social reformation. *El Centinela,* for instance, urged its readers to engage in the task of "self-reformation," to abandon the heritage of the past and to regenerate habits, ideas, and minds.[112] The paper even suggested encouraging the settlement of British and North American immigrants in uninhabited regions such as Patagonia, in the hope that men and women brought up in the more developed countries would import the cultural, political, and legal values of their native societies.[113]

Despite all these efforts, by the end of the 1820s the social foundation of a secure republic had not yet been achieved. Indeed, the Río de la Plata provinces would have to wait until the second half of the nineteenth century to become a republic populated by law-abiding citizens.

Anglo-American Models and the Argentine Republic

In the short term, the story developed in this essay is not the history of a successful process. But when we look beyond the failure to construct an effective national government in the Río de la Plata from the revolution of 1810 to 1827, we see that the steps later taken by the provinces to form the Argentine Republic reflected, in large part, the views of the group that had supported the adoption of Anglo-American models. Those views, nurtured by Atlantic intercourse, contributed to the constitutional and juridical background of the Argentine liberal politicians of the second half of the nineteenth century.

When the provinces of the Río de la Plata that had not broken off to form independent states (Bolivia, Paraguay, and Uruguay) ratified a federal constitution in 1853, the situation was completely different from that of the 1820s. The surviving provinces had explored the limits of sovereignty and were now more inclined to transfer part of their political power to a central government. In this new context, the ruling elite regarded the debates and proposals of its predecessors as an important economic, juridical, and institutional tradition upon which a new political culture could be established. Now the central government could act as a complex institution capable of shaping the local society—or at least its most dynamic sectors—according to North Atlantic patterns. To accomplish this would be a challenging and time-consuming task; and, in the meantime, as Juan Bautista Alberdi said, it would be necessary to accept an "imperfect freedom" and to postpone the expectation of enjoying the "complete republican freedom" that the North Americans enjoyed until the moment when the local people were as "rich, educated and developed" as those of New York, Boston, or Philadelphia.[114]

The need to educate the people was explained by Domingo Faustino Sarmiento, president of Argentina from 1868 to 1874. Sarmiento admired the United States and wanted Argentina to become a nation of farmers like those who had colonized the North American West.[115] Such views had a shared foundation in the earlier efforts of the Buenos Aires elite from 1810 to 1827. In the 1880s, liberal Argentine politicians believed that they were achieving the goals of the 1810 revolution, suspended while the Río de la Plata provinces had been distinct sovereign states. By the end of the nineteenth century, a liberal and republican tradition had been developed in Argentina, and those who followed this tradition perceived themselves to be the heirs of the generation who had fought against both imperial domination and provincial power in order to build the state and the nation.

As in the British North American colonies, many of the revolutionary actors in the Río de la Plata had seen themselves as the heirs of the Enlightenment, with all the potential as well as all the ambiguities thereby entailed.[116] The rights of men, the consent of the people as government's main source of legitimacy, freedom of expression—these concepts had characterized the intellectual repertoire of the elites engaged in American revolutions both North and South. They were embedded in a complex Atlantic network of intellectual, political, and economic exchanges that were continuous and increasingly far-reaching.

The role played by commerce clearly illustrates the way in which economics, philosophy, and politics interacted. By the end of the eighteenth century, Immanuel Kant believed, international commerce could be considered one of the foundations of perpetual peace. Nature had made nations different in their resources and requirements; therefore they needed each other to obtain the supplies they could not produce, a situation that helped guarantee peace among them.[117] A similar conception was anticipated by the 1776 treaty drafted by the Continental Congress that John Adams took to Europe. As Bernard Bailyn points out, this treaty expressed "the enlightened conviction that the free flow of commerce between nations would be advantageous to all, that neutral carriers should have freedom of the seas in times of war, that the definition of contraband should be severely limited, and there should be complete reciprocity in commercial rights and privileges between the inhabitants of the contracting powers."[118]

Hispanic American leaders had similar opinions. Andrés Bello—a Chilean who took part in the Venezuelan diplomatic mission to London from 1810 to 1820—stated that restrictions on international commerce damaged the people, depriving them of the advantages that would emerge from their reciprocal communication.[119] Sometimes, too, commercial networks bridged the gap between societies. In the case of the Río de la Plata, the expansion of commerce ensured that the habits and fashions of one society entered into another together with merchandise. The very attachment to certain articles—a fabric or iron objects—converted comfort into a new value. The settlement of overseas populations also contributed to spreading habits related to good manners and the general civility of social exchange.

Of course, the Atlantic exchanges did not suppress the singularity of each region, and they did not assume the absence of resistance to the circulation of foreign political models, habits, and values. In fact, there were many people who thought those models alien to their own society;

many local forces refused to accept the cultural and political patterns of the North Atlantic world.

But a group of the Buenos Aires elite maintained over many years its determination to go forward despite resistance—in a way, *because* of that resistance, which they viewed as proof of the Atlantic dynamics of the process in which they were engaged. Like other revolutionary elites, that of Buenos Aires believed that revolution triggers unforeseeable problems. Once reason had demolished the religious foundations of political power, how could men be governed? The answers evoked pessimistic images of human nature, and, echoing James Madison's statement about government being necessary because men were not angels, *El Censor* expressed regret that "it is impossible to maintain order without recourse to force. So unhappy is the human condition!"[120]

This pessimistic view hardly matched the principle of legitimacy grounded in the consent of the people. If "men were not angels," was it necessary to require *all* the people's consent? To deal with this problem, many proposals around the Atlantic world imposed restrictions on suffrage. The 1812 Cádiz constitution stipulated literacy as a prerequisite for citizenship—a plan that compelled Jefferson's admiration.[121] Many Hispanic American countries adopted a similar course, but the idea did not gain currency in the case of the Río de la Plata provinces because many members of the upper classes were themselves illiterate.[122]

If government was to be legitimated through the consent of the people, the risk of majorities ruling against minorities was significant. Madison said that a popular government allowed the majority to sacrifice the common good to the factional interest of the group, even if this group represented the greatest number.[123] By the mid-1810s, a similar opinion was held by the Buenos Aires elite, who believed that the problem lay in the structure of the legislative power. Because the legislative branch was supposed to represent the people's sovereign will, it was prone to "commit excesses" under the guise of accomplishing the majority's mandate.[124]

These problems being "Atlantic," so were the solutions. Aware of its provincialism, the Buenos Aires elite found in Europe and the United States the language to express vital questions and to provide answers to them. Inasmuch as the revolution had developed against the Spanish colonial legacy, the Río de la Plata was neither willing nor able to search in its own colonial past for the tools to shape a promising future. Quite the opposite of the North American founders, Buenos Aires revolutionary leaders saw their society not as the moral reserve of virtue, but rather as the repository of vices inherited from despotism.[125] Atlantic intercourse helped them to undertake the reformation of habits, behavior, and values considered to be crucial for the training of proper citizens, and to become acquainted with the institutional devices designed to build a free republic.

For the building of a republic, constitutionalism was, in a very real sense, an "Atlantic solution." Following the example of the United States, South American countries took the long constitutional path supplied with practical tools rather than simply theoretical principles. Yet the novelty of constitutionalism presented severe difficulties in establishing workable institutions, and the proposals of social, cultural, intellectual, and political transformation were unable to overcome the lack of strong links among the provinces and to remove the other obstacles that interfered with unification. The Río de la Plata had to wait twenty-five years before it could establish the institutional foundations of both the state and the nation, which by the middle of the nineteenth century had regained the Atlantic perspective inaugurated with the 1810 revolution.

12

The Atlantic Worlds of David Hume

EMMA ROTHSCHILD

The disposition of Enlightenment in Europe, which David Hume described as "a general, but insensible revolution" in the "minds of men," was considered at the time to be an oceanic condition. It was a "universal fermentation" in which "navigation had extended itself over the whole globe," as in Hume's description of the early seventeenth century, or a vast system of communication, in his description of his own times, in which "men naturally flock to capital cities, sea-ports, and navigable rivers," and "the minds of men, being once roused from their lethargy, and put into a fermentation, turn themselves on all sides."[1]

These ideas of changes in the mind, which are connected to changes in riverine and maritime shipping, are extremely elusive in the unphilosophical terms of later history. Enlightenment or "lights" was understood, in Hume's lifetime, in three main senses, which correspond, very approximately, to later historians' conceptions of the Enlightenment as a sect (of philosophers), as a milieu (of printers, booksellers, tutors, and translators), and as a disposition or condition of mind. I want to try, in what follows, to reconsider the new European dispositions of the eighteenth century, and their relationship to Atlantic commerce and communications, by looking at David Hume's own life, his own Atlantic worlds.

Hume was thought of in his lifetime, and for much of the nineteenth century, as the first great theorist of long-distance commerce, or of what one of his biographers described, in 1846, as "the social economy of the globe."[2] I will be concerned, in the first part of this essay, with Hume's own involvement with American and other Atlantic ventures, including his uncompleted effort to emigrate to Massachusetts ("Such a Romantic Adventure, & such a Hurry").[3] In the second part, I will consider some more general questions about the history of the Atlantic and the history of the European Enlightenment: about the ways in which Atlantic relationships extended into the interior of Scotland and other European countries; the extent to which these Atlantic relationships, which were continuous in so many respects with Asian and Indian Ocean connections of commerce, were at the same time distinctive, especially in respect of the ownership of land and slaves; and the connections between the Atlantic world and the Enlightenment, in Hume's own understanding of a disposition of mind, "fluctuating, uncertain, fleeting, successive and compounded."[4]

Public and Private Lives

Hume grew up a few miles inland from the small North Sea port of Berwick-upon-Tweed, in the estate of Ninewells in Berwickshire, which was his address for more than half his life, and where he wrote most of his two *Enquiries,* the *Dialogues concerning Natural Religion,* and almost all his essays and discourses.[5] The little port of Berwick was Hume's opening to the outside world. His earliest correspondence was about lending and sending books and about getting letters "by Berwick." His journeys, as a young man, were through Berwick; in 1739 he was detained in London "by contrary winds, which have kept all Berwick ships from sailing"; in 1751 it was by "Thomas Henderson, the Berwick Carrier . . . he puts up at James Henderson, Stabler," that he expected a copy of Strabo. Berwick was a source of family news; "I was in Berwick lately a Night, & going to a Shop next Morning to buy Something, the Shopkeeper told me he had a Lodger of my Name, whom upon Enquiry I found to be your Uncle the Captain," he wrote to his cousin Alexander in 1743. It was even, in 1751, the place to which he intended to remove, with his sister Katherine, upon the marriage of their older brother: "Katty & I have been computing in our turn; and the result of our deliberation is, that we are to take up house in Berwick."[6]

Berwick in the eighteenth century was a microcosm of long-distance relationships. It was in England, for one thing, and David Hume's (or the carrier's) short ride to Berwick down the valley of the Whiteadder involved crossing a frontier between two countries, two established religions, two systems of justice, and two regimes of customs and excise. Hume's own *History of England* was full of the ravages of the Scottish borders in the sixteenth and seventeenth centuries. In "the glorious aera of the union," in the words of a late eighteenth-century historian of the town—and in the image that was of such importance to Hume's philosophical ideas—Berwick was able to assume a new, commercial, and connected destiny.[7]

The town was situated, in the description of the eighteenth-century historian John Fuller, where the "transparent Tweed, with stately majesty . . . disembogues its waters into the German ocean." To the west were the Cheviot Mountains, of "Alpin or Andean rank." It lay on the great London and Edinburgh post road and on the sea route from Leith. Berwick was distinguished, above all, by the "very extensive and regular coasting trade now carried on between this port and London." There was a "perpetual hurry and bustle on the quay in loading and unloading smacks and other vessels." There were excise officers and tide waiters and collectors of customs, the impersonations of British revenue. There were Gravesend and Harwich ships and Berwick "smacks"; there was an old man, "one Home," who rode to London with "six horses loaded with salmon." By the middle of the century, Berwick was a center of the bookselling, book-smuggling, and book publishing trade: from editions of Locke and Montesquieu to *The Lady's, Housewife's, and Cookmaid's Assistant,* and a *Polite Familiar Letter-Writer,* which instructed the reader, in 1768, in how to "hold commerce with the inhabitants of the East and West Indies."[8]

The town was open, too, to the vast world of the "German Ocean," which lay before the eyes of the traveler who descended from Ninewells on the Chirnside road, past the hamlet called "Brow of the Hill." There were ships from the Baltic, and from Norway, Prussia, and Russia; there was a ship which came from Rotterdam with paper, chestnuts, and four thousand young trees; there were exports to Cádiz and Malaga. Berwick could not be "called a romantic or a smooth placid scene," as even Fuller acknowledged. It was bordered by coal pits, quarries, and brickeries, in "large confused heaps." Its marketplace, including the cattle market, was in the middle of the town, and "the blood runs in open gutters all the way from the shambles to the river." By the end of the eighteenth century there were "59 public houses." But it was a place of commerce and information, on two sides of a great river; "it exhibits London in miniature."[9]

Hume's first extended journey, at the age of 23, was to the larger seascape of the English Atlantic. "I was of a good Family," he wrote in his only autobiographical essay, "My Own Life," but one that "was not rich." His income from property, as late as 1751, was no more than £50 a year, and in February 1734 he was "tempted or rather forced to make a very feeble Trial for entering into a more active Scene of Life." He therefore set out to London, and on to Bristol, where he launched himself on a mercantile career, in the house of some "eminent Merchants" trading to the West Indies, as will be seen, in this high season of the Bristol trade in sugar and slaves.[10] Hume's new life lasted only for some four months. But his hopes, at first, had been high. His three opportunities, he wrote at the time, in one of the earliest of his many reflections on different possible lives, were to be a lawyer, a traveling tutor or "Governor," or a merchant. Since the law "appear'd Nauseous to me," and he disliked the prospect of "general Companies," "I therefore fixt my Choice upon a Merchant; & having got Recommendation to a considerable Trader in Bristol, I am just now hastening thither, with a Resolution to forget myself, & every thing that is past, to engage myself, as far as is possible, in that Course of Life, & to toss about the World, from the one Pole to the other, till I leave this Distemper behind me."[11]

It was after the unsuccessful summer in Bristol that Hume turned to *"philosophical discoveries,"* and to the work, the *Treatise of Human Nature,* of which he wrote to his cousin that its principles, if they were to "take place," "would produce almost a total alteration in philosophy." He proceeded to Paris; to Rheims, where his address was "Monsieur David Hume Gentilhomme Ecossais chez Monsieur Mesier au Peroquet verd," and where he proposed to find lodgings together with a friend from Bristol; and eventually, on his own, to the little town of La Flèche, on the river Loir, before it flows into the Loire, and to Nantes and the Atlantic.[12] He was far inland, once more, from the universe of what he described in the *Treatise* as "industry, traffic . . . travels, cities, fleets, ports." He could see, from his room, a vista of "mountains, and houses,

and trees," and a vaster vista of the imagination, as when the porter
mounted the stairs, to bring him a letter from a "friend, who says he is
two hundred leagues distant," "spreading out in my mind the whole sea
and continent between us, and supposing the effects and continu'd existence of posts and ferries, according to my memory and observation."[13]

By the autumn of 1737, Hume had returned to London and found a
printer for the *Treatise*. But the book "fell *dead-born from the Press*," as
he wrote in "My Own Life," and he returned to his mother and brother
in the country. He was not without misgivings, or "a certain shame-
facedness I have to appear among you at my years, without having yet a
settlement, or so much as attempted any."[14] But he was soon engaged,
once more, in the busy life of Berwick, Edinburgh, and now of Glasgow.
Through his "oldest and best friend," William Mure of Caldwell in
Renfrewshire, he came to know the commercial and official scenes of
the west of Scotland. "I shall come down early in the Spring to the Borders of the Atlantic Ocean, & rejoice the Tritons & Seagods," he wrote
to Mure in 1742, of a proposed visit to John Boyle, the Earl of Glasgow
and the heir to a fortune in shipping and the administration of Customs
and Excise; he acquired a "whole Circle of my West countrey Acquaintances."[15]

James Oswald of Dunnikier, Hume's other old and dear friend from
his period in Berwickshire, introduced him to the seaside life of the east
of Scotland. Mr. Oswald "has shown me the whole Oeconomy of the
Navy, the Source of the Navy Debt; with many other Branches of public
Business," Hume wrote to William Mure in 1744, after a visit to Oswald
near Kirkcaldy in Fife; and Oswald, like Mure, was a master of coastal
politics. He was Commissioner of the Navy for Scotland, parliamentary
manager of the Board of Trade, and an expert on Canadian affairs;
he represented the parliamentary constituency of the Dysart Burghs,
Kirkcaldy, Kinghorn, Dysart, and Burntisland, the "low, sea-salted, wind-
vexed promontory," with its "little towns, posted along the shore as
close as sedges, each with its bit of harbour," of which Robert Louis
Stevenson wrote that "History broods over that part of the world like
the easterly *haar.*"[16]

These Fife towns, in the course of the eighteenth century, were open
to the world. Burntisland by the 1790s offered "access, by sea, to every
quarter of the globe"; the square-rigged vessels of Dysart traded "from

London, Liverpool, and other English ports, to the Mediterranean, West
Indies, and America"; the Kirkcaldy ships were sometimes away at sea
for "3 or 4 years," and the Kirkcaldy customhouse, of which Adam
Smith's father, the older Adam Smith, had been the comptroller, managed the export and import duties for all the towns on the north side of
the Firth of Forth. Kinghorn, with its public ferry, had become a cosmopolitan place, in the description of the *Statistical Account*—one of the
dangerous, seductive seaports in which "all the banditti and vagabonds
of the country continually passing and repassing through this great
thorough-fair, and occasionally stopping, and lodging for days and weeks
together, cannot fail to poison the principles, and to corrupt the morals
of those with whom they mingle, and among whom they nestle."[17]

Hume's own Atlantic expedition took place in 1746. In the winter of
1745, he had spent a "melancholy & unsociable" period in Hertford-
shire, as companion to an unhappy young landowner, the Marquess of
Annandale. When his employment ended, he went to London, and some
days later he dispatched "my whole Baggage for Scotland." But "a few
hours before I was setting out for Edinburgh," he encountered a distant
relation, a proprietor of coal mines in the same seaside promontory of
Fife as the Oswalds, General James St. Clair. General St. Clair was at the
time preparing an expedition to Canada, and he offered the position of
secretary to his young kinsman. "Such a Romantic Adventure, & such a
Hurry, I have not heard of before," Hume wrote to another cousin, in a
letter sent from the naval base of Portsmouth, "before my departure for
America"; "I knew not a word of this Matter till Sunday last at Night."[18]

In Portsmouth, as the expeditionary force awaited "the first fair wind
[which] carries us away," Hume reflected on his future life in America.
The force was bound for Boston, where they were to spend the winter
before proceeding to Canada. It might be possible, Hume concluded, to
become an army officer in America at a sufficiently distinguished rank
(for "at my years I could not decently accept of a lower commission
than a company"); his prospect would be "to procure at first a company
in an American regiment, by the choice of the Colonies." But destiny
intervened once more, and General St. Clair's expedition was "detain'd
in the Channel, till it was too late to go to America." In one of the
changes of mind so characteristic of British (and French) policies during
the War of the Austrian Succession, the ministry then dispatched them

"to seek Adventures on the Coast of France." They had hoped, in Hume's later account, to receive detailed instructions from the secretary of state (the Duke of Newcastle), "who, by his office, is led to turn his eyes every where, and who lives in London, the centre of commerce and intelligence." But the orders that awaited them in Plymouth were less than instructive; they were to "make an attempt on L'Orient, or Rochefort, or Rochelle, or sail up the river of Bourdeaux; or . . . to sail to whatever other place on the western coast they should think proper."[19]

The general found himself, in Hume's description, to be "without intelligence, without pilots, without guides, without any map of the country to which he was bound, except a common map, on a small scale, of the kingdom of France, which his Aid-de-camp had been able to pick up in a shop at Plymouth." St. Clair "much questioned if there was in the fleet any one person who had been ashore on the western coast of France, except himself, who was once at Bordeaux." The officers responded to an inquiry about the coast of France, "as if the question had been with regard to the coast of Japan or California"; the expedition was even without money ("except a few chests of Mexican dollars, consigned to other uses"). But it was eventually determined, on the basis of the accompanying admiral's recollection of something he had "once casually heard" from a member of Parliament for Southwark, that their objective should be the Brittany town of Lorient.[20] Lorient, in this first worldwide war of commerce, was the principal port of the French Compagnie des Indes; and it was at Lorient that Hume's American expedition ended, in September 1746.

"The General sent a Summons to the Town, who seemed to prepare for their Defense, by burning all their Suburbs," Hume wrote on September 22 in a little notebook he kept on board ship. Three deputations, from the military, the town, and the "India Company," offered to surrender, if their houses were secured from pillage and the military were permitted to remove. These conditions were refused, and the expedition's "Engineers engag'd with a Mortar, & two 12 pounders to set the Town in a Flame, in one afternoon." But the weather, once more, did not favor the British. "Every Body much discourag'd, especially on account of the Rain, which fell all day as well as yesterday & the day before," Hume wrote on September 25; the engineers "in general shoud themselves confusd & ignorant in their Business. They forgot the Grate to heat their Ball." On September 30 the general proposed "some other attempt on the Coast of France," which the "Sea Officers unanimously declined."[21]

The expeditionary force was then ordered to Cork, which was the western extremity of its Atlantic adventure, and in January 1747 it was recalled to England. Hume listed the orders received in the course of the journey: ". . . 9. To disembark at Dover 10. To disembark at Gravesend 11. I omitted an Order to wait till further orders." He also listed the material detritus of the Atlantic adventure, with its ordering of rank and comfort: "One Trunk D. Hume Esq One Box Mr Hume's Books Box Paper Mr Hume One Trunk the General Canvas Bed One Trunk of the Generals with a Mat & a Bed Stead."[22] He stayed in London for a short time, "to see, if anything new will present itself," as he wrote to yet another kinsman. But by August 1747 he had returned to Ninewells and to the life of a "poor Philosopher," in the familiar conditions of Newcastle coastal shipping: "Our Ship was dirty: Our Accomodation bad: Our Company sick: There were four Spies, two Informers, & three Evidences who saild in the same Ship with us."[23]

A few months later, in February 1748, Hume set off again with General St. Clair, on this occasion to the less adventurous destinations of Carinthia and Turin, beginning with the "Helveot Sluice." ("I had the Misfortune to be excessively sick," he wrote to his brother; "Harwich & Helvoet are the general Images in Abridgement of all the Towns in the two Countries: Both of them small Sea Port Towns.") He was much interested in the new world of riverine travel: the "Ice-boats" on the Maese ("plump, down you go into the Water of a sudden"); the breadth of the Rhine at Cologne (which he compared to the Whiteadder, at Ninewells); the 80-foot boat, with three rooms, including "our Kitchen," on the Danube at Ratisbon; the Court of Chastity in Vienna, "who send all loose Women to the Frontiers of Hungary"; and the source of the Drave, which "falls into the Danube, & into the Black Sea." He formed a good impression of the scene: "Germany is undoubtedly a very fine Country, full of industrious honest People, & were it united it woud be the greatest Power that ever was in the World."[24] But the general's embassy came to an end with the Peace of Aix-la-Chapelle, which ended the War of the Austrian Succession in 1748, and by late 1749 Hume was back, once more, at Ninewells, with "my Brother at his Country house."[25]

Hume's circumstances changed very much for the better in 1752, with the publication of his *Political Discourses,* of which he wrote at the end of his life that it was "the only work of mine that was successful on the first Publication: It was well received abroad and at home."[26] With the *Discourses* Hume became famous, and eventually rich, and a figure in the sect of the French Enlightenment. It was in the *Discourses,* too, that he returned to the theory of empires, or to the world of industry, traffic, alliances, voyages, cities, fleets, and ports: to the Atlantic world of the eighteenth century.

The *Political Discourses* existed under that title for little more than a year. It was subsumed, by 1753, in Hume's *Essays and Treatises on Several Subjects,* and in the intricate publishing history of his various shorter works. But the title itself was an indication of Hume's philosophical purpose, of his intention, as in Machiavelli's *Discorsi* and James Harrington's *Political Discourses,* to which he refers in the concluding pages of the book, to revive speculation about principles of government.[27] These principles, in turn, were to a substantial extent principles of the government of economic connections, or of political economy. Commerce, luxury, money, interest, the balance of trade, the balance of power, taxes, public credit: these were the preoccupations of Hume's political masterpiece, and it was an investigation, above all, of the new circumstances of global commerce, a eulogy to "free communication and exchange."[28]

The idyll at the heart of the *Political Discourses* is of a peaceful exchange of commodities and ideas, in which "commerce is extended all over the globe," "innocent luxury" flourishes, "men naturally flock to capital cities, sea-ports, and navigable rivers," and the "middling rank of men" are respected. In this civilized world the "tempers of men are softened," and even government, once "human reason has refined itself by exercise," can become mild and moderate. "Millions of people," as in eighteenth-century Britain, can be "held together, in a manner so free, so rational, and so suitable to the dignity of human nature." Human nature is itself improved. "The minds of men, being once roused from their lethargy, and put into a fermentation, turn themselves on all sides," and "it is impossible but they must feel an encrease of humanity, from the very habit of conversing together, and contributing to each other's pleasure and entertainment." This was Hume's most extended evocation of the disposition of Enlightenment, and it was of profound importance to other idylls, including Condorcet's, of a generation later. Hume's concatenation of Enlightenment, in his discourse on luxury—"thus *industry, knowledge,* and *humanity,* are linked together by an indissoluble chain"—was the inspiration of Condorcet's inquiry of 1794, as to whether "nature links, by an indissoluble chain, truth, happiness and virtue."[29]

But the tranquil world of commerce—and this is the most important polemical point of the *Discourses*—was at the same time, for Hume, in deadly peril from the spirit of conquest and empire. The *Political Discourses* was a work of the moment, or of the interwar world of 1752, between the universally misunderstood treaty of Aix-la-Chapelle of 1748 and the new misunderstandings that led to the outbreak of the Seven Years' War in 1756. It was imbued with the recollection of the "late wars" and with the expectation of wars to come.[30] Its direst prospect was that these wars, with their conflicts in Cape Breton and Madras and Lorient, would be pernicious, in multiple respects, for the spirit of humanity.

"War is attended with every destructive circumstance; loss of men, encrease of taxes, decay of commerce, dissipation of money, devastation by sea and land," Hume wrote; it led inevitably to taxes; it was the outcome of "our own imprudent vehemence"; it tended, if funded by public borrowing, to "dissolution and destruction." The freedom of government was itself in peril in a world of imperial conquest. In the Roman republic, the public had been "almost in continual alarm"; the Roman Empire had declined not because of luxury but because of the "unlimited extent of conquest." In the American colonies, the British ruled over a system of domestic slavery as barbarous as that of ancient times. In the system of *"pressing of seamen"* into naval service, "a continued violence is permitted in the crown . . . the wild state of nature is renewed." The last paragraph of the *Political Discourses,* like the last paragraph of the *Wealth of Nations,* was an excoriation of imperial conquest: "the ruin of every free government."[31]

Hume's description of commercial exchange, and of its opposite or other, the world of colonial conquest, is an evocation, in part, of the Atlantic life he had observed or imagined in Berwick and Bristol and London. The *Political Discourses* includes a mass of details of commercial existence: the mines in America, the bullion of Cádiz, the rate of interest in Batavia and Jamaica, the expansion of paper money in the colonies, the taxation of brandy in the interest of the southern colonies, the provincial splendor of Bordeaux and Toulouse, the prices of bank stocks and India bonds. Its most extended metaphor is of the communication of commerce as an immense and global body of water. In the Atlantic ocean, money drains from the Indies to Spain and France; in the Asiatic commerce, "the immense distance of CHINA, together with the monopolies of our INDIA companies," cannot obstruct the flow of commerce; there is even a confluence of all oceans, and "were it not for the continual recruits, which we receive from AMERICA, money would soon sink in EUROPE, and rise in CHINA, till it came nearly to a level in both places."[32]

But the publication of the *Political Discourses* was also the opportunity by which Hume was introduced to a much vaster scene. It was through his description of public credit, above all, that his writings became known, like Voltaire's (in Johann Gottfried Herder's sarcastic phrase), "from Lisbon to Kamchatka, from Zembla to the colonies of India": "Hume! Voltaire! Robertsons! Classical spectres of the twilight!"[33] Hume's celebrated simile of war and finance—"I must confess, when I see princes and states fighting and quarrelling, amidst their debts, funds, and public mortgages, it always brings to my mind a match of cudgel-playing fought in a *China* shop"—was translated by the Abbé Raynal *("la boutique d'un fayencier")* and by Immanuel Kant *("in einem Porzellänladen").*[34] The *Discourses,* by 1754, had been published in two rival French translations; even Johann Gottfried Hamann, in Riga, translated Hume's writings on public credit.[35] It was through his writings, too, the *Discourses* and the *History of England,* that Hume finally came to live in Paris, that he became a philosophe in the service—or the gold brocade coat—of the British ministry.

Hume returned to official life in 1763, as a member of the household of the new British ambassador to France, with a pension of £200 a year for life, the expectation of becoming secretary of the embassy, and a suspicion that the ambassador, Lord Hertford, "thinks I may be useful to [his son] in his Studies." He found himself celebrated as an English philosophe, or as "one of the greatest geniuses in the world" (as he reported to Adam Ferguson). When he attended the ambassador to Versailles in November 1763, he was welcomed by the 9-year-old Duc de Berri (later Louis XVI), who said how much he had enjoyed reading "many passages in my works," by the 8-year-old Comte de Provence (later Louis XVIII), who said how much he looked forward to reading "my fine History," and by the 6-year-old Comte d'Artois (later Charles X), of whom Hume wrote to an Edinburgh friend, "I heard him mumble the word *Histoire,* and some other terms of panegyric."[36]

The world of French politics into which Hume settled, in the period of postwar exchange that followed the Treaty of Paris, was itself a universe of oceanic connections. Hume's own duties, in the extraordinary scene of inter-imperial exchange in which Canada was ceded by the French to the British, Louisiana by the French to the Spanish, Martinique by the British to the French, Grenada by the French to the British, and Florida by the Spanish to the British, were concerned to a great extent with maritime relationships. He wrote a memorandum to the French ministry about illicit cutting of timber in Newfoundland and illicit fishing in "intermediate seas" by the inhabitants of the French islands of St. Pierre and Miquelon; he investigated the jetties at Dunkirk and the legal proceedings, which extended to "Dunkirk, Calais & Boulogne," of a former merchant from New Hampshire; he wrote another memorandum about the devaluation of French paper money in Canada, and the "Hardship & Injustice" imposed on English merchants.[37] The embassy was solicited on behalf of two French ladies, proprietors in Grenada, who wished to take the oath of allegiance to the British Crown, and by the young daughter of a Swiss officer in Canada, who wrote from a refugee camp in the Charente that "the father enjoyed, like the daughter herself enjoys, the advantage of being of a nation that serves, indifferently, all the crowns which provide her with good conditions."[38] Hume was also engaged, as an intimate friend of the intendant Trudaine de Montigny ("You know, I lived almost with M. de Montigny and his Family," he wrote in 1766), in the British embassy's reporting of the tragedy of the French colonization of Cayenne, of which the economist Turgot's brother was the governor, and in which some nine thousand people died within a few months in 1764–1765, of epidemic disease, starvation, or despair.[39]

Even Hume's life as a philosophe in Paris was surrounded by the minutiae of colonial and oceanic existence. He first encountered Jean d'Alembert, who became his closest friend in Paris, and to whom he left £200 in his will, when D'Alembert wrote to him on behalf of "a poor Canadian family" who were living as refugees on an island off the Atlantic coast of France, and who wished to return to "English domination." Denis Diderot wrote to Hume to recommend a "jeune Pensylvain," who was a student of medicine, and a married couple, of whom the wife was placed by Hume as "gouvernante" in the home of Sir George Colebrooke, war contractor, husband of an Antigua heiress, proprietor in Grenada and Lanarkshire, and chairman, later, of the East India Company.[40] Benjamin Franklin, with whom Hume exchanged elaborate compliments at the time of Franklin's residence in Craven Street near Covent Garden, delighted Hume, on a later visit, by franking his letters, in his capacity as deputy postmaster general of the colonies.[41] Charles-Marie de la Condamine, the mathematician, Amazon explorer, and measurer of the degree of meridian at the equator, wrote to Hume in Paris in 1765 to ask for his help in respect of yet another young colonial, a "native of the province of Quito in America," who had fallen foul of "an Oydor of Quito (this is a very respected idol in Spanish America)" because he had refused to marry his daughter, and who was proceeding around Europe, seeking to enter the service of the French, the British, or the Portuguese.[42]

When Hume left Paris for England in January 1766 (this was his notorious journey with Jean-Jacques Rousseau, who insisted on "wearing the Armenian dress," and who "passed ten hours in the night time above deck during the most severe weather, when all the seamen were almost frozen to death"), his intention was to return to Edinburgh, and to live in retirement and indolence on the proceeds of his investments; "my four per cents in the Stocks," and the "long Annuities." But a year later, he was again in London, and again "from a Philosopher, degenerated into a petty Statesman."[43] This was his last public office, as undersecretary of state for the Northern Department (which was responsible for Russia and France, although not the American colonies), under the pa-

tronage of General H. S. Conway, the brother of his former patron Lord
Hertford, and the theorist, at the time of the Stamp Act crisis, of the
sentiments of the American colonists. He had become part of what
Edmund Burke described at the time as "Conways chain," in which
"His family get every thing."[44]

The new way of life, as Hume wrote to Hugh Blair, was "by no means
disagreeable. I pass all the Forenoon in the Secretary's House from ten
till three, where there arrives from time to time Messengers, that bring
me all the Secrets of this Kingdom, and indeed of Europe, Asia, Africa
and America." He was in touch with his new friends from Paris and his
old friends from Scotland. A distant cousin of the melancholy nobleman,
William Johnstone, who had changed his name to Pulteney, asked him
to write to France in respect of "a bond due by the French East India
Company, indorsed to me by the attorneys of my Brother, John Johnstone, at Calcutta." Then, in January 1768, Hume left office for the last
time, having requested "the Liberty, after my Dismission, of inspecting
all the public Records and all the Papers in the Paper-Office." He considered the possibility of going to live in Paris, but decided against it, in
part because he feared that he would be expelled ("after being twice employed by the English ministry in places of trust and confidence") when
the next war broke out between France and England. In August 1769 he
returned to Edinburgh and to the life he so cherished, of "reading and
sauntering and lownging and dozing, which I call thinking."[45]

Hume was an observer, in all these vicissitudes, these journeys by
ferry and barge and Newcastle shipping, of the Atlantic crises of the
middle of the eighteenth century, and the new crises of the times were
of profound importance to his historical and political ideas. "I am an
American in my Principles, and wish we would let them alone to govern
or misgovern themselves as they think proper," Hume wrote in 1775 to
his old friend William Mure, about a petition in Renfrewshire.[46] J. G. A.
Pocock has described these and other observations on empire as the
"dying thoughts of a North Briton," and Hume returned to the "late
war," and its "extremely frivolous object," in the revisions he made to
his *History of England* in the last months of his life. "Our late delusions
have much exceeded anything known in history, not even excepting
those of the crusades," he wrote of the national debt "in the present
year, 1776," in a footnote about Queen Elizabeth's revenues; "we have

even lost all title to compassion, in the numberless calamities that are waiting us."⁴⁷

This dismal view of imperial power was more or less uninterrupted, throughout the long midcentury of Hume's literary life, or since his *Political Discourses* of 1752. "O! how I long to see America and the East Indies revolted totally & finally," he wrote to another old friend, Sir Gilbert Elliot, in 1768; to the publisher William Strahan, in 1769, he anticipated "the total Revolt of America, the Expulsion of the English from the East Indies."⁴⁸

The forty years' war of the eighteenth century was in this sense the dominating circumstance of Hume's public life, as it was of so much of the political life of the late Enlightenment. If the period from the outbreak of the War of the Austrian Succession in 1739 to the end of the War of American Independence in 1783 is conceived of as a single conflict, with its interwar periods and its postwar periods and its periods of false or imagined or expected war, then it was this conflict that formed Hume's political ideas and the world of information in which he lived. It was a global conflict: the "most frivolous Causes," Hume wrote to Trudaine de Montigny in 1767, had during the last war "spread the Flame from one End of the Globe to the other"; the disputes between the Spanish and the English in the South Atlantic, he wrote to Strahan in 1771, threatened to throw "almost the whole Globe into a Ferment." It was also a war of intelligence, or of the failure of intelligence. "That horrible, destructive, ruinous War; more pernicious to the Victors than to the Vanquished," was "fomented by some obscure designing Men," he wrote to Trudaine, and it might have been prevented by "the Explication of a few Points."⁴⁹

The eighteenth-century wars have been described, as they were described at the time by Du Pont de Nemours and Adam Smith, as virtual or offshore conflicts, subjects of amusing conversation, in Paris or London, or of "the amusement of reading in the newspapers" about the exploits of distant fleets and armies. They were in this respect conflicts of information, in a world of what Herder described in 1774 as a *Papierkultur.*⁵⁰ But they were at the same time conflicts that transformed the financial organization of Europe and the North American colonies, in the empire of public credit that was Hume's great subject in his *Political Discourses,* as it was Du Pont's and Smith's great subject as well.

The wars also transformed the individual existences of the hundreds of thousands of young men who were subject, or who feared they might be subject, to the lotteries for the royal militia (which Hume's friend Turgot tried to reform in the Limousin), or to the pressing of seamen by which, in Hume's own description, "a continued violence is permitted in the crown."[51] They were distant conflicts, which imposed themselves, in multiple ways, on the interior lives of societies.

Hume was fascinated, from his earliest youth in Berwickshire, with information and intelligence, and with the sentiments of individuals in respect of different kinds of news. In the *Enquiry,* he compares the accounts of miracles to reports of impending marriages in country places and provincial towns; "the pleasure of telling a piece of news so interesting, of propagating it, and of being the first reporters of it, spreads the intelligence." The presumption of universal self-love, he says, is confuted by the pleasures of the imagination; "any recent event or piece of news, by which the fate of states, provinces, or many individuals is affected, is extremely interesting even to those whose welfare is not immediately engaged."[52] The discursive, inquisitive men and women who are at the heart of his description of human nature are continuously recounting and receiving information; they are also continuously looking for new sources of intelligence, and trying to decide whether pieces of information are true. They "love to receive and communicate knowledge"; they live in a "conversible World," in which everyone "mutually gives and receives Information."[53]

This was the world in which Hume himself lived, from the family news in Berwick in 1743 ("your Uncle the Captain"), to the debacle in the French Atlantic, to his own moment of maximum knowingness, in London in 1767, amidst the "Secrets of this Kingdom" and the public records "in the Paper-Office."[54] He was preoccupied, throughout his life, with postal privileges, with associations to get down newspapers from London, letters sent by the common carrier, and the "universal practice of opening all letters . . . a clerk in the post-office opens a letter, runs it over, and, finding it concerns only private business, forwards it presently."[55] In Paris, he was anxious for political news from England; you "promisd, to correspond," he wrote to William Strahan, and "I have long expected to hear from you and to learn your Sentiments of English

Politics." In London, with all his secrets, he was anxious for news of his old friends in Paris; he felt as isolated "as I should be in Westphalia or Lithuania," he wrote to the Comtesse de Boufflers.[56]

The new world of information was of dominating importance, more generally, to the politics of distance that was at the heart of Hume's philosophical and moral thought. The idea of distance (and the word "distance") is everywhere, in the *Treatise* and in the *Political Discourses.* The individual is surrounded by what Hume describes as "distance or outness (so to speak)"; he exists in a universe of near or distant objects, of which he has more or less reliable information, and to which he is connected in more or less accidental ways. The nearby is more important, in general, than the distant. But the relationships of contiguity and distance are very far from orderly, and distance in time has a more powerful effect on the imagination, for example, than distance in space. "Our situation, with regard both to persons and things, is in continual fluctuation; and a man, that lies at a distance from us, may, in a little time, become a familiar acquaintance"; in the immense universe of people and things and relationships, the very distant—or the objects at the very edge of our vision—can suddenly, dizzyingly, be transformed into the very near.[57]

These ideas of distance and connectedness were illustrated, even in the *Treatise,* by the relationships of the Atlantic world of commerce. The distance between Hume in the Loire Valley and his friend in Scotland was filled in imagination by posts and ferries; the uniformity of human existence was the outcome of "industry, traffic, manufactures, law-suits, war, leagues, alliances, voyages, travels, cities, fleets, ports." Individuals spent much of their lives in making judgments about other people, as "a merchant looks for fidelity and skill in his factor or super-cargo." Even "the greatest distance of place this globe can admit" was sometimes insufficient to distract the mind, and "a *West-India* merchant will tell you, that he is not without concern about what passes in *Jamaica.*"[58]

In the *Political Discourses,* Hume described a good sort of distance— the "great extent" of the Roman Empire under the Antonine emperors, which was for Hume (as it was later for Edward Gibbon and Adam Smith) the very image of a profound peace, or the mildness of a republican government in an "extensive country," which later so inspired James

Madison, and in which "the parts are so distant and remote, that it is very difficult, either by intrigue, prejudice, or passion, to hurry them into any measures against the public interest."[59]

But there was also a bad sort of distance. The imagination of distance, or the failure of imagination, was in foreign relationships far more insidious. It was subject, even more than in domestic politics, to the empire of chance. Of all the revolutions of the state, Hume wrote in 1742, "the foreign and the violent" were particularly unsusceptible of reasonable observation, because they were "more influenced by whim, folly, or caprice." "Foreign politics" were far more dependent on "accidents and chances, and the caprices of a few persons." They were dependent, too, on distant connections or on long chains of consequences and coincidences, endlessly imagined and endlessly disconcerted. The failure of imagination of distance was a cause—the most fatal of all causes—of errors in human conduct.[60]

The tenuous freedom of modern commercial societies was continuously at risk, in Hume's dismal prospect, from the evil opposing forces of enthusiasm or superstition, faction or corruption. But it was in the direst of peril in the conditions of empire and conquest. "Enormous monarchies are, probably, destructive to human nature," he wrote in his discourse on the balance of power; their wars, "carried on at a great distance," and their idiosyncratic combination of faction (in some colonies) and corruption (in others, or in the Asiatic luxury described by Sallust) were destructive of all political virtue. "Arbitrary Power can extend its oppressive Arm to the Antipodes; but a limited Government can never long be upheld at a distance," Hume wrote to William Strahan in 1775. Even the good distance of republican government in an "extensive country" would be destroyed by the bad distance of empire, as in the peroration of the *Discourses:* "extensive conquests, when pursued, must be the ruin of every free government."[61]

Empiricism and Dominion

The new distance of empire was destructive, even, of the innocuous pleasures of moral inquiry. There is a footnote in one of Hume's essays, "Of National Characters," that became a foundational text of late eighteenth- and nineteenth-century racism, and his sentiments regarding

African slavery have been considered, rightly, as one of the most disturbing evils of Enlightenment thought. "I am apt to suspect the negroes to be naturally inferior to the whites," Hume wrote, in a version of the essay prepared not long before his death; he likened the "one negroe" in Jamaica (Francis Williams, the Latin poet) who was supposed to be "a man of parts and learning," to "a parrot, who speaks a few words plainly."[62] Hume's footnote, as Henry Louis Gates has shown, inspired Kant to assert that "the Negroes of Africa have by nature no feeling that rises above the trifling," and Hegel to abandon the supposed universalism of Enlightenment: "the peculiarly African character is difficult to comprehend, for the very reason that in reference to it, we must quite give up the principle which naturally accompanies all *our* ideas—the category of Universality."[63]

Hume is not to be blamed for Hegel, and mid-eighteenth-century ideas of race are exceptionally difficult to make sense of (for several different reasons, including that they were so closely involved with theological positions and that they were, by the 1770s, in continual flux).[64] But Hume's footnote was very far from being insouciant, or unintended. It was not present in the earliest version of his essay on national characters, published in 1748; it was added in a new edition published in 1753; and it was revised, carefully, in the final version, in which the capacious assertion of white superiority of 1753—"I am apt to suspect the negroes, and in general all the other species of men (for there are four or five different kinds) to be naturally inferior to the whites"—was reduced to the assertion of black inferiority of 1776, "I am apt to suspect the negroes to be naturally inferior to the whites."[65] It was a statement by Hume about which he reflected, and which is difficult to understand.

Hume was apparently sincerely distressed by the institution of slavery; he wrote in his discourse on the populousness of ancient nations that "the remains which are found of domestic slavery, in the AMERICAN colonies" were such as to "trample upon human nature," and to "disgust us with that unbounded dominion."[66] But he was not, in the notorious footnote, expressing a view that had "as an excuse, either the prejudice of necessity, or the invincible error of a universal custom" (this was Condorcet's phrase, some years after Hume's death, in a comparison of the ancient and modern defenders of slavery).[67] Adam Smith, who was by the 1760s Hume's closest friend, was well known as a eulogist, in the *Theory of Moral Sentiments,* of the virtues of Africans; the first work ever published *about* Smith, in fact, was a pamphlet of 1764 in which he was accused, by the Virginian Arthur Lee (whom Hume had met in Paris in 1765), of having "exalted into heroes" the African slaves, and "debased into monsters" the American colonists.[68] The immorality of African slavery was the subject of intense discussion in Paris at the time Hume was living there as an English philosophe. It was at the center, in particular, of the drama over the French expedition to Cayenne, which so occupied Turgot, Hume's friend Trudaine de Montigny, and the British embassy, and which turned on the possibility of American colonization without slaves.

Even in his own lifetime, Hume's footnote was the subject of intense interest, of which he must to at least some extent have been aware. He was undoubtedly aware of the devastating criticism of his views by the Aberdeen philosopher James Beattie in the *Essay on Truth,* which was published in 1770, and to which he responded, at least indirectly, in his final revisions of the essay on national character. Another of his eloquent critics, the physician Benjamin Rush, was the "jeune Pensylvain" about whom Diderot had written to him some years earlier. Hume may even have followed the uses of his essay in the conflict of pamphlets over the famous Somerset case of 1772, which established, in a judgment by Lord Mansfield in favor of James Somerset, the slave of a Boston customs official, Charles Steuart, that there was no right of slave owners in England to transport their slaves by force to the other slave societies of the British Empire.

"In looking into Mr Hume's Essays," one of the opponents of James Somerset and the "Negroe Cause," Samuel Estwick, "Assistant Agent for the Island of Barbados," wrote in 1773, "I was made happy to observe the ideas of so ingenious a writer corresponding with my own"; he differed with Hume, however, in that he distinguished "man from man" not on the basis of understanding, but of *"the moral sense."* The great abolitionist Granville Sharp, James Somerset's patron, actually described Hume in 1776, in a response to Estwick, as the "first broacher of that uncharitable doctrine," that "Negroes are *'an inferior species of men.'*" "The learned Dr. Beattie, in his *Essay on Truth,* has fully refuted the insinuations of Mr. Hume," Sharp wrote, "so that Mr. Estwick's subsequent attempt, which was prompted only by the authority of Mr. Hume, needs no further confutation."[69]

Hume's footnote poses difficult questions, in these circumstances, about his idyll of commercial and civilized society. The late eighteenth-century idea of the disposition of Enlightenment was a composite of two different observations: first, about certain universal or natural conditions of the mind, including inquisitiveness, rationality, sociability, self-love, and the love of information; and second, about the particular historical circumstances in which these dispositions flourish or are repressed. Hume provided no very elaborate theory of the causal relationship between the historical circumstances and the universal conditions (or of the empirical foundations of his own "science of man"). But his footnote makes it clear that the universal dispositions were not, in his own view, really universal. Or rather, for Hume, on this as on numerous other occasions, the universal was something to be considered with the greatest circumspection, something insidious, almost ecclesiastical.

The footnote makes clear, too, the slightness of the empirical generalizations on which Hume's ideas of the mind were based. As James Beattie wrote of Hume's assertions, they would not, even if true, prove the point in question, "except it were also proved, that the Africans and Americans, even though arts and sciences were introduced among them, would still remain unsusceptible of cultivation." As to their truth, "no man could have sufficient evidence, except from a personal acquaintance with all the negroes that now are, or ever were, on the face of the earth. Those people write no histories; and all the reports of all the travellers that ever visited them, will not amount to any thing like a proof of what is here affirmed." In respect of the "empires of Peru and Mexico," meanwhile, "we know that these assertions are not true."[70]

Hume's skepticism, too, or his easiness in respect of a world without religious or rational order, comes to lose its charm in these remarks. For Beattie, the natural or universal equality of all human individuals was founded, in a quite straightforward way, on the nature of God. For some of Hume's friends and admirers, including Smith, Turgot, and Condorcet, it was founded on a more complicated conception of moral personality, a conception that was widely considered, by later critics of the eighteenth-century Enlightenment, to be almost religious. But it was also founded on at least the prospect of serious empirical investigation, on a theory of knowledge as well as a theory of nature. Hume, in this passage and in other, similar passages about class, seemed easily, or effortlessly, to forget the "natural equality" to which he referred from time to time. It was as though the sense of the dignity of human nature were not very secure, in the end, in the absence of religious or almost religious confidence.

Hume's description of the oscillating psychology of philosophical reflection, at the end of book 1 of the *Treatise*—"Where am I, or what? . . . I am confounded with all these questions, and begin to fancy myself in the most deplorable condition imaginable, inviron'd with the deepest darkness. . . . I dine, I play a game of back-gammon, I converse, and am merry with my friends. . . . [when] I wou'd return to these speculations, they appear so cold, and strain'd, and ridiculous, that I cannot find in my heart to enter into them any farther"—is one of the most engaging expressions of the experience of epistemological or metaphysical thought. But it is much less engaging as an expression of moral thought. The indolence of which Hume was so conscious—and "which appears in his philosophy as the most amiable vice with which Nature has in her benevolence blessed us," in Edgar Wind's description—is less than amiable if it is the morality of African slavery by which the philosopher is confounded, and which he then forgets in conversation with his friends.[71]

Even Hume's own personality comes to seem less charming in relation to the footnote and to his revisions of it. Hume is one of the individuals of the eighteenth century who is easiest to know, or to imagine one knows. He was interested in his own and his friends' "characters"; one of the merriments of Christmas, on the coast of Fife—"as a gambol of the season they agreed to write each his own character, to give them to Hume"—was to describe one's own personality. He described at great length the events of his inner life and his inner thoughts; he wrote a large number of letters, which survive, to his intimate friends; he had a large number of friends and an exceptional gift, much commented upon, for what he described as the virtue "that seems principally to ly among *Equals,* and is, for that Reason, chiefly calculated for the middle Station of Life. This Virtue is FRIENDSHIP."[72] His friends, too, were eager to describe what he was like. "Concerning [his] character and conduct there can scarce be a difference of opinion," Adam Smith wrote in his account of Hume's death; he was of "extreme gentleness," and "of good-nature and good-humour"; he was as near "to the idea of a perfectly wise and virtuous man, as perhaps the nature of human frailty will permit."[73]

Hume's footnote is of great interest, for all these reasons, in trying to understand his philosophical opinions and his "own character." The most convincing explanation, it seems to me, was the one suggested by Turgot in a letter of 1773 to Condorcet—namely, that Hume was "very insensitive." "I know that there are men who are very insensitive [*très peu sensibles*] and who are at the same time honest, such as *Hume, Fontenelle,* etc.; but they all have as the basis for their honesty *justice,* and even a certain degree of *goodness,*" Turgot wrote, à propos of the insensitivity of Helvétius.[74] Hume's footnote, from this perspective, was the expression of an insensitive empiricism into which he ventured from time to time. It was in the spirit, for example, of his assertion in the *Treatise* that "the skin, pores, muscles, and nerves of a day-labourer are different from those of a man of quality: So are his sentiments, actions and manners."[75] Hume was determined, in this passage as in the racist footnote, to demonstrate that observation is the only basis for generalization; that the universal and the uniform are endlessly elusive; and that the causes of sentiments are to do with social relationships, rather than with climate or with the nature of God. He was more interested in his continuing project of "subverting the whole sacred drama of Fall and Redemption" (in Colin Kidd's words) than in the lives of "the Africans and Americans."[76] He was entirely without interest, or so it seemed, in the exercise by which Smith, Turgot, and Condorcet were so intrigued, of imagining oneself to be someone else; a slave, or a day-laborer, or a woman in childbirth. He was also very little interested in evidence about these other people, or in the empirical investigations he described in his philosophical writings. He was honest, and good, and not at all *sensible.*

Hume's footnote is of great interest, too, in relation to the circumstances of his life and of his successive and oceanic milieux. For Hume's Atlantic milieu was a world full of slaves, of information about slaves, and of slaves' own information. His earliest Atlantic adventure, as a Bristol merchant's clerk in 1734, brought him to Bristol at the height of its dominance in the European-African-American slave trade, following the acquisition (at the end of another European war, and as negotiated by a bishop of Bristol) of the *asiento*, the right to supply slaves to the Spanish colonies. "His Master dealt in sugar," Josiah Tucker told the antiquarian and lawyer David Dalrymple, of Hume's period in Bristol.[77] The mercantile house of Michael Miller, in which he is reported to have been employed, was involved in the Jamaica trade; the Bristol parliamentary election of May 1734, while he was there, turned on Walpole's excise bill in respect of tobacco, and on processions of horsemen with "knots of gilded tobacco in their hats"; the Bristol newspapers, as throughout the century, included advertisements for slaves, rewards for the return of runaway slaves, and reports of slave rebellions.[78]

Even on his return to Scotland, and to the interior world of Berwickshire, Hume was surrounded by the consequences of the colonial economy. A substantial proportion of Hume's oldest friends, in the enlightened and commercial society of mid-eighteenth-century Scotland, were connected, indirectly or directly, to the Atlantic slave economy. William Mure was granted "the Reversion of the office of Receiver General of the Island of Jamaica" in 1763; James Oswald was the kinsman, and patron in office, of the West African and West Indian merchant dynasty of Richard Oswald; Oswald's son "Jemmy," of whom Hume sent news from Normandy ("very good Accounts of Jemmy in every Respect"), became secretary of the Leeward Islands.[79] The family of Sir James Johnstone, through whom Hume was connected to his melancholy employer of 1745, included seven sons, of whom five—in Bengal, Grenada, Dominica, Tobago, and Florida—became the owners of other individuals.[80]

These were not, even, distant ills. Hume's acquaintances lived off the wealth of slave property, and they lived in close proximity to slaves. Benjamin Franklin settled in Craven Street with an English landlady and two slaves.[81] James Grant, who was one of General St. Clair's secretaries, together with Hume, in the 1740s ("if he recovers his Health, he loses his Shape; & must always remain in that perplexing Dilemma," Hume wrote of him in 1750), returned to Sutherland with a retinue of attendants, a state coach, and a black cook.[82] One of the legal scandals of Hume's last period in Edinburgh was the divorce proceeding of Houston Stewart Nicholson against his wife Margaret in 1770. Nicholson was the brother-in-law of Sir William Maxwell of Springkell, a respected figure of the west of Scotland, a cousin of William Mure and a trustee of Alexander and James Johnstone, and the events in question took place at Maxwell's estate; one of the witnesses was "Latchimo, a negro," about whom the defendant objected "in respect he was a slave, and not a Christian," to which the pursuer countered that "there was no proper slavery known in this country," and "it was no objection to a witness that he was not a Christian; it was enough that he believed in a God and a future state."[83]

The "slave or servant of John Johnstone," one of the sons of Hume's friend Sir James Johnstone, was charged with child murder in Fife in 1771, a few miles from Adam Smith's home in Kirkcaldy, and sentenced, as a slave, by a court in Perth—"A criminal slave adjudged to be sold for behoof of the master," in the words of the headline in *The Scots Magazine*.[84] The case that eventually established that there was no slavery in Scotland was brought in 1774, in Perth and Edinburgh, by Joseph Knight, the slave of a kinsman of another of Hume's friends, Sir John Wedderburn. Even the Somerset case of 1772 involved a respectable figure in the official milieu of the Scottish Atlantic; Charles Steuart, the owner of James Somerset, was cashier and paymaster-general of the Customs Office in Boston, a creditor in the collapse of the Ayr Bank ("or Scotch Bank of Air, as John Bull's Sons affect to call it," as Steuart wrote to a Scottish friend in Boston, James Murray), a friend of Benjamin Franklin's son and the Johnstones' uncle, and the brother of an Edinburgh lawyer who was the son-in-law of the publisher of the *Caledonian Mercury*.[85] Scotland in the eighteenth century was not a slave society, or a slave-owning society. But it was a society in which Atlantic slavery was at the edge of Hume's and Mure's and the Oswalds' experience, and of their imagination.

The Atlantic and the Interior

To return, now, to the Enlightenment and the Atlantic. David Hume, as I have tried to suggest, lived in an Atlantic milieu, or in an uncertain and fleeting succession of Atlantic milieux. The world of the mid-eighteenth century, even for this indolent and uncommercial "philosophe," was an Atlantic world. He was familiar, from his earliest youth, with the bustling life of English, Scottish, and French ports; his friendships, also from his early period in Scotland, were with individuals whose interests and connections extended around the world; he was connected to the most extravagantly colonial of Scottish families; he set off to go to America himself, in the expedition of 1746 to Canada that ended in Lorient; the work of his which was most celebrated in his lifetime, the *Political Discourses* of 1752, was an extended investigation of oceanic commerce and conflict; he was concerned, in both of his official positions in "the English ministry," with Atlantic policies and with the Canadian and Equadorian connections of the French sect of Enlightenment; he lived, like so many others, in an information society, which was also a society of news and intelligence about the forty years' war of the mid-eighteenth century; he lived, too, in a society of Atlantic slavery.

Hume's life is an interesting illustration, for all these reasons, of the ways in which the Atlantic world of the eighteenth century extended far inland, into the interior of provinces and into the interior of individual existence. I have been concerned, in general, with Hume's "life and times," rather than with his "life and work," and I do not wish to suggest that the Atlantic scenes in which he found himself were of determining or decisive importance in respect of his philosophical, historical, or political ideas. (The *Treatise of Human Nature,* which he wrote in his mid-20s in the little inland town of La Flèche, is indeed one of the most extraordinary examples in the entire history of philosophy of the extent to which philosophical invention is the outcome of individual genius, and not of a cultural or intellectual "context.")[86] The subset of his political ideas—the economic ideas in the *Political Discourses*—with which I have been concerned were of great importance to his own literary career and to his reputation in the century following his death, although they have been of much less subsequent interest.[87] But it is his life, above all— a life that was well documented and for which the documentary evidence has survived reasonably well—that seems to me to provide such an intriguing glimpse of the Atlantic world of the eighteenth-century Enlightenment.

It would be difficult to sustain an argument that the circumstances of Hume's life constitute a "representative situation," or one of the "characteristic" or "typical" facts that have been the objective of so much social history.[88] But they were characteristic, at least, of his own circle of acquaintances, in the sometimes prosperous and sometimes unsettled

circumstances of lowlands Scotland in the middle of the eighteenth century. Hume's uneminent friends, like James Oswald and William Mure,
described very much the same sort of milieu as Hume himself. Their
own correspondence and manuscripts still exist (in part because of the
circumstance of their friendship with Hume), and they evoke the same
fluctuating world in which conversations veer from the philosophy of
mind to official positions in West Florida, or from a fine speech by
"Burck" on the "theory of colonys" to the addresses of merchants in
Berwick.[89]

The relationship between provincialism and Enlightenment in
eighteenth-century Scotland has been the subject of distinguished historical investigation.[90] But even within this open, inquisitive society,
Hume's individual circumstances were particularly conducive to a life of
tossing "about the World, from the one Pole to the other." He did not
belong to the "middling rank of men," or the "middle station of life," of
which he offered such amiable descriptions in his essays and in his *History of England*. He was a "Gentleman"; this is how he was identified in
the calendar that regulated so much of daily life in eighteenth-century
Edinburgh.[91] He was also the younger son of a very impoverished family, at a time when commerce still, in Scotland as in France, "derogated"
from the rank of gentlemanliness, in social relationships if not in law. He
had no more than three or four possibilities, as a young man, for leading
a seemly life in British society; and even the life of a tutor was replete
with ignominies of various sorts (as when the unhappy Lord Annandale
accused him of having suggested that he was treating him "like a servant"). So for Hume, as for so many of his friends in Scotland, official
employment was of even more than ordinary importance, and employment, above all, in the overseas world of the empire.

Hume's life was for all these reasons idiosyncratic. But at least some
of the circumstances of Hume's Atlantic world were universal, in the
sense that they impinged on the lives of almost everyone in mid-eighteenth-century England and Scotland and France. They were conditions
of the inner experience of commercial and colonial life, or of what Bernard Bailyn and Philip Morgan have described as its "lifeblood, its social, economic, intellectual, and cultural dimensions," as distinct from
the "skeleton," or the "structural framework of colonial life."[92] These
cognitive or psychological conditions of Atlantic life are particularly

difficult to imagine in regard to the influence of the Atlantic colonies
and commerce on individuals in Europe: on the millions of individuals
like Hume, who did not go to America, or to Africa. Colonial, or at least
North American, continental commerce and patronage, as Jacob Price
showed in an important article called "Who Cared about the Colonies?"
accounted for only a small proportion of British public and economic
life in the eighteenth century; colonial posts were a small percentage of
all offices, Americans and those with American experience were a small
percentage of all members of Parliament, exports were a small percentage of national income. But indicators of this sort, as Price also observed, convey only a partial impression of what the American or Atlantic colonies meant to the "nation as a whole."[93] It is in respect of this
more capacious sort of influence that the successive scenes of Hume's
life are so suggestive.

The seaside world of Berwick-upon-Tweed and Kirkcaldy, in particular, was replicated around almost the entire littoral of the British Isles,
and around at least some of the littoral of Portugal, France, Holland,
and the Baltic as well. One of the platitudes of eighteenth-century writings on commerce was that Britain owed its economic success to its
Meerlage, or its situation as an island surrounded by rivers and ports, in
which no point was more than 70 miles from the sea. This seaside and
riverine world, the bustling world of Berwick or the fluctuating world
of Kinghorn, was itself, as was also observed by innumerable contemporaries, a promiscuous scene. It was a place of carriers and porters. It was
open to the seas and open, too, to the rich and the poor. It was a place of
physical proximity and overheard news, in which "the sight of the ships
and the conversation and adventures of the sailors" enticed the young to
go to sea.[94] "This flux and reflux of strangers makes the Town of Gravesend and Milton always lively," a historian of the 1790s wrote of the port
of Gravesend, which was the destination of the Berwick smacks and to
which Hume's unhappy French expedition was ordered; "The Tiltboat,
like the grave, confounds all distinctions; high and low rich and poor,
sick and sound, are indiscriminately blended together."[95]

The accidents of Hume's life, including the months when he thought
he was on the point of departing for America, or when he was awaiting
the news of an official position, were also characteristic of the lives of
large numbers of other people. The particular opportunities that Hume

sought were reasonably lofty: a company in an American regiment, or the position of acting secretary and acting or de facto tutor in Lord Hertford's household in Paris. But there were tens of thousands of individuals in Britain who were waiting for positions, or opportunities, or destinies, and many of these destinies, in the middle of the eighteenth century, were connected to overseas events. The spirit of emigration that so exercised Hume's friends in Scotland in the last decade of his life, and that Hume himself described as a "frenzy of migrating to foreign countries," was one sort of connection: for the individuals who emigrated, and for the other individuals (like Hume) who thought about emigrating and who decided not to go, or were prevented from going, and even for the individuals who waited for news (or remittances, or inheritances) from their friends and families on the other side of the ocean.[96]

The spirit of war and conquest was a connection of a different sort. The wartime world of 1739 to 1783 was a virtual conflict, and it was also, for many hundreds of thousands of people, from Inverness to Madras, a war of imprisonment and death. In England or Scotland or France, the war began, for many, with the impressment into naval service that Hume described as an "irregular power," a "great violence and disorder," or with the lotteries for the militia in the inland provinces of France.[97] It unfolded in the brutality of military and naval life and in the existential uncertainty that even Hume experienced, in the discouragement of the Lorient expedition, or in Plymouth, Portsmouth, and Cork, waiting for orders of where to go. It extended, like the world of emigration, into the lives of the parents and friends of the impressed, the enlisted, and the imprisoned.[98] It ended in the postwar demobilization that Adam Smith described in the *Wealth of Nations,* of "so great a change in the situation of more than a hundred thousand men, all accustomed to the use of arms, and many of them to rapine and plunder."[99] Close to a million men, out of the prewar population of France of some twenty-five million, served in the armed forces during the Seven Years' War, and there were many more, like the rope carriers and the women selling wine in the great marine painter Joseph Vernet's views of Bordeaux, Rochefort, and La Rochelle, who were part of the military economy or who waited at home for news of defeat or victory or inheritance.[100]

The eighteenth-century world of news and information, even more generally, was for large numbers of people a universe of news about distant wars and distant opportunities. Hume was involved, again to an id-iosyncratic extent, in the *Papierkultur* of the times. But there were mul-tiple other sources of news (a "communication network made up of media and genres that have been forgotten," in Robert Darnton's de-scription), and these unconventional media were everywhere, even in the Scottish interior. The innkeepers and carriers whom Hume encoun-tered in Berwick, like "old Home" who rode to London with salmon from the Tweed, or Thomas Henderson, the carrier, and James Henderson, the stabler, were sources of news, for their own friends and connections as well as for the "conversible world" of passing philosophers. The sea-side itself was a sort of gazette. Hume's acquaintance Alexander Carlyle, when he and the other British students in Leiden in the winter of 1745 "were in great anxiety about the Rebellion," traveled all the way to Rot-terdam "to learn if they had heard anything by fishing-boats"; "having gone so far and brought back no news," they decided they would im-pose on the rest of the students, and would "frame a gazette," in the form of a "banker's private letter he had got by a fishing-boat."[101]

This multiplicity of sources of eighteenth-century information was a necessary but not a sufficient condition for the existence of Atlantic sen-timents. There is also the question, which is one of the most difficult of all historical questions, of what the news meant to individuals at the time. Isolation "is not a matter of distance or the slowness of communi-cation; it is a question of what a dispatch means to the recipient," as Perry Miller wrote of early New England, in a passage that John Clive and Bernard Bailyn quoted in their description of Scotland in the eigh-teenth century. The sentiment of Atlantic connectedness, too, was a matter of meaning, as well as information. The passions inspired by news of distant provinces were not always (as Hume observed in the *Enquiry*) particularly "strong and steady."[102]

But at least some of the circumstances of the mid-eighteenth-century world do suggest that the Atlantic news meant a great deal to large num-bers of people, as it meant a great deal to Hume. The question of the meaning of information is in fact an intensely Humean question, and Hume's own observations of the mind provide some sort of indication of what Atlantic information meant. "It is nothing but a mass, collec-tion, heap, or bundle, of different perceptions, or objects, that fleet away in succession, with inconceivable rapidity, perpetually changing, and perpetually in motion": this was James Beattie's summary of Hume's view of the soul, and one of Hume's enduring preoccupations was with why some of these objects and impressions were important to the individuals concerned, and some were not.[103] Hume undoubtedly believed, as Beattie surmised, that the relationships between objects and ideas, or meanings, were in part the outcome of chance (the seeds of things colliding by accident, in the images of Lucretius to which Hume returned so often). They were not orderly in a Stoical sort of way; the cognitive importance of events to individuals could not be arrayed in well-ordered concentric circles, from the nearest to the most distant relationships. But Hume did make various suggestions about why things have meaning, and they are interesting suggestions in relation to the Atlantic world of his own times.

The most evident reason for a distant event to be meaningful (or the reason "so obvious and natural," in Hume's own expression) is that it is connected to the individual's own life or interests.[104] It is distant only in space (or in space and time). Hume was surrounded, for most of his life, by pieces of information about the British colonies in North America. It is reasonable to assume that the information had much more meaning for him in the particular period—the late summer of 1746, in Plymouth and Lorient—when he was thinking about his own future life in Boston, or in Canada. It is reasonable, that is to say, to imagine Hume imagining what life would be like as the officer in command of "a company in an American regiment, by the choice of the Colonies"; it is fairly reasonable to assume that he afterwards thought about American news slightly differently, because of this earlier connection in the mind.

But these are very much the sorts of connections that were almost universal, or at least familiar, in the Scotland of the time. Some forty thousand people, or less than 5 percent of the population, left Scotland for North America in the 1760s and early 1770s; a very much larger proportion must have thought about leaving, or thought about why their friends and relations had left, and what had happened to them, or thought, even, about the consequences of the "frenzy of migrating."[105] These were all ways of thinking about the Atlantic world, and about what it meant. They were not ways of thinking peculiar to philosophers, or to the middle classes, or even to the servants of philosophers and petty officials, like Adam Smith's servant Robert Reid, who walked from Québec to Halifax in the winter of 1784 to become a coroner in New Brunswick, or Hume's own servant William Boyd, who acted as a sort of labor exchange of employment opportunities in the colonies.[106] Elizabeth Macdonald, a servant who set off to emigrate to North Carolina in 1773, told the customs officers in Shetland that "several of her Friends having gone to Carolina before her, had assured her that she would get much better service and greater Encouragement"; John McBeath, a shoemaker, was "encouraged to Emigrate by the Accounts received from his own and his Wife's Friends"; James Duncan, a farmer, believed he had "very promising Prospects by the Advices of his Friends in Carolina"; Alexander Morrison said that, "by the Reports from America, he is in hopes of bettering his Circumstances"; James Sinclair said, "he is informed land and Provisions are cheap."[107] This is indirect speech, or the words of the Shetland official; it is also the language of intention, information, and meaning.

Hume's picture of the mind is of a collection of objects and ideas, close by and distant, in time and space and imagination. One of the characteristics of the life of the mind is that distant events suddenly become proximate; they are at the edge of the mind's eye, as it were, and they suddenly come into view. There are many reasons that this should happen: because they remind one of something else, or because they make one feel compassion, or because they are colored with emotion, including the emotion of self-love. But this is what the Atlantic world was like, for very large numbers of people. Individuals were connected, by friendship and reports and prospects, to distant events; their ideas were colored by the fear of being impressed into service or ordered to the West Indies, or by the expectation of improvement, or news, or an American or East Indian inheritance. They reflected on the probabilities of good and difficult outcomes, and the process of reflection was itself a connection to distant events. The oceanic world was at the edge of the vision of almost everyone, as it was at the edge of David Hume's vision, in his childhood home in Berwickshire, or in his little room in La Flèche, as he looked toward the Loir, and to the Loire, and to Nantes and the Atlantic. It was, from time to time, at the center of almost everyone's view, as it is at the center, suddenly, of the view of the traveler who descends from Chirnside to Berwick, over the brow of the hill, to the vista of the "German Ocean."

A Confluence of Oceans

The view from the brow of the Berwickshire hills is toward Bremen and the Baltic, and the seaside gaze of the eighteenth century was a view out to sea, more than a view of the Atlantic Ocean. The Fife and Northumberland trade flowed into a vaster global commerce. The ship on which the emigrants who were questioned in Shetland left for North Carolina in 1773, the *Bachelor,* was from Kirkcaldy. Janet Schaw of Edinburgh, a friend of Lord Mansfield and his sister, left for Antigua and North Carolina in 1774 from Burntisland, with her brother, "Black Robt.," "my brother's Indian servant," and "poor Ovid," "our owners poor Devil of a Negro man . . . who was to be laid in Irons, 'till we were fairly out at Sea."[108] Gravesend was a port of origin for the East Indies and the West Indies alike. All the English East India Company's ships set out on a long Atlantic journey, and the French East India Company's home port—"L'Orient," or "The East"—was in the most westerly or Atlantic province of France. One of the well-established routes to India was via "the Brazils, in South America."[109] This was the communication of oceans that Hume and James Oswald imagined as a vast body of water, in which money sinks in Europe and rises in China.[110]

The East and West Indies were even in a political sense little more than a vast blur from the interior perspective of the Scottish provinces. They posed similar political dilemmas of government at a distance, as in Hume's histrionic anti-colonialism—"America and the East Indies revolted totally & finally"—or in the description of the upstarts of fortune in Bath, in Hume's friend Tobias Smollett's *Expedition of Humphrey Clinker:* "Clerks and factors from the East Indies, loaded with the spoil of plundered provinces; planters, negro-drivers, and hucksters, from our American plantations, enriched they know not how."[111] "What idea of Christianity must Indians conceive from our traders? What notions must the Africans entertain of our humanity?" the poet Richard Clarke asked in 1773, in a satire called *The Nabob,* which was in part about Hume ("this vile sophist, and the worst of men"): "When ills are distant, are they then your own?"[112]

This eighteenth-century sense of an indistinctly "Indian" empire is extremely difficult to imagine, after so many years of imperial organization. One of the most troublesome exercises of understanding, in the history of ideas, is to try to think oneself into the situation of individuals in the past who did not distinguish in any clear way between countries or conditions that are for ourselves, as later observers, self-evidently distinct. (It is closely related to the exercise of trying to imagine what it would be like not to know how a particular story—the story of the British Empire, for example, or of the revolt of the American colonies—was going to end, an exercise of thinking oneself into a vastly more imperfect knowledge of space, as well as of time.)

But it seems to have been the case that the British Empire in the Atlantic and the British Empire in the Indian Ocean were far less disconnected, in the minds even of mid-eighteenth-century officials, than they became in the post-revolutionary world, just as British America was far less distinctly divided into the slave societies of the West Indies and the slave-owning societies of the continental colonies.[113] The East and West Indies were both uncivil societies. One of the revelations of the postwar world of the 1760s and 1770s was indeed the discovery, with the East India Company scandals, that the British Empire was a ferment of cruelty and barbarism in the commercial "East," as well as in the slave-owning and slave-trading "West"; another was the erosion, with the extension of the empire to the Floridas and the Gulf of Mexico, of the distinction between the scorching and the less scorching America, or between the tropical America of the Spanish, and the vaguely remembered virtuous America of the seventeenth-century English settlers. It would be very helpful, a correspondent wrote to the *Gentleman's Magazine* in 1772, if "any curious gentleman, who lives in Florida, or any of the adjacent parts," could provide information "whether there are any lions in the forests of those places"; in Panama, he added, "the wildernesses there abound with wolves, tygers, and lions."[114]

The Atlantic and the Indian Ocean (or the Bay of Bengal) worlds were a blur even in the lives of individuals or families. Of the sons of Sir James Johnstone, three went to the East Indies, three went to the West Indies, and one went to both; two went to the colonies that later became the United States; one was a proprietor of French East India company bonds in Calcutta, a slave plantation in Grenada, a town plot in West Florida, and a million acres of land in New York; another was the commander of a convoy of East Indiamen, on the Atlantic-African route to India. James ("Ossian") Macpherson went to Florida with one of the

Johnstone brothers; he had earlier sought office in the third, interior frontier of mid-eighteenth-century Scotland—"giving *Fingall* the office of Inspector-General (or whatever it may be called,) of the Annexed Estates," as Lord Bute's brother wrote in August 1763 to William Mure; on his return from America, he devoted himself to Asia, as the minister in London of the Nabob of Arcot.[115] David Wedderburn, the brother of Hume's close friend Alexander Wedderburn, also went to Florida, where he was given the Choctaw name of *Fannimingo Mattaha,* and proceeded to the service of the East India Company in Bombay.[116] The poet William Julius Mickle, who was the Johnstones' first cousin and the translator of the *Lusiad,* the epic of the Portuguese Empire, was "on the point of setting out for Carolina" in 1765, or for "some settlement in the East or West Indies."[117] Hume's old friend Michael Ramsay wrote to him in Paris to complain about his own nephew, who "has entered into the rage of going to the E. or West Indies."[118] James Steuart, the Edinburgh lawyer, wrote to his brother, the owner of James Somerset, about his son's intention of "going out to the West or East Indies"; Charles Steuart's nephews eventually included a merchant in Tobago, a naval officer, a merchant in Grenada, and the assistant resident at the Court of the Nizam of Hyderabad.[119]

But there was a profound emotional and ideological difference, nevertheless, between the Atlantic and the East Indian worlds of commerce, as they were experienced in Europe in Hume's lifetime and in Hume's successive environments. The meaning of oceanic news can be visualized, as I have tried to suggest, in relation to two representations of space. One is of a world of information, of overheard conversations, orders, newspaper articles, rumors, amazing stories, reports of the price of land, conversations with stablers and salmon carriers, letters from one's "Wife's Friends." The other is of the cognitive world of the individual, who is connected to all this information from time to time, but for whom some of the information, and above all the information that influences his or her own circumstances and expectations, is of meaning, or in the center of the mind's eye.

The East Indian and the Atlantic worlds impinged in multiple respects on the lives of individuals in Scotland: on the individuals who were left behind when their brothers or sisters emigrated; or who were employed, as "writers" or writers' clerks, on the unending litigation inspired by colonial relationships; or who were dependent on the estates that changed hands, or names, in the flux of new fortunes; or who lived in fear (of the death of a distant friend) or hope (of inheritance). But the closest of these connections in the mind was the connection of opportunity, or of setting off into the new worlds of empire; and in this respect, at least, the Eastern and the Atlantic empires were far more distinct.[120]

The opportunities of office, in Hume's and the Oswalds' and the Johnstones' milieu of once or future gentlemen, were a matter, in substantial part, of family connections. They were relationships of corruption, in Hume's dichotomy of corruption and faction, rather than of faction. This was the case in the East Indies as in the West Indies and North America. But the procedures of departure were strikingly different, all the same. When one of the sons of Sir James Johnstone petitioned the "Honble the Court of Directors of the United East India Company" in 1753 to become a "writer" in the Indies, he included in his "Humble Petition" a certificate of baptism and a certificate of arithmetic and bookkeeping; the rhetoric of opportunity for this unfortunate young boy of 16 was that of a servant who "humbly prays your Honours," and "humbly hopes himself qualified."[121] To sail from Gravesend on an East Indiaman was to embark on a floating palace, and in a floating or virtual sovereignty, with its own constitution, its own examinations, its own political procedures, its own history, its own humility and grandeur. It was also to depart for a destination that was itself considered to be historical.

"This is the historical Age and this the historical Nation," Hume wrote to Strahan from Edinburgh in 1770, and the Atlantic world was far less historical, in Hume's and his friends' descriptions, than the world of the Asian empires, from Algiers to the China Sea.[122] There were histories of the colonies, even before Robertson's *History of America;* "every body has heard of the magnificence, good government, and ingenuity, of the ancient Peruvians," James Beattie wrote in his response to Hume's racist footnote.[123] But the oppressiveness of history, the sense of societies crushed under the weight of customs and chronicles and superstitions, or of what Adam Smith called "institutions," was a condition, above all, of the Eurasian landmass, of an immense territory of once-powerful empires, from the Alhambra to the Ottoman court and to the "Moguls" and "Moors" of India. A letter from an officer, printed in a

Military History of 1756 and 1757, depicts events in Bengal as unfolding at the extremity of this well-known world: "when *Calcutta* was taken by the *Moors* in *June* last . . . a Son of Sir *James Johnstone*, [was] killed amongst the rest. I mention these, as perhaps you know some of them."[124]

The East Indies, in this vast comparison of historicities, was a land full of kings, or of satraps, bashaws, nabobs, nizams, and emperors. It was governed, or misgoverned, or overgoverned. It was like the orient of Sallust's Asiatic luxury. The British in the East Indies were servants of the Company, and they were also, in the 1750s and 1760s, the servants of rich and established Asiatic rulers. They found themselves, like Robert Clive, a "Flower of the Empire" of Alamgir, the "Embroiderer of the Carpet of Magnificence."[125]

In North America, too, British officials were deeply involved over the course of several centuries in diplomatic or negotiated relationships with native American "kings" and sachems, the sort of negotiations in which George Johnstone, "Ossian" Macpherson, and David Wedderburn were involved in West Florida in 1765.[126] The north of the American continent, including the "West Indian" islands, was nonetheless imagined, even before the new American historiography of the post-revolutionary period, as an emptier land than the East Indies, a less historical land. "Between India and America no analogy can be drawn," Hume's friend William (Johnstone) Pulteney declared in the House of Commons in 1801. "Above all, America is uninhabited, and boundless tracks of fertile land were presented to the industry of the planter. India is one of the most populous countries on the globe, and every inch of ground is appropriated." "It was true," another orator added: "In America, every thing was wild and uncultivated. In India, every thing was made."[127]

This sense of the emptiness of America was of continuing importance in later ideologies of empire; as in J. R. Seeley's conclusion in his lectures on the expansion of England, a little over a century after Hume's death, that "India is all past and, I may almost say, has no future," while "in the colonies everything is brand-new. . . . There you have no past and an unbounded future."[128] But it was of immediate importance to the opportunities of eighteenth-century officials, and in particular because of a set of circumstances to do with the ownership of land that were essential to the Scottish historians' narratives of the progress of the human mind. A utopia, of which there were so many in and around the Atlantic, was a land without a location and without a history. It was a land, too, without property rights in land. The distinction between the exercise of rights of sovereignty in countries with no "fixed occupancy" (as in much of North America), in countries "within the jurisdiction of some known and acknowledged state" (as in Bengal), and in countries where "the sovereignty of which they were held, is become vacant, or is trans-ferred" (as in Florida and other former Spanish possessions), was at the heart of British imperial policy in the 1760s and 1770s. It was at the heart, too, of the transactions of Atlantic and Asiatic emigration.[129]

Men and a few women returned to Scotland with new riches from the East Indies and from the West Indies. But the men who came home with riches from the East, or who bequeathed their fortunes to their nieces and nephews, were proprietors of jewels or bonds or "paper" (including the bonds that were transmitted through Lisbon and through Paris, like the French East India Company bonds endorsed in Calcutta, about which William Johnstone Pulteney wrote to Hume in 1767).[130] The men who came home from the Atlantic world were proprietors of land: like Alexander Johnstone, of plantations and slaves and mills and boiling houses; or like James Macpherson: of a rectangular lot in Pensacola, West Florida, Lot 1 on Mansfield Street in this territory of imperial ces-sion, away from the "swamp" and next to the administrative offices.[131]

The romance of the ownership of land and slaves was in these respects one of the defining conditions of the Atlantic world, and one of the ways in which it was considered at the time to be most different from the world of the East Indies.[132] America was an uncivil society, less civil, at least until the widely described violence of the 1760s, than the socie-ties of British-Indian forts and Moghul dependencies. One of the earli-est gestures of independence, for thousands of the new American pro-prietors of the eighteenth century, was to buy themselves black slaves; one of the easiest routes to land tenure was to submit oneself to the long and oppressive arm of administration, as in "Ossian" Macpherson's geo-metrical property in Pensacola. But the idyll, in each case, was of owner-ship. Even Charles Steuart invoked a version of the beautiful language of the book of Micah—the language of John Dickinson's early revolution-ary polemics of the 1760s, "that they should sit every man under his vine, and under his fig-tree"—in a letter he wrote to James Murray, his friend in Massachusetts, about the legal proceedings in Lord Mansfield's courtroom, and "how the negroe cause goes on"; his friend, he imagined, was in the most different of circumstances, "in a genteel retreat under the shade of your own fig tree."[133]

The romance of land was important, above all, because it was a romance for the poor as well as for the rich. "As I was told, they went upon a principle of pride to North America, expecting to become lairds themselves in that supposed paradise," a Hamburg linen merchant said in the House of Commons in 1774 of the emigrants to North Carolina on the *Bachelor*.[134] The details of departure for the Atlantic colonies were ignominious and uncomfortable—a process, for tens of thousands of individuals, of indenture, indebtedness, undernourishment, misinformation, and seemingly endless waiting in ports and seaside towns. But it was a very different sort of transition from the departure for the East Indies. In Hume's own Scylla and Charybdis of dispositions, the Eastern empire represented corruption, and the Atlantic empire represented faction; the East represented superstition, and the American colonies enthusiasm; the shipping industry to the East Indies represented monopolistic power, and the shipping industry to North America, with its little ships from Fife towns and its "vile merchants in men," represented the unlimited competition of sects, or enterprises, or interests.

Atlantic Enlightenment

The historiography of the eighteenth century has been altered, in the past few years, by two important shifts of perspective, in space and in time. One is a change of point of view in a geographical sense, from a view of national histories to the histories of larger oceanic systems, and from a view of the American colonists, in particular, as looking to the West, to a view of native and other Americans "facing East from Indian Country." The second is a change of point of view in a historical or chronological sense, from a view of the 1760s and early 1770s as a pre-revolutionary period, to a view of these disrupted times as a postwar period, and even, as has been suggested here, of the entire pre-revolutionary epoch as a wartime world, from 1739 to 1783.[135]

These changes in perspective are very much in the spirit of the eighteenth-century Enlightenment and of the aspiration continually to change one's own perspectives and to see the world as it is seen by others. Sir William Meredith, one of the almost-American members of Parliament, the brother-in-law of a Boston war contractor, urged the House of Commons, at the height of the East India Company crisis of 1773, to "suppose, that it had been the fortune of Bengal to have conquered England, and that the East Indians were plundering here, as the Englishmen are plundering there"; to ask themselves if Indian justice would have looked the same from the perspective of England, if "three East Indian judges were to reside at the Land's-End in Cornwall," as English justice looked now from the perspective of India.[136] But I think that the two changes in perspective, in space and in time, can also suggest interesting ways of looking at the eighteenth-century Enlightenment itself, and at its history.

One way in which this can be done is by seeing the sect of Enlightenment, as they to a great extent saw themselves, as Atlantic or cosmopolitan figures.[137] Such a perspective restores the importance of some of the writings of the philosophes, conspicuous at the time, that have become far less so since the middle of the nineteenth century. I have been concerned, in this spirit, with Hume's *Political Discourses,* and with the concentration, throughout his political writings, on the evils of war. Several others of the English and French philosophes were intensely interested in global commerce and colonies; almost the entire extent of the *Wealth of Nations,* which Smith himself described as a "very violent attack . . . upon the whole commercial system of Great Britain," was concerned with long-distance relationships of various sorts.[138] To see the philosophers of the Enlightenment as pre-revolutionary figures, or as the predecessors of national revolutions (including the supposed revolution of freedom of commerce), is to lose sight of their own points of view, and their own preoccupations with the outside and oceanic world.

But there is a different and more profound sense in which the Enlightenment was oceanic, and even Atlantic. I said at the outset that the eighteenth-century understanding of Enlightenment as a disposition or a way of thinking was awkward for modern historians, and it was awkward even for Hume's or Voltaire's immediate followers. It was a composite, as has been seen, of two different sorts of observations, about the mind and about the circumstances of the mind. There were on the one hand certain universal or natural conditions of all individuals, including inquisitiveness, rationality, sociability, conversation, curiosity, self-love, and the love of information. These conditions were on the other hand influenced, even transformed, by social, legal, and economic circumstances. The drama of the process of transformation, in early modern Europe, was at the heart of Hume's own historical-philosophical narrative, in his *History of England* and in the *Political Discourses,* as it was of so many other histories of the human mind. He was writing, at one and the same time, a political history and a history of change in ideas and social relationships; and the history of social change was at one and the same time a history of the universal or the eternal and a history of the most fleeting or fluctuating of circumstances. This was Hume's own solution to the dilemmas of the science of man, as J. G. A. Pocock and Nicholas Phillipson have shown. It was in this context, of the transformation of the mind, that Hume used the unfamiliar word "enlightened"; this was the drama of Enlightenment.[139]

It is this drama that was so reduced by Hume's casual empiricism, so *"souillé,"* as in the expression Condorcet used of the "soiled virtues of antique peoples."[140] The universal dispositions were not really universal; they were not the dispositions of day-laborers; the "conversible World" was a condition of the "Part of Mankind, who are not immers'd in the animal Life."[141] The drama of the history of the human mind was reduced, too, by the imposing difficulties of the historical enterprise itself. These difficulties were epistemological as well as historiographical. Hume had no very convincing explanation of why certain conditions of mind were universal, except (in the words of one of the nineteenth-century critics of the Scottish Enlightenment) by "evolving from his own consciousness the circumstances and motives that diversify the employments of a nation."[142] He had no convincing empirical or historical explanation, either, of the causal relationships between institutions and dispositions: of the most important presumption of the science of man. The rhetoric of "the abstract science of human nature," with its sentiments, dispositions, senses, sensations, faculties, powers, and principles, is now one of the most archaic of all the idioms of eighteenth-century thought, and it came to seem archaic within a very few years of Hume's death.[143]

But the idea of Enlightenment is not archaic. The prospect that Hume described, or the idyll of civilized societies, tolerant, conversible, unviolent,

moderately good tempered and moderately equitable, loving to receive
and communicate knowledge, had been an aspiration of many earlier societies, in many different locations, and it is an aspiration for many individuals still. The historical transformation that Hume described, too—
the change in the social, cultural, commercial, political and legal circumstances of many parts of Europe and of the Europeans' overseas
world—is a historical event, something that really happened.

It is this composite idea of Enlightenment that is so evocatively and so
jarringly Atlantic. For one of the things that changed, in the course of
the eighteenth century, is that Hume's world of information and conversation, his conversible world, was diffused far more widely, in Europe
and elsewhere, than it had been before. One of the reasons for the
change was that far more individuals had the possibility, or the opportunity, of changing their own situations. There are many explanations for
the change in the disposition of Enlightenment, and many of them are
very much the sorts of explanations that were described at the time by
the sect of Enlightenment: the increased security of personal and property rights (at least in England); the diffusion of printing and the culture
of paper; the increase in education (at least in Scotland, and in Northern
Europe); the reform of "feudal residues" in civil law; the slow increase
in the standard of living; the respite from civil wars of religion.

But the consequence of these changes in circumstance, for the lives of
many millions of individuals, was an expansion of possibility. It had become possible, in eighteenth-century Europe, or very much easier, to
change one's own circumstances, to move one's residence, or one's settlement, or one's occupation, or one's condition, or one's country. The
characteristic observations of late eighteenth-century writings on commerce, about improving one's circumstances, or "bettering our condition," have been interpreted by modern observers as the platitudes of
universal self-interest. But they were very far from platitudes, in Hume's
and Smith's world; they were the assertion, rather, of the possibility of
social, legal, and psychological change.

The Atlantic economy, with its influence into the deepest interior of
European provinces, its magnetism, in Bernard Bailyn's expression, was
of critical importance to this drama of change.[144] Hume in his essay of
1748 on the original contract—it is another of his casually empirical and
in this case "classist" throwaway lines—asks, "Can we seriously say,

that a poor peasant or artizan has a free choice to leave his country, when he knows no foreign language or manners, and lives from day to day, by the small wages which he acquires?"[145] But tens of thousands of poor peasants really did have the choice, before the end of Hume's own lifetime, to leave their country and to move on. The distance between Hume's idyll of Enlightenment and the idyll of the younger philosophers of Enlightenment, of Smith's or Turgot's or Condorcet's imagination of the inner lives of the poor, the heroism of the unheroic, was in part the outcome of differences in sensitivity, or sensibility. But it was also the reflection of changes in the real world of the eighteenth century. The individuals in Scotland whom Hume described in 1741 as "the meanest slaving Poor" had always lived, as everyone always lives, in a world of ideas.[146] These ideas, by the end of his own life, were the subject of obsessive interest. "Every man has a right to his ideas," Hume's old opponent Lord Camden said in the House of Lords, in the course of the disputes over literary property of 1774 (in which Hume was enlisted in support of the rights of the booksellers, as against the licentiousness of Scotland, "over-run with a kind of literary packmen"); "but what if he speaks, and lets them fly out in private or public discourse? Will he claim the breath, the air, the words in which his thoughts are clothed? Where does this fanciful property begin, or end, or continue?"[147]

The emigrants on the *Bachelor* existed, in their own words, or in the words of the Shetland official, in a world of intentions and information and expectations and assurances. They were not themselves particularly poor; they had stock, or cattle, or friends who contributed the money to pay for their passage.[148] They were part of the Atlantic economy of news and information; they had received accounts, advices, and reports of conditions in North America; they had been sent letters by their children; they had been informed about the cost of land by their "Brothers in Law, already in America." The prosopography of these farmers' and weavers' lives is as complicated, and as dependent on the whims and winds of chance, as the prosopography of the Humes, and Homes, and Johnstones. They used the language of psychological conditions, of assurances and encouragement. They had theories of agrarian change and of the role of distilling in the consumption of corn. They had political theories, of the "oppressive" and the "arbitrary." They were the individuals of the enlightened imagination.

The eighteenth-century world of the Atlantic Enlightenment was a jarring combination of good and evil. In the *Wealth of Nations,* Adam Smith paraphrased the celebrated opening words of the Abbé Raynal's *Histoire des deux Indes,* about the discovery of America and of the sea route to India as the two greatest and most important events in the history of mankind, "uniting, in some measure, the most distant parts of the world." But he then, suddenly, changed perspective: "To the natives, however, both of the East and the West Indies, all the commercial benefits which can have resulted from those events have been sunk and lost in the dreadful misfortunes which they have occasioned."[149] This juxtaposition, of possibility and calamity, of perspectives in space and perspectives in time, was itself the continuing condition of Atlantic life. The emigrants on the *Bachelor* were men and women of the Enlightenment, and they were at the same time on the point of leaving the Enlightenment behind for the violence of the American interior and for the possibility of becoming, themselves, the owners of other individuals. The Atlantic world was "fluctuating, uncertain, fleeting, successive and compounded" for David Hume, and so it was for everyone else as well.

Notes
Acknowledgments
List of Contributors
Index

Notes

Introduction

1. Bernard Bailyn, *Atlantic History: Concepts and Contours* (Cambridge, Mass., 2005); see also Horst Pietschmann, "Atlantic History—History between European History and Global History," in *Atlantic History: History of the Atlantic System, 1580–1830,* ed. Pietschmann (Göttingen, 2002), 11–43; William O'Reilly, "The Atlantic World and Germany: A Consideration," in *Latin America and the Atlantic World,* ed. Renate Pieper and Peer Schmidt (Cologne, 2005), 35–56; and Silvia Marzagalli, "Sur les origines de l''Atlantic History,'" *Dix-huitième siècle* 33 (2001): 17–31.

2. Pietschmann, "Atlantic History," 43, 45.

3. For notable efforts to integrate Virginia's early history into the larger world, see Karen O. Kupperman, *The Jamestown Project* (Cambridge, Mass., 2007); April L. Hatfield, *Atlantic Virginia and Inter-Colonial Relations in the Seventeenth Century* (Philadelphia, Pa., 2004); Peter C. Mancall, ed., *The Atlantic World and Virginia, 1550–1624* (Chapel Hill, N.C., 2007). For parallel efforts in New England's historiography, see Carla Gardina Pestana, *The English Atlantic in an Age of Revolution, 1640–1661* (Cambridge, Mass., 2004); Francis J. Bremer and Lynn A. Botelho, eds., *The World of John Winthrop . . . 1588–1649* (Boston, 2005), esp. the introduction: "Atlantic History and the World of John Winthrop"; and Mark Peterson, *"Theopolis Americana,"* in this volume.

4. Jorge Cañizares-Esguerra, "Entangled Histories: Borderland Historiog-

raphies in New Clothes?" *American Historical Review* 112 (June 2007): 787.

5. Patrick O'Brien, "Historiographical Traditions and Modern Imperatives for the Restoration of Global History," *Journal of Global History* 1 (March 2006): 4–7, at 5; J. H. Elliott, *Empires of the Atlantic World: Britain and Spain in America, 1492–1830* (New Haven, Conn., 2006); Lara Putnam, "To Study the Fragments/Whole: Microhistory and the Atlantic World," *Journal of Social History* 39 (Spring 2006): 617.

6. Peter A. Coclanis, "Atlantic World or Atlantic/World?" *William and Mary Quarterly*, 3d ser., 63 (October 2006): 728, 739.

7. O'Brien, "Historiographical Traditions," 11; Kevin H. O'Rourke and Jeffrey G. Williamson, "When Did Globalization Begin?" National Bureau of Economic Research (NBER) Working Paper 7632 (2000), 26.

8. Björn Hettne, "Globalism, the New Regionalism and East Asia," *Selected Papers Delivered at the United Nations University, Global Seminar 1996,* ed. Toshiro Tanaka and Takashi Anoguchi (Hayama, Japan, 1996), n.p. [1, 2].

9. For a detailed example of the scattering of a single British family into the four corners of the globe, see Emma Rothschild, *The Inner Life of Empires* (Princeton, N.J., 2010); for an individual's intercontinental wanderings, see Linda Colley, *The Ordeal of Elizabeth Marsh* (London, 2007).

10. Donna Merwick, *The Shame and the Sorrow: Dutch-Amerindian Encounters in New Netherland* (Philadelphia, Pa., 2006), esp. chs. 3, 8–13; Coclanis, "Atlantic World or Atlantic/World?" 729; Alison Games, "Beyond the Atlantic: English Globetrotters and Transoceanic Connections," *William and Mary Quarterly*, 3d ser., 63 (October 2006): 689; Herbert S. Klein, *The Atlantic Slave Trade* (New York, 1999), 52–55, 89, quotation at 53.

11. Klein, *Atlantic Slave Trade*, quotations at 53, 89, 54.

12. Games, "Beyond the Atlantic," 682; Jürgen Osterhammel and Niels P. Petersson, *Globalization* (Princeton, N.J., 2005), 44–45. Cf. Geoffrey Parker, "Europe and the Wider World, 1500–1750: The Military Balance," in *The Political Economy of Merchant Empires: State Power and World Trade, 1350–1750*, ed. James D. Tracy (New York, 1991), 179; and Carla R. Phillips, "The Growth and Composition of Trade with the Iberian Empires, 1450–1750," in *The Rise of Merchant Empires: Long Distance Trade in the Early Modern World, 1350–1750*, ed. James D. Tracy (New York, 1990), ch. 2. The Philippines, in the history of early modern European expansion, seem to have been anomalous. The many islands

were only partly conquered and settled by the invading Spanish; the native population did not suffer a demographic catastrophe; there was no great influx of African slaves; and the areas colonized were dominated not by planters but by Crown and military officials and a veritable phalanx of friars and priests.

13. Phillips, "Growth and Composition of Trade," 55. For detailed studies of the commercial interactions among Portuguese, Dutch, and Asians, see Ernst Van Veen and Leonard Blussé, eds., *Rivalry and Conflict: European Traders and Asian Trading Networks in the Sixteenth and Seventeenth Centuries* (Leiden, 2005).

14. Osterhammel and Petersson, *Globalization,* quotations at 47.

15. The only candidate would seem to be Pierre Chaunu, who in his eleven-volume study of the Seville/Atlantic trade acknowledged Braudel's influence. But the master did not return the compliment, dismissing Chaunu's heroic labor as not only un-Braudelian but *deliberately* un-Braudelian. Chaunu's purpose, Braudel wrote, was "not at all the same as mine," was "easier to grasp . . . not the large-scale vista which I seek . . . [for this] he would have needed to widen his archival researches." Chaunu, Braudel declared, chose "of his own free will [*volontairement*] to remain within the boundaries of his own serial history, without taking any account of other series which might exist." And in any case, "is not this oceanic book too long, too discursive, in sum too hastily written? Pierre Chaunu writes as he speaks: if he had submitted his text to me, what arguments [*belles disputes*] we would have had." Fernand Braudel, *On History,* trans. Sarah Matthews (Chicago, 1980), 93, 96, 102. Cf. Braudel, "Séville et l'Atlantique (1504–1650)," *Annales* 18 (May–June 1963): 546, 552.

16. Nicholas Canny, "Atlantic History and Global History," in Pieper and Schmidt, *Latin America and the Atlantic World,* 26–28; cf. Canny, "Atlantic History: What and Why?" *European Review* 9 (October 2001): 399–411.

17. Canny, "Atlantic History and Global History," 29; Kenneth Pomeranz, *The Great Divergence: Europe, China, and the Making of the Modern World Economy* (Princeton, N.J., 2000), 4, 20, 23, ch. 6; C. A. Bayly, *The Birth of the Modern World, 1780–1914: Global Connections and Comparisons* (New York, 2004), 55; see also 59, 72.

18. Pieter Emmer, "In Search of a System: The Atlantic Economy, 1500–1800," in Pietschmann, *Atlantic History,* 169, 177; Coclanis, "Atlantic World or Atlantic/World?" 741, 731.

19. Peter A. Coclanis, ed., *The Atlantic Economy during the Seventeenth and Eighteenth Centuries: Organization, Operation, Practice, and Per-*

sonnel (Columbia, S.C., 2005), xii; Stanley J. Stein and Barbara H. Stein, *Silver, Trade, and War: Spain and America in the Making of Early Modern Europe* (Baltimore, Md., 2000), 72. Cf. Pieter Emmer, "Barriers within the Atlantic: Success and Failure of the Minor European Nations," in Pieper and Schmidt, *Latin America and the Atlantic World*, 263–277; Emmer and Wim Klooster, "The Dutch Atlantic, 1600–1800: Expansion without Empire," *Itinerario* 23, no. 2 (1999): 48–69.

20. Coclanis, *Atlantic Economy;* P. C. Emmer, O. Pétré-Grenouilleau, and J. V. Roitman, eds., *A "Deus Ex Machina" Revisited: Atlantic Colonial Trade and European Economic Development* (Leiden, 2006); Johannes Postma and Victor Enthoven, eds., *Riches from Atlantic Commerce: Dutch Transatlantic Trade and Shipping, 1585–1817* (Leiden, 2003); Daviken Studnicki-Gizbert, *A Nation upon the Ocean Sea: Portugal's Atlantic Diaspora and the Crisis of the Spanish Empire, 1492–1640* (New York, 2007).

21. Victor Enthoven, "An Assessment of Dutch Transatlantic Commerce," in Postma and Enthoven, *Riches from Atlantic Commerce,* 389–445: "On the basis of available data it now appears that, except perhaps for a short period around 1700, Dutch Atlantic trade during the *ancien régime* was more important for the Dutch economy than commerce with Asia" (445); Jan de Vries, "The Dutch Atlantic Economies," in Coclanis, *Atlantic Economy,* 18, 20: "historians have long been inclined to deprecate too much the importance of the New World to the Dutch Republic . . . the total value of the Dutch imports from the New World rose to approximately equal those from Asia by the 1770s."

22. Silvia Marzagalli, "The French Atlantic," *Itinerario* 23, no. 2 (1999): 79–83; Paul Butel, *The Atlantic,* trans. Iain H. Grant (New York, 1999), esp. 113–126, 149–160; Butel, "France, the Antilles, and Europe in the Seventeenth and Eighteenth Centuries: Renewals of Foreign Trade," in Tracy, *Rise of Merchant Empires,* ch. 4; James Pritchard, *In Search of Empire: The French in the Americas, 1670–1730* (New York, 2004), chs. 3–4.

23. David Eltis and David Richardson, "A New Assessment of the Transatlantic Slave Trade," in *Extending the Frontiers: Essays on the New Transatlantic Slave Trade Database,* ed. Eltis and Richardson (New Haven, Conn., 2008), 1, 2, 45.

24. At www.slavevoyages.org. The listed authors are David Eltis, David Richardson, Stephen Behrendt, and Manolo Florentino.

25. Stephen D. Behrendt, "Markets, Transaction Cycles, and Profits: Mer-

chant Decision Making in the British Slave Trade," *William and Mary Quarterly,* 3d ser., 58 (January 2001): 171–204.

26. Herbert S. Klein et al., "Transoceanic Mortality: The Slave Trade in Comparative Perspective," 101, and David Richardson, "Shipboard Revolts, African Authority, and the Atlantic Slave Trade," 74–76, both in *William and Mary Quarterly,* 3d ser., 58 (January 2001).

27. For comments on the large literature on African-American cultural persistence and considered critiques, see David Eltis, Philip Morgan, and David Richardson, "Agency and Diaspora in Atlantic History: Reassessing the African Contribution to Rice Cultivation in the Americas," *American Historical Review* 112 (December 2007): 1329, and Behrendt, "Markets, Transaction Cycles, and Profits"; cf. Lorena S. Walsh, "The Chesapeake Slave Trade: Regional Patterns, African Origins and Some Implications," *William and Mary Quarterly,* 3d ser., 58 (January 2001): 139–170; Walsh, "Issues and Questions in African-American History" (Report presented at the International Center for Jefferson Studies, Charlottesville, Va., 6 Oct. 2000).

28. John K. Thornton, *The Kongolese St. Anthony: Dona Beatriz Kimpa Vita and the Antonian Movement, 1684–1706* (New York, 1998), 99–101, 204–205. On the complex background of slave recruitment and the dehumanizing effect of "commodifying" African captives, see Stephanie E. Smallwood, *Saltwater Slavery: A Middle Passage from Slavery to American Diaspora* (Cambridge, Mass., 2007), esp. chs. 2, 6. The most vivid and wrenching account of the inhumanity of the Middle Passage is Marcus Rediker, *The Slave Ship: A Human History* (New York, 2007).

29. Klein, *Atlantic Slave Trade,* 58; Thornton, *Kongolese St. Anthony,* 102–103, 208–211.

30. Hancock, *Citizens of the World: London Merchants and the Integration of the British Atlantic Community, 1735–1785* (New York, 1995).

31. The full development of these themes will be published in Hancock, *Oceans of Wine: Madeira and the Organization of the Atlantic World, 1640–1815* (New Haven, Conn., 2009).

32. Cf. Hancock, "Self-Organized Complexity and the Emergence of an Atlantic Market Economy, 1651–1815," in Coclanis, *Atlantic Economy,* 30–71.

33. Jacob M. Price, "Summation," in *Atlantic Port Cities: Economy, Culture, and Society in the Atlantic World, 1650–1850,* ed. Franklin W. Knight and Peggy K. Liss (Knoxville, Tenn., 1991), 271; Anne Pérotin-Dumon,

"The Pirate and the Emperor: Power and the Law on the Seas, 1450–1850," in Tracy, *Political Economy of Merchant Empires,* 222–224; John Fisher, "Imperial 'Free Trade' and the Hispanic Economy, 1778–1796," *Journal of Latin American Studies* 13 (May 1981): 21–25; Frances Armytage, *The Free Port System in the British West Indies: A Study in Commercial Policy, 1716–1822* (London, 1953), 27–51.

34. Frank E. Manuel and Fritzie P. Manuel, *Utopian Thought in the Western World* (Cambridge, Mass., 1979), 334.

35. Bernard Bailyn, *The Peopling of British North America: An Introduction* (New York, 1986), ch. 1, esp. 32–34.

36. Hartmut Lehmann et al., eds., *In Search of Peace and Prosperity: New German Settlements in Eighteenth-Century Europe and America* (University Park, Pa., 2000), chs. 2–4, 7–10, 14; Renate Wilson, *Pious Traders in Medicine: A German Pharmaceutical Network in Eighteenth-Century North America* (University Park, Pa., 2000), 209.

37. Frederick B. Tolles, *Quakers and the Atlantic Culture* (New York, 1960), quotation at 29; Tolles, *The Atlantic Community of the Early Friends* (London, 1952); Rebecca Larson, *Daughters of Light: Quaker Women Preaching and Prophesying in the Colonies and Abroad, 1700–1775* (New York, 1999).

38. Paolo Bernadini and Norman Fiering, eds., *The Jews and the Expansion of Europe to the West, 1450–1800* (New York, 2001), 1–2, 347, 361, 513; quotations at 335, 337, and 346. On *conversos,* crypto-Judaism, and Jewish identity, see Miriam Bodian, "'Men of the Nation': The Shaping of *Converso* Identity in Early Modern Europe," *Past and Present* 143 (May 1994): 48–76.

39. James C. Boyajian, "New Christians and Jews in the Sugar Trade, 1550–1750: Two Centuries of Development in the Atlantic Economy," in Bernadini and Fiering, *Jews and the Expansion of Europe,* ch. 22, esp. 478, 479.

40. Thomas J. Müller-Bahlke and Jürgen Gröschl, eds., *Salzburg-Halle-North America* (Tübingen, 1999), xx.

41. The Halle mission in India has now been elaborately documented in Andreas Gross, Y. Vincent Kumaradoss, and Heike Liebau, eds., *Halle and the Beginnings of Protestant Christianity in India,* 3 vols. (Halle, 2006), quotation at 2:809, and summarized in D. Dennis Hudson, *Protestant Origins in India: Tamil Evangelical Christians, 1706–1835* (Grand Rapids, Mich., 2000), quotation at 22; E. Arno Lehmann, *It Began at Tranquebar* (Madras, 1956), 39, 48, 59. For a vivid example of the dif-

ficulties of conversion, see Hugald Grafe, "The First Indian Christians in Tranquebar," in Gross et al., *Halle*, 1:209–228, esp. 219.

42. J. Gabriel Martínez-Serna, "Instruments of Empire: The Jesuit-Indian Encounter in the New World Borderland," Working Paper no. 04011, Atlantic History Seminar, Harvard University, 2004, pp. 9, 7.

43. J. F. Moran, *The Japanese and the Jesuits: Alessandro Valignano in Sixteenth-Century Japan* (London, 1993), 2, 191, 192; Klaus A. Vogel, "European Expansion and Self-Definition," in *Cambridge History of Science*, vol. 3, ed. Katherine Park and Lorraine Weston (Cambridge, 2006), 829–830; Liam M. Brockey, *Journey to the East: The Jesuit Mission to China, 1579–1724* (Cambridge, Mass., 2007), 198–203; Andrew C. Ross, *A Vision Betrayed: The Jesuits in Japan and China, 1542–1744* (Edinburgh, 1994), 204; George Minamiki, *The Chinese Rites Controversy from Its Beginnings to Modern Times* (Chicago, 1985), 58–62, 69–72; cf. D. E. Mungello, ed., *The Chinese Rites Controversy, Its History and Meaning* (Nettetal, Germany, 1994), 3–28; Carole Blackburn, *Harvest of Souls: The Jesuit Missions and Colonialism in North America, 1632–1650* (Montréal, 2000), 130–131.

44. Ross, *Vision Betrayed*, 199, 198; Moran, *Japanese and the Jesuits*, 192; Nicholas Standaert, "Christianity Shaped by the Chinese," in *Cambridge History of Christianity*, vol. 6, ed. R. Po-Chia Hsia (Cambridge, 2007), 570.

45. Robert Morrissey, "The Terms of Encounter: Language and Contested Visions of French Colonization in the Illinois Country, 1673–1702," Working Paper no. 07007, Atlantic History Seminar, Harvard University, 2007, pp. 27, 33; Allan Greer, "Conversion and Identity: Iroquois Christianity in Seventeenth-Century New France," in *Conversion: Old Worlds and New*, ed. Kenneth Mills and Anthony Grafton (Rochester, N.Y., 2003), 191–192. See also Greer and Kenneth Mills, "A Catholic Atlantic," in *The Atlantic in Global History, 1500–2000*, ed. Jorge Cañizares-Esguerra and Erik Seeman (Upper Saddle River, N.J., 2006); Greer, "Towards a Comparative Study of Jesuit Missions and Indigenous Peoples in Seventeenth-Century Canada & Paraguay," in *Native Christians: Modes and Effects of Christianity among Indigenous Peoples of the Americas*, ed. Robin Wright and Aparecida Vilaca (Aldershot, England, 2008); José Gabriel Martínez-Serna, "Jesuit Frontiers and Indian Ethnogenesis in Seventeenth-Century Spanish America" (paper presented at the Tenth Anniversary Conference of the Atlantic History Seminar, Harvard University, 2005), 5.

46. Sabine MacCormack, *Religion in the Andes: Vision and Imagination in Early Colonial Peru* (Princeton, N.J., 1991), 290; Kenneth Mills, *Idolatry and Its Enemies: Colonial Andean Religion and Extirpation, 1640–1750* (Princeton, N.J., 1997), ch. 9, quotations at 284, 271. For an excellent summary of "Andean Christianities" as part of an "emerging Andean interculture," see Kenneth Mills, "The Naturalization of Andean Christianities," in Hsia, *Cambridge History of Christianity*, vol. 6, ch. 27.

47. For Cañizares-Esguerra's full exploration of the transcultural uses of typology and the theme of the Satanic engagement with the Americas, see his *Puritan Conquistadors: Iberianizing the Atlantic, 1550–1700* (Stanford, Calif., 2006), quotation at 98.

48. Jorge Cañizares-Esguerra, *Nature, Empire, and Nation: Explorations of the History of Science in the Iberian World* (Stanford, Calif., 2006), ch. 1, quotations at 4, 19, 20 (the chapter was first published as an essay, "Iberian Science in the Renaissance: Ignored How Much Longer?" *Perspectives on Science* 12 [Spring 2004]: 86–124); Eric H. Ash, *Power, Knowledge, and Expertise in Elizabethan England* (Baltimore, Md., 2004), 3, 142–145. Ash makes clear (ch. 5) how Bacon's "arguments in favor of an action-oriented, collaborative, state-sponsored institute of scientific culture" remained arguments, "a program for philosophical reform," rigidly hierarchical, with himself, the philosopher, at the top, "above the mean labors of those actually performing the experiments and supplying the observations for his philosophy." And he explains at length (15–16) that the new generation of Elizabethan "experts" remained humanists, writing books not to instruct master craftsmen in new skills and techniques but "to publicize their authors' mastery of the arts they addressed and to alter the very nature of those arts, elevating them above their traditional, vulgar, unlearned craft status to render them apt fields for leisurely study by a cultured, educated audience. . . . Mere craftsmen were increasingly seen as unequal to the task at hand. . . . [The expert's role] was not to practice the art in question but to *comprehend* it and to make it available and accessible to their patrons." It remained for the next generation—Hartlib's generation of engaged reformers and universal promoters of practical, mechanical, and agricultural arts—and the intellectuals of the new scientific academies to resume the applied research that the Spanish had begun in their passion to understand and control the New World.

49. Edgar Zilsel, "The Social Roots of Science" (1939), in *The Social Origins of Modern Science,* ed. Diederick Raven, Wolfgang Krohn, and Robert S.

Cohen (Dordrecht, The Netherlands, 2000), chs. 1, 2, quotations at 4, 5, 6; Rupert Hall, "The Scholar and the Craftsman in the Scientific Revolution," in *Critical Problems in the History of Science,* ed. Marshall Clagett (Madison, Wisc., 1969), 14–23, quotation at 16.

50. Antonio Barrera-Osorio, *Experiencing Nature: The Spanish-American Empire and the Early Scientific Revolution* (Austin, Texas, 2006), 6–8, 11.

51. Ibid., 133; Elliott, *Empires of the Atlantic World,* 333; Jorge Cañizares-Esguerra, "Spanish America: From Baroque to Modern Colonial Science," in *Cambridge History of Science,* vol. 4, ed. Roy Porter (Cambridge, 2003), ch. 31.

52. Barrera-Osorio, *Experiencing Nature,* 11; Emily Berquist, "Science and Nature in the Early Modern Iberian World: A Review Essay," *Itinierario,* 31, no. 3 (2007): 95–98.

53. Barrera-Osorio, *Experiencing Nature,* 11, 134.

54. J. C. Davis, *Utopia and the Ideal Society: A Study of English Utopian Writing, 1516–1700* (Cambridge, 1981), 313.

55. James McClellan, "Scientific Institutions and the Organization of Science," in Porter, *Cambridge History of Science,* 4:87–106; Bruce T. Moran, "Courts and Academies," in Park and Weston, *Cambridge History of Science,* 3:267–271; Steven Shapin, *The Scientific Revolution* (Chicago, 1996), 131–135.

56. Neil Safier, "Unveiling the Amazon to European Science and Society: The Reading and Reception of La Condamine's *Relation abrégée d'un voyage fait dans l'intérieur de l'Amérique méridionale* (1745)," *Terrae Incognitae: The Journal for the History of Discoveries* 33 (2001): 34–38.

57. Iris H. W. Engstrand, *Spanish Scientists in the New World: The Eighteenth-Century Expeditions* (Seattle, Wash., 1981), passim, quotation at 7; A.-M. Brenot, "Les voyageurs français dans la Vice-Royauté de Perou au XVIIIe siécle," *Revue d'histoire moderne et contemporaine* 35 (April–June, 1988): 245; Roger Mercier, "Les Francais en Amérique du Sud au XVIIIe siécle: la mission de l'Académie des Science (1735–1745)," *Revue française d'histoire d'Outre-mer* 56, no. 205 (1969); Daniela Bleichmar, "Atlantic Competitions: Botany in the Eighteenth-Century Spanish Empire," in *Science and Empire in the Atlantic World,* ed. James Delbourgo and Nicholas Dew (New York, 2008), ch. 9, esp. table 9.1; Safier, "Unveiling the Amazon," 39, 44, 47. On the "painful and hilarious" mishaps of La Condamine's voyage, see Jorge Cañizares-Esguerra in Porter, *Cambridge History of Science,* 4:735. For a comprehensive analysis of La Condamine's career, publications, and influence in the context of Euro-American exploration and science, see Neil Safier,

Measuring the New World: Enlightenment Science and South America (Chicago, 2008), esp. chs. 2, 3.

58. Alan Frost, "The Atlantic World of the 1780s and Botany Bay: The Lost Connection," North American Studies Lecture, La Trobe University, 2008; Roger Hahn, *The Anatomy of a Scientific Institution: The Paris Academy of Sciences, 1666–1803* (Berkeley, Calif., 1971), 90; Carlos M. Shaw, "*Terra Australis*—The Spanish Quest," in *Studies from Terra Australis to Australia,* ed. John Hardy and Alan Frost (Canberra, 1989), ch. 6; Safier, "Unveiling the Amazon," 44, 47.

59. The phrase is Thomas Mann's, referring specifically to his native corner of the German world, the city of Lübeck, with its access to the Baltic Sea, "once the threshold of the Hanseatic League." *Germany and the Germans* (Washington, D.C., 1945), 3.

60. Kuno Francke, "Cotton Mather and August Hermann Francke," *Harvard Studies and Notes in Philology and Literature* 5 (Boston, 1896): 60–63; Ernst Benz, "Ecumenical Relations between Boston Puritanism and German Pietism: Cotton Mather and August Hermann Francke," *Harvard Theological Review* 54 (July 1961): 162, 163; Benz, "Pietist and Puritan Sources of Early Protestant World Missions (Cotton Mather and A. H. Francke)," *Church History* 20 (June 1951): 51.

61. Benz, "Pietist and Puritan Sources," 29, 33, 34; Francke, "Mather and Francke," 61; Benz, "Ecumenical Relations," 171, 178.

62. Francke, "Mather and Francke," 60, 61; Mather, *Nuncia Bona e Terra Longinqua: A Brief Account of Some Good & Great Things a Doing for The Kingdom of God, in the Midst of Europe . . .* (Boston, 1705), 6–8.

63. Benz, "Ecumenical Relations," 165; Benz, "Pietist and Puritan Sources," 34, 38–39, 32, 41; Francke, "Mather and Francke," 64, 65, 62.

64. Benz, "Ecumenical Relations," 167, 168, 182–187; Benz, "Pietist and Puritan Sources," 49. For Mather's earlier statement of this theme, see his *Batteries upon the Kingdom of the Devil* (London, 1695).

65. Knight and Liss, *Atlantic Port Cities,* 3; Elliott, *Empires of the Atlantic World,* 333.

66. Susan M. Socolow, "Buenos Aires: Atlantic Port and Hinterland in the Eighteenth Century," in Knight and Liss, *Atlantic Port Cities,* quotation at 240; 246, 263, 264, 271, 272; Tulio Halperín Donghi, *Politics Economics and Society in Argentina in the Revolutionary Period* (Cambridge, 1975), 157, 169, 171ff. For an extended analysis of Buenos Aires's vital role in Spain's late colonial commercial regime—"the fulcrum of a modernizing empire," "a hub for a reconstituted early modern empire"—see

Jeremy Adelman, *Republic of Capital: Buenos Aires and the Legal Transformation of the Atlantic World* (Stanford, Calif., 1999), chs. 1, 3 (comparison with Boston, 20); and for the viceroyalty in the revolution from the merchants' point of view, see ch. 4.

67. Halperín Donghi, *Politics Economics and Society,* 189.

68. Jeremy Adelman, *Sovereignty and Revolution in the Iberian Atlantic* (Princeton, N.J., 2006), 208, 261–263, 281, 283–284, 300 (quotation at 263). For a comprehensive survey of these waves of turmoil, see Jaime E. Rodríguez O., *The Independence of Spanish America* (New York, 1998), 123–136; for an extended account, Halperín Donghi, *Politics Economics and Society,* passim.

69. David Bushnell, *Reform and Reaction in the Platine Provinces, 1810–1852* (Gainesville, Fla., 1983), chs. 1, 2; Klaus Gallo, *The Struggle for an Enlightened Republic: Buenos Aires and Rivadavia* (London, 2006), chs. 2, 3.

70. John Lynch, *Símon Bolívar: A Life* (New Haven, Conn., 2006), 12, 92, 94, 120, 121; Bernard Bailyn, *To Begin the World Anew* (New York, 2003), 145–147.

71. Rodríguez, *Independence,* 128–129.

72. Bernard Bailyn, *Voyagers to the West: A Passage in the Peopling of America on the Eve of the Revolution* (New York, 1986), 40–42, 26.

73. Bayly, *Birth of the Western World,* 55.

1. Ecology, Seasonality, and the Transatlantic Slave Trade

This essay builds on Stephen D. Behrendt, "Markets, Transaction Cycles, and Profits: Merchant Decision-Making in the British Slave Trade," *William and Mary Quarterly,* 3d ser., 58 (January 2001): 171–204. Unless noted otherwise, all transatlantic slave trade data are contained in the file of 34,941 slaving voyages in *Voyages: The Trans-Atlantic Slave Trade Database,* online at www.slavevoyages.org.

1. Efik was a dialect of the Ibibio language and the name of Egbo Young's ethnic group. D. Simmons, "An Ethnographic Sketch of the Efik People," in *Efik Traders of Old Calabar,* ed. Daryll Forde (London, 1956), 1.

2. The letter reads: "your may get them cargo Ready befor he come home dont kept hime Long and I think he gets Liverpool 15 or twenty day March": Egboyoung Offiong [Ekpenyong Ofiong] to "Gentleman," Old Calabar, 23 July 1783, DX/1304, Merseyside Maritime Museum (hereafter, MMM); translation by author. Egbo Young (born ca. 1740) was one of the forty to fifty Efik merchants who traded with British cap-

tains in the 1780s. He worked at Duke Town, the most powerful of the Efik villages that comprised "Old Calabar" in southeast Nigeria. Burrows's "tender"—a junior captain—was Thomas Sarratt.

3. Burrows purchased enslaved Africans and a "Quantity of Ivory and Palm Oil," as advertised later in a Liverpool gazette (*Liverpool General Advertiser*, 22 April 1784, p. 2). Efik merchants, known to Europeans as "Ekrikok," traded on the west bank of the Cross River and sold Burrows palm oil.

4. Two of the twenty extant Calabar documents, written in broken English, mention American markets. In a letter from about 1769, Orrock Robin John refers to "the Antiguas Country." In 1773 Robin John Otto Ephraim mentions "West India." See Paul E. Lovejoy and David Richardson, "Letters of the Old Calabar Slave Trade, 1760–1789," in *Genius in Bondage: Literature of the Early Black Atlantic,* ed. Vincent Carretta and Philip Gould (Lexington, Ky., 2001), 102, 105 (Letters 3, 5).

5. Such a timely return to Liverpool would allow Wickstead and his associates to continue their planned second venture to Calabar and to trade again with Egbo Young. A departure from Merseyside in June or July 1784 would place Burrows back at Old Calabar in season, furthering the chances that he would subsequently arrive in the West Indies in season. Burrows returned to Liverpool on 20 April 1784 on the *Edward;* the owners immediately advertised the ship for sale, and then purchased the ship *Lion* for Burrows's July venture to Old Calabar. His employers purchased a new ship to convert to a Guineaman.

6. For example: Ralph Davis, *The Rise of the English Shipping Industry in the Seventeenth and Eighteenth Centuries* (London, 1962), 279–285, 294; David W. Galenson, *Traders, Planters and Slaves: Market Behavior in Early English America* (New York, 1986), 33–37.

7. Letters often specify African markets and the best months to depart Europe and arrive in the Americas—but they do not mention what captains will be trading in African provisions or discuss slaving seasons. "The best Season for the Coast of New Callibar & Bonny is to leave England in May & June so as to have the vessels placed that they will arrive in these Islands about 1st to 10th Octobr & from thence to Janry or even middle of this month: by their falling in this manner the credits are not so long & the period for sales much the best." Frances and Robert Smith to James Rogers, Dominica, 22 Feb. 1788, C107/8, National Archives, London (hereafter, NA). Many other examples are contained in Elizabeth Donnan, ed., *Documents Illustrative of the History of the Slave Trade to America,* 4 vols. (Washington, D.C., 1930–1935).

8. Documented by the *Cornwall Chronicle* (Montego Bay, Jamaica), 10 Jan. 1784, two Jamaican Colonial Office records, and a list of slave sales from the Kingston firm Rainford, Blundell and Rainford. The month of arrival in Jamaica also can be inferred from the *Edward*'s muster roll and *Lloyd's List*. See www.slavevoyages.org, voyage 81141, sources.

9. Among African peoples forced into the transatlantic slave trade, 1520s–1866, perhaps only the youngest children had no familiarity with agricultural work. Of those who survived the Middle Passage, 95% would labor in tropical and subtropical regions in the Western Hemisphere, the large majority on lands growing cash crops and provisions. David Eltis, Frank D. Lewis, and David Richardson, "Slave Prices, the African Slave Trade and Productivity in the Caribbean, 1674–1807," *Economic History Review* 58 (November 2005): 673.

10. Thomas Thistlewood measured rainfall amounts in southwest Jamaica in 1783 and 1784: 3.4 inches in December 1783, 0.7 inches in January 1784, 2.8 inches in February, 3.9 inches in March, 2.7 inches in April, and 9.4 inches in May 1784, the start of the rainy season. Michael Chenoweth, "The 18th Century Climate of Jamaica Derived from the Journals of Thomas Thistlewood, 1750–1786," *Transactions of the American Philosophical Society* 93, no. 2 (2003): 56.

11. I accept that large-scale climate change in the Atlantic world had an impact on some seasonal patterns, but argue that such changes did not alter secular trends. James Searing notes how in Senegambia and the Western Sudan there was a significant wet period ca. 700–1100 and a dry period from 1630 to 1860. He states, though, that eighteenth-century evidence indicates that climate and rainfall patterns were "not significantly different from those of today." James F. Searing, *West African Slavery and Atlantic Commerce: The Senegal River Valley, 1700–1860* (New York, 1993), 5.

12. See, for example, H. H. Lamb, *Climate, History and the Modern World*, 2d ed. (London, 1995), 23–35.

13. Two air masses converge over the African tropics: monsoon winds from the Indian Ocean and a tropical continental air mass that moves south from the Sahara. This Intertropical Convergence Zone (the "doldrums") shifts north and south with the apparent motion of the sun, producing July–October rains in the African Atlantic north of the equator and January–April rains along much of the African coast south of the equator. See William Yaw Osei and Samuel Aryeetey-Attoh, "The Physical Environment," in *Geography of Sub-Saharan Africa*, ed. Samuel Aryeetey-Attoh (Upper Saddle River, N.J., 1997), 11–13, and P. R.

Crowe, "Wind and Weather in the Equatorial Zone," *Transactions and Papers (Institute of British Geographers)* 17 (1951): 23–76, for a general discussion, and Philip D. Curtin, *Economic Change in Precolonial Africa: Senegambia in the Era of the Slave Trade* (Madison, Wisc., 1975), 15, regarding Senegambia, the northerly limit of the Convergence Zone.

14. Cape Ann is a key navigational marker at 7°7N latitude and 13°1W longitude; Cape Formosa is at 4°30N latitude and 5°22E longitude.

15. Joseph C. Miller, *Way of Death: Merchant Capitalism and the Angolan Slave Trade, 1730–1830* (Madison, Wisc., 1988), 318–321.

16. After 1750, Havana (82°W) was the western-most major slaving market in the Atlantic world. Before 1750, the major westerly markets were Veracruz (96°W, prominent ca. 1595–1650) and Cartagena (75°W, prominent ca. 1550–1700).

17. Firms reminded their captains about the importance of timing ventures to leeward markets. As a Liverpool company wrote in 1768: "it does not answer to proceed from Barbadoes to [Maryland or Virginia] sooner than [the] beginning or middle of April; nor later than the Middle or End of July furthest." Powell & Co. to David Tuohy, Liverpool, 9 July 1768, 380 TUO 4/3, fol. 11, Liverpool Record Office. They also advised their captain that slave prices increased from Barbados to the Windward/Leeward Islands and then to Jamaica, but that the uncertainty of continued slave mortality in the Caribbean during the week-long voyage and the possibility that the Jamaica market would be glutted also had to be considered.

18. Lying 2 degrees north of the equator on December 29, 1611, van den Broecke wrote: "we had lain becalmed, for the most part, since the 11th of November, and had advanced what proved to be only 5 degrees." J. D. La Fleur, ed., *Pieter van den Broecke's Journal of Voyages to Cape Verde, Guinea and Angola (1605–1612)* (London, 2000), 86. Three weeks after sailing from Sierra Leone to Demerara, Captain Robert Hall of the *Eliza* steered into southerly winds that kept forcing him to sail above his mark. On August 12, 1805, he commented, "For these 16 Years I never did experience so much Southerly Winds." On August 29 Hall despaired: "I never experienced such Weathr in my life I am very doubtful of our fetching Demerary as we cannot get to the south[w]ard by any means." T70/1220, NA, journal of the *Eliza*, 22 July 1805. Hall did not sight Demerara until 20 September—a month later than he had anticipated.

19. From late December to early February strong dust-laden northeast trade winds, the harmattan, only occasionally hindered coastal navigation and

mooring along Upper Guinea and the Gold Coast. Departing the Gold Coast in February 1777, Captain Peleg Clarke sailed into a "tarnado" that damaged his masts, "So that in 2 Moments I was a compleat Wreck." Donnan, *Documents*, 3:329.

20. The North Atlantic hurricane season, usually dated August 1–November 1 by insurers, centered on the warmer waters of the Caribbean. Ceremonies in the Danish Caribbean on July 25 and October 25 marked days to pray for deliverance from hurricanes. C. G. A. Oldendorp, *History of the Mission of the Evangelical Brethren of the Caribbean Islands of St. Thomas, St. Croix, and St. John,* ed. Johann Jakob Bossard (Ann Arbor, Mich., 1987), 45. Tropical storms do not occur in the South Atlantic.

21. From detailed information on the later British slave trade, captains had an equal chance of running aground on African estuarial sandbars and of hitting reefs or encountering hurricanes.

22. The group of nine small islands, about 20 miles from the coast, known as the Iles de Los, "afford[ed] harbours and safe anchorages in deep water for ships of any burthen," which "lye here with the greatest safety in all weathers." Donnan, *Documents* 4:495, as described in 1794 by Joseph Hawkins, supercargo on board an American slave vessel. "The River Sierra Leone is in many Respects an important Station to a commercial Nation. Its Harbour is safe and commodious, and at all Times easy of Access; while there is no other River, for a vast Extent of Coast, into which Ships of large Burthen can enter." *British Parliamentary Papers,* 1801–2 (100), 2:23–24, statement of the chairman and Court of Directors of the Sierra Leone Company.

23. In late 1773 five London vessels "Arriv'd off the Barr of Senegal, but could not get in, being only seven Feet Water." In early October 1774 the "old Channel" was "forced open again by the Freshes, which came down very strong." *Lloyd's List,* 8 March 1774, 10 Jan. 1775. For details about the Senegal River and its bar, see *The Atlantic Navigator,* 4th ed. (London, 1854), 126. After the August–September rains, rising river levels and great surges of water dredged the estuary. In October 1610, near the Sette-Cama River between Mayoumba and Cape Lopez, van den Broecke wrote, "At this time of the year it is very difficult to enter the river, because in the dry season it gets silted up by the sea." La Fleur, *van den Broecke's Journal,* 77.

24. See, for example, *Memoirs of the Late Captain Hugh Crow of Liverpool* (1830; London, 1970), 62–63, 194–195; John Adams, *Remarks on the Country Extending from Cape Palmas to the River Congo* (1823; London, 1966), 99.

25. Only the Gold Coast trading posts Dixcove and Sekondi were accessible to small craft; the pounding surf forced all other vessels to anchor 2–3 miles off shore; Adams, *Remarks on the Country,* 159; J. J. Crooks, ed., *Records Relating to the Gold Coast Settlements from 1750 to 1874* (1923; London, 1973), 58. Cabinda Bay was the best anchorage between Cape Lopez and Luanda. Phyllis M. Martin, "Family Strategies in Nineteenth-Century Cabinda," *Journal of African History* 28, no. 1 (1987): 66. Coastal communities, seeking Atlantic commerce, did not develop if sandbars proved too dangerous. A sandbar blocked the mouth of the Kwanza River between Luanda and Benguela; Miller, *Way of Death,* 16.

26. For example: *The Complete Pilot for the Windward Passage; or, Directions for Sailing through the Several Passages to the Eastward of Jamaica* (London, 1789).

27. The Liverpool slaver *Garland* (voyage 81554) hit Cobbler's Rock (*Lloyd's List,* 24 April 1792), and the Liverpool slaver *Old Dick* (voyage 82963) hit Folly Reef (*Royal Gazette* [Kingston], 2–9 April 1796).

28. For rainfall in Upper Guinea, see George E. Brooks, *Eurafricans in Western Africa: Commerce, Social Status, Gender, and Religious Observance from the Sixteenth to the Eighteenth Century* (Athens, Ohio, 2003), 2–12.

29. Dorman and Bourke report rainfall from fifty-three coastal and island stations in the Atlantic world. Six stations experienced annual rainfall greater than 100 inches: Conakry, Guinea (181 inches); Cayenne, Guiana (151 inches); Harbel, Liberia (133 inches); Cristobal, Panama (132 inches); Puerto Cabezas, Nicaragua (123 inches); and Libreville, Gabon (121 inches). Rainfall in tropical Miami, by contrast, measured 60 inches. Clive E. Dorman and Robert H. Bourke, "Precipitation over the Atlantic Ocean, 30°S to 70°N," *Monthly Weather Review* 109 (March 1981): 557.

30. For monthly rainfall data in the Atlantic Ocean, 1979–2006 (illustrated graphically), see precip.gsfc.nasa.gov. For a discussion of rainfall amounts by Atlantic latitude band, see Dorman and Bourke, "Precipitation over the Atlantic Ocean," 554–563.

31. Richard Hakluyt, *The Principal Navigations, Voyages, Traffiques and Discoveries of the English Nation,* ed. Jack Beeching (1599; New York, 1987), 360–361.

32. Dorman and Bourke, "Precipitation over the Atlantic Ocean," 556; *New Scientist* 166, no. 2236 (29 April 2000): 64; Semyon A. Grodsky and James A. Carton, "Intertropical Convergence Zone in the South Atlantic and the Equatorial Cold Tongue," *Journal of Climate* 16 (February

2003): 731. As Simpson and Riehl state: "Regions of convergence have most rain; regions of divergence are driest. Over a large part of the oceans precipitation is as little as one-tenth of that in the equatorial zone." Robert H. Simpson and Herbert Riehl, *The Hurricane and Its Impact* (Baton Rouge, La., 1981), 40.

33. Kenneth F. Kiple and Brian T. Higgins, "Mortality Caused by Dehydration during the Middle Passage," *Social Science History* 13 (Winter 1989): 425–431, totals determined by body weight (hence they differ by age and gender).

34. Winneba fort was the best place for slave vessels to water on the Gold Coast. Adams, *Remarks on the Country*, 8, 159; Crooks, *Records Relating to the Gold Coast*, 58.

35. Three days after departing Sierra Leone in mid-1805, for example, Liverpool captain Robert Hall's sailors "Caught 150 Gallons water." T70/1220, NA, journal of the *Eliza*, 22 July 1805.

36. Kiple and Higgins do not discuss dehydration in the context of African trading regions or of seasonal rainfall on land or at sea; "Mortality Caused by Dehydration," 425–431. For shortages of water at Luanda and Benguela and dehydration on the subsequent Middle Passage, see Miller, *Way of Death*, 419–420.

37. Slave traders knew that it was important to purchase local foods with which Africans were familiar, as slaves often resisted eating. Discussing his voyage from Old Calabar to Barbados, Captain John Crean Hunt stated: "Our Yams have held out so that I have plenty on board for the remainder of the Passage[;] beans have not been forced on them." J. C. Hunt to James Rogers & Co., off Barbados, 11 May 1793, C107/59, NA. See also Ludewig Ferdinand Rømer, *A Reliable Account of the Coast of Guinea, (1760)*, ed. Selena Axelrod Winsnes (Oxford, 2000), 198.

38. B. W. Higman, *Slave Populations of the British Caribbean, 1807–1834* (Baltimore, Md., 1984), 215; Bonham C. Richardson, *The Caribbean in the Wider World, 1492–1992: A Regional Geography* (New York, 1992), 63.

39. The four main species in Nigeria: *D. rotundata, D. alata, D. cayenensis, D. esculenta*. Coursey estimated in 1967 that more than half of Nigerian yams at that time were *D. rotundata*. D. G. Coursey, *Yams: An Account of the Nature, Origins, Cultivation and Utilisation of the Useful Members of the Dioscoreaceae* (London, 1967), 22–24, 133–138. Historically, yams have been most important to Ibo of eastern and midwestern Nigeria (201–203).

40. For sugar, see the breakdown based on slave import data provided from

the estimates page at www.slavevoyages.org, assuming the following percentages of slaves disembarked in the Americas working first in sugar: Brazil, 25% ; Caribbean, 75%; Guianas, 75%; North America, 5%; non-Caribbean Spanish Americas, 5%. For percentages of plantation crops in the Caribbean, see David Eltis, "The Slave Economies of the Caribbean: Structure, Performance, Evolution and Significance," in *General History of the Caribbean: The Slave Societies of the Caribbean,* ed. Franklin W. Knight, 6 vols. (London, 1997), 3:110–114.

41. Richard B. Sheridan, *Sugar and Slavery: The Economic History of the British West Indies, 1623–1775,* 2d ed. (Kingston, Jamaica, 1994), 210, 231–232.

42. For useful maps depicting the geographic distribution of African crops, see George Peter Murdock, "Staple Subsistence Crops of Africa," *Geographical Review* 50 (October 1960): 523–540.

43. Coursey, *Yams,* 72; J. Alexander and D. G. Coursey, "The Origins of Yam Cultivation," in *The Domestication and Exploitation of Plants and Animals,* ed. Peter J. Ucko and G. W. Dimbleby (London, 1969), 419; S. Y. C. Ng, "Micropropagation of White Yam *(Dioscorea rotundata),*" in *Biotechnology in Agriculture and Forestry,* vol. 19: *High-Tech and Micropropagation III,* ed. Y. P. S. Bajaj (New Delhi, 1992), 136–137.

44. Sugar, grown unsuccessfully in Hispaniola, re-emerged there after 1515 when new mill equipment and laborers arrived from the Canary Islands and Madeira. By the late 1530s there were thirty-four mills, most concentrated near Santo Domingo. David Watts, *The West Indies: Patterns of Development, Culture, and Environment Change since 1492* (New York, 1987), 104, 112–113, 125; Genaro Rodríguez Morel, "The Sugar Economy of Española in the Sixteenth Century," and Alejandro de la Fuente, "Sugar and Slavery in Early Colonial Cuba," in *Tropical Babylons: Sugar and the Making of the Atlantic World, 1450–1680,* ed. Stuart B. Schwartz (Chapel Hill, N.C., 2004), 90, 102, 144. Morel cites a 1523 royal decree ordering a Hispaniola planter to operate his sugar mill "after Christmas day on the first day of spring"; 90. For Madeira and the Canaries, see Alberto Vieira, "The Sugar Economy of Madeira and the Canaries, 1450–1650," in Schwartz, *Tropical Babylons,* 42–84.

45. São Tomé's year-round rain in the southwest, high humidity, and constant temperatures allowed the cultivation of sugar every month. Farmers learned that they would produce the highest quality crystal, however, by planting in January and February, cutting cane by April/May, and then curing it during the summer, when dry easterlies passed over the island. Robert Garfield, *A History of São Tomé Island, 1470–1655: The Key to*

Guinea (San Francisco, Calif., 1992), 71–72. There are pronounced microclimates in São Tomé: parts of the southwest receive 160 inches of rain per year (110 inches in March–May); by contrast, São Tomé city, in the island's northeast, receives only 38 inches of rain annually.

46. C. Daryll Forde, "Land and Labour in a Cross River Village, Southern Nigeria," *Geographical Journal* 90 (July 1937): 29; W. B. Morgan, "The Forest and Agriculture in West Africa," *Journal of African History* 3, no. 2 (1962): 236; Phoebe Ottenberg, "The Afikpo Ibo of Eastern Nigeria," in *Peoples of Africa,* ed. James L. Gibbs, Jr. (New York, 1965), 7; Emea O. Arua, "Yam Ceremonies and the Values of Ohafia Culture," *Africa* 51, no. 2 (1981): 697–699. On 11 August 1785, Antera Duke and other Efik traders from Duke Town, Old Calabar, traveled 3 miles "to Aqua about King Aqua eating new yams." Stephen D. Behrendt, A. J. H. Latham, and David Northrup, *The Diary of Antera Duke: An Eighteenth-Century African Slave Trader* (New York, forthcoming). The farming schedule begins one or two months earlier in the drier northern lands on the yam belt. For the location of southern yams, see A. J. H. Latham, *Old Calabar, 1600–1891: The Impact of the International Economy upon a Traditional Society* (Oxford, 1973), 2–7.

47. B. W. Higman, *Slave Population and Economy in Jamaica, 1807–1834* (Mona, Jamaica, 1995), 21, 196. In 1774 Edward Long pointed out that "canes on the South side are ripe and fit to cut in the beginning of January; but the North side crops do not commence till about the latter end of March, or sometimes later. The greater frequency of rain, and cloudiness of the atmosphere . . . retard vegetation, and prevent the canes from coming earlier to maturity." Edward Long, *The History of Jamaica,* 3 vols. (London, 1774; repr. 1970), 1:358.

48. Planters residing in ecosystems with two rainy/dry seasons (such as in pockets of French Saint-Domingue) attempted to produce two crops a year. There were small monthly variations in the sugar production schedule in some islands, depending on specific land ecologies, water requirements, and labor supplies. Planters understood that even fields close to one another might produce varied sugar amounts and quality. Ward Barrett, "Caribbean Sugar-Production Standards in the Seventeenth and Eighteenth Centuries," in *Merchants & Scholars: Essays in the History of Exploration and Trade,* ed. John Parker (Minneapolis, Minn., 1966), 147–154.

49. In Saint-Domingue, the North Plain received 40% of its rain in November–January, percentages attained in the west in two mini–rainy seasons (April–May and August–October). In the colony's southern lands, 70%

of the 80 inches of annual precipitation fell in May–October. David
Geggus, "Slave Society in the Sugar Plantation Zones of Saint Domingue
and the Revolution of 1791–93," *Slavery and Abolition* 20 (August
1999): 33–34; www.worldclimate.com. Hispaniola has the most extreme
rainfall in the Greater Antilles. In Saint-Domingue, annual rainfall
ranges from 20 to 100 inches, linked generally to elevation and foliage.
Leo Alpert, "The Areal Distribution of Mean Annual Rainfall over the
Island of Hispaniola," *Monthly Weather Review* 69 (July 1941): 201–
204.

50. P. E. H. Hair, Adam Jones, and Robin Law, eds., *Barbot on Guinea: The
Writings of Jean Barbot on West Africa, 1678–1712,* 2 vols. (London,
1992), 2:674.

51. Simon Taylor to Robert Taylor, St. Thomas in the East, 9 Oct. 1799; Simon Taylor to Robert Taylor, St. Mary's, 29 Dec. 1803, Simon Taylor
Letter Book, Institute of Commonwealth Studies, University of London.

52. Woodville to Rogers, Liverpool, 10 Jan. 1791, C107/13, NA.

53. Early yams also do not store as well as those harvested at the end of the
rainy season. Coursey, *Yams,* 74, 85–88.

54. In the late 1600s Barbot stated that he had seen some yams that weighed
8–10 pounds. One hundred years later Captain Sherwood remarked
that his "good sound yams" averaged 7 pounds. Hair, Jones, and Law,
Barbot on Guinea, 2:460; Sheila Lambert, ed., *House of Commons Sessional Papers of the Eighteenth Century,* 145 vols. (Wilmington, Del.,
1975), 72:204, evidence of Sherwood before the Jamaica Assembly, 3
Dec. 1789. Captains calculated consumption rates of one-half yam per
African per day during a 90–120–day period and purchased 10,000–
50,000 tubers, thus indicating that they loaded tubers of varying maturity and species. The largest Nigerian yam, *D. alata,* the "Greater Yam,"
generally weighs 10–20 pounds, but tubers as heavy as 132 pounds
have been grown. Yams lose weight during dry-season storage as water
in tissues evaporates. Thus yams purchased in November would weigh
more than those purchased late in the season. Coursey, *Yams,* 46, 182–
183.

55. Millet and sorghum, grown in drier lands in Africa, but not in the Atlantic Americas, were the second most important African foodstuffs in the
transatlantic slave trade. As the slave trade pushed supply zones farther
inland, more and more Africans forced to the coast would have lived
in the drier African millet-sorghum belt. Slaving ships transported sorghum to the West Indies, but it disappeared from cultivation. C. Wayne

Smith and Richard A. Frederiksen, "History of Cultivar Development in the United States: From 'Memoirs of A. B. Maunder—Sorghum Breeder,' " in *Sorghum: Origin, History, Technology, and Production,* ed. C. Wayne Smith and Richard A. Frederiksen (New York, 2000), 193. Thus few Africans would have seen these familiar cereals in the Americas: none grew in the West Indies or along the Atlantic littoral.

56. Rice was the most important cereal in the Atlantic slaving world, production centering in West Africa, the Lowcountry of Carolina and Georgia, and in Suriname and Maranhão. African rice transplanted to the Americas with the slave trade. Limited rice production occurred in Maranhão floodplains in the early 1600s, but the cereal did not become a major export crop until the 1760s and 1770s. In South America, rice began in Suriname in the mid-1600s, was abandoned later in the century, and then re-emerged in the 1780s. In the tropical Carolina and Georgia Lowcountry rice became the principal eighteenth-century cash crop. Dauril Alden, "Late Colonial Brazil, 1750–1808," in *Colonial Brazil,* ed. Leslie Bethell (New York, 1991), 322–325; Judith A. Carney, *Black Rice: The African Origins of Rice Cultivation in the Americas* (Cambridge, Mass., 2001); Carney, "'With Grains in Her Hair': Rice in Colonial Brazil," *Slavery and Abolition* 25 (April 2004): 3–20; Carney, "Rice and Memory in the Age of Enslavement: Atlantic Passages to Suriname," *Slavery and Abolition* 26 (December 2005): 326–331.

57. K. B. Dickson, "Trade Patterns in Ghana at the Beginning of the Eighteenth Century," *Geographical Review* 56 (July 1966): 419–422.

58. Bruce F. Johnston, *The Staple Food Economies of Western Tropical Africa* (Stanford, Calif., 1958), 59, 91–92.

59. Dolores Koenig, "Social Stratification and Labor Allocation in Peanut Farming in the Rural Malian Household," *African Studies Review* 29 (September 1986): 108, 109, 114.

60. Minor trades in the Gambia River's tributaries began in late June when waters rose, thus assisting navigation and the transportation of slaves and commodities. Stephen D. Behrendt, "Markets, Transaction Cycles, and Profits: Merchant Decision Making in the British Slave Trade," *William and Mary Quarterly,* 3d ser., 58 (January 2001): 187.

61. For Senegambia, see Curtin, *Senegambia,* 17–18, where he differentiates among varieties of cereals and growing seasons along the extensive Senegal River.

62. Carney, "Rice and Memory," 332–335.

63. In late April 1750, Captain John Newton loaded 17,000 pounds of rice

on the Windward Coast. During two weeks in mid-December 1797, Captain James Rigby purchased 15,000 pounds of rice at Bassa, en route to the Bight of Benin. These captains purchased about 2 pounds of rice per African per day. Bernard Martin and Mark Spurrell, eds., *The Journal of a Slave Trader (John Newton), 1750–1754* (London, 1962), 42–49; F. William Torrington, ed., *House of Lords Sessional Papers,* Session 1798–1799, 3 vols. (Rahway, N.J., 1975), 3:89–90, evidence of James Rigby, 28 May 1799.

64. Peter Potter to William Davenport & Company, *Young Sisters,* 21 Feb. 1784, New Davenport Papers, MMM.

65. Purchasing rice on the Windward Coast in 1750, Liverpool captain John Newton remarked on 21 April that "the season [was] advancing fast" and on 30 April that "the season is so far advanced." Martin and Spurrell, *Journal of a Slave Trader,* 42–49.

66. In some years insufficient rains did not allow a second crop: "wee have had but little raine this yeare and that they shall have but on[e] cropp this yeare and . . . Corne will be verry deare." Richard Thelwall to the Royal African Company (RAC), Anomabu, 25 Sept. 1693, in *The English in West Africa: The Local Correspondence of the Royal African Company of England, 1681–1699,* ed. Robin Law, 3 parts (Oxford, 1997–2006), 1:140.

67. In late March African chiefs at "Little Commenda" on the Gold Coast "doe demand their customes as due at putting the corne in the ground." David Harper to RAC, Comenda, 30 March 1683, in Law, *English in West Africa,* 1:57. According to slave trader and fort official Archibald Dalzel, "The Dahomans, like the other inhabitants of tropical climates, plant twice a year, viz. at the vernal and autumnal equinoxes; after which, the periodical rains prevail. Indeed they may be said to reap four, or rather two double crops; for soon after the *maize* comes above ground, they plant *callavances* [chickpeas or beans] in the interstices between the rows; which practice gives fields a very beautiful appearance." Archibald Dalzel, *The History of Dahomy, An Inland Kingdom of Africa* (London, 1793; repr. 1967), v. The principal maize harvest occurred in July/August, and coastal Europeans commented in early July how they lacked corn: "Here is no corne to be gott at present, till new corne come which will be a month or thereabouts." Thomas Stephenson to RAC, Sekondi Fort, 9 July 1691, in Law, *English in West Africa,* 3:92. By late January, traders received chests of "old corn." Ralph Hassell to RAC, Anomabu, 27 Jan. 1687, in Law, *English in West Africa,* 2:195.

68. Maize arrived in São Tomé in the early 1500s, and transplanted to the African mainland a few decades later. Stanley B. Alpern, "The European Introduction of Crops into West Africa in Precolonial Times," *History in Africa* 19 (1992): 25.

69. Law, *English in West Africa,* 3:277.

70. According to a French fort administrator in 1697, a Senegal leader warned the French that "they should consider upon whom their trading posts in Senegal depended; he could expel them or starve them to death by forbidding his subjects to provide them with provisions." Searing, *West African Slavery,* 24, quoting Wolof leader Latsukaabe's warning to André Brüe.

71. On the later Middle Passage to Grenada, forty-five Africans died, deaths that Hume attributed to their rice diet. On his previous voyage, during the yam season, "we had not much Mortality." Torrington, *Lords Sessional Papers,* 3:138–139, evidence of Robert Hume, 31 May 1799.

72. Phyllis M. Martin, *The External Trade of the Loango Coast, 1576–1870: The Effects of Changing Commercial Relations on the Vili Kingdom of Loango* (London, 1972), 13; Lambert, *Commons Sessional Papers,* 71:8, evidence of James Fraser, 29 Jan. 1790.

73. Adams, *Remarks on the Country,* 161–162.

74. James Clemens & Co. to Captain William Speers, 3 June 1767, 380 TUO 4/2, fol. 3, Liverpool Record Office; Adams, *Remarks on the Country,* 162.

75. John Thornton, "Demography and History in the Kingdom of Kongo, 1550–1750," *Journal of African History* 18, no. 4 (1977): 512–529; John K. Thornton, *The Kingdom of Kongo: Civil War and Transition, 1641–1718* (Madison, Wisc., 1983), 36–37.

76. For example, on the *Hannah,* fitted out in July 1789 for 320 slaves from New Calabar, the firm Leyland and Molyneux purchased £25 of beans and £44 worth of rice. On their ship *Jenny,* fitted out in November 1792 for 283 slaves from the Congo River, they purchased £81 of beans and £52 worth of rice. Account books of the *Hannah* and *Jenny,* Anti-Slavery Collection, I, Clements Library, Ann Arbor, Mich. Undoubtedly, the captain sailing to New Calabar later purchased large quantities of African yams.

77. David Richardson, ed., *Bristol, Africa and the Eighteenth-Century Slave Trade to America,* 4 vols. (Bristol, 1986–1996), 4:195, on the slaver *Rodney;* Simon Taylor to Robert Taylor, Holland, Jamaica, 10 May 1806, Simon Taylor Letter Book.

78. David Eltis, "Fluctuations in Mortality in the Last Half Century of the Transatlantic Slave Trade," *Social Science History* 13 (Autumn 1989): 332–335.

79. For Africans who subsisted largely on yam diets—particularly those already weakened by protein-energy malnutrition and diseases such as kwashiorkor—being force-fed corn, rice, or beans would have increased risks of severe diarrhea and dehydration. See Michael C. Latham, *Human Nutrition in the Developing World* (Rome, 1997), 140–142; Kenneth F. Kiple, *The Caribbean Slave: A Biological History* (New York, 1984), 74–75.

80. In the years 1662–1807, 209 British slavers in the Bight of Biafra between July and December had an average slave mortality loss, later on the Middle Passage, of 16.3% (*sd* [standard deviation] .179). On 96 Guineamen slaving in this region from January to June, the average slave mortality loss on the passage was 22.9% (*sd* .191). On 79 French slaving voyages to the Bight of Biafra, 1710–1791, these seasonal differences were greater: 16.0% (*n* = 46; *sd* .129) and 33.4% (*n* = 33; *sd* .256), respectively. Within the Bight, Old Calabar stands out as a trading outlet of greatest Middle Passage mortality following the in- and out-of-crop seasons. For the British and French trades at Old Calabar: 18.6% (July–December, *n* = 70, *sd* .159); 32.4% (January–June, *n* = 51, *sd* .233). Slave mortality from Bonny had less seasonal variation: 15.6% (July–December, *n* = 99, *sd* .198) and 17.9% (January–June, *n* = 44, *sd* .149).

81. Galenson, *Traders, Planters and Slaves*, 35.

82. Behrendt, "Markets, Transaction Cycles, and Profits," 197.

83. William Butterworth [Henry Schroeder], *Three Years Adventures, of a Minor, in England, Africa, the West Indies, South-Carolina and Georgia* (Leeds, 1822), 28; Alexander Falconbridge, *An Account of the Slave Trade on the Coast of Africa* (London, 1788), 5–6.

84. Stephen D. Behrendt, "Crew Mortality in the Transatlantic Slave Trade in the Eighteenth Century," *Slavery and Abolition* 18 (April 1997): 49–71; Herbert S. Klein, Stanley L. Engerman, Robin Haines, and Ralph Shlomowitz, "Transoceanic Mortality: The Slave Trade in Comparative Perspective," *William and Mary Quarterly*, 3d ser., 58 (January 2001): 93–117.

85. BT98/44,94, NA. Eight sailors died from June 21 to October 5 at Old Calabar.

86. The most important observations: those of Samuel Gamble in 1793–1794, along the Rice Coast. See Bruce L. Mouser, ed., *A Slaving Voyage*

to Africa and Jamaica: The Log of the Sandown, *1793–1794* (Bloomington, Ind., 2002), 75–76.

87. As the West India missionary Christian Oldendorp stated in the mid-1700s: "Since the sole consideration in the purchase of slaves is their fitness to perform hard labor in the West Indian possessions of the Europeans, first priority is given to the strength, age, and the health of their bodies." Oldendorp, *History of the Mission,* 213.

88. Hair, Jones, and Law, *Barbot on Guinea,* 2:674.

89. Peter Potter to William Davenport & Co., Old Calabar, 23 July 1785, New Davenport Papers. Not surprisingly, merchants' instructions to captains trading at Old Calabar only for dyewood, palm oil, or ivory do not mention yam supplies. William Davenport & Co. to Captain William Begg, Liverpool, 17 May 1780, New Davenport Papers.

90. Richard Rogers to James Rogers & Co., Old Calabar, 20 July 1788, C107/12, NA. Barbot was told that a "ship that takes in five hundred slaves, must provide above a hundred thousand yams; which is very difficult, because it is hard to stow them, by reason they take up so much room." Hair, Jones, and Law, *Barbot on Guinea,* 2:689, 700, 709n53.

91. Peter Potter to William Davenport & Co., Old Calabar, 3 Nov. 1785, New Davenport Papers.

92. The following information, contained in Antera Duke's diary, may be found in Behrendt, Latham, and Northrup, *Diary of Antera Duke.*

93. European explorers and soldiers later learned the difficulties of traveling overland in Nigeria during the rainy season and thus marched in dry months. See E. A. Steel, "Exploration in Southern Nigeria," *Geographical Journal* 32 (July 1908): 6–11.

94. In October 1784 Burrows returned to Old Calabar in command of the Liverpool slaver *Lion.* On 22 October 1786 he died at sea, shortly before reaching the Cross River, in command of the *Renown.* BT98/47,349, NA.

95. The file contains information on monthly ship arrivals in specific American import regions for 20,350 voyages, 1527–1866, accounting for six million African migrants. From information on Middle Passage voyage time, one can estimate months when ships departed Africa. Analysis is based on a sample of 23,844 slaving voyages: there are 9,100 cases with a recorded African month of departure, and 14,744 cases when only the month of arrival in the Americas is given. From data on Middle Passage voyage length (from six weeks to four months, depending on regions of trade), African months of departure for those 14,744 voyages can be esti-

mated. Wind variability in the Atlantic might significantly extend the number of Middle Passage days, but I believe that the voyage samples are sufficiently large to demonstrate general trends.

96. G. Ugo Nwokeji, "African Conceptions of Gender and the Slave Traffic," *William and Mary Quarterly,* 3d ser., 58 (January 2001): 47–68.

97. Glenn Davis Stone, Robert McC. Netting, and M. Priscilla Stone, "Seasonality, Labor Scheduling, and Agricultural Intensification in the Nigerian Savanna," *American Anthropologist,* n.s., 92 (March 1990): 11.

98. An estimated 670,000 slaves shipped from the Bight of Biafra, 1750–1800: www.slavevoyages.org, estimates page.

99. K. Onwuka Dike and Felicia I. Ekejiuba, *The Aro of South-Eastern Nigeria, 1650–1850: A Study of Socio-Economic Formation and Transformation in Nigeria* (Ibadan, 1990); G. Ugo Nwokeji, "The Biafran Frontier: Trade, Slaves, and Aro Society, c. 1750–1905" (Ph.D. diss., University of Toronto, 1999), 97. The three authors note the importance of Bende and Uburu fairs organized by the Aro, but do not assign months to them or discuss slaves brokered at fairs.

100. David Wynford Carnegie, *Letters from Nigeria, 1899–1900,* ed. Ann O'Hear (Madison, Wisc., 1992), 58. One European observer in 1898 on the Niger River noted, "men and women were bought and sold at the rate of one hundred a-month until the Niger rising with the rains swept the market and slave-dealers' huts away." Harold Blindloss, quoted in Nwokeji, "Biafran Frontier," 204.

101. Miller, *Way of Death,* 672. Numerous slave owners from African hinterland to coast continually passed "dying slaves off to other owners" (xxi).

102. Bonny traders had matched Calabar's slave exports by the 1730s, and then exceeded them in all but one year from 1748 to 1776. During the 1760s and 1770s Bonny merchants exported twice as many slaves as Efik traders; in some years, 1776, for example, they tripled Calabar's total of 2,000 slave exports. In June 1780, after three years of reduced overseas business, Efik leaders wrote to Liverpool merchants to inform them that they "have Slaves Same a[s] Bonny or other place[s]." Lovejoy and Richardson, "Letters," 109.

103. Sample years include peacetime periods with approximately the same volume of the slave trade from Bonny, Old Calabar, and New Calabar. During years of Atlantic warfare, risk of capture from privateers and warships reduced the number of European slaving vessels. During the American Revolutionary War few slavers traded in the Bight of Biafra.

104. See note 95 regarding months of ship arrivals and departures. To esti-

mate the three- to five-month period by African region when captains loaded slaves, I followed David Eltis and David Richardson, "Productivity in the Transatlantic Slave Trade," *Explorations in Economic History* 32 (October 1995): 478.

105. Curtin, *Senegambia*, 109, 160, 273–274, 301–302; Martin A. Klein, *Slavery and Colonial Rule in French West Africa* (New York, 1998), 21.

106. Mouser, *Slaving Voyage*, 99–101.

107. Nathaniel Cutting Journal, 1–3 May 1790, Massachusetts Historical Society, Boston, Mass. From a sample of 2,939 voyages embarking 600,000 slaves in Upper Guinea, more ships (322) departed the coast in May with more slaves (67,000) than in any other month.

108. African merchants weighed "maintenance costs" against future slave prices. Curtin estimates that in the mid-1800s it cost £2.74 to keep a person alive for a year on millet, with an additional £3–4 for security, housing, and clothes. Since the slave might sell for £10–12, the costs to hold slaves represented half of the selling price. Curtin, *Senegambia*, 169.

109. Barbot identified the late December–early February "proper season" of the harmattan, strong dust-laden northeast trade winds that kept "all persons . . . white or black . . . confined to their houses." Though storms could hinder coastal navigation and mooring, he did not state that slave trades ended. Hair, Jones, and Law, *Barbot on Guinea*, 2:456–457, 560; Winsnes, *Reliable Account*, 18n11.

110. Law, *English in West Africa*, 1:10, 128, 147, 182–183, 189, 203, 318–319; 3:24n113.

111. Stephen D. Behrendt, "Human Capital in the British Slave Trade," in *Liverpool and Transatlantic Slavery*, ed. David Richardson, Suzanne Schwartz, and Tony Tibbles (Liverpool, 2007), 74.

112. The Slave Coast "consisted originally of the two kingdoms of Whydah and Ardrah, forming the most populous and best cultivated part of the African coast." Robert Montgomery Martin, *Statistics of the Colonies of the British Empire* (London, 1839), 528.

113. John Carter to the RAC, Whydah, 19 Sept. 1685, Carter to the RAC, Anomabu, 15 Feb. 1686, both in Law, *English in West Africa*, 2:326, 378. Law identifies the dry season as a time "when sailing conditions (especially landing and embarking through the surf at Whydah) were most favourable"; 326n24.

114. British captains shipped two-thirds of all Bight of Biafra slaves (80% before 1808). Of the slaves shipped from the Bight of Benin, 60% embarked on Portuguese or Brazilian vessels.

115. *The Strange Adventures of Andrew Battell, of Leigh, in Angola and the Adjoining Regions,* ed. E. G. Ravenstein (London, 1901), 7–53; La Fleur, *van den Broecke's Journal,* 53–102.

116. For a later example, Joachim John Monteiro, *Angola and the River Congo,* 2 vols. (London, 1875; repr. 1968), 1:40–49.

117. The five largest African slave-trading communities were Luanda, Benguela, Bonny, Ouidah, and Cabinda. From 1701 to 1810 at least one million slaves passed through Luanda, and a recent estimate for Benguela totals 388,700 slaves. David Eltis, Paul E. Lovejoy, and David Richardson, "Slave-Trading Ports: Towards an Atlantic-Wide Perspective," in *Ports of the Slave Trade (Bights of Benin and Biafra),* ed. Robin Law and Silke Strickrodt (Stirling, 1999), 20–25.

118. In general, see Miller, *Way of Death,* particularly 126–169. See also note 75 here and Jill R. Dias, "Famine and Disease in the History of Angola, c. 1830–1930," *Journal of African History* 22, no. 3 (1981): 351–355; Joseph C. Miller, "The Significance of Drought, Disease and Famine in the Agriculturally Marginal Zones of West-Central Africa," *Journal of African History* 23, no. 1 (1982): 29–54.

119. As Thornton writes, referring to the Gold Coast: "Large armies, however, had serious logistical problems, when soldiers had to come bringing their own food supplies and afterwards were required to live off the land. The logistical stresses of using armies of this type counted in several campaigns. The Akyem army broke off fighting in its war against a coalition of Fante, Asin and Akwamu in 1716 because the rainy season was not a good time to fight, as the people who bore arms were needed to work their fields. Similarly, in 1754 the war between Asante and a combined army from Denkyira, Twifo, Wasa and Akyem threatened the whole area with famine, as every able-bodied man was serving in the war and there was no one left at home to attend the crops. In 1760, Ouwsu Bore of Denkyira proposed the abandonment of their campaign in Asin for the same reason, that the men were needed to plant at home, and without this there would be famine. The army of Anlo was defeated by Popo in 1792 because it had to dispatch a significant portion of its forces back to fetch food, the army having run out, and Popo commanders took advantage of the situation to launch a successful attack." John K. Thornton, *Warfare in Atlantic Africa, 1500–1800* (London, 1999), 68.

120. Robert S. Smith, *Warfare and Diplomacy in Pre-Colonial West Africa,* 2d ed. (Madison, Wisc., 1989), 29; Andrew Hubbell, "A View of the Slave Trade from the Margin: Souroudougou in the Late Nineteenth-Century

Slave Trade of the Niger Bend," *Journal of African History* 42, no. 1 (2001): 27.

121. Gregory to RAC, 4 Sept. 1691, in Law, *English in West Africa,* 3:282.

122. The cavalry-based Oyo Empire conducted dry-season warfare in the Bight of Benin. The coastal states found it difficult, as Thornton says, "to resist cavalry armies, but because horses could not live for long in the south, those northern areas [in the Oyo Empire] where horses could be maintained could not sustain their power in the south once the dry season had passed." The rainy season also limited the effectiveness of fire and gunpowder weapons, and when the rains coincided with the planting season, military leaders kept men home to prevent famine. Thornton, *Warfare in Atlantic Africa,* 64, 68, 76. Firearms were effective only during the dry season, after soldiers burned grasses and bush to make clearings. Dike and Ekejiuba, *Aro of South-Eastern Nigeria,* 171.

123. Evidence of Wadstrom, *Report of the Lords of the Committee of Council* (London, 1789), Part I, Slaves.

124. Thornton, *Warfare in Atlantic Africa,* 81, 85, 87.

125. Walter Hawthorne, *Planting Rice and Harvesting Slaves: Transformations along the Guinea-Bissau Coast, 1400–1900* (Portsmouth, N.H., 2003), 109, 159, 169.

126. Jean Barbot, at River Sess (the Windward Coast, in modern-day Liberia) in December 1681/January 1682, did not trade for much ivory: "The blacks had a more urgent task, being engaged in sowing their rice." Hair, Jones, and Law, *Barbot on Guinea,* 1:268, 278.

127. Portuguese Crown regulations in the mid-1500s specified that ships sailing for Upper Guinea could depart Lisbon only between August and March, and should sail from the coast for Lisbon by May. These rules acknowledged that West African merchants transported commodities during the dry months; few itinerant merchants reached the coast during the June–September rains. John W. Blake, *European Beginnings in West Africa, 1454–1578* (New York, 1937), 13, 61, 131–132.

128. Hawthorne, *Planting Rice and Harvesting Slaves.*

129. Ranging from Senegambia (12.9%) to Loango-Ambriz (21.6%), as calculated from Table 1.3. Small-scale, irregular coastal raids may have occurred to meet the short-term demand from these captains.

130. One might suspect that African slave owners held children out of season, as they cost less to keep alive. Regional age/sex data per month, though limited, do not support significant seasonal differences in the numbers of children shipped overseas. It is reasonable to suppose, though,

that some brokers retained African children out of season, speculating that they would increase in age, strength, and value once captains arrived to bid for labor in season. Arguably those slaves purchased during the out-of-season, hungry months were debilitated and were later fed imported foods, which had a negative impact on their shipboard health (see notes 71, 79, 80).

131. Of course, if slaving vessels did not arrive, African owners risked provisioning and working slaves beyond their value. In the Upper Gambia River on May 20, 1797, explorer Mungo Park heard that no slaving vessel "had arrived for some months past." A group of Sera-Wolli slave traders, traveling west in a caravan with their slaves, decided to turn back, not having "the means of maintaining their slaves in Gambia, until a vessel should arrive; and were unwilling to sell them to disadvantage." Mungo Park, *Travels in the Interior Districts of Africa,* ed. Kate Ferguson Marsters (1799; Durham, N.C., 2000), 297.

132. Of the 10.7 million who survived the Middle Passage, 5.25 million African migrants worked in sugarcane, and perhaps 1.25 million toiled on tobacco, coffee, rice, indigo, cotton, and cacao estates. For sugar estimates and percentages of West India crops, see note 40. Of the major slave-important regions, Brazil, by 1800, had the "most diverse economic usage of slaves to be found in the Western Hemisphere." Perhaps "one quarter of all the slaves were to be found in plantations or mines." Herbert S. Klein, *African Slavery in Latin America and the Caribbean* (New York, 1986), 81–82. Another 1.5 million people worked on livestock pens, or on plantations producing maize, wheat, cassava, or forestry products. An estimated 1–1.25 million enslaved Africans worked in silver and gold mining, most before 1750. Brazilian gold, important particularly from 1690 to 1750, drew in perhaps 500,000 African workers. Alexandre Vieira Ribeiro, "The Transatlantic Slave Trade to Bahia, 1582–1851," in *Extending the Frontiers: Essays on the New Transatlantic Slave Trade Database,* ed. David Eltis and David Richardson (New Haven, Conn., 2008), 130–154, esp. 136–138. Household work, including ranching, occupied the lives of 750,000–1,000,000 African men, women, and children.

133. Cap-Français, the principal disembarkation center for French slaving vessels in northern Saint-Domingue, has the rainiest winter (60% of precipitation occurring in October–February); more enslaved Africans arrived in the April–June quarter than at any other West Indian import center, a fact linked not only to those months being drier but also to the port's diversified hinterland and its re-export slave trade. David Geggus,

"The French Slave Trade: An Overview," *William and Mary Quarterly,* 3d ser., 58 (January 2001): 126–128.

134. In Bahia there were two planting seasons, separated by heavy May rainfall: late February–early May; and early June–early September. Cutting and processing occurred from August to April—avoiding the rainy May–July months, which rotted cane, dampened firewood, and hindered cart transport. The intensive Bahia sugar industry kept mills operating eleven consecutive months, producing sugar loaves nine and a half months of the year. Stuart B. Schwartz, *Sugar Plantations in the Formation of Brazilian Society: Bahia, 1550–1838* (New York, 1985), 101–107. Soldier John Stedman marched in Suriname on December 11, 1774, "the very heart of the dry season." Richard Price and Sally Price, eds., *Stedman's Surinam: Life in an Eighteenth-Century Slave Society* (Baltimore, Md., 1992), 114.

135. Bahia was one region that grew large quantities of sugar and tobacco. The tobacco industry was centered in the Recôncavo, west of the Bay of All Saints. February–March rains signaled the planting season. Farmers sowed in May, transplanted three to four weeks later, weeded and pruned in July–August, and then harvested in September. By 1700 much of this tobacco was sweetened with molasses and herbs and shipped to the Bight of Benin. Bahia tobacco planters demanded new African farmers during the rainy winter and drier spring. Stuart B. Schwartz, "Plantations and Peripheries, c. 1580–c. 1750," in Bethell, *Colonial Brazil,* 100–104; Catherine Lugar, "The Portuguese Tobacco Trade and Tobacco Growers of Bahia in the Late Colonial Period," in *Essays Concerning the Socioeconomic History of Brazil and Portuguese India,* ed. Dauril Alden and Warren Dean (Gainesville, Fla., 1977), 32; B. J. Barickman, *A Bahian Counterpoint: Sugar, Tobacco, Cassava, and Slavery in the Recôncavo, 1780–1860* (Stanford, Calif., 1998), 97, 160; Michiel Baud and Kees Koonings, "*A lavoura dos pobres:* Tobacco Farming and the Development of Commercial Agriculture in Bahia, 1870–1930," *Journal of Latin American Studies* 31 (May 1999): 288–293. By the mid-1800s the leaf had moved south to Paraná, Santa Catarina, and Rio Grande do Sul, in latitudes 24–32°S, the location of Brazil's main tobacco industry today.

136. Behrendt, "Markets, Transaction Cycles, and Profits," 196; T. H. Breen, *Tobacco Culture: The Mentality of the Great Tidewater Planters on the Eve of Revolution* (Princeton, N.J., 1985), 46–53; Philip D. Morgan, *Slave Counterpoint: Black Culture in the Eighteenth-Century Chesapeake and Lowcountry* (Chapel Hill, N.C., 1998), 73–74, 164–169.

137. The first season's Carolina rice crop arrived at docks in November, and peak export months were January, February, and March. Most vessels sailing to Charleston to load rice departed England in September–November and returned between December and April. Morgan, *Slave Counterpoint,* 149–169; Kenneth Morgan, "The Organization of the Colonial American Rice Trade," *William and Mary Quarterly,* 3d ser., 52 (July 1995): 437, 444–448; *South-Carolina Gazette,* 25 Nov. 1732–2 Feb. 1734. Indigo also was packed for shipment by the late fall, merchants taking advantage of increased supplies of tonnage to carry off the dye crop.

138. Alden, "Late Colonial Brazil, 1750–1808," 322–325; Carney, "'With Grains in Her Hair,'" 3–20.

139. Lyman L. Johnson and Susan Migden Socolow, "Colonial Centers, Colonial Peripheries, and the Economic Agency of the Spanish State," in *Negotiated Empires: Centers and Peripheries in the Americas, 1500–1820,* ed. Christine Daniels and Michael V. Kennedy (New York, 2002), 69; J. A. B. Beaumont, *Travels in Buenos Ayres, and the Adjacent Provinces of the Rio de la Plata* (London, 1828), 18–21.

140. The South Carolina slave market would reopen temporarily, a fact unknown to Burrows in December 1783.

141. Ship captains needed to arrive in the Chesapeake between April and August or risk a substantial drop in the price of imported labor. According to Edmund Jenings of Virginia (1709): "When Negroes come in about the begining of the Summer, the planters are abundantly more fond of them, and will give greater price for them, because they are sure of the advantage of their labour in that years Crop, whereas Negros bought at the Latter end of the year, are of little Service till the next Spring, and this is the true reason of that difference of price." David W. Galenson, *White Servitude in Colonial America: An Economic Analysis* (New York, 1981), 91.

142. Charter groups of Africans from the Upper Guinea Coast may have introduced rice cultivation techniques to Carolina. See Carney, *Black Rice.*

143. For the period 1789–1792, Richardson calculates slave prices as follows: Sierra Leone (£17–£22), Gold Coast (£18–£21), Calabar (£12–£14), and Cameroons/Cape Lopez (£8–£12). See David Richardson, "Prices of Slaves in West and West-Central Africa: Toward an Annual Series, 1698–1807," *Bulletin of Economic Research* 43 (January 1991): 33–46.

144. The Portuguese first capitulated to British commercial dominance at Old Calabar, abandoning the slave trade in the Cross River between

1715 and the abolition of the British slave trade in 1807. From 1707 to 1715 at least thirty-one Portuguese vessels slaved at Old Calabar, but the number dropped to five from 1719 to 1738. There are no documented Portuguese slavers at Old Calabar again until 1809. The Portuguese could not compete against Bristol captains who moved into the Cross River slave trade after 1713. The French moved into Old Calabar in 1713–1716 (eleven ships), but the trade then dropped until 1763.

145. This migration peaked in the 1820s: at least 1,061 Portuguese Guineamen disembarked 376,000 "West-Central African" slaves in Brazil, the large majority of these people shipped from Luanda and Benguela into Rio de Janeiro.

146. The Dutch incursion into Portugal's South Atlantic slaving empire continued transatlantic shipping patterns: at least 104 Dutch-flagged slavers transported 24,000 Africans to Pernambuco between 1637 and 1645, the vast majority embarking at Luanda or Benguela. The Brazilian slave trade, 1822–1852, drew primarily on the traditional West-Central African supply centers, the major new migration being from Southeast Africa to Brazil. The Southeast African slave trade to Brazil accelerated after 1811 and during the subsequent forty years accounted for about 20% of all Brazilian slave imports. Most ships arrived first in Rio de Janeiro. Edward A. Alpers, "'Moçambiques' in Brazil: Another Dimension of the African Diaspora in the Atlantic World," in *Africa and the Americas: Interconnections during the Slave Trade,* ed. José C. Curto and Renée Soulodre-La France (Trenton, N.J., 2005), 44.

147. David Eltis, Stephen D. Behrendt, and David Richardson, "National Participation in the Transatlantic Slave Trade: New Evidence," in Curto and Soulodre-La France, *Africa and the Americas,* 25; Carney, "'With Grains in Her Hair,' " 12–15.

148. At the first peak of Old Calabar–Kingston trade in 1754–1755, for example, agents in southeast Jamaica also sold twenty-five slaving cargoes shipped from the Gambia River, Windward Coast, Cape Coast Castle, Anomabu, Benin, Ouidah, New Calabar, Bonny, and northern Angola. At the next peak in Old Calabar's trade with Kingston in 1793–1794, agents also sold slaves shipped from Gambia, Rio Nuñez, Iles de Los, Bance Island, Sierra Leone, Cape Mount, Bassa, Cape Coast Castle, Anomabu, Ouidah, Popo, New Calabar, Bonny, Gabon, Melimba, the Congo River, and Ambriz. The great African ethnic diversity in Jamaica's slave population, a diversity seen at the level of individual plantations, developed during the first two generations of British rule in

the island. Trevor Burnard, "The Atlantic Slave Trade and African Ethnicities in Seventeenth-Century Jamaica," in Richardson, Schwarz, and Tibbles, *Liverpool and Transatlantic Slavery*, 142–153.

149. In the mid-1700s Liverpool merchants began purchasing slaves at all African Atlantic markets from the Gambia River to northern Angola. In plantation sectors such as the Chesapeake, supplied first by London and Bristol merchants, Liverpool's move into the region ensured that the distribution of Africans into Maryland and Virginia became more varied geographically. Lorena S. Walsh, "Liverpool's Slave Trade to the Colonial Chesapeake: Slaving on the Periphery," in Richardson, Schwarz, and Tibbles, *Liverpool and Transatlantic Slavery*, 112–113.

150. Geggus, "French Slave Trade," 126–134, 137–138. To help explain specific importation patterns, Geggus focuses on slave prices (and hence on planter preferences for certain African ethnicities and males) and comparative planter wealth (richer sugar planters, poorer coffee and indigo planters). Crop seasons are important also, as French planters were more willing to purchase slaves from less-favored African regions, such as the Bight of Biafra, during crop harvests.

151. With detailed shipping information now available, more and more historians are attempting to "dissect the diaspora into a number of 'different population dispersals and regroupings,'" to examine "diasporic streams" and specific "linkages" or "connections." For "dispersals and regroupings," see Kristin Mann, "Shifting Paradigms in the Study of the African Diaspora and of Atlantic History and Culture," *Slavery and Abolition* 22 (April 2001): 7, quoting a 1996 paper presented by Paul Lovejoy. For "diasporic streams," see James H. Sweet, *Recreating Africa: Culture, Kinship, and Religion in the African-Portuguese World, 1441–1770* (Chapel Hill, N.C., 2003), 13. For "connections," see José C. Curto and Renée Soulodre-La France, "Introduction: Interconnections between Africa and the Americas during the Era of the Slave Trade," in their *Africa and the Americas*, 3; José C. Curto and Paul E. Lovejoy, eds., *Enslaving Connections: Changing Cultures of Africa and Brazil during the Era of Slavery* (Amherst, N.Y., 2004). Scholars looking for African cultural carryovers in the Americas have had more success studying Brazil than colonies in the British slaving world. See Philip D. Morgan, "Cultural Implications of the Atlantic Slave Trade: African Regional Origins, American Destinations and New World Developments," *Slavery and Abolition* 18 (April 1997): 122–145; Burnard, "Atlantic Slave Trade and African Ethnicities," 138–163, and the previously cited works on Brazil.

152. Geggus states that French Caribbean sugarcane planters "preferred Afri-

cans from the Bight of Benin, whose men and women were regarded as robust, good agriculturalists, and capable of taking charge of their own provision grounds." Geggus, "French Slave Trade," 128. British Gold Coast fort administrator John Hippisley believed that the African interior was "quite fruitful and verdant" and "extremely well peopled." He commented on the "populousness of Africa" because he witnessed monthly trades in human cargoes and foodstuffs. John Hippisley, *Essay on the Populousness of Africa* (London, 1764), 3; R. Mansell Prothero, "John Hippisley on the Populousness of Africa: A Comment," *Population and Development Review* 24 (September 1998): 609–612.

153. Commenting on the later British slave trade, Captain John Adams noted that competition on the Gold Coast drove up slave prices, "as to leave but little profit to the merchant, who was compelled to seek a better and cheaper market, which he found on the coast of Angola." Adams, *Remarks on the Country*, 217–218.

2. Kongo and Dahomey, 1660–1815

1. David Eltis, *The Rise of African Slavery in the Americas* (New York, 1999); Hugh Thomas, *The Slave Trade: The Story of the Atlantic Slave Trade, 1440–1870* (New York, 1997); Herbert Klein, *The Atlantic Slave Trade* (New York, 1999); Joseph E. Inikori, Don C. Ohadike, and A. C. Unomah, *The Chaining of a Continent: Export Demand for Captives and the History of Africa South of the Sahara, 1450–1870* (Mona, Jamaica, 1997).

2. Marina de Mello e Sousa, *Reis Negros no Brasil escravista: história da festa de coroação de rei congo* (Belo Horizonte, Brazil, 2002); Elizabeth W Kiddy, *Blacks of the Rosary: Memory and History in Minas Gerais, Brazil* (University Park, Pa., 2005); James H. Sweet, *Recreating Africa: Culture, Kinship, and Religion in the African-Portuguese World, 1441–1770* (Chapel Hill, N.C., 2003).

3. Weber's conception is primarily sociological; different definitions have emerged from other disciplines, including history, political science, and anthropology, and have been the subject of controversy among Africanists.

4. For a discussion of the controversy with regard to the Kingdom of Dahomey, see Robin Law, *The Slave Coast of Africa, 1550–1750: The Impact of the Slave Trade on an African Society* (Oxford, 1991), 70–104, a clear engagement with opponents of the vision of Africa as without states, as contended by Dov Ronen and Robert Ross.

5. Joseph C. Miller, "Central Africa During the Era of the Slave Trade,

1490s–1850s," in *Central Africans and Cultural Transformations in the American Diaspora,* ed. Linda Heywood (New York, 2002), 38–39, 41–42, quotation at 38, based on his interpretation of Jan Vansina, *Paths in the Rainforest: Toward a History of Political Tradition in Equatorial Africa* (Madison, Wisc., 1990), 146–158. In fact, Vansina does not present the image of village strongmen or "lords" as the operational principal of the region after the emergence of what he calls principalities in about 1200. Compare Miller, "Central Africa," 40–43, on Kongo to Vansina, *Paths in the Rainforest,* 155–158.

6. Calculated from the figures for the slave trade, 1680–1810, as presented in Klein, *Atlantic Slave Trade,* table A.1, p. 208. We have suggested that slaves from Kongo and its near neighbors made up about one-third of the West-Central African exports.

7. On the origins of Kongo, see John Thornton, "The Origins and Early History of the Kingdom of Kongo, c. 1350–1550," *International Journal of African Historical Studies* 34, no. 1 (2001): 89–120.

8. In this, Kongo shares features with ancient Muslim polities such as the Empire of Mali, whose heritage was also widely acknowledged in Senegambia and Sierra Leone.

9. Linda M. Heywood and John K. Thornton, *Central Africans, Atlantic Creoles and the Foundation of the Americas* (New York, 2007).

10. Hessisches Hauptstaatsarchiv, 171 Z 4306, Garcia II to Moritz van Nassau, 12 May 1642. The right side of the page in this original letter has been torn, obscuring some words of the titles, which can be restored by resorting to the Dutch translation of the same letter in Nationaal Archief Nederland, Oud West Indische Compagnie, 58 (no pagination).

11. Olifert Dapper, *Naukeurige beschrijvinge van Africa gewesten* (Amsterdam, 1668), 582.

12. Garcia II to Moritz van Nassau, 12 May 1642.

13. Decree of Garcia II, 19 Sept. 1648, in *Monumenta Missionaria Africana,* ed. António Brásio, 1st ser., 15 vols. (Lisbon, 1952–1988), 10:245.

14. John Thornton, *The Kingdom of Kongo: Civil War and Transition, 1641–1718* (Madison, Wisc., 1983), 38–55, for detailed discussion of the structure of the Kongo state and its rebellions, particularly during the reign of Garcia II.

15. Ibid.

16. Academia das Ciências de Lisboa (hereafter, ACL), MS Vermelho 296, "Viagem do Congo do Missioario Fr. Raphael de Castello de Vide, hoje Bispo de S. Thomé," 127 (this text comprises copies of four letters, dated 16 July 1781, 25 Sept. 1782, 29 Nov. 1783, 15 Sept. 1788).

17. Ibid., 151.

18. Raimondo da Dicomano, "Informazione sul regno del Congo . . . ," 1798, fol. 7, in António Brásio, "Documentario," *Studia* 34 (1972), original pagination marked. See also Governor of Angola, Manuel de Almeida e Vasconcelos, to Minister of Marine, 1794, in Carlo Toso, "'L'informazione sul Regno de Congo' di Raimondo da Dicomano," *L'Italia Francescana* (Rome, 1977), 90.

19. Marcellino d'Atri, "Giornate apostoliche fatte da me Fra Marcellino . . . nelle Messione del regni d'Angola e Congo . . ." (MS of 1702) in *L'anarchia congolese nel sec. XVII: la relazione inedita di Marcellino d'Atri*, ed. Carlo Toso (Genoa, 1984); this edition marks the original pagination, p. 139. The appearance of the word "emperor" in royal titles may suggest the advent of the Kikongo term *ntotila* as the title of the ruler, joining *ntinu*, which appears to be the earlier term. The root of *ntotila* contains the sense of gathering together and uniting.

20. Cherubino da Savona, "Congo 1775: Breve Raguaglio del Regno di Congo, e sue Missione scritto dal Padre Cherubino da Savona . . . ," at fol. 41, published, with original foliation marked, in Carlo Toso, "Relazioni inedite di P. Cherubono Cassinis da Savona sul 'Regno del Congo e sue Missioni,'" in *L'Italia Francescana*.

21. ACL, MS Vermelho 296, Castello de Vide, "Viagem," 130. The original of the first of the four letters (see note 15) is in Arquivo Histórico Ultramarino (Lisbon), Angola (hereafter, AHU), caixa [cx.] 64, doc. 56, and printed in *Annes do Conselho Ultramarino* 2 (1859–1860): 62–80; AHU, cx. 70, doc. 8, Afonso V to Governor of Angola, 11 April 1788.

22. Garcia V to Governor of Angola, 6 July 1803, in *Arquivos de Angola*, 2d ser., 19 (1962): 58; Garcia V to Governor of Angola, 1814, French edition and translation in Louis Jadin, "Recherches dans les archives et Bibliotheques de Italie et du Portugal sur l'ancien Congo," *Bulletin des séances, Academie royale des sciences coloniales* 2 (1956).

23. Da Savona, "Congo," fol. 42; AHU, cx. 50, doc. 65, Francisco Innocencio de Souza Coutinho to King, 4 March 1766.

24. Da Savona, "Congo," fols. 42–44.

25. ACL, MS Vermelho 296, Castello de Vide, "Viagem," 73.

26. Da Savona, "Congo" (1755), in António Brásio, "O problema de eleição e coroação dos Reis do Congo," *História e Missiológia: Ineditors e esparsos* (Luanda, 1973), 380.

27. Dapper, *Naukeurige Beschrijvinge*, 572.

28. John K. Thornton, *The Kongolese Saint Anthony: Dona Beatriz Kimpa Vita and the Antonian Movement, 1684–1706* (New York, 1998).

29. "Como veio a fe de Christo . . . ," published in *Boletim Oficial de Colonia de Angola* (1858).

30. The clan mottos, collected for the most part in the 1920s (though from older manuscript material in some cases) were edited by Jean Cuvelier, *Nkutama a mvila za makanda,* 4th ed. (1934; Matadi, Congo, 1972), 70 (for the motto relating to Afonso and his mother).

31. He adopted the title Redeemer because he had defeated the heretical Antonian movement; see Thornton, *Kongolese Saint Anthony.*

32. Pedro IV to Bernardo da Gallo, 28 March 1709, in Toso, "Relazioni inedite."

33. Manuel II to Giuseppe da Modena, 10 July 1723, in Jadin, "Recherches . . . sur l'ancien Congo," 396.

34. AHU, cx. 70, doc. 8, Afonso V.

35. Archivio de Propaganda Fide, Scritture Referite nelli Congressi, Congo (hereafter, APF: SRC Congo, 5), fols. 181–181v, Bernardino Ignazio d'Asti to Propaganda Fide, 12 Oct. 1749. Muconde was probably not her name, but the name of her province, Mukondo, which was traditionally a district ruled by a woman who had the title queen.

36. Da Savona, "Congo," passim.

37. ACL, MS Vermelho 296, Castello de Vide, "Viagem," 131–132.

38. Ibid., 127.

39. Ibid., 79–80.

40. Ibid., 127–128.

41. APF: SRC Congo, 5, fols. 230–230v, "Catalogo delle Missionari e PP auificanarii, che atualmte asistono in questi due Regni di Congo e Angola . . . 15 Dec. 1752." For an earlier assessement see d'Atri, "Giornate apostoliche fatte da me Fra Marcellino," passim.

42. Da Dicomano, "Informazione," fol. 2v.

43. APF: SRC Congo, 5, fol. 299v [Rosario del Parco]; "Informazione del Regno di Congo ed Angola," 1760.

44. Klein, *Atlantic Slave Trade,* table A.1, pp. 208–209.

45. John Thornton, "As guerras civis no Congo e o tráfico de escravos: a história e a demografia de 1718 a 1844 revisitadas," *Estudos Afro-Asiáticos* 32 (1997): 55–74, at 66–67.

46. The fullest treatment of Dahomey's origins is in Law, *Slave Coast.*

47. The authenticity of the document was questioned almost as soon as it reached England, and there has been considerable modern discussion of it. We have followed Robin Law's argument that, while the letter may not have been entirely authentic, it probably did represent Agaja's ideol-

ogy; see Robin Law, "Further Light on Bullfinch Lambe and the 'Emperor of Pawpaw': King Agaja of Dahomey's Letter to King George I of England, 1726," *History in Africa* 17 (1990): 211–216. Law prints a facsimile of the letter published in *The Parliamentary History of England* (1816), and we have followed its pagination.

48. Agaja to George I, Jan. 1726 from *Parliamentary History of England,* printed in Law, "Further Light," 84–85, spelling as in the original (which should be attributed to Lambe rather than to Agaja).

49. Pierre Verger, *Fluxo e refluxo do tráfico de escravos entre o Golfo do Benin e a Bahia de Todos os Santos dos séculos XVII a XIX* (Salvador, 2000), 283.

50. The chronicle was incorporated and published in Archibald Dalzel's *History of Dahomy, an Inland Kingdom of Africa* (London, 1793). John Adams, *Remarks on the Country extending from Cape Palmas to the River Congo* (1823; London, 1966), 52–55, thought of Abson as "more an Dahomean than a European" and that he spoke Fon fluently and had polygamous marriages into the Dahomean elite. Abson was very much a client of the king, being constantly in attendance at court, and was widely believed to put Dahomean interests above those of the English or other Europeans. We are thus inclined to believe his chronicle was a favored official view of the country's history during those years, though the printed version (edited by Dalzel for a European audience and to support the slave trade) makes snide asides and criticisms of Dahomey and the king.

51. Robert Norris, *Memoirs of the Reign of Bossa Ahádee, King of Dahomey an Inland Country of Guiney* (1789; London, 1968), 154–155.

52. Abson's Chronicle as printed in Dalzel, *History of Dahomy,* 181.

53. Ibid., 182.

54. Ibid., 217.

55. Ibid., 226.

56. As noted, Dalzel used the chronicle to show the warlike nature of Africans in the debate over the slave trade. Adandozan's letter, written for very different purposes, however, shows that the warrior chronicle was a favored genre and makes Abson's account seem more likely to reflect Dahomean rulers' interests.

57. Instituto Histórico e Geografico Brasileiro (IHGB), lata 137, pasta 62, Adandozan to King João of Portugal, 9 Oct. 1810, fols. 1–3, 5v–6.

58. William Snelgrave, *New Account of Some Parts of Guinea, and the Slave Trade* (London 1734), 129.

59. Law, *Slave Coast,* 327, quoting Pruneau and Guestard from the Archives Nationales de France.

60. Law, *Slave Coast,* 330.

61. Norris, *Memoirs,* 8.

62. Agaja to George I, 86.

63. Ibid., 87.

64. Ibid., 88.

65. Law, *Slave Coast,* 331–332.

66. Agaja to George I, 85.

67. Norris, *Memoirs,* 86.

68. Norris, *Memoirs,* and reprinted by Dalzel, *History of Dahomy,* 107–108.

69. Alberto da Costa e Silva, "Mémoria histórica sobre os cosumtes particulars dos Povos Africanos, com relação privativa ao Reino de Guiné, e nele com respeito ao Rei de Daomé, de Luís António de Oliveira Mendes," *Afro-Asia* 28 (2002): 251–292, original foliation marked, fol. 30.

70. Vicente Ferreira Pires, *Viagem de África em o Reino de Dahomé,* ed. Claudo Ribeiro de Lessa (São Paulo, 1957), 47–48.

71. Pires, *Viagem,* 77.

72. Dalzel, *History of Dahomy,* ix.

73. Oliveira Mendes, "Memoria," fol. 30.

74. Agaja to George I, 90.

75. Ibid.

76. Arquivo Publico do Estatdo de Bahia (APEB), Secção Colonial, Correspondência Recebida de Autoridades Diversas, maço 197, cx. 76, doc. 1, Agonglo to Governor of Bahia, 31 March 1790.

77. Ibid.

78. IHGB, Lata 137, pasta 62, doc. 1, Adandozan to King of Portugal, n.d. [ca. 1810].

79. APEB, Secção Colonial, Correspondência Recebida de Autoridades Diversas, maço 197, cx. 76, doc. 2, Agonglo to Fernando José, n.d. [ca. 1796].

80. Dalzel, *History of Dahomy,* 217–219, as reported in Abson's chronicle.

81. Pires, *Viagem,* 100.

82. Oliveira Mendes, "Memoria," fol. 30.

83. The Dahomean gods are described in detail in Pires, *Viagem,* 87–94.

84. On the incorporation of deities of conquered regions, see Law, *Slave Coast,* 333–334.

85. Agaja to King George I, 85.

86. Ibid., 88.

87. Adandozan to João Carlos de Bragança, 20 Nov. 1804, in Verger, *Fluxo*, 311.

88. For a full discussion of the early politics and relations, see Heywood and Thornton, *Central Africans, Atlantic Creoles*.

89. Ibid.; Linda Heywood, "Portuguese into African: The Eighteenth-Century Central African Background to Atlantic Creole Cultures," in Heywood, *Central Africans and Cultural Transformations*, 91–113, and Heywood, "The Angolan-Afro-Brazilian Cultural Connections," *Slavery and Abolition* 20 (April 1999): 9–23.

90. François-Joseph Pamphile de Lacroix, *Mémoires pour server à la revolution de Saint-Domingue*, 2 vols. (Paris, 1819), 1:253.

91. Suchou de Rennefort, *Histoire des Indes Orientales* (Paris, 1688), 208–209.

92. "De Statu Regni Congi," Brásio, *Monumenta* 3:505.

93. Henry Koster, *Travels in Brazil* (London, 1816), 273.

94. AHU Codice 1303, "Compromisso da Irmandade de Nossa Senhora dos Homens Pretos da Vila do Recife," 1782.

95. Koster, *Travels*, 274.

96. De Mello e Souza, *Reis Negros no Brasil escravista;* Marcelo McCord, *O Rosário de D. Antônio: Irmandades negras, alianças e conflitos na história social do Recife, 1848–1872* (Recife, 2005).

97. Arquivo Nacional Torre de Tombo, Inquisição de Lisboa, Processo 16001, pp. 2–3. For a discussion of this incident see Sweet, *Recreating Africa*.

98. Christian Georg Andreas Oldendorp, *Historie der caribischen Inseln Sanct Thomas, Sanct Crux und Sanct Jan: Kommentierte Edition des Originalmaunskriptes*, ed. Gundrun Meier et al., 4 vols. (Berlin, 2000–2002) 1:741–742.

99. Luiz Mott, *Rosa Egipcíaca: uma santa africana no Brasil* (Rio de Janeiro, 1993), 13; Will of Joana Machado, 6 March 1782, quoted from archival sources in Ouro Preto in Rodrigo Castro Rezende, "Africanos, Crioulos e Mestiços: a população de cor em algumas localidades mineiras no século XVIII e a construção de suas identidades," paper presented at XV Encontro Internacional das Populacionais, 18–22 Sept. 2006, available online at www.abep.nepo.unicamp.br. Castro Rezende contends that all the local identities were imposed by non-Africans, though in this case it seems more likely that a particular sovereign locality is intended.

100. Robin Law, "Ethnicities of Enslaved Africans in the Diaspora: On the Meanings of 'Mina' (Again)," *History in Africa* 32 (2005): 247–267.

101. Dalzel, *History of Dahomy*, introduction, v.

102. For the vocabulary, see Yeda Pessoa de Castro, *Falares africanos na Bahia: um vocabulário afro-brasileiro* (Rio de Janeiro, 2001), and a letter written by Africans from Dahomey in the Danish West Indies to the queen of Denmark in Ewe-Fon and Creole versions, in which the Ewe-Fon was the same as the Mina language in Brazil. In the Ewe-Fon version of the letter, they wrote, "Cabe my le ad ga Tome," while in the Creole version the words are, "Die tyd mi a wes na Poppo op Africa" (When I was in Dahomey/Poppo in Africa . . .). Both are printed in *Büdingische Sammlung einiger in die Kirchen-Historie* 1, no. 4 (1741): 485–487.

103. Mariza de Carvalho Soares, "A 'nação' que se tem e a 'terra' de onde se vem: categorias de inserção social de africanos no imperio português, século XVIII," *Estudos Afro-Asiaticos* 26 (2004): 303–330.

3. The Triumphs of Mercury

1. Daniel Rodgers, *Atlantic Crossings: Social Politics in a Progressive Age* (Cambridge, Mass., 1989), makes a case for the oceanic community being remarkably unified between 1875 and 1925. Jeffrey Williamson and Kevin O'Rourke argue much the same, and use the economists' test of price convergence to prove it. Kevin H. O'Rourke and Jeffrey G. Williamson, *Globalization and History: The Evolution of a Nineteenth-Century Atlantic Economy* (Cambridge, Mass., 1999), which builds upon several important papers and articles, including: Jeffrey G. Williamson, Kevin H. O'Rourke, and Timothy J. Hatton, "Mass Migration, Commodity Market Integration and Real Wage Convergence: The Late Nineteenth Century Atlantic Economy," National Bureau of Economic Research (NBER) Working Paper Series, Historical Working Paper 48 (1993); Kevin H. O'Rourke and Jeffrey G. Williamson, "When Did Globalization Begin?" Working Paper 7632 (2000), and Ronald Findlay and Kevin H. O'Rourke, "Commodity Market Integration, 1500–2000, Working Paper 8579 (2001), both in NBER Working Paper Series; Kevin H. O'Rourke and Jeffrey G. Williamson, "After Columbus: Explaining Europe's Overseas Trade Boom, 1500–1800," *Journal of Economic History* 62 (June 2002): 417–456.

2. George Day Welsh to ———, 13 March 1815, Private Collection, Funchal, Madeira. Welsh was born in Barbados but after 1783 had transferred his allegiance to the United States. In 1809, he was denied membership in Madeira's British Factory, in the precedent-making resolution that "no American subject can ever become a Member of this Factory."

Minutes of the British Factory, 21 Nov., 15 Dec. 1809, Blue Sea Chest, Blandy's Head Office, Funchal, Madeira.

3. Men and women began to think and act across the globe as well, although through 1815 the Atlantic remained the more important arena for connection.

4. On volumes of sugar and rum leaving the West Indies: John J. McCusker, *Rum and the American Revolution: The Rum Trade and the Balance of Payments of the Thirteen Continental Colonies*, 2 vols. (New York, 1981), 1:143–144, 208–209, 316, 329, and 2:891–895, 899–901, 905–906, 918–919, 939–944, 960–961; and McCusker, ed., *Essays in the Economic History of the Atlantic World* (London, 1997), chs. 7–8. For the numbers of ships, see Kenneth Morgan, *Bristol and the Atlantic Trade in the Eighteenth Century* (Cambridge, 1993); Christopher J. French, "The Trade and Shipping of the Port of London, 1700–1776" (Ph.D. diss., University of Exeter, 1980). The increase in London's sugar fleet can be surmised by comparing London marine lists for 1702–1704 and 1802–1804; bills of entry chronicling ships' cargoes do not survive in any significant continuous run for London, but comparison could be made to Bristol bills of entry for 1748 and 1780. The bills and lists are chronicled and described in McCusker, *European Bills of Entry and Marine Lists: Early Commercial Publications and the Origins of the Business Press* (New York, 1985), 36, 43, 52, 56–57, and "The Business Press in England before 1775," in McCusker, *Essays,* 162–167. The evolution of function can be glimpsed by comparing trade directories from the 1690s, the 1740s, and the 1790s. On the evolution of traders and their functions, not only growth but consolidation, generally, see Jacob M. Price and Paul G. E. Clemens, "A Revolution in Scale in Overseas Trade: British Firms in the Chesapeake Trade," *Journal of Economic History* 47 (March 1987): 1–43.

5. On technical innovation in British West Indian sugar planting, see J. R. Ward, *British West Indian Slavery, 1750–1834: The Process of Amelioration* (Oxford, 1988), 61–118, 261–273; in sugar refining, see Noel Deer, *The History of Sugar,* 2 vols. (London, 1949–1950); in rum distilling, see John McCusker, "The Business of Distilling in the Old World and the New World during the Seventeenth and Eighteenth Centuries," in *The Early Modern Atlantic Economy,* ed. John J. McCusker and Kenneth Morgan (New York, 2000), 204–211.

6. David J. Hancock, "Commerce and Conversation in the Eighteenth-Century Atlantic: The Invention of Madeira Wine," *Journal of Interdisciplinary History* 29 (Autumn 1998): 197–219.

7. Alan McGowan, *Tiller and Whipstaff—The Development of the Sailing Ship, 1400–1700* (London, 1981), and *The Century before Steam: The Development of the Sailing Ship, 1700–1820* (London, 1980).

8. David Hancock, "'A World of Business to Do': William Freeman and the Foundations of England's Commercial Empire," *William and Mary Quarterly,* 3d ser., 57 (January 2000): 3–34.

9. David Hancock, *Oceans of Wine: Madeira and the Organization of the Atlantic World, 1640–1815* (New Haven, Conn., 2009), chs. 5–6.

10. Ian K. Steele, *The English Atlantic: An Exploration of Communication and Community* (Oxford, 1986); Douglass C. North, "Sources of Productivity Change in Ocean Shipping, 1600–1850," *Journal of Political Economy* 76 (September–October 1968): 953–970; Gary M. Walton, "Sources of Productivity in American Colonial Shipping, 1675–1775," *Economic History Review,* 2d ser., 20 (1967): 76; Richard F. Dell, "The Operational Record of the Clyde Tobacco Fleet, 1747–1775," *Scottish Economic and Social History* 2 (1982): 7–8, 12; John M. Hemphill II, "Freight Rates in the Maryland Tobacco Trade, 1705–1762," *Maryland Historical Magazine* 54 (June 1959): 36–58, 153–187; Russell R. Menard, "Transport Costs and Long-Range Trade, 1300–1800," in *The Political Economy of Merchant Empires: State Power and World Trade, 1350–1750,* ed. James D. Tracy (New York, 1991), 228–275, esp. 254, 265, 268; Gary Walton, "Quantitative Study of American Colonial Shipping" (Ph.D. diss., University of Washington, 1966).

11. Jack Greene, *Negotiated Authorities: Essays in Colonial Political and Constitutional History* (Charlottesville, Va., 1994), 16, 23–24; Frederick Cooper, *Colonialism in Question: Theory, Knowledge, History* (Berkeley, Calif., 2005), 197.

12. On the state's control, see Michael Mann, "The Autonomous Power of the State: Its Origins, Mechanisms and Results," in *States in History,* ed. John A. Hall (Oxford, 1986), 122–123; John Brewer, "The Eighteenth-Century British State: Contexts and Issues," in *An Imperial State at War: Britain, from 1689 to 1815,* ed. Lawrence Stone (London, 1994), 65. Examples regarding early modern history as state history include: Brewer, *The Sinews of Power: War, Money, and the English State, 1688–1783* (New York, 1988), xi, xv–xvi, 252; John McCusker and Russell Menard, *The Economy of British America, 1607–1789* (Chapel Hill, N.C., 1985), 71–90, 331–350; Phyllis Deane, *The State and the Economic System* (New York, 1989); Daniel Baugh, "Maritime Strength and Atlantic Commerce: The Uses of 'A Grand Marine Empire,' " in Stone, *An Imperial State at War,* 188–194; Peter Miller, *Defining the Common*

Good (Cambridge, 1994); Christopher Bayly, "The First Age of Global Imperialism, c. 1760–1830," *Journal of Imperial and Commonwealth History* 26 (May 1998): 28–47.

13. Economists have long emphasized the role of decentralized markets in linking traders in their model of the world, and their work has highlighted other aspects of decentralization. The Viennese-born economist Friedrich von Hayek was among the early proponents of the idea that markets are successful because they aggregate dispersed agents' local and particular information. Friedrich A. von Hayek, "The Use of Knowledge in Society," *American Economic Review* 35 (September 1945): 519–530. Despite the fact that economists today are more skeptical of the informational efficiency of markets than Hayek was, the picture he painted—of dispersed buyers and sellers, acting in ignorance of each other and each other's information, using prices to infer the relative value of goods, and making decisions for themselves rather than by referring to a central monitor or authority—remains their canonical model. Even when the model only partially characterizes the historical reality, "decentralized decision-making processes" enabled "societies to maximize the efforts to explore alternative ways of solving problems." Douglass North, *Institutions, Institutional Change and Economic Performance* (New York, 1990), 80–81.

14. Richard Pares, *A West-India Fortune* (London, 1950), ch. 1; Hancock, *Oceans of Wine*, ch. 4.

15. Christopher Bayly, *Empire and Information: Intelligence Gathering and Social Communication in India, 1780–1870* (Cambridge, 1996); Michel Callon, "Some Elements of a Sociology of Translation: Domestication of the Scallops and the Fishermen of St Brieuc Bay," in *Power, Action and Belief: A New Sociology of Knowledge,* ed. John Law (London, 1986). The meaning of "network"—and so of "network analysis"—is at best imprecise, having been applied to a multiplicity of operations and situations at various times. Robert G. Eccles and Nitin Nohria, *Beyond the Hype: Rediscovering the Essence of Management* (Boston, 1992), 25–26. On the lack of a distinct, general theory, see Amalya L. Oliver and Mark Ebers, "Networking Network Studies: An Analysis of Conceptual Configurations in the Study of Inter-organizational Relationships," *Organization Studies* 19, no. 4 (1998): 549–583. Cf. Walter W. Powell and Laurel Smith-Doerr, "Networks and Economic Life," in *The Handbook of Economic Sociology,* ed. Neil J. Smelser and Richard Swedberg (Princeton, N.J., 1994), 368–402; Silvia Marzagalli, "The Establishment of a Transatlantic Trade Network: Bordeaux and the United States,

1783–1815," Working Paper no. 03006, Atlantic History Seminar, Harvard University, 2003, pp. 2–3; David Hancock, "The Trouble with Networks: Managing the Scots' Early-Modern Madeira Trade," *Business History Review* 79 (Autumn 2005): 467–492; Rosalind J. Beiler, "Dissenting Religious Communication Networks and European Migration, 1660–1710," this volume, note 4. The scholarship that deploys network analysis is voluminous: Jacob R. Marcus, *Early American Jewry* (Philadelphia, Pa., 1951); Bernard Farber, *Guardians of Virtue* (New York, 1972); Jerome H. Wood, Jr., *Conestoga Crossroads: Lancaster, Pennsylvania, 1730–1790* (Harrisburg, Pa., 1979), 93–112; Lorena S. Walsh, "Community Networks in the Early Chesapeake," in *Colonial Chesapeake Society*, ed. Lois G. Carr et al. (Chapel Hill, N.C., 1988), 200–241; Darrett Rutman and Anita Rutman, *A Place in Time: Middlesex County, Virginia, 1650–1750* (New York, 1984); Peter Bearman, *Relations into Rhetoric: Local Elite Social Structure in Norfolk England, 1540–1640* (New Brunswick, N.J., 1993); John Padgett and Christopher Ansell, "Robust Action and the Rise of the Medici," *American Journal of Sociology* 98 (May 1993): 1259–1319; Paul M. Hohenberg et al., *The Making of Urban Europe, 1000–1994* (Cambridge, Mass., 1995); Leos Müller, *The Merchant Houses of Stockholm, c. 1640–1800: A Comparative Study of Early-Modern Entrepreneurial Behavior* (Uppsala, 1998); R. Darrell Meadows, "Engineering Exile: Social Networks and the French Atlantic Community, 1789–1809," *French Historical Studies* 23 (Winter 2000): 67–102.

16. Business and trade lend themselves well to network analysis, given the detailed people- and place-oriented written accounts they produce. Good business histories have built their arguments around it: Mary B. Rose, *Firms, Networks and Business Values: The British and American Cotton Industries since 1750* (Cambridge, 2000); Silvia Marzagalli, *Les boulevards de la fraude: le negoce maritime et le Blocus continental, 1806–1813* (Villeneuve d'Ascq, 1999); Nuala Zahedieh, "Credit, Risk and Reputation in Late Seventeenth-Century Colonial Trade," *Research in Maritime History* 15 (1998): 53–74; Gillian Cookson, "Family Firms and Business Networks: Textile Engineering in Yorkshire, 1780–1830," *Business History* 39 (January 1997): 1–20. From such case-study discussion, a rudimentary general "theory" is emerging: Duncan J. Watts, *Small Worlds: The Dynamics of Networks between Order and Randomness* (Princeton, N.J., 1999); John F. Padgett, "Multiple Networks and Multiple Discourses," Santa Fe Institute Program, 1998, unpub. paper; Eric R. Wolf, "Kinship, Friendship, and Patron-Client Relations in

Complex Societies," in *The Social Anthropology of Complex Societies,* ed. Michael Banton (London, 1966), 1–22.

17. W. Ross Ashby, "Principles of the Self-Organizing Dynamic System," *Journal of General Psychology* 37 (1947): 125–128, and *Design for a Brain: The Origin of Adaptive Behavior,* 2d ed. (New York, 1960). The concept is grounded in the study of complex systems, also known as nonlinear, dynamical, adaptive, or networked systems. The most accessible introductions are: Roger Lewin, *Complexity: Life at the Edge of Chaos* (New York, 1992), and Grégoire Nicolis and Ilya Prigogine, *Exploring Complexity* (New York, 1989). On wider applicability, see W. Brian Arthur, "Inductive Reasoning and Bonded Rationality," and Paul Krugman, "Complex Landscapes in Economic Geography," both in *American Economic Review: Papers and Proceedings* 84 (May 1994): 406–411, 412–416; John H. Holland, "The Global Economy as an Adaptive Process," in *The Economy as an Evolving Complex System,* ed. Philip W. Anderson, Kenneth J. Arrow, and David Pines (Redwood City, Calif., 1987), 117–118.

18. Middletown is nowadays most famous as the site of the Three Mile Island nuclear power plant disaster in 1979. Frey's personal and business papers, hereafter designated simply as Frey Papers, are now privately held in Middletown.

19. Birth Register, Glatten Kirch (now part of the city of Sulz-am-Neckar), Freudenstadt, Württemberg, Germany: Johannes Georg Eberhardt, b. March 1, 1732; Anna Catharina Späth, who would marry Frey, b. August 10, 1730; *Pennsylvania Gazette,* 5 Oct. 1749; I. Daniel Rupp, *A Collection of Upwards of Thirty Thousand Names of German, Swiss, Dutch, French and Other Immigrants in Pennsylvania from 1727 to 1776,* 2d ed. (Philadelphia, Pa., 1876), 216 (Georg Eberharth, arriving in Philadelphia from Württemberg, via Amsterdam and Shields, on the ship *Jacob,* October 2, 1749, and swearing oath as Georg Eberhardt); Edward W. Hocker, *Genealogical Data Relating to the German Settlers of Pennsylvania and Adjacent Territory* (Baltimore, Md., 1980), 10, 15, 24; Ralph B. Strassburger, *Pennsylvania German Pioneers,* ed. William J. Hinke, 3 vols. (Norristown, Pa., 1934), 1:418 (Georg Eberhardt, taking an oath of loyalty to the government, at the State House). On immigration into Philadelphia in 1749, see Marianne S. Wokeck, *Trade in Strangers: The Beginnings of Mass Migration to North America* (University Park, Pa., 1999), 40, 44–45, 242. Wokeck estimates the number aboard the *Jacob* to be about 250, not 290.

20. On the grant of the land to the Fishers, see *Pennsylvania Archives,*

3d ser., 24:409–410: John Fisher receiving 691 acres from the colony pro-
prietors in February 1747; Warrant Register, Lancaster County, 16:66;
George Frey, Warrant and Survey Book, fols. 62–65, 97–100, Am. 294,
Historical Society of Pennsylvania (hereafter, HSP), Philadelphia. The
Fisher family is chronicled in Anna W. Smith, *Genealogy of the Fisher
Family, 1682 to 1896* (Philadelphia, Pa., 1896), 20, 35–36; copy of will of
George Fisher, George Fisher II Correspondence, 1801–1851, MG 68,
Pennsylvania State Archives (hereafter, PSA), Harrisburg. A comple-
mentary but not always accurate or unbiased source on Eberhardt and
the Fishers is the memoir of George Fisher, the son of the man who
granted Frey his lots and whose reminiscence is printed in C. H. Hutchinson, *The Chronicles of Middletown* (Middletown, Pa., 1906), 63–67.

21. Hocker, *Genealogical Data*, 10, 15, 24; Hutchinson, *Chronicles*, 63–64.
On redemption, see Wokeck, *Trade in Strangers*, 150–151.

22. Land warrant, granting 100 acres in Heidelberg Township, Berkshire
County, to John George Ehrhard, Ehrhard Baum Gartel, and Lodowick
Engel, 16 Oct. 1754, fol. 110, Proprietaries' Warrant Register, 1752–
1759, Records of the Bureau of Land Records, RG 17, PSA.

23. Charles F. Snyder, "The Penn's Creek Massacre," *Northumberland County
Historical Society Proceedings* 11 (1939): 147–173; William Schnure,
Selinsgrove Chronology, 2 vols. (Selinsgrove, Pa., 1918), 1:10; George F.
Dunkelberger, *The Story of Snyder County* (Selinsgrove, Pa., 1948), 81,
161. For mention by Frey, see Survey and Warrant Book, fol. 22, Am.
294, HSP.

24. For a brief account in Frey's own words, see Caveat of George Frey, entered into the Land Office on 7 April 1773; Survey and Warrant Book of
George Frey, fol. 22, Frey Papers.

25. The name may also have been given by a fellow German settler of the
same name who died without an heir in an earlier frontier massacre and
made Eberhardt his heir. As this account suggests, there is some confusion over name and identity. A Johan Eberhardt was in the area through
September 1755. A George Eberhard was living in the same area and was
said to have died with his family from an earlier massacre on October 5.
Yet, on October 20, a Georg Aberheart and a Georg Fry were said to
have survived the October 16 massacre. George Fry died the following year. *Minutes of the Provincial Council of Pennsylvania* (Harrisburg,
Pa., 1851), 6:648; Dunkelberger, *Story of Snyder County*, 81, 161, 164–
166, 214–215, 225; cf. Richard K. MacMaster, *Conscience in Crisis: Mennonites and Other Peace Churches in America, 1739–1789* (Scottdale,
Pa., 1979), 123, doc. 41, quoting *Pennsylvania Archives*, 8th ser., 5:3857–

3859. And a Georg Eberhardt was a sergeant in the militia in 1757. Georg Eberhardt (Heidelberg Township) to Conrad Weiser, 1 July 1757, Conrad Weiser Correspondence, 2:75, HSP. Finally, there is the chance that a John Everhart had previously lived under the name Bastian Remus, who married one Anna Maria, whom he abandoned before 1755, and who thereafter "passed under the name of John Everhart." *Pennsylvania Gazette,* 1 June 1758. The reconstruction offered here seems the most logical, inasmuch as it agrees with George Frey's later recollection and the greatest number of independent accounts.

26. Debra D. Smith and Frederick S. Weiser, eds., *Trinity Lutheran Church Records: Lancaster, Pennsylvania* (Apollo, Pa., 1995), 1:250, no. 115 (28 Dec. 1756). Anna Catharina Späth was born in Böffingen, Württemberg, on August 10, 1730, a daughter of Hans George Späth and Anna Maria Meyer, who had arrived in Lancaster in 1752. The father died right before the marriage. Frey Papers.

27. Frey does not appear on the Lancaster Borough tax rolls of 1750–1751, 1754–1755, or 1756–1757, but he does appear in 1759. At least three John Freys (Frey/Frei/Free) appear on Lancaster Borough tax lists that year: a butcher, a laborer, and a single man with no stated occupation. Frey does not appear on Lancaster County tax rolls of 1750, 1751, 1756, and 1759. The first county roll that lists him (and none exists for the 1760s) is 1771, when he owned 100 acres, a horse, and a cow, and paid the largest tax in Middletown; the following year, he paid the largest tax, and owned another cow. Tax Lists, Lancaster Borough, 1750–1751, 1754, 1756–1757, 1759; William H. Egle, ed., *Provincial Papers: Proprietary and State Tax Lists* (Harrisburg, Pa., ca. 1898). In the early years of using the surname "Frey," our subject sometimes used a first name of John (Johan), sometimes John (Johan) Georg(e), and sometimes Georg(e).

28. Advertisement, 9 Dec. 1776, Copy Book of Letters A (1773–1778), fol. 135, Frey Papers. On vacating Lot 98 for Lot 84 in 1768, Frey rented 98 out to the storekeeper John Williams, who during the early 1770s worked as a junior partner to Randle and John Mitchell of Philadelphia. The structure is described in detail in January 1774 when the Mitchells pulled out of backcountry trading and put the store up for sale. *Pennsylvania Gazette,* 10 Nov. 1773, 5 Jan. 1774. After acquiring Lots 87 and 88 along High Street, Frey owned nearly half of the entire block formed by Main, Pine, High, and Cross Streets.

29. On his own holdings, see Egle, *Provincial Papers: Proprietary and State Tax Lists, sub* Middletown for 1771, 1772, 1779, 1789, 1795, 1795–1799; *Pennsylvania Gazette,* 11 July 1781 (Upper Paxton Township, 300 acres).

On his management of the 300 acres he and four others acquired from Fisher, see Articles of Agreement, 26 Jan. 1765, Survey and Warrant Book, fols. 100–103, HSP. They paid £1,050 current *in toto* by January 12, 1772. In effect, Frey was landlord of 15% of the 276 town lots. On speculations, see *Pennsylvania Gazette*, 22 June (Lancaster), 9 Nov. (Northumberland) 1774, 26 Dec. 1781 (for 1773: Penn's Township, Northumberland, John Frey, 200 acres; Bald Eagle Township, Northumberland, George Frey, 1,100 acres; for 1774: Bald Eagle Township, Northumberland, George Fry, 1,800 acres; for 1776: Bald Eagle Township, Northumberland, George Frey, 1,200 acres), 9 April 1783 (Northumberland, George Frey, 1,550 acres), 28 May 1783 (Newbury Township, York). Cf. Survey and Warrant Book, fols. 34, 37, 51, 55, 58, 91, 123, 124, HSP.

30. As early as 1760, awareness of the possibility of developing a mill there existed. *Pennsylvania Gazette*, 6 Nov. 1760. Others were moving into milling at the same time Frey was considering it. In September 1775, Jehu Hollingsworth of Chester County, the twin of Frey's future partner John Hollingsworth of Newcastle County, and a third cousin of his agent Levi Hollingsworth of Philadelphia, was selling a tract of land on which he had erected a three-story, 32 × 40–foot limestone grist and shelling mill, "with three pair of stones and two [20-foot-high] water wheels . . . and a large dam," the previous spring. The mill could grind ten bushels a day. *Pennsylvania Gazette*, 27 Sept. 1775.

31. Warrant and Survey Book, fols. 127 (16 Feb. 1783), 131 (20 Dec. 1784), 144 (21 Dec. 1784), 145 (22 March 1785), HSP; Anon., "John Penn's Journal of a Visit to Reading, Harrisburg, Carlisle, and Lancaster, in 1788," *Pennsylvania Magazine* 3 (1879): 293–294; *Pennsylvania Packet*, 10 Oct. 1789; *Laws of the Commonwealth of Pennsylvania*, 3 vols. (Philadelphia, Pa., 1793–1797), 2:712–713 (1789).

32. On Frey's mid- and late-1760s purchasing, see Ledger B (1765–1773), Frey Papers. On Shippen & Burd's specialty retailing, see James Burd Account Book, Lancaster, April 1765–May 1769, 1: fol. 114, James Burd Business Records and Accounts, and Edward Shippen to James Burd, 4 Dec. 1766, 22 Jan., 9 June 1768; cf. 4 Dec. 1766, 29 May, 4 Aug. 1767 for loans of Frey's wagon to Shippen & Burd, Edward Shippen of Lancaster Letter Books, American Philosophical Society, Philadelphia (hereafter, APS). For activity in the 1770s, see Copy Book of Letters A, passim, Frey Papers.

33. Survey and Warrant Book of George Frey, Am 294, HSP; Ground Rent Book, 1770–1800, and Copy Book of Letters C (1781–1786), fols. 73–75;

Lancaster Deed Book N, p. 59, and Book O, p. 445, PSA; Ground Rent Book, 1770–1800, Frey Papers. On Frey's dealings with his tenants, some of whom were his close friends, see Frey to James Burd, 28 May 1782, Copybook of Letters C, fol. 80, Frey Papers.

34. Copy Book of Letters C; Ledger E (1776–1784); Ledger F (1782–1788), Frey Papers.

35. William Jenkins was the son of James Jenkins, Sr., and the brother of James Jenkins, Jr., both of Manheim, Pennsylvania. For Jenkins's connection to the Hill and Sanches firms, see Robert Bisset to Henry Hill, 15 May 1773, folder 5, Hill Family Manuscripts, Sarah A. G. Smith Family Papers, HSP; Joseph Gillis to Henry Hill, 2, 26 Aug., 20 Sept. 1783, fols. 14–16, Hill Family Manuscripts, John Jay Smith Family Papers "A," Library Company Collection, HSP. On the departure of the *Concord,* which left Philadelphia in June 1783 under Captain Atkinson with Frey's flour, see *Pennsylvania Packet,* 17 June 1783. The ship left Funchal soon after August 2, 1783, with 82 pipes aboard, 16 of which were consigned by Sanches & Co. and 60 by Lamar, Hill, Bisset & Co. *Saidas,* book 279, fols. 125r–127v, Arquivo Nacional, Lisbon, Portugal. The ship returned on September 19, 1783, with 70 pipes of its wine consigned to eleven different Philadelphia merchants, two of whom—Joyce Brothers and Aaron Levi—supplied Frey. Book of Entries, 1783, *sub* 19 Sept. 1783, PSA. See also Ledger F, fols. 91, 201, 249, and Copy Book of Letters C, fols. 183, 185, 202, 207, 302, Frey Papers, for the June 1784 departure. In 1785, Sanches declared bankruptcy in Madeira; in 1788, William Jenkins left the island and returned to Pennsylvania.

36. On post-1784 "flour for wine" adventures, see: Ledger F, Ledger [G] (1786–1790), and Ledger H (1790–1799), Frey Papers. On fur and skin ventures to England and northwest Europe, see Copy Book of Letters A, fols. 79, 85, and Ledger H, fol. 68, Frey Papers. For furs and skins, Frey dealt with fellow Württemberger Johannes Peter Webber, who had settled in London.

37. On the 1783 and later sales to Marylanders and Virginians, see Frey to Leonard Dorsey, Copy Book of Letters C, fols. 185, 202, 207, 218, 232, 291, 313, 317, 333, 447–448, and Ledger F, passim. See also Ledger F, fol. 201, Ledger H, fol. 68, Frey Papers. Cf. Letters to Miles & Wister, Copy Book of Letters A, fols. 27–29, 36–40, 51, 53, 79, 85, 93–96, 101, 113–114, 122–125, Frey Papers.

38. Copy Book of Letters A, passim, Copy Book of Letters C, passim, Frey Papers.

39. Daybook 2 (1 May 1773–28 Feb. 1774), and Daybook 16 (May 1800–

Feb. 1801), Ledgers D (1773–1774) and K (1797–1805), passim, Frey Papers. Cf. Philadelphians' internationalism, as evidenced in the accounts of the following retailers: Samuel Neave Ledger (1752–1756), HSP; Tench Francis Ledger & Invoice Book, 1759–1763, HSP; Mifflin & Massey Ledger A (1760–1763), HSP; John & Peter Chevalier Day Book, 1760–1766, HSP; Benjamin Fuller Papers, 1762–1799, 5 vols., HSP; Daniel Roberdeau Letter Book (1764–1771), HSP.

40. Kim M. Gruenwald, *River of Enterprise: The Commercial Origins of Regional Identity in the Ohio Valley, 1790–1850* (Bloomington, Ind., 2002), 62. Examples from other retailers' operations are abundant. Particularly good is one South Carolina store run by Joseph Kershaw. At his general store at Pine Tree Hill, 263 of the 291 items sold in 1775 were nonlocal in origin, and of those nearly half (42% of the total) were imports. Kershaw Account Book (1774–1775), Wisconsin Historical Society, Madison, Wisc.

41. Hancock, *Oceans of Wine*, ch. 6.

42. Max Savelle, *George Morgan: Colony Builder* (New York, 1932), 7. Cf. Charles Carroll to Wallace, Johnson & Muir, 20 March 1783, Charles Carroll of Carrollton Letterbook (1771–1783), fol. 62v, New York Public Library, New York; ――― to Elias Hasket Derby, 26 April 1787, Elias H. Derby Letters, box 11, fol. 6, Phillips Library, Essex Institute, Salem, Mass.; John Codman III to John Searle & Co., 6 April 1789, Codman Papers, Society for the Preservation of New England Antiquities, Boston, Mass.; Ludlow & Gould to Elias Hasket Derby, 26 April 1787, Elias H. Derby Letters, box 11, fol. 6.

43. *Pennsylvania Gazette*, 13 Sept. 1753, 26 June 1755, 26 July 1764; *Pennsylvania Chronicle*, 28 Jan. 1768; *Pennsylvania Gazette*, 26 March 1772; 12, 17 May, 21, 25 Aug. 1773, 11, 12 May, 23 Nov., 1774, 29 March, 2 May 1775; *Pennsylvania Journal*, 4 Jan., 29 March, 5, 12 April 1775. Postwar establishments are recorded in: *Pennsylvania Gazette*, 14 Jan., 28 April, 1 Sept. 1784; Francis White, *The Philadelphia Directory* (Philadelphia, Pa., 1785), 12, 38, 50, 76, 77; *Pennsylvania Gazette*, 17 Aug., 2 Nov. 1785, 2 Aug. 1786, 17 Feb. 1790, 2 Nov. 1791; *Federal Gazette*, 19 May, 13 Aug. 1790; Clement Biddle, *The Philadelphia Directory* (Philadelphia, Pa., 1791); *Federal Gazette*, 26 Jan. 1792; *Dunlap's American Daily Advertiser*, 1 May 1793, p. 4; *Pennsylvania Gazette*, 19 Oct. 1796. The first federal census for Philadelphia City and County listed no "wine merchants" in Southwark Town, but nine lived in the rest of the city. Edmund Hogan, *Prospect of Philadelphia and Check on the Next Directory*, part 1 (Philadelphia, Pa., 1795) listed twelve others. The third

federal census of 1810 listed no "wine merchants" at all (the descriptor may have been falling out of fashion), but it mentioned three owners of "wine stores." The anonymous *Philadelphia Directory* (Philadelphia, Pa., 1811) listed seven wine merchants, storekeepers, and shopkeepers, in addition to five proprietors of "liquor stores" selling wine. Subsequent references appear in *Poulson's American Daily Advertiser,* 13, 20 Oct. 1810. By 1814, there were at least ninety specialists offering drink to Philadelphians; see *Kite's Philadelphia Directory for 1814* (Philadelphia, Pa., 1814). On Frey's suppliers, cf. Copy Book of Letters A and C, Frey Papers.

44. William Smith was the first to open a liquor commission store in Philadelphia. *Pennsylvania Gazette,* 10 April 1766. Brokers rose in popularity toward the end of the war, and as a group continued to grow in the last few decades of the century. Ibid., 17 Nov., 1 Dec. 1779, and 27 June 1781; *Pennsylvania Packet,* 19 June 1781; *Independent Gazetteer,* 3 May 1783.

45. Peter Anspach to John Mitchell, 27 June 1774; Charles Hamilton to John Mitchell, 23 Sept. 1774; Book of Goods, 1773; John Reynolds to John Mitchell, 11 Aug. 1772; ———— to John Mitchell, 5 May 1774; John Taylor to John Mitchell, 15, 16 Aug. 1773; George Irwin to John Mitchell, 1 Dec. 1773; John Williams to John Mitchell, 29 June 1774; Murray & Connelly to John Mitchell, 8 Nov. 1772, 2, 15 Feb. 15, 1773; Charles Hamilton to John Mitchell, 15 April 1774: all in John Mitchell Papers, PSA; *Pennsylvania Gazette,* 26 Nov. 1774; Ledger (1770–1772), fols. 54, 60, John Mitchell Papers, PSA; John Williams' Daybook, 1773–1774, APS.

46. Sequestered John Mitchell Papers, 1762–1781, MG-92, PSA. On John and Randle Mitchell, see: Hannah B. Roach, comp., *Colonial Philadelphians* (Philadelphia, Pa., 1999), 83, 86, 115; F. Edward Wright, ed., *Abstracts of Philadelphia County, Pennsylvania Wills, 1763–1784* (Philadelphia, Pa., 1998), nos. 1594, 1674, and 1895; ibid., *1777–1790* (2004), nos. 2385, 2424, 2538, and 2548; and ibid., *1790–1802* (1896) *sub* Andrew Caldwell; *Pennsylvania Gazette,* 1 Jan., 30 May 1751, 2 Jan., 20 Sept. 1753, 1 Feb., 4 Oct. 1759, 18 Sept. 1760, 4 March 1762, 21 April, 24 Nov. 1763, 9, 16 Aug. 1764, 13 June 1765, 26 June 1766, 23, 30 June 1768, 2 May, 18 April, 10 Oct. 1771, 16 April, 28 Oct., 11 Nov. 1772, 31 March, 10 Nov. 1773, 20 April 1774, 13 Oct., 24 Nov. 1784; *Pennsylvania Chronicle,* 14 Oct. 1771, 3 Oct. 1772; *Pennsylvania Evening Post,* 30 July 1776, 17 Jan., 4 July, 1 Aug. 1778, Richard K. Showman, ed., *The Papers of General Nathanael Greene,* vol. 2 (Chapel Hill, N.C., 1980),

387–389, 460–461, vol. 3 (1983), 132, 273, 287, 303–311, 462, 470, 474, 477; W. W. Abbot, ed., *The Papers of George Washington*, Presidential Series, vol. 2 (Charlottesville, Va., 1987), 347–348, vol. 6 (1996), 101, vol. 7 (1998), 389; John Tobler, *The South-Carolina and Georgia Almanack* (Charleston, S.C., 1784, 1785); *South-Carolina Gazette*, 15 May, 19 June 1784; John Milligan, *The Charleston Directory* (Charleston, S.C., 1790), 26; *Charleston News and Courier*, 27 Jan. 1826.

47. Wine distributors seem to have blazed a trail in putting "brand marks" on the goods they moved. Paul Duguid, "Developing the Brand: The Case of Alcohol, 1800–1880," in *Enterprise & Society* 4 (September 2003): 405–441. Port and Champagne distributors followed the lead of Madeirans. Robert Bisset to Henry Hill, 9 May 1784, 9: fol. 53, John Jay Smith Family Papers "A," HSP.

48. Frey to Morgan Jenkins, 22 Jan. 1782, fol. 18; to Levi Hollingsworth, 24 April 1782, fol. 53; 23 Sept. 1782, fol. 119; to Benjamin Pulteney, 15 May 1782, fol. 69; 5 Oct. 1782, fol. 123; to Wister & Aston, 19 Dec. 1782, fol. 141: all in Copy Book of Letters C, Frey Papers.

49. Frey to Thomas Pulteney, Jr., 25 Jan. 1782, fol. 18; Frey to Benjamin Pulteney, 30 April 1782, fol. 62; 26 June 1782, fol. 89: all in Copy Book of Letters C, Frey Papers.

50. Copy Book of Letters C, Frey Papers.

51. Ledger B, and Copy Book of Letters C, Frey Papers.

52. The quotation is found in Thomas Wermuth, *Rip Van Winkle's Neighbors: The Transformation of Rural Society in the Hudson River Valley, 1720–1850* (Albany, N.Y., 2001), 61. See also Frey to Robert Patton, Copy Book of Letters A, passim; Day Book A (1774–1779), fol. 36; Day Book 5 (1775–1778), fol. 51; Copy Book of Letters [B] (1781–1782), *sub* 24 Feb. 1781, Frey Papers; *Pennsylvania Gazette*, 29 Sept. 1773.

53. Hancock, *Oceans of Wine*, ch. 8; Inventory Book, Frey Papers.

54. Ibid.

55. *Last Will and Testament of George Frey, Deceased* (n.p., 1806); Inventory of the Goods, Chattels, Rights and Credits . . . of George Frey, 4 June 1806, Frey Papers: the total value of the estate was $3,588; total value of mills, stores and contents, $624; total value of accounts, bonds, and notes both recoverable and desperate, $22,129. Frey had previously granted annuities to relatives in Germany and friends in Holland and the Cape Colony. The Freys had had at least one child, but he or she died from smallpox inoculation in 1780 or 1781. Frey to Dr. John Laning, 4 Feb. 1782, Copy Book of Letters C, fol. 21, Frey Papers.

4. Inter-Imperial Smuggling in the Americas, 1600–1800

1. Cf. Abbé Prévost, *Voyages du capitaine Robert Lade en differentes parties de l'Afrique, de l'Asie et de l'Amerique . . .* , 2 vols. (Paris, 1744), 1:51–55; Gregorio de Robles, *América a fines del siglo XVII: noticia de los lugares de contrabando* (Valladolid, 1980), 35, 81.

2. Piracy and smuggling are two different, although sometimes overlapping, forms of illegality, but acts of piracy are largely irrelevant to this study, since illegal trade, like legal trade, was usually conducted freely by the parties involved. As one historian has written: "Piracy and trading can be disguises for one another, and sometimes were, but usually piracy prevents the modicum of mutual trust which is necessary even between smugglers before an effective exchange of goods can be attempted." Murdo J. MacLeod, *Spanish Central America: A Socioeconomic History, 1520–1720* (Berkeley, Calif., 1973), 362. Smugglers could turn into pirates if states enforced the laws in colonies where connivance had been the rule: Anne Pérotin-Dumon, "The Pirate and the Emperor: Power and the Law on the Seas, 1450–1850," in *The Political Economy of Merchant Empires: State Power and World Trade, 1350–1750*, ed. James D. Tracy (New York, 1991), 196–227, at 199.

3. I do not discuss smuggling that took place within a single empire, although such breaches of imperial laws were not inconsequential. For instance, export duties levied in the British sugar-producing islands in the West Indies on produce bound for other British colonies were largely evaded. Frank Wesley Pitman, *The Development of the British West Indies, 1700–1763* (New Haven, Conn., 1917), 302–304. Likewise, the amount of tobacco leaving the Chesapeake for Great Britain was often understated or the cargo hidden completely. Arthur Pierce Middleton, *Tobacco Coast: A Maritime History of Chesapeake Bay in the Colonial Era* (Newport News, Va., 1953), 188–189. For tobacco smuggling into Great Britain, see Robert C. Nash, "The English and Scottish Tobacco Trades in the Seventeenth and Eighteenth Centuries: Legal and Illegal Trade," *Economic History Review* 35 (August 1982): 354–372. Under-registration of silver carried by the Spanish fleets returning to Europe was massive. Overall, fraud connected with the fleet that anchored in Portobelo in 1624 amounted to no less than 87% of the value of the commodities carried. Silver also disappeared into illegal intra-imperial circuits on the other end of South America. Between 1616 and 1625, Potosí silver with a value of at least 750,000 pesos was smuggled to Spain

via Buenos Aires. Enriqueta Vila Vilar, "Las ferias de Portobelo: apariencia y realidad del comercio con Indias," *Anuario de Estudios Americanos* 39 (1982): 275–336; Marie Helmer, "Comércio e contrabando entre Bahia e Potosí no século XVI," *Revista de História* (São Paulo) 4 (1953): 195–212, esp. 201; Harry E. Cross, "Commerce and Orthodoxy: A Spanish Response to Portuguese Commercial Penetration in the Viceroyalty of Peru, 1580–1640," *The Americas* 35 (October 1978): 151–167, esp. 154–156. See also Fernando Serrano Mangas, *Armadas y flotas de la plata, 1620–1648* (Madrid, 1989), 328–335. Smuggling of Brazilian gold within the Portuguese Empire was smaller, according to the 1733 estimate of Pedro de Almeida, the former governor of São Paulo and Minas Gerais. One-seventh was sent illegally to Lisbon, the Azores, and Portuguese trading stations in Africa or to other parts of Brazil: Ernst Pijning, "Controlling Contraband: Mentality, Economy and Society in Eighteenth-Century Rio de Janeiro" (Ph.D. diss., Johns Hopkins University, 1997), 14–15. For the role of the Canary Islands in Spanish smuggling of dry goods to Spanish America, see Agustín Guimerá Ravina, *Burguesía extranjera y comercio atlántico: la empresa comercial irlandesa en Canarias (1703–1771)* (Madrid, 1985), 380–383.

4. Thomas C. Barrow, *Trade and Empire: The British Customs Service in Colonial America, 1660–1775* (Cambridge, Mass., 1967), 136–137.

5. Angel López Cantos, "Contrabando, corso y situado en el siglo XVIII: una economía subterránea," *Anales: Revista de Ciencias Sociales e Historia de la Universidad Interamericana de Puerto Rico Recinto de San Germán*, n.s. 1, no. 2 (1985): 31–53, esp. 39.

6. Theodora Keith, "Scottish Trade with the Plantations before 1707," *Scottish Historical Review* 6 (1908): 32–48, esp. 39; César García del Pino, "El Obispo Cabezas, Silvestre de Balboa y los contrabandistas de Manzanilla," *Revista de la Biblioteca Nacional José Martí*, 3d ser., 17 (May–June 1975): 13–54, esp. 32–33; Celestino Andrés Araúz, *El contrabando holandés en el Caribe durante la primera mitad del siglo XVIII*, 2 vols. (Caracas, 1984), 1:126; Lance Grahn, *The Political Economy of Smuggling: Regional Informal Economies in Early Bourbon New Granada* (Boulder, Colo., 1997), 35.

7. Nathaniel Uring, *A History of the Voyages and Travels of Capt. Nathaniel Uring...* (London, 1726), 164–165.

8. *Peter Oliver's Origin and Progress of the American Rebellion: A Tory View*, ed. Douglas Adair and John A. Schutz (San Marino, Calif., 1963), 46.

9. Julius R. Ruff, *Violence in Early Modern Europe* (New York, 2001),

240; Olwen Hufton, *The Poor in Eighteenth-Century France, 1750–1789* (Oxford, 1974); Volker Jarren, *Schmuggel und Schmuggelbekämpfung in den preussischen Westprovinzen, 1818–1854* (Paderborn, 1992), 231.

10. Governor Alfonso de Castro to the King, Santo Domingo, 22 Nov. 1736, quoted in Antonio Gutiérrez Escudero, *Población y economía en Santo Domingo, 1700–1746* (Seville, 1985), 207; James Gregory Cusick, "Spanish East Florida in the Atlantic Economy of the Late Eighteenth Century," in *Colonial Plantations and Economy in Florida,* ed. Jane G. Landers (Gainesville, Fla., 2000), 168–210, esp. 174–175.

11. The Marquis of Fayet, governor of Saint-Domingue (1732–1737), wrote these words in 1733: Charles Frostin, *Histoire de l'autonomisme colon de la partie française de St. Domingue aux XVIIe et XVIIIe siècles: contribution à l'étude du sentiment américain d'indépendance* (Lille, 1973), 328. See also Jean Tarrade, *Le commerce colonial de la France à la fin de l'Ancien Régime: l'évolution du régime de "l'Exclusif" de 1763 à 1789* (Paris, 1972), 109.

12. Grahn, *Political Economy of Smuggling,* 84, 110. See also G. Earl Sanders, "Counter-Contraband in Spanish America: Handicaps of the Governors in the Indies," *The Americas* 34 (July 1977): 59–80, esp. 76.

13. Rafael Cartay A., *Ideología, desarrollo e interferencias del comercio caribeño durante el siglo XVII* (Caracas, 1988), 183.

14. I. A. Wright, "Rescates: With Special Reference to Cuba, 1599–1610," *Hispanic American Historical Review* 3 (August 1920): 333–361, esp. 357–359.

15. Virginia Bernard, *Slaves and Slaveholders in Bermuda, 1616–1782* (Columbia, Mo., 1999), 177.

16. Samuel G. Margolin, "Lawlessness on the Maritime Frontier of the Greater Chesapeake, 1650–1750" (Ph.D. diss., College of William and Mary, 1992), 420–421.

17. The Earl of Bellomont to the Lords of Treasury, New York, 25 May 1698, in John Romeyn Brodhead, *Documents Relative to the Colonial History of the State of New-York,* ed. E. B. O'Callaghan, vol. 4 (Albany, N.Y., 1854), 318. Not much had changed by the 1760s: Cathy Matson, *Merchants and Empire: Trading in Colonial New York* (Baltimore, Md., 1998), 277.

18. Caleb Heathcote to the Council of Trade and Plantations, 7 Sept. 1719, in *Calendar of State Papers: Colonial Series, America and West Indies, January 1719 to February 1720,* ed. Cecil Headlam (London, 1933), 217.

19. Joseph R. Frese, S.J., "Smuggling, the Navy, and the Customs Service, 1763–1772," in *Seafaring in Colonial Massachusetts,* Publications of the

Colonial Society of Massachusetts, 52 (Charlottesville, Va., 1980): 199–212, esp. 209–210. Thanks to Martin Hubley for pointing me to this article. For other cases see Pauline Maier, "Popular Uprisings and Civil Authority in Eighteenth-Century America," *William and Mary Quarterly*, 3d ser., 27 (January 1970): 3–35, esp. 9–10; Benjamin H. Irvin, "Tar, Feathers, and the Enemies of American Liberties, 1768–1776," *New England Quarterly* 76 (June 2003): 197–238, esp. 200.

20. León Trujillo, *Motín y sublevación en San Felipe* (Caracas, 1955), 23, 29–30, 45, 51, 67, 75, 80, 114; Roland Dennis Hussey, *The Caracas Company, 1728–1784: A Study in the History of Spanish Monopolistic Trade* (Cambridge, Mass., 1934), 115–117. The Porteous riots in Edinburgh in 1736 (fictionalized by Sir Walter Scott in *The Heart of Midlothian*), which were set off by the capture of three smugglers and the execution of one of them, constituted a parallel European case. Such revolts had some elements in common with the anti-customs riots that took place in the thirteen colonies from 1764 through 1775 and helped set the stage for the American Revolution. Several broke out over inter-imperial smuggling: Richard Maxwell Brown, "Violence and the American Revolution," in *Essays on the American Revolution*, ed. Stephen G. Kurtz and James H. Hutson (Chapel Hill, N.C., 1973), 81–120, esp. 97, 119; Adele Hast, *Loyalism in Revolutionary Virginia: The Norfolk Area and the Eastern Shore* (Ann Arbor, Mich., 1982), 14.

21. Pijning, "Controlling Contraband," 12–13; Privy Council to Francis Lord Willoughby. Whitehall, 11 March 1663, in *Documents Illustrative of the History of the Slave Trade to America*, ed. Elizabeth Donnan, 4 vols. (Washington, D.C., 1930–1935), 1:161–162; *Calendar of State Papers, Colonial Papers, 1685–1688*, ed. J. W. Fortescue (London, 1899), 54–55; Mr. Alured Popple to Mr. Attorney and Sollicitor General, 2 Feb. 1720, in Headlam, *Calendar of State Papers, January, 1719 to February, 1720*, 327, no. 537; Mr. Solicitor General to Mr. Popple. 4 Feb. 1720, in Headlam, *Calendar*, 346–347, no. 547; Frances Armytage, *The Free Port System in the British West Indies: A Study in Commercial Policy, 1766–1822* (London, 1953), 31–32.

22. Pijning, "Controlling Contraband," 42–43.

23. Adam Smith, *An Inquiry into the Nature and Causes of the Wealth of Nations*, ed. R. H. Campbell and A. S. Skinner, 2 vols. (1776; Oxford, 1976), 2:898. Benjamin Franklin would have agreed with Smith. He noted, "there is no kind of dishonesty into which otherwise good people more easily and frequently fall, than that of defrauding government of its revenues, by smuggling when they have an opportunity, or encourag-

ing smugglers by buying their goods." Franklin to the printer of the *London Chronicle,* 24 Nov. 1767, in *The Papers of Benjamin Franklin,* ed. Leonard Labaree (New Haven, Conn., 1970), 14:315–316.

24. Barrow, *Trade and Empire,* 144.

25. Herbert Eugene Bolton, *Texas in the Middle Eighteenth Century: Studies in Spanish Colonial History and Administration* (Berkeley, Calif., 1915), 410; Stewart L. Mims, *Colbert's West India Policy* (New Haven, Conn., 1912), 157, 285–286. Cf. Lucien-René Abénon, *La Guadeloupe de 1671 à 1759: étude politique, économique et sociale* (Paris, 1987), 121; Kenneth J. Banks, "Official Duplicity: The Illicit Slave Trade of Martinique, 1713–1763," in *The Atlantic Economy during the Seventeenth and Eighteenth Centuries: Organization, Operation, Practice, and Personnel,* ed. Peter A. Coclanis (Columbia, S.C., 2005), 229–251, esp. 246.

26. Grahn, *Political Economy of Smuggling,* 108, 112, 115.

27. Until then, the sale of offices had been limited to posts with no judicial or administrative duties, such as clerks and scribes. But, pressed for money, the Crown put higher offices up for sale as well, both at home and in the colonies. Horst Pietschmann, "Burocracia y corrupción en Hispanoamérica colonial: una aproximación tentativa," *Nova Americana* 5 (1982): 11–37, esp. 23–24.

28. MacLeod, *Spanish Central America,* 350–351. Spanish officials in the Andean region used another method to make money, forcing goods upon natives. This was the functional equivalent of smuggling in Atlantic America.

29. John Brewer, *The Sinews of Power: War, Money and the English State, 1688–1783* (London, 1989), 69; Sydney V. James, *Colonial Rhode Island: A History* (New York, 1975), 334. Robert Middlekauff, *The Glorious Cause: The American Revolution, 1763–1789* (New York, 1982), 63.

30. For Spanish America, see Zacarías Moutoukias, "Power, Corruption, and Commerce: The Making of the Local Administrative Structure in Seventeenth-Century Buenos Aires," *Hispanic American Historical Review* 68 (November 1988): 771–801, esp. 776.

31. Richard L. Bushman, *King and People in Provincial Massachusetts* (Chapel Hill, N.C., 1982), 158–161.

32. Jorge Juan and Antonio de Ulloa, *Noticias secretas de América (siglo XVIII),* 2 vols. (1748; Madrid, 1918), 1:228.

33. Cf. Tamar Herzog, *La administración como un fenómeno social: la justicia penal de la ciudad de Quito (1650–1750)* (Madrid, 1995), 151–152, 307–308.

34. Grahn, *Political Economy of Smuggling,* 143–144.

35. Fabrício Prado, "Colonia do Sacramente: Commerce, Authority and

Social Networks in the Eighteenth-Century Rio de la Plata Frontier," unpub. paper. I thank the author for sending me a copy.

36. Frostin, *Histoire de l'autonomisme colon,* 327n. For permits in the 1740s, see Jacques Mathieu, *Le commerce entre la Nouvelle-France et les Antilles au XVIIIe siècle* (Montréal, 1981), 212–213.

37. Pijning, "Controlling Contraband," 99–100, 104.

38. The trials took place in 1619–1622. Although in this particular case, the names of the smugglers make it hard to conclude that they were all Portuguese rather than Spanish, this type of collusion between officials and traders must have been widespread. Inge Wolff, "Negersklaverei und Negerhandel in Hochperu, 1545–1640," *Jahrbuch für die Geschichte von Staat, Wirtschaft und Gesellschaft Lateinamerikas* 1 (1964): 157–186, esp. 176.

39. Grahn, *Political Economy of Smuggling,* 96.

40. Archivo General de Simancas (Simancas, Spain) (hereafter, AGS), Estado 6351, statement by Christiaan Boom, 1732. Cf. Juan Carlos Solórzano, "El comercio de Costa Rica durante el declive del comercio español y el desarrollo del contrabando inglés: período 1690–1750," *Anuario de Estudios Centroamericanos* 20, no. 2 (1994): 71–119.

41. Abénon, *Guadeloupe,* 2:129.

42. Nationaal Archief (The Hague), Oud Archief Curaçao 808, fol. 453. Testimony of Eliao Israell and Eliao de Jacob Pereyra, Curaçao, 16 May 1738. Bribes were also a staple of the British Atlantic. Enumerated goods, which officially could be shipped only in British ships to Britain, would often go directly to Amsterdam after the ship stopped at Dover or Falmouth, where port officials were bribed, enabling the vessel to continue without making payments. Matson, *Merchants and Empire,* 84.

43. Fernando A. Novais, *Portugal e Brasil na crise do antigo sistema colonial (1777–1808)* (São Paulo, 1979), 80–82.

44. Kenneth R. Andrews, *The Spanish Caribbean: Trade and Plunder, 1530–1630* (New Haven, Conn., 1978), 181–187, 195.

45. Huguette Chaunu and Pierre Chaunu, *Séville et l'Atlantique, 1504–1650,* 8 vols. in 11 (Paris, 1955–1959), 4:180–181; Kenneth R. Andrews, ed., *English Privateering Voyages to the West Indies, 1588–1595* . . . (Cambridge, 1959), 339n.

46. Captain-general Pedro de Valdés to King Philip III, 18 July 1603, in García del Pino, "Obispo Cabezas," 34; *Een lief-hebber des vaderlandts, levendich discours vant ghemeyne lants welvaert voor desen de Oost ende nu oock de West-Indische generale compagnie aenghevanghen seer notable om te lesen* (Amsterdam, 1622); Andrews, *The Spanish Caribbe-*

an, 195. Some Dutch trade in these islands occurred in collaboration with Spaniards and Flemings based in Seville: Eddy Stols, "Gens des Pays-Bas en Amérique espagnole aux premiers siècles de la colonisation," *Bulletin de l'Institut historique belge de Rome* 44 (1974): 565–599, esp. 580.

47. Gemeentearchief Amsterdam (GAA), Notarieel Archief (NA) 195, fol. 181v, act of 16 March 1607. GAA NA 120, fol. 111v, act of 31 Aug. 1610; Chaunu and Chaunu, *Séville et l'Atlantique*, 4:347–348; Andrews, *English Privateering Voyages*, 384; Andrews, *The Spanish Caribbean*, 214, 227–230.

48. Christopher Ebert, "Dutch Trade with Brazil before the Dutch West India Company, 1587–1621," in *Riches from Atlantic Commerce: Dutch Transatlantic Trade and Shipping, 1585–1817*, ed. Johannes Postma and Victor Enthoven (Leiden, 2003), 49–75, esp. 70–71; Charles R. Boxer, "English Shipping in the Brazil Trade, 1640–1665," *The Mariner's Mirror* 37 (1951): 197–230.

49. Between 1621 and 1645, Spain naturalized 196 men, of whom 66 were Portuguese, 56 Flemish, and 25 Genoese: Antonio Domínguez Ortiz, "La concesión de 'naturalezas para comerciar en Indias' durante el siglo XVII," *Revista de Indias* 10 (1959): 227–239, esp. 231. As early as the 1560s, the Portuguese had been firmly entrenched in illegal trade in Spanish America: Paul E. Hoffman, *The Spanish Crown and the Defense of the Caribbean, 1535–1585: Precedent, Patrimonialism, and Royal Parsimony* (Baton Rouge, La., 1980), 120–121.

50. Chaunu and Chaunu, *Séville et l'Atlantique*, 4:569, 573–576.

51. Wright, "Rescates," 349–350.

52. Alice P. Canabrava, *O comércio português no Rio da Prata (1580–1640)* (São Paulo, 1944), 130–140.

53. Andrews, *The Spanish Caribbean*, 73; Enriqueta Vila Vilar, *Hispanoamérica y el comercio de esclavos: los asientos portugueses* (Seville, 1977), 179–180; Enriqueta Vila Vilar with Wim Klooster, "Forced African Settlement: The Basis of Forced Settlement: Africa and Its Trading Conditions," in *General History of the Caribbean*, vol. 2, *New Societies: The Caribbean in the Long Sixteenth Century*, ed. P. C. Emmer and Germán Carrera Damas (London, 1999), 159–179, esp. 165–166, 177–178.

54. Beatrix Heintze, "Das Ende des unabhängigen Staates Ndongo (Angola): Neue Chronologie und Reinterpretation (1617–1630)," *Paideuma* 27 (1981): 198–269, esp. 205–207. Smuggling of slaves and whitewashing of their returns in Angola continued into later decades: Frédéric Mauro, *Le Portugal et l'Atlantique au XVIIe siècle (1570–1670): étude*

économique (Paris, 1960), 176–177. For the role of Portuguese and Dutch New Christians in the smuggling of Potosí silver, see Jonathan I. Israel, *Diasporas within a Diaspora: Jews, Crypto-Jews and the World Maritime Empires (1540–1740)* (Leiden, 2002), 135–142.

55. Christopher Ward, *Imperial Panama: Commerce and Conflict in Isthmian America, 1550–1800* (Albuquerque, N.M., 1993), 130.

56. Vila Vilar, *Hispanoamérica*, 158, 208–209; Zacarías Moutoukias, *Contrabando y control colonial en el siglo XVII: Buenos Aires, el Atlántico y el espacio peruano* (Buenos Aires, 1988), 62, 65; Liliana Crespi, "Contrabando de esclavos en el puerto de Buenos Aires, durante el siglo XVII: complicidad de los funcionarios reales," *Desmemoria* (Buenos Aires) 7 (2000): 115–133.

57. Moutoukias, *Contrabando y control colonial,* 66. His absolute numbers are: 12,000–17,000 illegal slaves, 7,000 who had been whitewashed, and 6,000 legal captives. These figures pertain to the period 1586–1665.

58. Declaration by Henrick Coenraeds, The Hague, 22 Dec. 1636, in João de Laet, *Descrição das Costas do Brasil de João de Laet, 1637: Manuscrito da John Carter Brown Library, Providence,* ed. B. N. Teensma (Petrópolis, Brazil, 2007), 254–256.

59. Ibid., 259. Peter D. Bradley, *Society, Economy and Defence in Seventeenth-Century Peru: The Administration of the Count of Alba de Liste (1655–61)* (Liverpool, 1992), 45–46.

60. María Cristina Navarrete, *Historia social del negro en la colonia Cartagena, siglo XVII* (Santiago de Cali, 1995), 72.

61. Linda A. Newson and Susie Minchin, *The Portuguese Slave Trade to Spanish South America in the Early Seventeenth Century* (Leiden, 2007), 144–146. In 1634–1635, 1,017 slaves were registered and 2,310 were not: Nikolaus Böttcher, *Aufstieg und Fall eines atlantischen Handelsimperiums: portugiesische Kaufleute und Sklavenhändler in Cartagena de Indias von 1580 bis zur Mitte des 17. Jahrhunderts* (Frankfurt am Main, 1995), 158–161.

62. Geoffrey Parker and Lesley M. Smith, "Introduction," in Parker and Smith, *The General Crisis of the Seventeenth Century,* 2d ed. (London, 1997), 1–31, esp. 20.

63. Andrews, *The Spanish Caribbean,* 251.

64. Much of this paragraph appeared in Wim Klooster, *Illicit Riches: Dutch Trade in the Caribbean, 1648–1795* (Leiden, 1998), 50. The same methods were still in use in 1716: Ana Crespo Solana, *Entre Cádiz y los Países Bajos: una comunidad mercantil en la ciudad de la ilustración* (Cádiz, 2001), 238–239.

65. GAA NA 2793/47V-50 and 1135/398–399, acts of 19 Nov. 1659 and 20 Dec. 1660. See, for a case in which Dutch and Spanish investments balanced each other, Archivo General de Indias (AGI) (Seville), Indiferente General 1668, Esteban de Gamarra, Spanish ambassador, to the Crown, The Hague, 2 Feb. 1666. Cf. Manuel Bustos Rodríguez, *Burguesía de negocios y capitalismo en Cádiz: los Colarte (1650–1750)* (Cádiz, 1991), 36, 39–40, 59.

66. AGS, Estado 8388, fols. 55–56; AGI, Indiferente General 1668, Esteban de Gamarra, Spanish ambassador, to the Crown, The Hague, 26 July 1661 and 15 April 1664.

67. Klooster, *Illicit Riches,* 51–52. In the early seventeenth century, the Canaries had functioned as an illegal gateway for Spanish ships to destinations in the Portuguese Atlantic: Chaunu and Chaunu, *Séville et l'Atlantique,* 4:267–268.

68. GAA NA 47/96V, 48/21; AGI, Indiferente General 1668, Memorandum Consejo de Indias, Madrid, 16 Jan. 1664; Engel Sluiter, "Dutch-Spanish Rivalry in the Caribbean Area, 1594–1609," *Hispanic American Historical Review* 28 (May 1948): 165–196, esp. 173–174; Chaunu and Chaunu, *Séville et l'Atlantique,* 4:350; George F. Steckley, "The Wine Economy of Tenerife in the Seventeenth Century: Anglo-Spanish Partnership in a Luxury Trade," *Economic History Review* 33 (August 1980): 335–350, esp. 337–338; Manuel Herrero Sánchez, *El acercamiento hispano-neerlandés, 1648–1678* (Madrid, 2000), 72. The Portuguese had used the Canary Islands in a similar way in the third quarter of the sixteenth century: Andrews, *The Spanish Caribbean,* 72.

69. For instance, a ship that sailed to the Canaries in 1651 and returned to Amsterdam by way of Margarita and Caracas was baptized *The Holy Spirit and the Cross.* GAA NA 2156/62, act of 4 Dec. 1651.

70. This was the case with the *Engel Gabriel,* which sailed in ca. 1652 and 1658, and probably at some date in between those years. Israel, *Diasporas within a Diaspora,* 280–281; GAA NA 2859, fol. 248.

71. AGI, Indiferente General 1668, Esteban de Gamarra to the Spanish Crown, Nov. 1665.

72. Moutoukias, *Contrabando y control colonial,* 131, 143–146; Klooster, *Illicit Riches,* 53–54.

73. AGS, Estado 8394, fol. 62, Esteban de Gamarra to the Spanish Crown, Feb. 1665.

74. Conversely, the knowledge that no fleet was coming could invite large-scale smuggling. When the Dutch learned that no *flota* was dispatched in 1691, they sent thirty-two ships to Spanish America: AGS, Estado 4141, Memorandum of the Consejo de Estado, Madrid, 14 Feb. 1693.

75. AGI, Indiferente General 1668, Esteban de Gamarra to the Spanish Crown, unknown date. Cartay is wrong in asserting that when the *galeones* sailed from Spain to Portobelo in 1662 after a two-year lull in fleet activity, the Spanish colonies were so well provided with merchandise that the fleet returned to Spain without selling most of its cargo. Cartay, *Ideología, desarrollo e interferencias,* 179. See also Ward, *Imperial Panama,* 149–150.

76. Ward, *Imperial Panama,* 150.

77. Moutoukias, *Contrabando y control colonial,* 146–147, 152–153.

78. Wim Klooster, "Slavenvaart op Spaanse kusten: De Nederlandse slavenhandel met Spaans Amerika, 1648–1701," *Tijdschrift voor Zeegeschiedenis* 16 (1997): 121–140, esp. 123; Klooster, *Illicit Riches,* 106. Some slavers sailed without permission of the West India Company, which held the monopoly of the Dutch slave trade in this period. One example is the ship *Santa Catalina,* which arrived in Cartagena de Indias in 1669 from Ardra, where 440 slaves had been bought: Marisa Vega Franco, *El tráfico de esclavos con América: asientos de Grillo y Lomelín, 1663–1674* (Seville, 1984), 92n22, 174–175n28.

79. Vega Franco, *El tráfico de esclavos,* 176–177, 179.

80. Charles M. Andrews, *The Colonial Period of American History,* 4 vols. (New Haven, Conn., 1938), 4:36–37, 61–62.

81. The Privy Council to Francis Lord Willoughby. Whitehall, 11 March 1663, in Donnan, *Documents,* 1:161–162.

82. Claudia Schnurmann, *Atlantische Welten: Engländer und Niederländer im amerikanisch-atlantischen Raum, 1648–1713* (Cologne, 1998), 184.

83. Vincent T. Harlow, *A History of Barbados, 1625–1685* (Oxford, 1926), 263.

84. Philip Alexander Bruce, *Economic History of Virginia in the Seventeenth Century: An Inquiry into the Material Condition of the People, Based upon Original and Contemporaneous Records* (New York, 1907), 354–359.

85. Paul Butel, *Histoire de l'Atlantique: de l'antiquité à nos jours* (Paris, 1997), 131, 133.

86. Gérard Lafleur, "Relations avec l'étranger des minorités religieuses aux Antilles françaises (XVIIe–XVIIIe s.)," *Bulletin de la Société d'histoire de la Guadeloupe,* 57/58 (1983): 27–44, esp. 29; Mims, *Colbert's West India Policy,* 47.

87. Quoted in John C. Rule, "Louis XIV, Roi-Bureaucrate," in *Louis XIV and the Craft of Kingship,* ed. John C. Rule (Columbus, Ohio, 1969), 3–101, esp. 59.

88. Clarence J. Munford, *The Black Ordeal of Slavery and Slave Trading in the French West Indies, 1625–1715*, 3 vols. (Lewiston, N.Y., 1991), 2:378; Frostin, *Histoire de l'autonomisme colon*, 31, 62, 65.

89. Violet Barbour, *Capitalism in Amsterdam in the Seventeenth Century* (Baltimore, Md., 1950), 89–90; Nellis M. Crouse, *The French Struggle for the West Indies, 1665–1713* (1943; London, 1966), 4, 10–11; Paul Butel, *Les Caraïbes au temps des filibustiers, XVIe–XVIIe siècles* (Paris, 1982), 81–82, 97, 102; Frostin, *Histoire de l'autonomisme colon*, 267; Mims, *Colbert's West Indian Policy*, 326–327.

90. Governor Thomas Lynch to Lords of Trade and Plantations, Jamaica, 29 Aug. 1682, *Calendar of State Papers, Colonial Series, America and West Indies, 1681–1685*, ed. J. W. Fortescue (London, 1898), 284; Georges Scelle, *Histoire politique de la traite négrière aux Indes de Castille: contrats et traités d'assiento*, 2 vols. (Paris, 1906), 2:159; Curtis Nettels, "England and the Spanish-American Trade, 1680–1715," *Journal of Modern History* 3 (1931): 1–32, esp. 14; Nuala Zahedieh, "The Merchants of Port Royal, Jamaica, and the Spanish Contraband Trade, 1655–1692," *William and Mary Quarterly*, 3d ser., 43 (1986): 570–592, esp. 573, 581–584, 590; Héctor R. Feliciano Ramos, *El contrabando inglés en el Caribe y el Golfo de México, 1748–1778* (Seville, 1990), 61; MacLeod, *Spanish Central America*, 364, 367–369. English slavers also smuggled Africans into Puerto Rico in this period, mainly Mandinga from Upper Guinea, exchanging them for salted beef, pigs, tobacco, ginger, hides, and the dyestuff *achiote*: Luis M. Díaz Soler, *Historia de la esclavitud negra en Puerto Rico* (Río Piedras, 1965), 83.

91. Ward, *Imperial Panama*, 152–153.

92. Sir William Beeston to William Blathwayt, Jamaica, 18 March 1697, in Fortescue, *Calendar of State Papers, Colonial Series, 1681–1685*, 403.

93. Carl Bridenbaugh and Roberta Bridenbaugh, *No Peace beyond the Line: The English in the Caribbean, 1624–1690* (New York, 1972), 336–337. According to one estimate, only 5% of total produce was smuggled out of Barbados in the period 1660–1700: David Eltis, "New Estimates of Exports from Barbados and Jamaica, 1665–1701," *William and Mary Quarterly*, 3d ser., 52 (October 1995): 631–648, esp. 636.

94. Keith, "Scottish Trade with the Plantations," 44–45.

95. David R. Owen and Michael C. Tolley, *Courts of Admiralty in Colonial America: The Maryland Experience, 1634–1776* (Durham, N.C., 1995), 113–114.

96. Bernard Bailyn, *The New England Merchants in the Seventeenth Century* (1955; New York, 1964), 152–153; Earl of Bellomont to the Lords

of Trade, New York, 25 Nov. 1700, in Brodhead, *Documents Relative to the Colonial History,* 4:792.

97. Moutoukias, *Contrabando y control colonial,* 154, 157–158, 164–165; Mario Rodríguez, "Dom Pedro of Braganza and Colônia do Sacramonte," *Hispanic American Historical Review* 38 (May 1958): 179–208, esp. 190–191; Prado, "Colonia do Sacramonte." One historian has suggested that rigorous Spanish measures against smuggling were successful after 1691: Luís Ferrand de Almeida, *A Colónia do Sacramento na época da sucessão de Espanha* (Coimbra, 1973), 136, 150.

98. Privy Council reporting letter from the Earl of Carlisle, Governor of Jamaica, Whitehall, 28 May 1679, in *Acts of the Privy Council of England: Colonial Series,* ed. W. L. Grant (London, 1908), 1:835–836. The plan to transform Saint-Domingue into a smugglers' den was proposed by Louis de Pontchartain, Minister of Marine, in a letter to Jean-Baptiste Ducasse, the colony's governor: Frostin, *Histoire de l'autonomisme colon,* 67.

99. Frostin, *Histoire de l'autonomisme colon,* 340. Their main destination was Cap-Français in Saint-Domingue: Moreau de Saint-Méry, *Description topographique, physique, civile, politique et historique de la partie française de l'isle Saint-Domingue,* ed. Blanche Maurel and Étienne Taillemite, 3 vols. (Paris, 1958), 1:480.

100. Philippe Jacquin, *Les Indiens blancs: Français et Indiens en Amérique du Nord (XVIe–XVIIe siècle)* (Paris, 1987), 150–152; J. F. Bosher, *The Canada Merchants, 1713–1763* (Oxford, 1987), 182 (quote).

101. Richard Pares, *War and Trade in the West Indies, 1739–1763* (New York, 1936), 131; Rubén Silié, *Economía, esclavitud y población: ensayos de interpretación histórica del Santo Domingo español en el siglo XVIII* (Santo Domingo, 1976), 64; Carlos Daniel Malamud Rikles, *Cádiz y Saint Malo en el comercio colonial peruano (1698–1725)* (Cádiz, 1986), 48–49; "Colección Lugo: Recopilación diplomática relativa a las colonias española y francesa de la isla de Santo Domingo," *Boletín del Archivo General de la Nación* (Santo Domingo) 90–91 (1956): 407–408.

102. Frostin, *Histoire de l'autonomisme colon,* 266, 349–350. Cf. for trade in Puerto Rico: Chevalier de ***, *Voyages et avantures du Chevalier de ***,* 4 vols. (London, 1769), 2:166–167. The governor and intendant of Martinique complained that French slavers bypassed the island to sell the Africans at Saint-Domingue, whose settlers purchased them for 900 livres and sold them for 2,500 to the Spanish: Liliane Crété, *La traite des nègres sous l'ancien régime: le nègre, le sucre et la toile* (Paris, 1989), 226.

103. Crété, *La traite des nègres,* 260–261, 338–340; Ruud Paesie, "Lorrendrayen

op Africa: De illegale goederen- en slavenhandel op West-Afrika tijdens het achttiende-eeuwse handelsmonopolie van de West-Indische Compagnie, 1700–1734" (Ph.D. diss., University of Leiden, 2008), ch. 4. For examples of the Danish slave trade to Costa Rica in these years, see Russell Lohse, "Slave-Trade Nomenclature and African Ethnicities in the Americas: Evidence from Early Eighteenth-Century Costa Rica," *Slavery and Abolition* 23 (December 2002): 73–92.

104. Charles Frostin, "Les Pontchartrain et la pénétration commerciale française en Amérique espagnole (1690–1715)," *Revue historique* 498 (1971): 307–336, esp. 308, 323.

105. Scelle, *Histoire politique,* 2:301–302; Colin Palmer, *Human Cargoes: The British Slave Trade to Spanish America, 1700–1739* (Urbana, Ill., 1981), 85.

106. André Lespagnol, "Les malouins dans l'espace caraïbe au début du XVIIIe siècle: la tentation de l'interlope," in *Commerce et plantation dans la Caraïbe XVIIIe et XIXe siècles: actes du colloque de Bordeaux, 15–16 mars 1991,* ed. Paul Butel (Bordeaux, 1992), 9–25, esp. 11–15.

107. Fernando Jumar, "Le commerce français au Río de la Plata pendant la guerre de succession d'Espagne," in *La mer, la France et l'Amérique latine,* ed. Christian Buchet and Michel Vergé-Franceschi (Paris, 2006), 309–331, esp. 325–327.

108. Cf. the classic E. W. Dahlgren, *Les relations commerciales et maritimes entre la France et les côtes de l'Océan Pacifique (commencement du XVIIIe siècle)* (Paris, 1909).

109. Sergio Villalobos R., "Contrabando francés en el Pacífico, 1700–1724," *Revista de Historia de América* 51 (1961): 49–80, esp. 62; Sergio Villalobos, *Comercio y contrabando, en el Río de la Plata y Chile, 1700–1811* (Buenos Aires, 1965), 28–29; Carlos D. Malamud, "El comercio directo de Europa con América en el siglo XVIII," *Quinto Centenario* 1 (1981): 25–52, esp. 44; Simon Collier, *Ideas and Politics of Chilean Independence, 1808–1833* (New York, 1968), 36.

110. Malamud, "El comercio directo," 45. Another historian claims that the silver loaded by the French in Peru between 1700 and 1715 was valued at 400 million livres: Thomas J. Schaeper, *The French Council of Commerce, 1700–1715: A Study of Mercantilism after Colbert* (Columbus, Ohio, 1983), 225.

111. Malamud Rikles, *Cádiz y Saint Malo,* 78, 113.

112. Scelle, *Histoire politique,* 2:362–363, 365–366, 376–377, 401–402; John Lynch, *Bourbon Spain, 1700–1808* (Oxford, 1989), 57.

113. Pitman, *Development of the British West Indies,* appendix 2, 391–392; Frostin, *Histoire de l'autonomisme colon,* 353–354.

114. *Journal of the Commissioners for Trade and Plantations February 1708–9 to March 1714–5 Preserved in the Public Record Office* (London, 1925), 90; Leonard Woods Labaree, *Royal Instructions to British Colonial Governors, 1670–1776,* 2 vols. (New York, 1935), 2:728; Frostin, *Histoire de l'autonomisme colon,* 338–342; *J. L. Carstens' St. Thomas in Early Danish Times: A General Description of all the Danish, American or West Indian Islands,* ed. Arnold R. Highfield (St. Croix, V.I., 1997), xxxviii.

115. Governor Sir Bevill Granville to the Board of Trade, Barbados, 3 Sept. 1703, quoted in Pitman, *Development of the British West Indies,* 195, 222.

116. Kenneth J. Banks, *Chasing Empire across the Sea: Communications and the State in the French Atlantic, 1713–1763* (Montréal, 2002), 170; Frostin, *Histoire de l'autonomisme colon,* 345. Settlers were told by their government in 1716 that commerce with foreign colonies was taboo, except for trade with Spanish America, which yielded bullion: Jacques Petitjean Roget, *Le Gaoulé: la révolte de la Martinique en 1717* (Fort de France, 1966), 232; Pitman, *Development of the British West Indies,* 210n.

117. Geoffrey J. Walker, *Spanish Politics and Imperial Trade, 1700–1789* (Bloomington, Ind., 1979), 12; Nettels, "England and the Spanish-American Trade," 19.

118. Walker, *Spanish Politics,* 68, 71.

119. The high estimate is from George Nelson, "Contraband Trade under the Asiento, 1730–1739," *American Historical Review* 51 (October 1845): 55–67, esp. 61. See also Feliciano Ramos, *El contrabando inglés,* 31; and Stephen Alexander Fortune, *Merchants and Jews: The Struggle for British West Indian Commerce, 1650–1750* (Gainesville, Fla., 1984), 148.

120. Villalobos, *Comercio y contrabando,* 34–35.

121. Pares, *War and Trade,* 115.

122. The first claim was made in *Interesses de Inglaterra mal entendidos en la Guerra, que continuaba en 1704,* cited in Geronymo de Uztariz, *Theorica y practica de comercio y de marina, en diferentes discursos y calificados exemplares . . .* (Madrid, 1742), 67–68. See for the other estimate: G. V. Scammell, "'A Very Profitable and Advantageous Trade': British Smuggling in the Iberian Americas, circa 1500–1750," *Itinerario: European Journal of Overseas History* 24, no. 3–4 (2000): 135–172, esp. 161.

123. Grahn, *Political Economy of Smuggling*, 123, 127.

124. Scammell, "British Smuggling," 160.

125. Pares, *War and Trade*, 41; Feliciano Ramos, *El contrabando inglés*, 67; Barbara Potthast-Jutkeit, "Centroamérica y el contrabando por la Costa de Mosquitos en el siglo XVIII," *Mesoamérica: Revista del Centro de Investigaciones Regionales de Mesoamérica* 19 (1998): 499–516, esp. 503.

126. MacLeod, *Spanish Central America*, 370; Solórzano, "El comercio de Costa Rica," 108.

127. Klooster, *Illicit Riches*, 240; Wim Klooster, "Curaçao and the Caribbean Transit Trade," in Postma and Enthoven, *Riches from Atlantic Commerce*, 203–218, esp. 216–217. This picture is somewhat distorted, since intercolonial Spanish-American figures have not been discounted.

128. For example, in 1726–1730, Dutch imports from Curaçao amounted to 2,410,394 pounds against 1,140,950 pounds imported from all of Spanish America into Spain: Klooster, *Illicit Riches*, 240.

129. Ibid., 84–86, 175; Gutiérrez Escudero, *Población y economía en Santo Domingo*, 202–211. See also Neill Bothwell to William M. Knight, Santo Domingo, 15 June 1744, Letters of the Bright Family, vol. 4, fols. 244–247, Bright Family Papers, University of Melbourne Archives (Australia). Thanks to Stephen D. Behrendt for providing me with a copy of this document.

130. Pitman, *Development of the British West Indies*, 206.

131. Michael Jarvis, "'In the Eye of All Trade': Bermuda, Bermudians, and the Maritime Atlantic World, 1680–1800," unpub. MS, ch. 4; Pitman, *Development of the British West Indies*, 214–215.

132. John Jay TePaske, *The Governorship of Spanish Florida, 1700–1763* (Durham, N.C., 1964), 73.

133. John Robert McNeill, *Atlantic Empires of France and Spain: Louisbourg and Havana, 1700–1763* (Chapel Hill, N.C., 1985), 156, 269n44.

134. C. R. Boxer, "Brazilian Gold and British Traders in the First Half of the Eighteenth Century," *Hispanic American Historical Review* 49 (August 1969): 454–472, esp. 461–464. During the War of the Austrian Succession (1740–1748), the neutral Dutch carried large amounts of gold directly from Bahia, Pernambuco, and Rio de Janeiro: Michel Morineau, *Incroyables gazettes et fabuleux métaux: les retours des trésors américains d'après les gazettes hollandaises (XVIe–XVIIIe siècles)* (New York, 1985), 216–217.

135. Scammell, "British Smuggling," 153. The Dutch ambassador to Spain wrote in 1731 that the Spanish court considered Colônia and Curaçao

the main gates through which contraband entered Spanish America: NA, Collectie Fagel, Frans van der Meer to pensionary Stein, Antigola, 21 June 1731.

136. Prado, "Colonia do Sacramonte."

137. John G. Clark, *New Orleans, 1718–1812: An Economic History* (Baton Rouge, La., 1970), 142–143; Marcel Giraud, *A History of French Louisiana*, 5 vols. (Baton Rouge, La., 1991), 5:157–158.

138. Representation of the President, Council and Assembly of Jamaica to the Council of Trade and Plantations, 2 May 1735, in *Calendar of State Papers, Colonial Series, America and West Indies, 1735–1736*, ed. Arthur P. Newton (London, 1953), 425. Cf. Vera Lee Brown, "Contraband Trade: A Factor in the Decline of Spain's Empire in America," *Hispanic American Historical Review* 8 (May 1928): 178–189.

139. Grahn, *Political Economy of Smuggling*, 31.

140. Ibid., 59–60, 86.

141. Abénon, *Guadeloupe*, 1:278; Frostin, *Histoire de l'autonomisme colon*, 327n; Pares, *War and Trade*, 396–397; Banks, *Chasing Empire*, 35.

142. Pitman, *Development of the British West Indies*, 281–282; Pares, *War and Trade*, 396–397; Barrow, *Trade and Empire*, 142; Fred Anderson, *Crucible of War: The Seven Years' War and the Fate of Empire, 1754–1766* (New York, 2000), 578.

143. Patrick Villiers, *Marine royale, corsaires et trafic dans l'Atlantique de Louis XIV à Louis XVI* (Dunkerque, 1991), 430, 434–435; Pitman, *Development of the British West Indies*, 234; Crété, *La traite des nègres*, 233. Cf. Michel-René Hilliard d'Auberteuil, *Considérations sur l'état présent de la colonie française de Saint-Domingue: ouvrage politique et législatif; présenté au ministre de la marine*, 2 vols. (Paris, 1776–1777), 1:58; John Garrigus, *Before Haiti: Race and Citizenship in French Saint-Domingue* (New York, 2006), 37. The Jamaicans who established Saint-Domingue's first Masonic lodge in 1738 were probably indigo smugglers.

144. Rosario Sevilla Soler, *Santo Domingo tierra de frontera (1750–1800)* (Seville, 1980), 152.

145. Governor William Hart to the Board of Trade. St. Christopher, 15 Feb. 1726/7, in Donnan, *Documents*, 2:336–337; Middleton, *Tobacco Coast*, 191. Control of Saint Lucia was disputed between France and Britain until 1814, when Britain took the island.

146. *Proceedings and Debates of the British Parliaments Respecting North America 1754–1783*, ed. R. C. Simmons and P. D. G. Thomas, 6 vols. (Millwood, N.Y., 1982–1987), 2:578.

147. Governor William Mathew to Alured Popple, St. Christopher, 26 May 1737, in *Calendar of State Papers, Colonial Series, America and West Indies,* vol. 43, 1737 (London, 1963), 167, 170.

148. *Journal of the Commissioners for Trade and Plantations January 1749–1750 to December 1753 Preserved in the Public Record Office* (London, 1932), 129, 131.

149. C. E. Smith and C. V. H. Maxwell, "A Bermuda Smuggling-Slave Trade: The 'Manilla Wreck' Opens Pandora's Box," *Slavery and Abolition* 23 (April 2002): 57–86.

150. Frostin, *Histoire de l'autonomisme colon,* 626. Molasses production in Saint-Domingue came to 70,000 barrels per year in the 1770s: Hilliard d'Auberteuil, *Considérations sur l'état présent,* 1:317. After the French government allowed them to sell unwanted drink to foreigners, planters in the French colonies began filling barrels labeled "syrup" with sugar: Robert Louis Stein, *The French Sugar Business in the Eighteenth Century* (Baton Rouge, La., 1988), 78.

151. Elisha Brown, *Reftections [sic] upon the present state of affairs in this colony, offered to the consideration of the freeholders thereof* (Newport, R.I., 1759), 4. See for Hopkins's defense: Stephen Hopkins, *Governor Hopkins's vindication of his conduct, in relation to the sugars* (Newport, R.I., 1762); *Remarks on a late performance, sign'd, a freeman of the colony, in answer to a dialogue between the governor of the colony of Rhode-Island, and a freeman of the same colony* (Newport, R.I., 1762). Cf. James, *Colonial Rhode Island,* 321.

152. Hilliard d'Auberteuil, *Considérations sur l'état présent,* 1:285.

153. Thomas M. Truxes, *Irish-American Trade, 1660–1783* (New York, 1988), 114; James B. Hedges, *The Browns of Providence Plantations,* 2 vols. (Cambridge, Mass., 1952), 1:66.

154. These Africans were commonly those who could not be sold in the British islands; they probably included many Coromantees: David Geggus, "Sex Ratio, Age and Ethnicity in the Atlantic Slave Trade: Data from French Shipping and Plantation Records," *Journal of African History* 30 (1989): 23–44, esp. 35.

155. Pitman, *Development of the British West Indies,* 328; Tarrade, *Le commerce colonial,* 100, 111; John D. Garrigus, "Blue and Brown: Contraband Indigo and the Rise of a Free Colored Planter Class in French Saint-Domingue," *The Americas* 50 (October 1993): 233–263, esp. 244–245; Crété, *La traite des nègres,* 238; Banks, *Chasing Empire,* 170. One contemporary source estimated the annual flow of indigo alone from Saint-Domingue to Jamaica at £100,000: Hilliard d'Auberteuil, *Con-*

sidérations sur l'état présent, 1:281. See, for the opinion that the volume of slave smuggling has been exaggerated, Arlette Gautier, "Les origines ethniques des esclaves déportés à Nippes, Saint-Domingue, de 1721 à 1770 d'après les archives notariales," *Revue Canadienne des Études Africaines* 23 (1989): 28–39, esp. 33. For smuggling in Guadeloupe in this period, see Anne Pérotin-Dumon, *Être patriotique sous les tropiques: la Guadeloupe, la colonisation et la Révolution, 1789–1794* (Basse-Terre, 1985), 64–77.

156. One French source alleged that rice from Georgia and Carolina cost 15 to 18 livres per 100 pounds, a bargain compared to the 60 to 80 livres charged by French merchants. And flour arriving from New England and the mid-Atlantic region fetched 30 livres per barrel, much cheaper than French flour, which sold for 90 to 100 livres. Jean Baptiste Du Buc, *Lettres critiques et politiques, sur les colonies & le commerce des villes maritimes de France, addressées à G. T. Raynal* (Paris, 1785), 93–94.

157. Klooster, *Illicit Riches,* 103. In addition, British ships took around a thousand French vessels in the first four years of the war: James G. Lydon, *Pirates, Privateers, and Profits* (Upper Saddle River, N.J., 1970), 157–159.

158. Cf. Isaac Dookhan, *A History of the Virgin Islands of the United States* (n.p., 1974), 100; Thomas M. Truxes, "Transnational Trade in the Wartime North Atlantic: The Voyage of the Snow *Recovery,*" *Business History Review* 79 (Winter 2005): 751–780, esp. 756, 768–772. See, for the services of resident Protestant Frenchmen on behalf of merchants in Newport, Rhode Island: Frostin, *Histoire de l'autonomisme colon,* 601–602.

159. Banks, *Chasing Empire,* 178; Weuves, le jeune, *Réflexions historiques et politiques sur le commerce de France avec ses colonies de l'Amérique* (Geneva, 1780), 52–53; Allan Christelow, "Contraband Trade between Jamaica and the Spanish Main, and the Three Port Act of 1766," *Hispanic American Historical Review* 22 (May 1942): 309–343; H. J. Habakkuk, "Population, Commerce and Economic Ideas," in *The New Cambridge Modern History,* ed. A. Goodwin (Cambridge, 1965), 8:36.

160. Armytage, *Free Port System,* 31–64.

161. Neil R. Stout, "Goals and Enforcement of British Colonial Policy, 1763–1775," *American Neptune* 27 (1967): 211–220; Frese, "Smuggling, the Navy, and the Customs Service"; "The Court of Vice-Admiralty in Virginia and Some Cases of 1770–1775," ed. George Rees, *Virginia Magazine of History and Biography* 88 (July 1980): 301–337.

162. López Cantos, "Contrabando, corso y situado," 37; Memorandum by

Alexandro O'Reylly, 1765, in *Crónicas de Puerto Rico: desde la conquista hasta nuestros días, 1493–1955*, ed. Eugenio Fernández Méndez, 2d ed. (1957; San Juan, 1976), 237–269, esp. 245.

163. AGI, Caracas 932, annex to a letter by Juan de Goizueta and Vicente Rodríguez de Rivas, directors of the Compañía Guipuzcoana, to Julián de Arriaga, Madrid, 30 July 1771; Vicente de Amézaga Aresti, *Vicente Antonio de Icuza, comandante de corsarios* (Caracas, 1966), 189–198.

164. Enrique M. Barba, "Sobre el contrabando de la Colonia del Sacramonte (siglo XVIII)," *Investigaciones y Ensayos* 28 (January–June 1980): 57–76, esp. 60–61n3; Kenneth Maxwell, *Conflicts and Conspiracies: Brazil and Portugal 1750–1808*, 2d ed. (New York, 2004), 8–9.

165. Virginia Harrington, *The New York Merchant on the Eve of the Revolution*, (New York, 1935), 249–250; Barrow, *Trade and Empire*, 153; Matson, *Merchants and Empire*, 271–272, 299; *Letterbook of Greg & Cunningham, 1756–1757: Merchants of New York and Belfast*, ed. Thomas M. Truxes (Oxford, 2001), 88–89.

166. Carole Shammas, "How Self-Sufficient Was Early America?" *Journal of Interdisciplinary History* 13 (Autumn 1982): 247–272, esp. 265n. Cf. *The Beekman Mercantile Papers, 1746–1799*, ed. Philip L. White (New York, 1956), 685–694; Benjamin Woods Labaree, *The Boston Tea Party* (New York, 1964), 6–13; *John Norton & Sons, Merchants of London and Virginia: Being the Papers from their Counting House for the Years 1750 to 1795*, ed. Frances Norton Mason (New York, 1968), 213; K. G. Davies, ed., *Documents of the American Revolution, 1770–1783*, 21 vols. (Shannon, Ireland, 1971–1981), 3:80; Truxes, *Irish-American Trade*, 44–45.

167. Neil R. Stout, *The Royal Navy in America, 1760–1775: A Study of Enforcement of British Colonial Policy in the Era of the American Revolution* (Annapolis, Md., 1973), 44.

168. Margaret Ellen Newell, *From Dependency to Independence: Economic Revolution in Colonial New England* (Ithaca, N.Y., 1998), 267–269.

169. Allan Christelow, "French Interest in the Spanish Empire during the Ministry of the Duc de Choiseul, 1759–1771," *Hispanic American Historical Review* 21 (November 1941): 515–537, esp. 532.

170. Walker, *Spanish Politics*, 223.

171. Jean-François Landolphe, *Mémoires du Capitaine Landolphe, contenant l'histoire de ses voyages pendant trente-six ans, aux côtes d'Afrique et aux deux Amériques*, ed. J. S. Quesné, 2 vols. (Paris, 1823), 1:37–39; McNeill, *Atlantic Empires of France and Spain*, 200. Suriname received most of its horses from New England. Since molasses was the common means of payment, this trade was also illegal: Johannes Postma, "Breaching the

Mercantile Barriers of the Dutch Colonial Empire: North American Trade with Suriname during the Eighteenth Century," in *Merchant Organization and Maritime Trade in the North Atlantic, 1660–1815,* ed. Olaf Uwe Janzen (St. John's, Nfld., 1998), 107–131, esp. 128. See for the close commercial ties between Puerto Rico and Danish Saint Croix in the later eighteenth century: Waldemar Westergaard, *The Danish West Indies under Company Rule (1671–1754): With a Supplementary Chapter, 1755–1917* (New York, 1917), 220, 251, 314; Johannes Brøndsted, ed., *Vore gamle Tropekolonier,* 2 vols. (Copenhagen, 1953), 2:92.

172. Miguel Izard, *El miedo a la revolución: la lucha por la libertad en Venezuela (1777–1830)* (Madrid, 1979), 85, citing Angel López Cantos, *Don Francisco de Saavedra, segundo intendente de Caracas* (Seville, 1973), 102; Hilliard d'Auberteuil, *Considérations sur l'état présent,* 1:253n1. The latter's estimate is inflated because the mule trade with the Spanish Main was at least partially in the hands of merchants from Dutch Curaçao and Saint Eustatius, who would not have introduced such amounts of bullion into a French colony: Weuves, le jeune, *Réflexions historiques,* 54.

173. See for southern Cuba Feliciano Ramos, *El contrabando inglés,* 47, 55, 124–125, McNeill, *Atlantic Empires of France and Spain,* 197–200, and the account by a New York merchant about a venture in 1753 in Georgia Department of Archives and History (Atlanta), Colonial Records, Miscellaneous Bonds, Book R, deposition of Abraham Sarzedas, Hanover, Jamaica, 2 Sept. 1763. I thank Holly Snyder for providing me with a copy of this document. Cf. Peggy K. Liss, *Atlantic Empires: The Network of Trade and Revolution, 1713–1826* (Baltimore, Md., 1983), 46, and Theodore C. Hinckley, "The Decline of Caribbean Smuggling," *Journal of Inter-American Studies* 5 (January 1963): 107–121, esp. 114–117, for British policy during and right after the Seven Years' War.

174. Liss, *Atlantic Empires,* 82; John Caughey, "Bernardo de Galvez and the English Smugglers on the Mississippi, 1777," *Hispanic American Historical Review* 12 (February 1932): 46–58, esp. 50; Jack D. L. Holmes, "Some Economic Problems of Spanish Governors of Louisiana," *Hispanic American Historical Review* 42 (November 1962): 521–543, esp. 526–527.

175. Feliciano Ramos, *El contrabando inglés,* 233–234, 238.

176. MacLeod, *Spanish Central America,* 369. Indigo was also bought on the Mosquito Coast: Potthast-Jutkeit, "Centroamérica y el contrabando," 507.

177. Potthast-Jutkeit, "Centroamérica y el contrabando," 514; Scammell, "British Smuggling," 161.

178. Villiers, *Marine royale*, 682. Paul Wentworth to Lord Suffolk, Amsterdam, 5 Aug. 1777, in *Naval Documents of the American Revolution*, ed. William Bell Clark and William James Morgan, 10 vols. (Washington, D.C., 1964–1996), 9:548.

179. Authorization of specific foreign imports took place in Saint-Domingue in 1784, when three ports (Cap-Français, Port-au-Prince, and Les Cayes) were designated to replace the entrepôt of Môle Saint-Nicolas, which had been unable to handle all foreign traffic. From these ports, the French government also allowed molasses and rum to be exported. Decrees in 1786 and 1788 added tobacco, beer, and whale oil to the list of permitted foreign products: Blanche Maurel, *Cahiers de doléances de la colonie de Saint-Domingue pour les États généraux de 1789* (Paris, 1933), 70. Apart from a few ad hoc measures, the massive flour shipments from the United States were never legalized, however, leading to a feud between colony and mother country at the start of the French Revolution. In the last five months of 1789 alone, fifty-four ships from Philadelphia supplied flour: James Alexander Dun, "'What avenues of commerce, will you, Americans, not explore!' Commercial Philadelphia's Vantage onto the Early Haitian Revolution," *William and Mary Quarterly*, 3d ser., 62 (July 2005): 473–504, esp. 486.

180. Seymour Drescher, *Econocide: British Slavery in the Era of Abolition* (Pittsburgh, Pa., 1977), 195. After a dispute between the United States and France, various U.S. trading businesses chose Curaçao as their base in the late 1780s, using Dutch colors to gain access to Saint-Domingue's coffee and cotton: Klooster, *Illicit Riches*, 98.

181. Eric Willem van der Oest, "The Forgotten Colonies of Essequibo and Demerara, 1700–1814," in Postma and Enthoven, *Riches from Atlantic Commerce*, 323–361, esp. 359. Trade with the Caribbean accounted for 31.4% of all U.S. exports in 1790: John H. Coatsworth, "American Trade with European Colonies in the Caribbean and South America, 1790–1812," *William and Mary Quarterly*, 3d ser., 24 (April 1967): 243–266, esp. 248.

182. Liss, *Atlantic Empires*, 112.

183. New forms of smuggling, however, emerged, occurring for example along the border between the United States and Canada: Joshua M. Smith, *Borderland Smuggling: Patriots, Loyalists, and Illicit Trade in the Northeast, 1783–1820* (Gainesville, Fla., 2006).

184. Curaçao, he added, purchased substantial amounts of coffee. Venault de Charmilly, *Lettre à M. Bryan Edwards, membre du Parlement d'Angleterre, et de la Société Royale de Londres, colon propriétaire à la Jamaïque, en réfutation de son ouvrage, intitulé, Vues Historiques sur la colonie française de Saint-Domingue, etc. etc.* (London, 1797), 77; Julius Sherrard Scott III, "The Common Wind: Currents of Afro-American Communication in the Era of the Haitian Revolution" (Ph.D, diss., Duke University, 1986), 71; Armytage, *Free Port System,* 65.

185. David Patrick Geggus, *Slavery, War and Revolution: The British Occupation of Saint Domingue 1793–1798* (New York, 1982), 97, 231; Alan L. Karras, "Caribbean Contraband, Slave Property, and the State, 1767–1792," *Pennsylvania History: A Journal of Mid-Atlantic Studies* 64 (Summer 1997): 250–269, esp. 263–264. Under British occupation in 1794, the Navigation Acts applied to Saint-Domingue: Geggus, *Slavery, War and Revolution,* 134.

186. Harry Bernstein, *The Brazilian Diamond in Contracts, Contraband and Capital* (Lanham, N.J., 1986), 62–63; Joaquim Felício dos Santos, *Memórias do distrito diamantino da comarca do Sêrro Frio (Provincia de Minas Gerais),* 3d ed. (Rio de Janeiro, 1956), 206. Cf. Maxwell, *Conflicts and Conspiracies,* 100–102. In the 1810s, British traveler John Mawe wrote that "there is strong presumptive authority for stating that, since the first discovery of the mines, diamonds to the amount of two million sterling have thus found their way to Europe. . . ." John Mawe, *Travels in the Interior of Brazil, particularly in the Gold and Diamond Districts of that Country . . .* (London, 1812), 257.

187. Rudy Bauss, "Rio Grande do Sul in the Portuguese Empire: The Formative Years, 1777–1808," *The Americas* 39 (April 1983): 519–535, esp. 532–533; Jeremy Adelman, *Sovereignty and Revolution in the Iberian Atlantic* (Princeton, N.J., 2006), 72–74. In addition, thirty-one or thirty-two foreign ships entered the port of Rio de Janeiro on average in 1792–1800, but these included British whalers, which would not necessarily have engaged in illicit business. Pijning, "Controlling Contraband," 163. See also Jorge M. Pedreira, "From Growth to Collapse: Portugal, Brazil, and the Breakdown of the Old Colonial System," *Hispanic American Historical Review* 80 (November 2000): 839–864, esp. 853–860. According to one estimate, at least 22,000 slaves were illegally imported to Buenos Aires in the period 1750–1806, although foreign imports were legal between 1791 and 1796. If most of these Africans left for Potosí, the number who remained in Buenos Aires was also large, as suggested by the sixfold increase of the enslaved population from 1,276 in

1744 to 7,719 in 1810. Lyman L. Johnson, "The Competition of Slave and Free Labor in Artisanal Production: Buenos Aires, 1770–1815," *International Review of Social History* 40 (1995): 409–424, esp. 414; Susan M. Socolow, "Buenos Aires at the Time of Independence," in *Buenos Aires: 400 Years,* ed. Stanley R. Ross and Thomas F. McGann (Austin, Tex., 1982), 18–39, at 24. For the numbers of legally imported Africans, see the memorandum by Viceroy Nicolás de Arredondo to his successor, 16 March 1795, in *Memorias de los virreyes del Río de la Plata,* ed. Sigifrido A. Radelli (Buenos Aires, 1945), 394.

188. John Fisher, "The Imperial Response to 'Free Trade': Spanish Imports from Spanish America, 1778–1796," *Journal of Latin American Studies* 17 (1985): 35–78; Adelman, *Sovereignty and Revolution,* 156.

189. Jean Tarrade, "Le commerce entre les Antilles françaises et les possessions espagnoles d'Amérique à la fin du XVIIIe siècle," in Butel, *Commerce et plantation dans la Caraïbe XVIIIe et XIXe siècles,* 27–43, esp. 36; A. J. Pearce, "British Trade with the Spanish Colonies, 1788–1795," *Bulletin of Latin American Research* 20 (April 2001): 233–260, esp. 240, 243, 245, 249.

190. John Lynch, "The Origins of Spanish American Independence," in *The Independence of Latin America,* ed. Leslie Bethell (New York, 1987), 1–48, esp. 20–22. For the early stages of U.S. (contraband) trade with Spanish America, in particular Havana, see James A. Lewis, "Anglo-American Entrepreneurs in Havana: The Background and Significance of the Expulsion of 1784–1785," in *The North American Role in the Spanish Imperial Economy, 1760–1819,* ed. Jacques Barbier and Allan J. Kuethe (Manchester, England, 1984), 112–126.

191. John McCusker, for example, remarked that it "amounted to far less, relative to the total trade, than the sound and fury generated by such commerce would suggest. It is simply another instance of the disproportionate view of affairs induced by a concentration on aberrant behavior." John J. McCusker, "Rum and the American Revolution: The Rum Trade and the Balance of Payments of the Thirteen Colonies" (Ph.D. diss., University of Pittsburgh, 1970), 306.

192. Curtis Nettels, "British Mercantilism and the Economic Development of the Thirteen Colonies," *Journal of Economic History* 12 (Spring 1952): 105–114, esp. 110. See also Woody Holton, *Forced Founders: Indians, Debtors, Slaves, and the Making of the American Revolution in Virginia* (Chapel Hill, N.C., 1999), 46–61; and Margolin, "Lawlessness on the Maritime Frontier," 437.

193. The supporters of free trade at the Spanish court were consistently

eclipsed by other interests in the 1810s: Michael P. Costeloe, "Spain and the Latin American Wars of Independence: The Free Trade Controversy, 1810–1820," *Hispanic American Historical Review* 61 (May 1981): 209–234.

194. Quoted in Anthony Pagden, "Heeding Heraclides: Empire and Its Discontents, 1619–1812," in *Spain, Europe and the Atlantic World,* ed. Richard L. Kagan and Geoffrey Parker (New York, 1995), 316–333, esp. 331.

5. Procurators and the Making of the Jesuits' Atlantic Network

1. Felix Zubillaga and Agustín García Galán, who have looked closely at procurators, are two exceptions; Dauril Alden and Herman W. Konrad have emphasized procurators' economic role.

2. See Sean T. Perrone, "The Procurator General of the Castilian Assembly of the Clergy, 1592–1741," *Catholic Historical Review* 91 (January 2005): 26–59.

3. The Philippines province can also be considered as part of the Atlantic world, because all communication between Rome and Manila had to cross the Atlantic, then pass overland through New Spain to leave from Acapulco en route to Manila; this was also the case for the vice-province of the Mariana Islands. The French and Portuguese Jesuits in the Indian Ocean and Far East also had to cross the Atlantic, but followed the route around the Cape of Good Hope. The Italian and Central European provinces were not part of the Atlantic world per se, but participated in it through the colonial empires of Spain, Portugal, and France, and to a much lesser degree those of England and Holland. Ireland and Scotland were both Atlantic provinces in the strict sense, but they participated in the transatlantic Jesuit network in the same way as the Italian and Central European provinces.

4. Stuart B. Schwartz, "The Formation of a Colonial Identity in Brazil," and Anthony Pagden, "Identity Formation in Spanish America," both in *Colonial Identity in the Atlantic World, 1500–1800,* ed. Nicholas Canny and Anthony Pagden (Princeton, N.J., 1987), 15–50, 51–94.

5. The assistancies were Lusitaniae, Hispaniae, Galliae, Germaniae, and Italiae. For a descriptive chart, see the various printed catalogues of the order—for example, *Catalogus Personarum & Domiciliorum Societatis Iesu* (Mexico, 1751).

6. Joaquín María Domínguez, Charles O'Neil, and Manuel Guibovitch, *Diccionario histórico de la Compañía de Jesús: biográfico-temático* (hereafter, *Diccionario histórico*) (Rome, 2001), "Procurador," 3244–3245.

7. *Diccionario histórico*, "Procurador," 3244–3245.

8. Felix Zubillaga, "El Procurador de la Compañía de Jesús en la Corte de España," *Archivum Historicum Societatis Iesu* (hereafter, *AHSI*) 16 (1947): 13–22, 42; *Diccionario histórico*, "Procura de Misiones de la Antigua Compañía de Jesús," 3242–3244.

9. John W. O'Malley, *The First Jesuits* (Cambridge, Mass., 1993), 53.

10. David Weber, "Bourbons and Bárbaros: Center and Periphery in the Reshaping of Spanish Indians Policy," A. J. R. Russell-Wood, "Center and Periphery in the Luso-Brazilian World, 1500–1808," Elizabeth Mancke, "Negotiating an Empire: Britain and Its Overseas Peripheries, ca. 1550–1780," and Jack Greene, "Transatlantic Colonization and the Redefinition of Empire in the Early-Modern Era: The British-American Experience," all in *Negotiated Empires: Centers and Peripheries in the New World, 1500–1800*, ed. Christine Daniels and Michael V. Kennedy (New York, 2002), 79–104, 105–142, 235–266, 267–282.

11. The ministers who took the lead in expelling the Society from their monarch's domains and later were the main instigators of the Pope's suppression of the Company in 1773 were, respectively, the first ministers or favorites of the Portuguese king Joseph I, Sebastião de Melo, Marquis de Pombal; of the Spanish king Carlos III, Pedro Rodriguez Count of Campomanes; and of the French king Louis XV, Etienne François, Duc de Choiseul.

12. The Society had similar issues over jurisdiction with the three Catholic Atlantic powers: the Portuguese *padroado real,* the Spanish *patronato real,* and the Gallican rights of the French Church. All three regulated Crown–diocesan relationships, but papal bulls exempted the Society from most of these concordats.

13. O'Malley, *The First Jesuits,* 54.

14. Some Jesuit provinces existed more on paper than in reality, such as the Ethiopian province. Others were created as vice-provinces and split from existing provinces depending on ministerial potential as well as realities on the ground, while a few, such as the Malabar province and the Mariana vice-province, disappeared altogether.

15. Dauril Alden, *The Making of an Enterprise: The Society of Jesus in Portugal, Its Empire, and Beyond, 1540–1750* (Stanford, Calif., 1996), 75–77.

16. Ibid. I thank John Thornton and Linda Heywood for this and other invaluable information on the Jesuits in Portuguese Africa.

17. The direct involvement of the Portuguese Jesuits in the transatlantic slave trade was limited. They sold a few hundred slaves given to them by local leaders in the Angolan coast in order to build a college there in the

1590s. A *visitador* sent to inspect the Angolan enterprise suggested that the sale of slaves could be the economic foundation of that mission, but the Procurador do missões in Lisbon strongly objected to the scheme, a rejection confirmed by Father General Claudio Aquaviva (1581–1615) in 1604; Alden, *Making of an Enterprise,* 544–546. This is not to say that the Company did not buy slaves in Brazil brought by secular Portuguese, but the Company was not directly involved in the transatlantic transportation of slaves.

18. A. J. R. Russell-Wood, "Holy and Unholy Alliances: Clerical Participation in the Flow of Bullion from Brazil to Portugal during the Reign of Dom João V (1706–1750)," *Hispanic American Historical Review* 80 (November 2000): 824–825.

19. Zubillaga, "El Procurador de la Compañía de Jesús," 13–24; Agustín Galán García, *El "Oficio de Indias" de Sevilla y la organización económica y misional de la Compañía de Jesús* (Seville, 1995), 59 and 167.

20. King Sebastião died young in 1578, in a wild attempt to conquer what is today Morocco from the Turks, a scheme widely attributed to the influence on the king of his Jesuit confessor; Alden, *Making of an Enterprise,* 81–83.

21. The financing of the Atlantic missions of French Jesuit provinces was unique: the Caribbean missions had plantations for their operations. The missions of New France were subsidized by aristocratic donors, the rich Paris province, the sale of ginseng, and proceeds from the best-selling *Jesuit Relations.* Jesuits in New France could not sustain estates that produced agricultural surpluses as did their counterparts in Portuguese and Spanish America, the French Caribbean, and Maryland.

22. The other four French provinces were Toulouse, Champaign, Lyon, and Aquitaine.

23. Published originally during the seventeenth century, the *Relations* became some of the best-selling books on non-European peoples; they were republished in a bilingual edition during the 1890s by Reuben Gold Thwaites as *The Jesuit Relations and Allied Documents: Travels and Explorations of the Jesuit Missionaries in New France, 1610–1791,* 73 vols. (Cleveland, Ohio, 1896–1901), and in the twentieth century by Lucien Campeau as part of the Society's *Monumenta* series: *Monumenta Novae Franciae* (Québec, 2003).

24. Nicholas P. Cushner, *Why Have You Come Here? The Jesuits and the First Evangelization of the Americas* (New York, 2006), 187, 174.

25. Pierre Delattre and Edmond Lamalle, "Jésuites Wallons, Flamands, Français: Missionnaires au Paraguay, 1608–1767," *AHSI* 16 (1947): 98–

176. The German and Italian provinces participated in the transatlantic flow of personnel, goods, and funds in much the same way as the Belgian provinces—that is, through the Spanish, Portuguese, and French provinces' overseas efforts. On books from Flanders, see Galán García, *El "Oficio de Indias" de Sevilla,* 100.

26. *Diccionario histórico,* "Antillas holandesas," 194.

27. Wim Klooster, "Between Habsburg Neglect and Bourbon Assertiveness: Hispano-Dutch Relations in the New World, 1650–1750," in *España y las 17 Provincias de los Países Bajos: Una revisión historiográfica (S. XVI–XVIII),* ed. Ana Crespo Solana and Manuel Herrero Sánchez (Córdoba, 2002), 714–715; Cornelis Ch. Goslinga, *The Dutch in the Caribbean and in the Guianas, 1680–1791* (Dover, N.H., 1985), 259. I thank Wim Klooster for this and other invaluable information on the Dutch Jesuits.

28. Klooster, "Between Habsburg Neglect"; *Diccionario histórico,* "Antillas holandesas."

29. The Spanish terms were *rescatadores* and *encomenderos*—the latter not to be confused with the sixteenth-century meaning of the term, which referred to second-generation Conquistadors with semi-seigniorial rights over an Indian population.

30. The scandal is described in great detail in Dale Van Kley, *The Jansenists and the Expulsion of the Jesuits from France, 1757–1765* (New Haven, Conn., 1975), esp. 90–107; see also D. G. Thompson, "The French Jesuit Leaders and the Destruction of the Jesuit Order in France, 1756–1762," *French History* 2 (September 1988): 237–263, and Thompson, "The Lavalette Affair and the Jesuit Superiors," *French History* 10 (June 1996): 206–239.

31. For example, only a year apart the Company co-published Andrés Perez de Ribas's *Historia de los triunfos de nuestra Santa Fe* (Madrid, 1645) and Alonso de Ovalle's *Historica relacion del reino de Chile* (Rome, 1646). These two books described the missions of the Society in the northern and southern frontiers of the Spanish Empire in the Americas. Copies were found throughout the colleges of the Society, thus helping to diffuse ethnographical knowledge.

32. Pierre-François-Xavier Charlevoix, *Histoire et description générale de la Nouvelle France* (Paris, 1744) and *Histoire du Paraguay* (Paris, 1756). He did, however, spend some time in Italy as a Procureur à Rome.

33. José de Acosta, *Historia natural y moral de las Indias* (Seville, 1590).

34. For a multifaceted look at the rather eccentric work of this scholar, see the essays in Paula Findlen, ed., *Athanasius Kircher: The Last Man Who Knew Everything* (New York, 2004).

35. Galán García, *El "Oficio de Indias" de Sevilla*, 98–100.

36. "Fatura delas Piezas q ban en la flota del Cargo de Don Pedro Corbete, que partio de Cádiz a 12 de Julio de 1673," Archivo de la Provincia de Mexico de la Compañía de Jesús (hereafter, AHPM), section III, box 38, doc. no. 1505-A. A few years later when he wrote the triennial report of his tenure as procurator, he explained that he was personally responsible for the expenses of a sixth crate, full of chocolate, which he had sent to Rome possibly to curry favor with the curia: "Advertencia a la carta quenta que va con esta en la qual solo se ponen los gastos que causaron los cinco caxones de libros de mi quenta, no las partidas que debo del caxon de Chocolate que se remitio a Roma," 14 Oct. 1678, AHPM, section III, box 38, doc. no. 1505; both accounts were written in Mexico by Procurator Burgos.

37. Archivo General de la Nación, Mexico City (hereafter, AGN), *Jesuitas*, vol. 1, no. 33, exp. no. 74, fol. 214.

38. Parras library inventory from AGN, *Temporalidades* 64 (August 1767).

39. Peter Masten Dunne, *Andrés Pérez de Ribas: Pioneer Black Robe of the West Coast, Administrator, Historian* (New York, 1951).

40. Paula Findlen, "A Jesuit's Books in the New World: Athanasius Kircher and His American Readers," in her *Athanasius Kircher*, 329–364, at 346–347.

41. E. J. Burrus, "Sigüenza y Góngora's Efforts for Readmission into the Jesuit Order," *Hispanic American Historical Review* 33 (August 1953): 387–391.

42. Findlen, "A Jesuit's Books." For Sigüenza y Góngora, see Irving Leonard, *Baroque Times in Old Mexico: Seventeenth-Century Persons, Places, and Practices* (Ann Arbor, Mich., 1959), and *Don Carlos de Sigüenza y Góngora: A Mexican Savant of the Seventeenth Century* (Berkeley, Calif., 1929). For Kino, see Herbert Eugene Bolton, *Rim of Christendom: A Biography of Eusebio Francisco Kino, Pacific Coast Pioneer* (Tucson, Ariz., 1984).

43. Octavio Paz, *Sor Juana Inés de la Cruz, o, las trampas de la fé* (Mexico City, 1982), 357–386.

44. Findlen, "A Jesuit's Books"; Hugues Didier, "Antonio Vieira: un predicador portugués frente a la oratoria sagrada española," *Criticón* 84–85 (2002): 233–243. Even the Jesuits in Parras had Portuguese and Spanish copies of Vieira's sermons: AGN, *Jesuitas*, vol. 1, no. 33, exp. no. 30. The best treatment of Sor Juana, her work, and her intellectual world is Paz, *Sor Juana Ines de la Cruz*.

45. Nicholas P. Cushner, *Jesuit Ranches and the Agrarian Development of Argentina, 1650–1767* (Albany, N.Y., 1983), 49–65.

46. Magnus Mörner, *The Political and Economic Activities of the Jesuits in the La Plata Region: The Hapsburg Era* (Stockholm, 1953), and Barbara Ganson, *The Guaraní under Spanish Rule in the Rio de la Plata* (Stanford, Calif., 2003).

47. Cushner, *Why Have You Come Here?* 184–190.

48. Alden, *Making of an Enterprise,* 416–429; Nicholas P. Cushner, *Lords of the Land: Sugar, Wine, and Jesuit Estates of Coastal Peru, 1600–1767* (Albany, N.Y., 1980); Celia López-Chávez, "Con la cruz y con el aguardiente: la empresa vitivinícola Jesuita en el San Juan colonial," and Ana María Rivera Medina, "Estado, productores, e intermediarios: la vitivinicultura en el 'país de cuyum' siglo XVIII," both in *Universum* (Talca, Chile) 20, no. 2 (2005): 82–107, 198–233; Raúl Sánchez Andaur, "Viticultores Jesuitas en el Obispado de Concepción (Chile)," *Universum* 21, no. 1 (2006): 92–103.

49. Galán Garcia, *El "Oficio de Indias" de Sevilla,* 97. In what must be a typographical error, Galán Garcia says this transaction occurred in 1548, but the Order did not send its first missionaries to Brazil until the next year, and the primary source he uses is dated 1585, so the correct date must be 1584.

50. Russell-Wood, "Holy and Unholy Alliances," 824.

51. Steven J. Harris, "Jesuit Scientific Activity in the Overseas Missions, 1540–1773," *Isis* 96 (March 2005): 71–79; Margarita Artschwager Kay, "The Florilegio Medicinal: Source of Southwest Ethnomedicine," *Ethnohistory* 24 (Summer 1977): 251–259.

52. Steven J. Harris, "Long Distance Corporations, Big Science, and the Geography of Knowledge," *Configurations* 6 (Spring 1998): 14–17.

53. Galán Garcia, *El "Oficio de Indias" de Sevilla,"* 98–99.

54. Alden, *Making of an Enteprise,* 312n60.

55. Russell-Wood, "Holy and Unholy Alliances."

56. Ibid., 824.

57. Some of the transfers were "horizontal" within the network, and not always within the same assistancy. See Luke Closey, "The Early Modern Jesuit Missions as a Global Movement," Working Papers from the World History Workshop Conference Series, 2005, paper no. 3 (University of California, Multi-Campus Research Unit). The transfer of bullion to Rome seems to have been a particular personal obsession of Campomanes in Spain, though its importance to imperial finances was

marginal. See Stanley J. Stein and Barbara H. Stein, *Apogee of Empire: Spain and New Spain in the Age of Charles III, 1759–1788* (Baltimore, Md., 2003), 232.

58. Geoffrey Holt, "The Fatal Mortgage: The English Province and the Père La Valette" *AHSI* 38, no. 76 (1969): 464–478. The fate of the English Jesuits was different from that of their French, Portuguese, and Spanish counterparts, all of whom were exiled to the Papal States and their properties confiscated when the order was suppressed. Ironically, the Jesuits of the English province fared better than those of other Atlantic provinces. The Jesuits in England kept most of their possessions (though some property was confiscated by the French Crown), and even flourished. The various districts of the English province became independent of each other, retaining control of their own properties and finances to support the priests who worked in them. In 1778 their work was recognized by papal brief, and they were allowed to keep community life until 1803, when they were aggregated into the Russian Jesuits, who had never been suppressed. The Jesuits in Maryland, under the name Corporation of Roman Catholic Clergymen, founded Georgetown College and resumed the name of the Society in 1805.

59. *"prohibido darles sugetos que no son españoles"*: "Las dilatadas y trabajosas misiones de Cinaloa, Parras, Tepeguanes, Tarahumaras, Siera de San Andres, de San Ignacio, y Topia . . . ," AHPM, section III, box 41, doc. no. 1667.

60. Galán Garcia, *El "Oficio de Indias" de Sevilla*, 121.

61. "Lettres diverses, adressés au R. P. Jean de Laberville, tauchant les Missions des Illinois," Jacques Gravier, 5 March 1702, in *The Jesuit Relations and Allied Documents*, vol. 66, doc. no. 178, puffin.creighton.edu/ jesuit/relations.

62. Alden, *Making of an Enterprise*, 628.

63. *Diccionario histórico*, "Procura de Misiones," 3242–3243; see also Alden, *Making of an Enterprise*, esp. ch. 12, "The Fiscal Administration of an Enterprise," 298–318.

64. David Weber, *The Spanish Frontier in North America* (New Haven, Conn., 1992), 60–74.

65. Felix Zubillaga, "El Procurador de Indias Occidentales de la Compañía de Jesús," *AHSI* 22, no. 43 (1953): 367–417, esp. 369–374; for a history of the Florida mission, see Weber, *The Spanish Frontier*.

66. Chile and Marianas remained vice-provinces through the seventeenth century; for the place of the Philippines, see note 3.

67. This branch office of the Procurator of the West Indies in Madrid should

not be confused with the post of Court Procurator created in 1570, though the two coordinated their specialized tasks at court.

68. Galán García, *El "Oficio de Indias" de Sevilla,* 84–110; Zubillaga, "El Procurador de Indias Occidentales."

69. *Diccionario histórico,* "Procura des Misiones," 3243–3244; Galán García, *El "Oficio de Indias" de Sevilla,* ch. 7: "El Hospicio de Indias: una necesidad en una nueva empresa," 163–182.

70. Galán García, *El "Oficio de Indias" de Sevilla";* Zubillaga, "El Procurador de Indias Occidentales."

71. Quoted in Zubillaga, "El Procurador de Indias Occidentales," 394–398.

72. In "Instruczion para los Procuradores de las Indias oczidentales que residen en Sevilla y Madrid y para los que seran embiados de aquellas Provincias y para los Provinciales de unos y de otros," Juan Pablo Oliva, Rome, 3 Jan. 1668. Certified by Joan de Ribedenayra in Seville on 20 March 1668, AHPM, section III, box 37, doc. no. 1487.

73. In "Instruccion para los Procuradores de las Indias Occidentales en Sevilla y Madrid ordenada por N. M. R. P. Miguel Angel Tamburini, confirmando con alguna mayor explicacion las ordenes dados en diversos tiempos por N. N. P. P. Generales Claudio Aquaviva, Mucio Vitteleschi, Gosvino Nikel, Juan Pablo Oliva, y Thirso Gonzales," by Miguel Angel Tamburini, Rome, 22 June 1709, AHPM, section III, box 37, doc. no. 1486.

74. "Catalogo de las cosas q lleba encomendadas del P. Pedro Antonio Diaz, Provincial de esta Nueba España el P. Lorenzo de Albandro, Procurador a Roma," 27 May 1663, AHPM, section III, box 37, doc. no. 1478.

75. *"concluir el pleyto de los diezmos que segun el emplazamiento que se hizo a las cathedrales de las Indias estara ya para sentenciarse":* "Dos negocios principales lleva a su cargo el Procurador que se embia por esta Provincia a las Cortes de Madrid y Roma," Nov. 1674, AHPM, section III, box 37, doc. no. 1479.

76. "Ynstruccion a los Padres Procuradores en algunos puntos que sean de obrar en Madrid y Roma," P. Bernardo Pardo, 4 June 1681, AHPM, doc. nos. 1480 and 1481; "Para la conduccion de los sugetos. Ynstruccion de P. Provincial a los P. Pedro de Echagoain y Bernabe Francisco Gutierrez, Procuradores a Roma, acerca de los negocios que son de su cargo para su mejor especion." Bernardo Pardo, 6 June 1681, AHPM, doc. no. 1669.

77. "Instruccion q da el P. Andres Nieto Provincial de la Provincia de la Nueba España de la Compañia de JESUS a los Padres Nicolas de Segura y Juan Ignacio de Uribe Procuradores de dicha Provincia a la Curia Romana," signed by Provincial Andres Nieto and his secretary Joseph

Barba, Mexico City, 13 Nov. 1726, AHPM, section III, box 41, doc. no. 1670.

78. "Instruccion queda el P. Joseph Barba Provincial de la Provincia de Nueba España de la Compañia de JESUS a los P. Procuradores Juan de Guendulain y Andres Xavier Garcia, Procuradores de dicha Provincia a la Curia Romana," signed by Provincial Joseph Barba and his secretary Francisco Xavier Ferndandez, 3 Feb. 1734, AHPM, section III, box 41, doc. no. 1671; "Instruccion que da el P. Christobal de Escobar y Llamas Provincial de la Provincia de Nueba España de la Compañia de IHS a los P. Procuradores Pedro de Echavarri y Joseph Maldonado Produradores de dicha Provincia a la Curia Romana," signed by Provincial Christobal de Escobar and his secretary Agustin Carta, 8 Oct. 1743, AHPM, section III, box 41, doc. no. 1672.

6. Dissenting Religious Communication Networks and European Migration, 1660–1710

I would like to thank Peter Busch, Shirley Leckie, and Derek Russell for their useful comments on this essay at critical points in my attempts to conceptualize the project.

1. Mary Maples Dunn and Richard S. Dunn, eds., *The Papers of William Penn* (hereafter, *Penn Papers*), vol. 1, *1644–1679* (Philadelphia, Pa., 1981), 439; Norman Penney, ed., *The Short Journal and Itinerary Journals of George Fox* (New York, 1925), 239.

2. William I. Hull, *Benjamin Furly and Quakerism in Rotterdam* (Lancaster, Pa., 1941), 46; Ethyn Kirby, *George Keith, 1638–1716* (New York, 1942), 37.

3. By "Pietist," I mean the various seventeenth-century European religious groups that called for reforms by stressing individual piety and devotional life. I am including participants in the "Frommigkeitsbewegungen" of the seventeenth century as well as Halle Pietism in the 1690s and early 1700s, especially before its integration into the Prussian Lutheran church. Martin Brecht and Johannes van den Berg, eds., *Geschichte des Pietismus*, vol. 1: *Der Pietismus vom siebzehnten bis zum frühen acthzehnten Jahrhundert* (Göttingen, 1993), 1–9; Jonathan Strom, "Problems and Promises of Pietism Research," *Church History* 71 (2002): 536–554; Hartmut Lehmann, "Erledigte und nicht erledigte Aufgaben der Pietismusforschung: Eine nochmalige Antwort an Johannes Wallmann," *Pietismus und Neuzeit* 31 (2005): 13–20.

4. For a good discussion of communication network theory, see Renate

Pieper, *Die Vermittlung einer Neuen Welt: Amerika im Nachrichtennetz des Habsburgischen Imperiums, 1493–1598* (Mainz, 2000), 1–68.

5. "Transnational" is used according to early modern definitions that focused on ethnic and cultural characteristics and the political boundaries of territories rather than in the sense of modern nation-states.

6. Rosalind J. Beiler, "Bridging the Gap: Cultural Mediators and the Structure of Transatlantic Communication," in *Atlantic Communications: The Media in American and German History from the Seventeenth to the Twentieth Century*, ed. Norbert Finzsch and Ursula Lehmkuhl (Oxford, 2004), 45–64.

7. Michael Driedger, *Obedient Heretics: Mennonite Identities in Lutheran Hamburg and Altona during the Confessional Age* (Aldershot, England, 2002), 82–106. For two recent syntheses of the extensive literature on "confessionalization," the process through which German territorial leaders used official churches to transform society and cultural identity, see Ute Lotz-Heumann, "The Concept of 'Confessionalization': A Historiographical Paradigm in Dispute," *Memoria y Civilizacion* 4 (2001), 93–114, and Thomas Kaufmann, "Einleitung," *Interkonfessionalität-Transkonfessionalität-binnenkonfessionelle Pluralität: Neue Forschungen zur Konfessionalisierungthese*, ed. Kaspar von Greyerz et al. (Gütersloh, Germany, 2002), 13–14.

8. Barry Reay, *The Quakers and the English Revolution* (New York, 1985), 103–122; Hugh Barbour, *The Quakers in Puritan England* (New Haven, Conn., 1964), 234–256; Carla Gardina Pestana, *The English Atlantic in the Age of Revolution, 1640–1661* (Cambridge, Mass., 2004), 154–155.

9. See especially the essays in Fred Van Lieburg, ed., *Confessionalism and Pietism: Religious Reform in Early Modern Europe* (Mainz, 2006).

10. Jon Butler, *The Huguenots in America: A Refugee People in a New World Society* (New York, 2003); Bertrand Van Ruymbeke, *From New Babylon to Eden: The Huguenots and Their Migration to Colonial South Carolina* (Columbia, S.C., 2005); Van Ruymbeke and Randy J. Sparks, eds., *Memory and Identity: The Huguenots in France and the Atlantic Diaspora* (Columbia, S.C., 2003).

11. Nanne van der Zijpp, "The Dutch Aid the Swiss Mennonites," in *A Legacy of Faith: A Sixtieth Anniversary Tribute to Cornelius Krahn*, ed. Cornelius J. Dyck (Newton, Kansas, 1962), 145–151.

12. Bernard Bailyn has argued that migration to British North America was "an extension outward and an expansion in scale of domestic mobility in the lands of the immigrants' origins, and the transatlantic flow must be viewed within the context of these *domestic* mobility patterns." Bernard

Bailyn, *The Peopling of British North America: An Introduction* (New York, 1986), 20.

13. Although the English term "Anabaptist" is fairly neutral, European Mennonites preferred the terms "Mennoniten," "Taufgesinnten" (German), or "Doopsgezinden" (Dutch) because, aside from the first generation, they were not baptized as children and rebaptized as adults but rather practiced "believer's baptism." Driedger, *Obedient Heretics,* 1.

14. Richard K. MacMaster, *Land, Piety, Peoplehood: The Establishment of Mennonite Communities in America, 1683–1790* (Scottdale, Pa., 1985), 19–21; Donald F. Durnbaugh, *The Believer's Church: The History and Character of Radical Protestantism,* 2d ed. (Scottdale, Pa., 1985), 64–74.

15. MacMaster, *Land, Piety, Peoplehood,* 21–24; James Lowry, trans. and ed., *Hans Landis: Swiss Anabaptist Martyr in Seventeenth Century Documents* (Millersburg, Ohio, 2003), 1–13.

16. Alastair Hamilton, Sjouke Voolstra, and Piet Visser, *From Martyr to Muppy: A Historical Introduction to Cultural Assimilation Processes of a Religious Minority in the Netherlands: The Mennonites* (Amsterdam, 1994), vii–xi; Cornelius J. Dyck, ed., *An Introduction to Mennonite History* (Scottdale, Pa., 1967), 89–102; MacMaster, *Land, Piety, Peoplehood,* 24–25.

17. Cornelius Krahn, *Dutch Anabaptism* (Scottdale, Pa., 1981), 253–254; MacMaster, *Land, Piety, Peoplehood,* 26–28.

18. Dieter Hangebruch, "Krefeld unter oranischer und unter preußischer Herrschaft," in *Krefeld: Die Geschichte der Stadt,* vol. 2, *Von der Reformationszeit bis 1794,* ed. Reinhard Feinendegen and Hans Vogt (Krefeld, 2000), 191–192; see also Jeremy D. Bangs, trans., *Letters on Toleration: Dutch Aid to Persecuted Swiss and Palatine Mennonites, 1615–1699* (Rockport, Maine, 2004), doc. no. 15, pp. 104–107.

19. Gemeentearchief Amsterdam (hereafter, GA), 565, A #1405 (a), as translated in Bangs, *Letters on Toleration,* doc. no. 96, p. 248.

20. 19 Dec. 1671, GA, 565, A, #1248, copies of original documents on microfilm at the Lancaster Mennonite Historical Society (hereafter, LMHS), Lancaster, Pa. Unless otherwise noted, all GA documents referred to were read at the LMHS. Rosalind J. Beiler, "Information Networks and the Dynamics of Migration: Swiss Anabaptist Exiles and Their Host Communities," in *Religious Refugees in Europe, Asia and North America (6th–21st Centuries),* ed. Susanne Lachenicht (Münster, 2007), 81–91.

21. "Deacons" in the Dutch Mennonite church were lay leaders assigned to take care of the physical needs of the congregation. They oversaw poor relief and church finances. Mary Sprunger, "Rich Mennonites, Poor

Mennonites: Economics and Theology in the Amsterdam Waterlander Congregation during the Golden Age" (Ph.D. diss., University of Illinois at Urbana-Champaign, 1993), 34–35.

22. Bangs, *Letters on Toleration,* 22–29.

23. Accounts, 1659–1661, GA, 565, A #1194, as translated in Bangs, *Letters on Toleration,* doc. no. 31, pp. 136–146.

24. 20 Jan. 1672, GA, 565, A, #1116, as translated in Bangs, *Letters on Toleration,* doc. no. 110, pp. 268–269.

25. 12 April 1690, GA, 565, A, #1127; 15 July 1690, GA, 565, A, #1130.

26. 19 Dec. 1671, GA, 565, A, #1248; GA, 565, A #1400–1406; van der Zijpp, "Dutch Aid," 139–140; MacMaster, *Land, Piety, Peoplehood,* 27.

27. 2 Feb. 1672, GA, 565, A, #1410; 28 Feb. 1672, GA, 565, A, #1412.

28. 6 April 1672, GA, 565, A, #1196.

29. 2 Nov. 1671, GA, 565, A, #1405. For locations of the Palatine Mennonite congregations who participated in aiding the refugees, see Harold S. Bender, ed., "Palatine Mennonite Census Lists, 1664–1774," *Mennonite Quarterly Review* 14 (1940): 5–40.

30. 19 Dec. 1671, GA, 565, A, #1248.

31. Meinrad Schaab, *Geschichte der Kurpfalz,* vol. 2, *Neuzeit* (Stuttgart, 1992), 136–138.

32. Petition of the Mennonite ministers in Kriegsheim, 31 Oct. 1660, Badisches Generallandesarchiv, Karlsruhe, Germany (hereafter, GLA), 77/4336a, 63.

33. Petition of the Mennonites in the Palatinate, 26 Nov. 1680, GLA 77/4337. For a translation of Karl Ludwig's original decree allowing Mennonites to settle in the Palatinate, see Edict, 17 Aug. 1664, in Bangs, *Letters on Toleration,* doc. no. 85, pp. 236–237.

34. Ralf Klötzer, "Verfolgt, geduldet, anerkannt: Von Täufern zu Mennoniten am Niederrhein und die Geschichte der Mennoniten in Krefeld bis zum Ende der oranischen Zeit (ca. 1530–1702)," in *Sie kamen als Fremde: Die Mennoniten in Krefeld von den Anfängen bis zur Gegenwart,* ed. Wolfgang Froese (Krefeld, 1995), 34–36; Peter Kriedte, *Proto-Industrialisierung und großes Kapital: Das Seidengewerbe in Krefeld und seinem Umland bis zum Ende des Ancien Régime* (Bonn, 1983), 221–224.

35. GA, 565, A, #1427, #1752, #1753, #1759, #1760, #1761; see also Archiv der Mennonitengemeinde Krefeld, 80/4/5–8, 80/4/12, 80/4/14–16, Stadtarchiv, Krefeld, Germany (hereafter, Stadtarchiv Krefeld]); Klötzer, "Verfolgt," 48.

36. William Braithwaite, *The Beginnings of Quakerism,* 2d ed. (New York, 1970), 307–309; Barbour, *Quakers in Puritan England,* 254–256, suggests

that early Quakerism was more a movement (like a revival or renewal movement) than a religious sect.

37. Barbour, *Quakers in Puritan England,* 33–71, 94–126; Frank C. Huntington, Jr., "Quakerism during the Commonwealth: The Experience of the Light," *Quaker History* 71 (1982): 69–88. For a review of the literature on Quaker origins, see H. Larry Ingle, "From Mysticism to Radicalism: Recent Historiography of Quaker Beginnings," *Quaker History* 76 (1987): 79–94.

38. The name "Society of Friends" was not used until after the restoration of the Stuart monarchy when Quakers increasingly worked to define their practice and organizational structures. Braithwaite, *Beginnings of Quakerism,* 44, 73; Hugh Barbour and J. William Frost, *The Quakers* (New York, 1988), 25–35.

39. Kenneth L. Carroll, "American Quakers and Their London Lobby," *Quaker History* 70 (1981): 22; Huntington, "Quakerism during the Commonwealth," 69–70; Frederick B. Tolles, *Quakers and the Atlantic Culture* (New York, 1960), 1–35; Pestana, *The English Atlantic,* 130–131.

40. Barbour and Frost, *The Quakers,* 3–24; Barbour, *Quakers in Puritan England,* 70–71, 207–233; Christopher Hill, *The World Turned Upside Down: Radical Ideas during the English Revolution* (New York, 1972), 186–215; Carroll, "American Quakers," 22.

41. Barbour and Frost, *The Quakers,* 65–66; Craig Horle, *The Quakers and the English Legal System, 1660–1688* (Philadelphia, Pa., 1988), 65–159.

42. Braithwaite, *Beginnings of Quakerism,* 98–110; Tolles, *Quakers and the Atlantic Culture,* 21–35.

43. Swarthmore MSS, Library of the Society of Friends, London (hereafter, LSF). For an overview of the collection and an index to the volumes including personal letters, see the typescript calendar, Geoffrey F. Nuttall, *Early Quaker Letters from the Swarthmore Mss. to 1660* (London, 1952). The Swarthmore collection is only one portion of early Quaker correspondence. These letters do not include formal epistles (letters of exhortation) and other published literature that Quakers produced during the period.

44. William Ames, Utrecht, to Margaret Fell, 17 April 1657, MS box E, James Bowden's Copies of Letters of Early Friends, European Section, 14, LSF.

45. Kate Peters, *Print Culture and the Early Quakers* (New York, 2005), 15–42.

46. Barbour and Frost, *The Quakers,* 66–69.

47. N. C. Hunt, *Two Early Political Associations: The Quakers and the Dissenting Deputies in the Age of Sir Robert Walpole* (Oxford, 1961), 1–17.

48. Horle, *Quakers,* 161–253.

49. *Penn Papers,* 1:24–26; Elton Trueblood, *Robert Barclay* (New York, 1968), 61–77; Kirby, *George Keith,* 19–34.

50. Frederick Tolles and E. Gordon Alderfer, eds., *The Witness of William Penn* (New York, 1980), 63–105; Melvin Endy, *William Penn and Early Quakerism* (Princeton, N.J., 1973), 137–141.

51. 24 July 1660, GLA 77/4336a, 54; 18 Aug. 1660, GLA 77/4336a, 48; 19 Aug. 1660, GLA 77/4336a, 57; 4 Sept. 1660, GLA 77/4336a, 59–60; 26 Oct. 1660, GLA 77/4336a, 62; Paul Michel, "Täufer, Mennoniten und Quäker in Kriegsheim bei Worms," *Der Wormsgau* 7 (1965–1966): 43–44; William I. Hull, *William Penn and the Dutch Quaker Migration to Pennsylvania* (Philadelphia, Pa., 1935), 266–291; Braithwaite, *Beginnings of Quakerism,* 414.

52. Peter Hendriks, Amsterdam, to Roger Longworth, 4 June 1680, Etting Collection, Misc. MSS, 4:9, Historical Society of Pennsylvania (hereafter, HSP); 14 July 1680; 7, 26, 31 Aug. 1680, GLA 77/4337.

53. William Caton, *A Journal of the Life of that Faithful Servant and Minister of the Gospel of Jesus Christ, William Caton* (London, 1689), 63, 64–71; William Ames, Kriegsheim, to George Fox, 14 Feb. 1661, and William Ames, Frankfurt an der Oder, to Margaret Fell, 18 April 1661, both MSS box E, James Bowden's Transcripts of Letters of Early Friends, European Section, 11, 6; William Caton, Rotterdam, to Margaret Fell, 27 Aug. 1661, Swarthmore MSS 1, 322, Trans. 1, 458; Stephen Crisp, *A Journal of the Life of Stephen Crisp,* in *A Memorable Account of the Christian Experiences, Gospel Labors, Travels and Sufferings of that Ancient Servant in Christ Stephen Crisp in his Books and Writings Herein Collected* (London, 1695), 28–30; William Penn, Mannheim, to Karl Ludwig, Elector of the Palatinate, 25 Aug. 1677, *Penn Papers,* 1:451–454.

54. Peter Hendriks, Amsterdam, to Roger Longworth, 4 June 1680, Etting Collection, Misc. MSS, 4:9.

55. Hull, *William Penn,* 196–204.

56. Barbour, *Quakers in Puritan England,* 55–61.

57. Account of his travels in Germany and Holland written from Frankfurt in 1661. Taken from "Letters, Followed by account of John Stubbs & William Caton's Journey to Holland," Portfolio 1/10, LSF.

58. William I. Hull, *The Rise of Quakerism in Amsterdam, 1655–1665* (Philadelphia, Pa., 1938), 17–177.

59. Wilhelm Hubben, *Die Quäker in der deutschen Vergangenheit* (Leipzig,

1929), 61–105; Sünne Juterczenka, "Von Amsterdam bis Danzig: Kommunikative Netze der europäischen Quäkermission im 17. und frühen 18. Jahrhundert," in *Atlantic Understandings: Essays on European and American History in Honor of Hermann Wellenreuther,* ed. Claudia Schnurmann and Hartmut Lehmann (Hamburg, 2006), 139–158; J. Z. Kannegieter, *Geschiedenis van de vroegere Quakergemeenschap te Amsterdam, 1656 tot begin negentiende eeuw* (Amsterdam, 1971).

60. Johannes van den Berg, "Die Frömmigkeitsbestrebungen in den Niederlanden," in *Geschichte des Pietismus,* 1:99–105; Aart de Groot, "Jean de Labadie" in *Orthodoxie und Pietismus,* ed. Martin Greschat (Stuttgart, 1982), 191–203.

61. Hull, *Benjamin Furly,* 31. William Penn converted to Quakerism in 1666–1667. Melvin B. Endy, *William Penn and Early Quakerism* (Princeton, N.J., 1973), 93–98.

62. Trueblood, *Robert Barclay,* 84–85.

63. Penn's journal of this journey is in *Penn Papers,* 1:425–508. See also Hull, *William Penn,* 64–106.

64. Hull, *William Penn,* 21–31; F. Ernest Stoeffler, *The Rise of Evangelical Pietism* (Leiden, 1971), 162–169; Trueblood, *Robert Barclay,* 84–87. For Penn's correspondence with Labadie's followers, see *Penn Papers,* 1:215–219.

65. Stoeffler, *Rise of Evangelical Pietism,* 229. The literature on Spener and German Pietism is vast. For a brief overview and a good synthesis, see the multivolume series edited by Martin Brecht et al., *Geschichte des Pietismus* (Göttingen), esp. vols. 1 and 2.

66. Andreas Deppermann, *Johann Jakob Schütz und die Anfänge des Pietismus* (Tübingen, 2002), 81–206; Elizabeth Fisher, "'Prophesies and Revelations': German Cabbalists in Early Pennsylvania," *Pennsylvania Magazine of History and Biography* 109 (1985): 302–306.

67. *Penn Papers,* 1:447.

68. Ibid., 447–456; Fisher, "'Prophesies and Revelations,'" 316; Hull, *William Penn,* 132–139; Deppermann, *Johann Jakob Schütz,* 322–327.

69. Martin Brecht, "Philipp Jakob Spener, sein Programm und dessen Auswirkungen," in Brecht et al., *Geschichte des Pietismus,* 1:278–289. For Spener's extensive correspondence network, see Johannes Wallmann, ed., *Briefe aus der Frankfurter Zeit, 1666–1686,* vol. 1, *1666–1674* (Tübingen, 1992), and vol. 2, *1675–1676* (Tübingen, 1996).

70. Deppermann, *Johann Jakob Schütz,* 222–336; Fisher, "'Prophesies and Revelations,'" 299–333.

71. See, for example, *Penn Papers,* 1:215–219, 448–451, 459–463; Marjorie

Nicolson, *Conway Letters: The Correspondence of Anne, Viscountess Conway, Henry More, and Their Friends, 1642–1684* (New Haven, Conn., 1930), 309–436; Trueblood, *Robert Barclay*, 64–67, 74–75, 84–92; Deppermann, *Johann Jakob Schütz*, 322–327.

72. Gary Nash, *Quakers and Politics: Pennsylvania, 1681–1726*, new ed. (1968; Boston, 1993), 4–10; John E. Pomfret, *Colonial New Jersey: A History* (New York, 1973), 22–48.

73. *Penn Papers*, 1:452–453.

74. Nash, *Quakers and Politics*, 8–9; Sally Schwartz, *"A Mixed Multitude": The Struggle for Toleration in Colonial Pennsylvania* (New York, 1988), 12–35; Mary K. Geiter, *William Penn* (London, 2000), 33–44.

75. William Penn, New York, to William Blathwayt and Francis Gwyn, 21 Nov. 1682, in *William Penn and the Founding of Pennsylvania, 1680–1684: A Documentary History*, ed. Jean R. Soderlund et al. (Philadelphia, Pa., 1983), 190.

76. Nash, *Quakers and Politics*, 11–28.

77. Julius F. Sachse, *Daniel Falckner's Curieuse Nachricht from Pennsylvania: The Book That Stimulated the Great German Immigration to PA in the Early Years of the XVIII Century* (Lancaster, Pa., 1905), 9–12; Julius F. Sachse, "Address of Julius F. Sachse," *The Pennsylvania-German Society Proceedings and Addresses* 7 (1897): 157–164; Hull, *Benjamin Furly*, 68–76. Sachse's work tends to be hagiographic and should be used with caution. I have tried, whenever possible, to verify the information he supplies by reading the original sources he cites or other historians who corroborate his interpretation by relying on original sources.

78. Richard S. Dunn and Mary Maples Dunn, *The Papers of William Penn*, vol. 2, *1680–1684* (Philadelphia, Pa., 1982), 81; Soderlund et al., *William Penn*, 58–66; Albert C. Myers, ed., *Narratives of Early Pennsylvania, West New Jersey and Delaware, 1630–1707* (New York, 1912), 201. For Penn's views on toleration, see Schwartz, *"A Mixed Multitude,"* 12–22.

79. Patrick Erben, "Promoting Pennsylvania: Penn, Pastorius and the Creation of a Transnational Community," *Resources for American Literary Study* 29 (2003–2004): 25–65.

80. Beiler, "Bridging the Gap," 54–56; MacMaster, *Land, Piety, Peoplehood*, 35–41.

81. Hull, *William Penn*, 253.

82. Sachse, *Daniel Falckner's Curieuse Nachricht*, 10–11; Samuel Pennypacker, "The Settlement of Germantown, PA and the Causes Which Led to It," *Pennsylvania Magazine of History and Biography* 4 (1880), reprinted in *Historical and Biographical Sketches* (Philadelphia, Pa., 1883),

11–12; Marion D. Learned, *The Life of Francis Daniel Pastorius* (Philadelphia, Pa., 1908), 122–123. For the debate among historians about whether the original settlers of Germantown were Quakers or Mennonites and German or Dutch, see Charlotte Boecken, "'Dutch Quaker' aus Krefeld, die (Mit)Gründer Germantowns 1683?" *Die Heimat* 53 (1982): 23–31.

83. Schwartz, "*A Mixed Multitude*", 25–26; Hull, *William Penn*, 207–232; Dieter Pesch, ed., *Brave New World: Rhinelanders Conquer America— The Journal of Johannes Herbergs* (Kommern, Germany, 2001), 25–31.

84. Deppermann, *Johann Jakob Schütz*, 327–335; Francis Daniel Pastorius, "Beehive," as quoted in Learned, *Pastorius*, 110; Francis Daniel Pastorius, "Res Propriae—Common Place Book, 1685–1716," 7, Papers of Francis Daniel Pastorius, 1651–1719, HSP.

85. Power of Attorney, Frankfurt, 2 April 1683, Papers of Francis Daniel Pastorius, 1651–1719. For a discussion of the different names used by the company of investors, see Learned, *Pastorius*, 120, 140. In the early years, Pastorius referred to the company as the "High German Company," "High German Society," "German Company," "German Society," and "German Company or Society." In Pennsylvania and after the investors reorganized in 1686, Pastorius referred to them as "the Frankfurt Company." The investors in Germany referred to themselves as the "Pennsylvania Company."

86. *Penn Papers*, 2:490, 591–597; Learned, *Pastorius*, 126–148; Deppermann, *Johann Jakob Schütz*, 327–335; "Grund- und Lager-Buch," AM 3713, HSP; Marianne Wokeck, "Francis Daniel Pastorius," in *Lawmaking and Legislators in Pennsylvania: A Biographical Dictionary*, vol. 1, *1682–1709*, ed. Craig Horle et al. (Philadelphia, Pa., 1991), 586–590; Hull, *William Penn*, 290–292, 336–337; Harold S. Bender, "The Founding of the Mennonite Church in America at Germantown, 1683–1708," *Mennonite Quarterly Review* 7 (1933): 238–246.

87. See, for example, *Copie, eines von einem Sohn an seinen Eltern auss America, abgelassenen Brieffes/ Sub dato Philadelphia, den 7. Martii 1684*, City Library of Zurich (facsimiles in Koenneken MSS and in Learned, *Pastorius*, 124); *Sichere Nachricht auss America, wegen der Landschafft Pennsylvania/ von einem dorthin gereissten Teutschen/ de dato Philadelphia den 7. Martii 1684*, City Library of Zurich (facsimile in Learned, *Pastorius*, 128); and a series of letters to his family and the society published in *Umstandige geographische Beschreibung der zu allerletzt erfundenen Provintz Pensylvaniae, in denen end-grantzen Americae in der West-Welt gelegen,/ durch Franciscum Danielem Pas-*

torium . . . Worbey angehencket sind einige notable Begebenheiten,/ und bericht-schreiben an dessen Herzn Vattern Melchiorem Adamum Pastorium, und andere gute Freunde (Frankfurt, 1700). For an overview of Pastorius's promotional literature, see Albert Myers, *Narratives of Early Pennsylvania, West New Jersey, and Delaware* (New York, 1912), 353–448.

88. Julius Sachse, *Letters Relating to the Settlement of Germantown in Pennsylvania, 1683–4 from the Könneken Manuscript in the Ministerial Archiv of Lübeck* (Lübeck and Philadelphia, 1903), v–vi. Sachse reproduced in facsimile form the original Dutch and German manuscript copies of the letters as well as English translations; Sachse, *Letters*, 7–29. For connections between Könneken, Jawert, and the Saalhof Pietists, see Ernst Fritze, "Adelheit Sybilla und der Maler Johann Heinrich Schwartz in Lübeck," *Zeitschrift des Vereins für Lübeckische Geschichte und Altertumskunde* 71 (1991): 81–123.

89. Deppermann, *Johann Jakob Schütz,* 322–327, 381–384; Fisher, "'Prophesies and Revelations,'" 318–320.

90. An account of their journey is recorded in Johannes Kelpius, "Original Journal," 1694–1708, AM 0880, HSP. It is translated in Julius Sachse, ed., "The Diarium of Magister Johannes Kelpius," in *Pennsylvania: The German Influence in Its Settlement and Development* (Lancaster, Pa., 1917). Sachse's translation contains errors and should be used with care.

91. Fisher, "'Prophesies and Revelations,'" 299–333; Jon Butler, "Magic, Astrology, and the Early American Religious Heritage, 1600–1760," *American Historical Review* 84 (1979): 317–346; Bailyn, *Peopling,* 123–125; Julius Sachse, *The German Pietists of Provincial Pennsylvania* (1895; New York, 1979), 11–27, 43–48; 219–250.

92. Jacob Bruno Wigers, London, to Henry July Elers, Halle, 3 May 1699, Hauptarchiv B71a, s. 69–74, Archiv der Franckesche Stiftung, Halle, Germany (hereafter, AFSt).

93. Falckner, Lübeck, to August Hermann Francke, Halle, 26 Aug. 1691, Francke Nachlaß, 32/11:3 [10902]; Falckner, Lüneberg, to August Hermann Francke, Halle, 8 Feb. 1692, Francke Nachlaß 32/11:4 [10903]; Falckner, Hamburg, to August Hermann Francke, Halle, 27 Jan. 1693, Francke Nachlaß 32/11:5 [10904], Staatsbibliothek zu Berlin—Preussischer Kulturbesitz, Berlin.

94. Sachse, *Falckner's Curieuse Nachricht,* 22–38, 45–245. One copy of Falckner's original manuscript is in Hauptarchiv D85: S.469–597, AFSt.

95. Philip Otterness, *Becoming German: The 1709 Palatine Migration to New York* (Ithaca, N.Y., 2004), 25–29; Georg Fertig, *Lokales Leben,*

atlantische Welt: Die Entscheidung zur Auswanderung vom Rhein nach Nordamerika im 18. Jahrhundert (Osnabrück, 2000), 101–105. Fertig argues that the early literature about Pennsylvania was not intended to recruit additional immigrants. Documentary evidence, however, suggests otherwise—at least for Falckner's pamphlet. See Jacob Bruno Wigers, London, to Henry July Elers, Halle, 3 May 1699, Hauptarchiv B71a, s. 69–74, AFSt; [n.a.], Jena, to Francke, Halle, 1 Jan. 1700, Hauptarchiv D84: 194–195, AFSt.

96. GA, 565, A, #1746–1783 (section titled "Voorspraak bij de Overheid").
97. GA, 565, A, #1746.
98. Petition of the Mennonites in the Palatine Electorate, 26 Nov. 1680, GLA 77/4337.
99. GA, 565, A, #1749, #1750, #1751, #1752, #1753, #1755; Archiv der Mennonitengemeinde Krefeld 80/4/7, 80/4/10, 80/4/11, Stadtarchiv Krefeld.
100. For a good discussion of poor relief in the Amsterdam Mennonite churches, see Sprunger, "Rich Mennonites, Poor Mennonites," 34–35.
101. Van der Zijpp, "Dutch Aid," 138–140.
102. 22 Jan. 1710, GA, 565, A #1255; Cornelius J. Dyck and Dennis Martin, eds., *Mennonite Encyclopedia* (Hillsboro, Kansas, 1955–1990), 4:378.
103. Van der Zijpp, "Dutch Aid," 146–147. George Ritter was the son of Jacob Ritter and Magdalena Gouttes who was baptized August 8, 1667. He was a druggist by profession who, by 1708, was also listed as a merchant. See William J. Hinke, trans. and ed., "Letters Regarding the Second Journey of Michel to America, February 14, 1703, to January 16, 1704 and His Stay in America till 1708," *Virginia Magazine of History and Biography* 24 (1916): 297; and Charles Kemper, ed., "Documents Relating to Early Projected Swiss Colonies in the Valley of Virginia, 1706–1709," *Virginia Magazine of History and Biography* 29 (1921): 7.
104. Feb. 24, 1710, GA, 565, A #1756.
105. Letter from the States General to the Government of Bern, 15 March 1710, English translation of copy in Hendrik Toren's notebook, GA, 565, A #1009, pp. 39–40, LMHS. See also copy in GA, 565, A #1758.
106. Van der Zijpp, "Dutch Aid," 147.
107. 30 March 1710, GA, 565, A #1258.
108. Van der Zijpp, "Dutch Aid," 147.
109. J. G. de Hoop Scheffer, "Mennonite Emigration to Pennsylvania," *Pennsylvania Magazine of History and Biography* 2 (1878): 124–125; June 1710, GA, 565, A #1261.
110. 25, 26 April, 14 May, 2, 15 July 1710, GA, 565, A #1009.

111. 15 July 1710, GA, 565, A #1009.

112. Van der Zijpp, "Dutch Aid," 149; GA, 565, A # 1266, 1270, 1271, 1274, 1277, 1278, 1279, 1280, 1283, 1286, 1294, 1295, 1296, 1307, 1308, 1310, 1313, 1773.

113. Benedict Brechtbuhl, Mannheim, to Abraham Jacobs, Amsterdam, 4 April 1711; GA, 565, A #1324.

114. 25, 26 April, 14 May, 2, 15 July 1710, GA, 565, A, #1009; Otterness, *Becoming German*, 67–68.

115. GA, 565, A # 1287, 1288, 1290, 1293.

116. Van der Zijpp, "Dutch Aid," 150.

117. GA, 565, A #1317, 1326.

118. Ibid., A #1321; 1334.

119. Ibid., A #1339.

120. Van der Zijpp, "Dutch Aid," 150–151; GA, 565, A# 1321, 1334, 1339.

121. GA, 565, A# 1321, 1334, 1339.

122. Toren's notebook, GA, 565, A, #1009.

123. *Mennonite Encyclopedia*, 4:738–739.

124. James Dayrolle, The Hague, to Secretary Boyle, 25 June 1709, State Papers (SP) 84/232, 144–145, Public Records Office/National Archives, Kew Gardens, London (hereafter, PRO/NA). Additional documents concerning the 1709 migration are in SP 44/107, SP 84/232, 233, 234, Colonial Office (CO) 5/1049, 1084, CO 388/76, PRO/NA. For a recent study of this migration, see Otterness, *Becoming German*.

125. Craig W. Horle et al., eds., *The Papers of William Penn*, vol. 4, *1701–1718* (Philadelphia, Pa., 1987), 673–676.

126. William J. Hinke, trans. and ed., "Report of the Journey of Francis Louis Michel from Berne, Switzerland, to Virginia, October 2, 1701–December 1, 1702," *Virginia Magazine of History and Biography* 24 (1916): 1–43, 113–141, 274–303; Klaus Wust, "Palatines and Switzers for Virginia, 1705–1738: Costly Lessons for Promoters and Emigrants," *Yearbook of German-American Studies* 19 (1984): 43–55; Colonial Office 5/289, 5/1315, 5/1316, PRO/NA.

127. GA, 565, A #1339.

128. Otterness, *Becoming German*, 37–88.

129. Rosalind J. Beiler, "Distributing Aid to Believers in Need: The Religious Foundations of Transatlantic Migration," *Pennsylvania History* 64, Special Supplemental Issue (1997): 79–84.

130. Alison Olson, *Making the Empire Work: London and American Interest Groups, 1690–1790* (Cambridge, Mass., 1992), 51–75; Hunt, *Two Early Political Associations*, 1–48, 113–129.

131. Vincent H. Todd, ed., *Christoph von Graffenried's Account of the Founding of New Bern* (Raleigh, N.C., 1920), 18; Otterness, *Becoming German,* 37–56.

132. Bernard Bailyn, *Atlantic History: Concept and Contours* (Cambridge, Mass., 2005), 81–101; Carla Gardina Pestana, "Religion," in *The British Atlantic World, 1500–1800,* ed. David Armitage and Michael Braddick (New York, 2002), 69–89.

133. Beiler, "Distributing Aid," 76–77; Marianne S. Wokeck, *Trade in Strangers: The Beginnings of Mass Migration to North America* (University Park, Pa., 1999), 59–112.

7. Typology in the Atlantic World

1. Leonhard Goppelt, *Typos: The Typological Interpretation of the Old Testament in the New* (1939), trans. Donald H. Madvig (Grand Rapids, Mich., 1982); John J. O'Keefe and Russell R. Reno, *Sanctified Vision: An Introduction to Early Christian Interpretation of the Bible* (Baltimore, Md., 2005); James Samuel Preus, *From Shadow to Promise: Old Testament Interpretation from Augustine to the Young Luther* (Cambridge, Mass., 1969); Erich Auerbach, "Figura" (1944), in Auerbach, *Scenes from the Drama of European Literature* (New York, 1959), 11–71.

2. On typological readings of classical myths, see Hugo Rahner, *Greek Myths and Christian Mystery,* trans. Brian Battershaw (1957; New York, 1971); authors such as Theodolphus (*Ecloga,* ca. 800), Bernard of Utrecht (*Kommentar,* late thirteenth century), and Petrus Berchorius (*Ovidius moralizatus,* ca. 1350), for example.

3. See the French translation of the *Speculum Humane Salvationis* by Jehan Mielot, "Le miroir de l'humaine salvation," University of Glasgow Library, MS Hunter 60 (T.2.18), fol. 43v. Biblical references: Judith: Vulgate, Jth. 1–16; Jael: Judg. 4:17–22, Judg. 5:24–27; Tomyris: Herodotus, *The History,* trans. George Rawlinson (New York, 1862), 1:201–214.

4. H. David Brumble, *Classical Myths and Legends in the Middle Ages and Renaissance: A Dictionary of Allegorical Meanings* (Westport, Conn., 1998); and Don C. Allen, *Mysteriously Meant* (Baltimore, Md., 1970). See, for example, Georg Witsel, *Parallela: Affinia quaedam, et aliquo modo correspondentia exnostris, hoc est, Sacris & Gentilium libris* (Mainz, 1544); Jacques Hugues, *Vera historia Romana sev Origo Latii vel Italiae ac Romanae vrbis e tenebris longae vetustatis in lucem producta* (Rome, 1655); Johannes Henricus Ursinus, *Analectorum sacrorum* (Frankfurt, 1658–1660); Zachary Bogan, *Homerus Hebraizōn: sive, Comparatio*

Homeri cum Scriptoribus Sacris quoad normam loquendi (Oxford, 1658);
James Duport, *Homeri poetarum omnium seculorum facilè principis
Gnomologia, duplici parallelismo illustrata uno ex locis S. Scripturae,
quibus gnomae Homericae aut propè affines, aut non prorsùs ab similes*
(Cambridge, 1660); Filippo Picinelli, *Lumi riflessi; o, Dir vogliamo
concetti della Sacra Bibbia osservati ne i volumi non sacra, studii eruditi*
(Milan, 1667); Johannes Hoffmann and Andreas Rötel, *Deorum gentilium
praecipuorum origines ex Sacra Scriptura derivatus* (Jena, 1674); Johann
Bompart, *Parallela sacra et profana; sive, Notae in Genesin* (Amsterdam,
1689); and Eccardus Leichnerus, *Opuscula quae ad historiam
philologiam sacram spectant* (Rotterdam, 1700).

5. Jorge Cañizares-Esguerra, *Puritan Conquistadors: Iberianizing the Atlantic, 1550–1700* (Stanford, Calif., 2006), 35–36. The discussion of the
Castellanos frontispiece borrows from my description there.

6. F. A. March, *Latin Hymns with English Notes* (New York, 1883), Third
Ambrosian Hymn *(De sanctis martyribus),* lines 19–20 (p. 23). My
thanks to Paul Shore for calling my attention to this image.

7. Unless otherwise noted, biblical quotations are from the King James version when in English and from the Vulgate version when in Latin. Dan.
14:26: "... io diruptus est draco."

8. Rev. 19:15–16: "Rex regum et Dominus dominantium."

9. Ps. 40:1–3 [Vulg. 39:2–4]: "Expectans expectavi Dominum et intendit
mihi / Et exaudivit preces meas et eduxit me de lacu miseriae et de luto
fecis et statuit super petram pedes meos et direxit gressus meos. / Et
inmisit in os meum canticum novum carmen Deo nostro videbunt multi
et timebunt et sperabunt in Domino" (I waited patiently for the Lord;
and he inclined unto me, and heard my cry. / He brought me up also out
of an horrible pit, out of the miry clay, and set my feet upon a rock, and
established my goings. / And he hath put a new song in my mouth, even
praise unto our God: many shall see it, and fear, and shall trust in the
Lord).

10. Ps. 52:8 [Vulg. 51:10]: "ego autem sicut oliva fructifera in Domo dei"; 86
[Vulg. 85]: 9: "omnes gentes quascumque fecisti venient et adorabunt co-
ram te Domine et glorificabunt nomen tuum"; 97 [Vulg. 98]:2: "notum
fecit Dominus salutare suum in conspectus gentium revelavit iustitiam
suam."

11. Matt. 11:28: "Venite ad me omnes"; John 10:16: "Alias oves habeo
que non sunt ex hoc ovili et ilias oportet me adducere et vocem meam
audient."

12. Isa. 49:18: "leva in circuitu oculos tuos et vide omnes isti congregati sunt

venerunt tibi vivo ego dicit Dominus quia omnibus his velut ornamento vestieris et circumdabis tibi eos quasi sponsa"; Ps. 45:3–4 [44:5]: "specie tua et pulchritudine tua et intende prospere procede et regna propter veritatem et mansuetudium et iustitiam et deducet te mirabiliter dextera tua."

13. Tacitus, *The Histories,* trans. Clifford H. Moore (Cambridge, Mass., 1943), bk. IV, 74 (2:144–146): "Neque quies sine armis, neque utrumque sine tributes": "Regna bellaque per Gallias semper fuere donec in nostrum ius concederetis. nos, quamquam totiens lacessiti, iure victoriae id solum vobis addidimus, quo pacem tueremur; nam neque quies gentium sine armis neque arma *sine stipendiis neque stipendia sine tributis* haberi queunt" (There were always kings and wars throughout Gaul until you submitted to our laws. Although often provoked by you, the only use we have made of our rights as victors has been to impose on you the necessary costs of maintaining peace; for you cannot secure tranquility among nations without armies, nor maintain armies without pay, nor provide pay without taxes).

14. Dan. 11:2: "et nunc veritatem annuntiabo tibi Ecce adhuc tres reges stabunt in Perside et quartus ditabitur opibus nimiis super omnes et cum invaluerit divitiis suis concitabit omnes adversum regnum Graeciae" (And now will I shew thee the truth. Behold, there shall stand up yet three kings in Persia; and the fourth shall be far richer than they all: and by his strength through his riches he shall stir up all against the realm of Greece).

15. "Et alioqui nullum justis genus reditus, quam quod terra, coelum, annus refert." Pliny the Younger, *Letters,* trans. William Melmoth (Cambridge, Mass., 1947) bk. IX.37 (p. 264).

16. 1 Paralipomenom 9:21; 2 Chronicles 9:21: "siquidem naves regis ibant in Tharsis cum servis Hiram semel in annis tribus et deferebant inde aurum et argentum et ebur et simias et pavos" (For the king's ships went to Tarshish with the servants of Huram: every three years once came the ships of Tarshish bringing gold, and silver, ivory, and apes, and peacocks).

17. Job 38:22: "numquid ingressus es thesauros nivis aut thesauros grandinis aspexisti" (Hast thou entered into the treasures of the snow? or hast thou seen the treasures of the hail). Jer. 10:13: "Ad vocem suam dat multitudinem aquarum in caelo et elevat nebulas ab extremitatibus terrae fulgura in pluviam facit et educit ventum de thesauris suis" (When he uttereth his voice, there is a multitude of waters in the heavens, and he

causeth the vapours to ascend from the ends of the earth; he maketh lightnings with rain, and bringeth forth the wind out of his treasures).

18. *Juvenal and Persius,* trans. G. G. Ramsay (Cambridge, Mass., 1930), bk. XIV, 304 (p. 286): "misera est magni custodia census"; Pliny, *Letters,* bk. IX.37 (p. 264): "at hoc magnam fides acres oculos numerosas manus poscit."

19. Isa. 2:7: "repleta est terra argento et auro et non est finis thesaurorum eius" (Their land also is full of silver and gold, neither is there any end of their treasures).

20. "quidquid conspicuum pulchrumque est aequore, toto res fisci est": *Juvenal and Persius,* bk. IV, 54–55 (p. 60).

21. Macrobius, *The Saturnalia,* trans. Percival Vaughan Davies (New York, 1969), II, 4, 31: "paucos denarios protulit quos principi daret."

22. Arica: "omnes pensitare debunt," *Codex Iustinianus,* ed. Paul Krueger, in *Corpus Iure Civilis,* ed. Paul Krueger et al., 3 vols. (Berlin, 1954), 2:10.16.4; Paitia: "Unusquisque sciat quid debeat susceptoribus dare," *Codex Iustinianus,* 10, 72. 9; Castrovirreina: "neque commento tribute attingat"; Cailoma: "multus in arca fiscus": Juvenal's *Satires,* 14.260; Vilcabamba: "Fisci volumus legale custodire compendium": Cassiodorus, *Variae,* ed. Theodor Mommsen (Berlin, 1961), I. XVIIII.1 (p. 24); Oruro: "adpendam arcariis gazae tuae": Esther 3:9; Chiquiavo: "reddite ergo quae sunt Caesaris Caesari": Matt. 22:21.

23. Ps. 74:4: "liquefacta est terra et omnes qui habitant in ea *ego confirmavi columnas eius diapsalma*"; [KJ 73:(3)]: "The earth and all the inhabitants thereof are dissolved: I bear up the pillars of it."

24. Horace, *Satires, Epistles and Ars Poetica,* trans. H. Rushton Fairclough (Cambridge, Mass., 1966), bk. II, 2.100–101 (p. 144): "ego vectigalia magna divitiasque habeo tribus amplas regibus."

25. Francisco Stasteny, "La capilla de la Inmaculada Concepción en Lima," in *La tradición clásica en el Perú virreinal,* ed. Teodoro Hampe Martínez (Lima, 1999).

26. Gen. 49:15: "subposuit umerum suum ad portandum factusque est tributis serviens."

27. In 1622 in New Spain the Discalced Carmelite Antonio Vazquez de Espinosa applied the curse of Issachar more widely to explain the servile condition of all Amerindians. Antonio Vázquez de Espinosa, *Descripción de la Nueva España* (1622; Mexico City, 1944), 41–45. In *Luz y methodo de confesar idolatras y destierro de idolatrías* (Puebla, 1692), Diego Jaime Ricardo de Villavicencio presented the destruction of the

temple of Jerusalem and the Diaspora of the Israelites as prefigurations of the plight of the Aztecs under Spanish rule (Cortés being the fulfillment of Moses). He also cited passages of the Pentateuch as prefigurations of the tribute that would be imposed on the Aztecs as a result of their idolatry.

28. Deut. 20:11: "cunctus populus qui in ea est salvabitur et serviet tibi sub tribute."

29. On the *requerimiento,* see Rolena Adorno, *The Polemics of Possession in the Spanish American Narrative* (New Haven, Conn., 2007), 265; and *Colección de documentos inéditos relativos al descubrimiento, conquista y organización de las antiguas posesiones españolas de América y Oceanía,* 42 vols. (Madrid, 1864–1884), 1:443–444.

30. The literature on Protestant uses of typology is vast but is often focused on the Puritans. Yet Anglicans, Scottish Presbyterians, Quakers, and indeed nearly every other group also deployed typology. See Alfred A. Cave, "Canaanites in a Promised Land: The American Indian and the Providential Theory of Empire," *American Indian Quarterly* 12 (Autumn 1988): 277–297; Sacvan Bercovitch, ed., *Typology and Early American Literature* (Amherst, Mass., 1972); Paul Stevens, "'Leviticus Thinking' and the Rhetoric of Early Modern Colonialism," *Criticism* 35 (Summer 1993): 441–461; Avihu Zakai, *Exile and Kingdom: History and Apocalypse in the Puritan Migration* (New York, 2002).

31. "Carolus redux Magnae spes altera Britaniae"; Matt. 5:9: "Beati pacifici"; 2 Sam. 22:51: "Deo Turris salutum Regi sui"; Ps. 147:19–20.

32. Heb. 11[13]: "These all died in faith, not having received the promises, but having seen them afar off, and were persuaded of them, and embraced them, and confessed that they were strangers and pilgrims on the earth. [14] For they that say such things declare plainly that they seek a country. [15] And truly, if they had been mindful of that country from whence they came out, they might have had opportunity to have returned. [16] But now they desire a better country, that is, an heavenly: wherefore God is not ashamed to be called their God: for he hath prepared for them a city."

33. Prov. 16:10: "divinatio in labiis Regis."

34. His commota fugam Dido sociosque parabat.

> conveniunt, quibus aut odium crudele tyranni
> aut metus acer erat; navis, quae forte paratae,
> corripiunt onerantque auro; portantur avari
> Pygmalionis opes pelago; dux femina facti.

(Moved hereby, Dido made ready her flight and her company. Then assemble all who felt towards the tyrant relentless hatred or keen fear; ships, which by chance were ready, they seize, and load with gold; the wealth of grasping Pygmalion is borne overseas, the leader of the work a woman.) *Aeneid,* trans. H. Rushton Fairclough, 2 vols. (Cambridge, Mass., 1938), I, 360–364 (1:266, 267)

35. Sic Venus, et Veneris contra sic filius orsus:

> "nulla tuarum audita mihi neque visa sororum—
> o—quam te memorem, virgo? namque haud tibi voltus
> mortailis, nec vox hominem sonat; o dea certe!"

(Thus Venus; and thus in answer Venus's son began: "none of thy sisters have I heard or seen—but by what name should I call thee, O maiden? For thy face is not mortal nor has thy voice a human ring; O godess surely!") *Aeneid* I.325–27 (1:262–265).

36. "O terque, quaterque, beati": *Aeneid* I.94 (1:246); "Ostendent terries hunc tantum fata, nec ultra esse sinent": *Aeneid* VI, 869 (1:568); "Ego dixi dii estis et filii Excelsi omnes, vos autem sicut homines moriemini" (Ps. 81:6–7; KJ, Ps. 82).

37. "universa vanitas omnis homo vivens diapsalma" (Ps. 39:5), and "advena sum apud te et peregrinus sicut omnes patres mei" (Ps. 39:12).

38. "Sic mare, sic terras fero et offero, praedico coelum"; "Hic et ubique manet, monet, et movet omnia Pixis" (Hic maneo, haec moneo, Est orbis, at urbis opus); "Is peregre estq domi. Terras fer fertur as astra."

39. Neil Kamil, *Fortress of the Soul: Violence, Metaphysics, and Material Life in the Huguenots' New World, 1517–1751* (Baltimore, Md., 2005).

40. For Puritan typological readings of nature, see Christopher Lukasik, "Feeling the Force of Certainty: The Divine Science, Newtonianism, and Jonathan Edwards's 'Sinners in the Hands of an Angry God,'" *New England Quarterly* 73 (June 2000): 222–245; Stephen J. Stein, "Jonathan Edwards and the Rainbow: Biblical Exegesis and Poetic Imagination," *New England Quarterly* 47 (September 1974): 440–456.

41. Jaime Lara, *City, Temple, and Stage: Eschatological Architecture and Liturgical Theatrics in New Spain* (Notre Dame, Ind., 2004). Historians have usually attributed the grid plans to Renaissance urban ideologies seeking to drive the message of sharp differences of rationality between the civilization of the Europeans and the alleged barbarism of the natives. On the grid plan as an epiphenomenon of Renaissance imperial ideologies, see Valerie Fraser, *The Architecture of Conquest: Building in the Viceroyalty of Peru, 1535–1635* (New York, 1990); Ezek. 40–48.

42. David Brading, *Mexican Phoenix: Our Lady of Guadalupe—Image and Tradition across Five Centuries* (New York, 2001), esp. 160; see also Cañizares-Esguerra, *Puritan Conquistadors*, 202–203.

43. Gen. 3:15: "conteret caput tuum"; Matt. 8:27: "venti et mare oboediunt olli."

44. It is drawn from Ps. 147:19–20: "Qui adnuntiat verbum suum Iacob: iustitias et iudicia sua Israhel. / Non fecit taliter omni nationi, ei iudicia sua non manifestavit eis" (He shewed his word unto Jacob, his statutes and his judgments unto Israel. / He hath not dealt so with any nation: and as for his judgments, they have not known them).

45. Although Dee's volume predates it, Castellanos's book and its imagery came to be known among English "conquistadors" as well as among the Spanish. In a treatise recounting a trip to the coast of Guiana in 1596 to recover samples of gold (a voyage undertaken immediately on the heels of Walter Raleigh's first trip in 1595), Lawrence Kemys, Walter Raleigh's learned lieutenant, turned to Castellanos's epic to identify the numerous Spanish expeditions to Guiana and thus to persuade Elizabeth that there was something worth conquering in the New World. "Heere follow the names of those worthie Spaniardes that have sought to discover and conquere Guiana, extracted out of Juan de Castellanos clerigo"; in Lawrence Kemys, *A Relation of the Second Voyage to Guiana* (London, 1596), appendix.

46. Carlos Sigüenza y Góngora, *Teatro de virtudes políticas que constituyen a un príncipe: advertidas en los monarcas antiguos del Mexicano Imperio, con cuyas efigies se hermoseó el Arco triunfal que la . . . Ciudad de México erigió para . . . recibimiento del . . . Virrey Conde de Paredes, Marqués de La Laguna . . .* (Mexico City, 1680).

47. On Guaman Poma as supporting the later argument of Bartolome de Las Casas that authority should devolve to indigenous rulers in the Americas, see Adorno, *The Polemics of Possession*, ch. 2. For interpretations of this image of Guaman Poma, see Sabine MacCormack, *On the Wings of Time: Rome, the Incas, Spain, and Peru* (Princeton, N.J., 2007), 227–236; and Ramón Mujica Pinilla, "Arte e identidad: Las raíces culturales del barroco perunao," in *El Barroco Peruano*, ed. Ramon Mujica Pinilla, 2 vols. (Lima, 2002), 1:6–8.

48. Joseph-François Lafitau, *Mœurs des sauvages américains comparées aux mœurs des premiers temps* (Paris, 1724).

49. Sigüenza y Góngora, *Teatro de virtudes políticas*, 15, 4.

50. Andrea Alciato, *Emblematum liber* (Augsburg, 1531), the first and most

widely known book of emblems—depictions of mottos, images, and verse.

51. Sigüenza y Góngora, *Teatro de virtudes políticas*, 122, 131.

52. I have tried elsewhere to trace such circulation in the early modern Atlantic world; see Cañizares-Esguerra, *Puritan Conquistadors;* "Entangled Histories: Borderland Historiographies in New Clothes?" *American Historical Review* 112 (June 2007): 787–799; and "The Core and Peripheries of Our National Narratives: A Response from IH-35," *American Historical Review* 112 (December 2007): 1423–1432.

53. Friedrich Ohly, "The Cathedral as Temporal Space: On the Duomo of Siena" (1977), in *Sensus Spiritualis: Studies in Medieval Significs and Philology of Culture*, trans. Kenneth J. Northcott (Chicago, 2005), 136–233; Richard K. Emmerson, "Figura and the Medieval Typological Imagination," in *Typology and English Medieval Literature*, ed. Hugh T. Keenan (New York, 1992).

8. A Courier between Empires

Research for this essay was supported by the Andrew W. Mellon Foundation, which funded a postdoctoral fellowship at the University of Pennsylvania's Penn Humanities Forum in 2006–2007, and the International Seminar on the History of the Atlantic World at Harvard University, which supported my research in Rio de Janeiro and São Paulo in fall 2007. My sincere thanks to Bernard Bailyn, Júnia Furtado, Íris Kantor, the members of the Johns Hopkins University History Seminar, and colleagues in the history department at the University of British Columbia for their carefully considered comments and criticism on earlier drafts.

1. *Correio Braziliense, ou Armazém Literário* (London, 1808–1822). The presence of the Portuguese court in Rio de Janeiro from 1808 to 1821 has been the subject of several publications, including Kirsten Schultz, *Tropical Versailles: Empire, Monarchy, and the Portuguese Court in Rio de Janeiro, 1808–1821* (New York, 2001), and Patrick Wilcken, *Empire Adrift: The Portuguese Court in Rio de Janeiro, 1808–1821* (London, 2005).

2. "Hipólito" may appear to be an awkward shorthand for Hipólito da Costa, but it has become accepted usage to speak of him not as da Costa (which has nearly no identifying value in a culture where such surnames abound) but rather by using his first name, Hipólito. Though scholars have shied away from bombastic proclamations about Hipólito such as that by Francisco Adolfo de Varnhagen, who wrote that "no statesman did as much to prepare Brazil for the formation of a constitutional em-

pire than the illustrious editor of the *Correio Braziliense*," it is still
generally accepted that Hipólito's role in influencing the contours of imperial rule during the critical years of 1808–1822 was significant, if not
necessarily unparalleled. On Hipólito's participation in events leading
to Brazil's independence from Portuguese rule, see Rolando Monteiro,
Hipólito da Costa e a independência (Rio de Janeiro, 1979).

3. Among the effects of this restricted view of the Enlightenment, attributed to a generation of scholars including Peter Gay and Ernst Cassirer,
was the exclusion of nearly any intellectual developments taking place
beyond France, Britain, Germany, or Italy. For the iconic example from
this generation, see Peter Gay, *The Enlightenment: An Interpretation*,
vol. 1, *The Rise of Modern Paganism* (1966; New York, 1995), 3–20. Especially glaring in their approach was the limited role given to ideas that
circulated beyond the Pyrenees, an oversight replicated even by more
contemporary scholars attempting to escape from the restricted and limited views espoused by Gay, Cassirer, Carl Becker, Franco Venturi, and
others. See, for instance, Gertrude Himmelfarb, *The Roads to Modernity: The British, French, and American Enlightenments* (New York,
2004). But even historians of the Iberian empires did not necessarily
challenge such views. For many, seeing these regions as passive recipients of French ideas allowed them to participate in the Enlightenment
as well. For historians of colonial Latin America in particular, book
lists and correspondence that demonstrated the presence of subversive
French authors in local libraries were sufficient to show that there was a
correlation between European philosophical movements and subsequent
revolts across the ocean. Bradford Burns's study of the Luso-Brazilian
Azeredo Coutinho is a case in point: "José Joaquim de Cunha de
Azeredo Coutinho contributed to the introduction of the Enlightenment into colonial Brazil," Burns wrote, "and, thus, unintentionally, albeit significantly to Brazilian independence." E. Bradford Burns, "The
Role of Azeredo Coutinho in the Enlightenment of Brazil," *Hispanic
American Historical Review* 44 (May 1964): 145–160. In the case of
Spanish America, historians such as Roland Hussey sought out "traces
of French Enlightenment" in the discourse of Creoles, clerics, and refugees, emphasizing a vibrant if occasionally contraband book trade between Europe and the Americas or contacts made through scientific
expeditions carried out by Europeans in the New World. See Roland D.
Hussey, "Traces of French Enlightenment in Colonial Hispanic America," in *Latin America and the Enlightenment*, ed. Arthur P. Whitaker

(Ithaca, N.Y., 1961), 23–52. Likewise, in Portuguese America, the intellectual origins of revolts and conspiracies from Bahia to Vila Rica were often understood in relation to French political ideologies, even though the underlying social conditions and interpretations of these movements frequently bore little relation to how they might have been formulated or perceived in Old Regime France. On the *Conjuração dos Alfaiates,* see Guilherme Pereira das Neves, "Bahía, 1798: Une lecture coloniale de la Révolution française," in *L'image de la Révolution française,* ed. Michel Vovelle (Paris, 1989); on the Inconfidência Mineira, see the classic study by Kenneth Maxwell, *Conflicts and Conspiracies: Brazil and Portugal, 1750–1808* (New York, 2004).

4. John Wilton Appel, *Francisco José de Caldas: A Scientist at Work in Nueva Granada* (Philadelphia, Pa., 1994); Jeanne Chenu, *Francisco José de Caldas, un peregrino de las ciencias* (Madrid, 1992); John E. Woodham, "The Influence of Hipólito Unanue on Peruvian Medical Science, 1789–1820: A Reappraisal," *Hispanic American Historical Review* 50 (November 1970): 693–714; Jorge Cañizares-Esguerra, "How Derivative Was Humboldt?" in *Colonial Botany: Science, Commerce, and Politics in the Early Modern World,* ed. Londa Schiebinger and Claudia Swan (Philadelphia, Pa., 2004), 148–168; Anthony Pagden, *Spanish Imperialism and the Political Imagination* (New Haven, Conn., 1998), 148–165. In an important study of Unanue's utopian thought, for instance, Cañizares-Esguerra has shown how an emphasis on commerce and subjugation during the Incan and colonial periods allowed for the emergence of conservative and even reactionary elements in the "enlightened" programs of some of Peru's most revered intellectuals of the Independence era. See Jorge Cañizares-Esguerra, "La Utopía de Hipólito Unanue," in *Saberes andinos: ciencia y tecnología en Bolivia, Ecuador y Perú,* ed. Marcos Cueto (Lima, 1995).

5. Other figures of what Kenneth Maxwell has called the "Generation of the 1790s" included the naturalist José Bonifacio de Andrada e Silva, the jurist Tomás Antônio Gonzaga, Francisco José de Lacerda e Almeida, who carried out important studies in Angola and Mozambique, and the native of Minas Gerais José Joaquim de Cunha de Azeredo Coutinho, who became interested in physiocracy after studying in Coimbra. See Maxwell, "The Generation of the 1790s and the Idea of Luso-Brazilian Empire," in *Colonial Roots of Modern Brazil,* ed. Dauril Alden (Berkeley, Calif., 1973), 107–144; Maria Odila Leite da Silva Dias, "Aspectos da Ilustração no Brasil," in her *A interiorizacão da metrópole e outros*

estudos (Rio de Janeiro, 2005); Fernando Novais, *Portugal e Brasil na crise do antigo sistema colonial (1777–1808)* (São Paulo, 1979), ch. 4; and Burns, "The Role of Azeredo Coutinho," 145–160.

6. For the most complete biographical study of Dom Rodrigo, see Andrée Mansuy-Diniz Silva, *Portrait d'un homme d'état: D Rodrigo de Souza Coutinho, comte de Linhares, 1755–1812*, 2 vols. (Lisbon, 2002–2006).

7. Rodrigo de Sousa Coutinho, as cited in Maria Beatriz Nizza da Silva, "O pensamento científico no Brasil na segunda metade do século XVIII," *Ciência e Cultura* 40 (September 1988): 862. On Sousa Coutinho's reforms, see Maria de Lourdes Viana Lyra, *A utopia do poderoso imperio: Portugal e Brasil, bastidores de politica, 1748–1822* (Rio de Janeiro, 1994), esp. 61–105. Translations from the Portuguese are my own, unless otherwise noted.

8. José Mariano da Conceição Veloso, *O Fazendeiro do Brazil*, as cited in Viana Lyra, *A utopia do poderoso imperio*, 84.

9. Hipólito was likely involved in Masonic activities prior to his departure for Philadelphia, but to date no hard evidence has surfaced that would corroborate this hypothesis. Indeed, there are few references to Hipólito's contact with Freemasons while in Philadelphia, which is interesting as a yardstick of the extent to which he understood his journal as a public, rather than a private, document. One enticing comment refers to his journey to New York. He recalls reading an article in the *Aurora* about the "lodges of the free-masons, that I cut out and kept as a curiosity." Hipólito da Costa, *Diário da Minha Viagem a Filadélfia, 1798–1799* (Lisbon, 2007) (hereafter, Hipólito da Costa, *Diário*), 19 April 1799. For a study of freemasonry in the North Atlantic, see Jessica Harland-Jacobs, "'Hands Across the Sea': The Masonic Network, British Imperialism, and the North Atlantic World," *Geographical Review* 89 (April 1999): 237–253. See also the classic study by Margaret Jacob, *Living the Enlightenment: Freemasonry and Politics in Eighteenth-Century Europe* (New York, 1991).

10. Recent studies of Hipólito, few since the mid-1950s, have almost exclusively focused attention on the political content and government ideology espoused in the *Correio Braziliense*. See, for example, Jane Herrick, "The Reluctant Revolutionist: A Study of the Political Ideas of Hipolito da Costa (1774–1823)," *The Americas* 7 (October 1950): 171–181; Maria Beatriz Nizza da Silva, "União sem sujeição," in *Hipólito José da Costa e o Correio Braziliense*, ed. Alberto Dines and Isabel Lustosa (São Paulo, 2002), vol. 30, bk. 1: 515–552; Lúcia Maria Bastos P. Neves, "Invasões em Portugal: A corte na América e o *Correio*

Braziliense," Observatório da Imprensa, no. 234 (22 July 2003), www .observatoriodaimprensa.com.br. One exception to this trend is Paulo Roberto de Almeida, "Um Tocqueville *avant la lettre:* Hipólito da Costa como *founding father* do americanismo," *Achegas.net: Revista de Ciência Política* 9 (July 2003), www.achegas.net.

11. Recent scholarship has emphasized the important role that Hipólito's Philadelphia sojourn played in the journalist's broader career. For discussions of Philadelphia's many influences on the young Hipólito, see Marco Morel, "Entre estrela e satélite," and Paulo Roberto de Almeida, "O nascimento do pensamento econômico brasileiro," both in Dines and Lustosa, *Hipólito José da Costa e o Correio Braziliense,* 269–320, 323–370; and, more recently, Tânia Dias, "A escrita diária de uma 'viagem de instrucão,'" *Escritos: Revista da Casa de Rui Barbosa* 1 (2007): 17–42; and Thais Helena dos Santos Buvalovas, "O 'Diário da minha viagem para Filadélfia': impressões de um ilustrado luso-brasileiro na América (1798–1799)" (MA thesis, University of São Paulo, 2007).

12. Nicholas Robson, *Hints for a General View of the Agricultural State of the Parish of Saint James, in the Island of Jamaica* (London, 1796). My thanks to Philip Morgan for providing this reference.

13. Rodrigo de Sousa Coutinho, "Para Hippolito José da Costa," reproduced in "Biografia de Hippolito José da Costa Pereira Furtado de Mendonça," *Revista do Instituto Histórico e Geográfico de São Paulo* 17 (1912): 254–256.

14. According to Joel Fry, curator of the Bartram Botanical Garden, this description corresponds to the cases of botanical specimens that the Bartrams prepared for shipment overseas. It is quite possible that the shipment was prepared by them.

15. On the *estrangeirados* and efforts to reform the sciences in Portugal during the Enlightenment, see Ana Carneiro, Ana Simões, and Maria Paula Diogo, "Enlightenment Science in Portugal: The Estrangeirados and Their Communication Networks," *Social Studies of Science* 30 (August 2000): 591–619. On Pombal's reforms and their influence on the natural sciences in particular, see João Carlos Pires Brigola, *Colecções, gabinetes e museus em Portugal no século XVIII* (Lisbon, 2003).

16. Such were the poet and lawyer Cláudio Manoel da Costa, originally from Minas Gerais, who matriculated in Coimbra in 1749, and José Joaquim de Cunha de Azeredo Coutinho, a native of Rio de Janeiro and the future author of the *Ensaio economico sobre o commercio de Portugal e suas colonias* (1794), who entered the school of canon law in

1775, just when the reforms instituted by Pombal were beginning to be felt. Among Hipólito's university contemporaries were Alexandre Rodrigues Ferreira, a native of Bahia, who was chosen to lead a decade-long "philosophical voyage" through Amazonia (1783–1792), and Manuel Galvão da Silva, Joaquim José da Silva, and João da Silva Feijó, all Brazilians who in the last two decades of the eighteenth century were sent on scientific expeditions to, respectively, Angola, Mozambique, and Cape Verde. These expeditions are studied in William J. Simon, *Scientific Expeditions in the Portuguese Overseas Territories (1783–1808) and the Role of Lisbon in the Intellectual-Scientific Community of the Late Eighteenth Century* (Lisbon, 1983). Finally, another cohort of enlightened thinkers whose names could be found on the student rosters at Coimbra during this period would play a role in the revolts and conspiracies in Minas Gerais and elsewhere. They included José Alvares Maciel, Ignácio José de Alvarenga Peixoto, and Manuel Inácio da Silva Alvarenga (the last of whom founded the "Sociedade Literária do Rio Janeiro" in 1786). They benefited from the new Cartesian orientation of the university, access to the renovated laboratories and gardens, and the use of a medical amphitheater and astronomical observatory.

17. José António de Sá, *Compendio de observaçoens,* as cited in Brigola, *Colecções,* 221.

18. On Peale's museum, see Sidney Hart and David C. Ward, "The Waning of an Enlightenment Ideal: Charles Willson Peale's Philadelphia Museum, 1790–1820," *Journal of the Early Republic* 8 (Winter 1988): 389–418; David R. Brigham, "'Ask the Beasts, and they Shall Teach Thee': The Human Lessons of Charles Willson Peale's Natural History Displays," *Huntington Library Quarterly* 59, no. 2/3 (1996): 182–206.

19. Hipólito returned frequently to Peale's museum, despite the low esteem in which he appears to have held it. On April 12, 1799, he observed in the museum a wooden bridge with only one span and two machines, one of which was useful in bringing fertilizer out to the fields. Later in the year, on November 16, he attended Peale's inaugural (and largely autobiographical) lesson on natural history, at which time he also observed a machine to put holes in bombs, a topic about which he would compose a report when back in Portugal. Hipólito da Costa, *Descrição de uma máquina para tocar a bomba a bordo dos navios* (Lisbon, 1800).

20. Hipólito da Costa, *Diário,* 28 Dec. 1798.

21. On late eighteenth-century Philadelphia and its French connections, see Frances Childs, *French Refugee Life in the United States, 1790–1800*

(Baltimore, Md., 1940); François Furstenberg, "U.S. and French Atlantic Connections: The Case of French Émigrés in Philadelphia, c. 1789–1803," unpub. paper (2002).

22. Papers of Robert Liston, 1796–1800, National Library of Scotland (microfilmed).

23. Hipólito da Costa to Rodrigo de Sousa Coutinho, "Memória sobre a viagem aos Estados-Unidos," *Revista do Instituto Histórico e Geográfico Brasileiro* 21 (1858): 351.

24. Hipólito da Costa, *Diário,* 25 Jan. 1799.

25. There were four principal botanical gardens in Philadelphia at the time of da Costa's visit: the garden at Gray's Ferry; Bartram's Garden; William Hamilton's Woodlands; and Fair Mount Gardens, known at the time as Lemon Hill.

26. It is possible that Hipólito met Parke when he visited the "public library" established by Franklin on December 28, a mere two weeks after his arrival in Philadelphia. On Thomas Parke, see Whitfield J. Bell, Jr., "Thomas Parke, M.B., Physican and Friend," *William and Mary Quarterly,* 3d ser., 6 (October 1949): 569–595. Hipólito also accompanied Parke on his rounds at the Pennsylvania Hospital in early March. There, he observed with interest the cleanliness of the establishment and the division into separate wards by gender and illness. Patients with venereal diseases and mental illnesses were placed into separate spaces that Hipólito indicates he did not visit.

27. On Marshall's botanical activities, see Louise Conway Belden, "Humphry Marshall's Trade in Plants of the New World for Gardens and Forests of the Old World," *Winterthur Porfolio* 2 (1965): 107–126.

28. Letter from Thomas Parke to Humphry Marshall, 26 Feb. 1799, Historical Society of Pennsylvania, Philadelphia, Pa.

29. Marshall's *Arbustum americanum* was the first text to describe the sugar maple tree as *Acer saccharum,* rather than using the Linnaean term, *Acer saccharinum,* as did Hipólito, Benjamin Rush, and, of course, Linnaeus. For a discussion of Hipólito's publication of the *Descripção da arvore assucareira,* and its binomial classification by naturalists and systematizers, see A. F. Günther Buchheim, "A Rare Portuguese Monograph on the Sugar-Maple Tree," *Archives of Natural History* 18 (June 1991): 185–189.

30. Frans A. Stafleu, review of Humphry Marshall, *Arbustum americanum: The American Grove* in *Taxon* 17 (August 1968): 427.

31. Joseph Ewan and Nesta Dunn Ewan, *Benjamin Smith Barton: Natural-*

ist and Physician in Jeffersonian America (St. Louis, Mo., 2007). It is possible that he and Barton had met the night before at Peale's inaugural museum lecture, an event that Barton was likely to have attended.

32. Hipólito da Costa, *Diário,* 11 April 1799.

33. Wiles joined Bligh on his circumnavigation and was later charged with caring for the Liguanea garden in Jamaica. See William Fawcett, "The Public Gardens & Plantations of Jamaica," *Botanical Gazette* 24 (November 1897): 347.

34. Letter from Hipólito da Costa to Tench Coxe, 14 Jan. 1800, Historical Society of Pennsylvania. It is possible that Hipólito was referring here to the Manufacturing Society in Philadelphia, of which Coxe was the secretary.

35. Tench Coxe, *A View of the United States of America* . . . (Philadelphia, Pa., 1794), 77.

36. Ibid., 78.

37. This shipment of books, sent by Hipólito on June 1, 1800, was accompanied by twenty-seven seeds, including the *Acer canadensis,* the *Juniperus virginiana,* and the *Magnolia tripetala,* among others. Hipólito da Costa, *Copiador e registro das cartas de ofício,* no. 18, Biblioteca Municipal de Évora.

38. James Anderson, *Five Letters to Sir Joseph Banks . . . on the Subject of Cochineal Insects* (Madras, 1787).

39. Hipólito da Costa, *Diário,* 21 Nov. 1799.

40. These views were expressed most concisely in Souza Coutinho's treatise on the "most appropriate political system for our Court to embrace for the maintenance of its vast possessions, especially those of America." See Rodrigo de Souza Coutinho, "Systema politico que mais convém que a nossa corôa abrace para a conservação dos seus vastos Dominios, particularmente dos da América," reproduced in Marcos Carneiro de Mendonça, *O Intendente Câmara, 1764–1835* (Rio de Janeiro, 1933), 277–299.

41. In her recently completed master's thesis, defended at the University of São Paulo in December 2007, Thais Buvalovas has argued that it is unlikely—according to inconsistencies encountered in an analysis of several sources written by Hipólito himself—that he in fact traveled to Mexico. See Buvalovas, "O 'Diário.' " For the purposes of the present essay, however, we will keep open the possibility that what Hipólito wrote was legitimate, although a more detailed examination of the archival record may eventually indicate that such a journey was indeed more fiction than fact.

42. Hipólito da Costa, "Memória sobre a viagem," 363.

43. Hipólito da Costa, *Copiador e registro das cartas,* no. 3.

44. Hipólito da Costa, "Memória sobre a viagem," 364.

45. Letter from Rodrigo de Sousa Coutinho to João Felipe de Fonseca, 4 Feb. 1800, Arquivo Histórico Ultramarino, Reino, Caixa 158A. Many thanks to Júnia Ferreira Furtado for providing this citation.

46. Hipólito da Costa, "Memória sobre a viagem," 361.

47. On the Nantucket whaling industry in the seventeenth and eighteenth centuries, see Daniel Vickers, "Nantucket Whalemen in the Deep-Sea Fishery: The Changing Anatomy of an Early American Labor Force," *Journal of American History* 72 (September 1985): 277–296; and Edward Byers, *The Nation of Nantucket: Society and Politics in an Early American Commercial Center* (Boston, 1987).

48. Hipólito da Costa, *Diário,* 11 Dec. 1798.

49. Ibid., 30 April 1799.

50. Hipólito da Costa, "Description of the City of Lisbon; shewing the Utility of constructing the Houses, and paving the Streets of Cities, with Marble, Limestone, or other Calcareous Materials, in Preference to Silicious Materials, or Bricks of Clay," *The Medical Repository of Original Essays and Intelligence* 3, no. 1 (1799), article 1 (n.p.).

51. This work was never completed. On Conceição Veloso's participation in the early scientific academies in Rio, see Maria de Fátima Nunes and João Carlos Brigola, "José Mariano da Conceição Veloso (1742–1811)— Um frade no universo da natureza," in *A Casa Literária do Arco do Cego* (Lisbon, 1999), 54–56.

52. José Mariano da Conceição Veloso, *Fazendeiro do Brazil,* vol. 1 (Lisbon, 1798).

53. I will be treating the relationship between Conceição Veloso and Hipólito da Costa in a forthcoming article.

54. For a discussion of the Arco do Cego and Conceição Veloso's role, see Robert Wegner, "Livros do Arco do Cego no Brasil colonial," *História, Ciências, Saude—Manguinhos* 11 (2004): 131–140.

55. "Portaria sobre a fuga do prezo Hypolito Joze da Costa," *Santo Ofício, Conselho Geral,* Instituto dos Arquivos Nacionais Torre do Tombo (Lisbon), bk. 358, fol. 8.

56. Hipólito da Costa, *Correio Braziliense,* 1:3.

57. José Joaquim de Cunha de Azeredo Coutinho, *Ensaios Econômicos . . . de Azeredo Coutinho,* as cited in Viana Lyra, *A utopia do poderoso imperio,* 87.

58. Maxwell, "Generation of the 1790s," 143.

59. In his classic account of the history and development of Brazilian literature, the literary scholar Antonio Candido attempted to set forth the parameters of what he called "Nossa Aufklärung" (Our Enlightenment), a specifically Brazilian version of the European Enlightenment that for Candido had happily coincided "with a moment in which the move beyond colonial status opened up the possibility of realizing the dreams of intellectuals"; Brazilian independence, according to Candido, was "the greatest goal of the enlightened movement and its principal expression." Antonio Candido, *Formação da literatura brasileira,* 2 vols. (São Paulo, 1959), 1:238. Candido and many of his generation saw the process by which Brazil was transformed from colonial rule to an independent nation as one whose contours were shaped by the political ideologies of individuals such as Hipólito da Costa.

60. On the journals and gazettes circulating in Rio de Janeiro from the time of Dom João VI's arrival through the independence period, see Maria Beatriz Nizza da Silva, *A Gazeta do Rio de Janeiro, 1808–1822: cultura e sociedade* (Rio de Janeiro, 2007); and Isabel Lustosa, *Insultos impressos: a guerra dos jornalistas na Independência (1821–1823)* (São Paulo, 2000).

61. Hipólito da Costa, *Correio Braziliense,* 3:175.

62. Ibid., 2:475.

63. Ibid.

64. Ibid., 13:95–96. This paragraph summarizes the analysis found in Candido, *Formação da literatura brasileira,* 1:251.

65. For a detailed discussion of the passage of Eusébio de Queiroz's anti-slave-trade bill, see Leslie Bethell, *The Abolition of the Brazilian Slave Trade: Britain, Brazil and the Slave Trade Question* (Cambridge, 1970), esp. 327–341.

66. For the most thorough recent account of the origins of British abolitionism, see Christopher Brown, *Moral Capital: Foundations of British Abolitionism* (Chapel Hill, N.C., 2006).

67. Hipólito da Costa, "Escravatura no Brazil," *Correio Braziliense* 29 (1822): 574.

68. Ibid., 614.

69. Ibid.

70. The only missing phase in the process by which Hipólito moved from the inner sanctum to the outer periphery of imperial control was, in fact, the period in which he converted to the Masonic cause. Rodrigo de Sousa Coutinho was a Freemason as well, and it is possible that, when his fortunes flagged within the imperial hierarchy, so did those of

Hipólito. As a rule, Hipólito avoided discussing his Masonic links in his Philadelphia diary, leading one to doubt further the extent to which his journal reflects a mimetic account of his thoughts and experiences while in North America. Documents that may shed light on such an essential moment of his transformation have not yet been uncovered; although Hipólito explained clearly that he joined the Masonic order while in Philadelphia, there is reason to suspect that he had already nourished contacts in Portugal. See Buvalovas, "O 'Diário.' " He gave as his reason for joining the Masonic order "the general estimation in which Masonic societies are held in America, where individuals of almost every degree of respectability, both as to rank and talents, enroll themselves as members." He went on to say that the opposition to an otherwise esteemed order "was the powerful motive that raised my curiosity, and induced me to seek admission into the society." Hipólito da Costa, *A Narrative of the Persecution of Hippolyto Joseph da Costa Pereira Furtado de Mendonça, a Native of Colonia-do-Sacramento on the River La Plata; Imprisoned and Tried in Lisbon, by the Inquisition, for the Pretended Crime of Free-Masonry* (London, 1811), 25.

71. Mecenas Dourado, *Hipólito da Costa e o Correio Braziliense* (Rio de Janeiro, 1957), 638–641; *Correio Braziliense* (1822), 29:609.

72. *Correio Braziliense* 29 (1822): 609.

73. For some recent and instructive examples of how extra-European spheres can be integrated into eighteenth-century thought across traditionally conceived geographic and ideological boundaries, see Laurent Dubois, "An Enslaved Enlightenment: Re-Thinking the Intellectual History of the French Atlantic," *Social History* 31 (February 2006): 1–14; François Furstenberg, "The Significance of the Trans-Appalachian Frontier in Atlantic History," *American Historical Review* 113 (June 2008): 647–677; Gillian Weiss, "Barbary Captivity and the French Idea of Freedom," *French Historical Studies* 28 (2005): 231–264; Alyssa Goldstein Sepinwall, *The Abbé Grégoire and the French Revolution: The Making of Modern Universalism* (Berkeley, Calif., 2005); Paul Cheney, *Revolutionary Commerce: The Political Economy of Colonial Expansion and the French Monarchy* (Cambridge, Mass., forthcoming); James Delbourgo, *A Most Amazing Scene of Wonders: Electricity and Enlightenment in Early America* (Cambridge, Mass., 2006); and Neil Safier, *Measuring the New World: Enlightenment Science and South America* (Chicago, 2008).

74. *Correio Braziliense* 29 (1822): 610.

9. Scientific Exchange in the Eighteenth-Century Atlantic World

My thanks to the National Science Foundation (NSF) for supporting portions of this work under Grant No. 0723597. Any conclusions are mine and do not necessarily reflect the views of the NSF. I also thank the participants of the Atlantic History Seminar's June 2007 conference, and especially Bernard Bailyn, for their helpful comments. Some material is reprinted by permission of the publisher from my *Plants and Empires: Colonial Bioprospecting in the Atlantic World* (Cambridge, Mass., 2004).

1. Pierre-Louis Moreau de Maupertuis, *Vénus physique: suive de la lettre sur le progrès des sciences,* ed. Patrick Tort (1752; Paris, 1980), 164.

2. Bruno Latour, *Science in Action: How to Follow Scientists and Engineers through Society* (Cambridge, Mass., 1987), ch. 6. But see Roy MacLeod, ed., *Nature and Empire: Science and the Colonial Enterprise,* special issue of *Osiris* 15 (Chicago, 2000); "Focus: Colonial Science," ed. Londa Schiebinger, *Isis* 96 (March 2005): 52–87; and James Delbourgo and Nicholas Dew, eds., *Science and Empire in the Atlantic World* (New York, 2008). Also of interest in this context is Jorge Cañizares-Esguerra and Erik R. Seeman, eds., *The Atlantic in Global History, 1500–2000* (Upper Saddle River, N.J., 2007).

3. Richard Drayton, *Nature's Government: Science, Imperial Britain, and the "Improvement" of the World* (New Haven, Conn., 2000), 92; Antonio Barrera, "Local Herbs, Global Medicines: Commerce, Knowledge, and Commodities in Spanish America," in *Merchants and Marvels: Commerce, Science, and Art in Early Modern Europe,* ed. Pamela H. Smith and Paula Findlen (New York, 2002), 163–181, esp. 174; Antonio Barrera-Osorio, *Experiencing Nature: The Spanish American Empire and the Early Scientific Revolution* (Austin, Texas, 2006); Harold Cook, "Global Economies and Local Knowledge," in *Colonial Botany: Science, Commerce, and Politics in the Early Modern World,* ed. Londa Schiebinger and Claudia Swan (Philadelphia, Pa., 2005), 100–118; Harold Cook, *Matters of Exchange: Commerce, Medicine, and Science in the Dutch Golden Age* (New Haven, Conn., 2007); Richard Grove, *Green Imperialism: Colonial Expansion, Tropical Island Edens and the Origins of Environmentalism, 1600–1860* (New York, 1995), 78, 89–90.

4. Samuel Wilson, ed., *The Indigenous People of the Caribbean* (Gainesville, Fla., 1997); William Keegan, "The Caribbean, Including Northern South America and Lowland Central America: Early History," in *Cambridge World History of Food,* ed. Kenneth Kiple and Kriemhild Conee Ornelas, 2 vols. (Cambridge, 2000), 2:1260–1278, esp. 1262, 1269–1271; Barrera, "Local Herbs," 166–167.

5. Noble David Cook, *Born to Die: Disease and New World Conquest, 1492–1650* (New York, 1998), 23–24; Irving Rouse, *The Tainos: Rise and Decline of the People Who Greeted Columbus* (New Haven, Conn., 1992), 169; David Henige, "On the Contact Population of Hispaniola: History as Higher Mathematics," *Hispanic American Historical Review* 58 (May 1978): 217–237; Peter Hulme, *Colonial Encounters: Europe and the Native Caribbean, 1492–1797* (London, 1986), 60, 67.

6. Edward Long, *The History of Jamaica*, 3 vols. (London, 1774), 1:6.

7. Jean-Baptiste-René Pouppé-Desportes, *Histoire des maladies de Saint Domingue*, 3 vols. (Paris, 1770), 3:59. Pierre Barrère also provided Latin, French, and "Indian" names for plants, but he did not call his listing a *pharmacopoeia*: Pierre Barrère, *Essai sur l'histoire naturelle de la France équinoxiale* (Paris, 1741).

8. Pierre Barrère, *Nouvelle relation de la France équinoxiale* (Paris, 1743), 204.

9. Charles-Marie de La Condamine, "Sur l'arbre du quinquina" (28 Mai 1737), *Histoire memoires de l'Academie Royale des Sciences* (Amsterdam, 1706–1755), 330. On the tradition of animals using herbs to heal themselves, see L. A. J. R. Houwen, "'Creature, Heal Thyself': Self-Healing Animals in the *Hortus sanitatis*" (unpub. lecture, Department of English, Ruhr-Universität Bochum, Germany).

10. Pouppé-Desportes, *Histoire des maladies*, 3:81; Long, *History of Jamaica*, 2:380; Robert James, *A Medicinal Dictionary*, 3 vols. (London, 1743–1745), 1: preface.

11. [Nicolas-Louis Bourgeois], *Voyages intéressans dans différentes colonies françaises, espagnoles, anglaises, etc.* (London, 1788), 67; [Anon.], *Histoire des désastres de Saint-Domingue* (Paris, 1795), 47.

12. Michael Craton, *Searching for the Invisible Man: Slaves and Plantation Life in Jamaica* (Cambridge, Mass., 1978), 54; John Gabriel Stedman, *Stedman's Surinam: Life in an Eighteenth-Century Slave Society*, ed. Richard Price and Sally Price (Baltimore, Md., 1992), 63.

13. [Bourgeois], *Voyages*, 458, 470. For others who admired slave medicine, see James Grainger, *An Essay on the More Common West-India Diseases* (Edinburgh, 1802); Bertrand Bajon, *Mémoires pour servir à l'histoire de Cayenne et de la Guiane française* (Paris, 1777–1778), 1:vii, 351–352 (I thank Emma Rothschild for calling this wonderful source to my attention); and Richard B. Sheridan, *Doctors and Slaves: A Medical and Demographic History of Slavery in the British West Indies, 1680–1834* (New York, 1985), 80–82.

14. Judith Carney, "African Traditional Plant Knowledge in the Circum-Caribbean Region," *Journal of Ethnobiology* 23 (Fall/Winter 2003): 167–185; [Bourgeois], *Voyages*, 470.

15. Sir Gavin de Beer, *Sir Hans Sloane and the British Museum* (New York, 1975), 41–42. Knight is cited in Sheridan, *Doctors and Slaves*, 81.

16. Michel-Étienne Descourtilz, *Flore pittoresque et médicale des Antilles, ou, histoire naturelle des plantes usuelles des colonies françaises, anglaises, espagnoles et portugaises*, 8 vols. (Paris, 1833), 1:16–17; Nicolas Philibert Adelon et al., eds. *Dictionaire des sciences médicales*, 60 vols. (Paris, 1812–1822), 14: s.v. "femme," 654.

17. David de Isaac Cohen Nassy, *Essai historique sur la colonie de Surinam* (Paramaribo, 1788), 64.

18. Hans Sloane, *A Voyage to the Islands Madera, Barbados, Nieves, St. Christophers, and Jamaica; with Natural History, etc.*, 2 vols. (London, 1707–1725), 1:xiii–xiv.

19. Long, *History of Jamaica*, 2:381.

20. James E. McClellan III, *Colonialism and Science: Saint Domingue in the Old Regime* (Baltimore, Md., 1992), 178. I thank Emma Spary for calling this example to my attention.

21. [Bourgeois], *Voyages*, 487. Philippe Fermin, *Traité des maladies les plus fréquentes à Surinam et des rèmedies les plus propres à les guérir* (Amsterdam, 1765), preface; for a similar point, see Bajon, *Mémoires*, 1:361.

22. Grainger, *Essay on the More Common West-India Diseases*, 70.

23. Nicolás Monardes, *Joyfull Newes out of the Newe Founde Worlde*, 2 vols., trans. John Frampton (1577; London, 1925), 1:136–137; J. Worth Estes, "The European Reception of the First Drugs from the New World," *Pharmacy in History* 37 (1995): 10; Alonso de Ovalle, of the Company of Jesus, "An Historical Relation of the Kingdom of Chile," in *A General Collection of the Best and Most Interesting Voyages and Travels*, trans. and ed. John Pinkerton, 17 vols. (London, 1808–1814), 14:38; La Condamine, "Sur l'arbre du quinquina," 329; Neil Safier, "Unveiling the Amazon to European Science and Society: The Reading and Reception of La Condamine's *Relation Abrégée d'un voyage fait dans l'intérieur de l'Amérique méridionale* (1745)," *Terrae Incognitae: The Journal for the History of Discoveries* 33 (2001): 33–47.

24. [Bourgeois], *Voyages*, 487; Philippe Fermin, *Description générale, historique, géographique et physique de la colonie de Surinam*, 2 vols. (Amsterdam, 1769), 1:209.

25. Nicolas Joseph Thiery de Menonville, *Traité de la culture du nopal et de*

l'éducation de la cochenille dans les colonies françaises de l'Amérique (Cap-Français, 1787), 1:14; Sloane, *Voyage*, 1:liv–lv.

26. William Eamon, *Science and the Secrets of Nature: Books of Secrets in Medieval and Early Modern Culture* (Princeton, N.J., 1994), 4–5.

27. Jaime Jaramillo-Arango, *The Conquest of Malaria* (London, 1950), 79.

28. Carl Thunberg, *Travels in Europe, Africa and Asia, performed between the years 1770 and 1779*, 4 vols. (London, 1795), 2:286; Jean-Paul Nicolas, "Adanson et le mouvement colonial," in *Adanson: The Bicentennial of Michel Adanson's 'Familles des plantes'*, ed. George Lawrence (Pittsburgh, Pa., 1963), 440; Adam Smith, *An Inquiry into the Nature and Causes of the Wealth of Nations*, ed. Edwin Cannan, 2 vols. (1776; Chicago, 1976), 1:69.

29. Lisbet Koerner, "Women and Utility in Enlightenment Science," *Configurations* 3 (1995): 251; David Mackay, *In the Wake of Cook: Exploration, Science, and Empire, 1780–1801* (London, 1985), 15; R. G. Latham, ed., *The Works of Thomas Sydenham*, 2 vols. (London, 1848–1850), 1:82.

30. S. W. Zwicker, *Breviarium apodemicum methodice concinnatum* (Danzig, 1638), cited in Justin Stagl, *A History of Curiosity: The Theory of Travel, 1550–1800* (Chur, Switzerland, 1995), 78; Margaret Hannay, "'How I These Studies Prize': The Countess of Pembroke and Elizabethan Science," in *Women, Science and Medicine, 1500–1700*, ed. Lynette Hunter and Sarah Hutton (Stroud, England, 1997), 109–113, 67–76.

31. Charles de l'Escluse [Carolus Clusius], *Rariorum aliquot Stirpium, per Pannoniam, Austriam, et vicinas . . . historia* (Antwerp, 1583), 345; see also Jerry Stannard, "Classici and Rustici in Clusius' Stirp. Pannon. Hist. (1583)," in *Festschrift anlässlich der 400 jährigen Widerkehr der wissenschaftlichen Tätigkeit von Carolus Clusius (Charles de l'Escluse) im pannonischen Raum*, ed. Stefan Aumuller (Eisenstadt, 1973), 253–269. Sydenham is quoted in de Beer, *Sir Hans Sloane*, 25.

32. Her cure was published in "Mrs. Stephen's Cure for the Stone," *London Gazette*, 16 June 1739, n.p. See also Stephen Hales, *An Account of Some Experiments and Observations on Mrs. Stephen's Medicines for dissolving the Stone* (London, 1740); James Parsons, *A Description of the Human Urinary Bladder . . . to which are added Animadversions on Lithontriptic Medicines, particularly those of Mrs. Stephens* (London, 1742); Arthur Viseltear, "Joanna Stephens and the Eighteenth Century Lithontriptics: A Misplaced Chapter in the History of Therapeutics," *Bulletin of the History of Medicine* 42 (1968): 199–220. It was common in the period for governments to buy the secret of useful cures for "public util-

ity"; see Lawrence Brockliss and Colin Jones, *The Medical World of Early Modern France* (Oxford, 1997), 622–623.

33. William Withering, *An Account of the Foxglove, and Some of Its Medical Uses* (Birmingham, England, 1785), 2–10.

34. Koerner, "Women and Utility," 250–251. On the exceptional Africans who received degrees from European universities in the eighteenth century, see Londa Schiebinger, *Nature's Body: Gender in the Making of Modern Science* (1993; New Brunswick, N.J., 2004), 191–196, 200.

35. Sheridan, *Doctors and Slaves*, 37–40; James Thomson, "Remarks on Tropical Diseases," *Edinburgh Medical and Surgical Journal* 18 (1822): 31–48; James Thomson, *A Treatise on the Diseases of Negroes, as They Occur in the Island of Jamaica; with Observations on the Country Remedies* (Jamaica, 1820), 151–156.

36. Thomson, *Treatise*, 147; John Williamson, *Medical and Miscellaneous Observations, Relative to the West India Islands*, 2 vols. (Edinburgh, 1817), 2:19.

37. James Thomson, "Observations and Experiments on the Nature of the Morbid Poison called Yaws, with Coloured Engraving of the Eruption," *Edinburgh Medical and Surgical Journal* 15 (1819): 321–328, esp. 326.

38. Williamson, *Medical and Miscellaneous Observations*, 2:146; William Wright, *Memoir of the Late William Wright, M.D.* (Edinburgh, 1828), 401; Thomas Trapham, *A Discourse of the State of Health in the Island of Jamaica* (London, 1679), 113–114; Benjamin Moseley, *A Treatise on Sugar with Miscellaneous Medical Observations*, 2d ed. (London, 1800), 184; Alexander Anderson, archives, Linnaean Society of London, MSS Drawer 30, MS no. 616, "Medical observations," no. 145; Sheridan, *Doctors and Slaves*, 87–88. See also Moseley, *Treatise on Sugar*, 187.

39. Thomson, "Observations and Experiments," 321; Williamson, *Medical and Miscellaneous Observations*, 2:143.

40. Thomas Dancer, *The Medical Assistant; or Jamaica Practice of Physic* (1801; Kingston, 1819), 187–188; William Hillary, *Diseases in the Island of Barbados* (London, 1766), 346.

41. Moseley, *Treatise on Sugar*, 184–187.

42. Thomson, "Observations and Experiments," 321; Wright, *Memoir*, 411.

43. "Medical News," *Medical and Philosophical Commentaries* by a Society in Edinburgh 2 (1774): 90–92. See also Sheridan, *Doctors and Slaves*, 87.

44. Wright, *Memoir*, 411; Hillary, *Observations*, 341. Richard Shannon also noted African cures for yaws: *Practical Observations on the Operation and Effects of Certain Medicines in the Prevention and Cure of Diseases*

to which Europeans are Subject in Hot Climates, and in these Kingdoms (London, 1794), 382–383.

45. Dancer, *Medical Assistant*, 190; Thomson, "Observations and Experiments," 322.

46. Bryan Edwards was informed by one of his slaves from a village near Anamaboe (in present-day Ghana) that the natives on the Gold Coast inoculated their children against yaws by infusing infectious matter into the thigh; infants suffered a slight disorder that saved them from the disease later in life. Bryan Edwards, *The History, Civil and Commercial, of the British West Indies*, 5 vols. (1793; London, 1819), 2:81. James Maxwell also reported that black mothers inoculated their children, *Observations on Yaws* (Edinburgh, 1839), 22–23. Unless otherwise noted, references in this section are to Thomson, "Observations and Experiments," 321–328, and "Remarks on Tropical Diseases," 31–48.

47. *Report of the Lords of the Committee of Council appointed for the consideration of all matters relating to trade and foreign plantations; submitting . . . the evidence . . . collected in consequence of His Majesty's order in Council, . . . 11th of February 1788, concerning . . . trade to Africa, and particularly the trade in slaves; and the effects . . . as well in Africa and the West Indies, as to the general commerce of this Kingdom* (London 1789), part 3, no. 15: "What impedes the natural increase of negro slaves?"; Wright, *Memoir*, 401; Hillary, *Observations*, 344; also Grainger, *Essay on the More Common West-India Diseases*, 55–56.

48. Williamson, *Medical and Miscellaneous Observations*, 146. "Negroes well clothed and fed, possessing the comforts which a good master and their own industry ensure them, have every chance of going through the disease without suffering material inconvenience"; "Lettre écrit à M Portal, de l'Academie Royale des Sciences, par M. Macgrudan, Médecin à la Jamaïque, sur l'inoculation du pains," *Journal de physique, de chimie, d'histoire naturelle et des arts* 1 (1773): 37–47.

49. Wright, *Memoir*, 408; Lettre écrit à M Portal," 37–47; Dancer, *Medical Assistant*, 190.

50. Dancer, *Medical Assistant*, 308.

51. Thomson, "Remarks on Tropical Diseases," 35–36. Jamaican physicians John Quier and others asked similar questions concerning smallpox. Quier generally inoculated infants born to mothers who suffered smallpox while pregnant, but he reported one case of an infant girl who developed her immunity to smallpox while in the womb. [Donald Monro, ed.], *Letters and Essays . . . by Different Practitioners* (London, 1778), 103–104.

52. Williamson, *Medical and Miscellaneous Observations,* 2:146.

53. Thomson "Remarks on Tropical Diseases," 44.

54. Jerome Handler, "Slave Medicine and Obeah in Barbados, ca. 1650 to 1834," *New West Indies* 74 (2000): 57–90; see also Robert Renny, *A History of Jamaica* (London, 1807), 171.

55. Moseley, *Treatise on Sugar,* 190–205, quotation at 194; Thomson, *Treatise,* 9; *Report of the Lords of the Committee of Council* (1789), part 3; materials for the next several paragraphs are drawn from this report. See also Jerome Handler and Kenneth Bilby, "On the Early Use and Origin of the Term 'Obeah' in Barbados and the Anglophone Caribbean," *Slavery and Abolition* 22 (August 2001): 87–100; Vincent Brown, "Spiritual Terror and Sacred Authority in Jamaican Slave Society," *Slavery and Abolition* 24 (April 2003): 24–53.

56. John Gregory, *Lectures on the Duties and Qualifications of a Physician* (London, 1772), 147–148.

57. Winthrop Jordan, *White over Black: American Attitudes toward the Negro, 1550–1812* (Chapel Hill, N.C., 1968), 12, 242. See also Marie-Hélène Huet, *Monstrous Imagination* (Cambridge, Mass., 1993).

58. John Haygarth, *Of the Imagination, as a Cause and as a Cure of Disorders of the Body: Exemplified by Fictitious Tractors, and Epidemical Convulsions* (Bath, 1800), 2–3. On Perkins's tractors, see James Delbourgo, *A Most Amazing Scene of Wonders: Electricity and Enlightenment in Early America* (Cambridge, Mass., 2006), ch. 7.

59. Haygarth, *Of the Imagination,* 4, 6–24, 28.

60. Smith, cited in ibid., 10–11, 16, 29–30.

61. *Report of the Lords of the Committee of Council* (1789), part 3, nos. 22–27; Spooner in Saint Christopher and Grenada; Adair in Antigua.

62. Ibid.

63. Williamson, *Medical and Miscellaneous Observations,* 1:97–98.

64. Moseley, *Treatise on Sugar,* 194; Thomson, *Treatise,* 9.

65. *Report of the Lords of the Committee of Council* (1789), part 3, Stephen Fuller in Jamaica.

66. Ibid., paper delivered by Mr. Rheder, Jamaica. Reprinted in Edwards, *History,* 2:117–119.

67. Edward Bancroft, *An Essay on the Natural History of Guiana in South America* (London, 1769), 371–374.

68. Pierre Campet, *Traité pratique des maladies graves* (Paris, 1802), 55.

69. Bancroft, *Essay,* 3.

70. Pierre Pelleprat, *Introduction à la langue des Galibis* (Paris, 1655), 3;

see also Juan Pimentel, "The Iberian Vision: Science and Empire in the Framework of a Universal Monarchy, 1500–1800," in MacLeod, *Nature and Empire,* 26; La Condamine, "Sur l'arbre du quinquina," 340; Charles-Marie de La Condamine, *Relation abrégée d'un voyage fait dans l'interieur de L'Amérique Méridionale* (Paris, 1745), 53–55; Alexander von Humboldt (and Aimé Bonpland), *Personal Narrative of Travels to the Equinoctial Regions of the New Continent, during the Years 1799–1804,* trans. Helen Williams, 7 vols. (London, 1814–1829), 3:301–303.

71. Humboldt, *Personal Narrative,* 5:431.
72. Jean-Baptiste Leblond, *Voyage aux Antilles: d'île en île, de la Martinque à Trinidad, 1767–1773* (1813; Paris, 2000), 138.
73. Cited in Robin Blackburn, *The Making of New World Slavery: From the Baroque to the Modern, 1492–1800* (London, 1997), 281.
74. Charles de Rochefort, *Histoire naturelle et morale des Iles Antilles de l'Amérique* (Rotterdam, 1655), 449.
75. James Currie, *Medical Reports on the Effects of Water, Cold and Warm, as a Remedy in Fever and other Diseases* (1797; London, 1805), v–vi.
76. Williamson, *Medical and Miscellaneous Observations,* 1:171.
77. Jean Barthélemy Dazille, *Observations sur le Tétenos* (Paris, 1788), preface.
78. Antonio Lafuente, "Enlightenment in an Imperial Context: Local Science in the Late Eighteenth-Century Hispanic World," in MacLeod, *Nature and Empire,* 155–173, esp. 161.
79. McClellan, *Colonialism and Science,* 236.
80. This is a topic that I intend to examine in greater detail.
81. Benjamin Moseley, *A Treatise on Tropical Diseases; or on Military Operations: and on the Climate of the West,* 3d ed. (London, 1792), 510–511; Moseley, *Treatise on Tropical Diseases,* 4th ed. (London, 1803), 407–408, 128–129; Grainger, *Essay on the More Common West-India Diseases,* 57; James Lind, *An Essay on Diseases Incidental to Europeans in Hot Climates* (London, 1768), 129–131.

10. *Theopolis Americana*

1. Sewall's edition was probably David Pareus, *A Commentary upon the Divine Revelation of the Apostle and Evangelist John,* trans. Elias Arnold (Amsterdam, 1644).
2. M. Halsey Thomas, ed., *The Diary of Samuel Sewall, 1674–1729,* 2 vols. (New York, 1973), 1:91 (hereafter, *Sewall Diary*).

3. John Winthrop, "A Modell of Christian Charity," in *The Winthrop Papers*, 7 vols. to date (Boston, 1929–), 2:295; Oliver Wendell Holmes, *The Autocrat of the Breakfast Table* (Boston, 1891), 125.

4. A few men with Boston connections, such as John Humfry and Robert Sedgwick, took an interest in these Caribbean ventures, but on the whole Cromwell's call for Puritans to abandon New England and focus their efforts on the West Indies met with remarkable indifference. For a recent discussion, highlighting the ways in which these figures lay outside the New England mainstream, see Louise A. Breen, *Transgressing the Bounds: Subversive Enterprises among the Puritan Elite in Massachusetts, 1630–1692* (New York, 2001).

5. For an overview of Boston's relations with the Stuart monarchs in this period, see Mark Peterson, "Boston Pays Tribute: Autonomy and Empire in the Atlantic World, 1630–1714," in *Shaping the Stuart World, 1603–1714: The Atlantic Connection*, ed. Allan I. Macinnes and Arthur H. Williamson (Leiden, 2006), 311–336.

6. The most thorough and cogent summary of this transformation can be found in Owen Stanwood, "The Protestant Moment: Antipopery, the Revolution of 1688–1689, and the Making of an Anglo-American Empire," *Journal of British Studies* 46 (July 2007): 481–508. I am grateful to Professor Stanwood for allowing me to read an advance copy of his essay.

7. See Mark A. Peterson, *The Price of Redemption: The Spiritual Economy of Puritan New England* (Stanford, Calif., 1997).

8. Bernard Bailyn, *The New England Merchants in the Seventeenth Century* (Cambridge, Mass., 1955).

9. On Belcher's career, see Michael C. Batinski, *Jonathan Belcher, Colonial Governor* (Lexington, Ky., 1996); "Jonathan Belcher," in Clifton K. Shipton, *Sibley's Harvard Graduates* (Cambridge, Mass., 1933), 4:439–448. The scholarship on Cotton Mather is far too voluminous to be cited here, but for general biographies, see David Levin, *Cotton Mather: The Young Life of the Lord's Remembrancer, 1663–1703* (Cambridge, Mass., 1978), and Kenneth Silverman, *The Life and Times of Cotton Mather* (New York, 1984). Among the better more-specialized studies of aspects of Mather's career are Richard F. Lovelace, *The American Pietism of Cotton Mather: Origins of American Evangelicalism* (Grand Rapids, Mich., 1979), and Michael P. Winship, *Seers of God: Puritan Providentialism in the Restoration and Early Enlightenment* (Baltimore, Md., 1996).

10. On Andrew Belcher's career and Jonathan's upbringing, see Batinski, *Jonathan Belcher*, 3–9; and Shipton, "Jonathan Belcher." Bailyn, in *New England Merchants*, 195–197, describes Andrew Belcher and his descendants as "prototypes of the ascending merchant families in the late seventeenth and early eighteenth centuries."

11. Batinski, *Jonathan Belcher*, 4–11.

12. Jonathan Belcher, "A Journal of My Intended Voyage and Journey to Holland, Hannover, &c, July 8, 1704 to October 5, 1704" (hereafter, Belcher Journal), MS, Massachusetts Historical Society, Boston (hereafter, MHS).

13. For a thorough discussion of this subject, see C. D. Van Strien, *British Travelers in Holland during the Stuart Period* (Leiden, 1993).

14. For a general study of colonial British American travelers in a somewhat later period, see Susan Lindsey Lively, "Going Home: Americans in Britain, 1740–1776" (Ph.D. diss., Harvard University, 1996).

15. For the effect of the tumultuous Anglo-Dutch relations of the seventeenth century on British travelers to the Netherlands during Queen Anne's reign, see Van Strien, *British Travelers in Holland*, 8–13.

16. On Andrew Belcher's role in the rebellion against Andros, see Robert Earle Moody and Richard Clive Simmons, eds., *The Glorious Revolution in Massachusetts, Selected Documents, 1689–1692* (Boston, 1988), 4–5, 54, 60–64, and passim.

17. Belcher Journal, 14–16. On the House of Nassau and the construction of Dutch patriotism, see Simon Schama, *The Embarrassment of Riches: An Interpretation of Dutch Culture in the Golden Age* (New York, 1997), 51–125.

18. Belcher, in fact, declined the college trustees' suggestion that the building be named "Belcher Hall," preferring to honor "the immortal Memory of the glorious King William the 3d. who was a Branch of the illustrious House of Nassau": Batinski, *Jonathan Belcher*, 170; see also Annie Haven Thwing, *The Crooked & Narrow Streets of the Town of Boston* (Boston, 1920), 228, 237–241.

19. For instance, in 1716 Andrew Belcher joined a group of like-minded church members in dissuading the newly arrived royal governor, Samuel Shute, from attending a dance hosted by the organist of the Anglican King's Chapel; see *Sewall Diary*, 2:838. On the general subject of Puritan hostility to Anglican culture in Boston, see Peterson, *The Price of Redemption*, 173–184.

20. Ebenezer Pemberton, *Advice to a Son: A Discourse at the Request of a*

Gentleman in New-England, upon his Son's going to Europe (London, 1705). Belcher took time while in London to arrange for the publication of Pemberton's sermon.

21. Belcher Journal, 26.

22. In describing the lives of the diplomats at Hanover, Belcher writes, "the English gentlemen there . . . spend most of their time in reading, indeed there is little else to do, a Court life, being very Idle; Dressing and diversion is all their care & concern and they live in an entire oblivion of Religion and will (I fear) insensibly fall into atheism, they never go to any Chh nor mind Sunday any more than any other day." Belcher Journal, 53, 118–125.

23. On Boston's growing prominence as a shipping center, see Bernard Bailyn and Lotte Bailyn, *Massachusetts Shipping, 1697–1714* (Cambridge, Mass., 1959), 20–21; for population estimates, see Carl Bridenbaugh, *Cities in the Wilderness: The First Century of Urban Life in America, 1625–1742* (New York, 1971), 143–144; Gary Nash, *The Urban Crucible: The Northern Seaports and the Origins of the American Revolution*, abridged ed. (Cambridge, Mass., 1986), 33–34.

24. Nash, *Urban Crucible*, 34–39; G. B. Warden, *Boston, 1689–1776* (Boston, 1970), 60–79; Elizabeth E. Dunn, "'Grasping at the Shadow': The Massachusetts Currency Debate, 1690–1751," *New England Quarterly* 71 (March 1998): 54–76.

25. Belcher Journal, 23–24. For a discussion of the significance of stock exchanges for the creation of cosmopolitan culture, see Margaret C. Jacob, *Strangers Nowhere in the World: The Rise of Cosmopolitanism in Early Modern Europe* (Philadelphia, Pa., 2006), 66–94. On market reform in Boston, see Warden, *Boston*, 53–54, 76–77, 106–107, 117–121.

26. During the crisis over paper money and banking schemes of 1740–1741, a crisis that would ultimately end his term as royal governor of Massachusetts, Belcher issued a proclamation denouncing the so-called Land Bank, which might "defraud Men of their Substance," and praised the rival Silver Bank, saying that its notes were "of service to the people as a medium in commerce, for they are truly & really equal to gold and silver to the possessors": Batinski, *Jonathan Belcher*, 142. See also Dunn, "'Grasping at the Shadow,'" 61–66; Rosalind Remer, "Old Lights and New Money: A Note on Religion, Economics, and the Social Order in 1740 Boston," *William and Mary Quarterly*, 3d ser., 47 (October 1990): 566–573.

27. Belcher Journal, 19, 28–30. On Dutch charity and philanthropy in the seventeenth century, see Van Strien, *British Travelers in Holland*, 134–

136, 191–198; Schama, *Embarrassment of Riches,* 570–579; Sheila D. Muller, *Charity in the Dutch Republic: Pictures of Rich and Poor for Charitable Institutions* (Ann Arbor, Mich., 1985). On the development of the Boston "spinning school" in the 1730s as a means of poor relief, see Eric G. Nellis, "Misreading the Signs: Industrial Imitation, Poverty, and the Social Order in Boston," *New England Quarterly* 59 (December 1986): 486–507. During Belcher's decade as Massachusetts governor in the 1730s, Boston's systems for poor relief, education, and charity received a major overhaul; see Nash, *Urban Crucible,* 78–79, Warden, *Boston,* 101–126; Bridenbaugh, *Cities in the Wilderness,* 392–394; Horace E. Scudder, "Life in Boston in the Provincial Period," in *The Memorial History of Boston,* ed. Justin Winsor, 4 vols. (Boston, 1882), 3:458–461.

28. Belcher Journal, 16. Baron Johann Kaspar von Bothmer would later play an important role as the Hanoverian Elector's representative in Britain, ensuring George I's peaceful accession to the British throne when the death of Queen Anne stirred considerable speculation about the possibility of a challenge from the Stuart pretender; see Ragnhild Hatton, *George I, Elector and King* (Cambridge, Mass., 1978), 97, 107–109, 147–151.

29. See Maria Kroll, *Sophie, Electress of Hanover: A Personal Portrait* (London, 1973), esp. 183–247 on court life at Herrenhausen during the era of Belcher's visits.

30. Belcher Journal, 41–47.

31. Ibid., 45.

32. Ibid., 42, 46. Belcher described the scene as follows: "While we were talking with him [the Elector George] a servant came in and whisper'd to him, that Capt Bouche was come express from the Army and just arriv'd. He immediately retir'd and we waited half an hour between hope and fear 'till his return, ye Electress gave over play and went into her closet, being a little frighted, because of her son in the Army, at length the Elector came in again and told us the good news, of the French and Bavarians being intirely defeated by our Army" (42).

33. Ibid., 55. For portraits of George's Turkish servants, Mahomet and Mustapha, see Joyce Marlow, *The Life and Times of George I* (London, 1973), 71.

34. Jonathan Belcher to John White, 27 Dec. 1704, MS, Belknap Papers, MHS; Julius H. Tuttle, "Note on the Portrait of the Electress Sophia of Hanover," *Publications of the Colonial Society of Massachusetts* 20 (Boston, 1920): 96–103.

35. Other Bostonians who encountered Catholics and Jesuits in more trying circumstances include Benjamin Colman, who was captured by French privateers and held in French jails, where he argued with a "Romish priest" before his eventual exchange; Jeremiah Dummer, who engaged in a Latin debate on theology with the rector of the Sorbonne at Paris's church of St. Sulpice; John Williams, taken captive during the attack on Deerfield in 1704, who spent much of his time in captivity arguing with the Jesuits in Montréal and Québec; and John Nelson, Boston merchant, who was taken captive and held at the Bastille while conducting complex diplomatic negotiations during the War of the Spanish Succession. See Ebenezer Turell, *Life and Character of the Reverend Benjamin Colman* (Boston, 1749), 5–14; "Jeremiah Dummer," in Shipton, *Sibley's Harvard Graduates,* 4:464; John Williams, "The Redeemed Captive Returning to Zion," in *Puritans among the Indians: Accounts of Captivity and Redemption, 1676–1724,* ed. Alden T. Vaughan and Edward W. Clark (Cambridge, Mass., 1981), 183–196; Richard R. Johnson, *John Nelson, Merchant Adventurer: A Life between Empires* (New York, 1991).

36. Belcher Journal, 57–61. On the history of the monastery at Lambspring and its connections to the English Benedictines and to the later Stuarts, see Dom Bennet Weldon, *Chronological Notes Containing the Rise, Growth and Present State of the English Congregation of the Order of St. Benedict* (London, 1881), 184–186, 189–193, 232–233, and appendix VIII, 23–27.

37. Belcher Journal, 63–68; emphasis in original. For a contemporary description of the Hartz silver mines, see Georg Henning Behrens, *The Natural History of the Hartz Forest* (London, 1730).

38. The furnishings of the king of Prussia's palace were so lavish that, in Belcher's words, "it put me in mind of the Queen of Sheba, who when she had seen Solomon's glory, it is said there was no more spirit in her": Belcher Journal, 73. The queen of Prussia was Sophia's only daughter and favorite child, Sophia Charlotte, known as "Figuelotte," whose death in 1705 was a crushing blow to her mother; see Kroll, *Sophie, Electress of Hanover,* 206–212.

39. For a useful overview of the many facets of Leibniz's career, see Nicholas Jolley, ed., *The Cambridge Companion to Leibniz* (Cambridge, 1995); Joachim Vennebusch, *Gottfried Wilhelm Leibniz, Philosopher and Politician in the Service of a Universal Culture* (Bad Godesburg, Germany, 1966).

40. Belcher Journal, 76–78.

41. On Leibniz's interest in and experience with alchemy, see Roger Ariew,

"G. W. Leibniz, Life and Works," in Jolley, *The Cambridge Companion to Leibniz*, 20–21, 41n11. For a valuable introduction to the place of alchemy in the early modern scientific world and the role played in it by an early graduate of Harvard College, see William R. Newman, *Gehennical Fire: The Lives of George Starkey, an American Alchemist in the Scientific Revolution* (Cambridge, Mass., 1994). According to Newman, Harvard students in Belcher's era would have been exposed to alchemical theories of matter in the college's natural philosophy curriculum, especially from the use of Charles Morton's *Compendium of Physics,* which was introduced in 1687 (*Compendium physicae ex authoribus extractum* [n.p., 1687]). Throughout Belcher's lifetime, alchemical theses were publicly defended at the college's annual commencement exercises; see 32–39.

42. Batinski, *Jonathan Belcher,* 16–18.

43. Jonathan Belcher to "Dear Brother," 16 Nov. 1708, Belcher Miscellany, Princeton University Library, Princeton, N.J. I am grateful to Michael Batinski for supplying me with this reference. Little else is known of the fate of this Indian servant, though the story raises intriguing possibilities. The boy's name may have been derived from classical mythology, where Io was the name of a servant girl taken by Zeus as a lover, transformed into a heifer because of Hera's jealousy, then eventually restored to human form and elevated to the status of the gods (Hercules was her descendant). Perhaps Belcher bestowed this name on the Indian servant expecting him to be similarly transformed through contact with royalty. In any case, this story, when set alongside the narrative of the unfortunate hautboy player, gives us insight into Belcher's views on servitude and slavery, power and despotism. What redeemed the otherwise slavish relationship between the Indian servant and the princess, or, for that matter, what redeemed Belcher's own servile relationship with the princess, was the quality of Christian charity that infused it. The Elector might be a tyrant and the oboe player a scoundrel, but servitude need not require brutality, or so Belcher sincerely believed.

44. Here Belcher would prove to be mistaken—Frederick died while still Prince of Wales, leaving his son to succeed to the throne as George III.

45. Jonathan Belcher to "Dear Brother," 16 Nov. 1708. This medal, which Belcher described as "a pretty pocket piece with her face on one side, which she desired I would accept as a mark of her respect," was a copy of the one Sophia had made for Lord Macclesfield, the English ambassador who in 1702 had arrived to present her with official news of the Act of Settlement; see Kroll, *Sophie, Electress of Hanover,* 202–203, 220,

which shows a copy of the medal, facing p. 237. The medal's reverse depicted a distant ancestor of Sophia's and matriarch of the Guelph dynasty, Matilda (1156–1189), daughter of Henry II of England, who married the Duke of Saxony. When the Holy Roman Emperor in 1180 attempted to confiscate the duke's lands in Brunswick, the duke resisted, and the couple sought refuge in England. The choice of Matilda for this commemorative medal was meant as a reminder of the ancient ties between England and Germany and their mutual resistance to imperial domination.

46. Hugh Amory and David D. Hall, eds., *A History of the Book in America*, vol. 1, *The Colonial Book in the Atlantic World* (New York, 2000).

47. For a social and cultural history of the scholarly community of early modern Europe, see Anne Goldgar, *Impolite Learning: Conduct and Community in the Republic of Letters, 1680–1750* (New Haven, Conn., 1995).

48. For a theoretical discussion that introduces the idea of material objects as "distributed personhood," see Alfred Gell, *Art and Agency: An Anthropological Theory* (Oxford, 1998).

49. Cotton Mather contributed numerous observations and articles to the Royal Society in London, in return for which he was elected to membership.

50. On Increase Mather's continuing belief in the providential interpretation of comets, and for the suggestion that his approach lacked the rigor of contemporary European scientific investigators, see Robert Middlekauff, *The Mathers: Three Generations of Puritan Intellectuals, 1596–1728* (New York, 1971), 140–143; Winship, *Seers of God*, 63, 180n44; Michael G. Hall, *The Last American Puritan: The Life of Increase Mather, 1639–1723* (Middletown, Conn., 1988), 165–174.

51. The complete title of *Kometographia* went on to explain that the treatise included information on "the place in the heavens where they [comets] were seen, their motions, forms, duration; and the remarkable events which have followed in the world, so far as they have been by learned men observed." In Steven Shapin's summary of Bacon's position, "the condition for a proper natural philosophy was its foundation in a laboriously compiled factual register of natural history—a catalog, compilation, and collation of all the effects that could be observed in nature." See Shapin, *The Scientific Revolution* (Chicago, 1996), 85.

52. Ibid., 59, 65.

53. Recent work by Theodore D. Bozeman reinforces this idea of the Puri-

tan movement's continuity with aspects of Roman Catholic piety and discipline; see *The Precisianist Strain: Disciplinary Religion and Antinomian Backlash in Puritanism to 1638* (Chapel Hill, N.C., 2004), 63–144.

54. Hall, *The Last American Puritan*, 44–46; Robert Kingdon and Michel Reulos, "'Disciplines' réformées du XVIe siècle françaises: une découverte faite aux Etats-Unis," *Bulletin de la Société de l'histoire du protestantisme français* 130, no. 1 (1984): 69–86.

55. [Isaac la Peyrère], *Men before Adam, A System of Divinity* (London, 1656), 18.

56. See Anthony Grafton, "Isaac La Peyrère and the Old Testament," in his *Defenders of the Text: The Traditions of Scholarship in the Age of Science, 1450–1800* (Cambridge, Mass., 1991), 204–213; Richard Popkin, *Isaac La Peyrère (1596–1676): His Life, Work, and Influence* (Leiden, 1987).

57. Steven Shapin and Simon Shaffer, *Leviathan and the Air Pump: Hobbes, Boyle, and the Experimental Life* (Princeton, N.J., 1985), was the seminal work in this vein; others include Bruno Latour, *We Have Never Been Modern* (Cambridge, Mass., 1993); Mario Biagioli, *Galileo, Courtier: The Practice of Science in the Culture of Absolutism* (Chicago, 1993); and Lorraine Daston and Katharine Park, *Wonders and the Order of Nature, 1150–1750* (New York, 1998).

58. See Newman, *Gehennical Fire*.

59. For a discussion of the role of honor, religion, and gentility in the making of social authority among early modern scientific practitioners, see Steven Shapin, "Who Was Robert Boyle? The Creation and Presentation of an Experimental Identity," in his *The Social History of Truth: Civility and Science in Seventeenth-Century England* (Chicago, 1994), 126–192.

60. Margaret Jacob offers a comparable argument in *Strangers Nowhere in the World*, 41–65, that alchemical forms of scientific investigation were driven underground in England after 1660, because the religious and political radicalism of many alchemical practitioners of the 1640s and 1650s was no longer acceptable in Restoration England. Jacob offers a comparison with France, where alchemy continued to thrive well after 1660, to demonstrate the significance of political forces in the construction of communities of knowledge in England, but an equally strong case could be made through comparison with New England, where alchemical thought and practice continued to thrive beyond the reach of Restoration politics and royal authority.

61. The best explication of this worldview, shared by clergy and ordinary

folks alike, can be found in David D. Hall, *World of Wonders, Days of Judgment: Popular Religious Belief in Early New England* (New York, 1989).

62. For accounts of the smallpox crisis, see Ola Elizabeth Winslow, *A Destroying Angel: The Conquest of Smallpox in Colonial Boston* (Boston, 1974); John B. Blake, *Public Health in the Town of Boston, 1630–1822* (Cambridge, Mass., 1959), 52–98; Perry Miller, *The New England Mind: From Colony to Province* (Cambridge, Mass., 1953), 345–366; Silverman, *Life and Times of Cotton Mather,* 336–363; Margot Minardi, "The Boston Inoculation Controversy of 1721–1722: An Incident in the History of Race," *William and Mary Quarterly,* 3d ser., 61 (January 2004): 47–76. My account of the crisis draws on all these sources.

63. These reports were: Emmanuel Timoni, "An Account, or History, of the Procuring the Small Pox by Incision, or Inoculation: as It Has for Some Time Been Practised at Constantinople," Royal Society of London, *Philosophical Transactions* 29, no. 339 (1714): 72; and Jacobus Pylarini, "Nova & Tuta Variolus Excitandi per Transplantationem Methodus, Nuper Inventa & in Usum Tracta," *Philosophical Transactions,* no. 347 (1716): 393–399.

64. Thomas Bartholin, "Historia Medica de Variolis, Anno 1656, Hafniae Epidemiis," *Cista Medica Hafniensis* (Copenhagen, 1662), 590–591. Cotton Mather's marginal notations can be found in the copy held by the American Antiquarian Society.

65. *New England Courant,* 7, 14 Aug. 1721; *Boston Newsletter,* 24 July 1721.

66. *Diary of Cotton Mather,* 2 vols., MHS, *Collections,* 7th series, vols. 7–8 (Boston, 1911–1912), 2:23. The earliest English version of Francke's reports on the progress of his efforts at Halle was entitled *Pietas Hallensis: or, an Abstract of the Marvellous Footsteps of the Divine Providence,* trans. A. W. Boehm (London, 1707).

67. For background on the life of Francke and the evolution of the Halle institute, see Gary R. Sattler, *God's Glory, Neighbor's Good: A Brief Introduction to the Life and Writings of August Hermann Francke* (Chicago, 1982); F. Ernest Stoeffler, *German Pietism during the Eighteenth Century* (Leiden, 1973), 1–88. On the development of Cotton Mather's correspondence with Francke, see Kuno Francke, "Cotton Mather and August Hermann Francke," in *Harvard Studies and Notes in Philology and Literature* 5 (Boston, 1896): 57–67; Kuno Francke, "The Beginning of Cotton Mather's Correspondence with August Hermann Francke," *Philological Quarterly* 5 (July 1926): 193–195.

68. This letter was published the following year as Crescentio Mathero, *De Successu Evangelij apud Indos in Nova-Anglia epistola ad cl. virum D. Johannem Leusdenum . . .* (London, 1688).

69. Cotton Mather, *Triumphs of the Reformed Religion in America: The Life of the Renowned John Eliot* (London, 1691). This was the second edition of Mather's work, which had first appeared earlier that year in Boston, published by Joseph Brunning. Another London edition appeared from John Dunton in 1694, the text was reprinted again in Mather's *Magnalia Christi Americana* (London, 1702), and further editions were produced in Bristol and London in 1755 and 1820; see Thomas J. Holmes, *Cotton Mather: A Bibliography of His Works,* 3 vols. (Cambridge, Mass., 1940), 3:1124–1130.

70. Richard Baxter, perhaps the leading figure in English dissent and ecumenical Pietism in the latter half of the seventeenth century, was reading Mather's *Life of Eliot* on his deathbed, and was temporarily revived by it; see Holmes, *Cotton Mather,* 1129. The first edition of Gordon's geography was intended by its preface to be merely a guide to "that most Pleasurable and Useful Science," handy for the merchant, sailor, soldier, or even the clergyman who wanted to travel in his imagination to the Holy Land. By 1699, the revised version had clearly developed an evangelical purpose—the preface was now directed toward "the younger Sort of our Nobility and Gentry," to channel their idle time toward pious ends. The section on New England now included, for the first time, a description of John Eliot's work among the natives, and a lengthy new appendix to the work summarized the holdings of European powers in "Asia, Africk, and America" and offered "some Reasonable Proposals for the Propagation of the Blessed Gospel in all Pagan Countries." See Patrick Gordon, *Geography Anatomiz'd: or, A Compleat Geographical Grammar* (London, 1693), "To the Reader"; cf. Gordon, *Geography Anatomiz'd: or The Compleat Geographical Grammar* (London, 1699), preface, 346, 391–402.

71. Gordon, a chaplain in the Royal Navy and a fellow of the Royal Society, joined the SPCK in its founding year and three years later went to America as one of its first missionaries. His geography text was adopted widely in English public schools, and "contributed greatly to the stirring of conscience which led to the foundation of the S.P.C.K. and the S.P.G."; W. K. Lowther Clarke, *Eighteenth Century Piety* (London, 1944), 91–95. Gordon's *Geography* also influenced Cotton Mather's "Desiderata," a list of proposals for "general services for the Kingdom of God among mankind," with which he concluded his *Bonifacius;* see

Cotton Mather, *Bonifacius: An Essay upon the Good* (Boston, 1710), ed. David Levin (Cambridge, Mass., 1966), 139 (although in this modern edition, the author of Gordon's *Geography* is misidentified, n. 2).

72. W. O. B. Allen and Edmund McClure, *Two Hundred Years: The History of the Society for Promoting Christian Knowledge, 1698–1898* (New York, 1970), 7.

73. W. R. Ward, *The Protestant Evangelical Awakening* (New York, 1992), 302–307; on Boehm's career, see Arno Sames, *Anton Wilhelm Böhme: Studien zum ökumenischen Denken und Handeln eines halleschen Pietisten* (Göttingen, 1990).

74. Upon Boehm's death in 1722, Newman wrote in a letter to Cotton Mather, "In him I have lost one of my dearest and intimate companions, and every place where I used to enjoy him seems desolate as if one half of me was gone to the grave"; Henry Newman to Cotton Mather, 31 Aug. 1722, quoted in Allen and McClure, *Two Hundred Years*, 231–233; see also Leonard W. Cowie, *Henry Newman: An American in London, 1708–1743* (London, 1956), 47.

75. Samuel Newman, first minister of the town of Rehoboth, Massachusetts, was the author of the largest and most comprehensive biblical concordance written in any modern European language until the nineteenth century, a work that went through many editions; see Cotton Mather, "Bibliander Nov-Anglicus, The Life of Samuel Newman," in *Magnalia Christi Americana* (London, 1702; repr. New York, 1972), bk. 3: 113–116.

76. Cowie, *Henry Newman*, 195–222.

77. See Francke, "Mather's Correspondence with August Hermann Francke," 193–194; Cotton Mather, *Nuncia Bona e Terra Longinqua: A Brief Account of Some Good & Great Things a Doing for the Kingdom of God, in the Midst of Europe* (Boston, 1715). Mather's text, together with an edited version of Francke's Latin original, are published together in Kuno Francke, "Further Documents Concerning Cotton Mather and August Hermann Francke," *Americana Germanica* 1, no. 4 (1897): 32–66.

78. Francke, "Further Documents," 51–52. A loose English translation of Francke's letter to Mather was published by A. W. Boehm in a revised edition of *Pietas Hallensis*; see August Hermann Francke, *Pietas Hallensis: or, An Abstract of the Marvellous Footsteps of Divine Providence*, trans. A. W. Boehm (London, 1716), 56ff. Increase Mather's letter to Johannes Leusden had actually been published at Utrecht in 1693 in an expanded version that appended a discussion of missions to the East Indies to Mather's description of New England missions, then the whole enlarged

work was translated into German and published at Halle in 1696; for a copy of this rare work, see Increase Mather, *Ein Brieff von dem glucklichen Fortgang des Evangelii bey den West-Indianern in Neu= Engeland an den beruhmten Herrn Johann Leusden* (Halle, 1696), Houghton Library, Harvard University, Cambridge, Mass.

79. *Diary of Cotton Mather,* 2:332–333, 563.

80. Cotton Mather, *India Christiana: A Discourse Delivered unto the Commissioners for the Propagation of the Gospel among the American Indians* (Boston, 1721). At the end of this pamphlet, Mather reprinted his correspondence with Ziegenbalg and Gründler, including both the Latin originals and English translations on facing pages, 62–87.

81. *Diary of Cotton Mather,* 2:193, 335–336, 348, 364, 400, 490, 497–499.

82. Cotton Mather, *Bonifacius,* ed. Levin, 138–142.

83. For an overview of the impact of continental Pietism on Cotton Mather's work, see Ernst Benz, "The Pietist and Puritan Sources of Early Protestant World Missions (Cotton Mather and A. H. Francke)," *Church History* 20 (June 1951): 28–55; Benz, "Ecumenical Relations between Boston Puritanism and German Pietism: Cotton Mather and August Hermann Francke," *Harvard Theological Review* 54 (July 1961): 159–193; and Lovelace, *American Pietism of Cotton Mather.*

84. Lovelace, *American Pietism of Cotton Mather,* 73–109.

85. Benz, "Pietist and Puritan Sources."

86. See Cotton Mather, *Theopolis Americana: An Essay upon the Golden Street of the Holy City: Publishing, A Testimony against the Corruptions of the Market=Place, with some Good Hopes of Better Things to be yet seen in the American World* (Boston, 1710), 21–23. Mather's essay was dedicated to Samuel Sewall, who had published a decade earlier Boston's first antislavery tract, *The Selling of Joseph: A Memorial* (Boston, 1700). In addition to his own text, Sewall had arranged for a Boston edition of an antislavery exchange taken from the proceedings of London's Athenian Society; see *The Athenian Oracle, The Second Edition, Printed at London, 1704, Vol. 1. P. 545–548. Quest. Whether Trading for Negroes i.e. carrying them out of their own Country into perpetual Slavery, be in it self Unlawful, and especially contrary to the great Law of Christianity* (Boston, 1705).

87. On the Huguenots, see Cotton Mather, *A Letter Concerning the Terrible Suffering of our Protestant Brethren, on board the French King's Galleys* (Boston, 1701); Jon Butler, *The Huguenots in America: A Refugee People in New World Society* (Cambridge, Mass., 1983); J. F. Bosher, "Huguenot Merchants and the Protestant International in the Seventeenth

Century," *William and Mary Quarterly*, 3d ser., 52 (January 1995): 77–102; Charles C. Smith, "The French Protestants in Boston," in Winsor, *Memorial History of Boston*, 2:249–268. For an overview of German refugee migrants to North America in the eighteenth century, see A. G. Roeber, "'The Origin of Whatever Is Not English among Us': The Dutch-speaking and the German-speaking Peoples of Colonial British America," in *Strangers within the Realm: Cultural Margins of the First British Empire*, ed. Bernard Bailyn and Philip D. Morgan (Chapel Hill, N.C., 1991), 237–244; Roeber, *Palatines, Liberty, and Property: German Lutherans in Colonial British America* (Baltimore, Md., 1996); Philip Otterness, *Becoming German: The 1709 Palatine Migration to New York* (Ithaca, N.Y., 2004).

88. This obsession with combating international Catholicism turned up, among other places, in the frequent hopeful rumors that spread through Boston of the death of Louis XIV of France, along with ongoing reports of Louis's persecution of Protestants; see *Sewall Diary*, 1:92, 102, 176, 267, 330–331, 365, 492. Sewall even gave friends copies of the revocation of the Edict of Nantes; *Sewall Diary*, 2:393.

89. Paul Dudley, *An Essay on the Merchandize of Slaves & Souls of Men, with an Application thereof to the Church of Rome* (Boston, 1731). The title page of Dudley's tract listed the author only as "a Gentleman," but at the time of his death in 1751, Dudley left Harvard College an endowment to sponsor an annual lecture, and every four years, the "Dudleian Lecture" was to be given with the aim of "detecting and convicting and exposing the Idolatry of the Romish Church, Their Tyranny, Usurpations, damnable Heresies, fatal Errors, abominable Superstitions, and other crying Wickednesses in their high Places"; see Shipton, "Paul Dudley," in *Sibley's Harvard Graduates*, 4:52–53.

90. Mather wrote to Ziegenbalg, the Halle missionary in India, "Great and Grievous and never enough to be bewailed, has been the Scandal given in the Churches of the Reformation; in that so very little, yea, next to nothing, has been done in them, for the Propagation of a Faith, which breathes nothing but the most unexceptionable Wisdom and Goodness; . . . while at the same time, the Church of Rome, strives with an Unwearied and Extravagant Labour, to Propagate the Idolatry and Superstition of Antichrist, and advance the Empire of Satan. And the Missionaries and Brokers of that Harlot, are indeed more than can be numbred." See Mather, *India Christiana*, 64; see also Mather, *Bonifacius*, ed. Levin, 138.

91. Inspired by the German Pietists, especially Johann Arndt's *Vier Bucher*

vom Wahren Christentum, trans. A. W. Boehm (London, 1712), Mather attempted to reduce the fundamentals of Christianity to fourteen *axiomata evangelii aeterni,* and later reduced these fourteen to an even more simplified three points, consisting of belief in the divine trinity as the world's creator to whom mankind owes obedience; belief in Jesus Christ's sacrificial atonement as the sole basis for human salvation; and upholding the golden rule as a guide to human relations. See Mather, *India Christiana,* 64–74; Benz, "Pietist and Puritan Sources," 43–46.

92. On Leibniz's quest for the philosophical basis of a universal human language, see Donald Rutherford, "Philosophy and Language in Leibniz," in *The Cambridge Companion to Leibniz,* 224–269; Olga Pombo, *Leibniz and the Problem of a Universal Language* (Münster, 1987). On the general movement in early modern Europe to find a universal language as a means to repair the rifts in Christendom, cultivate commerce, and facilitate scientific discourse, see James Knowlton, *Universal Language Schemes in England and France, 1600–1800* (Toronto, 1975).

93. Cotton Mather, *Nuncia Bona e Terra Longinqua: A Brief Account of Some Good & Great Things a Doing for the Kingdom of God in the Midst of Europe* (Boston, 1715), in Kuno Francke, "Further Documents," 61–62.

94. Encouraging reform efforts in this vein was the main purpose of Mather's *Bonifacius: An Essay Upon the Good.*

95. Mather's efforts as a healer spanned his infamous involvement in witchcraft and possession in the 1680s and 1690s, to his famous promotion of smallpox inoculation in the 1720s. Although modern historiography tends to separate these efforts into "bad" superstition and "good" science, Mather's endeavors to understand and heal human maladies were all of a piece. For a view of his medical opinions late in his career, see Cotton Mather, *The Angel of Bethesda,* ed. Gordon W. Jones (Barre, Mass., 1972); on alchemy and medicine in New England during Mather's lifetime, see Mather's biographical sketch of the younger John Winthrop entitled "Hermes Christianus," in *Magnalia Christi Americana,* bk. 2:30–33; Newman, *Gehennical Fire,* 28, 32–40; see also Patricia A. Watson, *The Angelical Conjunction: The Preacher-Physicians of Colonial New England* (Knoxville, Tenn., 1991), and Walter Woodward, *Prospero's America: John Winthrop, Jr., Alchemy, and the Creation of New England Culture* (Chapel Hill, N.C., forthcoming).

96. Early eighteenth-century Boston clerical writings in this vein include Cotton Mather, *Lex Mercatoria: or, The Just Rules of Commerce Declared* (Boston, 1705); Benjamin Colman, *Some Reasons and Arguments*

offered to the Good People of Boston . . . for the setting up Markets in Boston (Boston, 1719); Thomas Prince, *Vade Mecum for America: or, A Companion for Traders and Travelers* (Boston, 1731).

97. Mather, *Theopolis Americana,* 42–43.

98. *Diary of Cotton Mather,* 2:333; see also Mather, *Bonifacius,* 15; Cotton Mather, *Shaking Dispensations: An Essay upon the Mighty Shakes, which the Hand of Heaven, hath given, and is giving, to the World; with some Useful Remarks on the Death of the French King* (Boston, 1715); Silverman, *Life and Times of Cotton Mather,* 303.

99. Batinski, *Jonathan Belcher,* 45–53.

100. For an overview of the Salzburg crisis, see Ward, *Protestant Evangelical Awakening,* 93–115.

101. George Fenwick Jones, ed., *Henry Newman's Salzburger Letterbooks,* Wormsloe Foundation Publications 8 (Athens, Ga., 1966).

102. George Fenwick Jones, ed., *Detailed Reports on the Salzburger Emigrants Who Settled in America . . . Edited by Samuel Urlsperger,* vols. 1–3, 1733–1736, Wormsloe Foundation Publications 9–11 (Athens, Ga., 1968–1972), 1:188–189; 2:vii, xxi, 14; 3:xix, 1. Benjamin Colman's letter to Urlsperger is omitted from volume 3 of Jones's modern edition of the Salzburger reports, but can be found in the original text, Samuel Urlsperger, *Der Ausfuhrlichen Nachrichten von der Koniglich-Gross-Britannischen Colonie Saltzburgischer Emigranten in America* (Halle, 1741), a copy of which is in Houghton Library, Harvard University.

103. "Travel Diary of Commissioner Von Reck," in Jones, *Detailed Reports,* 1:116–134; see especially 119–120 (on Philadelphia), 122–123 (on New York), 127–130 (on Belcher and Boston), and 122–123, 126–127 (on slavery and the slave trade).

104. Frances Yates, *The Rosicrucian Enlightenment* (London, 1972), 1–29.

105. Ibid., 171–205.

106. Samuel Sewall's own contribution to New England millennialism included *Phaenomena quaedam Apocalyptica ad aspectum Novi Orbis configurata; Or, some few lines towards a description of the New Heaven As It makes to those who stand upon the New Earth* (Boston, 1697), with a second edition in 1727; also Sewall, *Proposals Touching the Accomplishment of Prophecies Humbly Offered* (Boston, 1713). See also James Holstun, *A Rational Millennium: Puritan Utopias of Seventeenth-Century England and America* (New York, 1987).

107. On Sophia's ancestry and her pride in her Palatine origins, see Kroll, *Sophie, Electress of Hanover,* 21–51.

108. Ward, *Protestant Evangelical Awakening.*
109. Cotton Mather, *Theopolis Americana,* 50.

11. The Río de la Plata and Anglo-American Political and Social Models, 1810–1827

1. These questions are carefully analyzed by François-Xavier Guerra, who writes that the Habsburg monarchy had built its legitimacy on a complex network of reciprocal rights and obligations underlying the links between the king and the kingdom. This network could not be eliminated—at least not from people's imagination—by the Bourbon monarchy, though it made great efforts to establish a model of authority structured on a binary power relationship. See Guerra, *Modernidad e independencias: ensayos sobre las revoluciones hispánicas* (Madrid, 1992), 55–79.

2. Pilar González Bernaldo, for instance, referring to the obstacles that Bolívar tried to overcome in creating Gran Colombia—unsuccessfully, for Gran Colombia was dissolved in 1830—states that Creole elites faced the difficulty of founding a modern nation without any historical and cultural precedents that would permit the transfer of monarchical legitimacy to the rising republics. See Bernaldo, "Pedagogía societaria y aprendizaje de la nación en el Río de la Plata," in *De los imperios a las naciones,* ed. Antonio Annino, Luis Castro Leiva, and François-Xavier Guerra (Zaragoza, 1994), 451–469, at 452.

3. In Hispanic America, an intense debate arose in the revolutionary context, because the so-called modern interpretation of popular sovereignty, which supposed the free association of individuals, was confronted with a traditional view that "the people" referred to a corporate entity, such as cities having a cabildo and their hinterland. In Spanish there is, besides, an additional element of confusion, because the translation of "people" is "pueblo," which can refer to an abstract group of individuals but also means "village." So villages having a cabildo claimed what they believed were their sovereign rights. See José C. Chiaramonte, *Ciudades, provincias, estados: orígenes de la nación Argentina, 1800–1846* (Buenos Aires, 1997), 111–178.

4. Darío Roldán, "La cuestión de la representación en el origen de la política moderna: una perspectiva comparada (1770–1830)," in *La vida política en la Argentina del siglo XIX: armas, votos y voces,* ed. Hilda Sábato and Alberto Lettieri (Buenos Aires, 2003), 25–43; Bernard

Bailyn, *American Constitutionalism: Atlantic Dimensions* (London: Institute of United States Studies, 2002), 15.

5. The population of the hinterland of the city was similar. See Tulio Halperín Donghi, *Revolución y guerra: formación de una élite dirigente en la Argentina criolla* (Buenos Aires, 1972), 74.

6. In Hispanic America, *criollo* (Creole) was "a Spaniard born in America"—that is, a descendant of a family of Spanish origins; it did not refer to racial hybridization.

7. Session of 8 March 1813, in Emilio Ravignani, *Asambleas constituyentes argentinas,* 7 vols. (Buenos Aires, 1937–1940), 1:21.

8. Junta de Historia y Numismatica Americana, *Gaceta de Buenos Aires,* 6 vols. (Buenos Aires, 1911) (hereafter, *Gaceta de Buenos Aires*), 3:48 (24 Jan. 1812).

9. See, for instance, José Antonio Aguilar Rivera, *En pos de la quimera: reflexiones sobre el experimento constitucional atlántico* (Mexico, 2000).

10. John P. Robertson and William P. Robertson, *Cartas de Sudamérica* (Buenos Aires, 2000), 84.

11. See *Biblioteca de Mayo: Colección de obras y documentos para la historia argentina—La Lira Argentina, La Abeja Argentina, El Censor, Mártir o Libre, El Observador Americano, El Independiente, La Estrella del Sud, El Centinela,* 20 vols. (Buenos Aires, 1960), 7: introduction, 5735–5736.

12. Un Inglés (anonymous), *Cinco años en Buenos Aires (1820–1825)* (Buenos Aires, 1985), 89.

13. Camilla Townsend, *Tales of Two Cities: Race and Economic Culture in Early Republican North and South American—Guayaquil, Ecuador, and Baltimore, Maryland* (Austin, Tex., 2002), 105–108.

14. *El Censor,* in *Biblioteca de Mayo,* 8:7021 (20 March 1817).

15. Alexander Caldcleugh, *Viajes por América del Sur: Río de la Plata, 1821* (Buenos Aires, 1943), 55.

16. John Andrews, *Viajes de Buenos Aires a Potosí y Arica en los años 1825 y 1826* (Buenos Aires, 1920), 122.

17. Alexander Gillespie, *Buenos Aires y el interior* (Buenos Aires, 1985).

18. *Gaceta de Buenos Aires,* 1:507–508 (15 Oct. 1810); Un Inglés, *Cinco años en Buenos Aires,* 45.

19. John M. Forbes, *Once años en Buenos Aires, 1820–1831* (Buenos Aires, 1956), 214.

20. Samuel Haigh, *Bosquejos de Buenos Aires, Chile y Perú* (Buenos Aires, 1950), 34, 104–105; Henry M. Brackenridge, *La independencia argentina: viaje a América del Sur por orden del gobierno americano, los años 1817 y 1818 en la Fragata 'Congress'* (Buenos Aires, 1999), 72.

21. John Miller, ed., *Memorias del General Miller* (Buenos Aires, 1998), 155.

22. Robert Proctor, *Narraciones del viaje por la cordillera de los Andes, y residencia en Lima, Perú, en los años 1823 y 1824* (Buenos Aires, 1920), 42–43. San Martín, entitled the "liberator of Argentina, Chile and Peru" by twentieth-century Argentine historiography, retired from the Hispanic American public scene after an 1823 interview with Simón Bolívar in Guayaquil. After the interview, he settled for a short time in Mendoza—the province he had governed while organizing the Chilean campaign—and then traveled to France, where he lived until his death in 1850.

23. Robertson and Robertson, *Cartas de Sudamérica*, 209.

24. Brackenridge, *La independencia argentina*, 140; Un Inglés, *Cinco años en Buenos Aires*, 75–84, 105–114, 43; Haigh, *Bosquejos*, 25.

25. Un Inglés, *Cinco años en Buenos Aires*, 109.

26. Camilla Townsend shows how in Guayaquil tertulias were supposed to "bring enlightenment" and gathered the most prominent men and women of the city. See Townsend, *Tales of Two Cities*, 73.

27. Caldcleugh, *Viajes por América del Sur*, 34.

28. Haigh, *Bosquejos*, 29–30.

29. The role of women in tertulias is also highlighted by Camilla Townsend, in the case of Guayaquil. See Townsend, *Tales of Two Cities*, 73.

30. Robertson and Robertson, *Cartas de Sudamérica*, 384, 385.

31. Un Inglés, *Cinco años en Buenos Aires*, 165–166.

32. Ibid., 20.

33. Haigh, *Bosquejos*, 40; Un Inglés, *Cinco años en Buenos Aires*, 164–166.

34. Robertson and Robertson, *Cartas de Sudamérica*, 207.

35. *Los amigos de la patria y de la juventud* (Buenos Aires, 1961), 3:84 (15 Feb. 1816).

36. José Antonio Wilde, *Buenos Aires, desde setenta años atrás* (Buenos Aires, 1977), 79.

37. *Los amigos de la patria y la juventud*, 3:84 (15 Feb. 1816).

38. *El Censor*, in *Biblioteca de Mayo*, 8:6949 (5 Dec. 1816).

39. *El Centinela*, in *Biblioteca de Mayo*, 9, part 2:8607–8610 (no. 42).

40. *Argos* (Buenos Aires, 1910), 13 (no. 2); 44 (no. 7).

41. Robertson and Robertson, *Cartas de Sudamérica*, 395.

42. Caldcleugh, *Viajes por América del Sud*, 60.

43. Un Inglés, *Cinco años en Buenos Aires*, 115.

44. Pazos Kanki, *Letters on the United Provinces of South America* (New York, 1819), 15.

45. Ibid., 44, 83–85.

46. See Bernard Bailyn, *To Begin the World Anew: The Genius and Ambiguities of the American Founders* (New York, 2003), 5.

47. Noemí Goldman, "Libertad de imprenta, opinión pública y debate constitucional en el Río de la Plata (1810–1827),"in *Prismas, Revista de historia intelectual* 4 (2000): 12–34.

48. *Gaceta de Buenos Aires,* 2:318 (22 April 1811).

49. See Jorge Myers, "Ideas moduladas: lecturas argentinas del pensamiento político europeo," *Estudios Sociales* 26 (2004): 166.

50. In the latter case, people viewed North Atlantic intellectual production through a double mediation: the reviews and the newspapers, which were "reviewers" of the reviews.

51. By the middle of the 1820s, there were more than 140 reviews in London alone. George L. Nesbitt, *Benthamite Reviewing: The First Twelve Years of the* Westminster Review, *1824–1836* (New York, 1934), 15–16.

52. In his autobiography, Blanco White said that he did not remember exactly how many copies the Foreign Office actually bought. Antonio Garnica, ed., *Autobiografía de Blanco White* (Seville, 1975), 189.

53. The Foreign Office usually bought a hundred copies of *El Español* and endeavored to get five hundred more copies spread via British traders. David Brading, *Orbe indiano: de la monarquía católica a la república criolla, 1492–1867* (Mexico City, 1991), 586.

54. *Gaceta de Buenos Aires,* 2:713 (3 Sept. 1811).

55. Manuel Moreno Alonso, *Blanco White: la obsesión de España* (Seville, 1998), 523.

56. *El Censor,* 8:7227–7228 (13 Nov. 1817).

57. Ibid., 8:7131–7135 (24 July 1817).

58. Ibid., 7:5802 (18 Feb. 1812).

59. Ibid., 8:7401–7403 (6 June 1818).

60. *Gaceta de Buenos Aires,* 5:524 (22 Nov 1818).

61. See, for instance, the response to an article from a New York newspaper that appeared in *El Censor,* 8:7257 (12 Dec. 1817).

62. *Gaceta de Buenos Aires,* 1:263 (7 Aug. 1810).

63. *El Observador Americano,* in *Biblioteca de Mayo,* 9:7655 (30 Aug. 1816).

64. *El Censor,* 8:7079 (22 May 1817).

65. Pazos Kanki, *Letters on the United Provinces,* 122.

66. See Brackenridge, *La independencia argentina,* 286. Occasional bookstore announcements that appeared in newspapers also help us learn what the Buenos Aires elite read. For instance, in *La Prensa Argentina* we can find that the *Encyclopedie,* Montesquieu's *Complete Works,* and a *History of North America* were sold in the local bookstores. See *La*

Prensa Argentina, in *Biblioteca de Mayo,* 6244 (8 Oct. 1816), and 6251 (15 Oct. 1816).

67. Brackenridge, *La independencia argentina,* 164.
68. Ibid., 286.
69. *Gaceta de Buenos Aires,* 4:405 (18 Nov. 1815).
70. *El Censor,* 8:7302 (5 Feb. 1818).
71. We know this through the documentation of the political trial of Bernardo de Monteagudo for noncompliance with the mandate he had received when he was appointed a delegate to the 1813–1815 Assembly. The cost of the public trial was paid with the property taken from Monteagudo, which included books. Reconstructing the circulation of books is a major problem for Argentine historiography of the early nineteenth century, because Río de la Plata society did not have a tradition of keeping records on such aspects of local life. Thus, the reconstruction is only partially achieved through sources of information that for European and North American cultural or intellectual history are peripheral, such as wills—in cases where a legacy included books—or, as in the example above quoted, legal action. Autobiographies scarcely mentioned reading or discussing books.
72. *El Español,* vol. 1:411–437; 2:329–334; 8:23–37, 109–146. The project on the freedom on the press written for Venezuela on Miranda's request was not published, though part of it was rewritten for the work that Bentham published in 1821, *The Elements of the Art of Packing, as Applied to Special Juries, Particularly in the Cases of Libel Law.* That project can be found in *Manuscritos autógrafos de Jeremy Bentham,* Biblioteca Americana Diego Barros Arana, tier 2, shelf 25, vol. 17 (Caracas, Venezuela).
73. *Abeja Argentina,* in *Biblioteca de Mayo,* 6 (Aug.–Dec. 1822, June and July 1823).
74. *El Centinela,* in *Biblioteca de Mayo,* 9:8394.
75. *Gaceta de Buenos Aires,* 3:14 (15 Nov. 1811).
76. Letters from the government of Buenos Aires to the British ambassador before the Portuguese Court in Río de Janeiro, Lord Strangford, 14 June 1810, 10 Aug. 1810, in *Correspondencia de Lord Strangford y de la estación naval británica en el Río de la Plata con el gobierno de Buenos Aires* (Buenos Aires, 1941), 16, 23.
77. *Gaceta de Buenos Aires,* 3:108 (24 March 1812).
78. *El Censor,* 2:5761 (14 Jan. 1812).
79. Ibid., 6:5793 (11 Feb. 1812).
80. *La Prensa Argentina,* 13:5985 (5 Dec. 1815).

81. Letter from Manuel Belgrano—one of the most important leaders of the Río de la Plata revolutionary process, and envoy to London—read at the Secret Sessions of the 1816–1819 Congress. In Ravignani, *Asambleas constituyentes argentinas,* 1:482.

82. Neptali Carranza, *Oratoria argentina: recopilación cronológica de las proclamas, discursos, manifiestos y documentos importantes que legaron a la historia de su patria argentinos célebres, desde el año 1810 hasta 1904,* 5 vols. (Buenos Aires, 1905), 1:116. Manuel Belgrano supported the idea of crowning a descendant of the Inca, in a system whose king would "reign but not govern."

83. *El Censor,* 56:6868 (19 Sept. 1817).

84. *El Observador Americano,* 5:7681 (16 Sept. 1816).

85. Ibid., 9:7706 (14 Oct. 1816).

86. *El Independiente,* in *Biblioteca de Mayo,* 9:7748 (29 Sept. 1816).

87. Ibid., 13:7812 (8 Dec. 1816).

88. *Gaceta de Buenos Aires,* 2:486 (10 Jan. 1811).

89. Bailyn, *American Constitutionalism,* 15.

90. Marcella Ternavasio, "Division of Powers and Divided Sovereignty: The U.S. Experience in the River Plate Periodical Press during Independence, 1810–1820," paper presented at the Tenth-Anniversary Conference of the International Seminar on the History of the Atlantic World, Harvard University, 2005.

91. By 1810, a translation into Spanish of the U.S. Constitution was circulating in Buenos Aires. It was said to have been translated by an English merchant settled in the city. See Merle Simmons, *La revolución norteamericana en la independencia de hispanoamérica* (Madrid, 1992), 71. In 1812, Bernardo de Monteagudo, in his newspaper *El grito del Sud,* suggested publishing both the Constitution and the Articles of Confederation. See *El grito del Sud,* 2 vols. (Buenos Aires, 1961), 1:161,170 (20 Oct. 1812).

92. *El Observador Americano,* in *Biblioteca de Mayo,* 5:7680 (16 Sept. 1816).

93. "Friendship league" was the concept used by the groups that opposed the settlement of a centralized government, which were led by José Gervasio de Artigas, a political and military leader of the Banda Oriental (present-day Uruguay), a region that had belonged to the viceroyalty of the Río de la Plata but after 1810 refused to be subordinated to Buenos Aires. See Ravignani, *Asambleas constituyentes argentinas,* 6:634. The adversaries of this position characterized the proposal as "federative," when in fact it was closer to a confederation than a federation.